Theo

**SIC**

A
series
edited by
Slavoj Žižek

SIC stands for psychoanalytic interpretation at its most elementary: no discovery of deep, hidden meaning, just the act of drawing attention to the litter-ality [*sic!*] of what precedes it. A *sic* reminds us that what was said, inclusive of its blunders, was effectively said and cannot be undone. The series SIC thus explores different connections to the Freudian field. Each volume provides a bundle of Lacanian interventions into a specific domain of ongoing theoretical, cultural, and ideological-political battles. It is neither "pluralist" nor "socially sensitive"; unabashedly avowing its exclusive Lacanian orientation, it disregards any form of correctness but the inherent correctness of theory itself.

# Theology and the Political

*The New Debate*

CRESTON DAVIS,

JOHN MILBANK,

AND

SLAVOJ ŽIŽEK,

EDITORS

*With an*

*Introduction by*

*Rowan Williams*

SIC **5**

DUKE UNIVERSITY PRESS   Durham and London 2005

© 2005 Duke University Press

All rights reserved

Printed in the United States

of America on acid-free paper ∞

Typeset in Dante by

Tseng Information Systems, Inc.

Library of Congress Cataloging-

in-Publication Data appear

on the last printed page of

this book.

In memoriam
Charles Péguy
1873–1914
and
Francis J. Fagan
1907–1980

# Contents

Acknowledgments

THIS VOLUME is the result of the "Ontologies in Practice" conference hosted by the University of Virginia on September 12–15, 2002. I would like to acknowledge all the folks who have made the "Ontologies in Practice" conference and this volume a reality: Ward Blanton, Christopher W. Haley, Judith Revel, Matteo Mandarini, Rowan Williams, David Marshall, Lauren Winner, Melissa Herwaldt Riches, Aaron Riches, Conor Cunningham, Molly Bosscher Davis, Steven L. Jones, Pamela D. H. Cochran, Helen Ashley, Libby Moore Slade, Peter Slade, Tom Higgens, Matthew Gibson, Melissa S. Linton, Doug Burgess, Basit Koshul, Auroie Portet, Steven M. Neumeister, and Frances Garrett. I would especially like to acknowledge Rocco Gangle's invaluable encouragement and labors in helping organize and executing many aspects of the conference.

Thanks to the participants in the conference, Willis Jenkins, Justin Holcomb, Peter Ochs, Phillip Blond, Mary-Jane Rubenstein, Jamie K. A. Smith, Charles Mathewes, Jason Smick, Rocco Gangle, Eleanor Kaufman, Duane Barron, Brian Britt, Alex Gil, Janell Watson, Regina Schwartz, Antonio Negri, John Milbank, Joseph Prabhu, Abdulaziz Sachedina, Ruth Groenhout, Mohammad Azadpur, Kenneth Surin, Michael Hardt, and Slavoj Žižek.

I would like to especially acknowledge those organizations who generously gave financial and material support to the conference. Charles Marsh of the Project on Lived Theology; Skip Burzumato of the Center for Christian Study; Deans Duane Osheim and Peter Brunjes of the University of Virginia Graduate School of Arts and Sciences; Dean Edward Ayers and Heidi Winter of the University of Virginia School of Arts and Sciences; Robert Jackson; Vice-President's Office of Students' Affairs at the University of Virginia; Gene Block, University of Virginia Vice-President and Provost, and Laura Hawthorne of the Provost's Office; President of the University of Virginia, John Casteen III; the Center on Religion and Democracy; the University of Virginia Graduate Student Council; Nicholas Issac Graber-Grace, Laurel Anne Woodworth, and Lela A. Graham of Critical Mass; Michael Levenson and June Webb of the University of English department; and finally, Harry Gamble, Linda Hunt, and Laura Troutman of the Religious Studies department.

Special thanks is owed to the Centre of Theology and Philosophy at the University of Nottingham.

I would like to express appreciation to my fellow editors John Milbank and Slavoj Žižek for their help, support, and above all humor throughout all phases of this project. They have made this project a sheer delight. And finally, I would like to thank Molly Bosscher Davis for her help and support with this project and beyond. — CRESTON DAVIS

The editors and publisher also wish to thank the following for permission to reprint previously published material.

Katie Halliday of Taylor and Francis Ltd., kindly allowed us to reprint Eleanor Kaufman's article, "'To Cut Too Deeply and Not Enough': Violence and the Incorporeal," originally published in *Parallax* 9 (2003): 14–27; www.tandf.co.uk/journals.

Robert E. Wood, editor of the *American Catholic Philosophical Quarterly*, granted permission to reprint Conor Cunningham's article, "Lacan, Philosophy's difference, and Creation From No One" originally published in *American Catholic Philosophical Quarterly* 78, no. 3 (summer 2004): 445–479.

Catherine Pickstock's "Modernity and Scholasticism: A Critique of Recent Invocations of Univocity," first appeared in *Antonianum* LXXVII (2003): 3–46. Reprint permission was kindly granted by Lluis Oviedo.

Theology and the Political

*Rowan Williams* | Introducing the Debate:
Theology and the Political

UNDERLYING ALL THE very varied essays in this volume is a set of issues about how we understand human action. And what the essays have in common, I believe, is a conviction that the fundamental requirement of a politics worth the name is that we have an account of human action that decisively marks its distance from assumptions about action as the successful assertion of will. If there is no hinterland to human acting except the contest of private and momentary desire, meaningful action is successful action, an event in which a particular will has imprinted its agenda on the "external" world. Or, in plainer terms, meaning is power; Thrasymachus in the *Republic* was right, and any discourse of justice is illusory.

Some contemporary voices appear to be content with something very like this. What several of the voices here represented argue, implicitly or explicitly, is that this is to subvert the very idea of intelligible action—and that this is not a simply intellectual problem (in the restricted sense that the word *intellectual* sadly has these days). Meaningful action is action that is capable of contributing to a system of communication, to symbolic exchange. If meaningful action is successful action, it is precisely action that does not invite response (and thus potentially critique, revision, the revisiting of the terms of original engagement); it has succeeded in setting the terms of future act and discourse in accordance with a specific disposition of will. It does not require understanding.

When we act intelligibly—and this is common ground for Augustine, Hegel, Marx, and a good many equally unlikely bedfellows—we expose ourselves to the process of language. That is to say, we claim to have offered a *representation* of something prior in such a way as to introduce that prior and shaping reality into a continuing narrative of uncovering through response and question. I do something that I believe meaningful, and so I state my faith that what molds that action and constitutes its intelligible content (i.e., what can be communicated and can mold further action) is capable of reproduction in different form—sufficiently different to guarantee that another action is not repetition but further unfolding through representation of a content not exhausted by my action and determination alone. Common ground for Augustine, Hegel, and Marx, I suggested. For Augustine because human beings are created in the image of God, driven by desire of God to seek God in all things and not to rest in any finite object; language becomes a system of signs reinforcing the awareness of lack that stands at the heart of all human identity and thus moves us through an endless series of displacements and provisional understanding as we grow corporately in wisdom. For Hegel, because the act of thinking is itself an advance into the position that must be negated in order for universal intelligibility to take up and supersede the individual assertion of a view or perspective. For Marx, because the only way to a universal ownership of what is accorded value—and thus the only way to truthful apprehension of the world, as opposed to the slavery self-created by the unconscious inhabitants of a society dominated by a single class—is by the historical conflict in which the means of production are made to be no longer a possession and a tool of unilateral power for some over others.

It would not be easy to make a single vision out of these three (and all the others who are discussed here), and such is not the purpose of these essays. I read them as offering a concentrated attack on a whole variety of ways in which the idea of meaningful action as successful assertion hides in philosophies, theologies, and social projects—how the implicit nihilism of this idea pervades so much of modernity and the menagerie of intellectual styles known as postmodernity. To the extent that popular liberal and pluralist thought assumes with blithe unawareness a basic model of meaningful action in terms of assertion, it assumes a final social unintelligibility, an ultimate inability to make sense of each other's actions (which involves understanding so as to query and reexpress)—and thus raises the specter of the purest fascism, an uncriticizable exercise of social power in the name of a supposed corporate assertion.

One of the things that this book suggests in place of this barbarism could be summed up as a conviction about action as *testimony* (I think especially of some of Ricoeur's work here, as well as Merleau-Ponty's). Action witnesses, makes present in representation, and invites engagement with structures that have nothing to do with will; action is most intelligible in this perspective when least assertive in the crude sense, most meaningful when least concerned to dominate. For the religious philosopher, there are numerous categories available—especially martyrdom as the most distinctive instance of witness by the opposite of success. For the Christian believer, the core conviction is that the most densely "intelligible" action in the world's history, the event that most radically provokes new language, new possibilities, comprehensive self-questioning or *metanoia*, is the self-exposure of Jesus Christ to death at the hands of political and religious meaning makers. By no means all the writers here represented subscribe to religious or Christian allegiance, but the question all address is one that, properly grasped, insists upon a conversation with theology—theology as the discipline that follows what is claimed as the supreme act of testimony, and thus the supremely generative and revisionary act of all human history: the cross for Christians, the gift of Torah and communal identity for Judaism. Theology occurs, for Christians and in some sense for Jews also, in the wake of certain absences of what ordinarily passes for meaning (remember the unrepresentable nature of the Jewish God), absences that for complex reasons produce distinctive stagings of social possibility and linguistic revolutions. Theology claims that what intelligible action is "after" is divine action whose gratuitousness (or love) motivates and activates an unlimited process of representation without simple repetition (and thus posits irreducible human and other diversities).

This "new debate" is inescapable if we are determined to avoid the end of intelligibility. That end is not the inauguration of a *jouissant* pluralism but something more sinister, all the more so for being clothed in liberal dress. If this book stirs some recognition of just how "late" the late modern and late capitalist world has become in the countdown to social dissolution and the triumph of infinite exchangeability and timeless, atomized desire, it will have performed a function we need to see as necessary.

PART I | Revolution and
Theological Difference

*Terry Eagleton*  |  Tragedy and Revolution

OEDIPUS, BROKEN AND BLIND, stands before Colonus. As he once gave an answer to the Sphinx, his presence now poses a question to the nearby city of Athens. Is it to gather this unclean thing to its heart, or cast it out as so much garbage? Just as Oedipus himself, solver of riddles, detected the image of humanity—itself the ultimate conundrum—in the Sphinx's portrait of a monster with four legs, two legs, and then three, so Athens is being asked to recognize the image of the human in this monstrosity at its gates. Four, two, and three in one is the enigma of identity and difference, the garblings and doublings of incest, the scrambling of subject positions, the giddy exchange of symbolic roles. Oedipus is the *pharmakos* at the threshold, the impossible homeopathy of poison and cure. He is both guilt and innocence, king and beggar, stranger and brother. Indeed, the very tragic theater in which he appears, according to its earliest theorist, is itself a kind of homeopathy, a catharsis in which we take a pinch of the noxious ingredients of pity and fear in order to purge ourselves of these poisons. Now, however, Oedipus must wait while Theseus, ruler of Athens, weighs the perils of excluding the sacred against the dangers of assimilating the polluted. Since the *pharmakos* is both in one, holy and defiled, contradiction incarnate, this is scarcely a simple choice.[1]

Tragedy is said to be about pity and fear, and pity and fear are a question of identity and alterity. We can, it would seem, pity only what is akin to us, just as we fear what is strange. Both are political notions: pity enjoyably cements the social bond from the inside, while fear austerely reinforces it against external threats and is what we feel in the presence of authority.

For another vein of aesthetics, this sadomasochistic fusion of pleasure and horror, the daunting delights of an infinite sovereignty, goes by the name of the sublime. Only if our imaginary social bonds are founded upon the Real, upon a certain horror at the heart of the social itself, will they prove sufficiently durable. Only if the Furies are installed within the city-state itself will it be secure—which is to say that only if the terrorism of the law is turned inward as well as outward, to become domesticated as hegemony as well as armed and helmeted as military might, will the social contract stand. Oedipus himself will end up as such a tutelary power, his death made fruitful for the future life of the polis, so that his death-in-life existence, once embraced by the city, will prove fertile for its flourishing. "Surely a just God's hand will raise him up again," exclaim the Chorus.

A tragedy like that of Oedipus, however, also turns Aristotle's logic of pity and fear on its head, scrambling its dichotomies by showing us that nothing is more fearful and opaque than ourselves and those akin to us, and nothing more pitiable than a humanity deformed alarmingly out of recognition. It is, indeed, only when we are "out" of recognition that we are fully "in" it. Confronted with the parricidal Oedipus, the demented Lear, or the tortured Christ, we are asked to couple these classical responses to tragedy together and come to pity what we fear. It is not just a matter of pitying whatever is still human in these poignant figures, whatever residual humanity has survived their monstrosity, but of feeling for them in that very deformity, grasping them as most human when unhuman, and hence of seeing them in the Real rather than the Imaginary. It is to perceive that what is most intimately human about them is also what is most frightful to gaze upon, and that no power can enable us to look upon them and live but an answering inhumanity in ourselves. The moment of recognition of this more-and-less-than-human in ourselves is the moment traditionally known as repentance.

These, then, are not men travestied, dehumanized, violently disfigured, but signs of the violent disfiguration that is humanity itself. In inviting the vagrant Oedipus into the city, Theseus is not simply divining a blessing within an apparent curse but recognizing in this beggarly sovereign an image of the monstrosity of himself and his city. When it comes to human affairs, the aberrant is the normative. What more graphic image of power than the powerless, since tyrant and vagrant are both beyond the law? And what could more forcefully testify to the failure of power, and so to its ironic kinship with the dispossessed, than the flayed, butchered bodies of its victims?

"I come to offer you a gift—my tortured body—a sorry sight," Oedipus tells Theseus, "But there is value in it more than beauty." Truth is unaesthetic, a mangled body; it reminds us of beauty only by negation. The cynic is the one for whom value is so much shit, whereas it is in shit—the detritus of a repressive social order—that the revolutionary finds value. The Fool is a figure who hovers somewhere between the two. Sophocles's meditation on Oedipus broods upon impossible arithmetical calculations—on incestuous paradoxes of two or more in one, of one plus one making four or more, on defacements and illegibilities at the heart of the symbolic order. Incest lays bare the guilty secret of that order, which is that all of its places must be arbitrarily interchangeable simply for it to function. Like any structure, the price it pays for working all by itself is the perpetual possibility of transgression, which is to say the possibility of not being itself at all. Incest is an abomination that confounds essential boundaries and obscenely commingles distinct categories; yet since desire itself does nothing less, the vilified, accursed Oedipus, as Freud will later instruct us, is simply representative of the way of the world, the social unconscious, the truth that transgression is our routine business. Incest is the Real of the symbolic order, to which Sophocles's art will place us in an imaginary relation.

Incest presses through the logic of the symbolic order to the point of a surreal, scandalous deconstruction, which is at once a garbling of all orthodox social relations and the unspeakable truth of them. If you are to be free to mutate the roles of, say, husband and father, then there is nothing in the structural grammar of the symbolic order itself to rule out the hybridity of being your own mother's spouse. Comedy seizes on this recognition as well, noting as it does that desire is no respecter of rank or difference and playing off our anxiety that social order will thereby be undermined against our deliciously vindictive desire for exactly that. Shakespeare's *King Lear*, in a way not entirely removed from Sophocles, rings changes on the tragic calculus of more, less, all, something and nothing, of ciphers, creative surpluses, and destructive superfluities, notions that resound through the poetry and the play just as they run as a riddling subtext beneath some of Shakespeare's other works.

Incest, monstrosity, is the place where exact calculations and distinctions break down, and so also is the wager of Theseus as he stands before this besmirched parody of his own kingship. Oedipus himself knows that an unspeakable power for good will flow from welcoming the immigrant, embracing the excremental remainder, assimilating into the political order the sign of its own nonidentity. To do this, however, is not to be "inclusive" (that magical postmodern word) but to encompass what that order is forced to exclude simply to be itself and thus to transform it beyond recognition. The astonishing irony of class society is that this excluded remnant is not some postmodern margin or minority, but the actual majority. This power for good, or magnificent flourishing of life, is known as sacrifice, the dialectical movement by which the very dissolution of the unclean thing becomes fertile and life-bearing. In modern political parlance, it goes by the name of revolution—the project, in Marx's words, of a class which is the dissolution of all classes, a total loss of humanity in the name of a total gain of one, and which thus represents in its very decomposition the shape of the classless future.

To acknowledge this thing of darkness as one's own, whatever name it happens to go under, is to throw the projective act of scapegoating into reverse, confessing that this savage travesty of humanity was cast out of the city not because it was alien but because it was far too familiar. A similar interplay of the alien and overintimate characterizes the act of incest. The scapegoat or *pharmakos* must be shifted from the metonymic to the metaphorical register—from being that fragment of the polis on which the people project their crime and guilt, driving it out and thereby disavowing it, to being the mirror in which they can recognize themselves for the monsters that they are ("Man" is the answer to the Sphinx's riddle), and by that recognition transcend their own deformity.

The scapegoat wins our compassion because it is the terrifying Real in the humanizing shape of suffering flesh and blood. But it is also suffering flesh and blood *as* the Real, as dehumanized and atrociously disfigured, and thus as placing so implacably anonymous a demand on our own humanity that only that within ourselves which is beyond the personal—whatever it is that lies nonsubjectively at the root of our subjectivity, rather than simply falls within its frame—can hope to answer to it at all adequately. Only the ruthless abstraction of love, which is no respecter of persons because it attends equally to the needs of any old person, could suffice to repair the ravages of a desire that is similarly indifferent to individuals in its impeccably egalitarian ambition to maim and madden them all. Only a Real that was beyond humanity, and so terrible but at the same time friendly to humanity, could prove sufficient.

Love differs in this sense from friendship, or indeed from the "romantic" version of itself, both of which are nothing if not particular. But this is not to contrast an abstract universalism with a sensuous specificity, in that hoariest of all antitheses to which the solution (we know it even before the words are out) is art. For one thing, particularism in these postmodern times is itself a full-bloodedly universal creed, just as nationalism is a thoroughly international phenomenon, and a highly parochial view of the world has come to be known as globalization. A universalized particularism is postmodernism's goal, whereas justice and charity involve that very different condition, a particularized universalism.

This is universal insofar as everyone has a claim to love and justice, but this claim is empty unless it is this or that individual's uniquely particular being that is granted recognition, and his or her irreducibly specific need attended to. Every individuality must be acknowledged, regardless of whose individuality it is. As far as that goes, any old individuality will do. When it comes to difference, one has to be grandly indifferent. This is why neither early-bourgeois abstraction nor late-bourgeois particularism will do—a traditional enough socialist case, to be sure, since socialism has insisted all along that the universal commonwealth must be constructed in and through the developed, uniquely individual powers and capacities bequeathed to us as an opulent heritage by middle-class society. One can tell the difference between a Marxist and a postmodernist by the former's unabashed admiration for the bourgeoisie.

In any case, there can surely be no genuine opening of our eyes to the particular, no grasping the situation as it actually is in all its densely determinate reality, which does not at some level implicate a kind of infinity—whether in the Christian sense that this hard-headed realism, pace the bankers and burghers, is the most difficult thing in the world and possible only by the power of grace (a novel variant on the ancient theme that virtue and knowledge have an internal bond), or simply as a kind of Kierkegaardian marveling at the fact that things are eternally given as what they are—that in purely gratuitous style God fashioned you and not someone else. In this perspective, individuality is the claim of the infinite on the finite, the mind-shaking mystery of the uniquely self-identical. To see eternity in a grain of sand is to see a grain of sand, not to see through it. Being is the way to see beings, not an entity to be seen in itself. To discern the workings of a nonsubjective Real in the subject is to see the subject as it is, constituted to its core by what is unnervingly alien to it. To understand political oppression is to grasp that this particular group of men and women is what it uniquely is exactly by virtue of its place in some more universal context. To say that those with freckles or ponytails are not oppressed as such is to say that their distinctive features can be understood well enough without recourse to such a global setting.

To return to the scapegoat: sacrifice, pace the right-thinking liberal, is not an evil to be kept to a minimum but an action that grows more beneficent the more it is universalized. For sacrifice to be general and reciprocal is just what a communist ethics urges. It is for each to find his or her life in being the means of life for others, to adapt the language of *The Communist Manifesto* a little. Shakespeare's *Measure for Measure* recognizes that a reciprocal scapegoating and condemnation can be flipped over at a stroke, with no momentous alteration of structure, into a community of forgiveness—induced, as it were, to cancel all the way through, as a futile round of tit-for-tat or moral exchange-value gives way to a mutual forbearance. Sacrifice is the authentic alternative to the bogus ruling-class conspiracy of pity and fear, by which an imaginary, endlessly circular sympathy for those identifiably of one's own kind (one that in fact depends on their abstract exchangeability) is buttressed by the intimidatory terrors of the Real.

Sacrifice, seen as the inner structure of authentic social relations, replaces fear of the death-dealing alien with the more fruitful death of the act of self-giving. Only on a universal "death" of that kind can a community of the living be durably founded. Such a death retains all the uncanny force of the Real, in contrast to the liberal humanist illusion that the social bond can be cemented by sympathy alone, but at the same time it helps to unburden the Real of its terrors. Death is now in the service of life, as the very form of an emancipated sociality, rather than life pressed into the service of a deathly annihilation. We observe the latter in the unstaunchable capitalist will, which can conceive of nothing more vigorous, dynamic and bouncily robust than itself, and which would be outraged to be informed that it is in reality a form of ascetic otherworldliness.

"Am I made a man in the hour when I cease to be?" Oedipus cries, pondering the tragic or revolutionary reversal by which genuine power can spring only from humanity's embrace of its own shitlike negativity. Only less can become more; only humanity at its nadir can be redeemed, since if what is redeemed is not the worst then it would not be a question of redemption. This is why the dispossessed are the sign of the future, a negative image of utopia. They testify to that future simply by what they are and so stay faithful to the ban on fashioning graven images of it, manufacturing blueprints, idols, and fetishes. "Nothing will come of nothing," Lear warns Cordelia, but the truth turns out to be just the opposite. In the arithmetic of redemption, two negatives make a positive: only by knowing that you are nothing, like the Fool, redoubling your negativity in ironic self-awareness, can you achieve an ironic edge over the fools who believe themselves to be boundless. Only by tracing the limits of one's finitude from the inside can one transcend it. Pace the paranoid Lear, something will come *only* from nothing, a founded identity spring only from an openness to death and destitution; but this truth is so terrible that it proves hard to survive it, so that Lear has no sooner passed from the illusory nothingness of "all" to a lowly but determinate "something" than he passes into nothingness once more.

It would be a mere inversion of this process to see the dispossessed as passing *tout court* from nothingness to power. "We once were naught, we shall be all," chant the proletariat in the *Internationale*—but there can be no authentic revolution if the "all" in question is simply what you lacked when you were naught. It is a question not just of restoring Oedipus to his king-ship, but of his transcending this status to achieve a form of sovereignty that, like Jesus's carnivalesque, mock-heroic entry into Jerusalem, transforms the very meaning of the term. Had Lear struggled through, this would no doubt have been the measure of his achievement as well. The revolutionary pas-sage from naught to all, like that from all to naught, involves a change in the meaning of the terms themselves, so that the power of the proletariat is not of the same species as the power that it overthrows. Lenin makes the point in *The State and Revolution* by insisting that what is at stake in the workers' struggle is not a change of state power but a transfiguration of the state itself.

It is not just a matter of appropriating an existing power and turning it to new ends, but neither is it a matter of disclaiming power altogether. Only the privileged liberal can afford to do that. Or, indeed, the privileged Lear of the play's first scene, who imagines in his megalomaniac fashion that he can divest himself of his sovereignty while remaining untouched in his au-thority. It is rather that the power that has passed through weakness is not one of substance with the power that thrust it there. The signifier "power" conceals a change in substance; hence the difference between a superstitious view of sacrifice and a revolutionary one. In the former case, you consume the flesh of the sacrificial victim in order to brim yourself full of its mysteri-ous strength, drawing life directly from its death. In the latter case, what you identify with (in the case of the Christian Eucharist, by literally absorbing it into your flesh as nourishment) is the transfigurative power of the victim's very weakness, the scapegoat of living death, not as a creature slain in order that you may hijack its vital force and live more vigorously at its expense. There is no simple passage from death to life here, but rather a movement from a living death (that of the destitute, the scapegoat) to a life that can flourish all the more richly because it has absorbed this death into itself in the form of an abiding awareness of human frailty, neediness and dependency. Only the political action that maintains this fidelity to failure can bear fruit. Only in the knowledge that failure is definitive of us can we succeed.

In the tragic calculus of all, something, and nothing, there can be no such thing as a global identity. They told me I was everything, the repentant Lear reflects bitterly, but it was false: "I am not ague-proof." What has forced him into a sense of finitude is the fragility of the body. Power can wreak the dam-age it does because it is bodiless, swaddled from material need by a thick skin of property and privilege. When we are out of our senses, we are out of our mind. Now Lear has to "see feelingly," think with the body, just as the blinded Gloucester must smell his way to Dover. One cannot be human without overreaching the body (hubris is what makes us human), yet this is also the source of our inhumanity. The contradictions of an Oedipus, who like the rest of us has knowledge only by virtue of the flaw that blinds him to the secret sources of his own flesh, come to a head in our own day in the military generals who can bomb at will because they are too remote to smell the burning flesh of their victims. But to speak of original sin as *felix culpa* is to remind ourselves that this blind spot is also the source of our creativity, as Oedipus or Gloucester can see only when they are eyeless.

A global identity of the kind the United States is intent on achieving today is an oxymoron, since there are none so blind as those who see only themselves. The most narcissistic nation is the one with its gunboats in every continent. You cannot roll over difference in the name of securing your identity, since in doing so you scupper the very conditions of identity itself. Like Oedipus, the West ends up blinded by an enormous knowledge, undone by its own forensic powers. Nothing more graphically illustrates this paradox than its confrontation with Islamic fundamentalism, in which one crazed textual literalness (Texan) encounters another (Taliban). The less the West is able to decipher its own bloodstained image in the monstrosity of terrorism, to discern the fruits of its own political actions in this festering despair, the more it can complacently define terrorism as absolute otherness; but the more it does this, the more justified it feels in suppressing the liberties and violating the rights of its own citizenry, thereby losing grip of its own dog-eared liberal-democratic identity and turning into an image of what it opposes, which, one need hardly add, is exactly what its opponents hope to achieve. What swifter way of forcing the West once more into fascism than driving it to defend its democratic freedoms?

Yet terrorism is far from absolutely other. Like most moral obscenities, it begins at home. As a self-conscious cult of political violence, a specialized form of politics all of its own rather than just the kind of common ravaging and plundering that runs back into the mists of time, terrorism is a thoroughly modern phenomenon, one which comes to birth at the origin of European middle-period modernity, the French Revolution. For Hegel, that revolution was the triumph of absolute freedom, or "freedom in a void," as he scathingly called it. It was the very epitome of bourgeois liberty — the fantasy of a freedom so utterly absolved of constraint that it could not even bear to be restricted by itself and thus turned logically to devouring itself once it had consumed its enemies.

Such liberty is bound to be self-destructive because it harbors a virulent hatred of material limit and so cannot tolerate even its own concrete self-realization. The force that drives this most crassly materialist of all social order is secretly antimaterialist, horrified by the unfinishedness and impurity of matter, enraptured by annihilation. It is, in a word, the death drive, a ferociously pure idealism in love only with itself, which accumulates for the sake of the obscene pleasure of voiding and negating, and which is known admiringly by Western ideology as the all-affirmative will. Bourgeois society itself, Hegel recognizes, is the ultimate anarchist, the very figure of what it fears. The destruction form it protects itself springs straight from its heart. This is literally so today, when Islamic terrorism represents a Western violence come home to roost, the familiar reimagined as the abominable and outlandish, market forces reconfigured as the monstrous.

Tragic or revolutionary: the terms are more usually contrasted than coupled. For tragedy is supposed to be the most patrician of all the art forms, heroic and high-minded, more preoccupied with the death of princes than with anything as drably quotidian as car smashes or concentration camps. The aesthetics of tragedy are seized less by human suffering than by its sublime transcendence. For this cadet-corps ideology, only *affirmative* suffering passes muster as the genuine tragic article, as opposed to the merely miserable or drearily dejected. Only that anguish which is exultant and auratic need apply for tragic status, just as only a humor that steers clear of belly laughs may qualify for classical French theater. No artistic form, at least according to its conservative champions, is more fastidiously pure, rank-conscious, remorselessly idealist, or jealous of its honor. Tragedy is life-enhancing rather than dispirited — a quality that proves precious to those ruling classes for whom pessimism is somehow subversive. In few places has this been truer than in the United States, that profoundly antitragic culture (though the source, so to speak, of tragedy in others) whose ideological orthodoxy regards skepticism as a thought crime and negativity as unpatriotic.

The exaltation of suffering in much classical tragic theory is at root a device for disavowing it. What it refuses to countenance is that tragedy, so to speak, is itself tragic. It is indeed true, as Yeats observes, that nothing can be sole or whole that has not been rent; but one might at least have the decency to add, in order to distinguish this Christian and Marxist orthodoxy from the Boy Scout syndrome, that it would be far preferable if this were not the case. If tragedy is a kind of value, then it is the kind of value we could do without, rather as it is a crying shame that we ever had to have anything called socialism. What we have in the theory of tragedy is for the most part an ideology, which is thus exactly the opposite of what is taking place in *Oedipus, Lear*, or *Death of a Salesman*. It is, moreover, for the most part a sort of religious ideology, in all the most objectionable senses of the word.

It is not only the modern age that makes an ideology out of tragedy. As a state apparatus, tragic art was harnessed to political dominion from the outset. For Aristotle's *Poetics*, it performs the politically vital service of draining off from the polis a perilous surplus of pity and fear, both socially enfeebling emotions. It is a kind of public therapy for a citizenry in danger of emotional flabbiness. The anti-ideological version of this is something like the crucifixion of Jesus, that sublime tragic scenario in which it is neither a question of our morbidly indulging nor briskly dispelling our pity and fear, but—absurdly—of the scapegoat himself taking compassion on us and pleading fearfully that the punishment we deserve for this cowardly political murder should not fall on our heads.

The reason Jesus himself gives to get us off the hook is, exactly, our ideological mystification—the fact that we cannot possibly know what we are doing, any more than any historic event can know itself other than in retrospect. By which time, of course, it cannot be undone, so that the knowledge is in a strict sense useless. We live forward and understand backward. Establishing a symbolic solidarity with this kind of scapegoat means accepting his pity by coming to have pity for ourselves, confessing our weakness and thus being freed from guilt. To grasp that this monster is of our own making is not just to acknowledge that it is we who have reduced him to this lamentable condition, but that in doing so we have turned him into a living image of ourselves.

To be able to look upon this frightful image of ourselves and live is to confess that the power by which we have brought the world to such a sorry pass is in fact no genuine power at all, but the reflex of frailty. It is to recognize that aggression, dominion, hatred, and greed have their root in fear. To discern the lineaments of true power in weakness—in the political actions of those who have nothing much left to lose—also involves discerning the pathos and bogusness of the power they challenge, even though it might well end up by blowing us all to pieces. Jesus is the figure of the *anawim*, the destitute or shit of the earth, those whose fate is to be divested even of themselves; but it is not just a question of acknowledging our responsibility for this fate, as class-society might confess in a spasm of self-recrimination that hunger and poverty are its own creations. It is only when we recognize our own countenance, rather than just our own actions, in the disfigured and dispossessed, when we acknowledge that their weakness signifies the fundamental failure of our own power system, that we can shift from liberal guilt to revolutionary politics.

Tragedy in the epoch of modernity has fulfilled rather different ideological functions from those proposed by Aristotle. For one thing, it has acted as a secularized or aestheticized version of theodicy. If tragedy is the art form that plucks affirmation, even joy and ecstasy, from human anguish, then it promises to offer yet another account—this time one conveniently unexplicated, shown rather than said—of the problem of evil. In fact, a great deal of tragic art is either silent on this score, or like much ancient tragedy stubbornly refuses to let the gods off the hook. Far from making suffering seem cosmically explicable, it allows its raw shrieks to resound unredemptively around the stage. It is for the most part tragic theory, not tragic practice, that seeks to reconcile us to our suffering as mysteriously providential, in notable contradiction to the attitude of the New Testament. For the New Testament, it would seem that suffering is an evil that, if it cannot be repaired, is best avoided. If you cannot avoid it, then that is an evil as well—which is not to say that the confrontation may not issue in some good. It is preferable, however, not to have to snatch value from the jaws of pain and heartache if you can conceivably do otherwise. It is only because the world is as oppressive as it is, and will seek to destroy you if you challenge it in the name of justice, that such avoidance is sometimes tragically possible.

For some of its apologists, tragedy is also a displaced form of religion in being a trace of the numinous in a naughty world, a residue of the mysterious, mythological, and metaphysical in a disenchanted age. It can talk of the transcendent without the embarrassment of having to put a name to it, hijack its high-toned glamour while ditching its tedious doctrine. Tragedy is where the gods, blood guilt, cosmic destiny, and the mystery of evil can still find a precarious foothold—and find it, moreover, in yet another ideological function of the tragic, in the form of a critique of modernity as such. Tragedy is the mythology that upbraids a modernity from which myth has been banished. As an aristocrat among art forms, it does what the aesthetic in general accomplishes in the modern period, but in a way that is exalted, writ large, raised to the second power. To claim, as critics frequently do, that tragedy is the most precious of aesthetic forms is really to propose that it is most typical or paradigmatic of the arts in the age of modernity, a distillation of their very essence and function.

In its unfathomable depths and starkly absolutist claims, tragic art is an antidote to the callow rationalism of modern culture, a critique of hubristic Reason. It represents the dark underside of Enlightenment, the obscurely suggestive shadow cast by an excess of light. Its gods, princes, and virile protagonists recall us to a heroic era before we lapsed into the squalor of democracy and the catastrophe of egalitarianism. Tragedy celebrates the sovereignty of power and fate over human agency, unmasking sentimental humanitarianism for the contemptible sham that it is. In disdain of all brittle doctrine of progress, it rubs our noses in the eternally irreparable. No mere medicine could patch up Philoctetes's foot, no social engineering retrieve Phaedra from her doom. Tragedy in this view of it is the most unabashedly

Tory of modes, valuing wisdom over knowledge, eternity over history. In affirming human powers in a way beyond the ken of the petit bourgeois suburban scientists, it also humbles them before some transcendent truth. Man has a dignity beyond the political mob or the scientific laboratory, but one entirely compatible with reverent submission. He is autonomous enough to rebut the scientific determinists, but subject to cosmic law in a way that equally confounds their middle-class colleagues, the liberal individualists.

Indeed, the question of freedom and determinism is another of tragedy's ideological functions, at least in the eyes of the great German theorists of the mode from Hegel and Hölderlin to Schelling and Schlegel.

Tragedy is an aesthetic solution to a philosophical contradiction — to the Kantian dualism of phenomenal determinism and noumenal freedom. Here, perhaps, is one solution to the puzzle of why tragedy, that most absolutist, aristocratic, antireformist of modes, should loom so large in the thinking of a buoyantly progressivist bourgeoisie, if by no means quite so large in its dramatic practice. Why does the topic crop up in the work of one modern European philosopher after another, from Schopenhauer to Sartre? One might do worse than respond that it is an answer (though, once again, more as a showing than a saying) to the problem of how we are apparently at once free and unfree.

Like any interesting philosophical problem, this is not of course in the first place a philosophical problem. It runs right to the heart of a bourgeois social order for which the political realm — one of freedom as a collective self-determination — is at loggerheads with the economic domain, in which we are shuttled around like so many inert bits of matter by unmasterable market forces. A knowledge of necessity is the dream of the human sciences, since then we would be able to calculate our actions more exactly and hence be more free to realize our projects. The fantasy of the stockbroker is to be able to foresee the behavior of others while remaining impenetrably unpredictable himself, appropriating Kant's noumenal realm for himself while consigning his competitors to the phenomenal. Yet such predictive knowledge is also the ruin of freedom, which thrives on the incalculable. This is why the American movie *Minority Report* must finally dismiss such precognition as the enemy of freedom rather than the enablement of it. Freedom and order are not really compatible. The human sciences are necessarily self-undoing, scuppering the very liberty whose conditions they investigate.

One might also post the question of freedom and unfreedom in a familiar Marxist form. Why is it that in these social conditions, our apparently free actions are confiscated from us, congeal into iron laws, and come to confront us in unrecognizable form as an implacable destiny? By what fatal mechanism does freedom warp into the image of its opposite, just as equality veers on its axis to become exploitation? This, to be sure, is scarcely a question peculiar to capitalism, though it is one mightily magnified there. Among other things, it is the cri de coeur of Oedipus himself, who discovers like the rest of us that the other returns an estranging response to the question of who he is. Philippe Lacoue-Labarthe argues that Oedipus, before becoming with Freud the "figure of desire," was the figure of the scientist or philosopher (epistemorphilia can be assumed to unite the two).[2] He is thus, one might claim, the allegorical signifier of the West twice over, first as daylight and then as darkness. Oedipus is knowledge at the end of its tether, the transparently obvious ruin of self-transparency, the starkest possible illumination of the obscurely unfathomable roots of selfhood. It is only after Kant has revealed the contradictions into which human reason falls when it seeks to transgress its own limits that Oedipus, with his hubristic hunger for a knowledge which will finally blind him, stages his reappearance in philosophy, with Hegel, Hölderlin, Schelling, Schlegel, and their confreres.

Yet tragedy is not just a salutary upbraiding of Enlightenment, a matter of traditionalist prudence against an upstart bourgeois eagerness. On the contrary, it is both the realization and the ruin of Enlightenment, which is no doubt one reason why it proves so alluring to a German philosophy as conscious of the baffling of Enlightenment in its national history as of its pressing relevance to it. On this view, tragedy portrays the defeat of the protagonist, crushed by a sublime Reason that brooks no rebellion. Yet in bowing to this Absolute, or indeed in resolutely embracing it in the manner of Shakespeare's Antony or Kleist's Prince Friedrich von Homberg, the tragic protagonist both obediently ratifies that Law and reveals at the same time a freedom that raises him to equality with it—which demonstrates, in fact, that his resolute submission is itself the secret work of the very Law or Reason that seems so oppressive.

If the insurgent hero's Oedipal strike against the name of the father is punished by death and destruction, hence expiating his guilt, it is also what ushers him into mature equality with that Law. His very failure yields us a glimpse of an infinite order of freedom and justice—one that, as in the Kantian sublime, can be illuminated only by negation, in the devouring flames that lay bare the hero's finitude. The power to relinquish one's creaturely existence could only spring from beyond it, so that the hero, as both priest and sacrificial victim, presides over the ritual of his own destruction with an authority that outlives it. The freedom by which he accepts his own finitude disproves it at a stroke. The act of being able to draw a limit to one's power must inevitably be self-undoing. The tragic act is in this sense a performative contradiction, transcending in its very freedom the limit to which it submits. Vulgar determinism is elevated to the rather more august status of providence, and the deepest liberty lies in a knowledge of necessity. The Absolute graciously permits the hero to struggle against his doom and in doing so pays tribute to his freedom. Without transgression, the Law is out of business.

If this promises to resolve the Kantian schism of freedom and determinism, it is because what seems an oppressive fate turns out to be Reason itself in phenomenal disguise, but also because what seems to be submission to this Law is in fact freedom. By choosing the inevitable in a spirit of *amor fati*, running toward one's death (as Shakespeare's Antony vows that he will) as a bridegroom to a lover's bed, one reclaims it for human liberty, making one's destiny one's decision. Nothing more cogently demonstrates your freedom than the act of gratuitously giving it away. Reason, moreover, has always already incorporated the hero's free action into its majestic teleology, and Necessity itself turns out to have the free self-determination of a subject. Tragedy also dismantles the distinction between freedom and necessity in a different sense, by demonstrating, all the way from Antigone to Willy Loman, that the commitments that most deeply constitute the self are not really of the kind it can easily choose. There is an inner as well as an outer necessity, a moral as well as a material destiny, as the ancient Greeks were well aware. There is a sense in which we are most free when we have no choice — when not to do what we must do is to violate the selfhood that is the very source of freedom.

It is not hard to read in this version of tragedy the allegory of a prematurely insurgent bourgeoisie — one conscious of the truth that political absolutism is still too powerful to break, but which can console itself with the knowledge that Reason is secretly on its side and will bring it to fruition in the fullness of time. Schiller's *Don Carlos* ends on just such a note. Neither is it difficult to see in this theory of tragedy a secularized version of the theology of the Crucifixion, to which it is faithful in almost every detail. For Schelling, the paradox of law and liberty is most graphically revealed when the tragic protagonist is an innocent figure who gratuitously embraces guilt and punishment, demonstrating his freedom through the loss of it. Indeed, the oxymoronic figure of the guilty innocent is the very stuff of tragedy from Oedipus onward. Yet it is also possible to decipher in this model of tragedy the dialectical movement by which, for the Georg Lukács of *History and Class Consciousness*, the working class comes to transcend its own commodity-like status in the act of confronting this very degradation, so that only a consciousness which has actively taken on the ultimate status of thinghood or sheer meaningless materiality can redeem that facticity as a general condition. Which is to say, for orthodox Marxist doctrine, that only an immanence can become transcendence.

Scapegoats, blood sacrifice, hubris, the *anawim*: no discourse could be less archaic, no language more insistently relevant to our political world. The postmodern discourse that might find all this a touch mythological or metaphysical is for the same reason embarrassed by talk of revolution. What we face, politically speaking, is a choice between one kind of death-in-life and another. On the one hand, there is a hubristic Western will, a form of "bad" infinity, shimmering with the hectic vitality of the terminally diseased. It is a form of life secretly in love with annihilation, and all that saves it from evil is the fact that it genuinely mistakes this nihilism for energy. Evil is far more clear-eyed about the matter: it knows that the point is to unmask the portentous sham of all apparent vitality by searching out the nothingness at its heart and reveling in it, creating even more of the stuff by destroying for the sheer delight of it. The imperial Western will is the death drive in the guise of the life-giving.

On the other hand, there is the alternative form of death-in-life which is the existence of the dispossessed, who know that only a life which has passed through death, finitude, and failure and continues to nourish these things at its heart has any final chance of flourishing. In the meantime, the West continues to prove incapable of tragedy. It cannot recognize its own visage in the raging fury at its gates. It is unable to decipher the symptoms of weakness and despair in that fury and therefore is capable only of fear rather than pity.

*Notes*

1   I have discussed these questions more fully in *Sweet Violence: The Idea of the Tragic* (Oxford: Oxford University Press, 2003).
2   See Philippe Lacoue-Labarther, "Oedipus as Figure," *Radical Philosophy*, no. 118 (2003): 7–17.

| Creston Davis and | Metanoia: The Theological |
| Patrick Aaron Riches | Praxis of Revolution |

AFTER THE GIVEN FAILURE of Soviet scientific materialism and the seeming triumph of capitalist hegemony, socialism by its own force must (re)turn to the theological. Socialism, as the true and beautiful alternative to capitalist barbarism, must recapture the force of its own political desire. To do so, it must finally and irrevocably jettison its alliance with modernity, progressivism, and atheism. Socialism's theological turn is necessarily the (re)turn to political desire as spontaneous liberation. It is the sanctification of the political body and the redemption of political time.

However, it is not enough simply to show that socialism must abandon its reliance on modernity's negative postulant of being.[1] To accomplish this would only recapitulate the same problematic and thereby destroy the site of a genuinely revolutionary politic. What we here propose is the cultivation of an immanent operation that can enact truth materially. This immanent operation is a political praxis, a kind of revolutionary "Constantinianism."[2] Our argument seeks to recover the intrinsically revolutionary implications of Christianity that have recently attracted the scrutiny of Marxists like Alain Badiou, Slavoj Žižek, Antonio Negri, and others. The horizon of this thesis is indebted therefore to an uncanny realignment. We argue that it is within this realignment that Christianity emerges with an uncompromising theopolitical praxis that outflanks the current liberal deadlock. This operation will show how a Christian revolutionary praxis is irrevocably rooted in being itself and therefore exposes the shortcomings of rival ontological articulations, including the Marxian dialectic. This means that any political praxis that is materially grounded in the name of the Event[3]—as an ontological, universal condition—must be recast as the material intersection of the transcendent with the immanent. The Event cannot be dematerialized: it is neither immanent "myth" nor transcendent History. Rather, the Event is here the kenotic in-breaking of the God-man, the Christ. The Event is the enactment in time of the overpowering and universalizing force of divine gift, perpetually distributed through being itself, and repeated nonidentically yet perfectly in the Mass.

The Event, cast in this light, outwits both the reified Logic of capital and the transcendental nature of idealism. It is the eternal rupture in time and the constitution of all time in the perpetual life of the Logos and the Pneumos through the Incarnation.[4] The rupture in the middle of time, which is the ontological ground of all time and eternity, is the Trinitarian work of the second and third persons. As John Damascene holds, the Spirit proceeds from the Father to rest on the Son.[5] This *rest* of the Pneumos, its alighting on the body of the Logos, is the Incarnational Event. The Pneumos rests on Jesus in Mary's womb, alights on him at his baptism, and raises his body from the dead. In this way the Incarnation enfolds the annunciation, the baptism, and the transfiguration into the singular Event of Resurrection, the Pneumatic work whereby the Spirit gives the Son what the Apostle Paul calls a "spiritual body" (1 Cor. 15:34).[6] Posited in this way, the Event is inescapably ontological—it cannot be limited as "myth" or History because it explodes, by excess, the categories of both. The Event is simultaneously the moment of immanent rupture and the eternity of transcendent fulfillment—it is the creative overdetermination of all material and bodily things. The Event is perpetual. It is replayed in the Pentecostal outpouring whereby the Pneumos alights on the bodies of those faithful to the Event, remaking them into the body of Christ, the Spirit-bearing community of the Church. And the ontological continuation of this rupture in the Event is repeated in the Mass by the consecration (or *epiclesis*) whereby the Pneumos continually descends on the elements, making them *more* than bread and wine, making them the very body and blood of the Logos. The Event is Creation, the Father speaking the Logos and in-breathing the Pneumos. And the Event is the rupture in time, the Incarnation, the Resurrection, and the Consummation of Christ's body in the Church. The Event is the repeated mobilization of matter and bodies as the Logos by the Pneumos. In this way the Church is repeated as the concretization of the Event, as the relationship of God with God-self, overflowing himself and lifting all humanity and the cosmos up into the Trinitarian life through the Event.

This Event sketches a doubling and redoubling of the middle, the *rest*, reconfiguring a noncollapsible relation to beginning and end through itself as middle-time. This is to be contrasted with Gilles Deleuze and Félix Guattari's rhizome, which, for them, "has no beginning or end" and only returns eternally to itself as middle qua middle.[7] In contrast to the rhizome, theological temporality ultimately moves up to the necessity of Incarnation through which revolutionary moments take hold on all levels of reality — stones, trees, animals, and all created matter become self-transcending modalities as the world awakens to, and is completed in, their perfected natures. As Saint Paul writes: "For we know that the whole creation groaneth and travaileth in pain together until now. And not only they, but ourselves also, which have the first fruits of the Spirit, even we ourselves waiting for the adoption, to wit, the redemption of our body" (Rom. 8:22–23). In this instance, the human being (among other beings) moves beyond her or his immanent nature — and this in contradistinction to Deleuze's "desubjectified body."[8] Deleuze writes that we "do not even know what a body can do, we talk about consciousness and spirit and chatter on about it all, but we do not know what a body is capable of, what forces belong to it or what they are preparing for."[9] The theological economy of being-as-gift, however, is a double-divine movement of God, who ruptures the immanent plane by the Logos and fuses it inextricably with transcendence by the Pneumos. This gives meaning beyond knowledge to all that a body can do and identifies the force that belongs to the body in the transcendent movement that alights upon it. This excess is possible because there is always something beyond the existent thing, beyond its apparent givenness. The irruptive and mediating mode of the theurgic Event allows eternity to rest on time (as the Spirit rests on the body of the Son) and so the Event is irreducible to a mode of historical representation that forecloses history within itself. The passing of immanent history — of time that repeats itself in the Nietzschean eternal return — can only relegate the subject to passivity because it cannot produce but only reproduce the already given. This necessarily posits the political as a stasis — unchangeable — and so neutralizes all positive political potentiality.

We propose that the subject, always here a theopolitical revolutionary subject, in order to be, must participate in the pluralization of being. And so the subject, if the subject is to be real, must participate in remaking the present reality beyond what it is, as more than it is, thereby liberating it from its reductive, empirical capture. We will show this first by locating a cosmic mediation that structures the emergent conditions in which the Christian, revolutionary subject takes hold in the world by a Metanoic (re)turn to the Event. This cosmic mediation will necessarily be positioned in the "between" of transcendence and immanence such that both become more than their definable parts. Armed with the beauty of a theopolitical subjectivity, we will, in the second part of the first section, show the severe limitations of Marxian materialism, which far from giving an ontological labor power, actually reproduces capitalist being. Finally, in the second section, we will show how different ontological articulations, equivocal, dialectical, univocal, do not supply the necessary ground for a true political subject to take hold in the world. Here it will be shown that a theological articulation of analogical being gives way to the truth of political life.

### Divine Synthesis, or Metanoia and the Political Praxis

Socialist praxis necessitates the operation of a mediating term among different modes of being. It therefore signals a noncollapsible participatory movement within a cosmic mediation (of the Logos and Pneumos) at all levels of hierarchical being: God, angels, humans, nonrational animals, plants, stones, and all the rest.[10] This metaphysical hierarchy gives actual difference to the cosmos, refusing the banality of secular "equality," which is nothing more than homogeneous reproduction of the commodity form. Because there is real difference and because there is a way of relating all things to everything else through noncollapsible mediation, then a socialist praxis can be seen as a divine, human, constitutive power—desire—expressible within the social plane of creation by fusing the particular human with universal humanity as wrought by the incarnate Logos. This constitutive power refuses every attempt to conceive of humanity as removed from creation and is therefore at odds with secular Christianity and atheistic Marxism. This is to demand that socialism be rooted in an ontology that fuses the revolutionary project to the world. To do this is to finally make revolutionary socialism really materialistic (what Marx never completely accomplished). At the same time it is to restate the position of orthodox Christianity that reads transcendence as grounded in the immanent without remainder, as Logos. To do this is to realize that in Christianity immanence is fully revealed in the Incarnation. To proclaim this afresh is to refuse two atheistic and neutralizing tendencies. The first would trap the transcendent outside the world, in the manner of a Creator who once having made creation could not touch the created work, forcing the creaturely search for the divine to necessarily become a flight from the world. The second tendency is to pantheistically trap God within the immanent, draining the divine of transcendent otherness and so collapsing immanence into itself and destroying the possibility of the immanent being known in terms of any relation that could give it depth. Installing an irreducible mediation between transcendence and immanence lays the groundwork for a political turn that unites being with the subject. It is our claim that this turn is inexhaustively revolutionary, in that it cannot be expressed as Gnostic political pietism, or as violent German idealism, and so guards itself against the tendencies of authoritarianism. Thus, a mediating term necessarily irrupts from an ontological recognition that to heed the divine injunction — "on earth as in heaven" — is to embody the desire to overturn the conditions of an unjust world and to recognize that this ontological desire is an inescapable requirement of desiring the one true God.

To name a mediating term requires first a return to the axiom that expresses the relationship between revelation and revolution as mutually exclusive: revelation is transcendent, whereas revolution is immanent. In both cases the issue is sundered and related to an absolute temporal irruption. Yet this axiomatic polarization of the purely immanent against the purely transcendent cannot really enact the politics of the Mass (or masses), and so cannot fully *turn*. What this axiom expresses is an incompleteness, a short circuit, for it leaves the subject either at the altar rail of the church waiting for the "dismissal" ("Go in peace to love and serve the Lord"), or living in a world sundered from the eucharistic feast.

The question of this chapter, therefore, is: Where is the material continuity between the revelationary and the revolutionary interruptions of time? Our response is that the condition of the Event actually mediates being to beings in three specific and interdependent ways: (1) creational irruption, (2) soteriological irruption, and (3) eschatological irruption. By this logic, the Event is read as that which constitutes, saves, and liberates by the eternal singular/universal Incarnation and Resurrectional interruption of both time (fused to eternity) and matter (infused with Pneumos). Even more, it is to argue for a fulfillment by which the axiom is exploded, as category, in order to accommodate the Event. Beyond revolution as pure immanent interruption and revelation as pure transcendent interruption, there is a third "time" within time. This third "time" alone can give real time beyond the perpetual return to the same, what is expressed in the cry of Ecclesiastes: "I have seen all the works that are done under the sun; and, behold, all *is* vanity and vexation of spirit" (1:14). This temporal structure of the third "time" is taken up within the intertwining of transcendence and immanence, the universal and the particular.

This nondualistic recognition of the Event is practically named *metanoia*, the Greek word for repentance, literally "change of *nomos* [mind/as body]." Theophan the Recluse calls it "a radical change for the better, a sudden change of will, a turning from sin towards God . . . a painful change of will."[11] Metanoia is the total recentering of being by (re)turning to being-as-gift, which is belonging to the Event. The metanoic (re)turn to the Event is the mode whereby the subject is formed, and not the subject alone, but the subject in common faithfulness with the whole community of the Event. It is radical, sudden, painful, and breaks open the self at home with the ego. Here it is useful to invoke the work of the Russian Orthodox theologian Vladimir Lossky, who helps elucidate the nature of the metanoic turn, its materiality, and its personal integrity. In his work *The Mystical Theology of the Eastern Church*, while recounting the stages of divine union as outlined by Isaac the Syrian, Lossky writes of metanoia as "the gateway of grace"[12] — and so a move into the gift of being itself. Metanoia is not a stage left behind, an "event" relegated to passivity by the distance of the past tense, but rather an ontological constitution in the Event itself. And here the Event is that which is eternally realized in the perpetual, non-identical reenactment of Mass. Lossky writes: "It is in fact not a stage, but a condition which must continue permanently." By metanoia, the gift of revelation becomes revolution through a practice of communal forgiveness, which is, in John Milbank's words, "the uninterrupted flow of the one initial Creation."[13] By this move, the Event is repositioned by metanoia as "the gift of time" in time, representing a cosmic-theurgic movement that repeats itself in history as "permanent revolution." Metanoia is henceforth the nonnegative recentering, the absolute (re)turn of all desire to being. As such, metanoia is the ontological (re)turn to the Event as constitutive of eternity and life itself.

The Event is the horizon in which metanoia takes hold. It is the happening by which the subject realizes her/himself as subject. By this operation, the Event short-circuits Louis Althusser's Ideological State Apparatus[14] and the interpolation of the subject by the ideology of Empire, grounding the subject in the real material conditions of being itself. And so metanoia, constituted in the Event, is a direct refusal of empire and the ontological agon that it perpetuates. And this is perfectly uttered by Jesus, when he begins his ministry with the words, "Repent: for the kingdom of heaven is at hand" (Matt. 4:17). Time is here interrupted, the empire of Caesar is revealed as parody, and the true kingdom arrives with the Logos. In the face of this radix (radicality) the only response is metanoic: to repent and believe the royal herald of the True King. Metanoia is thus the recentering of praxis, which in the doing proclaims what Jesus speaks to Pilate before his crucifixion: "My kingdom is not of this world" (John 18:36). By this move, the Holy Fool is installed as the vanguard revolutionary, because the Fool lives already as if the world is turned upside down, as if the empire has no hold on reality.[15] The injunction of the Event stands the world on its head, as Mary proclaims in the *Magnificat*: "He hath put down the mighty from *their* seats, and exalted them of low degree. He hath filled the hungry with good things; and the rich he hath sent empty away" (Luke 1:52–53).

Metanoia is a questioning beyond the stasis of self. Thus any "Christianity" that claims the faith can stand "outside the political," that seeks to squeeze the faith into the "individual" and wants to separate eschatology from the social, cannot claim the Logos in orthodox faithfulness. Any accommodation to the antipolitics of individualism is a secularized perversion of orthodoxy. Salvation is communistic metanoia. It is constituted in the Event as the death of the individual and birth of the member into the body of Christ. This is why Greek Orthodox theologian Christos Yannaras argues that "the greatest heresy of our age is pietism."[16] It is because the pietist seeks salvation for himself or herself, supposing it to be an issue outside the Church, outside the recreation of the cosmos, and so an immaterial issue of individual morality. This liberal heresy, argues Yannaras, "undermines the ontological truth of Church unity and personal communion."[17] Indeed, pietism undermines ontology all together, and so it is more than a disavowal of Christian orthodoxy, it is a turn to a dualistic atheism. In contradistinction, the Church's orthodoxy is necessarily grounded in a communistic ontology, wherein, as the Apostle Paul argues, the turn to God is the action not of an "individual" but of the whole body of the Church through Christ. Paul writes: "As by the offence of one *judgment came* upon all men to condemnation; even so by the righteousness of one the *free gift came* upon all men unto justification of life" (Rom. 5:18). And so Christianity contends that participation in the Godhead is the vocation intended for humanity, and in this way there is, as the Church Fathers maintained, no such thing as an "individual" getting "saved."

However, this is not to say that the universal must overtake the particular person, erasing the particularity of his or her identity. To the contrary, the Event as universal secures and establishes the possibility of the particular because the Event is the constitution of difference itself. Without the universal, the particular (as "individual") would become her or his own subjective universal, which would necessarily foreclose the possibility of particularity and personhood, installing in their place the "individual" as homogeneous universal. It is therefore necessary to secure a universal grounded in a particular of excessive heterogeneity—this is precisely what the Incarnational Event does. Thus Lossky makes clear that for Christianity—where there is no "individual"—there is only the *person*, constituted in a manner likened to Trinitarian hypostases. And so each person shares one common nature and realizes uniqueness in terms of relation and love for the other, in the commune of humanity. Lossky writes: "Here each person exists not by excluding others, not by opposition to the 'Not-I,' but by a refusal to possess the nature for himself."[18] Salvation is thus found only in the Church's reenactment and (re)turn to the universal accomplishment of the Logos, as the Event that enables the Church to participate communally in the life of the Holy Trinity by the descent of the Pneumos.

The gospel—metanoia: the kingdom of heaven is at hand!—is unarguably cast by Paul, in his letters, as a confrontational challenge to the authenticity of Caesar's empire. This is why Milbank writes, "the hypostatic descent of the Spirit inaugurated on earth a counter-polity exercising a counter-sovereignty."[19] Paul's message is that the counterpolity of the Pneumos, founded by the countersovereignty of the Logos, constitutes the Real Kingdom. Paul proclaims that the powers and principalities of this world are no more than a parody of this Real Kingdom, which has arrived in Christ through the Event. Naming the empire a "parody" refuses two positive manners of casting the empire: first, the empire cast as a positive claim that protects its citizens against evil (terrorism, instability, chaos, violence, and such); and second, the positive critical dualism that imagines the empire as the embodiment of a positive evil. For Paul the casting of the empire as parody is done ultimately to outwit the latter, the positive posit of evil (it can thus be read anachronistically in contrast to Kant's "potent principalities"). Now to follow Paul with any conviction is to acknowledge that the Lordship of Jesus Christ is positioned by him as a radical refusal of empire, and a declaration that, by the Event, the empire is nothing more than the ancien régime. When Paul announces the gospel—the "good news"; he is not preaching an esoteric mystery cult or some standard of morality and piety—Paul is making a royal proclamation: Jesus is *Lord*! And this announcement of the Lordship of Christ is simultaneously an announcement that Caesar is not, that Caesar's claim of Lordship is a parody of the truth. Empire is nothing more than legal fiction. When Paul speaks of the Event, he echoes, and so subverts, the language of Roman imperialism.[20] Indeed, the "*evangelion* of Caesar" was a standard jingle of imperial Rome, an ancient Roman version of the American bumper sticker extolling the "Power of Pride." At the time of Paul's letters, the official *evangelion*—the Gospel of Caesar—was the normative and only legal "gospel," the "good news" of the Emperor's self-aggrandizement, the propaganda of empire ideology. And the Lordship Caesar claimed was not neatly confined to a "secular" realm; it was a claim of Lordship that reached for divinity—Caesar was called "son of the gods"—and this *reach* was in a manner akin to Adam's grab for the apple, in order that, as the serpent tells him, "ye shall be as gods" (Gen. 3:5). The "Lord" of the Roman empire thought divinity a thing to be grasped. And what is more, Caesar demanded by force of law and army that every knee bend and every tongue confess that he was Lord. Hence, when Paul sets Christ up as the true Lord, Caesar is revealed as the parodic inversion of Christ on every level. Jesus is the Lord, "Who, being in the form of God, thought it not robbery to be equal with God: But made himself of no reputation, and took upon him the form of a servant" (Phil. 2:6). So Paul's theology of the Event is, in N. T. Wright's words, "overtly counter-imperial theology."[21]

For Paul, metanoia is a speech of rupture that does more than just call empire into question, it names it the ancien régime. The Church is constituted precisely on this political move. The gospel is political subversion. And regaining the bite of this theopolitical subversion is part of our task here. Anyone who reads Paul under the malaise of post-Enlightenment reason, imagining that "politics" can be kept neatly separate from "religion," ought to recall that Paul died a martyr's death, and before he was killed, he was accused of treason for proclaiming the Lordship of Christ. The Roman authorities charged Paul with breaking Roman law, proclaiming a rival lord, doing, as the Acts of the Apostles puts it, "contrary to the decrees of Caesar, saying that there is another king, one Jesus" (17:7). And the politics of Paul's gospel was the normative implication for all of early Christianity, terribly realized in the frequency of Christian martyrdom at the hands of the Roman authorities. Hence in the early Christian community there is not the slightest hint of dualism, no liberal divide between the "political" and the "religious." Against this background Tertullian can write with tremendous force: "The blood of the martyrs is the seeds of the church" (sanguinis Martyrum semen christianorum).[22] The empire was killing Christians because they were political dissidents, who, by constituting themselves in the Event, claimed: "When they [the empire] shall say, Peace and safety; then sudden destruction cometh upon them" (1 Thess. 5:3). Destruction will come on the empire, because the Event has already exposed it as legal fiction. Here we do well to recall the martyrdom of Polycarp, the second-century Bishop of Smyrna, who, for refusing the Lordship of Caesar, was seen as antiempire and so murdered for treason. When Polycarp was called and questioned for the last time before the proconsul, the proconsul urged him to confess Caesar as Lord. But Polycarp refused. He responded to the proconsul that there is only one Lord, Jesus: "if you flatter yourself that I shall swear by the Fortune of Caesar, as you suggest, and if you pretend not to know me, let me frankly tell you: I am a Christian!"[23]

Metanoia, as Christian praxis, is inseparable from declaring the empire dead. And if the empire is dead, then fidelity to it is death itself. The early Anglican Bishop Lancelot Andrewes, in an Ash Wednesday sermon, wrote: "Repentance itself is nothing else but redire ad principia, 'a kind of circling,' to return."[24] Andrewes here forces an ontological operation. Metanoia for him is nothing connected to piety, narrow morality, or a private realm of "religion." Metanoia for Andrewes is a real (re)turn to first principles. As such, the circling to first principles is that action of constitution in the Event, recognizing the Event as the foundation of all eternity and creation—which is tantamount to claiming that all eternity begins in the Event, the Logos, its Incarnation and Resurrection by the Pneumos. The Event is the Logos itself, in its deepest Pneumatic materiality, seen in immanence and transcendence intertwining. As Saint John writes, "That which was from the beginning, which we have heard, which we have seen with our eyes, which we have looked upon, and with our hands have handled, of the Word [Logos] of life" (1 John 1:1). The Event is material, and its materiality, as the rupture in time, is, in fact, the beginning of all materiality and the creation of all things, and so, as Žižek puts it, "the Event emerges *ex nihilo*."[25] Ex nihilo the Event emerges, yet its transcendence is to be touched and handled. Paul writes in his letter to the Colossians, that in the Event of Jesus "is the image of the invisible God, the firstborn of every creature: For by him were all things created" (1:15-16). So the Event of the Logos is the transcendent made immanent, through which all things hidden are revealed, the invisible is manifest in its full brightness by the descent of the Pneumos. This visibility of things otherwise opaque explains why Badiou argues, "For Paul, the Event has not come to prove something; it is pure beginning."[26] In other words, the Event is rupture because the Event is materialized and makes visible the constitution of all things as created and yet more than contingent. The materialization of the cosmos is shot through with a Pneumatic infinity within which the rupture is less a break than a mending of the world in its true unfolding. Hence, the Event is universal, and in the Logos the religious-politico-cosmic is held together in a Pneumatic unity of irreducible multiplicity. In this regard, Lancelot Andrewes could not have been more right: metanoia to the Event is *redire ad principia*, because the Event *is* the first principle that arrives in the middle as the beginning and end of time.

The material Event is the constitution of subjectivity, unveiled in the metanoia to the Man-God. As Badiou argues, "it [the Event] is not a question of knowledge, but of the advent of a subject."[27] So the subject is not only defined by the Event but realizes subjective force and praxis through "fidelity" to the Event. This is why Rowan Williams, commenting on the work of Sergei Bulgakov, writes that God's creation is "a *task* for humankind . . . an environment to be humanized."[28] Humanization begins with the human environment itself, as in the Event humanity sees not only the image of God, but the true image of universal/divinized humanity in Christ. Only in the praxis of the *task* is the subject realized. As the Apostle James writes, "But wilt thou know, O vain man, that faith without works is dead?" (2:20). Subjectivity is therefore constituted by a *faith in task*. As such, fidelity to the Event is a material participation in the ground of our being. The *task* is thus part of the metanoia, it is cooperation in the Event, it is the manifestation of faith—the ontological realization of the subject in (re)turn to the first principle.

The Church, as the community founded by the Event, is the *polis* of which empire is a parody. The ecclesial *task* is continual and total metanoia—"permanent revolution." Far from being immune or outside politics, the Church *is politics itself.* The entire praxis of the Church, centered on the (re)turn to the Event, makes the Church a pilgrim community, continually searching for the ground of its own immanent/transcendent foundation. Milbank writes, "The Church is the brotherhood and sisterhood of the Grail: of those ceaselessly questing for the Eucharist which is the source of the Church, and so perpetually questing for the Church itself."[29] As the Church continually quests for itself, it is in fact questing through creation and the cosmos, for the ground of all beseeching. As such, the Grail is the symbol of compassion and forgiveness, for it requires Love and gives the same. At the heart of the legend is the question of the Grail: *What is your wound?*[30] Likewise this question is at the heart of the Church and it binds together the suffering of its members in Christ's own passion, and particularly to the wound in his side, the wound from which the Church and all creation are born. Hence the search for the Holy Grail is simultaneously *the* material move and *the* ontological (re)turn to the Event. By this ontological-materialism the Event again declares that the empire is the ancien régime.

The operation of a mediating term (a "third") is therefore a praxis of political metanoia. Political metanoia is a religiously revolutionary proclamation that Christ is Lord. Political metanoia will not be trapped in the old agon of socialist revolution, with its prescripted "class conflict as liberation," legitimizing violence and so installing within its political project the seed of nihilism. Political metanoia is a distinctly Christian ontology of revelation and repentance as "permanent revolution," founded in gift and wound. And so it completes and fuses revolution and revelation in the singular and universal materiality of the Pneumos resting on the Logos.

### From Metanoia to the Marxian Immaterial

In *Dialectic of Enlightenment*, Horkheimer and Adorno write that despite the excessive array of seemingly different products and modes of entertainment in late capitalist society, "culture now impresses the same stamp on everything . . . a system which is uniform as a whole and in every part."[31] Beneath the seeming diversity of things in a capitalist economy lies a tendency toward a homogenous mode of reproduction and exchange tied to the commodity and its fetishization. This is the landscape of the disenchanted world, a homogeneous world of seeming difference. As Badiou puts it, "Everything that circulates falls under the unity of a count . . . [or] only what lets itself be counted in this way can circulate."[32] And Georg Lukács writes: "The mathematical analysis of work-processes denotes a break with the organic, irrational and qualitatively determined unity of the product."[33] The object of exchange takes on more and more the characteristics of the instrumentalist gaze, which seeks to subject it always to the encompassability of the quantifiable count. This disenchantment is the indicator of the commodity as the structuring principle of capitalism. In the excessive commodification of late capitalism, Horkheimer and Adorno identify the "culture industry" as that which interpolates all culture and consciousness into the commodity form and its monotonous return of the same, that is, the nondifferent. They write, "The whole world is made to pass through the filter of the culture industry."[34] Here, intoxicated with the malaise of commodification, "real life is becoming indistinguishable from the movies."[35]

The disenchantment of the world observed by Horkheimer and Adorno is the suppression of the bodily and the material beneath the fetishized and reified form of capitalist reality. Yet it would be a mistake to think of the fetishized form as a simple "disenchantment." Rather, it is best viewed as a perverted enchantment, for the culture industry is the mass production of fantastical simulacrums. Indeed, the fetishization of commodities is, as Marx rightly observes, a fantastic and mysterious thing. So, as Graham Ward suggests, the deepening of commodification is an ever-deepening reversal of Max Weber's "disenchantment-by-technological-advancement" — commodity fetishism is "re-enchantment."[36] In the same way as the commodity character of the object of exchange imposes a fantastic meaning over the object, so the culture industry imposes a fantastic reality over the real. In Lacanian terms, the Signifier is over the Signified, S/s — this, in commodified culture, is its fantastic homogeneity. Žižek refers to this enchanting concealment of homogeneous repetition as "Virtual Reality." Under this condition, the simulacrum is consumed and reality is left untouched. Žižek writes, "Virtual Reality simply generalizes this procedure of offering a product deprived of its substance: it provides reality itself deprived of its substance, of the hard resistant kernel of the Real — just as decaffeinated coffee smells and tastes like real coffee without being the real coffee. Virtual Reality is experienced as reality without being so."[37] The commodity thus is a simulacrum, a parody of the real, and so a legal forgery of the material value it embodies — the commodity is the empire. As legal forgery, commodity and empire persist in so far as the law of exchange is obeyed and reproduced. So the commodity's vapid and disembodied reality relies on its fetishized form. And though haunted by its material history, the commodity form of the thing submerges that material history beneath the totalizing yoke of exchange-value. The object of exchange's univocal "Value" as commodity provides the legal fiction for an array of seeming difference in the guise of empty simulacrums.

If there is a single point where Marxian materialism falters, it is in its inability to be *really material*. In fact, we submit that Marxism is not material enough. The subjective world is rightly seen by Marx as perverted and subjected to the law of the commodity form, so here the fissure between the subjective and objective is noticed; yet Marx's analysis strangely resists overcoming the commodity's antimony. Marx, in his effort to rescue the laboring subject from objective enslavement, posits all reality in the power of a subject set *over* the object. He sees the definite social relationship between subjects that assumes the fantastic form of a relation between things and rather crudely posits that the enslavement of the subject can be overcome by standing the commodity relationship on its head. This emphatically *cannot* overcome the subject/object problematic because it does not really seek to do so; and this because, for Marx, the producer is the only proper reality. The immanent world of material things, in Marxian terms, is always, and only, an objectification of the one who produces—which is to place a limit on the material by confining its immanent meaning to production without remainder. This self-enclosed operation consequently forecloses the possibility of transcendent meaning. The object always, by this Marxian scheme, needs to be submitted to its one and univocal real: the subjective producer. But is this not a radical disavowal of the material? Has not the material here been hijacked by an a priori determination of the object from the secret "high ground" of the subject? With this move Marx relegates the object of exchange to absolute passivity. The material is stripped of meaning; the object is divided by separating its existence (as a thing) from its actual mode of production. Hence for Marx the goal of socialist exchange is merely to invert capitalist exchange, to make exchange a social relationship that requires no recourse to objective/material content.

Thus, we argue that a more radical turn from capitalism must seek a deeper materialism—a materialism infused with transcendent meaning, where the Pneumos is understood as resting on and growing from within matter. And this deeper materialism must be rooted in a robust theological ontology. The radical turn (the truly revolutionary turn) is not only a transcendent, nonreductive materialism, but also a turn that perceives the material (in its fullest immanence) as an integrated part of the whole of creation.

Sergei Bulgakov makes the theomaterialist turn. In *Philosophy of Economy* he asserts, "We cannot stop at acknowledging this physical communism of being, for the universe is characterized not only by a general correspondence, a continuity and connectedness of the world of physical matter, but also by a certain relation between living, or organized, matter and nonliving, or dead, matter or, in other words, between organic and inanimate matter."[38] Bulgakov's move helps us to see that a real materialism can be given only in its ontological integrity, as something beyond its own self-subsistent (*causa sui*) actuality. In this manner, he beats Heidegger to the question of an ontological difference that is established between Being and beings. Bulgakov provides the common link that relates *essents* (beings) and *essent* (Being) without collapsing them into each other. Indeed, Bulgakov is able to escape Heidegger's (and later Derrida's) nihilistic error of placing being under erasure, which does not signal an end to metaphysics, but, to the contrary, radically reinvents metaphysics. Bulgakov is able to escape this representational ontology by invoking an analogical difference that explains the relationship among beings by explaining the relationship between God and creation, which unleashes an ineluctable common communion among all things created. Furthermore, this "physical communism of being" rightly refuses the fetishized and disembodied idol and instead seeks to venerate the material as an icon of divine being.

Thus the mode of human production, which Marx prioritizes, needs to be reread as a participatory mode of production within the divine creation of the cosmos. When the cosmos is envisaged as a priori to the mode of human production, then it is simultaneously recast as gift. Knowledge is therefore predicable only in terms of the source of the plenitude of being. Marx, in figuring human production as that action which imbues the material with meaning, imposes a drastic and problematic limit on the material. What the critique of capitalism needs, therefore, is to move more deeply into materialism, and to see all matter as itself created by God and as more than mere contingency or limitation of power.

Marxism's correct critique of the immaterial nature of the commodity is destabilized by its own immanent and delimited ontology, an ontology problematically grounded in a transcendentalist condition. For in fact, Marx's ontology of "species being" is founded on an anthropocentric structure rooted in German idealism. In this regard, his ontology cannot account for an active operation exterior to its own logical determination of what is possible beyond *human* labor power. Therefore the Marxian ontology is not robust enough to complete the transition from commodity culture to a fully materialized socialism.

Thus far we have argued for a revolutionary theopolitical subject beyond Marx. This theopolitical subject does not rely upon a self-enclosed immanent ontology. The theopolitical subject is given life by the Giver of all life. So the subject is already caught up in an infinite production, a process of becoming by the logic and concrete re-creation of the metanoic turn to the Event of the Christ in time. What remains is to positively and rigorously assess the different ontological modes of existence that give rise to a politics of truth.

### The Rise of the Political Subject: Being and Back Again!

Metanoia as a politic is the community of the Grail striving to be in Christ in a manner bringing harmony in *real* noncollapsible difference, difference that unfolds in peace. Therefore metanoia is bound to a modality of being that expresses difference through itself as a way of participating in the paschal vindication of the Event. Metanoia is possible only within a theologic of mediation in which a nonrepresentable — a "third" — is continually alighting. As Hans Urs von Balthasar conceives, "in the Eucharist the hour of Christ's birth remains a permanently present reality"[39] — which sets into play the perpetual potentiality of the metanoic act. In the Eucharist, the continual mediated participation in the Event is actualized, the ontological (re)turn to the Incarnation and Resurrection is made. This is partly to agree and partly to modify Badiou's notion of the Event as *indifferent to difference*, or a benevolence that tolerates difference. It is to agree with Badiou that particularity cannot be determinative, for if it is made so, the particular determinative necessarily tyrannizes all other difference, subjugating or eradicating them before the particular alights (the installation of a particular/preferred difference always risks affecting the collapse of real heterogeneity under a homogenizing particular). But it is also to modify Badiou by stating that the Event constitutes difference beyond the supremacy of any particular difference. The Event therefore favors not particularity but universal difference and must therefore seek a mode of being that can express *difference as the actual condition of material revolution*. This will be done by assessing four different ontological modes of being, beginning with the equivocal.

EQUIVOCAL BEING

To understand the meaning of a term first requires access to a word or "sign" and second requires a thing to which that word refers, a "signified." To be equivocal is to switch meanings so that the voice doubles between two or more meanings that cannot be reduced to a prior unity eliminating the double. In other words, the equivocal voice speaks in a forked-tongued manner, out of both sides of its mouth. Equivocation makes the meaning of a single "sign" mean two things at the same time without any arbitration between the two *different* things that have been forced under the single "sign." Take a famous philosophical example of equivocation, the "dog." Spinoza, describing the equivocal, employs the "dog" with orientation to both the hyperterrestrial star and the terrestrial animal.[40] The same word, "dog," is used, but because there is no community of "meaning" that links the two dogs together through a prior unity, then we say that the term is used equivocally.

When being is spoken equivocally it appears within an ever-shifting horizon of purely repeating-doubling that transcends the ground of self-cause (*causa sui*). This pure repeating-doubling determines itself in a substantive process vis-à-vis a contingency that rests always on something outside itself in order to be. In other words, the equivocal "thing" can never hold itself long enough to be a "thing" and is therefore vulnerable and open to external dominion or determination by an outside force. By this move it is clear that equivocal becoming, as a process of doubling and redoubling, is a radical exterior determination in the form of an indeterminate. What is more, this "determinate-indeterminate" becomes the self-transcending process that folds back into the indeterminate because, as William Desmond states, "the indeterminate continues again and again [in order] to renew itself in both."[41] This "both" — the determinate and the indeterminate — is constituted within a structural indefinite that mediates both poles as the interlude of being. And this interlude of being itself is consequently so concerned to resist the determination of being, as such, that it risks overcoding being in the becoming of pure irruption. But here it cannot be avoided: to posit being as equivocal is to subvert equivocity itself, because equivocity cannot think being in positive terms, terms that hold being long enough for it not to be determined by an outside despotism. For to think equivocally, to mobilize a single signifier in order that two different signifieds be signified at once, paradoxically forces a signifying difference — this signifying difference is the only way both signifieds can be thought at once. And here the equivocal signifying difference requires a move that is already beyond itself. The equivocal mode is therefore necessarily transcended, either by a mode of being that overcomes the "equivocal" name or by an outside "indeterminate determinant" that reiterates the "equivocal" in order to foreclose genuine becoming.

## DIALECTICAL BEING

Dialectical being provides a mode of mediating the difference of two poles in a manner that at first seems to overcome the equivocal aporia through a synthesis of difference. The synthesis of difference, however, is established through an interplay that is shaped, not by difference itself, but by—and only by—the *similitude* of each pole. In this way the difference of beings is subsumed into a homogenized likeness, derived from the sameness of the two poles. And so the dialectic is conditioned by its own internal logic: the search for a synthesis that resolves difference in a synthetic likeness. Thus, the essential difference of each pole in the dialectic is subsumed under the resolving synthesis so that what remains is form without depth. The surface literally overtakes depth in a ghostly fashion. In this way the dialectic risks loosing sight of difference altogether because it can only read difference as the prior condition of synthetic resolution. In this way the dialectical mode is a process of self-mediation and determination, which organizes "difference as sameness" by a process of spacializing the difference of beings by negating the depth of particular difference.

The movement of being under the dialectic is hindered and lapses into a negativity, as can be seen in the thought of Hegel himself. Hegel's dictum —*Omnis determinatio est negation*[42]—sets in motion a logic by which being *cannot be* until it first eliminates its opposite, nonbeing. This is the founding operation of the dialectical mode—it is dialectical because it is premised on the basic movement between opposites, being and nonbeing, immediacy (sense experience) and mediation. And because this mode of being begins on this foundational antagonism—an antagonism it can only overcome through homogenization of difference in the synthesis—it therefore relegates itself (as mode) to the essential negativity of eliminating difference. And so the dialectic seeks to negate whatever difference cannot be assimilated into its own unfolding, imposing a dramatic limit on being as such. The effect of this limit achieves a definite quality of "pure presence" whereby the seeming reality of a thing is determined without remainder. What this move essentially forecloses is the possibility that a thing might have a meaning *beyond* what the dialectic can apprehend. And so the thing, in the dialectical mode, risks being determined by its capacity to be dissolved through the dialectic into something exterior to itself. In this way, being overcomes itself in the dialectical mode through a process of limitation. Yet the dialectical transformation is not from something into something beyond, from one thing into another that is in excess of itself; it is rather a transformation from something into nothing *as* something.[43] Nihilo is here cast as something, not through a positive creation or recreation, but through a negation of difference that is cast as prior to being.

In positing the universal intelligibility of being in the synthetic resolution of difference, the dialectical mode tends toward a plastic venue in which difference is posited as a projection of false reality. Difference is therefore given only as a return to the nondifferent, which mimics the logic Marx identified in the commodity form (as is shown above). For difference in capitalism is always, and only, given in terms of a ghostly pure surface, thoroughly abstracted from corporality. Capitalism, like (or *as*) the dialectic, is abstract exchange that mediates the nondifferent with other forms of the nondifferent. That is to say, being, under the dialectic of capital, is thrown into the hopper of being that mass produces all things in the same terms as everything else. Therefore, the dialectic posit of universal intelligibility cannot finally be founded and trips upon a logical unfolding that repeats itself in absolute unproductive terms—that is, the Žižekian "Real."

What is needed is an ontological understanding of being that produces a positive unfolding—giving and sustaining real difference even as it unfolds and permeates all things. In this exact sense being as production must already and inherently be creating a political horizon, and this for two reasons: first, because production must return something in excess of itself, expressing different and new possibilities; and second, because the power to produce must always be present and available at the fundmental level of life. This positive unfolding, this sense of being as production, provides a capacity for "third"-term mediation, a capacity required for the metanoic (re)turn to first principles. Being needs to be read as unstoppable creation, as that in which infinite power resides. This is Kenneth Surin's notion of "constitutive power," which in his terms, "provides a basis for the construction of solidarities, worlds in which a new kind of politics can find its raison d'etre ... beyond capitalism."[44] This shapes being as unfolding through nonmediated thought. Being and thought here conjoin in such a way that political knowledge and being both pursue a fundamental and ineluctable revolutionary project that is not guilty of relying on ideological faithfulness to an ideal, nor is this process encumbered by the mediation of subjects within the state form.

UNIVOCAL BEING

Here we arrive at a notion of being that is determinative and univocal. Deleuze writes, "Being is Voice that . . . is said in one and the same 'sense' of everything about which it is said."[45] Invoking the univocal, Deleuze, Negri, and Surin unleash a transhistorical desiring of the single voice of being. They here draw on medieval nominalist theology, which holds a conviction of self-coherence for the world (and this in contrast to the scholastic mode, which understands the world as that which cannot finally explain itself). By the univocalist conception of being, desire does not constitute any lack—to move does not require positing a void filled only in the moving, nor does desire require a sedentary law that holds being back. Desire itself produces. In this sense, univocal being expresses a revolutionary effect that enters and disrupts the social fabric. There is a radical overturning of all things, shot through with an absolute immanence that perpetually overturns itself and designates a nomadism of singularities. By the univocalist reading, production and re-production are read as the expression of an ontological power prior to the secondary expression of labor arrested within the capitalist repetition of the nondifferent—that is, literally, the production of nothing. In this manner, as Surin says, "The conditions that enable capital to survive are the selfsame conditions that generate a countervailing constituent power that brings forth the agents and forces needed to resist it."[46] Hence, from the univocal perspective, it is necessary to shift the constitutive power of labor from the capitalist mode of nonproduction to a mode of pure production of real difference.

Surin's point instructively reveals univocity's stress on sameness, a same-ness that appears to unfold in a manner not unlike capitalism's reproduc-tion of nondifference—only for Surin and Negri, being returns nonidenti-cally to its prior cause. This nonidentical return to the prior cause happens primarily because, paradoxically, there is no prior cause—there is only the virtual cause. And so the virtual cause is self-cause, and becoming is the ex-pression of being in radical and substantial difference.[47] An ineluctable force of production is therefore at the heart of univocal being. Difference for Surin and Negri is therefore guaranteed, and it emerges in the world as the world without relying on any indirect route of mediation. Difference, in the singu-lar univocal sense, is absolute, for its being relies on nothing prior to itself.

And yet this univocal turn to nothingness—in which difference *is*—per-forms a reductive operation that, in fact, limits overdetermination to a fini-tude. And by limiting overdetermination in this way, a rigid determination of both being and thought is installed and breaks the essential mediation of being. The process of becoming is here posited as *the mode of being*, as it en-acts a reductivity that ultimately collapses rigid determinations prior to their unfolding. Here it must be stated that there is a clear risk that pure differ-ence in univocal becoming never truly arrives at a process of differentiation at all. Difference is exposed as masking real difference. Further, this limit-ing of overdetermination to the realm of immanent finitude, the insistence that becoming is the singular mode of being, consequently posits a radical in-difference at the heart of being itself. And this in-difference at the heart of Univocal being risks folding back into the prior unity of the One because it is unable to really articulate a productive production. And so univocal being is forced to reproduce the already produced, taking the form of a mechanical austerity that overcodes the connections among things in complacency. It is little wonder that Deleuze and Guattari are obsessed with desiring machines that can only return to a prior identity in a vicious cycle that never produces anything external to its own immanent operation. The difference is really in-different, and the Deleuzian register is relegated to speaking more about physics than being, as Badiou rightly argues.[48] This radical indifference at the core of univocal being is a matter of concern, in that it threatens to disarm the irruption of difference and so yield to the capitalistic axiomatic of identity. Unable to speak of producing outright — creating on its own terms — the univocal position cannot resist empire, cannot name it the ancien régime. Metanoia cannot here take hold, because under the univocal logic the return is necessarily a turn to the same and so is without an instantiation that moves from potentiality into act. For metanoia is itself an ontological discernment and orientation toward an original communication of radical otherness that plurivocally exceeds the terms of the immanent univocal mode.

ANALOGICAL BEING

And thus we are turned to the metaxological.[49] The force of this argument must necessarily merge with being as analogous, as the expression of difference given from the "between," issuing as a mediating "third." Here the mediation of difference and identity, sameness and otherness, can remain committed to the ambiguities of the middle. Being as analogous is often — but in our opinion wrongly — attributed to Aristotle either through his principle of kinesis, *omne quod movetur ab alio movetur* (all that is moved is moved by another),[50] or through his doctrine of analogy that moves between genus and species.[51] And it has been claimed that here, in these two Aristotelian principles, Thomas Aquinas derives his notion of analogical being. However, it cannot be altogether correct to posit that Aristotle's kinesiological principle alone shapes the core of Aquinas's conception of the nature of causality and ontology. Though it is true that Aquinas employs the immanent operation of cause and effect, his causal immanence is always imbued with a Neoplatonic-metaphysical sensibility, to which his commentaries on *Liber de causis*[52] and Dionysius necessarily bear witness.[53] It may need to be restated, however, that this Neoplatonic sensibility complicates how Aquinas uses Aristotle, and therefore Aquinas's kinesiology cannot be simply characterized as "Aristotelean" without doing it certain violence.[54]

For Aquinas, the categorical register of the becoming of being is dominated by an immanent mode of efficient and final causality, such that expressive being remains restricted through an a priori catalog of generic causality. And for him, this generic causality overcodes a definable, or representable, first principle. For Aristotle, on the other hand, the source of being is reserved and unfolds through a strict dualism structured between "every" being and "first" being—the consequences of which create a vacillation of uncertainty that irrupts between a composite substance and its abstracted form. The emergent problematic for Aristotle is therefore an inability to account for that which participates in composite substance—that is, an inability to account for the abstract form without exhausting the meaning of the first principle through material effects. For does not the permanence of corporal first essence (*ousia*) presuppose an unmoved mover, which guarantees materiality in the first place? Aristotle invokes the ousia in order to give conceptual content to the activation of all material substance, yet for him this first essence cannot be known outside a causal modality of vulgar materialist activation. For Aristotle, if there is to be material animation, there must first be a nonmaterial first principle, which cannot be accounted for through itself and so is constituted only by tracing the antecedent cause backward until it deadends in the first uncaused cause. But here Aristotle's causal logic forces its opposite, namely an uncaused first principle that is engulfed in materiality and installed as *the* accounted for, determinant principle. Thus the immanent force of Aristotle's (meta)physics stalls by appealing to a transcendent nonmaterial and representable first principle by which the world apprehends its motion. Thought and substance remain divorced by the switched logic of cause that determines the uncaused. In other words, the problematic of the discord between substance and thought remains for Aristotle exactly because substance can be thought only through a mediated and transcendent mode of causality that turns the first principle of the unmoved mover into a thoroughly representable principle. Hence the transcendent mode that Aristotle appeals to is really a disguised immanent operation of causality: the first cause in Aristotle is in some sense caused by another (the secondary material), and if that is the case, then the first cause is really a caused, uncaused cause. And if the first cause is really a caused, uncaused cause, then Aristotle is more properly located with a univocal mode as *causa sui*. What this amounts to is that Aristotle's ontology activates a quasi-immanent operation, and yet, on a different level, acts as if there is a real break between substance and thought, which can be constituted only within a dialectical horizon.[55]

The basic problematic of the Aristotelian aporia is overcome through the Christian theology of difference (and this in radical contrast to Suarez's "metaphysical" route, which conceives of being as entirely exhausted within the immanent domain of univocity). Establishing difference theologically is establishing difference analogically. It is to speak of difference in the manner of Aquinas, as he writes in the *Summa theologica*: "In analogical terms a word taken in one signification must be placed in the definition of the same word taken in other senses."[56] Thus difference can be in relation without being collapsed into sameness. Here the "to be" is fully determined by the first principle, which itself remains indeterminable—a nonrepresentable object or being grounded not upon that which it creates but on the difference its being makes. For this reason Aquinas considers the name *I AM THAT I AM* [HE WHO IS] the most perfect name for God. Aquinas writes, "this name HE WHO IS [*I AM THAT I AM*], determines no mode of being, but is indeterminate to all; and therefore it denotes the *infinite ocean of substance*."[57] And to know this unrepresentable source, as John Milbank rightly states, it is necessary to have knowledge through "a negative *élan*, and a flight of *eros*,"[58] which links up with the metanoic operation, because this attraction is the (re)turn of desire toward the gift of being, that is, being mediated through gift. Knowledge is therefore like an erotic attraction that resides at the heart of being, always exceeding finitude in divine love. Now knowledge and being as love in real difference merge and (re)turn beyond themselves as *more* than themselves. That is why Žižek is both right and wrong when he suggests that we must always dissolve epistemology and ontology because sundering these always "separate[s] us from the way reality really is."[59] For this fusion, according to Žižek, takes place only within a Hegelian mode that, again, makes what we know—and therefore what *is*—knowable only through a self-mediating constitution of the dialectic that rejects all difference which cannot be subsumed into its own unfolding.

By this move Žižek places himself in contradistinction to Aquinas, for whom the finitude of our natures and limitation of our reason is overcome in love and grace. As Aquinas states, "The knowledge which we have by natural reason contains two things: images derived from the sensible objects; and the natural intelligible light. . . . Now in both of these Human knowledge is assisted by the revelation of grace. For the intellect's natural light is strengthened by the infusion of gratuitous light."[60] And so knowledge is worked out in the light of revelation, as God's gratuitous love/grace. Accordingly, for Aquinas, knowledge can always transcend the limit of knowing the object qua object, and this in contrast to Žižek, who can account for human epistemic limitation only by resting the "incomplete" on the "actualization of the underlying virtual process of Becoming"[61] that remains entirely devoid of a real cause external to itself. And this exposes the contradiction of both the Hegelian and the univocal mode in a single breath. Because there "really" is, for Žižek, an "incompleteness" or finitude for humans, but it relies on the presumption that there is no real contingency of being, that the cause is itself uncaused. That is, for Žižek, the "virtual" self-identical process of becoming is itself an immanent cause. Being is substantial and therefore contingency is cancelled out all the way down, unless, of course, one wishes to install a field of false contingency (i.e., ideology), in which case epistemology is once again sundered from ontology. This is to realize that one cannot arrive at a radical temporal and epistemological contingency from a univocal ontology even if you sneak Hegel in through the back door.

Analogical difference is always material, not in terms of an immanent difference of "things" constituted simply by contrast, but rather in terms of the heterogeneous difference of potentiality in material act. This is because the material object is always *more* than it seems, always in *excess* of immanent difference: it is constituted in the Event and so imbued with transcendent potentiality. Hence the material world, pregnant with the grace of Christ, is transfigurable beyond the bounds that would seem to mark one thing as isolated from another. This means that difference needs to be figured within materialism as the mediation of the immanent and the transcendent, and so indivisible on all levels. Difference now marks a flux wherein things can morph into other things and reconstitute themselves by change and becoming. This is difference beyond stasis, and so a difference in relation to being that outwits the deadlock of equivocity, the sameness of the dialectic and the limit of univocity, in an eschatological process of transfiguration toward the divine. And moreover, this cosmic sense of difference leaves nothing untouched by the transfiguration of a particular, which now must be read as always a transfiguration of the whole of creation. As Athanasius pervasively argues, "For He alone, being Word [Logos] of the Father and above all, was in consequence both able to recreate all, and worthy to suffer on behalf of all. . . . He thus would make death to disappear from [humanity] as utterly as straw from fire."[62] And the perfect example of this recreation of all is the Pentecostal outpouring of the Pneumos, by which the Church is made the body of Christ. This is the coming of peace to all material creation. At the outpouring, all material creation is raised up in God: the soil is told to be glad and rejoice, the animals of the fields are told not to fear, the people are told that God, for their vindication, "will cause to come down for you the rain, the former rain, and the latter rain in the first *month*" (Joel 2:23), that the threshing floor will be full of grain, and "ye shall eat in plenty, and be satisfied" (2:26). It is from within this materialism that God says: "I will pour out my spirit upon all flesh; and your sons and your daughters shall prophesy, your old men shall dream dreams, your young men shall see visions" (2:28). The Pneumos's alighting has constituted the Church and transfigured it into the very body of Christ. This is how revelation is, in the tradition of Christianity, utterly grounded in materialism; and so, difference and revolution must necessarily be materially constituted in the outworking of creation ex nihilo.

Analogical difference therefore remains the only mode of being that arrives at a finitude capable of transcending itself. It alone overcomes the crisis of capitalism, the fissure between subject and object. By this mode of being, the finite is shown to be transcending itself through the noncollapsible difference of divine eros that flows through the world. Being is here read through the unfolding of creation's irreducible difference. As Aquinas argues:

> We must say that the distinction and multitude of things come from the intention of the first agent, who is God. For he brought things into being in order that His goodness might be communicated to creatures, and be communicated by them; and because His goodness could not be adequately represented by one creature alone, He produced many and diverse creatures, that what was wanting to one in the signification of the divine goodness might be supplied by another. . . . Hence the whole universe together participates in divine goodness more perfectly, and signifies it better than any single creature whatever.[63]

This integrity of difference among things—the material form of God's goodness—becomes the very condition of desire, the difference between things participating in the figure of erotic delight. In this way desire is an embodied movement merging in the love of other differences, and so increasing desire all the more. Thus Augustine posits desire as an infinite yearning that cannot be fulfilled or terminated—desire is itself the realization of the unencompassability of divine goodness expressed in the infinite heterogeneity of God's creation. That is why desire is in some sense both always already, and yet not quite ever finally, fulfilled. And the glory of God, now made manifest in the irreducible difference of the world, prompts a movement of longing toward the present, but never finally graspable, love of God-self. This love is never satisfied or attained in the mode of a complacent stasis. It is an ever-present longing, a (re)turn in difference through the world into God. Augustine writes that "whatever else appeals to the mind as being lovable should be directed into that channel into which the whole current of love flows."[64] And this current, or what we are calling desire, is, for Augustine, the infinite bodily unfolding into God-self: "'I am the way, and the truth, and the life'; that is, you are to come through me, to arrive at me, and to remain in me."[65] So from this we can say that God's goodness is signified in the differences of all things that prompt our desire through bodies, matter, the cosmos, and all creation to the perpetual and eternal production of love for Love.

God is love and God is three in one, and all materiality is a participation in this constant yearning of God for God-self. As Rowan Williams writes:

> It is as if the *ser* [essence] of the Godhead is being identified with the formal patter of indwelling itself—not with a "nature" beyond or behind the three, but with the movement of one into another in desire.

In one sense therefore, love itself is the *esencia* of God . . . "a single love unites the three, a love which we may recognize as the divine essence." The love specifically uniting Father and Son is . . . the love that is the "excess" of what each desires in the other.[66]

As such, materiality can be figured as part of both the desire and excess of God's own love. And this desire and excess, realized in creation, makes it possible for God to be both the giver of all and the subject who receives all through the gift of love, the gift by which the world becomes more than its givenness. This structures an ontological politics of power and love that gives way to metanoia and faithfulness to the Event. By the mode of analogical being, transcendence and immanence are shown as expressible only through the irreducible mediation of differences that coexist without collusion. This means that actual immanence has been acknowledged, that materialism has finally been fused to the transcendent and made *infinitely materialistic* — and this in a manner more immanent than Negri's "absolute immanence."[67] Materialism can here be recovered because it is finally cast as only *being* because it is the *excess* of transcendent love — the irreducible difference overflowing from the Holy Trinity. And so matter is capable of anything because it is grounded in an infinite power that far exceeds the limit of materiality as such. The impossible condition is always and already inscribed in creation itself.

This impossible condition is the radical contingency of being and metanoia is participation in the impossible. Analogy rests and reads the impossible. The Impossible irruption is the theurgic Event, it is rest and revolution — the Pneumos alighting on the Logos — the Incarnation, Resurrection, and Consummation of the Church and the cosmos. With the condition of the impossible inherently inscribed within the field of creation, it is reasonable to demand the impossible. Anything can be: the children of Abraham are raised up from stones, the Red Sea splits open as a gate of liberation, the wall of Jericho comes tumbling down, the lion and the lamb lie down together, the poor reclaim the earth, the trees clap their hands. The Impossible is more possible than the return of the identical. Suddenly creation itself overthrows the power of military empire, already naming it the ancien régime. "I tell you that, if these should hold their peace, the stones would immediately cry out" (Luke 19:40). The one faithful to the Event is the saint of revolution.

## Notes

1    This negative ontology is identifiable in the founding articulations of the secular, in which the unrepresentable ground of *esse* is entirely sundered from the world, so that being is cast into purely representable terms. This negative ontology casts the world as its own

self-referring foundation, and because secular being is determined by what is purely representable, being, as a pure concept of minimal propinquity, is forced to actively negate its opposite, nonbeing. So, being is said in terms of its act of negating its rival, nothingness, within the plane of immanence. By this, negative ontology requires: (a) a relation to nonbeing, and (b) the act of negating nonbeing in order to be.

2    The term *revolutionary "Constantinianism"* is in no way meant to be read as an invocation of state Christian authoritarianism or any kind of nostalgia for old Christianity-triumphalism. The excesses of a pure Constantinian imperialist state are obvious distortions of the weakness of Christ's way, and so revolutionary "Constantinianism" is as much a theological revolt against state Constantinianism as it is against capitalist empire. Revolutionary "Constantinianism" is here used in a manner that seeks to reclaim Christian politics as a praxis unashamedly committed to the Logos as the foundation of all political discourse, while at the same time it is revolutionary and so committed to a rigorously antiauthoritarian (re)turn to the Eucharist. So this use of "Constantinianism" seeks not only to threaten capitalism, but also to destabilize a certain strain of romantic, Christian authoritarianism that would use a notion of the Constantinian to underwrite the secular empire and its violence (as has become fashionable in conservative American Catholic circles that support the American "War on Terror"). In terms of the word *revolution*, it should be clear that a Christian revolution, established through the Event of the Logos as Eucharist, will necessarily have to tread carefully between radicalism and pacifism. However, it is not altogether clear if Christians should be "pacifists." Yet in Christian political praxis there may very well be a prima facie requirement of nonviolence. This raises the question: To what extent is Christianity confined to a nonviolent praxis? This question is immediately located within the thought of the theologian Stanley Hauerwas, who insists that "Christian politics will always be strange because the Christian believes that there are worse things than dying" (ethics lecture, spring term, 1998, Duke Divinity School). But this stance, as Hauerwas asserts, does not mean that the Christian necessarily must accept passivity: "The peace Christians desire, pray for, and receive cannot help but create instability in a world based on the assumption that violence is our ultimate weapon against disorder." (*The Peaceable Kingdom* [London: Notre Dame, 1983], 144. To the contrary, accepting passivity in the face of evil might in fact be a collusion with evil—it gives evil more than its share of being. Contrary to the Death of God theology of the 1960s, passivity is not what Christ chooses—Christ chooses a radical and revolutionary praxis of nonpassivity, expressed in the brokenness of the poor. It is therefore a praxis that is not reducible to violence. Further, Christianity must choose a power in weakness, as imitation of Christ, who, though he was in the form of God, thought divinity not a thing to be grasped, and so emptied himself for love on a cross.

3    Our notion of the Event is indebted to Ray Brassier and Alain Badiou. Badiou's definition of the event has three core components: (1) The nominating intervention that decides an undecidable. When one decides that something undecidable took place, no one knows what happened. The event is not an experience, it's an axiom. Only through the truth procedure does one come to know what happened by transforming the possibilities of the situation in such a way that what was previously unthinkable becomes thinkable. (2) The deductive fidelity that discerns between indiscernibles. Fidelity to an undecidable means you have no available cognitive criteria by which to discriminate between what follows and what does not follow from the eventally decision. It is a choice made in the absence of all information about the consequences of choosing that X follows from or is deductively

connected to the event. One deduces without knowing how to verify those deductions. (3) The "forcing" (a term Badiou takes from mathematician Paul Cohen) that allows one to know what will have been the case—and what was previously unknowable according to the state of the situation—by drawing the deductive consequences of the evental decision in a way that reconfigures the extant parameters of cognitive possibility within the situation. It is through forcing that one invents the conditions for the criteria through which it becomes possible to know what will be knowable or thinkable when one transforms the structural limits of what is currently knowable or thinkable according to the state of the situation. We would like to thank Ray Brassier for his conversation on these points.

4    The following argument of the relationship between the Logos and Pneumos (specifically that what the Spirit does is rest on the body of the Son and befriend matter) is indebted to Eugene F. Rogers Jr., and particularly what he has articulated in his forthcoming book *After the Spirit*. Rogers's pneumatology has materialist/transcendent implications and has informed our conceptualization of the Event. Rogers writes: "To think about the Spirit, you have to think materially, because, in Christian terms, the Spirit has befriended matter . . . for Christ's sake on account of the incarnation . . . God is trapped neither within nor outside of the world: so the Son may assume a body, and the Spirit indwell one, not abstractly, but for a purpose: to catch the whole world up into their common life with the Father." Eugene F. Rogers Jr., *After the Spirit* (Grand Rapids, Mich.: Eerdmans, 2005), 76 of typescript.

5    John Damascene, *Orthodox Faith* 1:8. Rogers, *After the Spirit*, 11 of typescript.

6    All scriptural quotations are from the Authorized King James Version, unless otherwise noted.

7    Gilles Deleuze and Félix Guattari, *A Thousand Plateaus: Capitalism and Schizophrenia*, trans. Brian Massumi (Minneapolis: University of Minneapolis Press, 1987), 25.

8    See Samira Kanash, "415 Men: Moving Bodies; or, The Cinematic Politics of Deportation," in *Deleuze and Guattari: New Mappings In Politics, Philosophy, and Culture*, ed. Elanor Kaufman and Kevin Jon Heller (Minneapolis: University of Minnesota Press, 1998), 133.

9    Gilles Deleuze, *Nietzsche and Philosophy*, trans. Hugh Tomlinson (New York: Columbia University Press, 1983), 39.

10   See Aristotle, *Metaphysics*, G, II, 1003 a 33.

11   Saint Theophan the Recluse, *Turning the Heart to God*, trans. Ken Kaisch and Igumen Ioana Zhitsov (Ben Lomond, Scotland: Conciliar, 2001), 2.

12   Vladimir Lossky, *The Mystical Theology of the Eastern Church* (Crestwood, N.Y.: St. Vladimir's, 1976), 204.

13   John Milbank, *Being Reconciled* (New York: Routledge, 2003), 49.

14   Louis Althusser, "Ideology and the Ideological State Apparatus (Notes Towards a Investigation)," in *Lenin and Philosophy and Other Essays*, trans. Ben Brewster (New York: Monthly Review, 2001), 85–126.

15   Cf. Stanislas Breton, *The Word and the Cross*, trans. Jacquelyn Porter (New York: Fordham University Press, 2002).

16   Christos Yannaras, *The Freedom of Morality*, trans. Elizabeth Briere (Crestwood, N.Y.: St. Vladimir's, 1984), 126.

17   Ibid., 121.

18   Vladimir Lossky, *In the Image and Likeness of God*, ed. John H. Erickson and Thomas H. Bird (Crestwood, N.Y.: St. Vladimir's, 2001), 106.

19   John Milbank, *Being Reconciled*, 105.

20  The following argument is indebted to the work of N. T. Wright. See *Resurrection and the Son of God* (Minneapolis: Fortress, 2003), 568–79; and *What Saint Paul Really Said* (Grand Rapids, Mich.: Eerdmans, 1997).

21  Wright, *The Resurrection and the Son of God*, 225.

22  Tertullian, *Apology*, 50.13.

23  "The Martyrdom of Polycarp," in *Ancient Christian Writers No. 6.*, trans. James A. Kleist (New York: Newman, 1948), 10:1.

24  Lancelot Andrewes, *Lancelot Andrewes: Selected Writings*, ed. P. E. Hewison (Manchester: Fyfield, 1995), 69.

25  Slavoj Žižek, *The Ticklish Subject: The Absent Centre of Political Ontology* (London: Verso, 1999), 130.

26  Alain Badiou, *Saint Paul: The Foundation of Universalism* (Stanford, Calif.: Stanford University Press, 2003), 49.

27  Ibid.

28  Rowan Williams, *Sergei Bulgakov: Toward a Russian Political Theology* (Edinburgh: T&T Clark, 1999), 126.

29  Milbank, *Being Reconciled*, 105. This notion of the Church as "the Grail community" is owed originally to Catherine Pickstock. See John Milbank and Catherine Pickstock, *Truth in Aquinas* (New York: Routledge, 2001), 111.

30  We would like to acknowledge Steven Neumeister for pointing out this connection. See Wolfram von Eschenbach, *Parzival*, trans. A. T. Hatto (New York: Penguin, 1980), 394–95.

31  Max Horkheimer and Theodor Adorno, *Dialectic of Enlightenment*, trans. John Cumming (New York: Continuum, 1994), 120.

32  Badiou, *Saint Paul*, 10.

33  Georg Lukács, *History and Class Consciousness*, trans. Rodney Livingston (Cambridge: MIT Press, 1999), 88.

34  Horkheimer and Adorno, *Dialectic of Enlightenment*, 12.

35  Ibid., 126.

36  Graham Ward, *True Religion* (Oxford: Blackwell, 2003), 129.

37  Slavoj Žižek, *The Puppet and the Dwarf: The Perverse Core of Christianity* (Cambridge: MIT Press, 2003), 96.

38  Sergei Bulgakov, *Philosophy of Economy: The World as Household*, trans. Catherine Evtuhov (New Haven, Conn.: Yale University Press, 2000), 96.

39  Hans Urs von Balthasar, *The Moment of Christian Witness* (San Francisco: Ignatius, 1987), 42.

40  William Desmond, *Being and the Between*, trans. Richard Beckley (Albany: State University of New York Press, 1995), 87.

41  William Desmond, *Being and the Between*, 179.

42  Hegel, *Science of Logic*, trans. A. V. Miller (Highlands, N.J.: Humanities Press, 1969), 113.

43  See Conor Cunningham's brilliant study of nihilism in which he makes the case for sustaining nihilism in a divine synthesis of being and non-being that cannot be reducible to either pole. *Genealogy of Nihilism: Philosophies of Nothing and the Difference of Theology* (London: Routledge, 2002).

44  Kenneth Surin, *"Delire* Is World-Historical": Political Knowledge in *Capitalism and Schizophrenia*," Polygraph 14 (2003): 139.

45  Gilles Deleuze, *The Logic of Sense*, ed. Constantin V. Boundas, trans. Mark Lester with Charles Stivale (New York: Columbia University Press, 1990), 179.

46  Surin, "'*Delire* Is World-Historical,'" 139.

47   For a great discussion on being as substantial (and not contingent), see Hardt, *Gilles Deleuze*, esp. 2–10.

48   See Alain Badiou, *Deleuze: The Clamor of Being*, trans. Louise Burchill (Minneapolis: University of Minnesota Press, 2000).

49   This concept comes from William Desmond.

50   One ought to approach any simple Aristotelian-cum-Aquinas alliance at the level of causality and ontology with caution. Indeed Aquinas sought to resolve the Aristotelian ontotheology by "deriving," as John Milbank aptly put it, "the 'is' of temporal/spatial beings *entirely* from the first principle, but a principle no longer conceived as itself a representable object or being (as with Aristotle), which would depend for its foundation upon what it is supposed to found." see Milbank's essay, "Only theology Overcomes Metaphysics" in John Milbank, *The Word Made Strange: Theology, Language, Culture* (Cambridge, Mass.: Blackwell Publishers, 1997), 41.

51   Gilles Deleuze, for instance, reads theology as grounded in analogical being à la Aristotle. Deleuze writes that analogy "rests essentially upon a certain complicity between generic and specific differences" which results in the problem of always determining the particular through the general (matter and form). *Difference and Repetition* (New York: Columbia University Press, 1994), 38. This means that all individuals, via analogical being, can be constituted only by what is already determined, from the general level, as conforming to the principle of individuation, according to Deleuze. In other words, Deleuze thinks that analogy never gets you to the particular because it remains wedded to the general movement located between genera and species. But it is clear from what we have already established that Aristotle's analogy is short-circuited by his ontotheology, which hinders one from accessing the particular in itself. Yet Deleuze never sees the radical shift in Aquinas's ontology that possesses a nonrepresentational source of all being, allowing the particular to be inherently noncollapsible into a general configuration.

52   Jean-Pierre Torrell, O.P., for example, argues that through the *Liber de causis* "Thomas found himself directly linked through Proclus to the Platonic heritage." *Saint Thomas Aquinas*, vol. 1, *The Person and His Work*, trans. Robert Royal (Washington, D.C.: Catholic University, 1996), 128.

53   See Fran O'Rourke, *Pseudo-Dionysius and the Metaphysics of Aquinas* (New York: E. J. Brill, 1992).

54   See M. D. Chenu, O.P., *Toward Understanding Saint Thomas*, trans. A. M. Landry, O.P., and D. Hughes, O.P. (New York: Henry Regner, 1964), 110, 203–30, 304–10.

55   This paragraph is indebted to the thinking of John Milbank.

56   Thomas Aquinas, *Summa theologica*, trans. Fathers of the English Dominican Province, 1a. q.13, a.10.

57   *Summa theologica*, 1a. q.13, a.11.

58   John Milbank, *The Word Made Strange: Theology, Language, Culture* (Oxford: Blackwell Publishers, 1997), 41.

59   Slavoj Žižek, *Organs without Bodies: On Deleuze and Consequences* (New York: Routledge, 2004), 56.

60   Aquinas, *Summa Theologica*, 1a. q.13, a.12.

61   Žižek, *Organs without Bodies*, 56.

62   St. Athanasius, *On the Incarnation* (Crestwood, N.Y.: St. Vladimir's Orthodoxy Theological Seminary, 1953), 33–34.

63   Aquinas, *Summa Theologica*, 1a. q.47, a.2 (translation slightly modified).

64 Augustine, *De doctrina Christiana*, XXII.21.

65 Augustine, *De doctrina Christiana*, XXXIV.38.

66 Rowan Williams, "The Deflections of Desire: Negative Theology in Trinitarian Disclosure," in *Silence and the Word: Negative Theology and Incarnation*, ed. Oliver Davies and Denys Turner (Cambridge: Cambridge University Press, 2002), 118.

67 Antonio Negri, *The Savage Anomaly: The Power of Spinoza's Metaphysics and Politics*, trans. Michael Hardt (Minneapolis: University of Minnesota Press), 1991.

*Slavoj Žižek*     The "Thrilling Romance
of Orthodoxy"

GILBERT KEITH CHESTERTON's basic matrix is that of the "thrilling romance of orthodoxy": in a properly Leninist way, he asserts that, far from being boring, humdrum and safe, the search for true orthodoxy is the most daring and perilous adventure (exactly like Lenin's search for the authentic Marxist orthodoxy — how much less risk and theoretical effort, how much more passive opportunism and theoretical laziness is in the easy revisionist conclusion that the changed historical circumstances demand some "new paradigm"!): "People have fallen into a foolish habit of speaking of orthodoxy as something heavy, humdrum, and safe. There never was anything so perilous or so exciting as orthodoxy."[1] Recall the deadlock of sexuality or art today: is there anything more dull, opportunistic, and sterile than to succumb to the superego injunction of incessantly inventing new artistic transgressions and provocations (the performance artist masturbating on stage or masochistically cutting himself, the sculptor displaying decaying animal corpses or human excrement), or to the parallel injunction to engage in more and more "daring" forms of sexuality. And one cannot but admire Chesterton's consistency: he deploys the same conceptual matrix — that of asserting the truly subversive, even revolutionary, character of orthodoxy — also in his famous "Defense of Detective Story," in which he remarks how the detective story

keeps in some sense before the mind the fact that civilization itself is the most sensational of departures and the most romantic of rebellions. When the detective in a police romance stands alone, and somewhat fatuously fearless amid the knives and fists of a thief's kitchen, it does certainly serve to make us remember that it is the agent of social justice who is the original and poetic figure, while the burglars and footpads are merely placid old cosmic conservatives, happy in the immemorial respectability of apes and wolves. The police romance is based on the fact that morality is the most dark and daring of conspiracies.[2]

It is not difficult to recognize here the elementary matrix of the Hegelian dialectical process: the external opposition (between law and its criminal transgression) is transformed into the opposition, internal to the transgression itself, between particular transgressions and the absolute transgression which appears as its opposite, as the universal law.[3] One can thus effectively claim that the subversive sting of Chesterton's work is contained in the endless variation of one and the same matrix of the Hegelian paradoxical self-negating reversal—Chesterton himself mockingly characterizes his work as the variation on a "single tiresome joke."[4] And what if, in our postmodern world of ordained transgression, in which the marital commitment is perceived as ridiculously out of time, those who cling to it are the true subversives? What if, today, straight marriage is "the most dark and daring of all transgressions"? This, exactly, is the underlying premise of Ernst Lubitsch's *Design for Living* (1933, based on a Noel Coward play): a woman leads a satisfied, calm life with two men; as a dangerous experiment, she tries single marriage; however, the attempt miserably fails, and she returns to the safety of living with two men.

In the very last pages of *Orthodoxy*, Chesterton deploys the fundamental Hegelian paradox of the pseudo-revolutionary critics of religion: they start with denouncing religion as the force of oppression which threatens human freedom; however, in fighting religion, they are compelled to forsake freedom itself, thus sacrificing precisely that which they wanted to defend—the ultimate victim of the atheist theoretical and practical rejection of religion is not religion (which, unperturbed, continues its life), but freedom itself allegedly threatened by it: the atheist radical universe, deprived of religious reference, is the gray universe of egalitarian terror and tyranny:

> Men who begin to fight the Church for the sake of freedom and humanity end by flinging away freedom and humanity if only they may fight the Church. . . . I know a man who has such a passion for proving that he will have no personal existence after death that he falls back on the position that he has no personal existence now. . . . I have known people who showed that there could be no divine judgment by showing that there can be no human judgment. . . . We do not admire, we hardly excuse, the fanatic who wrecks this world for love of the other.

But what are we to say of the fanatic who wrecks this world out of hatred for the other? He sacrifices the very existence of humanity to the non-existence of God. He offers his victims not to the altar, but merely to assert the idleness of the altar and the emptiness of the throne. . . . With their oriental doubts about personality they do not make certain that we shall have no personal life hereafter; they only make certain that we shall not have a very jolly or complete one here. . . . The secularists have not wrecked divine things; but the secularists have wrecked secular things, if that is any comfort to them.[5]

The first thing one should add to it today is that the same holds for the advocates of religion themselves: how many fanatical defenders of religion started with ferociously attacking the contemporary secular culture and ended up forsaking religion itself (losing any meaningful religious experience). And is it not that, in a strictly homologous way, the liberal warriors are so eager to fight the antidemocratic fundamentalism that they will end by flinging away freedom and democracy themselves if only they may fight terror? They have such a passion for proving that the non-Christian fundamentalism is the main threat to freedom that they are ready to fall back on the position that we have to limit our own freedom here and now, in our allegedly Christian societies. If the "terrorists" are ready to wreck this world for love of the other, our warriors on terror are ready to wreck their own democratic world out of hatred for the Muslim other. Jonathan Alter and Alan Dershowitz love human dignity so much that they are ready to legalize torture — the ultimate degradation of human dignity — to defend it.

When Alan Dershowitz not only condemns what he perceives as the international community's reluctance to oppose terrorism, but also provokes us to "think the unthinkable," like legalizing torture, changing the laws so that, in exceptional situations, courts will have the right to issue "torture warrants," his argumentation is not as easy to counter as it may appear.[6] First, torture "unthinkable"? Is it not going on all the time everywhere? Second, if one follows Dershowitz's utilitarian line of argumentation, could one not also argue for the legitimacy of terror itself? In the same way one should torture a terrorist whose knowledge can prevent the death of many more innocent people, why not fully condone terror, at least against military and police personnel waging an unjust war of occupation, if it can prevent violence on a much larger scale? Here, then, we have a nice case of the Hegelian opposition of In-itself and For-itself: "for itself," with regard to his explicit goals, Dershowitz is, of course, ferociously attacking terrorism — however, "in itself or for us," he is succumbing to the terrorist lure, since his argumentation against terrorism already endorses terrorism's basic premise.

More generally, does the same not hold for the postmodern disdain of great ideological causes, for the notion that, in our post-ideological era, instead of trying to change the world, we should reinvent ourselves, our whole universe, by engaging ourselves in new forms of (sexual, spiritual, aesthetic) subjective practices? As Hanif Kureishi put it in an interview apropos his *Intimacy*: "twenty years ago it was political to try to make a revolution and change society while now politics comes down to two bodies in a basement making love who can recreate the whole world." When confronted with statements like this, one cannot but recall the old lesson of critical theory: when we try to preserve the authentic intimate sphere of privacy against the onslaught of instrumental/objectivized "alienated" public exchange, privacy itself changes into a totally objectivized, "commodified" sphere. Withdrawal into privacy means today adopting formulas of private authenticity propagated by the recent cultural industry, from taking lessons in spiritual enlightenment and following the latest cultural and other fashions to engaging in jogging and bodybuilding. The ultimate truth of withdrawal into privacy are public confessions of intimate secrets on TV shows—against this kind of privacy, one should emphasize that, today, the only kind of breaking out of the constraints of "alienated" commodification is to invent a new collectivity. Today, more than ever, the lesson of the novels of Marguerite Duras is actual: the way—the only way—to have an intense and fulfilling personal (sexual) relationship is not for the couple to look into each other's eyes, forgetting about the world around, but, while holding hands, to look together outside, at a third point (the cause for which both are fighting, in which both are engaged).

The ultimate result of globalized subjectivization is not that "objective reality" disappears, but that our subjectivity itself disappears, turns into a trifling whim, while the social reality continues its run. One is tempted to paraphrase here the famous answer of the interrogator to Winston Smith who doubts the existence of the Big Brother ("It is You who doesn't exist!"): the proper reply to the postmodern doubt about the existence of the ideological big other is that it is the subject itself who doesn't exist. No wonder that in our era whose basic stance is best encapsulated by the title of a recent Phillip McGraw bestseller, *Self Matters*, teaching us how to "create your life from the inside out," finds its logical supplement in books with titles like *How to Disappear Completely*—manuals about how to erase all traces of one's previous existence and "reinvent" oneself completely.[7] It is here that one should trace the difference between Zen proper and its Western version: the proper greatness of Zen is that it cannot be reduced to an "inner journey" into one's "true self"; the aim of the Zen mediation is, quite on the contrary, a total voidance of the self, the acceptance that there is no self, no "inner truth" to be discovered. What the Western Buddhism is not ready to accept is thus that the ultimate victim of the "journey into one's self" is this self itself. And, more generally, is this not the same lesson as that of Theodor Adorno's and Max Horkheimer's *Dialectic of Enlightenment*? The ultimate victims of positivism are not confused metaphysical notions, but facts themselves; the radical pursuit of secularization, the turn toward our worldly life, transforms this life itself into an "abstract" anemic process—and nowhere is this paradoxical reversal more palpable than in the work of de Sade, where the unconstrained assertion of sexuality deprived of the last vestiges of spiritual transcendence turns sexuality itself into a mechanic exercise lacking any authentic sensual passion. And is not a similar reversal clearly discernible in the deadlock of today's Last Men, "postmodern" individuals who reject all "higher" goals as terrorist and dedicate their life to survival filled with more and more refined and artificially excited/aroused small pleasures?

In psychoanalysis, perhaps the supreme case of such reversal is the emergence of the so-called anal character: what begins when the small child refuses to cede his excrements on demand, preferring to keep them for themselves, since he does not want to be deprived of the surplus enjoyment of doing it in his own terms, ends as the grown-up figure of the miser, a subject who dedicates his life to hoarding his treasure and pays for it the price of an infinitely stronger renunciation: he is allowed no consumption, no indulging in pleasures, everything must serve the accumulation of his treasure. The paradox is that, when the small child refuses "castration" (ceding of the privileged detachable object), he takes the path that will end in his total self-castration in the real—his refusal to cede the surplus object will condemn him to the prohibition of enjoying any other object. In other words, his rejection of the demand of the real parental other (to behave properly in the toilet) will result in the rule of an infinitely more cruel internalized superego other that will totally dominate his consumption. And this brings us to Chesterton's principle of conditional joy: by way of refusing the founding exception (the ceding of the excessive object), the miser is deprived of *all* objects.

Perhaps the ultimate version of this paradoxical reversal in Chesterton is the one between magic and reality: for Chesterton, reality and magic are far from being simply opposed—the greatest magic is that of reality itself, the fact that there really is out there such a wonderful rich world. And the same goes for the dialectical tension between repetition and creativity: one should discard the wrong notion that repetition means death, automatic mechanical movement, while life means diversity, surprising twists. The greatest surprise, the greatest proof of the divine creativity, is that the *same* thing gets repeated again and again:

The sun rises every morning. I do not rise every morning; but the variation is due not to my activity, but to my inaction. . . . it might be true that the sun rises regularly because he never gets tired of rising. His routine might be due, not to a lifelessness, but to a rush of life. . . . A child kicks his legs rhythmically through excess, not absence, of life. Because children have abounding vitality, because they are in spirit fierce and free, therefore they want things repeated and unchanged. They always say, "Do it again"; and the grown-up person does it again until he is nearly dead. But, perhaps, God is strong enough to exult in monotony. It is possible that God says every morning, "Do it again" to the sun.[8]

This is what Hegel calls the dialectical coincidence of the opposites: monotony is the highest idiosyncrasy; repetition demands the highest creative effort. Does Chesterton thereby not provide the clue for the strange Aztec ritual of offering human sacrifices so that the sun will rise again next day? This attitude becomes comprehensible the moment one is able to perceive the infinite effort that has to sustain such an endless repetition. Perhaps the fact that, apropos of this miracle of continuous repetition, he inadvertently uses the term "gods,"[9] is crucial: is this attitude of perceiving repetition not as a blind automatism, but as a miracle of the highest effort of the will, not profoundly pagan? At a different level, the same point was made long ago by intelligent Marxists: in the "natural" course of the events, things change, so the truly difficult thing to explain is not social changes but, on the contrary, stability and permanence. Not why did this social order collapse, but how did it succeed to stabilize itself and persist in the midst of general chaos and change. Say, how it is that Christianity, the hegemonic ideology of medieval times, survived the rise of capitalism? And does the same not hold for anti-Semitism: the true mystery to be explained is its persistence through so many different societies and modes of production—we find it in feudalism, capitalism, socialism?

For Chesterton, the basic Christian lesson of fairy tales is contained in what he mockingly calls the "Doctrine of Conditional Joy": "You may live in a palace of gold and sapphire, if you do not say the word 'cow.' "; or, "You may live happily with the King's daughter, if you do not show her an onion. The vision always hangs upon a veto."[10] Why, then, does this seemingly arbitrary singular condition always limit the universal right to happiness? Chesterton's profoundly Hegelian solution is: to "extraneate" the universal right/law itself, to remind us that the universal Good we gain access to is no less contingent, that it could have been otherwise: "If Cinderella says: 'How is it that I must leave the ball at twelve?' her godmother might answer, 'How is it that you are going there till twelve?'"[11] The function of the arbitrary limitation is to remind us that the object itself the access to which is thus limited is given to us through an inexplicable arbitrary miraculous gesture of divine gift, and thus to sustain the magic of being allowed to have access to it: "Keeping to one woman is a small price for so much as seeing one woman. . . . Oscar Wilde said that sunsets were not valued because we could not pay for sunsets. But Oscar Wilde was wrong; we can pay for sunsets. We can pay for them by not being Oscar Wilde."[12]

Chesterton approaches here the renunciation necessary to happiness. When, exactly, can a people be said to be happy? In a country like Czechoslovakia in the late 1970s and 1980s, people in a way effectively *were* happy: three fundamental conditions of happiness were fulfilled there. (1) Their material needs were basically satisfied—not *too* satisfied, since the excess of consumption can in itself generate unhappiness. It is good to experience a brief shortage of some goods on the market from time to time (no coffee for a couple of days, then no beef, then no TV sets): these brief periods of shortage functioned as exceptions which reminded people that they should be glad that the goods were generally available—if everything is available all the time, people take this availability as an evident fact of life and do not longer appreciate their luck. Life thus went on in a regular and predictable way, without any great efforts or shocks, one was allowed to withdraw into one's private niche. (2) A second extremely important feature: there was the other (the Party) to be blamed for everything that went wrong, so that one did not feel really responsible—if there was a temporary shortage of some goods, even if there was stormy weather that caused great damage, it was "their" guilt. (3) And, last but not least, there was an Other Place (the consumerist West) about which one was allowed to dream, and even visit sometimes—this place was just at the right distance, not too far, not too close. This fragile balance was disturbed—by what? By *desire*, precisely. Desire was the force that compelled the people to move beyond—and end up in a system in which the large majority is definitely *less* happy.

Happiness is thus, to put it in the terms of Badiou, not a category of truth, but a category of mere Being, and, as such, confused, indeterminate, inconsistent (recall the proverbial answer of a German immigrant to the United States who, when asked "Are you happy?" answered: "Yes, yes, I am very happy, *aber gluecklich bin ich nicht*." It is a PAGAN category: for pagans, the goal of life is to live a happy life (the idea to live "happily ever after" is already a Christianized version of paganism), and religious experience or political activity themselves are considered the higher form of happiness (see Aristotle) —no wonder Dalai Lama himself is having such a success recently preaching around the world the gospel of happiness, and no wonder he is finding the greatest response precisely in the United States, this ultimate empire of the (pursuit of) happiness. In short, "happiness" is a category of pleasure principle, and what undermines it is the insistence of a beyond of the pleasure principle.[13]

In strict Lacanian sense of the terms, one should thus posit that "happiness" relies on the subject's inability or unreadiness to fully confront the consequences of its desire: the price of happiness is that the subject remains stuck in the inconsistency of its desire. In our daily lives, we (pretend to) desire things which we do not really desire, so that, ultimately, the worst thing that can happen is for us to get what we "officially" desire. Happiness is thus inherently hypocritical: it is the happiness of dreaming about things we really do not want. When today's Left bombards the capitalist system with demands that it obviously cannot fulfill (Full employment! Retain the welfare state! Full rights to immigrants!), it is basically playing a game of hysterical provocations, of addressing the master with a demand that will be for him impossible to meet and will thus expose his impotence. However, the problem with this strategy is not only that the system cannot meet these demands, but also that those who enounce them do not really want them to be realized. Say, when the "radical" academics demand full rights for the immigrants and the opening of the borders to them, are they aware that the direct implementation of this demand would, for obvious reasons, inundate the developed Western countries with millions of newcomers, thus provoking a violent racist working-class backlash that would then endanger the privileged position of the very academics? Of course they are aware of it, but they count on the fact that their demand will not be met—in this way, they can hypocritically retain their clear radical conscience while continuing to enjoy their privileged position. In 1994, when a new wave of emigration to the United States was in the making, Fidel Castro warned the United States that, if they do not stop inciting Cubans to immigrate, Cuba will no longer prevent them doing it—which the Cuban authorities effectively did a couple of days later, embarrassing the United States with thousands of unwanted newcomers. Is this not like the proverbial woman who snapped back at the man making macho advances on her: "Shut up, or you will have to do what you are boasting about!" In both cases, the gesture is that of calling the other's bluff, counting on the fact that what the other really fears is that one would fully meet his demand. And would the same gesture not throw into a panic also our radical academics? The old '68 motto *Soyons realistes, demandons l'impossible!* acquires here a new cynical-sinister meaning that, perhaps, displays its truth: "Let us be realists: we, the academic Left, want to appear critical, while fully enjoying the privileges the system is offering us. So let us bombard the system with impossible demands: we all know that these demands will not be met, so we can be sure that nothing will effectively change and we will maintain our privileged status quo!" If one accuses a big corporation of particular financial crimes, one exposes oneself to risks that can go up to murder attempts; if one asks the same corporation to finance a research project about the link between global capitalism and the emergence of the hybrid postcolonial identities, one stands a good chance of getting hundreds of thousands of dollars.

Conservatives are therefore fully justified in legitimizing their opposition to radical knowledge in the terms of happiness: knowledge ultimately makes us unhappy. Contrary to the notion that curiosity is inborn to humans, that there is deep in each of us a *Wissenstrieb*, the drive to know, Jacques Lacan claims that the spontaneous attitude of a human being is "I don't want to know about it" — a fundamental resistance against knowing too much. Every true progress in knowledge has to be bought by a painful struggle against our spontaneous propensities — is today's biogenetics not the clearest proof of these limits of our readiness to know? The gene responsible for Huntington's disease is isolated, so that each of us can learn precisely not only if he will get Huntington's, but also when he will get it. The onset of the disease depends on a genetic transcription mistake — the stuttering repetition of the "word" CAG in the middle of the gene: the age at which the madness will appear depends strictly and implacably on the number of repetitions of CAG in one place in this gene (if there are forty repetitions, you will get the first symptoms at fifty-nine, if forty-one, at fifty-four . . . if fifty, at twenty-seven). Good living, bodily fitness, the best medicine, healthy food, family love and support can do nothing about it — pure fatalism, undiluted by environmental variability. There are yet no cures, we can do nothing about it.[14] So what should we do when we know that we can submit ourselves to testing and thus acquire a knowledge that, if positive, tells us exactly when we will get mad and die? Can one imagine a clearest confrontation with the meaningless contingency determining our life?

Huntington's disease thus confronts us with a disturbing alternative: if there is in my family a history of this disease, should I take the test that will tell me if (and when) I will inexorably get the disease or not? What solution? If I cannot bear the prospect of knowing when I will die, the (more fantasmatic than realistic) ideal solution may seem to be the following one: I authorize another person or institution whom I trust completely to test me and *not to tell me the result*, simply to kill me unexpectedly and painlessly in my sleep just before the onslaught of the fatal illness, if the result was positive. However, the problem with this solution is that I *know that the Other knows* (the truth about my illness), and this ruins everything, exposing me to hor-rifying gnawing suspicion.

Lacan drew attention to the paradoxical status of this knowledge about the Other's knowledge. Recall the final reversal of Edith Wharton's *Age of Innocence*, in which the husband who for long years harbored illicit passionate love for Countess Olenska learns that his young wife all the time *knew* about his secret passion. Perhaps this would also offer a way to redeem the unfortunate *The Bridges of Madison County*: if, at the film's end, the dying Francesca were to learn that her allegedly simple-minded, down-to-earth husband knew all the time of her brief passionate affair with the *National Geographic* photog-rapher and how much this meant to her, but kept silent about it in order not to hurt her. Therein resides the enigma of knowledge: how is it possible that the whole psychic economy of a situation radically changes not when the hero directly learns something (some long repressed secret), but when he *gets to know that the other* (whom he mistook for ignorant) *also knew it all the time* and just pretended not to know to keep up appearances—is there anything more humiliating than the situation of a husband who, after a long secret love affair, all of a sudden learns that his wife knew about it all the time, but kept silent about it out of politeness or, even worse, out of love for him?

Is then the ideal solution the opposite one: if I suspect that my child may have the disease, I test him *without him knowing it* and then kill him pain-lessly just before the onslaught? The ultimate fantasy of happiness would be here that of an anonymous state institution doing this for all of us with-out our knowledge—but, again, the question pops up: do we know about it (about the fact that the other knows) or not? The way to a perfect totalitarian society is open. There is only one way out of this conundrum: what if what is false here is the underlying premise, the notion that the ultimate ethical duty is that of protecting the Other from pain, of keeping him in protective ignorance? So when Habermas advocates constraints on biogenetic manipu-lations with reference to the threat they pose to human autonomy, freedom and dignity,[15] he is philosophically "cheating," concealing the true reason of why his line of argumentation appears convincing: what he is really referring to is not autonomy and freedom, but happiness—it is on behalf of happiness that he, the great representative of the tradition of the Enlightenment tra-dition, ended up at the same side as conservative advocates of blessed igno-rance. It is in this sense that the Christian doctrine "not only discovered the law, but it foresaw the exceptions":[16] it is only the exception that allows us to perceive the miracle of the universal rule. And, for Chesterton, the same goes for our rational understanding of the universe:

The whole secret of mysticism is this: that man can understand everything by the help of what he does not understand. The morbid logi-
cian seeks to make everything lucid, and succeeds in making everything
mysterious. The mystic allows one thing to be mysterious, and everything else becomes lucid. . . . The one created thing which we cannot
look at is the one thing in the light of which we look at everything. Like
the sun at noonday, mysticism explains everything else by the blaze of
its own victorious invisibility.[17]

Chesterton's aim is thus to *save reason through sticking to its founding exception*: deprived of it, reason degenerates into a blind self-destructive skepticism, in short, into total *irrationalism*. This was Chesterton's basic insight
and conviction: that the irrationalism of the late nineteenth century was the
necessary consequence of the Enlightenment's rationalist attack on religion:

The creeds and the crusades, the hierarchies and the horrible perse-
cutions were not organized, as is ignorantly said, for the suppression of
reason. They were organized for the difficult defense of reason. Man,
by a blind instinct, knew that if once things were wildly questioned, reason could be questioned first. The authority of priests to absolve, the
authority of popes to define the authority, even of inquisitors to terrify:
these were all only dark defenses erected round one central authority,
more undemonstrable, more supernatural than all—the authority of a
man to think. . . . In so far as religion is gone, reason is going.[18]

The problem here is: is this "Doctrine of Conditional Joy" (or, to put it
in Lacanese: the logic of *symbolic castration*) effectively the ultimate horizon
of our experience? Is it that, in order to enjoy a limited scope of actual freedom, one has to endorse a transcendental limitation to our freedom? Is the
only way to safeguard our reason to admit an island of unreason in its very
heart? Can we love another person only if we are aware that we love God
more? It goes to Chesterton's credit that he spelled out the properly *perverse* nature of this solution apropos paganism; he turns around the standard
(mis)perception according to which the ancient pagan attitude is that of the
joyful assertion of life, while Christianity imposes a somber order of guilt
and renunciation. It is, on the contrary, the pagan stance that is deeply melancholic: even if it preaches a pleasurable life, it is in the mode of "enjoy it
while it lasts, because, at the end, there is always death and decay." The message of Christianity is, on the contrary, that of infinite joy beneath the de-
ceptive surface of guilt and renunciation: "The outer ring of Christianity is
a rigid guard of ethical abnegations and professional priests; but inside that
inhuman guard you will find the old human life dancing like children, and

drinking wine like men; for Christianity is the only frame for pagan free-dom."[19] Is not J. R. R. Tolkien's *The Lord of the Rings* the ultimate proof of this paradox? Only a devout Christian could have imagined such a magnificent pagan universe, thereby confirming that *paganism is the ultimate Christian dream*. Which is why the conservative Christian critics who recently expressed their concern at how books and movies like *The Lord of the Rings* or the Harry Potter series undermine Christianity through their message of pagan magic miss the point, the perverse conclusion which is unavoidable here: You want to enjoy the pagan dream of pleasurable life without paying the price of melancholic sadness for it? Choose Christianity! We can discern the traces of this paradox up to the well-known Catholic figure of the Priest (or a Nun) as the ultimate bearer of the sexual wisdom. Recall what is arguably the most powerful scene of *The Sound of Music*: after Maria escapes from the von Trapp family back to the monastery, unable to deal with her sexual attraction toward Baron von Trapp, she cannot find peace there, since she is still longing for the baron; in a memorable scene, the Mother Superior summons her and advises her to return to the von Trapp family and try to sort out her relationship with the baron. She delivers this message in a weird song, "Climb Every Mountain," whose surprising motif is: Do it! Take the risk and try everything your heart wants! Do not allow petty considerations to stand in your way! The uncanny power of this scene resides in its unexpected display of the spectacle of desire, which renders the scene literally *embarrassing*: the very person whom one would expect to preach abstinence and renunciation turns out to be the agent of the fidelity to one's desire.[20] Significantly, when *The Sound of Music* was shown in (still Socialist) Yugoslavia in the late 1960s, this scene—the three minutes of this song—was the only part of the film censored (it was cut out). The anonymous Socialist censor thereby displayed his profound sense for the truly dangerous power of Catholic ideology: far from being the religion of sacrifice, of renunciation to earthly pleasures (in contrast to the pagan affirmation of the life of passions), Christianity offers a devious stratagem to indulge in our desires *without having to pay the price for them*, to enjoy life without the fear of decay and debilitating pain awaiting us at the end of the day. If we go to the end in this direction, it would even be possible to sustain that therein resides the ultimate function of Christ's sacrifice: *you can indulge in your desires and enjoy, I took the price for it upon myself!* There is thus an element of truth in a joke about what is the ideal prayer of a young Christian girl to Virgin Mary: "O thou who conceived without having sinned, let me sin without having to conceive!" in the perverse functioning of Christianity, religion is effectively evoked as a safeguard allowing us to enjoy life with impunity.

The impression that we do not have to pay the price is, of course, misleading here. The price we effectively pay is desire itself: in succumbing to this perverse call, we compromise our desire. We all know the feeling of tremendous relief when, after a long period of tension or abstention, one is finally allowed to "let it go," to indulge in hitherto forbidden pleasures—this relief, when one can finally "do what one wants," is perhaps the very model (not of realizing, but) of compromising one's desire. That is to say, for Lacan, the status of desire is inherently ethical: "not to compromise one's desire" ultimately equals "do your duty." And this is what the perverse version of Christianity entices us to do: betray your desire, compromise with regard to the essential, to what really matters, and you are welcome to have all the petty pleasures you are dreaming about deep in your heart! The fundamental structure here is not so much that of "Conditional Joy" (you can have "it" on condition of some "irrational" contingent exception/prohibition), but, rather, that of the fake sacrifice, of pretending not to have "it," to renounce "it," in order to deceive the big Other, to conceal from it that we *do* have it. Let us take the example of Jeannot Szwarc's *Enigma* (1981), one of the better variations on what is arguably the basic matrix of cold war spy thrillers with artistic pretensions à la John le Carré; it tells the story of a dissident journalist-turned-spy who emigrated to the West and is then recruited by the CIA and sent to East Germany to get hold of a scrambling/descrambling computer chip whose possession enables the owner to read all communications between KGB headquarters and its outposts. However, small signs tell the spy that there is something wrong with his mission, that East Germans and Russians were already in advance informed about his arrival—so what is going on? Is it that the Communists have a mole in the CIA headquarters who informed them of this secret mission? As we learn toward the film's end, the solution is much more ingenious: the CIA already possesses the scrambling chip, but, unfortunately, Russians suspect this fact, so they temporarily stopped using this computer network for their secret communications. The true aim of the operation was the attempt by the CIA to convince the Russians that they do not possess the chip: they sent an agent to get it and, at the same time, deliberately let the Russians know that there is an operation going on to get the chip; of course, the CIA counts on the fact that the Russians will arrest the agent. The ultimate result will thus be that, by successfully preventing the mission, the Russians will be convinced that the Americans do not possess it and that it is therefore safe to use this communication link. The tragic aspect of the story, of course, is that the mission's failure is taken into account: the CIA wants the mission to fail; the poor dissident agent is sacrificed in advance for the higher goal of convincing the opponent that one doesn't possess his secret. The strategy is here to stage a search operation in order to convince the other (the enemy) that one does not already possess what one is looking for—in short, one feigns a lack, a want, in order to conceal from the Other that one already possesses the *agalma*, the Other's innermost secret. Is this structure not somehow connected with the basic paradox of symbolic castration as constitutive of desire, in which the object has to be lost in order to be regained on the inverse ladder of desire regulated by the Law? Symbolic castration is usually defined as the loss of something that one never possessed; the object-cause of desire is an object that emerges through the very gesture of its loss or withdrawal. However, what we encounter in the case of *Enigma* is the obverse structure of feigning a loss. Insofar as the other of the symbolic law prohibits jouissance, the only way for the subject to enjoy is to feign that he lacks the object that provides jouissance, to conceal from the Other's gaze its possession by way of staging the spectacle of the desperate search for it. This also casts a new light on the topic of sacrifice. One sacrifices not in order to get something from the Other, but in order to dupe the Other, in order to convince him or it that one is still missing something: jouissance. This is why obsessional neurotics experience the compulsion repeatedly to accomplish their compulsive rituals of sacrifice—in order to disavow their jouissance in the eyes of the Other. And does, at a different level, the same not hold for the so-called woman's sacrifice, for the woman adopting the role of remaining in shadow and sacrificing herself for her husband or family? Is this sacrifice not also false in the sense of serving to dupe the Other, of convincing it that, through the sacrifice, the woman is effectively desperately craving to obtain something that she lacks? In this precise sense, sacrifice and castration are to be opposed: far from involving the voluntary acceptance of castration, sacrifice is the most refined way of disavowing it, of acting as if one effectively possesses the hidden treasure that makes me a worthy object of love.

Is the way out of this predicament, then, to pass from the Doctrine of Conditional Joy to the Doctrine of *Unconditional* Joy as exemplified by the mystical experience, and which is the exact status of this unconditional jouissance? Is it only presupposed, imputed by the hysteric to the perverse Other—the "subject supposed to enjoy," or is it accessible in moments of mystical encounters of the Real? The crucial question here is: how does this Doctrine of Conditional Joy relate to the Paulinian suspension of our full commitment to terrestrial social obligations (live your life in the *as if* mode—"from now on, let even those who have wives be as though they had none, and those who mourn as though they were not mourning, and those who rejoice as though they were not rejoicing, and those who buy as though they had no possessions")? Are they two versions of the same principle? Are they not, rather, two *opposed* principles? In the Doctrine of Conditional Joy, the exception (be home at midnight, etc.) allows us fully to rejoice, while the Paulinian *as if* mode deprives us of the ability fully to rejoice by way of displacing the external limit into an internal one: the limit is no longer the one between rejoicing life and its exception (renunciation), it runs in the midst of rejoicing: one has to rejoice *as if we are not rejoicing.* The limit of Chesterton is clearly perceptible in his insistence on the need for firm eternal standards: he ferociously opposes the "false theory of progress, which maintains that we alter the test instead of trying to pass the test."[21] In his usual way, in order to prove his point, Chesterton enumerates a series of brilliant examples of the self-refuting inconsistency of modern critical intellectuals: "A man denounces marriage as a lie, and then denounces aristocratic profligates for treating it as a lie. He calls a flag a bauble, and then blames the oppressors of Poland or Ireland because they take away that bauble. The man of this school goes first to a political meeting, where he complains that savages are treated as if they were beasts; then he takes his hat and umbrella and goes on to a scientific meeting, where he proves that they practically are beasts."[22] Here, in effect, we jump from establishing that a concrete example fails the test (savages are treated like beasts, not as men; aristocrats treat marriage as a lie) to the universal conclusion that the very notion which enabled us to measure the falsity of a particular case is in itself already false (man as such is a beast, an animal species; marriage as such is a lie). In rejecting this universalization, Chesterton implicitly rejects the Hegelian self-negation that is also the fundamental procedure of the Marxian critique of ideology—recall Brecht's famous "What is the robbery of a bank compared to the founding of a new bank?" or the good old "property is theft" (i.e., the passage from the theft of some particular property to the notion that property as such already is theft). Similar reversals abound in the first chapter of *The Communist Manifesto*: from prostitution as opposed to marriage to the notion of (the bourgeois) marriage itself as a form of prostitution, and so on. In all these cases, Marx applies Hegel's insight (first articulated in the Introduction to the *Phenomenology of Spirit*) according to which, when the particular does not fit its universal measure, one should change the measure itself: the gap between the universal normative notion and its particular cases is to be reflected back into this notion itself, as its inherent tension and insufficiency—however, does Chesterton's basic matrix not involve the same gesture of self-negating universalization? Is not the "truth" of the opposition between Law and its particular transgressions that the Law itself is the highest transgression?

Therein resides not only the limit of Chesterton, but, more radically, the limit of the perverse solution which forms the very core of the "really-existing Christianity": with modernity proper, one can no longer rely on the preestablished dogma to sustain our freedom, on the pre-established Law/Prohibition to sustain our transgression—this is one of the ways to read Lacan's thesis that the big Other no longer exists. Perversion is a double strategy to counteract this nonexistence: an (ultimately deeply conservative, nostalgic) attempt to install the law artificially, *with the desperate hope that we will then take this self-posited limitation "seriously,"* and, in a complementary way, a no less desperate attempt to codify the very transgression of the law. In the perverse reading of Christianity, God first threw humanity into sin *in order to* create opportunity for saving it through Christ's sacrifice; in the perverse reading of Hegel, the Absolute plays a game with itself—it first separates itself from itself, introduces a gap of self-misrecognition, *in order to* reconcile itself with itself again. This is why today's neoconservative desperate attempts to reassert "old values" are also ultimately a failed perverse strategy of imposing prohibitions that no longer can be taken seriously. More precisely: when, exactly, did prohibitions lose their power? The answer is very clear: with Kant. No wonder Kant is *the* philosopher of freedom: with him, the deadlock of freedom emerges. That is to say, with Kant, the standard Chesterton solution—the reliance on the pre-established obstacle against which we can assert our freedom—is no longer viable, our freedom is asserted as autonomous, every limitation/constraint is thoroughly *self-posited*. This is also why one should be very attentive in reading Kant *avec* Sade: Lacan's ultimate thesis[23] is not that the Sadean perversion is the "truth" of Kant, more "radical" than Kant, that it draws out the consequences Kant himself did not have the courage to confront; on the contrary, the Sadean perversion emerges as the result of the Kantian compromise, of Kant's avoiding the consequences of his breakthrough.

Far from being *the* seminar of Lacan, his *Ethics of Psychoanalysis* is rather the point of deadlock at which Lacan comes dangerously close to the standard version of the "passion of the Real."[24] Do the unexpected echoes between this seminar and the thought of Georges Bataille, *the* philosopher of the passion of the Real, if there ever was one, not unambiguously point in this direction? Is Lacan's ethical maxim "do not compromise your desire" (which, one should always bear in mind, was never used again by Lacan in his later work) not a version of Bataille's injunction "to think everything to a point that makes people tremble,"[25] to go as far as possible—to the point at which opposites coincide, at which infinite pain turns into the joy of the highest bliss (discernible on the photo of the Chinese submitted to the terrifying torture of being slowly cut to pieces), at which the intensity of erotic enjoyment encounters death, at which sainthood overlaps with extreme dissolution, at which God himself is revealed as a cruel Beast? Is the temporal coincidence of Lacan's seminar on the ethics of psychoanalysis and Bataille's *Eroticism* more than a mere coincidence? Is Bataille's domain of the sacred, of the "accursed part," not his version of what, apropos *Antigone*, Lacan deployed as the domain of *ate*? Does Bataille's opposition of "homogeneity," the order of exchanges, and "heterogeneity," the order of limitless expenditure, not point toward Lacan's opposition of the order of symbolic exchanges and the excess of the traumatic encounter of the Real? "Heterogeneous reality is that of a force or shock," says Bataille.[26] And how can Bataille's elevation of the dissolute woman to the status of God not remind us of Lacan's claim that Woman is one of the names of God? Not to mention Bataille's term for the experience of transgression—impossible—which is Lacan's qualification of the Real. It is this urge to "go to the end," to the extreme experience of the impossible as the only way of being authentic, which makes Bataille *the* philosopher of the passion of the Real—no wonder he was obsessed with Communism and Fascism, these two excesses of life against democracy, which was "a world of appearances and of old men with their teeth falling out."[27]

Bataille was fully aware of how this transgressive "passion of the Real" *relies on prohibition*, which is why he was explicitly opposed to the "sexual revolution," to the rise of sexual permissivity that began in his last years: "In my view, sexual disorder is accursed. In this respect and in spite of appearances, I am opposed to the tendency which seems today to be sweeping it away. I am not among those who see the neglect of sexual interdictions as a solution. I even think that human potential depends on these interdictions: we could not imagine this potential without these interdictions."[28] Bataille thus brought to its climax the dialectical interdependence between law and its transgression—"system is needed and so is excess," as he liked to repeat: "Often, the criminal himself wants death as the answer to the crime, in order finally to impart the sanction, without which the crime would be *possible* instead of being *what it is*, what the criminal wanted."[29] This, also, was the reason he ultimately opposed Communism: he was for the excess of the revolution but feared that the revolutionary spirit of excessive expenditure will be afterward contained in the new order, even more "homogenous" than the capitalist one: "the idea of a revolution is intoxicating, but what happens afterward? The world will remake itself and remedy what oppresses us today to take some other form tomorrow."[30]

This, perhaps, is the reason why Bataille is strictly premodern: he remains stuck in this dialectic of the law and its transgression, of the prohibitive law as generating the transgressive desire, which forces him to the debilitating perverse conclusion that one has to install prohibitions in order to be able to enjoy their violation—a clearly unworkable pragmatic paradox. (And, incidentally, was this dialectic not already fully explored by Paul in Romans, in the famous passage on the relationship between Law and sin, on how Law engenders sin, which is the desire to transgress it?) Bataille is unable to perceive the consequences of the Kantian philosophical revolution: the fact that *the absolute excess is that of the Law itself*—the Law intervenes in the "homogeneous" stability of our pleasure-oriented life as the shattering force of the absolute destabilizing "heterogeneity." At a different level, but no less radically, the late capitalist "permissive" society in the thrall of the superego injunction "Enjoy!" elevates excess into the very principle of its "normal" functioning, so that one is tempted to propose a paraphrase of Brecht: "What is a poor Bataillean subject engaged in his transgressions of the system compared to the late capitalist excessive orgy of the system itself?" (And it is interesting to note how this very point was already made by Chesterton: orthodoxy itself is the highest subversion, serving the Law is the highest adventure.)

It is only in this precise sense that the otherwise journalistic designation of our age as the "age of anxiety" is appropriate: what causes anxiety is the elevation of transgression into the norm, the lack of the prohibition that would sustain desire. This lack throws us into the suffocating proximity of the object-cause of desire: we lack the breathing space provided by the prohibition, since, even before we can assert our singularity through our resistance to the norm, the norm in advance enjoins us to resist, to violate, to go further and further. One should not confuse this norm with regulations of our intersubjective contacts: perhaps, in no period in the history of humankind, interactions were so closely regulated; however, these regulations no longer function as the symbolic prohibition—they rather regulate modes of transgression themselves. So when the ruling ideology enjoins us to enjoy sex, not to feel guilty about it, since we are not bound by any prohibitions whose violations should make us feel guilty, the price we pay for this absence of guilt is anxiety. It is in this precise sense that, as Lacan put it, following Freud, anxiety is the only emotion which does not deceive: all other emotions, from sorrow to love, are based on deceit. Again, back to Chesterton, when he writes that "Christianity is the only frame for pagan freedom," this means that, precisely, this frame—the frame of prohibitions—is the only frame within which one can enjoy pagan pleasures: the feeling of guilt is a fake enabling us to give ourselves to pleasures—when this frame falls away, anxiety arises.

It is here that one should refer to the key distinction between the object of desire and its object-cause. What should the analyst do in the case of a promiscuous woman who regularly practices one-night stands, while complaining all the time how bad and miserable and guilty she feels about it? The thing *not* to do, of course, is to try to convince her that one-night stands are bad, the cause of her troubles, signs of some libidinal deadlock—this way, one only feeds her symptom, which is condensed in her (misleading) dissatisfaction with one-night stands. That is to say, it is obvious that what provides the true satisfaction to the woman is not promiscuity as such, but the very accompanying feeling of being miserable—therein resides her "masochistic" enjoyment. The strategy should thus be, in the first step, *not* to convince her that her promiscuity is pathological, but, on the contrary, to convince her that there is nothing to feel bad or guilty about: if she really enjoys one-night stands, she should continue doing them without any negative feelings. The trick is that, when she will be confronted with one-night stands *without* what appears to be the obstacle preventing her to fully enjoy them, but is effectively the *objet a*, the feature which allows her to enjoy them, the only feature through which she can enjoy them, one-night stands will lose their attraction and became meaningless. (And if she will still go on with her one-night stands? Well, why not? Psychoanalysis is not a moral catechism: if this is her way of enjoyment, why not?) It is *this* gap between object and object-cause that the subject has to confront when the prohibition falls away: is she ready to *directly* desire the obstacle as such?[31]

## Notes

1   Gilbert Keith Chesterton, *Orthodoxy* (San Francisco: Ignatius Press, 1995), 107.

2   Gilbert Keith Chesterton, "A Defense of Detective Stories," in *The Art of the Mystery Story*, ed. H. Haycraft (New York: Universal Library, 1946), 6.

3   What is the (in)famous Hegelian triad? Three friends have a drink at a bar; the first one says: "A horrible thing happened to me. At my travel agency, I wanted to say 'A ticket to Pittsburgh!' and I said 'A picket to Tittsburgh!'" The second one replies: "That's nothing. At breakfast, I wanted to say to my wife 'Could you pass me the sugar, honey?,' and what I said was 'You dirty bitch, you ruined my entire life!'" The third one concludes: "Wait till you hear what happened to me. After gathering the courage all night, I decided to say to my wife at breakfast exactly what you said to yours, and I ended up saying 'Could you pass me the sugar, honey?'"

4   Chesterton, *Orthodoxy*, 15.

5   Ibid., 146–47.

6   Alan Dershowitz, *Why Terrorism Works* (New Haven, Conn.: Yale University Press, 2002).

7   See Doug Richmond, *How to Disappear Completely and Never Be Found* (Secausus, N.J.: Carol Pub. Group, 1995). This book belongs to the series of how-to manuals that effectively form a refreshing obscene double of the "official" manual like those of Dale Carnegie: books which directly address our publicly inacceptable desires—other titles in the series include: *Cheaters Always Prosper*, *Advanced Backstabbing and Mudslinging Techniques*, *Revenge Tactics*, and *Spying on Your Spouse*.

8   Chesterton, *Orthodoxy*, 65–66.

9   Ibid., 66.

10  Ibid., 60.

11  Ibid., 62.

12  Ibid., 63.

13  What one should not forget is that both the theory of inscrutable divine Grace and materialism share their opposition to the notion of Providence (of the ultimate balance between virtues and happiness guaranteed by God): both Grace and materialism leave the connection of virtue and happiness to chance.

14  See Matt Ridley, Genome (New York: Perennial, 2000), 64.

15  See Jürgen Habermas, Die Zukunft der menschlichen Natur (Frankfurt am Main: Suhrkamp 2001).

16  Chesterton, Orthodoxy, 105.

17  Ibid., 33.

18  Ibid., 39.

19  Ibid., 164.

20  Years ago, an ironic review aptly characterized The Sound of Music as a movie about a stupid nun who would be allowed to lead her happy monastic life if her Mother Superior were not to invite her to her room and start to shout at her hysterically about the need to climb every mountain.

21  Chesterton, Orthodoxy, 40.

22  Chesterton, Orthodoxy, 47.

23  See Jacques Lacan, "Kant avec Sade," in Ecrits (Paris: Editions du Seuil, 1966).

24  See Jacques Lacan, The Ethics of Psychoanalysis (New York: Routledge, 1992).

25  Michel Surya, Georges Bataille (London: Verso Books, 2002), 479.

26  Georges Bataille, Visions of Excess (Manchester: Manchester University Press, 1985), 154.

27  Surya, Georges Bataille, 176.

28  Georges Bataille, Oeuvres completes (Paris: Gallimard, 1971–88), 3:512.

29  Ibid., 12:296.

30  Ibid., 12:232.

31  One should refer here to the distinction, found in Franz Rosenzweig, between the neighbor (der Naechste) and the "near/proximate thing" (das Naechste): the neighbor is the intriguing object of desire, in front of us, while "the near thing" is the (object) cause of desire, that which, from within us, from behind our back, out of our sight, pushes us toward the object, making it desirable, accounting for the urgency in our approach to the object. (I owe this reference to Eric Santner, of course.)

*Conor Cunningham* | Nothing Is,
Something Must Be:
Lacan and Creation
from No One

There is no cake, there is cake

USING THE WORK OF Lacan[1] but with reference to a number of other philosophers, this article argues eight main theses: first of all, non-Platonic philosophical construction follows after a foundational destruction; second, that
philosophy generally has a nothing outside its text, one that allows for the
formation of that text — for example, Kant forms the text of phenomena only
by way of the noumenal; third, that this transcendental nothing renders all
identities ideal, however that is conceived, an example being Alain Badiou's
notion of "belonging," one derived from the work of Georg Cantor and Paul
Cohen; fourth, that a consequence of this ideality is mereological nihilism;
fifth, due to this mereological nihilism any existent is only ever an aggregate,
an aggregate of some base element, or "stuff" — a position that returns such
philosophy to that of the ancients; six, this collapses idealism and materialism into each other, a collapse marked by what is referred to throughout
as an impossible monism. Moreover, this impossible monism is a result of
philosophy's constant production of a bastard trinity — a dual monism, as it
were. Seven, that there are two models of difference evident in non-Platonic
philosophy: the first is that of a block, with difference cut into it — like Swiss
cheese, as it were, and second, a flux which we seek to arrest with local
regimes of stability; last of all, that theology suggests the possibility of another difference, namely, a peaceable one.

It may be wise at this point to clarify what is meant by the term *impossible
monism*. Elsewhere I have argued that non-Platonic philosophy tends to gen-

erate dualisms that are concomitantly monist, and that this monism was at times named, ignored, or methodologically presupposed.[2] I employed Jastrow's figure of the duck-rabbit to communicate this idea. For there, we are left forever oscillating between two aspects, duck or rabbit—while the One upon which they are made manifest remains forever beyond our attention. Doing so, maybe, because its reality consists only in its aspectual expression; incidentally, Lacan's psychotic appears to reside between the duck and the rabbit. Toward the end of the essay it will be argued that Badiou and Gilles Deleuze adopt a similar position to Lacan. This impossible monism can be summed up as—nothing is, so something must be, for only if nothing is *as* something, will an impoverished immediacy be avoided, one that would require the thought of transcendence for it to be otherwise. Indeed, an example of this necessity is to be found in the Plotinian One, which is *epekeina noeseos*. For this One *must* produce one necessary effect, yet the eternity of this necessity renders this effect contemporary with the One, as it is in the end the impossible self-production of this One. Consequently, "l'un n'est pas," yet "il y a de l'un," as both Lacan and Badiou insist.

Philosophy's understanding of difference tends to arise from, or is generated by, an originary negation. In other words, difference, or construction, comes only after a certain destruction. Consequently, it is possible to argue that positive projects carried out in the name of such philosophy are based on destruction. As Claude Evans, here talking about Husserlian phenomenology, has put it: "Correlative to the method of *Abbau* is the method of 'Aufbau.'"[3] And Heidegger appears to concur when he tells us that "construction in philosophy is necessarily destruction, that is, deconstruction."[4] This destruction (*Destruktion, Abbau,* or *Zerstürung*) can come in many forms, an important example being the phenomenological reduction—the *epoché,* a suspension that leads, according to Edmund Husserl, to "World-annihilation" (*Weltvernichtung*), an annihilation that merely repeats Hegel: "The world is nullified."[5] This nullification, or annihilation, is what Husserl's collaborator Eugen Fink calls a "deworlding," one initiated by a radical *epoché.*[6] This later manifests itself in Sartre's notion of "aneantisant," which for him, following Kojève's reading of Hegel, characterizes consciousness. Interestingly, Derrida tells us, "In everything I try to say and write *epoché* is implied."[7]

The argument goes like this: generally there is a preceding unity in philosophy that is devoid of intelligence as it is before the presence of any "Text," so to speak, whether we call it *nous* or indeed the finite, that is, particular difference, as is the case with Hegel. A consequence of this situation is that there is no community between being and thought. As Lacan argues, "The Discordance between knowledge and being is my subject" (*Seminar XX,* 120).

Of course it could be pointed out that it would be wise to reject any Parmenidian equation of being and thought for fear of monism. But as we shall see, theology does not have to fear, for in positing a community between being and thought (as someone like Augustine does, for instance, when he insists that the true is that which is) there is no bastard trinity, that is, a dualistic opposition that slides into monism—or a One that expresses itself as two. Returning to philosophy—if, then, the philosophical text tends to follow after being, doing so because being and thought do not present us with an ontological community, then all intelligibility will be born from some sort of negation, or violence, as thought will have to impose itself. As Michael Dummett says, regarding Gottlob Frege, "The world does not come to us articulated in any way; it is we who, by the use of our language, *impose* a structure on it."[8] This inarticulate being is what Husserl calls "dumb experience,"[9] or as Lacan puts it, "dumb reality" (*Seminar VII*, 55). I shall employ the work of Jacques Lacan as an example of what I take to be a pervasive logic in philosophy when it is divorced from the theological. I use Lacan because I find in his work the voice of many philosophers, for example, Sartre and Heidegger, but most of all Hegel. Indeed according to Pierre Trotignon, all Lacan does is rewrite Hegel; other commentators such as Jean Wahl concur.[10] Yet Lacan himself admits as much insofar as he declares that Alexandre Kojève is his absolute master because he introduced Hegel's work to him.[11]

In Lacan, we can see that he, following Sartre, who in turn follows Kojève, argues that being, which he variously calls *das Ding*, the real and indeed the mother, lacks all Logos. The thing, which for Lacan, being is, as will be shown, does not afford difference because it is too much, a "full positivity," as Sartre calls it;[12] Lacan echoes this: "By definition, the real is full" (*Seminar IV*, 218). It is only by negating this One—by lacking it—that difference, that is, thought is possible. In other words, being—the Real—must be "decompressed," to put it in Sartrean terms. Lacan refers to this negation as the "murder of the Thing" (*Ecrits*, 104). By murdering the Thing, things can exist, as it were; here we have the strict opposition between being and thought. Lacan sums up this opposition by rewriting Descartes's dictum *cogito ergo sum*: "I think where I am not, I am where I do not think" (*Ecrits*, 166), a rewriting that strongly echoes Paul Valéry: "I think, therefore, I am not." Badiou repeats this understanding when he asks: "How will I, as someone, continue to exceed my own being? Which might also be said as: How will I continue to think?"[13]

Consequently, "truth is akin to Death," as Lacan puts it (see *Ecrits*, 145). And here we see the influence of Hegel for whom death was the "absolute master," as he himself insisted.[14] This assertion caused Kojève to refer to

Hegel's philosophy as one of "death,"[15] bequeathing to those who would follow a legacy of negation, arguably one he had inherited from Plotinus, whom
Hannah Arendt refers to as Hegel's "strange predecessor."[16] Lacan tells us
that "the being of language is the non-being of objects" (Ecrits, 263). We can
easily discern this legacy, one initially inherited from Kojève, in Maurice
Blanchot when he says: "The word gives me what it signifies, but first it suppresses it . . . it is the absence of that being, its nothingness."[17] Indeed, according to Blanchot "speech is tied to an absence of being"[18] but a "pure absence
wherein there is nevertheless a fulfillment of Being."[19] Consequently, Lacan
calls a word a "presence made of absence" (Ecrits, 65). Similarly, Blanchot
tells us that "language begins only with a void";[20] both Lacan and Blanchot
are here merely echoing Kojève, who argued that for Hegel "Being does not
speak" and is made to speak only by what he calls "subtraction," which he
likens to murder.[21] Interestingly, Badiou also considers ontology to be a matter of subtraction, because "being is anterior to language,"[22] indeed he also
considers being as a retroactive fiction, while Lacan speaks of a "retroactive
effect" (l'après-coup) (Seminar XX, 108). For Kojève, the concept "being" is
only possible by what he terms a "remembrance of being."[23] He is here speaking about the gap between a concept or a signifier, and that which is signified,
the object. According to Kojève, the concept of being is articulated only in
the absence of being, otherwise the difference intelligence requires will not
be forthcoming. In other words, signification, or intelligibility, requires a gap,
a space of difference, so that noesis is possible, and such difference can occur
only in the absence of that about which a concept seeks to speak. For the
concept, or the signifier, must step in and become that about which it means
to speak, and this is possible only if the signified is absent. Furthermore, any
concept (Kojève gives the example of "dog") just to function requires a particular betrayal, one that Kojève likens to murder. This betrayal, or murder,
is obvious, for the concept "dog" is precisely not any particular dog. Indeed,
the concept must subtract from the reality of any particular dog, and so exclude specificity. Instead, beings are captured within what one could call the
"true lie" of a successful conceptualization or signification. Again we see why
Lacan describes a word as a "presence made of absence" (Ecrits, 65). And
here we are still very much with Hegel when he tells us that being consists
in "not being what it is and being what it is not (das nicht zu sein, was es ist,
und das zu sein, was es nicht ist),"[24] a situation repeated by Badiou, as we shall
see below. As Lacan makes clear, a corollary of this is that "The signifier already considers [the subject] dead" (Seminar III, 180). Hence our very identity
is based on loss: "I identify myself in language, but only by losing myself in
it" (Ecrits, 86). With Blanchot, Kojève's "dog" becomes a "cat," for he tells us

that when we utter the word *cat* "death speaks."[25] This means that the existence dogs, cats or subjects have is the "Being of non-being" (*être de non-étant*, *Ecrits*, 300). Or as W. V. O. Quine puts it, "Caesar designates Caesar, and Rabbit denotes Rabbit, whatever they are."[26] Consequently, we who speak live "a life that is dead," as Lacan puts it (*Seminar II*, 232), or as Mallarmé says; "I am perfectly dead": this brings to mind Damien Hirst's installation *Some Comfort Gained by the Acceptance of the Inherent Lies in Everything*, which is, to a degree, a progeny of Magritte's "Ceci n'est pas une pipe."

As a result, according to Lacan, the reality of our words serves only to let the silence of the real appear: "The cry does not stand out against a background of silence, but on the contrary makes the silence emerge as silence" (*FFC*, 26). This is Lacan's doctrine of creation ex nihilo, one that he insists provides the opportunity for the complete elimination of God (see *Seminar VII*, 213). How? Well, we as creatures, as that which lives, do so without being. Hence there is now no need for God, for creation is from nothing to such a degree that it exceeds the need for a creator, doing so because it does, in one sense, not only come from nothing but remains so, as it is only the effect, or fabrication, of the signifier: "Every real signifier is, as such, a signifier that signifies nothing" (*Seminar III*, 185). But this nothing, like Heidegger's *das Nicht* or Badiou's void, is not simply negative: "Nothing, perhaps?—not perhaps nothing, but not nothing" (*FFC*, 64); or as Heidegger puts it, much to the annoyance of Rudolf Carnap: "nothing nothings" (*Das Nichts selbst nichet*).[27] As Bruce Fink says, "The word has wrought him or her from nothingness, and he or she can be spoken of, talked about, and discoursed upon—yet remains beingless."[28] I shall return to this below. First let me repeat some salient points, doing so in an effort to elucidate them.

For Kojève, Sartre, Lacan, et al., thought follows after being, after the murder of the thing—the real—which is indistinct, as it is "without fissure" (*Le réel est sans fissure*).[29] It is as if we would starve because our mouths are too full to swallow. Hence we exist only in what Lacan calls the lack of being: "All that exists lives only in the lack of being (*manque-à-être*)" (*Seminar VII*, 294); a formulation that Sartre, echoing Kojève's Hegel, had already articulated: "The being of a lack and as lack, it lacks being."[30] This lack is common to most philosophies that do not understand there to be an otherwise than monistic, nonviolent community of being and thought. In the absence of such a community thought is based on, or generated by, what could be called a trauma. For example, Dummett speaks of "slicing up the world."[31] Similarly, Lacan talks of the function of the cut, which is the cut the sign induces in the Real (see *Ecrits*, 299). Likewise Foucault: "Knowledge is not made for comprehension, it is made for cutting."[32] Badiou speaks of a "formal carving";[33] indeed, for him "every number is in the place of a cut,"[34] just as language causes "a split in existence."[35] This negation, this lack, one predicated on there being nothing outside the text, leads to what Badiou calls the "desubstantialization of truth,"[36] one that had already occurred in the work of philosophers such as Carnap, which we can witness when he tells us "The concept and the object are the same. This identity does not signify a substantialization of the concept, however, but, on the contrary, rather a 'functionalization' of the object."[37] In this way, all truth is only that of the text, something Carnap later came to believe. As Delacampagne says: "Carnap . . . abandoned a theory of truth according to which truth is determined by the correspondence of statements with reality in favor of one that made it reside instead in the internal coherence of statements with each other."[38] This is not too dissimilar to Lacan when he insists "I always speak the truth."[39] In other words, because thought and being are incongruous, "truth," as Spinoza had already insisted, is its own criterion;[40] something which Badiou echoes: "There are no criteria for truth."[41] Consequently, a version of "pragmatism" rules the day; if we do communicate, that is, signify, such an act will bring with its own genesis a "real" significance — one that is coterminous with that genesis. As Quine says, "any statement can be held to be true," moreover "every opinion is revisable."[42] Why? Because, as he argues, "the totality of knowledge . . . is man-made."[43] Consequently, we are involved in what Wilfred Sellars might call "a self-correcting enterprise," one that precludes any translation from the epistemic into the non-epistemic, as Donald Davidson might put it.

It seems that outside the text there is nothing, chaos, the void, or the indeterminate, as Derrida, Deleuze, Badiou, and Dummett insist respectively. Indeed, it should be noted that this idea of a pure text stems from the complete opposition of thought and being, for this accommodates the notion of truth-in-itself. An idea developed by Leibniz, whose bid for a universal *mathesis*, afforded by a *lingua characteristica*, was later to influence Bernard Bolzano, leading him to speak of representation-in-itself or propositions-in-themselves (*Setze an sich*), in the search for a pure logic (*reine Logik*) of ideal objectivities (*Gegenstendlichkeiten*). The desire for such a logic was to animate the work of many nineteenth-century thinkers such as Rudolf Lotze and Alexius Meinong, not to mention Giuseppe Peano, whose system of notation called "pasigraphy," was an attempt to "note everything," and indeed Frege's *Begriffschrift*, an ideography, is itself an attempt at *mathesis*. Of course, such ideas were not confined to what we now refer to as analytical philosophy, for Husserl, following Descartes, also pursued a *mathesis* of experience in his bid to view essences (*Wesenserschauung*). A consequence of which was the confining of truth to an almost Fregean notion of sense, and so to a pure

Text. As Dermot Moran says, with Husserl's understanding of *epoché*, "all questions regarding the true referent of an expression are excluded."[44] Indeed, Husserl says as much when he tells us, "The real relation [*das reale Verheltnis*], previously meant as actually existing, is destroyed,"[45] this of course echoes medieval nominalism, and more recently Badiou, whose entire philosophy is based on a denial of relations. Such "destruction" is but the result of Hegel's and Husserl's call for "world annihilation" (*Weltvernichtung*).

In Lacan, we can see that he negates the thing—the real—by murdering it with the letter, or the word (see *Écrits*, 848). He articulates the formation of thought by way of language, in terms of what he calls the primordial law of incest. The law, which is for him the name-of-the-father (*le nom du père*), divides up being by way of a primordial No: *le non du père* (see *Seminar VII*, 65, and *Seminar III*, 93). This prohibition affords us the functional, yet, in one sense, ontologically fictional, idea of a reality. In this way, the Oedipus complex is the birth of language as such. This is the regime of the symbolic, only as it murders the thing, holding back the real, so preventing our absorption—as we shall see below, this is also the case for Badiou. Yet, as we already know, because reality is predicated on negation, on lack, we lose ourselves in the very finding. To repeat: we exist but do so only by lacking being—we only are in being dead, so to speak. But this death is the very possibility of thought, of signification, for its rigor mortis is the ideality required to arrest the flux. In Husserl this ideality is afforded by repeatability (*Wiederholbarkeit*), because the required ideality, according to Derrida, "does not exist in the world," and so it depends purely on "repetition."[46] As was mentioned above, this was also the case for Kojève, for whom the concept of being is an act of mourning. Moreover, we can see that all "words" chant this originary loss. The word murders the thing—being—and this violence is then repeated as the very possibility of every word: words are, then, the murder of things. We negate the One, rather audaciously, then negate everyone, and this is our existence scratched out within the rubble of a thoughtless being—one that is murdered (Hegel, Kojève, Lacan, and Blanchot) destroyed (Husserl, Fink and Heidegger), decompressed (Sartre), deconstructed (Derrida), desubstantialized, or rendered inconsistent (Badiou).

We see this enabling death in every signifier by way of what Lacan refers to as the "time-lag" (*decalage*) that each involves, for the foundational subtraction takes time (see *Écrits*, 67). This means that our words or concepts, as functional idealities, take time to "ossify" enough to provide symbolization. More importantly, this "time-lag" is merely an echo of the ontological gap between thought and being, which becomes the gap between words and things. Here we return to the point made above, each word and all thoughts operate only by not being that which they might be thought to signify. In other words, only by signifying nothing, there being nothing outside this philosophical text—it being predicated on saying No to the thing, or in Badiou's case, the One—can we actually have sense, which is to say that all sense lacks ontological reference, or that any reference there might be thought to be, is wholly inscrutable, as Quine insists.[47] As a result, "The sign creates the thing signified," as Bourdieu says.[48] A sentiment to a degree echoed by Hilary Putnam when he tells us: "Objects do not exist independently of conceptual schemes."[49] Quine puts it rather more decisively, "No entity without identity," as "reference is nonsense except relative to a system of coordinates."[50] Moreover, such coordinates arise only within what Sellars calls "logical space."[51] Indeed Sellars argues that "all awareness of sorts, resemblances, facts etc., in short all awareness of abstract entities—indeed all awareness, even of particulars—is a linguistic affair."[52] It is for this reason that Quine states "there are no facts of the matter."[53] Just as for both Derrida and Deleuze there is no perception, or if there is it is hallucinatory.[54] What this gives rise to is the development of certain meontological moves, the grounding of this philosophical text in negation. For example, being becomes grounded in nonbeing (*meon*), or what Eugen Fink referred to as "constitutive pre-being" (*Vor-Sein*).[55] Why is this? According to Fink, "The mundane concept of the Absolute is an ontological concept, i.e., means a totality of that which is existent, the phenomenological concept of the Absolute can be characterized as non-ontological."[56] For this reason Fink seeks to develop what he calls a "meontic philosophy of absolute spirit";[57] one that is in search for the "not-existent" (*nichtseiend*).[58] To escape the mundane, and so approach the absolute, this philosophical text must reside within the No, the foundational negation, about which we have already spoken. This No can easily be discerned in the work of Hegel, for example when he tells us that "division [*Entzweiung*] is the source of the need for philosophy."[59] This No appears in many guises. For example, in Lacan it is the No to being, which affords us the being of nonbeing, as we saw above. He also tells us that meaning comes from nonmeaning (see *Écrits*, 508), sense from non-sense (see *Écrits*, 158). This is also the case for Deleuze, for he also argues that sense comes from nonsense,[60] while thought comes from what he calls nonthought,[61] just as the philosophical arrives by way of nonphilosophy.[62] Interestingly, Foucault discerns the operation of what he also refers to as a nonphilosophy in the work of Jean Hyppolite: "The non-philosophy of philosophy itself."[63] So too with Derrida, who seeks to follow Fink's exhortation to move beyond the ontological, the mundane, doing so by moving beyond every origin, by saying No to an origin, having instead *différance* as "non-origin," because it is a "non-concept,"[64] involving what he calls "nonmeaning," or "non-knowledge" (*non-savoir*).[65] As Lawlor says, "Derrida will appropriate from Levinas the notion of the wholly other in order to designate the system which is not a being, the system of nonsense."[66] Because for Derrida, again as Lawlor makes clear, philosophy must not only be determined as "non-mundane and non-existence, but also be determined as non-present."[67]

This meontic text, to use Fink's phrase, paradoxically manifests itself, as intimated above and elaborated upon below, in the generation of what could be termed a "pure text," one that does not speak of being—for thought and being are incongruous, but also because it is the "nothing" outside the text that enables the generation of intelligence. Here again is the foundational negation. This nonexistent also seems to guide the formation of the text that analytical philosophy constructs, because such constructions appear only within the rejection of being as such, as we saw was the case for Carnap, but also, all those philosophical texts that speak of propositions-in-themselves, pure logic, and so on, as mentioned above. This text relies on a "forgetting" of being, for such texts depend on ignoring the excess, or reference, of being, so that the universe of "sense" can construct a world composed of predicates, properties, data, or indeed names in a Badiouian sense. Again there is nothing outside the text. And are not logicism, physicalism, and behaviorism examples of pure texts, that is, abstractions (as Hegel had already implied regarding materialism)? Consequently, does the methodological artificiality of these philosophical texts not present us with what Delacampagne calls "scientific versions of Esperanto"?[68] And does a similar nominalism not also appear in the pure text of molecular biology? A text that, according to Doyle, leaves us as "meat puppets run by molecular machines . . . [which is] the transformation of the organism into an effect of a univocal language of life, an Esperanto of the molecule."[69] Hence it is not surprising to hear philosophers such as Nelson Goodman speak of world making, a feat achieved by the hermetic functioning of such "pure texts," hence his advocacy of what is termed "irrealism." To some degree, then, do we not here witness a coming together of analytical and continental philosophy? Each appears to coalesce around a shared "tradition," or logic, one that we could call "idealism," and it was idealism that Jacobi referred to as "nihilism" in his open letter to Fichte. And do we not discern the presence of such idealism in, for example, the "linguistic turn" prevalent in both philosophies, philosophies that generally stem from Frege and Husserl, who emerged from a similar milieu as progenitors of two parallel traditions? In this way, idealism is the name of much Western philosophy, and postmodern philosophers like Derrida are but modern examples of it. Lawlor appears to be correct when he says that "Derrida departs from the tradition of phenomenology not because he rejects the belief in meaning as ideal unities, but because he believes in meaning as ideal unities. For Derrida, everything depends on Husserl's concept of the noema."[70]

The Romanian writer Émile Cioran warns of the "temptation to exist," which is, according to Valéry, "the flaw in the great diamond." Rightly so, it seems. We already know that for Lacan we are simply the epiphenomena of signifiers, for he argues that "men, women and children are but signifiers" (*Seminar XX*, 33). Why? Because "the letter kills," here echoing Poe, but Lacan continues, "we learn this from the letter" (*Écrits*, 848). And this means that any negativity we deem in such a situation is a gift of that situation, so to speak. In other words, we lack being, but such lack gives birth to us, it is the womb of our difference, as it were, because "there is no such thing as a pre-discursive reality" (*Seminar XX*, 32). Moreover, creation arises, Kojève argues, only by negating the given—being—a negation that ends not in nothingness but in creation.[71] For it is our language, our nomination, which Lacan says makes a hole, and it is this hole, this hollowing out, that generates difference.[72] Lacan gives the example of a vase, which, according to him, receives its "existence" because of the hole in its middle: Lacan derives this example from both Heidegger and Kojève; incidentally, for Badiou our nomination does not bore a hole, but affords a counting-as-one; in other words, it affords collections.

For Lacan, then, existence is a temptation, and we must not be fooled by it, for the pleasure of life's wine brings its own sclerosis, so to speak. Yet we must not look at Lacan as if he is any different from those who had come earlier, especially Hegel. Because for Hegel we, the finite, are not, ontologically speaking; we exist only as an ideal, a piece of the whole held together by the minimal consistency of an ideality, one that from the very possibility of its articulation suspends the whole—or works only in the suspension of the whole.[73] We are ideals, signifiers, just as an entity such as a tomato is not real, only the thing is real: the true is the whole, as Hegel insists. But this whole has to result, at least in terms of the absolute; yet this is also the case for Badiou and Deleuze, as shall be argued below. This state of affairs might be more understandable if we think of an innocuous entity such as a teddy bear. Now, the contrived features that conjure up what we would refer to as the face of the toy is like reality—the realm of the symbolic—indeed, Lacan calls reality a "grimace of the real."[74] Yet the silent inertia of the matter itself—this speechless lump—is the real; Heidegger's notion of the broken tool may well bring a similar understanding to mind. To speak of the teddy bear we use the difference, the reality; the features afford us that by way of exclusion. In other words, we achieve form only by concentrating on the face and ignoring all else. We suspend or lack the whole, so making a cut in the "lump," this lump being itself an abstraction from a greater lump, the whole; or we make a "slice of the multiple" count as one, as Hallward puts it in relation to Badiou.[75] Consequently, objects are always otherwise than their given names. Hence to speak of a particular entity we must kill not only the real thing, but also any particular thing that falls under the shadow of linguistic attention. This is, it seems, the Hegelian and Husserlian nullification of the world, which is, for Badiou, to say no to "the All." And this is what Lacan calls the "structuring function of the lack" (FFC, 29). To repeat: the word murders the thing, words kill things; the gap between being and thought reappears between thoughts and things, to the extent that there is now a pure text, with literally nothing outside it — sense is now its own concern. As Lacan says, "There is only Being due to speaking."[76] Consequently, he speaks of the "void that is in the verb 'to be'" (Ecrits, 168). But we may start to discern certain pressures building up in this logic. For example, in one sense there cannot be any simple "linguistic idealism" because there is always one thing that remains prelinguistically asserted, namely, language itself. Language, then, becomes the thing-in-itself, it being naively presumed, and spoken of and employed with little hesitation. So even if we follow someone like Donald Davidson and reject scheme-content dualism, and so deny the possibility of a neutral nature or material lying behind conceptual schemes — schemes that cut their sense into it, such cutting will reappear in the sectioning and regimentation that language itself suffers — as we shall see, this is also the case for Badiou's multiplicity.

We can begin to realize that if language arises from the murder of the thing, being predicated on its nihilation, its decompression, destruktion, deconstruction, desubstantialization, subtraction, or suspension, then language becomes the new thing, which means the original gap reappears: language is subtracted from being, but now words subtract from things, yet also from the new thing, namely, language. Hence every articulation, that is, signification, must upon its own utterance give way to language, the new thing-in-itself. Consequently, any allocated name is based on a violent exclusion. In other words, for language, thought is otherwise than being, so it inhabits by default an illegitimate place under the sun. It is little wonder, then, that William Burroughs insists that "to speak is to lie, to live is to collaborate";[77] or to use Lyotard's somewhat more pithy assertion, "To speak is to fight."[78] A corollary of this is that identity can only be constructed, built up (Aufbau) from pieces, which are themselves pieces of pieces, and so on. In this way, the construction that follows after the ontological destruction can only be a constructivism, in other words, an idealism. Such destruction

(*Zerstürung*) and construction (*Aufbau*) is but the result of the originary opposition between being and thought, with its concomitant negation: *non*-being. This leads some philosophers (for example, F. W. J. Schelling, Sartre, Lacan, Blanchot, Žižek, and Badiou, to mention but a few) to deem that which is outside thought as excremental, a horrific remainder. This remainder is the aforementioned gap between thought and being, the real and reality. For the desired *mathesis*, the *characteristica universalis*, can succeed only by excluding, or ignoring, the sheer givenness of being. This "thoughtless sludge"—*l'Être sauvage* (wild being), to employ Maurice Merleau-Ponty's phrase—is now behind each and every name, thought, protocol statement, or representation, threatening to escape its "prison" and pour over the constructed boundaries of "sense," disrupting the language game. Consequently, every name must battle that which exceeds it—the named, or the real. This battle, indeed war, is what we now see in postmodern philosophy. We witness it in the rather schizophrenic approach to naming it displays. On the one hand, naming is necessary because being is thoughtless; on the other hand, this means that all names are violent, because they are imposed. Moreover, all names are narcissistic because they "wish to be the only name," as Düttmann puts it.[79] But, of course, narcissism then becomes the only name. We see in this understanding of signification, meaning, and truth, the fundamental violence of this philosophy's being. So postmodernism tells us that all names are false, so all are violent, and this then becomes the name that governs our existence.

Returning to Lacan, we saw above that for him the thing was murdered, and so symbolization became possible, difference could arise. It was mentioned earlier that he characterizes the thing in terms of the mother, while language, the symbolic, was the father—the law that says No, so generating the appearance of difference, sides, edges, and so on. Indeed, Oedipus had been Lacan's hero from the start, for it was Oedipus who asked, "Am I man at the hour I cease to be?" and this, of course, concurs with Lacan's notion that we only are as we lack being. Yet the Oedipus complex is quite troubling at an ontological level, for the simple reason that we can start to realize that any prohibition is actually a description. In other words, it is not that one should not have sex with the mother, but that one cannot. As Lacan himself insists, there is no such thing as a sexual relationship (see *Seminar XX*, 12). As a result we will begin to see that this is because all difference is but nominal. The father, the law that says No, is in effect the mother in trousers, as it were, because s-he is the real and the real does not have any real difference, which is to say, all is the mother so how could one have any sex, there not being two? In this way, it is better to consider the mother and the father as mutual aspects of the one real thing. But—and here is the crux—the real and reality (the symbolic) are also in this way but aspects of a mutual one, an impossible monism. Lacan is forced to admit as much, though only obliquely. According to him, "it is the lack of the lack which makes the real" (FFC, xii). Furthermore, Lacan tells us that the real must "yield" to the symbolic, what Badiou calls "the moving of the real."[80] Why must it? Before answering, let us note that at the same time he tells us that "the thing speaks of itself" (Ecrits, 121). Furthermore, we are told to discern the real by way of impasse. He says, "The real can only be inscribed on the basis of an impasse of formalization" (Seminar XX, 93). Incidentally, this is what Badiou endeavors to do. Lacan continues, "The limits, the points of impasse, of dead ends, show the real yielding to the symbolic" (Seminar XX, 93; emphasis mine). Indeed, he tells us that "the real is said between words, between the lines" (Seminar XX, 119). Consequently, we must, he insists, "be attentive to the un-said that lies in the holes of the discourse, but this does not mean we are to listen as if to someone knocking on the other side of a wall" (Ecrits, 93); this may be why Lacan thinks that the real is knotted. Now, if we are to look between the words, or in the holes of discourse, something strange occurs. We know that language is a lack of being, as it "bores a hole into being," as Sartre puts it.[81] But if language is in effect a hole, surely the holes in its discourse would be the silent solidity of compressed being, being in itself, the thing? So, like the mother and the father of the Oedipus complex, the real and reality (the symbolic) are mutual aspects. But of what? Here we return to Fink's understanding of Husserl's phenomenology.

Lawlor says that according to Fink's understanding of Husserlian phenomenology, "One passes out of the world to what is absolute (nonbeing) and that one remains with the world (being) because the world is rediscovered as lying within the absolute."[82] This is why Fink, as we saw above, speaks of a meontic philosophy of the absolute. And is it not true that Lacan's being of nonbeing is strictly analogous to this nonmundane absolute, this nothing which is? Furthermore, we can see that Badiou follows this line exactly, for he says no to the all, deeming it inconsistent and it is this inconsistent, this pas tout, that Žižek argues is Badiou's Lacanian real.[83] Badiou says No to the One because he deems it inconsistent—in other words, it cannot be counted or unified. A consequence of which is, as he says, that "without One, nothing is" (echoing Parmenides),[84] and Badiou means this with a particular strength, but this seems only to repeat Lacan who, as we saw earlier, says "Nothing, perhaps? Not perhaps nothing, but not nothing" (FFC, 64). Nothing is, in a strong sense; this is Fink's meontic philosophy of the Absolute, which we know he calls nonbeing. Indeed, because being is, according to Fink, a "moment of the absolute" and the absolute is nonbeing, then we can begin to see why such philosophy desubstantializes truth.[85] And this desubstantial-ization is pervasive; from, say, John Locke, for whom truth belongs only to propositions, to A. J. Ayer. This is a sentiment repeated, of course, in analyti-cal philosophy's general insistence that truth, meaning, or sense belong only to language — an insistence that can be witnessed in the variety of deflation-ary approaches such philosophy takes to the concept of truth. For example, disquotationalism renders truth purely a matter of language, or even a pro-sentential understanding of truth that in some sense deems truth redundant. Here we witness thought become being, and so paradoxically we are back with Parmenides. Interestingly, we can witness this paradox in Badiou. For he asserts, on the one hand, that "being is anterior to Language," yet the consequence of this is that he concurs with Parmenides by asserting that "thinking and being are the same thing."[86] The presupposition here is that ontologically, that is, in terms of *esse*, we do not exist, so Badiou is somewhat in agreement with Cioran, who we know deems existence a temptation, and we are returned to Kojève, Lacan, Sartre, and Blanchot, according to whom we are the living dead, cadavers that speak — or rather, cadavers because we speak, for only in speaking can death acquire sense, that is, significance. In other words, death is an event purely of the signifier, and the subject is that event and this is what Lacan calls the "fabricated signifier" (*Seminar VII*, 120). Moreover, according to Lacan, the very emptiness induced by the signifier, its lack of being, facilitates the idea of filling what can now be perceived as empty (here we can recall the example of the vase). For this reason, as men-tioned earlier, Lacan advocates a creationist doctrine, one that is not only atheist, but consubstantial with thought itself, and this is the move we see Badiou make when he equates thought and being. For this reason the subject is not a being toward death, as Heidegger argues, but a being from death — creation ex nihilo.

To repeat: being and thought are in opposition; thought then negates being, but then we find that being is but a moment of the absolute which is nonbeing, so being is twice negated. Consequently, thought now stands in for being, tempting us into existence by conjuring up signifiers "thick" enough to make idealized moments, which subsist for a time: such "thick" signifiers are akin to what Lacan calls *point de capiton*. We now can see that the real and reality, being and thought, infinite and finite, mother and father, are but aspects of the absolute, namely, "nonbeing," and the movement we see is but the self-movement of this meontic One. For this reason it is not sur-prising that Derrida tells us that for Husserl "passage is the absolute"; a pas-sage named *différance* in his own philosophy.[87] So, keeping the Neoplatonic notion that "from one comes one" in mind, can we not begin to see that from one comes the One? In other words, difference is a "result" (in a Hegelian sense) of the self-mutilation of a masochistic monism—the Absolute. To put it starkly, it is like flogging a dead horse with its tale until the force of the blows gives the appearance of movement and the wounds that of difference.

What characterizes this One, the absolute who is nonbeing, or the passage between being and Non-being, is a certain necessity. As Žižek says, "The Lacanian name for such an entity that is simultaneously necessary and impossible is, of course, the real"[88] or "the impossible real-thing," as he puts it elsewhere.[89] Indeed, it is because the real is impossible, as Lacan insists it is (see FFC, 167), that it presents itself or approaches only by way of the thing, or the object a—this is what Richard Boothby calls the "real of das Ding."[90] The necessity that the real involves is manifest also in Plotinus's One beyond being, who necessarily produces one effect, which in the end is something of a self-production. For the One on its own would be but an "unbroken whole," to employ Plotinus's own phrase;[91] just as for Lacan everything is "originally confused" (Ecrits, 65)—and of course Hegel's infinite requires the production of its one effect—namely, the finite. So it is little surprise to see this One, the absolute who is nonbeing—a non to being—reappear in Lacan, for whom the real is "knotted" with reality; nothing with something, nonbeing. According to Lacan, the real is beyond symbolization, but this is, of course, to leave itself open to being symbolized as that which is beyond symbolization; so too the One beyond being. Consequently, the real must produce reality, with which it is not to be identified, and not not to be identified—here echoing Hegel's understanding of the infinite in relation to the finite.

Let me elaborate on the nature of this One by alluding to two allegories. In Kafka's Before the Law, the man from the country sits before the law, in doing so he intimates the relationship between reality and the real, or indeed the One and the many. For example, we must ask, "What is before the law?" Well, we know that the man is before the law, yet from a slightly different angle, we can also say that the law itself is before the law. This simply means that the law is constituted only by the man remaining outside, as this affords division—an inside and an outside. In other words, the man who fails to enter the law, remaining forever before it, is the advent or possibility of the law, as his exclusion offers itself as a constitutive limit. But this means that the law is in some sense before itself, and so is lawless. Schelling makes a similar point, as Wolfram Hogrebe makes clear: "Something or other is the pre-rational spur of the rational. There is meaning only because there is madness."[92] So the law requires a certain contamination just to operate, what Peter Dews calls a "proto-ontological inconsistency,"[93] one which Žižek calls a "pathological stain,"[94] indeed for him the subject is possible only because it is impossible—for if we were purely ourselves, that is, pure subjectivity, then there would be only blank nothingness. This we see is why the One must produce an effect. Consequently, the One is in a similar predicament to the law, for the One cannot, in a sense, be One on its own. In other words, you cannot have your cake and eat it: if you eat the cake there is no longer a cake, it is broken, but without eating it, then the cake as an idea is pure emptiness. Indeed, it is for this reason that being, or the One, is for Lacan and company retroactive, as I mentioned above. In this way, to have cake, there cannot be a cake; alternatively, only in eating the cake can the cake be thought, or the One, the cake, is merely the result of a Cambridge change, its reality being only in the pieces. In other words, the pieces, or slices, give rise to the idea of the One, they allow it to be thought. This is what Lacan calls *extimité*, the excluded interior: the One and its one necessary effect (see *Seminar VII*, 101). As Boothby says, "In the encounter with *das Ding* the subject comes into relation with an aspect of the real that is at once inside and outside itself."[95] This *extimité* is the very impossibility of the real. An impossibility that leads Bruce Fink to say that "the real . . . does not exist."[96]

The One is, then, the result of a particular anguish. As Lacan says, "A privileged object, which has emerged from some primal separation, from some self-mutilation induced by the very *approach* of the real" (*FFC*, 83; emphasis mine). The approach of the real gives rise to what he elsewhere calls "primal masochism" (see *Seminar I*, 172–174). What is crucial is that this is not the real, rather it is only ever the *approach* of the real, its beginnings. In other words, the approach of the One as one is its beginning to be one: the would-be-one. It is for this reason that Lacan refers to the One as "the One-missing" (*l'Une-en-moins, Seminar XX*, 129). Indeed he asks: "Is the One anterior to discontinuity? I don't think so" (*FFC*, 26). Why not? Well, Lacan also says that "the signifier alone guarantees the theoretical coherence of the whole as whole" (*Ecrits*, 126). This is what he calls the "not whole" (*pas-tout*) (*Seminar XX*, 7). Indeed, Lacan says elsewhere that "there is no whole, nothing is whole."[97] And this is why Badiou says there is "no All,"[98] or that the "whole inconsists."[99] Similarly, the law can only approach itself because of the constitutive contamination. But that which this self-mutilation affords (the object, *das Ding*, or even *nous*) is the embodiment of a desire to return to that from which it came. This should not surprise us too much, for if it is there so that the "source" can be what it is, then it is only aspectually different from that source. In this way, the One is like a mirror, but because it is alone it cannot be what it is, for there is nothing else for it to reflect and so *be* a mirror; interestingly, Schelling argues that "the possible world appears to God as if in a mirror."[100] It is for this reason that we are not only before the law, but we are also before the "bar." Because for Lacan, as Jean-Luc Nancy and Philippe Lacoue-Labarthe argue, "the Bar is foundational, originary," hence the other is barred.[101] The other is not itself, because there is "no other of the other" (*Ecrits*, 311). For this reason, "there is no full other," as Yannis Stravrakakis argues.[102] Hence the other is traumatic, and the other is the would-be-one—it is, then, a matter of *Nachträglichkeit*.

*Nous*, or the object, which arises from this primordial need, is like an eye. But when this eye looks into the mirror it will wish to return, to lose itself. As Judith Butler says: "For both Lacan and Deleuze, ontological unity is primary, and only becomes interrupted through the advent of cultural law . . . which results in . . . relentless dissatisfaction. The unity or absolute presence then becomes the tacit but fundamental project of desire. The Hegelian effort to transvaluate or supersede all negativity into an all encompassing Being remains the constitutive desire of these ostensible post-Hegelian positions."[103] Butler is both wrong and right about Deleuze—we shall return to him below. Regarding Lacan, Boothby says, "The Real is experiencable only in the loss of an imaginary unity."[104] For Lacan, the thing, or the object that comes from the One, is, as he says, "That which in the real, the primordial real, I will say, *suffers* the signifier" (*Seminar VII*, 118; emphasis mine). The One suffers the signifier, but in so doing, it can be the mirror that it is, so to speak. But then the desire for absorption is all the more strong, for the object is ontologically not the One—a piece of it as such; being but a function of the cut (*coupure*). In Borges's allegory—*The Fauna of the Mirror*—the mirror people, who are ignored by those outside, will one day get their revenge, and this is, in a sense, the One's anger at the object's tolmatic audacity, its presumption of being, or even that being is—for only the One is really real. The revenge is double edged, though. For example, in Bataille's *Story of the Eye*, the protagonist attempts a form of acephality, so as to end the reign of detached reason, challenging its sovereignty. The character Simone takes the eye of the dead priest and puts it into her vagina, thus returning to the primal, at least according to Bataille. But here, then, is the vicious, or violent, circle—for the eye is first ripped from the face of the unseeing One, just so that it can reflect, but such sight drives the One, in a sense, to reabsorb the difference now cognized. Similarly for Lacan, on the one hand, "The Real is that which always comes back to the same place," and on the other, the "object is by nature a refound object" (*Seminar VII*, 118). Furthermore, "Our starting point, the point we keep coming back to, since we will always be at our starting point, is that every real signifier . . . signifies nothing" (*Seminar III*, 185). Moreover such a situation is the "signifier's presence in the real" (*Seminar III*, 119). Hence, as Boothby argues, "The object is at once filled with content and formally empty."[105] This, then, is the retroactive effect (*l'après coup*) that the real is.

Now, those who argue that in such Neoplatonist gods there is only monism are wrong to the degree that they concentrate only on the pronominal aspect—in other words, that which is contractive. They who discern creation proper pay more attention to the predicative—that which is expansive. Both are, of course, wrong, for this divinity fails on both counts. First of all, there is no monism, because the One, as an opaque mirror, so to speak, cannot *be* one, hence it is always beyond being. And second, it cannot create because all that does arrive is but the One's own realization. This is the absolute necessarily resulting, as we see with Hegel's God. We know that according to Lacan, the "Real must yield to the symbolic," and in so doing, the real "distinguishes itself." Yet conversely, as Lacan makes clear: "The symbolic, directing itself towards the real, shows us the true nature of *object a*" (*Seminar XX*, 93, 95). And it must be remembered that the object is the real. Hence it is not too surprising when Fink says that "Lacan's is a dialectic between part and whole with a twist: the whole is never whole."[106] For this reason, Žižek says that the "Real-Thing is really another name for the void,"[107] just as Lacan tells us that the "Real is a hole."[108] Consequently, the One says of its one necessary effect: *Wo Es war, soll Ich werden.* Or as Lacan expresses it: "The Lack of the lack makes the real"—the real must be made (*FFC*, xii).

As noted above, Butler posits a pre-Oedipal thing for Deleuze, and this is of course incorrect, just as there is no incestuous thing for Badiou—hence there is no simple desire for reabsorption. But this does not necessarily distinguish either of them from Lacan, at least on the reading offered here. Why not? Simply put, this thing is retroactive, just like the cake that subsists, as it were, only within its own consumption, its own impossibility. Indeed, it is arguable that this impossible monism appears in both Deleuze and Badiou and for a similar reason. Above I mentioned Bataille's heroine placing the eye, as an egg, into her vagina. Deleuze and Guattari also speak of an egg: "The BWO is the egg. But the egg is not regressive; on the contrary it is perfectly contemporary."[109] As is indeed the case with the cake! Now, this is important if such philosophy is to avoid a suicidal death drive. And it is important to avoid this; otherwise pluralism will not equal monism, as both Deleuze and Guattari insist it does.[110] Because if this equation does not work, there will be only pure immediacy. If that were the case, then nothing would not be *as* something, and this impoverished state could allow for a conception that afforded difference, and this conception might entertain the idea of transcendence. Now, if there is absorption then what we can conclude is that there is not really monism proper. Because to insist on absorption is to insinuate an empty One, as it were. Consequently, only by having a monism that does not demand absorption can there be a plenitudinal monism. So those who, in the name of Deleuze, for instance, insist on pure destruction are actually fake monists as such. For they have in this pure negativity, by default, constructed a crack in the monism, as they have exceeded it, doing so because they are able to limit it—in other words, monism can, then, only be negative. Badiou and Deleuze appear to realize this, hence the latter warning against unlimited destratification, for example. Indeed, this is why Badiou argues against the semblance of equivocity, instead casting his vote with univocity. For if equivocity were true, then utter destruction could well be advocated, but univocity at least gives the appearance that it avoids this. More importantly, the awareness of a need to allow for a less than negative characterization of monism, or indeed the void, can disclose four tendencies in their respective philosophies. First of all, the presence of an impossible monism, one that is inherently Neoplatonic, as there is an overriding necessitarianism, and the accompanying principle of "from one comes one"; second, the positing of a basic element, a "stuff," a substance; third, a "nothing outside their text," governing its formation; and lastly, mereological nihilism.

Regarding necessity, Deleuze tells us: "Something in the world *forces* us to think."[111] He continues, "Difference *must* be shown differing."[112] Likewise, Badiou: "Necessity is always a result";[113] moreover, as Hallward says, "the One is not, precisely because ones, unifications come to be as results."[114] Furthermore, as Deleuze insists, "The whole is not a closed set. The whole *creates* itself."[115] How, we might ask, does it do this? Well, for one thing, it must *produce* multiples, so to speak, that which is counted-as-one. In other words, the pure multiple's one necessary effect is the generation of the "count-as-one." For without this, the pure multiplicity will be a pure immediacy and such an immediacy may well reintroduce the idea of unity, doing so through the back door, as it were. As Hallward puts it, for Badiou "pure multiplicity *must not* itself be made consistent."[116] If it were, the One would return as the pure flux. Now, the introduction to this article mentioned that there were two models of difference available to the philosophical text, generally speaking. The first is the block into which we dig our meaningful holes, while the second is the flux that must be arrested if sense is to be forthcoming. What is interesting about the impossible monism in Lacan, Badiou, and indeed Deleuze is that the flux must, as it were, perform a citizen's arrest on itself—hence the masochistic eye ripped from the face, or the cake consumed, so allowing for the idea of the cake but one that is retroactive and so impossible. As Deleuze puts it: "Self-differentiation is the movement of a virtuality which actualizes itself. Life differs from itself."[117]

Badiou employs the axiom of extensionality so as to develop "belonging" (written ∈) as the only predicate of existence. In so doing, he will, he hopes, have the nothing *as* something: the void as the multiple of nothing. Badiou seeks pure presentation, something incidentally Virilio warns against, and this presentation is a structured presentation of multiplicity: we shall see that this "pure" presentation is indeed impure as it involves necessity.[118] The problem with the axiom of extensionality, wherein the members of a set have priority over the set, is that it leaves us bereft of a structuring principle, as Hallett argues. Indeed, according to him, for us to then say that sets exist is nothing but a "bald statement."[119] Yet this is mereological nihilism, affording only identity by way of aggregation. Badiou proudly indicates such a stance when he tells us that "identity is never anything other than an arrest of movement," a position which is corollary of his employment of extensional sets, by way of the axiom of choice, so as to accommodate his use of "belonging" as the sole predicate of existence.[120] But for Deleuze identity involves a "slowing down,"[121] or as he puts it elsewhere, "We exist only in contemplation—that is to say, in *contraction*."[122] Accordingly, difference is achieved only by arresting the flux, for we must "section" chaos, "wresting" sense from it.[123] So "man must constitute himself through the *repression* of the germinal flux."[124] Now, two things come together here: first, the governing nothing outside this philosophical text, and second, the base element. For Deleuze it is chaos, or life, which must be arrested or differed so as to avoid pure immediacy, hence something forces thought. As Deleuze says regarding science, art, and philosophy, they "cast planes over the chaos,"[125] while for Badiou it is the void, the inconsistent multiplicity that is arrested. Consequently, this void appears very much mediated, as it is, in a sense, contemporary only with the arresting. It is indeed the empty set, or rather the emptying set, for it is this emptying that affords the constitution of sets—no doubt this is a diabolic anaplerosis, for it fills by emptying. Moreover, as Hallward says, for Badiou "inconsistency is the *stuff* of every consistent presentation," or "substance" as he also refers to it.[126] This is indeed Badiou's base element.

Now, what arises is the problem of collapse. For example, for the Stoics such a threat arose from conflagration (*ekpyrsois*), for there, the universe resolves itself into creative fire, yet cosmic regeneration or palingenesis requires the interaction of this creative fire with precosmic moisture. As one commentator asks, "Whence comes the moisture?"[127] Such relations of differentiation are tensional, but in so being a stronger force, one that may collapse them into empty nothingness, always haunts such systems. For Badiou and Deleuze this is also the case. We know that for them life differs, or the multiple inconsists. Likewise, the "cake eats itself," but as the piece is it and the cake cannot now be discerned, absorption is eluded. But real difference is not forthcoming. When Deleuze, for instance, adopts the use of infinitives from the Stoics so as to avoid propositions, this use lapses into merely the splitting of infinitives, emulating the "split infinity," that is, the impossible monism of such philosophy. For example, "to green" must accommodate "to really green"; if not, then a pure atomism arises, one that affords a strange unicity, one that paradoxically resembles Parmenides's monism; incidentally, this unicity appears in Hume, for he has the object and subject as bundles of perceptions, which means that any single perception becomes a Parmenidian "one" all of its own. But more importantly, for Deleuze life *must* differ—here advocating a positive conception of power similar to that developed by Foucault.

Yet such power *must* split. For example, "the will-to-power" is problematic. As power cannot be itself on its own, as it were, just as Plotinus's One cannot. Power requires will, yet the converse is true. "To power" becomes "to will power," but this is also, then, "to power will"—likewise "to differ" becomes "to actually differ," or "to really multiply," and so ensure that the multiplicity avoids consistency. But this splitting of infinitives leads not to a simple inconsistency, but to an insistent and persistent inconsistency. It must be remembered that Badiou is keen to be rid of the finite as an original principle, and it is this which Žižek criticizes him for, fearing that the real can be discerned only through mortality. But the finite and infinite divide reappears, in the guise of the consistent and the inconsistent. For difference is had by the mediation afforded by consistency, one that prevents the multiplicity coagulating into one pure flux, as it were. Yet just as for Hegel, the absolute is in truth the in-finite, so the multiple is the in-consistent.

This means the ideal identities afforded by such mereological nihilism, our aggregation of their base elements, everything is but an instantiation of an invisible void, and this is no longer Badiou's void; as it is relegated to one side of a dialectic, so too Deleuze's life. And this dialectic, or this dualism, is threatened by a concomitant third—one that may render difference nominal, and so induce pure immediacy. Consequently, their impossible monism ceases, as equivocity is all that is forthcoming. This is a univocity of nonbeing. In this way, Badiou's philosophy of "pure presentation" is akin to Hegel's idealism, which is one of re-presentation. Just as Hegel's infinite results by the necessary production of the finite, which is of course the necessary production of only one effect, and so again is the self-production of the One, so too does Badiou's pure multiplicity, which has to induce the constant re-presentation of multiplicities that will count as one, a provision underwritten by their ontological untruth. So they, like Hegel's finite beings and Lacan's symbolizations, are successful failures. In effect they say "I am," so providing the requisite consistency, as is the case with Derrida's understanding of the sign's iterability, yet they in truth say "I am not"; just as the sign says "I am not what I signify, yet I only am by signifying what I am not." This need involves each monism in an "ergetic" becoming, as each One, or No One, is left forever, like a Sisyphus, to rise and fall between the poles of nothing and something. As Deleuze insists, rather than there being a theatre of the Oedipus complex, there is instead a factory as "everything is production,"[128] though one must ask—does this include production? Hence our infinitives and infinities split: "to *actually* produce." Nothing is, so something *must* be, and this something must signify the nothing; the no-thing of the text. Here, then, is the impossible desire of the impossible One—who can construct difference only by ontological misrecognition (*méconnaissance*). This leaves difference as the violent fruit of a perpetual dialectic between narcissism and self-loathing, a dialectic we can maybe name *Spaltung*. As Baudelaire puts it, "I am the wound and the knife." One is here reminded of Barnett Newman's series of paintings entitled *Onement*, or Badiou's "oneification."

So, then, according to Lacan's somewhat Hegelian text, all existence is but the manifestation of a One that bitterly lacerates its plump body in impotent anger. This One (who is always missing), this absolute who is *nonbeing*, must pass into being—the world, yet at the same time, this world is negated by the One. Consequently, this is the self-generation and negation of the No One, the nothing that *must* be *as* something. By contrast, for Theology the "body of Truth" receives such mutilation only by those who ask: "What is Truth?" as did Pilate, rather than "Who is Truth?" Badiou does in the end ask what, rather than who, for he names the void, in that he substantializes it. This is the "symptom of his situation," to use Žižek's phrase. Moreover, this situation is that of a purely secular state. For Badiou does indeed fill the void, doing so with the carcass of a dead God, a God he *must* keep "inexistent"; this, then, is the state of his situation. Badiou is not, then, a "guardian of the void," which he thinks philosophers should be; rather, he is a guard, like the one in Kafka's allegory. But this God was only ever his, or his ancestors', for instance, Plotinus's. He mistakenly thinks that infinity was central to theology, and this is not at all the case, whether historically or systematically. Maybe he made this mistake because of his dislike of tradition, hence his metaphysics is oblivious that it stands in a line running through Avicenna, Scotus, Suarez, Wolff, and so on. Yet just as Johann Hamann chastised Kant for his "purisms of Reason," maybe Badiou must be asked about his "purisms of truth," which give rise to the "adolescent" notion of a pure event, as Catherine Pickstock puts it.[129] Interestingly, we can here discern the difference between the impulse we witness in modernism from that which we see in postmodernism, and between difference as a block, requiring negation, and as flux, needing arrest. Furthermore, we can here maybe intimate a third model of difference, however briefly, one advocated by theology.

Modernism, in one sense, is motivated by a sense of overcoming limits, as it tries to push beyond the labels and words, being ever more innovative, whether that is in literature, music, or art. For example, modern art seeks to present the "object" in new ways, and it does not matter if such efforts are iconoclastic, anarchic, or even vicious, they are still governed by the idea of excess—so someone like Bataille is still modernist, at least in this sense. As is, of course, Adorno, who seeks the "truth" of the nonconceptual, that which is heterogeneous to thought. Yet so also does Deleuze, who seeks to "smash" restrictions and so aggregate new "blocs of sensation."[130] Badiou is just as typical, at least in this regard, because his guiding premise is that "everything that is consensual is suspect."[131] Hence his "inaesthetics" seeks to be a pure and new presentation of the pure *il y a*; this is what Hallward calls "Badiou's essentially modernist emphasis on the new and exceptional." So these modernists, they who discern limits and seek to transcend them, reconfiguring the given, are like climbers, making their way up over a high, high obstacle, muscles shaking under the strain, sweat, maybe even blood falling. But postmodernism changes the camera angle, moving back, until we see that this obstacle is a brick wall in the middle of an unremarkable field. We cannot, then, simply climb over a wall, one built just that morning, and think we have actually gotten somewhere later that afternoon. Indeed, this wall is like the markers, the signifiers, or concepts with which we seek to arrest the flux. But —and here is the crucial point—the *more is less*. In other words, to climb over the wall, or get behind the label, is to realize that there is nothing there, and that sense, or indeed meaning, is arbitrary, something we maybe should have suspected when we realized that sanity requires insanity, the law lawlessness, and so on. When we climb over the wall all we discover is nominalism. Consequently, we are left not with Freud's *da/fort* game, instead there is the mindless presence only of *da da da da*. As Malcolm Bowie argues, "The noise of da da da . . . this is the language of prophecy moving towards final emptiness";[132] or Mallarmé: "Nothing but the place will have taken place."[133]

Such a situation is a corollary of the two prevalent models of difference, as both presume violence as the very possibility of thought. Consequently, difference results from cutting, slicing, arresting, repressing, contracting, splitting, subtracting, and so on. Such anguished gymnastics are the outcome of pure immanence, for the only purity in such an understanding is that this immanence will indeed be pure with regard to the immanent, except, of course, the see-*saw* motion of impossible monism as it consumes itself in an endless production. By contrast, theology understands difference neither as a given block, nor as a given, yet endless flux. Yet theology does present difference as both specific and open. But still there is no given into which we can plunge our blades, or corral into meaningful sections. Divine simplicity precludes any such understanding regarding creation, and in this way, the Creator/creation relation is the true even of two, about which Badiou speaks and indeed seeks. It is little surprise, then, that Lacan, Badiou's master, suggests that "if no religion is true, Christianity comes closest to the form of truth,"[134] and that Badiou echoes this: "All the parameters of the doctrine of the event are thus laid out in Christianity."[135] The true reason for this is, I suggest, that theology is properly Trinitarian, rather than generating bastard trinities, which the introduction to this essay suggested was prevalent in non-Platonic philosophies. For example, Badiou's dualism consistent/inconsistent, like Hegel's finite/infinite, hides, as it were, a third figure, which is the very *movement* between these two perpetual aspects; Hegel names this *Geist*, while Spinoza names it substance, it being the third between God or nature. This is also the case for Deleuze's chaos that becomes sectioned, or the life that differs — between these two lies the third, upon which we cannot, it seems, fix our cognitive gaze. But such bastard trinities preclude nonviolent difference. Consequently, the politics of such difference remains reactive rather than creative. For instance, Badiou's events are solely intelligible, somewhat paradoxically, in terms of the "state" within which they are not counted; an event is a breakdown in the count. Yet this is deeply unsatisfactory because in an almost Hegelian sense, what counts, is counted or discounted, or what inconsists, consists, or is consisting, remains dependent on a perspective, the location of which is now utterly relative. Hence the call for pure events is marked by a distinct impurity — for the purity arises only from being free of that which they reject, or exclude.

According to theology, there is a nonreductive community between being and thought, to the degree that thought is not less than being, it does not fall short, as if it simply failed, for being induces thought, doing so because being is the beyond *of* thought — it is thought's beyond. Indeed, Parmenides hinted at such a notion when he tells us that "thought is excess" (*to gar pleon esti noema*). In this way, can we not come to understand that unless we have been thought, that is, unless we subsist as the lived nonidentical repetition of divine thought, then we will lapse into either of the two problematic models of difference. In being thought by God, being called into existence, I am the recollection of that call — the being of being thought by God. Such *anamnesis* prevents any subsequent hemorrhage of finitude into indefinite multiplication. For the specific is recalled, so it turns (*metanoia*) to hear this call, halting its slide into the dark night of purely negative determination, perpetual epistemic investigation, or absolute singularity—Ockham's *res absolutae*. For creation is this specific other, or difference, which is the fruit of the Father's delight in the Son. Now, what it seems must be understood is that there is only difference because of love: difference is subalternate to love. Let us take the myth of the Fall as instructive. There we see the problem of difference first raise its head. For one can venture that it was not the breaking of God's instruction that caused the Fall. Instead, it seems that it was the very idea of knowledge apart from God that was the Fall. For this idea, this concept of a separate *gnosis*, and an autarchical, epistemic realm, as it were, was indeed the Fall. Why? Because the immanent requires the mediation of transcendence to afford it peaceful distinction. But when the immanent turns to a separate realm to secure its identity, there is a lapse into pure immanence. And it is here that all Derrida's problems concerning the gift, and so on, occur. Not because all giving is contaminated by self-interest, but because donor, donee, and donation fail to achieve distinction except by violent insistence. So in this way the gift I seek to give you is ripped from the whole, strapped together and parceled up with wrappers of exclusive subtraction— in other words, a Badiouian event. Indeed, there is no this or that, no me or you, so to give is always the playing out of a violent myth, that of the given. Like Hegel's finite, the truth of such being, is nonbeing. We must, then, be otherwise than *this* being.

The world is gone, I have to carry you.—Paul Celan

## Notes

1    Throughout this article I shall refer to the main works of Lacan by way of abbreviation in the main text as follows: Jacques Lacan, *Ecrits*, trans. A. Sheridan (London: Routledge, 1977), hereafter *Ecrits*; the French version, Jacques Lacan, *Écrits* (Paris: Seuil, 1966), hereafter *Écrits*; Jacques Lacan, *Seminar I: Freud's Papers on Technique*, trans. John Forrester (New York: Norton, 1988), hereafter *Seminar I*; *The Seminar of Jacques Lacan, Book II: The Ego in Freud's Theory and in the Technique of Psychoanalysis 1954–1955*, trans. S. Tomaselli (New York: Norton, 1991), hereafter *Seminar II*; Jacques Lacan, *The Seminar of Jacques Lacan, Book III, 1955–1956*, trans. R. Grigg (London: Routledge, 1993), hereafter *Seminar III*; Jacques Lacan, *Seminar IV, La relation d'object* (Paris: Seuil, 1994), hereafter *Seminar IV*; Jacques Lacan, *The Four Fundamental Concepts of Psychoanalysis*, trans. A. Sheridan (London: Vintage, 1998), hereafter FFC; Jacques Lacan, *The Ethics of Psychoanalysis, Book VII, 1959–1960*, trans. D. Porter (London: Routledge, 1992), hereafter *Seminar VII*; Jacques Lacan, *Seminar XX, On Feminine Sexuality: The Limits of Love and Knowledge*, trans. Bruce Fink (New York: Norton, 1998), hereafter *Seminar XX*.

2   See Conor Cunningham, *Genealogy of Nihilism* (London: Routledge, 2002).

3   Claude Evans, "Phenomenological Deconstruction: Husserl's Method of *Abbau*," *Journal of the British Society for Phenomenology* 21 (1990): 19.

4   Martin Heidegger, *The Basic Problems of Phenomenology*, trans. Albert Hofstadter (Bloomington: Indiana University Press, 1982), 23. During his debate with Ernst Cassirer at Davos (March 17–April 6, 1929), Heidegger employed the word *Zerstürung* rather than *Abbau*, which is a much stronger, indeed violent, notion of negation. Heidegger later tried to stop the publication of the text that used *Zerstürung*, a text that he had handed out at that time; see Ernst Cassirer and Martin Heidegger, *Debat sur le kantisme et la philosophie* (Davos, mars 1929), ed. Pierre Aubenque (Paris: Beauchesne, 1972), 24.

5   G. W. F. Hegel, *The Logic*, trans. William Wallace (Oxford: Clarendon, 1975), 82.

6   Edmund Husserl, *Ideas Pertaining to a Pure Phenomenology and to a Phenomenological Philosophy, First Book*, trans. F. Kersten (Dordrecht: Kluwer, 1982), first book, section 49, 109–112. Also see Eugen Fink, "The Phenomenological Philosophy of Edmund Husserl and Contemporary Criticism," *The Phenomenology of Husserl*, ed. R. O. Elveton (Chicago: Quadrangle Books, 1970), 133. Fink also employs the stronger version of destruction (*Zerstürung*, 93).

7   Jacques Derrida, "Hospitality, Justice and Responsibility," *Questioning Ethics: Contemporary Debates in Philosophy*, ed. Richard Kearney and Richard Dooley (London: Routledge, 1998), 81.

8   Michael Dummett, *Frege: Philosophy of Language* (London: Duckworth, 1973), 504.

9   See Edmund Husserl, *Cartesian Meditations*, trans. D. Cairns (The Hague: Martinus Nijhoff, 1960), 38.

10   For Trotignon and Wahl, see Jean-Luc Nancy and Philippe Lacoue-Labarthe, *The Title of the Letter: A Reading of Lacan*, trans. Francois Raffoul and David Pettigrew (Albany: SUNY Press, 1992), 130. Also see Malcom Bowie, *Lacan* (London: Fontana, 1991), 95, where he suggests that there is a strong Hegelian undercurrent in Lacan's work.

11   Jacques Lacan, "Luetourdit," *Scilicet* 4 (1973): 9.

12   Jean-Paul Sartre, *Being and Nothingness*, trans. H. Barnes (London: Routledge, 2000), 22–23.

13   Alain Badiou, *L'Être et l'événement* (Paris: Editions du Seuil, 1988), 45.

14   G. W. F. Hegel, *The Phenomenology of Spirit*, trans. J. B. Ballie (New York: Harper Colophon Books, 1967), 237; interestingly, this passage is missing in A. V. Miller's translation of the same text.

15   Alexandre Kojève, *Introduction à la lecture de Hegel* (Paris: Gallimard, 1947), 539.

16   Hannah Arendt, *The Life of the Mind*, vol. 2, *Willing* (New York: Harcourt Brace Jovanovich, 1978), 44.

17   Maurice Blanchot, "La littérature et le droit à la mort," in *De Kafka à Kafka* (Paris: Gallimard, 1981), 36.

18   Ibid., 37.

19   Maurice Blanchot, *L'Entretien infini* (Paris: Gallimard, 1969), 307.

20   Blanchot, "La littérature et le droit à la mort," 38.

21   Alexandre Kojève, *Introduction to the Reading of Hegel*, ed. Allan Bloom, trans. James Nicholas (Ithaca, N.Y.: Cornell University Press, 1980), 143.

22   Alain Badiou, *L'Être et l'événement* (Paris: Editions du Seuil, 1988), 538.

23   Kojève, *Introduction to the Reading of Hegel*, 143, n. 34.

24   Quoted by Kojève, ibid., 200.

25   Blanchot, "La littérature et le droit à la mort," 37. One could wonder if Kojève's "dog" and Blanchot's "cat," find a precursor in the "horse" we find in the work of Avicenna and Duns Scotus; see Cunningham, *Genealogy of Nihilism*, 10 and 36.

26   W. V. O. Quine, "Reply to Robert Nozick," *The Philosophy of W. V. Quine*, ed. Lewis Edwin Hahn and Paul Arthur Schilpp (La Salle, Ill.: Open Court, 1986), 367.

27   Martin Heidegger, *Pathmarks*, ed. W. McNeill (Cambridge: Cambridge University Press, 1998), 90.

28   Bruce Fink, *The Lacanian Subject* (Princeton, N.J.: Princeton University Press, 1995), 52.

29   Ibid., 182.

30   Sartre, *Being and Nothingness*, 102.

31   Michael Dummett, *Frege: Philosophy of Language* (London: Duckworth, 1973), 407.

32   Michel Foucault, "Nietzsche, genealogie et l'histoire," in *Hommage à Jean Hyppolite* (Paris: Presses Universitaires France, 1974), 160.

33   Alain Badiou, *Court traite d'ontologie transitoire* (Paris: Seuil, 1998), 149.

34   Alain Badiou, *Le Nombre et les Nombres* (Paris: Seuil, 1990), 176.

35   Badiou, *L'Être et l'événement*, 58.

36   Ibid., 149.

37   Quoted by Michael Friedman, *A Parting of the Ways: Carnap, Cassirer, and Heidegger* (Chicago: Open Court, 2000), 77.

38   Christian Delacampagne, *A History of Philosophy in the Twentieth Century*, trans. M. B. DeBevoise (Baltimore: Johns Hopkins University Press, 1999), 109.

39   Jacques Lacan, "Television," trans. D. Hollier, R. Krauss, and A. Michelson, *October* 40 (1987): 7.

40   Benedictus De Spinoza, *Ethics*, trans. A. Boyle (London: Everyman, 1993), 71.

41   Alain Badiou, "Six Propriétés de la vérité," *Ornicar*, no. 32 (January 1985): 64.

42   W. V. O. Quine, *From a Logical Point of View* (New York: Harper and Row, 1953), 42–43.

43   Ibid.

44   Dermot Moran, *Introduction to Phenomenology* (London: Routledge, 2000), 156.

45   Edmund Husserl, *Ideas Pertaining to a Pure Phenomenology and to a Phenomenological Philosophy, First Book*, trans. F. Kersten (Dordrecht: Kluwer, 1983), first book, section 88, 215.

46   See Jacques Derrida, *Speech and Phenomena*, trans. David. B. Allison (Evanston, Ill.: Northwestern University Press, 1973), 58.

47   See W. V. O. Quine, *Ontological Relativity and Other Essays* (New York: Columbia University Press, 1969).

48   P. Bourdieu, *Language and Symbolic Power* (Cambridge: Polity, 1991), 207.

49   Hilary Putnam, *Reason, Truth and History* (Cambridge: Cambridge University Press, 1981), 52.

50   W. V. O. Quine, "Ontological Relativity," in *Ontological Relativity and Other Essays* (New York: Columbia University Press, 1969), 48.

51   Wilfred Sellars, *Science, Perception and Reality* (London: Routledge, 1963), 169.

52   Wilfred Sellars, *Empiricism and the Philosophy of Mind* (Cambridge, Mass.: Harvard University Press, 1997), 63.

53   W. V. O. Quine, *Words and Objections: Essays on the Work of W. V. Quine*, ed. Donald Davidson and Jakko Hintikka (Dordrecht: D. Reidel, 1969), 303.

54   "There never was any perception," Derrida, *Speech and Phenomena*, 103; "Every perception is hallucinatory," Gilles Deleuze, *The Fold: Leibniz and the Baroque*, trans. Tom Conley (London: Athlone, 1993), 93.

55  Eugen Fink, *Sixth Cartesian Meditation*, trans. Ronald Bruzina (Bloomington: Indiana University Press, 1995), 149.

56  Ibid., 142.

57  Ibid., 1.

58  Ibid., 91.

59  G. W. F. Hegel, *The Difference Between Fichte's and Schelling's Systems of Philosophy*, trans. Walter Cerf (Albany: SUNY Press, 1988), 1.

60  See Gilles Deleuze, *The Logic of Sense*, trans. M. Lester and C. Stivale (New York: Columbia University Press, 1990), 71–73.

61  Gilles Deleuze and Felix Guattari, *What Is Philosophy?*, trans. G. Burchell and H. Tomlinson (London: Verso, 1994), 59.

62  Ibid., 218; see also François Laruelle, *Philosophie et nonphilosophie* (Liège: Mardaga, 1989).

63  Michel Foucault, "Hommage à Jean Hyppolite," *Revue de métaphysique et de morale*, no. 2 (1969): 135.

64  Jacques Derrida, quoted in Richard Kearney, *Dialogues with Contemporary Continental Thinkers* (Manchester: Manchester University Press, 1984), 110.

65  Jacques Derrida, *Writing and Difference*, trans. A. Bass (Chicago: University of Chicago Press, 1978), 261.

66  Leonard Lawlor, *Derrida and Husserl: The Basic Problem of Phenomenology* (Bloomington: Indiana University Press, 2002), 244.

67  Ibid., 22.

68  Delacampagne, *A History of Philosophy in the Twentieth Century*, 104.

69  Richard Doyle, *On Beyond Living* (Stanford, Calif.: Stanford University Press, 1997), 36 and 42.

70  Leonard Lawlor, *Derrida and Husserl: The Basic Problem of Phenomenology* (Bloomington: Indiana University Press, 2002), 236, n. 8.

71  Kojève, *Introduction à la lecture de Hegel*, 492.

72  Jacques Lacan, quoted by François Regnault, "Art after Lacan," *Lacanian Ink*, no. 2001, 51.

73  See G. W. F. Hegel, *The Logic*, trans. William Wallace (Oxford: Clarendon, 1975), 180.

74  Lacan, "Television," 10.

75  See Peter Hallward, *Badiou: A Subject to Truth* (Minneapolis: University of Minnesota Press, 2003), 217–18.

76  Jacques Lacan, *Seminar XXI, January 15, 1974*, quoted in Fink, *The Lacanian Subject*, 182.

77  William Burroughs, *Nova Express* (New York: Grove, 1992), 14–15.

78  Jean-Francois Lyotard, *Postmodern Condition: A Report on Knowledge*, trans. Fredric Jameson (Minneapolis: University of Minnesota Press, 1985), 10.

79  Alexander Düttmann, *The Gift of Language*, trans. A. Lyons (London: Athlone, 2000), 100.

80  Alain Badiou, "Théorie axiomatique du sujet: Notes du cours 1996–1998," 14.1.98, quoted in Hallward, *Badiou*, 15.

81  Jean-Paul Sartre, *Being and Nothingness*, trans. H. Barnes (London: Routledge, 2000), 88 and 79.

82  Leonard Lawlor, *Derrida and Husserl: The Basic Problem of Phenomenology* (Indiana: Indiana University Press, 2002), 13.

83  See Slavoj Žižek, *The Ticklish Subject: The Absent Centre of Political Ontology* (London: Verso, 1999), 166.

84  See Badiou, *L'Être et l'événement*, 41.

85  Fink, *Sixth Cartesian Meditation*, 141, 144.

86    Badiou, *L'Être et l'événement*, 538, 49.

87    Jacques Derrida, *Edmund Husserl's "Origin of Geometry": An Introduction* (Lincoln: University of Nebraska Press, 1989), 165.

88    Slavoj Žižek, "The Abyss of Freedom," in *Ages of the World* (Ann Arbor: University of Michigan Press, 1997), 53.

89    Slavoj Žižek, *The Fragile Absolute* (London: Verso, 2000), 171, n. 73: "Lacan replaces the Kantian noumenal thing with the impossible real Thing."

90    Richard Boothby, *Freud as Philosopher: Metapsychology after Lacan* (New York: Routledge, 2001), 215.

91    Plotinus, *Enneads*, trans. S. Mackenna (London: Penguin Books, 1991), Iv. 8, 6.

92    Wolfram Hogrebe, *Prädikation und Genesis* (Frankfurt am Main: Suhrkamp, 1989), 114.

93    Peter Dews, *The Limits of Disenchantment* (London and New York: Verso, 1995), 134.

94    Slavoj Žižek, *For They Know Not What They Do* (London: Verso, 1991), 89.

95    Boothby, *Freud as Philosopher*, 205.

96    Fink, *The Lacanian Subject*, 25.

97    Jacques Lacan, "Radiophone," *Silicet* 2–3 (1970), quoted in Fink, *The Lacanian Subject*, 129.

98    See Badiou, *L'Être et l'événement*, 159–60.

99    Peter Hallward, *Badiou*, 367.

100    See Robert Brown, *The Later Schelling* (Lewisburg, Pa.: Bucknell University Press, 1977), 227.

101    Jean-Luc Nancy and Philippe Lacoue-Labarthe, *The Title of the Letter*, trans. F. Raffoul and D. Pettigrew (Albany: SUNY Press, 1992), 112.

102    Yannis Stavrakakis, *Lacan and the Political* (London: Routledge, 1999), 46.

103    Judith Butler, *Subjects of Desire* (New York: Columbia University Press, 187), 217.

104    Boothby, *Freud as Philosopher*, 149.

105    Ibid., 290.

106    Fink, *The Lacanian Subject*, 98.

107    Slavoj Žižek, *Welcome to the Desert of the Real* (New York: Wooster, 2001), 8.

108    Jacques Lacan, *Seminar XII*, quoted by François Regnault, "Art after Lacan," *Lacanian Ink* 19 (2001): 52.

109    Gilles Deleuze and Félix Guattari, *A Thousand Plateaus: Capitalism and Schizophrenia*, trans. B. Massumi (Minneapolis: University of Minnesota Press, 1987), 164.

110    Ibid., 20.

111    Gilles Deleuze, *Difference and Repetition*, trans. P. Patton (New York: Columbia University Press, 1994), 139.

112    Ibid., 56.

113    Badiou, *Court traité d'ontologie transitoire*, 138.

114    Hallward, *Badiou*, 63.

115    Gilles Deleuze, *Cinema 1: The Movement-Image*, trans. H. Tomlinson and B. Habberjam (Minneapolis: University of Minnesota, 1986), 10.

116    Hallward, *Badiou*, 82.

117    Gilles Deleuze, "Bergson's Concept of Difference," trans. M. MacMahon, *The New Bergson*, ed. John Mullarkey (Manchester: Manchester University Press, 1999), 51.

118    See Paul Virilio, *The Art of Fear*, trans. J. Rose (New York: Continuum, 2003).

119    Michael Hallett, *Cantorian Set Theory and Limitation of Size* (Oxford: Oxford University Press, 1984), 303.

120    Alain Badiou, "Topos, ou Logiques de l'onto-logique: Une Introduction pour philosophes, tome 1" (1993), quoted in Hallward, *Badiou*, 305.

121  See Deleuze and Guattari, *What Is Philosophy?*, 118.

122  Deleuze, *Difference and Repetition*, 74.

123  See Deleuze and Guattari, *What Is Philosophy?*, 156.

124  Gilles Deleuze and Felix Guattari, *Anti-Oedipus: Capitalism and Schizophrenia*, trans. R. Hurley, M. Sheen, and H. R. Lane (Minneapolis: University of Minnesota Press, 1983), 190.

125  See Deleuze and Guattari, *What Is Philosophy?*, 202.

126  Hallward, *Badiou*, 83.

127  Michael Lapidge, "Stoic Cosmology," in *The Stoics*, ed. J. Rist (Berkeley: University of California Press, 1978), 183.

128  Deleuze and Guattari, *Anti-Oedipus*, 4.

129  See Catherine Pickstock, "Modernity and Scholasticism," in *Antonianum* 78, fasc. 1 (2003): 3–46.

130  Deleuze and Guattari, *What Is Philosophy?*, 167.

131  Alain Badiou, *Abrégé de métapolitique* (Paris: Seuil, 1998), 90.

132  Malcolm Bowie, *Lacan* (London: Fontana, 1991), 87.

133  See Stephen Mallarmé, *Un coup de dés jamais n'abolira le hasard* (Paris: Librairie Gallimard, 1914).

134  Quoted by Badiou in *L'Être et l'événement*, 235.

135  Ibid.

*Regina Mara Schwartz* | Revelation and Revolution

He does not fill me up with goods, but compels me to goodness, which is better than goods received. — Emmanuel Levinas, *Collected Philosophical Papers*

Though he'd been sick for years, the rebbe's death came as a shock to the community. Some Lubavitchers, like Lieberman, started the process of accepting the reality that their messiah in waiting was gone. "Sure I felt disappointment, but you have to move on," Lieberman says. "What can one say other than that life is not always what you want it to be?"

But many clung stubbornly to their faith, insisting that the rebbe never really died or that the process of redemption was under way and that the rebbe would soon return and be revealed as the messiah. "Exactly how this is going to come about we really don't know," Rabbi Cohen says. "What we do know is that if you open your eyes, you can see that bit by bit it's coming to pass." — *New York Times Magazine*, Sept. 21, 2003

WHILE ALAIN BADIOU's real target is elsewhere — the hypocrisy of multi-cultural theorists or those who believe the only absolute is evil — he launches a critique in his *Ethics* against Emmanuel Levinas, reducing the philosopher's understanding of alterity to an ontological one (the other as the cultural other) and claiming that Levinas needs an ontological God (a supreme being) to ground his ethics. "This false love, which claims that the subject annihilates himself in a direct relation to the transcendence of the Other, is nothing more than narcissistic pretension."[1] One of the ironies of the politics of philosophy is that a thinker with such a passionate political commitment to emancipation as Emmanuel Levinas has been condemned as a spokesman for a liberalism whose investment in ethics is only to conserve the status quo while assuaging the conscience of the oppressor. But writing always in the shadow of the Nazi horror, Levinas developed a philosophy of ethics and of a subject constituted by ethics whose revolutionary potential has been occluded. This is the result, in part, of his having been coupled with Derrida; indeed, a hybrid entity, Levinasian-Derridean (virtually hyphenated) has emerged in the work of many commentators who have, in turn, taken their cue from Derrida himself—who in his enthusiasm has appropriated Levinas. Nonetheless, we should not allow a philosopher of such consequence to be read only through the lenses of another philosopher who has his own strong purposes. Here, I will try to retrieve the radical potential of his concept of revelation, one that has been obscured by its entanglement with the political opposition to a debased understanding of "alterity."

In Badiou's account, "contemporary ethics kicks up a big fuss about 'cultural' differences. Its conception of the 'other' is informed mainly by this kind of differences. Its great ideal is the peaceful coexistence of cultural, religious, and national 'communities,' and the refusal of 'exclusion'." Of course there are these differences, that is common sense, but "they hold no interest for thought . . . since differences are what there is, and since every truth is the coming-to-be of that which is not yet, so differences are then precisely what truths depose, or render insignificant."[2] But in the name of the "Law of founding alterity," proponents of ethics say it is "the 'recognition of the other' [as against racism, which would deny this other] or 'the ethics of differences'" (against substantialist nationalism, which would exclude immigrants or sexism, which would deny feminine-being), or "multiculturalism" (against the imposition of a unified model of behavior and intellectual approach).[3] Levinas does not equate alterity with cultural difference or race, and when pressed, he resisted that equation, even saying in an oft-quoted and oft-misunderstood remark, that the Arab is not the Other. Neither is the Other grounded in a substantialist nationalism; Levinas is continually suspicious of the state, even avoiding defining Israel in the substantialist sense: "So defined [as men constituted by the obligation to other men] . . . the heirs of Abraham are of all nations." Furthermore, in Levinas's work, alterity is not an inchoate concept devoid of context. Reacting against the problems that follow from Husserl's claim that the other is ultimately inaccessible, that we are condemned by our intentionality to what is virtually an endless narcissism of our own projections, Levinas refuses to exile the other to a vague unapproachable distance. Instead, the face of the other is always a specific person who appears before us in a specific situation calling us to responsibility: "One only comes into relation with what is other, infinite and transcendent when we interact with another human being in their specificity."[4]

The confusion seems to arise from many of his critics[5] when his language becomes theological; for instance, Badiou complains, "in order to be intelligible, ethics requires that the Other be in some sense carried by a principle of alterity which transcends mere finite experience. Levinas calls this principle the 'Altogether-Other' and it is quite obviously the ethical name for God. . . . There can be no finite devotion to the non-identical if it is not sustained by the infinite devotion of the principle to that which subsists outside it. There can be no ethics without God the ineffable."[6] Why, then, does Levinas take such pains to place his notion of God in the human ethical act? "In my relation to the other, I hear the Word of God. It is not a metaphor; it is not only extremely important; it is literally true."[7] In fact, Levinas comes remarkably close to inverting Badiou's formula, to saying not that there can be no ethics without God, but that there can be no God without ethics, for God appears only in the face of the Other. "The sentence in which God gets mixed in with words is not "I believe in God." It is the "here I am" said to a neighbor to whom I am given over, by which I announce peace, that is, my responsibility for the other."[8] As Kevin Hart summarizes, in Levinas "'the good beyond being' refers to the transcendence of the other person, not the transcendence of the deity. So transcendence is first and foremost to be conceived in ethics, not theology, and is to be considered by way of affirmation of what is outside consciousness, the other person, than as a rigorously consequent negation of all that that is predicated about the divinity."[9]

Badiou's critique does not accord with Levinas's understanding of Judaism as (1) the universal children of Abraham who are committed to charity or (2) the work of remaining faithful to the revelation, that is, engaging of acts of justice or (3) the other as not just another person, nor others in the sense of the infinite diversity of humanity, nor God as Being, but radically other, in the sense of something incomprehensible to me and hence uncontrollable by me. This otherness is best understood as a transcendence that breaks into our world, rupturing it and calling us to a new order, the order of responsibility, or (4) God is present only in the face of the other person, or (5) not only must the state answer to justice, but justice must answer to a prior Law, of charity or love. Perhaps because Levinas was an orthodox Jew and a Talmudic scholar (and in that capacity believed to be conservative), the remarkably radical nature of his thought is not always apparent. Even Badiou has to admit that "For the honour of philosophy, it is first of all necessary to admit that this ideology of a 'right to difference,' the contemporary catechism of goodwill with regard to 'other culture' are strikingly distant from Levinas's actual conception of things."

If Badiou had chosen to search for their common ground, he might have observed that Levinas fights ontology, including a God of Being, as persistently as he does in his thinking on the Event, and that moreover, Levinas's ethics is grounded not in a limitation of evil but in the command of a positive good.[10] For Levinas, "love is originary."[11] While, for Badiou, love is one of the orders of fidelity to an event—art, politics, science, love—he also gives it prominence of place: "The subject has to be given in his labor, and not only in his sudden emergence. 'Love' is the name of that labor."[12] Both embrace a particular universalism, a truth open to all but embraced by each, and both invoke an infinite or void, a rupture that breaks into the current state of things with the urgency of truth or revelation. As Levinas describes revelation, it is specific and universal (and here Badiou should approve): "Is not the personal—that is, the unique 'of itself'—necessary to the breach and the revelation taking place from outside?"[13] Levinas quotes a text from Exodus in this regard which, in prescribing how to make the Ark of the Tabernacle, specifies that poles be used for transporting the Ark: " 'The poles shall remain in the rings of the Ark; they shall not be taken from it.' The Law carried by the Ark is always ready to be moved. It is not attached to a point in space and time, but is continuously transportable and ready to be transported."[14]

But there is another way in which Badiou creates a straw man instead of getting at the impulse impelling Levinas. Impatient as he is with Levinas for grounding his ethics in a transcendent alterity, he nonetheless says it is even worse when ethics is not moored by religion. So while Levinas is guilty of the first sin, a religiously based ethics, he is at least not explicitly accused of the second, an ethics devoid of religion. Here too, Badiou unwittingly finds common ground with Levinas despite his protests—in religion. For he sees in Paul the exemplar of the truth procedure, that is, a subject who is constituted by the extraordinary Event—for Paul, the Resurrection—who is faithful to this Truth by engaging in its dissemination—the "work of love" is the Good News. Noting that Badiou's ultimate example of an Event is drawn from religion and not from one of his four categories of events: art, science, politics, and love, Žižek reveals Badiou as "endorsing the homology" that is so familiar between revolutionary Marxism and messianic Christianity, adding that "Badiou can also be read as the last great author in the French tradition of Catholic dogmaticists from Pascal and Malebranche on."[15] Nonetheless, Badiou explicitly claims to turn to Paul without himself having any faith in his declaration. One may well wonder if he indicts himself when he speaks of that move disparagingly: Badiou's invective for this recourse to religion without faith includes "pious language without true piety, a spiritual supplement for incompetent governments, and a cultural sociology preached, in line with the new-style sermons, in lieu of the late class struggle."[16]

Eagleton has also discerned that "Badiou's thought runs in the same theoretical grooves as some of the very acolytes of otherness he most scathingly opposes . . . he rejoins some of his political and theoretical enemies on the distinctly un-Kantian ground of the non-conceptualisable, revelatory, irreducibly singular, evental, subject-constituting character of truth."[17] Despite their differences—Badiou's Lacanian inheritance, Levinas's phenomenological one; Badiou's atheism and Levinas's religious belief—in the end, I will argue that Badiou and Levinas share the same theological structure. Both understand revolution as beginning and continuing in revelation. Furthermore, that theological structure cannot be disentangled from the political one.

## Caricatures of the Other

With Paul, the difference between Levinas and Badiou widens: if, for Badiou, fidelity to the Event is exemplified by proselytizing, if this act of converting, of political organization, is the work of love, for Levinas, fidelity to the Event means living according to its command of assuming responsibility for the other: "Truth—the knowledge of God—is not a question of dogma . . . but one of action, as in Jeremiah 22. . . . That is our universalism."[18] This in turn widens into their political differences: Badiou, seeing Paul as exemplary in his community building by conversion, is willing to run the attendant risks of totalitarianism and fundamentalism. Levinas, fearing totality with its connotations of intolerance and fascism, would be faithful to Revelation without any attempt to convert others. This is not an indifference to truth on the one hand, nor embracing a private truth or mysticism on the other. What follows from the Revelation at Sinai is a rigorous concept of the collective life, the political life, although one would learn this, surprisingly, from Badiou. This is indeed a new universal—not the empire (ancient Near Eastern or otherwise) that insists on fidelity on pain of destruction—but a universal in which each person acts in accord with their apprehension of a revelation, a revelation of responsibility—not of resurrection. In Badiou, being faithful to the Truth-Event requires speaking that truth, persuading others of that truth, organizing it politically—only then is it universal. For Levinas, the universal truth of revelation issues in a completely different regard for the other: he is not the object of persuasion, he is the one for whom I am responsible.

Badiou is intolerant of this position, seeing it as ushering in the fakery of liberalism. After Badiou has reduced alterity to an ontological construct and thereby can argue contemptuously that "infinite alterity is quite simply *what there is* . . . every modern collective configuration involves people from everywhere, who have their different ways of eating and speaking, . . . such is the way of the world" (emphasis mine),[19] and when he pauses from ranting about those hypocritical multiculturalists who are really deeply intolerant of difference—"foreigners are only tolerable so long as they 'integrate' themselves into the magnificent model presented to them by our pure institutions"[20]—he embraces, without embarrassment, Paul the proselytizer.

Badiou holds up the example of Paul for his universalism; to be more precise, the "universal particularity" he exemplifies for him. Of course, Paul's soteriology is not universal, requiring as it does faith in Christ: Jews and Gentiles alike who do not subscribe are lopped off. But Badiou would argue that it has the potential for a universalism—anyone can believe. The problem is that this is no less true of his supposed foil, Judaism: anyone can receive the justice of the covenant by obeying the commandments, as Jesus so well understood (Matt. 5:17). I will argue here that just as Badiou constructs a falsified Levinas whom he can oppose, despite (or perhaps because of) the profound similarities between their thought, so too their genuine difference—how they understand the revelation of the Law—is built upon another falsification, this one by Paul, whose reading of the Hebraic understanding of the law is the condition for a strategic opposition.

Badiou's interesting summary of Paul makes the best case: "When the subject as thought accords with the grace of the event . . . he, who was dead, returns to the place of life. He regains those attributes of power that had fallen onto the side of the law and whose subjective figure was sin. He rediscovers the living unity of thinking and doing. This recovery turns life itself into a universal law. *Law returns as life's articulation for everyone, path of faith, law beyond law.* This is what Paul calls love" (emphasis mine).[21] Here, in Badiou's account of Paul, we could also glean an excellent description of the revelation in the Hebrew Bible—although Badiou does not see it as such (although Paul probably does). Neither literal, pharisaical, nor a yoke of bondage, not offered only to an exclusive community of blood, but "breaking" upon a situation, it renders it completely incomprehensible in its former terms—the criterion for Badiou's Truth-Event. The revelation is indeed a law beyond Law. For Levinas, revelation is "the moment the word of God is heard is in the encounter with the Other, a double expression of weakness and strict, urgent requirement . . . there is an election there because that responsibility is inalienable."[22] It is "the commandment . . . ordering responsibility for the other: beyond ontology."[23] This does not remotely resemble the prescriptive understanding of the law, as Levinas points out: "The picture that one has of the prescriptive—which is reduced to the pettiness of rules to be respected or to the 'yoke of the law'—is not a true picture."[24]

There is a reason why Badiou fails to see Revelation in this light. "Truth," writes Badiou, "is diagonal relative to every communitarian subset; it neither claims authority from, nor (this is obviously the most delicate point) constitutes any identity. It is offered to all, or addressed to everyone, without a condition of belonging being able to limit this offer, or this address."[25] His project seeks to mobilize a universal singularity against both prevailing economic abstractions and "against communitarian or particularist protest." Paul offers him a way out of what we have come to think of as "identity politics" or communities forged around some substantialist identity. This is where he seems to place Judaism, with his inferences becoming stronger until they become explicit. The absolute singularity of truth means that it cannot fall under the category of law: "It will be necessary to proceed at once via a radical critique of Jewish law, which has become obsolete and harmful."[26] One assumes he means that the Law is "obsolete and harmful" according to Paul, although he does not endeavor to correct him. Indeed, this Paul is the hero of Badiou's story of ethics.

Badiou's reading of Paul's reading of Judaism—as a substantialist community requiring a condition of belonging to have access to its truth—does not hold up. I have labored to show that the substantialist identities associated with Judaism—whether a community of land, of blood, of shared history, or of state—do not delimit Judaism, not even in its founding text, the Hebrew Bible; I should say especially not there.[27] Those identities are repeatedly challenged by the ethical imperative to care not only for the widow and the orphan (those who do not belong) but also for the stranger, by the injunction that Israel be "the light to the nations," by a covenant promise made to Abraham and from thence to all the peoples of the world. "In the cave that represents the resting place of the patriarch and our mothers, the Talmud also lays Adam and Eve to rest: it is for the whole of humanity that Judaism came into the world."[28] The understanding of the Law as "obsolete and harmful" is not shared by Jesus when he asserts, "Do not imagine that I have come to abolish the Law or the Prophets. I have come not to abolish but to complete them. . . . Therefore the man who infringes even one of the least of these commandments and teaches others to do the same will be considered the least in the kingdom of heaven; but the man who keeps them and teaches them will be considered great in the kingdom of heaven" (Matt. 5:17), or even by Paul, who repeatedly acknowledges that the covenant of faith inheres in the Law: "Do we mean that faith makes the Law pointless? Not at all: we are establishing the Law" (Rom. 3:31).

Badiou is not alone. These caricatures—the people as a tribe, the law as a yoke, ritual as a prescription—these damaging descriptions of Judaism attributed to Paul by so many produce a "reading which depicts him attacking

Judaism as an inferior, mechanistic, commercialized religion" (and Boyarin notes the coincidence between this portrayal of Paul and that of anti-Semitic Europe),[29] a reading in which Paul presents the Law as, on the one hand, leading to the conviction of inadequacy "because of its alleged requirement that it be kept in its entirety for salvation," and, on the other hand, to the extent that the commandments are kept, leading to self-righteousness. In this reading of Paul, Judaism emerges as "a dry, spiritually deadly legalistic mentality."[30] Despite all the efforts to correct this picture by a fairer account of Judaism, by Krister Stendahl, W. D. Davies, and E. P. Sanders, among others, Badiou dangerously concurs with the old reading to make his own points about Paul as the particular universal par excellence.

Paul's reading of the Law is far more subtle and complex than this castigation as obsolete and harmful. Giorgio Agamben is a careful reader of Paul who sees that Paul has discovered the internal tension that inheres within the Law itself, in Pauline terms, between the "Law of works" and the "Law of faith," in Hebraic terms, the covenant on the flesh and the covenant on the heart. This tension can be traced to Paul's reading of the covenant, first given to Abraham in faith, before he was circumcised, and before the Mosaic law. But the Mosaic law is not simply dead: if it is no longer needed, that is because it has been fulfilled. "The messianic is not the destruction of the law, but the deactivation of the law, rendering it unobservable," observes Agamben, quoting the pericope in 2 Corinthians 3:12–13 that says the messiah is "telos tou katargoumenou, or fulfillment out of that which has been deactivated."[31] Avoiding the usual trap of finding Paul incoherent and self-contradictory on the Law, Agamben notes instead that the opposition is between the "normative and promissive" aspects within nomos itself: "It is this dialectic within the law that Paul refers to by means of the binomial epag-gelia/nomos (the first corresponding to faith, the second to works.)"[32]

Not for nothing does Paul often cite the law approvingly and describe its fulfillment in Christ. Not for nothing does he invoke the Revelation of the Covenant in Exodus to describe the creation of his own subjectivity in I Corinthians: "By the grace of God I am what I am" (1 Cor. 15:10). Interestingly, Acts describes Ananias, the one who gives Paul his new sight, as a "devout follower of the Law and one highly thought of by the Jews living there" (Acts 22:12). Paul does not mention that Ananias is also a Christian (Acts 9:10) or allude to his vision (Acts 9:10–16). While the seemingly contradictory statements Paul makes on the law—it kills but it is good—have prompted debate on how Paul regards the Law since Origen, the most convincing arguments share the conclusion that his impulse is not to reject the Law but to include pagans in it. This involves his drawing distinctions between the "works of Law" that have come to function as identity markers for Jewishness and are therefore exclusionary—circumcision, food laws, and Sabbath—and the Law. According to James Dunn, for Paul "the covenant is no longer to be identified or characterized by such distinctively Jewish observances as circumcision, food laws and Sabbath. Covenant works had become too closely identified as Jewish observances, covenant righteousness as national righteousness . . . God's purposes and God's people have now expanded beyond Israel according to the flesh, and so God's righteousness can no longer be restricted in terms of works of the law which emphasize kinship at the level of the flesh."[33] Boyarin concurs, noting the compelling example: "For neither circumcision counts for anything nor uncircumcision, but keeping the commandments of God" (1 Cor. 7:19).[34] Interestingly, Paul contrasts circumcision not to faith here, as we might naively anticipate, but to keeping the commandments, because for Paul, true faith and obedience to the Law are not opposed, but one and the same. This is clarified in Romans: "It is a good thing to be circumcised if you keep the Law; but if you break the Law, you might as well have stayed uncircumcised. If a man who is not circumcised obeys the commandments of the Law, surely that makes up for not being circumcised?" (Rom. 2:25-26).

Acknowledging his deep debt to Jeremiah, Paul joins him in rejecting the appearances of piety in favor of real obedience, that is, rejecting prescriptions in favor of a passionate commitment to justice. Jeremiah's Temple sermon showed Paul the way:

> Put no trust in delusive words like these: This is the sanctuary of Yahweh, the sanctuary of Yahweh, the sanctuary of Yahweh! But if you do amend your behavior and your actions, if you treat each other fairly, if you do not exploit the stranger, the orphan, and the widow, if you do not shed innocent blood in this place, and if you do not follow alien gods, to your own ruin, then here in this place I will stay with you. . . . Yet here you are, trusting in delusive words, to no purpose! Steal, murder, commit adultery, perjure yourselves . . . and then come presenting yourselves in this Temple that bears my name, saying: "Now we are safe"—safe to go on committing all these abominations! Do you take this Temple that bears my name for a robbers' den? (Jer. 7:4-11)

To bolster his universalism, Paul turns to spirituality. The spiritual law is not opposed to the law of God; it *is* that Law. "It is death to limit oneself to what is unspiritual; life and peace can only come with concern for the spiritual. That is because to limit oneself to what is unspiritual is to be at enmity with God: such a limitation never could and never does submit to God's Law" (Rom. 8:6-7).

But as a Jew well-versed in the Law, Paul also knew its powerful summary in the Torah, after the recounting in Deuteronomy of the giving of the law to Moses. Moses is speaking, enjoining the people to remember the law by remembering its revelation: "And now, Israel, what does Yahweh your God ask of you? Only this: to fear Yahweh your God, to follow all his ways, to love him, to serve him with all your heart and all your soul, to keep the commandments and laws of Yahweh that for your good I lay down for you today" (Deut. 10:12–13). What does this Law amount to? The commandments are not concerned with the subject, but with the other, the other person and the divine Other. Enjoining responsibility, as Levinas emphasizes: they are not to murder another, to steal from him, or slander him, that is, kill him with words. These are prefaced by requirements to be faithful to this law, to the Giver of this law, and not to stray from it to false truths, to idols. Moses continues, "Circumcise your heart then and be obstinate no longer, for your God is never partial, cannot be bribed. It is he who sees justice done for the orphan and the widow, who loves the stranger and gives him food and clothing. *Love the stranger then, for you were strangers in the land of Egypt*" (Deut. 10:12–20; emphasis mine). Deuteronomy demands justice to the needy, and no markers of identity, no circumcision of the mere flesh, will suffice. Jeremiah presses on this demand: "See, the days are coming—it is Yahweh who speaks—when I am going to punish all who are circumcised only in the flesh: Egypt, Judah, the sons of Ammon, Moab, and all who cut the corners of their hair who live in the desert. For all of these are uncircumcised, and the whole House of Israel too, are uncircumcised at heart" (Jer. 9:25–26). Paul, then, does not innovate, does not add good news to Judaism when he says, "To be a Jew is not just to look like a Jew, and circumcision is more than a physical operation. The real Jew is the one who is inwardly a Jew, and the real circumcision is in the heart—something not of the letter but of the spirit" (Romans 2:28–29). This much was already firmly part of the Covenant: "Circumcise yourself for Yahweh; off with the foreskin of your hearts (men of Judah and inhabitants of Jerusalem) lest my wrath should leap out like a fire . . . in return for the wickedness of your deeds" (Jer. 4:4). One can only wonder how this consonance with—indeed, imitation of—Jeremiah can sustain the reading of Paul as anti-Semitic. He is, rather, a Jew who echoes both the Mosaic covenant and its prophetic interpretation to the letter: "It is not listening to the Law but keeping it that will make people holy in the sight of God" (Rom. 2:13).

This is clearly not the whole story, for Paul also writes, "Now we are rid of the Law, freed by death from our imprisonment, free to serve in the new spiritual way and not the old way of a written law" (Rom. 7:6). Where does Paul pull away from his tradition? Not his messianism, not his spirituality, not

his universalism. All of these have ample precedent. I see his swerve occurring when he turns to the question of justice. He sees justice satisfied by the
process of justification; this grants salvation and the right to inherit eternal
life by having faith in Christ without having to perform the Law. The spirituality of the law is not the same as the doctrine of justification by faith that
Paul slips in subsequently: justification satisfies justice precisely when—and
this is important—it should not be satisfied. Justice is a demand, and it per-
severes—without being satisfied—as surely as hope does. By justification,
does Paul mean the works of the Law or the Law of faith? Here, Paul's rhetoric allows him to make what I regard as a genuinely radical claim: justification through Christ not only surpasses identity markers but fulfills justice
itself, the Law. In justification, Christ imputes his merit onto sinful man, and
so his faith suffices. Christ has done the work, paid the price, for him: "one
man, Jesus Christ, will cause everyone to reign in life who receives the free
gift that he does not deserve, of being made righteous" (Rom. 5:17).[35]

Luther, among the many who felt mightily relieved by this doctrine, draws
the conclusion that Paul points toward: human beings are depraved, they
cannot be just, the demand of justice is impossible for them, and they are delivered from their state of sin only by faith in Christ (Rom. 3:23). According
to Paul, "Both Jew and pagan sinned and forfeited God's glory, and both are
justified through the free gift of his grace by being redeemed in Christ Jesus
who was appointed by God to sacrifice his life so as to win reconciliation
through faith. In this way God makes his justice known; first, for the past,
when sins went unpunished because he held his hand, then, for the present
age, by showing positively that he is just, and that he justifies everyone who
believes in Jesus" (Rom. 3:24-26). Here we see how justice has elided into justification. Justice is no longer the gift of the covenant, the enjoining of human
beings to love that gift and keep its injunctions to be just; justice has taken
on a new meaning: it refers to whether the subject is worthless, condemned
to punishment, and the "justice of God" is not the grace of the covenant—
responsibility toward the stranger, the widow, and orphan—it is rather the
response of God to our sinful nature. Our agency as a subject, as a political
subject, is no longer the issue—Paul is quite explicit about this, citing the
case of the man who works for wages and earns his due as the old justice;
whereas, the man who has only faith in the one who justifies him is the new
order, adding that a man is happy if God considers him righteous, irrespective of good deeds (here he quotes Psalms 32:1-2 for authority, but it does not
say this). And now my critique of Badiou deepens, for the reason he holds
Paul up as the example, par excellence, of the particular universal is his political commitment: Paul, in complete fidelity to his truth-event, proclaimed it
unswervingly. This is the political agent, for Badiou; this is the subject consti-

tuted by the truth-event. But by means of this undeniably formal approach, leaving behind the content of Paul's good news, dismissing it as a fantasy that makes no difference to his structural argument, Badiou leaves himself open to a serious problem. Paul has bequeathed to us not the political subject that the Revelation of the Law offers, but a justified subject whose political life and ethical choices are *indifferent* to his salvation. With much confidence, Paul said that if I am circumcised and do not obey the law I am not righteous. One wonders what Paul would say if, instead, I have faith in Christ and fail to obey the law — am I still righteous? Yes, indeed, that is his point.

## Revelation

Badiou has defined politics as "the production of subjectivity in the position of truth." While the thought of Lacan informs this formula, it stands on its own, for the work of politics is productive — in the first place, productive of a subject who, having experienced an event in a situation that alters it conclusively, is faithful to that truth, and second, whose fidelity to that truth is *enacted* in a procedure by which this subject acts on behalf of that truth. The structure of dominance that prevailed in a situation, "the state" of the situation, is no longer inevitable; a new possibility is opened, heretofore (in the terms of the former situation) unthinkable, impossible. As Hallward describes it,

> Such a truth-procedure can begin only with some sort of break with the ordinary situation in which it takes place — what Badiou calls an *event*. An event has no objective or verifiable content. Its "happening" cannot be proved, only affirmed and proclaimed. Event, subject, and truth are thus all aspects of a single process of affirmation: a truth comes into being through those subjects who maintain a resilient *fidelity* to the consequences of an event that took place *in* a situation but was not *of* it.[36]

The theological vocabulary — and it is Badiou's which Hallward invokes — is explicit. "An evental fidelity is a real break (both thought and practised) in the specific order within which the event took place[37] . . . 'Break' because what enables the truth-process — the event — meant nothing according to the prevailing language and establish knowledge of the situation."[38] Such events are irreducibly singular and the fidelity to them is equally particular.[39] Like the Event for Badiou, revelation offers an alternative knowledge to philosophy for Levinas. Revelation ruptures the order of positive being, establishes a relation with exteriority "which, unlike the exteriority with which man surrounds himself whenever he sees knowledge, does not become simply the content of interiority, but remains 'uncontainable,' infinite and yet still maintaining a relation. . . . . it is precisely within this relation that man becomes his 'self': designated without any possibility of escape, chosen, unique, non-interchangeable and in this sense, free."[40]

While Badiou has called this the truth-event, I hear it resounding as something else, something one could argue is synonymous with his Event, that is, revelation. As a thought-experiment, then, let us do what Badiou has not done: read the Revelation in Exodus in Badiou's terms. In this way, we may discover places where his vision and that of Levinas intersect in fruitful ways. For Badiou, a subject is summoned into being by a response of persistent fidelity to an eternally enduring "truth-event which breaks disruptively, unpredictably, into the given in all of its irreducible, incommunicable singularity, beyond all law, consensus, and conventional understanding."[41] If this is not a description of revelation, what is? Badiou would argue that ethics is not the revelation of truth, but an ongoing process, that is, the process of remaining faithful to it. As Eagleton summarizes, "It is a question of 'persevering in the disruption,' a phrase which clips together both innovation and continuity, visionary crisis and dogged consistency, or what in Badiou's language would be the 'immortal' and the 'mortal.' . . . He wants, in short, to insert the eternal into time, negotiate the passage between truth event and everyday life, which is what we know as politics."[42] Levinas would call this revelation and justice, not politics; Badiou would call it truth. And because the difficulty and uncertainty of being faithful to the event—of being just—preoccupies both the rest of the biblical narrative after the revelation (and human history), it is understood as a process indeed.

While Badiou has no difficulty associating the Event with the Christ-event, he is notably less interested in the radical revelation that marks the earlier Sinai event. And yet this revelation beautifully exemplifies his demands: the narrative describes the production of subjectivity in the position of truth, the creation of subjects who are faithful to the event—and we are also given dire warnings of pseudo-events. I hardly need to rehearse the aura of the exceptional that fills the narrative of the Sinai revelation, the radical break from the ordinary from life as they knew it—Moses leads them not only out of Egypt, out of their habitual slavery, but even out of their camp in the wilderness, where they are subjected to the terrifying sound and light show:

> now at daybreak on the third day there were peals of thunder on the mountain and lightning flashes, a dense cloud, and a loud trumpet blast, and inside the camp all the people trembled. Then Moses led the people out of the camp to meet God; and they stood at the bottom of the mountain. The mountain of Sinai was entirely wrapped in smoke, because Yahweh had descended on it in the form of fire. Like smoke from

a furnace . . . louder and louder grew the sound of the trumpet. Moses
spoke, and God answered him with peals of thunder" (Exod. 19:16–19).

God appears in the form of fire and speaks in thunder. The form of fire is indistinct; the voice of thunder is unintelligible. This is not a deity who is easily
reduced to a being, or for that matter, to any concept of being. The Truth
has no place in the prior situation: under its terms, it is the void, unname-
able, unthinkable. And the subject who is created by this truth-event does
not exist prior to it. Interpreted, since Rudolph Otto, as *mysterium tremen-
dum*, or the idea of the holy, this demarcation of the place of the event also
points clearly to its break with the prior situation: "Yahweh said to Moses,
'Go down and warn this people not to pass beyond their bounds to come and
look on Yahweh, or many of them will lose their lives.' . . . Moses answered,
'The people cannot come up the mountain of Sinai because you warned us
yourself when you said, "Mark out the limits of the mountain and declare it
sacred" ' " (Exod. 19:21–24). Badiou emphasizes the power that results from a
truth: "A truth punches a 'hole' in knowledges, it is heterogeneous to them,
but it is also the sole known source of new knowledges."[43]

The atmosphere at Sinai trembles with something else, with threat, with
violence—but why? The people tremble before this God, begging Moses to
intercede lest they die (Exod. 20:19). Not only the message but also the mes-
senger is unbearable. Moses's face is radiant from this encounter with God,
and he must veil himself for others to stand it. Only before God and before
the elders, to whom he communicates this startling justice, is he unveiled.
Why is the revelation of the law accompanied by such fury? With the entry of
the demand for justice, the world changes decisively. Justice commands the
hearer to a terrifying moment of decisiveness: will he accept this call to justice, or turn away? The first answer is univocal and affirmative: when Moses
relates the words of God to the people "all the people said with one voice,
'All that he has spoken we will do; we will obey' " (Exod. 24:3, 7).

> The term evoking obedience here ["we will do"] is anterior to that
> which expresses understanding ["we will listen"] and in the eyes of the
> Talmudic scholars is taken to be the supreme merit of Israel, the "wis-
> dom of an angel." . . . This obedience cannot be reduced to a categorical
> imperative in which a universality is suddenly able to direct a will. It is an
> obedience, rather, which can be traced back to the love of one's neigh-
> bor: . . . a love that is obeyed, the responsibility for one's neighbor.[44]

Revelation is "a love that is obeyed": "Do not boil a kid in its mother's milk."[45]
Fidelity to this event proves to be difficult—a "difficult freedom," as Levinas refers to it. The wrong paths soon beckon. According to Badiou, there

are three ways to betray the Event: disavowal, trying to follow old patterns as if nothing had happened; false imitation of the event of truth; and a direct "ontologization" of the event of truth, its reduction to a new positive order of being. The Exodus narrative depicts the ancient Israelites betraying the revelation in every sense. They doubt the validity of event, murmuring "Is Yahweh with us or not?" (Exod. 17:7) and disbelieving: "You have brought us to this wilderness [not to emancipate us] but to starve this whole company to death!" (Exod. 16:3). They give their allegiance to a pseudo-truth, and they reduce their emancipation to an order of being signaled by creating an idol of gold: "They have been quick to leave the way I marked out for them; they have made themselves a calf of molten metal and worshipped it and offered it sacrifice. 'Here is your God, Israel,' they have cried, 'who brought you up from the land of Egypt!'" (Exod. 32:8–9). "Ontologization" is offered up as the danger of idolatry, of betrayal, of evil: "You know how prone these people are to evil," laments Aaron (Exod. 32:23). For Badiou, "to fail to live up to a fidelity is Evil in the sense of betrayal.⁴⁶ From one perspective, this is also the idolatry Paul engages in with reference to the Sinai event. By reducing it to prescriptions, to a positive law with rules, he refuses the event of revelation, and he does so contrary to Jesus, who, like Moses, is faithful to that revelation: "I come not to oppose the Law but to fulfill it." For his purposes, Paul engages in three different contradictory betrayals of the Sinai event: he denies the enormity of its importance, he ontologizes it (as a system of universal rule making), and then after reducing its significance, he claims it is oppressive (the yoke of the law).

When the revelation is betrayed in this way, it is destroyed (as the old Law becomes dead for Paul). When the people of Israel are unfaithful to the Event, it disappears for them. The narrative depicts this as the destruction of the tablets, the destruction of the laws of justice. Instead of Badiou's model, the Pauline example of subjectivity as a sudden conversion that renders the new subject nonexistent before, the Hebrew subject is more complex: first he declares fidelity to the event, faith to the revelation—"all that he commands we will do, we will obey"—and then, despite the intention of fidelity, despite these promises, he backslides, betraying the true event with a false one (idolatry), falling victim to a failure of courage—"because there were no graves in Egypt, did you take us to die in the wilderness?" (Exod. 14:11). Paul well understood this subject and classified it as death: "Though the will to do what is good is in me, the performance is not, with the result that instead of doing the good thing I want to do, I carry out the sinful things I do not want. When I act against my will, then, it is not my true self doing it, but sin which lives in me" (Rom. 7:18–20). In Paul's terms, this is not a subject, this is sin.

But in the Exodus narrative, Moses is offered in contrast to this widespread response as embodying unswerving fidelity and missionary zeal on behalf of the truth, so that his subjectivity is set in relief against the backsliding people who were given but cannot bear the difficulty of the truth. Moses demands fidelity to the Revelation, and only that fidelity—and *no substantialist identity*—will constitute the future community. Those who refuse become the enemy—not only to God, in Levinas's reading, but to emancipation: "Gird on your sword, every man of you, and quarter the camp from gate to gate, killing one his brother, another his friends and another his neighbor" (Exod. 32:27). The Marxist Badiou need not frame Paul as Lenin; he could have turned to Moses as a revolutionary leader: his priesthood of believers is formed at the cost of brothers and sons (Exod. 32:29). The Revelation starts a revolution.

But Moses demands fidelity to what? On the U.S. Supreme Court building, a frieze in the east portico depicts Moses, among other historical lawgivers, holding up two tablets; the tablets are blank. The entrance door to the building's courtroom also has two tablets with the Roman numerals I through X on them, but no words. When the law-giving is renewed, instead of the finger of God writing on the tablets, Moses does the writing, and the voice of God—never reified in stone—becomes the foundation of the oral Law, with authority equal to the written one. What he says is what the rabbis puzzle over. If what God offers is not merely a series of prescriptions, "the yoke of law," what does he confer in this breach with the past, and what is asked of the new subject? In fact, there is hardly any positive "content" in the Revelation as such, even in the Exodus narrative. Levinas argues that in the living interpretation of the revelation, what is asked is fidelity not to any positive law, but to justice: the prior world is ruptured by the radical entry of the demand for justice. Just as the first "decalogue" (Exod. 20) rehearses the need for fidelity to the lawgiver and respect for the other, so the renewed "ten words" (Exod. 34) concern remaining faithful—the demand of allegiance, to remember allegiance, to commemorate allegiance—with warnings and promised rewards. What is required is fidelity to the truth of revelation; hence, the warning is made again and again, in different ways, against false truth, idolatry. "You shall bow down to no other God" (Exod. 34:14), "you shall make yourself no gods of molten metal" (Exod. 34:17); and you shall remember the feast of unleavened bread that commemorates the exodus from the prior condition; you shall dedicate your first-fruits to god, dedicate a day in every week to God, the festival of harvest, three more days a year—that covers the "ten words" that are the terms of the covenant, all except for the last sublime metaphor for injustice: "You shall not boil a kid in its mother's milk." What gives life cannot be used to deal death.

Despite Badiou's charges that Levinasian ethics lacks a politics, Levinas has seen this revolutionary aspect of the revelation, and by turning away from the understanding of the subject as solipsistic but as constituted by its responsibility for another, by justice, Levinas has delineated an understanding of the subject that is not only preeminently social but also political. Up to a point—the delimiting point is Levinas's palpable suspicion of the political. Levinas's distrust of the state is the distrust of someone who has endured the state crimes of the Nazis. "The police official does not have time to ask himself where the Good is and where the Evil; he belongs to the established power. He belongs to the State, which has entrusted him with duties. He does not engage in metaphysics; he engages in police work."[47] He fears that if in order to fight evil we adopt the tactics of politics, we would find ourselves in the service of the state. "How can we engage responsibly in political action when we cannot be sure about the nature of evil, about what is evil? Interpreting the rabbis, he writes that for Rabbi Eleazar, "unquestionably violent action against Evil is necessary. And we shall soon see that this violence takes on all the appearances of political action."[48] But he sees the rabbi seeking deeper understanding, insisting on asking how do you recognize evil? For Levinas, here "lies the difference between a police action at the service of the established State and revolutionary action."[49]

This suspicion of the state does not condemn Levinas, as Žižek would have it, to a pre-political ethics. Žižek has divided his critique of ethics into its traditional, modern, and postmodern forms:

> What they all share is a *reduction of the political*, some version of pre-political ethics: there is no politics proper in a closed community ruled by a traditional set of values [the premodern]; universalists ground ethics in a proceduralist a priori of discursive (or distributive) ethics [modern]; "dispersionists" condemn politics as unifying, totalitarian, violent, and so on, and assume the position of ethical critics who reveal (or voice) the ethical Wrong or Evil committed by politics, without engaging in an alternative political project.[50]

Usually Levinas is regarded as falling in the third category, postmodern, in part because he has been associated with poststructuralism, in part, because of his deep distrust of totalitarian regimes. But he could be more precisely— and equally wrongly—categorized as a premodern who rehabilitates tradition, invoking substantialist community in his invocation of Judaism. I hope I have corrected that mistaken reading by now. In fact, Levinasian ethics is not prepolitical in any of the senses that Žižek elaborates. I would argue instead that, if anything, his ethics is postpolitical, not only because he lived through and took account of the Nazi horror, but also because it is after explicitly engaging politics in his work that he embraces an ethics that goes beyond politics—not an alternative to politics, but an ethics he believes works when politics fails, and so an ethics that politics must answer to.

When Levinas explicitly distinguishes between the heirs of Abraham, the universal family of humanity, and the state, he does so nervously, knowing that this will make some readers unhappy, adding, "it is suggested by the text. Let not the worshippers of the state, who proscribe the survival of Jewish particularism, be angered!"[51] "There is more in the family of Abraham than in the promises of the State. It is important to give, of course, but everything depends on how it is done. It is not through the State and through the political advances of humanity that the person shall be fulfilled, which of course, does not free the State from instituting the conditions necessary to this fulfillment. But it is the family of Abraham that sets the norms."[52] Privileging the "children of Abraham" over the state, Levinas takes pains to qualify that community as not a blood group (this is not "petit-bourgeois racism and particularism").[53] So who are the heirs of Abraham? "Those to whom their ancestor bequeathed a difficult tradition of duties toward the other man, which one is never done with, an order from which one is never free. . . . So defined, the heirs of Abraham are *of all nations*: any man truly man is no doubt of the line of Abraham" (emphasis mine).[54]

### Justice and Charity

If Badiou creates a falsified Levinas as Paul creates a falsified Hebraic Revelation—if I am right that this is because a more honest picture would make them concur with their antagonists more than differ from them—where have we arrived? That is, what is the relation of theology to politics? Of revelation to revolution? To approach this question, I want to turn not to the constitution of the subject (Badiou's preoccupation) or the constitution of the community (Paul's preoccupation), because in the end these entities may be more indifferent for their political ends than these leaders imagine. Instead, I want to turn to the question of justice, for it seems to me that this is the vital political concern.

In his work, Levinas offers a radical corrective to the procedural justice embraced by so much political theory: "Justice cannot be reduced to the order it institutes or restores, nor to a system whose rationality commands, without difference, men and gods, revealing itself in human legislation like the structures of space in the theorems of geometricians, a justice that Montesquieu calls the 'logos of Jupiter' recuperating religion within this metaphor, but effacing precisely transcendence."[55] For Levinas, justice is the call to responsibility and this justice must hold institutions of justice to account.[56] He does not underestimate the violence of justice, the violence of making judgments when what is called for is responsibility to every other: "There is a certain measure of violence necessary in terms of justice; but if one speaks of justice, it is necessary to allow judges, it is necessary to allow institutions and the state; to live in a world of citizens, and not only in the order of the Face to Face."[57] But he continues, careful to make justice flow from and answer to relation of charity, the true source of justice. "Love must always watch over justice."[58] Like Badiou, rather than accept a negative justice, one that only limits violence—Badiou speaks of the weakness of human rights as stemming from this negative understanding of justice—he urges a positive vision of justice that springs from charity. He continues:

> It is in terms of the relation to the Face or of me before the other that we can speak of the legitimacy or illegitimacy of the state. A state in which the interpersonal relationship is impossible, in which it is directed in advance by the determinism proper to the state, is a totalitarian state. So there is a limit to the state. Whereas, in Hobbes's vision—in which the state emerges not from the limitation of charity, but from the limitation of violence—one cannot set a limit on the state.[59]

His clearest enunciation follows: "Justice itself is born of charity. They can seem alien when they are presented as successive stages; in reality, they are inseparable and simultaneous, unless one is on a desert island."[60]

Despite their realms of compatibility, there is one place where Levinas avoids the charge that can be made against the event in Badiou—what is to distinguish the true event from the fake one, the positive revolution from, say, the Nazi horror? Levinas is careful to speak of revolution "not as formal, not as the overthrow of a given order" but defined by its content, by values: "Revolution takes place when one frees man; that is, revolution takes place when one tears man away from economic determinism."[61]

> It is not enough to be against a cause, one must be in the service of one. I do not think that revolutionary action is to be recognized by the massiveness of victorious street demonstrations. The fascists knew more successful ones. Revolutionary action is first of all the action of the isolated man who plans revolution not only in danger but also in the agony of his conscience . . . in the double clandestinity of the catacombs and of conscience. In the agony of conscience that risks making revolution impossible: for it is not only a question of seizing the evil-doer but also of not making the innocent suffer. In this also is to be found the difference in Jewish thought between the police and revolutionary politics.[62]

In the end, one wonders if Badiou's emphasis on structure, even the structure of subjectivity as fidelity to the truth-event is sufficient. He cannot speak of "content" because it is contingent upon the situation and each situation has its unique truths. But to speak of the force of truth as a rupture that reorganizes all knowledges, of a commitment to a truth that was heretofore hidden from view, does not, as Badiou himself recognizes, shield one from embracing a heretofore unseen horror. "I was then obliged to admit that the event opens a subjective space in which not only the progressive and truthful subjective figure of fidelity but also other figures every bit as innovative, albeit negative . . . take their place."[63] This is why Levinas distrusts metaphysics and must put ethics before it. Levinas embraces "a thought thinking more — or thinking better — than it thought according to truth."[64] Love is this More. Levinas tells us that upon reading Descartes's third *Meditations of First Philosophy*, he asked himself "whether all that was dear to the love of 'the-love-of-wisdom,' or the love that is the philosophy of the Greeks, was the certainty of fields of knowledge directed toward the object, or the even greater certainty of reflection on these fields of knowledge; or whether knowledge beloved of and expected from philosophers was not, beyond the wisdom of such knowledge, the wisdom of love, or wisdom in the guise of love. Philosophy as love of love."[65] Reason alone does not and cannot dictate goodness.

In "Loving the Torah More than God," Levinas engages an anonymous text that offers itself as a document written during the final hours of the Warsaw Ghetto resistance by one "Yossel, son of Yossel."[66] Doubts flow from his agony: "What can this suffering of the innocents mean? Is it not proof of a world without God, where only man measures Good and Evil?" But these "murmurings" do not issue in any idolatry or atheism; they take a very different turn from the generation lost in the wilderness. Instead of betraying the revelation in the midst of this horror, "Yossel, son of Yossel experiences the certainty of God with a new force, *beneath an empty sky.*" This is not paradox nor blind faith, nor has despair driven him to irrationality. Levinas reads the empty sky as the opportunity for a full conscience: "If he is so alone, it is in order to take upon his shoulders the whole of God's responsibilities." An absent God becomes most immanent internally. God is no protector or savior but is internalized as a moral principle that guides action. Humanity must create a just world. The Godless are redefined as those who do not have this. "The condition of the victims in a disordered world — that is to say, in a world where good does not triumph — is that of suffering." And this condition offers us a God who abandons man, abandons the just man. "But this God Who hides His face and abandons the just man to a justice that has no sense of triumph, this distant God, comes from within." He quotes Yossel: "I am happy to belong to the most unhappy people on earth, for whom the Torah represents all that is most lofty and beautiful in law and morality. . . . Now I know that you are really my God, for you could not be the God of those whose actions represent the most horrible expression of a militant absence of God." Empty sky, full conscience. Levinas understands the wellsprings of Yossel's "confidence that does not rely on the triumph of any institution: it is the internal evidence of morality supplied by the Torah."[67]

If the Revelation offers the gift of justice, it can be either accepted or refused, as the human history of failure and agony confirm. Neither Levinas in "Difficult Freedom" nor the Hebrew Bible ever underestimate how difficult this gift of justice is. If the Bible portrays humanity as persistently failing, it also insists that the radical entry of justice into the world cannot be compromised with cheap solutions—what it calls idolatry. The gift of grace in Paul works differently, imputing righteousness through the death of Christ. This gift of righteousness is received through belief in the resurrected Christ, compensating for the inadequacy of the human being to live up to the injunctions of the law, to satisfy the demands of justice. This imputed righteousness can make one feel better about his sinful self, even grant a new redeemed self, although he has done nothing to earn this relief from self-loathing, this escape from sin. What the gift of justice does, on the other hand, is present one with the harsh reality that only acts of justice performed by the subject, and only by him, can help to create a just world and only this can relieve despair. There is no other way out. And this is what makes the covenantal demand of justice ultimately political: while Revelation is a radical rupture into the status quo, it does not offer a miraculous solution to human pain.

## Notes

1    Alain Badiou, *Saint Paul: The Foundation of Universalism*, trans. Ray Brassier (Stanford: University of California Press, 2003), 90.

2    Alain Badiou, *Ethics: An Essay on the Understanding of Evil*, trans. Peter Hallward (London: Verso, 2001), 26–27.

3    Badiou, *Ethics*, 20.

4    Emmanuel Levinas, *Nine Talmudic Readings*, trans. Annette Aronowicz (Bloomington: Indiana University Press, 1990), pp. 43–44.

5    Strong critiques of Levinas can be found in John Milbank, "The Soul of Reciprocity," *Modern Theology* 17:3 (July 2001): 334–391; *The Word Made Strange* (Oxford: Blackwell, 1998), 36–54, and Gillian Rose, *The Broken Middle* (Oxford: Blackwell, 1992), 247–307.

6    Badiou, *Ethics*, 22.

7    Emmanuel Levinas, *Entre Nous: Thinking-of-the-Other*, trans. Michael B. Smith and Barbara Harshav (New York: Columbia University Press, 1998), 110.

8    Emmanuel Levinas, "God and Philosophy in Collected Philosophical Papers," trans. Alphonso Lingis (Boston: Martinus Nijhoff, 1987), 170.

9 Kevin Hart, "Forgotten Sociality," in *Discerning the Australian Social Conscience*, ed. Frank Brennan (Sydney: Jesuit, 1999), 4.

10 For Badiou, ontology is mathematics: "Pure presentation as such, abstracting all reference to 'that which' — which is to say, then, being-as-being, being as pure multiplicity — can be thought only through mathematics," *Ethics*, 127.

11 Levinas, *Entre Nous*, 108.

12 Badiou, *Saint Paul*, 91–92.

13 Levinas, "Revelation in the Jewish Tradition," in *Beyond the Verse*, trans. Gary D. Mole (London: Athlone Press, 1994), 133.

14 Ibid., 134.

15 Slavoj Žižek, *The Ticklish Subject: The Absent Centre of Political Ontology* (London: Verso, 1999), 141–42.

16 Badiou, *Ethics*, 23.

17 Terry Eagleton, *Figures of Dissent* (London: Verso, 2003), 249–50.

18 Emmanuel Levinas, *Difficult Freedom: Essays on Judaism*, trans. Sean Hand (Baltimore: Johns Hopkins University Press, 1990), 172.

19 Badiou, *Ethics*, 25, 27.

20 Badiou, *Saint Paul*, 8.

21 Ibid., 87–88.

22 Levinas, *Entre Nous*, 108.

23 Ibid., 199.

24 Levinas, *Beyond the Verse*, 135.

25 Badiou, *Saint Paul*, 14.

26 Ibid., 15.

27 Regina Schwartz, *The Curse of Cain: The Violent Legacy of Monotheism* (Chicago: University of Chicago Press, 1997).

28 Levinas, *Difficult Freedom*, 176.

29 Daniel Boyarin, *Radical Jew: Paul and the Politics of Identity* (Berkeley: University of California Press, 1994), 40.

30 Ibid., 41.

31 Giorgio Agamben, "The Fifth Day," in *Le Temps qui reste: Un commentaire de l'Epître Aux Romains*, trans. Judith Revel (Paris: Rivages, 2000), 9, 156.

32 Ibid., 6 and 151; "un element normative et un element promissif," 151.

33 James Dunn, 1990, 197, 200 in Boyarin, *Radical Jew*, 54.

34 Boyarin, *Radical Jew*, 54.

35 I am aware that current scholars of Paul do not find the Lutheran reading, of imputing righteousness to man, in Paul. Paul's meaning may well include a broader understanding of grace, in which the power to conduct a virtuous life is granted by Christ.

36 Peter Hallward, introduction to Badiou, *Ethics*, x.

37 Badiou, *Ethics*, 42.

38 Ibid., 43.

39 See Badiou, *Ethics*, 42–44.

40 Levinas, *Beyond the Verse*, 148.

41 Alain Badiou, *Saint Paul: The Foundation of Universalism*, trans. Ray Brassier (Stanford: Stanford University Press, 2003).

42 Eagleton, *Figures of Dissent*, 250.

43 Badiou, *Ethics*, 70.

44   Levinas, "Revelation in the Jewish Tradition," in *Beyond the Verse*, 146–47.
45   Exodus 23:19.
46   Badiou, *Ethics*, 71.
47   Levinas, "Judaism and Revolution," in *Nine Talmudic Readings*, 110.
48   Ibid., 109.
49   Ibid., 110.
50   Žižek, *The Ticklish Subject*, 171.
51   Levinas, *Nine Talmudic Readings*, 100.
52   Levinas, *Nine Talmudic Readings*, 99–100.
53   Ibid., 113.
54   Levinas, *Nine Talmudic Readings*, 113.
55   Levinas, *Beyond the Verse*, 107.
56   Levinas, *Otherwise Than Being: Or Beyond Essence*, trans. Alphonso Lingis (Pittsburgh: Duquesne University Press, 1998), 16.
57   Levinas, *Entre Nous*, 105.
58   Ibid., 108.
59   Ibid., 105.
60   Ibid., 107.
61   Levinas, *Nine Talmudic Readings*, 102.
62   Ibid., 110.
63   Badiou, *Ethics*, lvii.
64   Levinas, *Entre Nous*, 200, "Preface to the German Edition of *Totality and Infinity*."
65   Levinas, *Entre Nous*, 200.
66   Levinas, *Difficult Freedom*, 143.
67   Ibid., 144.

*Philip Goodchild* | Capital and Kingdom:
An Eschatological Ontology

MODERN POLITICAL THEORY has largely confined the scope of the political to the acts of human subjects, groups, and institutions in their mutual relations with each other. Such a humanistic metaphysics of power overlooks the ways in which the scope of merely human relations of power—such as provision, production, reproduction, possession, association, representation, legislation, jurisdiction, normalization, violence, promise, threat, selection, persuasion, funding, reason, knowledge, morality, piety, and attracting or giving attention—are delimited by extrahuman powers. For human power is dependent upon the availability of a material power. This is evident both in the dependence of the human will on the nutrition and sustenance of the human body, as in the contemporary famine in Zimbabwe, where regions that have supported the Movement for Democratic Change are deprived of access to grain—political will cannot be sustained for long by a diet of roots, bark, and leaves—and in the wider dependence of the economic system on ecological cycles that provide minerals and energy, that reproduce plant and animal life, and that absorb waste.[1] Moreover, the formal political and economic spheres are also dependent upon a much wider "social resources economy," consisting of subsistence agriculture, forms of social cooperation, a common cultural inheritance of arts and skills, and unpaid labor in household, caring, and community services.[2] The world operates more by the power of "kindness and compassion," exercised largely by women, than by formal relations of power. The direct dependence of human politics on a much wider sphere is also evidenced in the looming hydrocarbon energy crisis: now that oil production, which provides 38 percent of the world's primary energy, is due to peak within a decade, and gas production, which provides 24 percent of the world's primary energy, is due to peak in twenty years' time,[3] political decisions will necessarily be taken on the basis of the need to preserve access to and use of energy supplies, that is, to preserve the ability to make political decisions against political and physical risks.[4] Such a choice is no choice. Rising prices due to resource depletion and falling rates of oil production will soon shatter the global economy, rendering, among other things, the literature on "globalization" of merely historical interest.[5] Economic and ecological collapse are increasingly no longer exceptions to the steady progress of development, or the "internal contradictions" of a start-stop capitalism, but the norm against which islands of stability have to be preserved as exceptions.

There is, however, a second nonhuman determination of politics that invades the human will in quite a different way: the politics of money. Slavoj Žižek describes the self-enhancing circulation of capital as "Real . . . in the precise sense of determining the very structure of material social processes."[6] The point, as I shall argue in what follows, is that capitalism is not merely a description of what capitalists believe or do, but a systemic force of abstraction that is "objective" and anonymous. Any ontology linked to contemporary political practice must explore the sense of this spectral "Real."[7] Then Žižek tells us that the "abstraction" of capital is not merely one of the misperception of social (and ecological) reality and its real relations of production (and provisioning), as already indicated, but one of overlooking the inexorable "abstract" spectral logic of capital that determines what occurs in social reality:

> In short, the highest form of ideology lies not in getting caught up on ideological spectrality, forgetting about its foundations in real people and their relations, but precisely in overlooking this Real of spectrality, and pretending to address directly "real people with their real worries." Visitors to the London Stock Exchange are given a free leaflet which explains to them that the stock market is not about some mysterious fluctuations, but about real people and their products — *this* is ideology at its purest.[8]

Unless we raise ontological questions of the nature, force, and arising of the "Real," we risk having our social reality determined in practice by the abstract spectral logic of capital.

All forms of critical theory in the broadly Kantian tradition contest the naive and disavowed metaphysics of a dominant positivism that begins with the "real facts" established by science, or the facts about "real people" —

a metaphysics allied to the commodification of knowledge that eliminates temporal and social relations as well as spontaneity from being. Questions of ontology become central to demystifying claims of an apolitical sphere of "objective reality." Ontology thus informs practice. Yet all "historical ontologies"[9] that reintroduce temporal and social relations into thought differentiate themselves from such an inauthentic positivism that depends on the eternal truth of facts, however atomized or temporary, by invoking how matters operate in practice. Here we come to an extraordinary paradox: the practice of critique is informed by ontology, while ontology is informed by the practice of critique. And the persistent question emerges: can the Real, even within capitalism, be exhausted by practice, by what happens, by temporal and social relations?

Indeed, in attempting to determine a viable practice—a credible socialism, liberation, or revolution—or in attempting to determine a "true" ontology, one runs the risk of constructing a merely theoretical opposition to the mystifications of positivism, while, in one's social reality, by means of participation in social exchange, one bears witness to the uncanny fact that one's theory simply appears to one as naively, factually true in a positivist sense—or, even worse, one acquiesces in commodification simply by choosing a political strategy or ontology from the theoretical options available on the basis of taste (or, once chosen, justifying it by reasons internal to that strategy or ontology, which amounts to the same), pending the resolution of their interminable debates. The fundamental challenge facing all critical strategies and historical ontologies is a version of the naturalistic fallacy: less the problem of attempting to derive an "ought" from an "is" (there being strategies to overcome this, such as Spinoza's derivation of ethics from ontology), but the problem of responding to an "ought" with an "is" (for example, choosing Spinoza's ontology because it lends a strategy for overcoming the naturalistic fallacy), and thus repeating the positivist commodification of truth.

There are three issues at stake: does the adoption of a theoretical strategy or historical ontology have any bearing on the power of the Real, if this is mediated objectively through what we do, irrespective of what we think? Does the adoption of a "revolutionary praxis" effectively contest the power of the Real—if that power is spectral, rather than subject to resistance or seizure? And what, in the Real, actually mediates our ontology and our social practice, if we fail to uncover the truth of the Real?

To dualistically oppose a true ontology or a viable practice to the Real of capital repeats Žižek's predicament of "ideology at its purest." This is certainly true if one overlooks the exploitation of resources, animals, and cheap labor that feed, clothe, and service contemporary intellectual labor; it is also true if one overlooks the distinctive power of the Real. Even those who re-place "real people with their worries" with the most sophisticated critical ontology or with the hope for revolutionary events, if their practice is effec-tively determined by the spectral Real of capital, then "they know not what they do." Then the mutual dependence of ontology and practice, far from instantiating the virtuous circle of "revolutionary praxis," becomes a vicious ideological circle that perpetuates our enslavement. What I wish to draw at-tention to is the political impotence of all dualisms, for unless a mediation is given, then the dominant mediation in practice, capital, will fill the gap. My suspicion, to be explored in what follows, is that just as communism (whether ideal or "actually existing socialism") belongs within capitalism as such, disavowing its conditions of possibility in the unlimited productivity that belongs to capitalism itself,[10] so also socialism and political strategies of liberation, along with historical and critical ontologies, not only exist solely within capitalism but are dependent on capitalism for their concepts of free-dom, practice, universality and temporality through which they posit them-selves.[11] In short, any future utopian "kingdom," whether of ends, of social-ism, or of a true ontology, may simply function as an ideological fantasy of capitalism, like the American dream. An ontology that counterposes being and becoming, essence and existence, or ontology and practice, will remain forever incomplete, unaware of its conditions of possibility.

Thus the only true critique is an immanent critique of the actually exist-ing mediation between ontology and practice. It is a matter of exploring the historical particularity of the universal mediator, as well as the universality of this historical particular. It is a question of accepting the force of mediation and learning the secret of its power so that, by introducing a small difference at the beating heart of reality, the entire world becomes transformed. This is the inquiry which we shall follow.

## The Metaphysics of Money

There is but a single ontological problem: "What is money?" This is a prob-lem that we do not yet know how to pose, since only the politics of money can tell us the meaning of essence. Yet, once posed, an investigation of money may yield four ontological dimensions, a considerable advance on the vari-ant dualisms of ontology and practice: money as substance, money as tem-poral flow, money as credit, and money as fiat.

According to Aristotle, a substance selected for use as money had two properties: intrinsic usefulness, and portability.[12] Money as substance would thus appear to be a deterritorialized use-value. Such a substantialist view of money has had an enduring history in metalist theories of money and the linking of monetary value to the gold standard; it endures in contemporary economics insofar as it is assumed that money is sought for its *use*, not in itself, but as a means of payment or store of value.[13] A truly Copernican revolution took place, however, in 1526: Nicolaus Copernicus, the Polish priest and famous astronomer, argued in his *Treatise on Debasement* that it was the total amount of currency in circulation that determined the level of prices and the buying power of the currency. His radical new insight was that coins had already become simply tokens of value.[14] This Copernican insight was not fully understood by Isaac Newton, who devised the gold standard in 1717,[15] nor by Immanuel Kant, who drew on the example of money in his pocket to illustrate the claim that existence is not a predicate — he wrongly presumed that one cannot acquire real money by merely thinking about it.[16] Modern textbooks of economics, however, adopt a desubstantialized metaphysics by specifying the intrinsic value of money as its use: its fourfold function as medium of exchange, unit of account, store of value, and standard for deferred payments.

Let us examine the function of medium of exchange: Karl Marx's exemplary analysis of the emergence of the money-form as a token, the universal equivalent, charts both the nature of this function, and the emergence of universality as such. For a thought that embraces all beings and exchanges its representations for them is a universal equivalent, like the moneyform. And just as it is entirely different to exist in thought than to exist in reality, to have an exchange-value is entirely different from having a use-value. Extraordinary though Marx's analysis is, both as an account of commodity fetishism as the central component of ideology,[17] and for a universal logic of symbolization,[18] it was constructed as an initial stage in an immanent critique of bourgeois political economy, and may thus be wedded to presuppositions and categories that have yet to be tested by immanent critique. In particular, the logic of exchange rests on a naturalistic metaphysics of property: that land, commodities, fixed capital, and money are always the property of some named individual or corporation, and thus subject to exchange, in spite of the temporal, social, and ecological relations that make the existence of such "property" possible. The universal gives us formal, not real, existence. Now Marx, in his famous critique of primitive accumulation by means of the enclosure of property, demonstrated not only that the freedom to buy and sell land was founded upon the freedom of others to starve, but that money itself is a vital condition of expropriation:[19] the enclosures were made for the sake of making a profit. Thus the formal metaphysical categories of property and exchange appeal to a naturalistic metaphysics that overlooks temporal, social, and ecological relations—property being a social fiction that ensures rights without responsibilities, neglecting any obligations of inheritance of the past and preservation for the future. Yet more than this, if money is the condition for the capitalist category of property, then money is itself the condition of the illusions of both exchange and the money-form. Money becomes self-positing. Thus the Marxian account of the genesis of the money-form does not exhaust the ontology of money.

Turning to the function of money as a unit of account, we may note that Copernicus's insight led to the quantity theory of money (developed by the likes of John Locke and David Hume, among others): that prices of commodities are a function of the relative scarcity or abundance of money (prices multiplied by quantity of goods is equal to money multiplied by velocity of circulation). As both a commodity and unit of account, the value of that unit is thus a variable determined by scarcity. Yet the quantity theory still depends on the naturalistic illusion that money is a finite being. The dual role of money as both commodity and unit of account, however, enables a further feature of money to emerge, at odds with the quantity theory, for a commodity whose value is determined by its scarcity may be subject to speculation. Just as speculation in land and property leads to both an inflation of prices beyond their "use-value," and accumulation by the few as against distribution among the many,[20] so speculation in money and financial products both inflates the amount of financial wealth in circulation and maintains its relative scarcity among most consumers. Thus speculation removes global restrictions on the acquisition of wealth in monetary form arising from the quantity theory, as well as enabling individuals to pursue the acquisition of monetary wealth as a means to all other goals. Finite being is replaced by unlimited becoming. Since economic reality is actually determined by speculation, it is economics, rather than speculation on unlimited becoming, that is illusory. Moreover, once money becomes the means through which all demands are satisfied, the demand for money takes priority over all other demands. For demand is effective only when it is backed up by money, and the best way to maximize the effectiveness of one's demands is to increase one's store of money. Under conditions of speculation, money simply becomes interest-bearing capital, "M-M," money that gives birth to money. Money "in its most fetishised form" becomes the true nature of money, for the current value of any asset, whether fixed or variable capital, depends mainly on expectations about its future performance and expected yield, including its yield from speculative inflation. Thus far from money being a substance, or even a fixed, nominal quantity, it is a differential rate, a deterritorialized and decoded flow, with no intrinsic meaning. It is an unlimited "good," accountable to no one and determined by no one.

Money also functions as a standard for deferred payments. Marx was aware that the greater part of money in circulation was composed of bills of exchange: promises to buy a certain quantity of goods in the future at a certain price, in principle the basis for contemporary checks as well as "futures."[21] Indeed, to the extent that bills of exchange circulate, and may ultimately balance each other out by the compensation of credits and debts, then, as Marx says, "they serve absolutely as money, since no transformation into actual money takes place."[22] The unique metaphysical status of money, here, is that with no other commodity can a claim to the commodity serve the same purpose as the thing itself.[23] Money is no longer identifiable as a commodity. Now, we can analyze the bill of exchange into the following components: in the first place, the bill is created by someone taking a liability upon themselves. It is a contract. While effective demand is backed by money, the bill of exchange is backed entirely by trust. The demand is rendered effective when the receiver trusts that the commitment will be honored. Yet the bill can count as money, and circulate more widely, only if it is also accepted by a third party: that is, a banker (or credit card company) who will advance the sum by "discounting the bill," so that the recipient can buy the resources to produce and deliver the goods on time. Now the trust that the contract will be fulfilled need not rest entirely on good faith, credit, or the honor of the one who undertakes the liability; it may also rest on the social forces that ensure that contracts will be honored, including legal forces of the state, or, prior to that, religious beliefs that God may punish the dishonest. Thus a bill of exchange is composed of separable social components of demand, liability, trust, and the power to enforce contracts.

Money is thus the social complex of credit. This is also true in the case of speculation. Financial value depends on an imagined future. This imagined future is transcendent to current reality, and, furthermore, the future never comes. For, even if there is a stock market crash, the value of any asset still depends on projections about its future. In this respect, financial value is essentially a degree of hope, expectation, or credibility. Being transcendent to material and social reality, yet the pivot around which material and social reality is continually reconstructed, the value of money is essentially religious. To believe in the value of wealth is to believe in a promise that can never be realized; it is a religious faith. Yet one only has to act as though one believes in it, and by some miracle, it becomes true—for others may treat money in the same way, accepting it in exchange. This miracle is the very illusion that short circuits the truth of being in favor of the Real. Here, ontology is mediated to practice on the basis of credit.

The final supposed function of money is as a store of value, but money is much more than this. Once money becomes deterritorialized from its encoded representation in paper money, then it acquires a new metaphysical status. For the logic of the bill of exchange is repeated in all forms of credit, whether these are deposits in bank accounts, overdrafts, loans, or other credit instruments. It even bears the secret of paper money itself, when constituted as a promise to pay the "real sum of money," metallic or otherwise. Now, on the one hand, one has to "believe in practice" in a naturalistic metaphysics in order to enter into a credit arrangement, trusting that the credit instrument will be exchanged for "real money" in the future, or that a bank note can be exchanged for gold. On the other hand, bank notes need never be redeemed. Marx was therefore able to distinguish the twofold business of banks: the circulation of capital and the circulation of currency.[24] "Pocket money" that circulates as a physical commodity is not the same as "bookkeeping money": banks do not lend the money that is deposited with them; they *create* deposits and bank notes.[25] For, as Marx noted, a large sum of credits and debts between banks may cancel each other out, the difference being settled in the Clearing House.[26] The full consequence of this, explored by the English economic reformer Clifford Hugh Douglas, and in a parallel development placed at the critical point of Gilles Deleuze and Félix Guattari's theory of capitalism, is that money can be created at will, independently of production in the "real economy," so long as there is demand, liability, and trust.

Douglas's principal contribution was to demonstrate that while production and technology increase the amount of "real wealth" available, there is not a corresponding increase in "purchasing power" unless this takes the form of the creation of money. Businesses are thus involved in two separate activities: the production and distribution of goods, and the distribution of purchasing power through salaries, wages, and dividends.[27] Yet while businesses create "real wealth," banks are involved in the creation of money. Douglas was first struck by an accounting problem while working as the assistant superintendent of Farnborough aircraft factory in 1916. If each corporation pays a certain amount of its income to its workers in wages, a certain amount to its suppliers, and a certain amount to its shareholders in profits, then the workers would never receive sufficient income to buy the commodities that they produce, because money is put aside for the depreciation of plants, costs are always higher than wages, and there can never be a circular flow of money. For if a portion of the commodity price goes to paying off loans at interest, then there will never be enough money in the economy to purchase the goods — the money paid back to the banks is cancelled.[28] There is a structural problem of oversupply in a closed, global economy that can be addressed only from a single source: in order to be able to afford the goods for sale in an economy, that economy has to borrow money from the future.

Money is created by fiat in the form of credit, but such money belongs ultimately to the banks and will be repaid to them. One borrows money only if one believes that one will be able to make a sufficient sum to repay the loan with interest. For money is not created at the point of the creation of goods, the production of wealth; instead, economies are deflationary, suffering from a shortage of buying power, and this shortage is temporarily overcome by an ever-increasing spiral of debt. Such debt can be serviced only if more money is borrowed from the future, while at the same time production is increased through economic growth. The economic system is thus locked into a spiral of growth and debt—a spiral that can be sustained as long as there are no external obstacles to economic growth, but a spiral that could have devastating consequences as soon as ecological limits to growth are reached.

Banks create money by the creation of liabilities, that is, of debts: the granting of credit by a financial institution is thus the creation of a mortgage on future production.²⁹ Since one can "make money" through real production only if someone else creates money by entering into a liability, then, in order to pay off one's debts, one is enslaved to expanding future production. The whole economic system functions as a massive spiral of debt.³⁰ Moreover, instead of creating money where demand most urgently needs to be made effective, banks make loans or create money where it is most likely to yield a profit. Given the practice of offshore banking, and the deregulation of credit controls in line with existing financial practice, there is little political control over banking. For in an economy governed by debt, to restrict banking practices would threaten a fragile, competitive financial system.³¹ Whether it is government, business, or consumer debt, the political significance of the creation of money is that we are all mortgaged to the future, all slaves to debt—whether this is personal debt, or contracted by the businesses and governments on which we depend—and thus we are all compelled to enter into contracts that we might otherwise responsibly avoid, in order to honor our liabilities. Douglas's radical new insight is that, in spite of appearances, it is not our desires for consumption or wealth that determine our behavior, as though society operated by a pleasure principle or a will to power; it is slavery to debt. We must consume more, we must make profits, so that we can pay off our debts.

The tragedy of the neglect of Douglas and the social credit movement is that it has obscured this theoretical description of our condition as debt slavery: debt slavery and the demands of competition explain the creation of the capitalist system, the organization of society for the sake of production for profit, on the basis of the creation of liabilities in the form of bills of exchange, and later by banks;³² they explain why such a system depends on continual forced growth, through primitive accumulation, colonial expansion, globalization, and privatization of public services; they explain why such a system, which aims at profit alone and cannot take much account of the needs of subsistence and sustainability except as a drain on "wealth-creating" production, has produced such an extensive dispossession of people from their means of subsistence as well as an ecological crisis that may destroy most life forms on the planet; they explain why neoclassical economics, depending on the naturalistic metaphysics of a circular flow model of money, justifies extreme inequality because of the presumed "naturalness" of the economy, while at the same time never coming into contact with economic reality at any point; and they explain why, when economic expansion is curtailed by limitations to the global supply of primary energy, an economic system constructed out of unfulfilled liabilities and unpayable debts based on the promise of expansion will simply collapse in a way we have never seen before—probably within a couple of decades.

Let us return, then, to our question, "What is money?" What is striking is that the "true nature" of money is revealed only progressively through history, and since history has yet to end, we cannot yet be sure what money will have been. Money first appeared to be a valuable and portable commodity. Following the Copernican revolution, however, money was recognized as a physical token, defined less by its intrinsic value than by its acceptability. Money became "any medium which has reached such a degree of acceptability that no matter what it is made of, and no matter why people want it, no one will refuse it in exchange for his product"[33]—an illustration of "consumer sovereignty"[34] that is identical with producer slavery. The quantity of such a physical token was limited only by its acceptability. In principle, then, this shift enabled the growth of the production of goods for the sake of profit, rather than the provisioning of goods for the sake of utility, because it removed the "natural" boundaries to economic growth. Yet there remained social limits to the acceptability of token currency. In the third place, once a bill of exchange, a pure statement of demand rendered effective by being backed by a liability, comes to stand for and be treated as money, then money is simply effective demand. Agrarian and industrial capitalism could not expand until production for the sake of profit was equaled by effective demand.[35] In the fourth place, the physical token, the bill of exchange, becomes represented as a mathematical quantity in a sight deposit through the banking system. This enabled clearing balances to cancel each other out, and banks to lend money far in excess of their reserves—like a consumer taking out several mortgages on the same property.[36] Again, the growth in available currency can stimulate economic growth, provided that credit is backed not merely by securities, but also by liabilities as a mortgage on future production. In the fifth place, once money has become a mathematical variable, speculation determines the value of money by a differential rate of growth in value.

It is not enough to distinguish, then, between real and abstract money, for each form of abstraction remains real. The dualistic distinction between the real and the abstract is merely an effect of a naturalistic metaphysics that draws a sharp distinction between "money, on the one hand, and legal claims to money and operation in money on the other."[37] More significant than such dualism are differentiations based on modes of arising. Frances Hutchinson, Mary Mellor, and Wendy Olsen, in their important work *The Politics of Money*, which combines Marxist, Institutionalist, Social Credit, eco-feminist, and contemporary radical economics, make a sharp distinction between provisioning and production, between the demands of subsistence and the demands of speculation, between the "economic" and the "chrematistic." Where neoclassical economics fails is in its assumption that all productive activity is for the sake of a finite utility, without recognizing that capitalism itself is chrematistic rather than economic—production increasingly being geared toward an unlimited growth in profits (economists often invoke the naturalistic metaphysics implied in the quantity theory of money to refute this, without noting that the actual contrast between the rate of growth of money, $M_4$, and the rate of economic growth, GDP, overturns the quantity theory). A society driven by money, banking, and credit becomes "*the* critical feature of modernity."[38] Now, if money is effective demand, then it becomes far more politically important to control the creation of money, which has largely been for private profiteering, power struggles, and excessive consumption, than to control the means of production *as defined by capitalism*.[39] Hutchinson, Mellor, and Olsen do not define capitalism as commodification of labor power, or production for the sake of profit, however; instead, borrowing a description from Ellen Meiksins Wood, they claim that the distinctive and dominant characteristic of the capitalist market is its compulsion in two senses: "First, that material life and social reproduction in capitalism are universally mediated by the market, so that all individuals must, in one way or another enter into market relations in order to gain access to the means of life; and second, that the dictates of the capitalist market—its imperatives of competition, accumulation, profit maximization, and increasing labor productivity—regulate not only all economic transactions but social relations in general."[40] In addition to economic demands for the provisioning of households, and chrematistic demands for speculative profits, capitalism is actually determined by nonhuman "market imperatives." Let us emphasize that these three are separate metaphysical drives: the householders' *conatus*, which seeks substance or utility; the speculators' will to power, which seeks unlimited becoming; and the impersonal market imperative, driven by debt. Here, money is no longer merely a commodity, a means of making demands effective, or a system of accounting, speculation, or credit: the truth of money is its own nonhuman imperative. And it is such market imperatives that any viable political strategy must address.

Hutchinson, Mellor, and Olsen follow C. H. Douglas in recommending a national dividend so as to achieve economic democracy, where the demands of all are effective.[41] The basis for this is the separability between credit and liability: Douglas defines true credit as "the effective reserve of energy belonging to the community," or the dynamic capacity of the community to deliver goods and services as and when required.[42] In short, credit is identified with fixed capital—that is, the inheritance of resources, knowledge, skills, machines, and plants, reclaimed as a common inheritance upon which a dividend is payable, rather than being subject to private appropriation. Such capital is productive power, or a speculation on production, as defined by capitalism. I therefore have some reservations about both the justice of this recommendation, and, if instituted, its ability to redeem all from debt slavery and gear production to the demands of sustainability and subsistence. My concerns are twofold: first, credit is not capital—it does not belong directly to the sphere of productive forces—and second, liability may function as the condition of possibility of credit when justice may not. The history of the rise and dominance of capitalism, from the failure of peasant uprisings in sixteenth-century England, through Third World independence movements, to contemporary anti-IMF riots, demonstrates how inexorably capitalism has succeeded in overriding any resistance based on claims for justice. Justice, liked fixed capital, is extraordinarily malleable, for those in power may believe in the justice of appropriation, if it increases productivity; they may believe in the natural justice of the market to reward enterprise, if this is inherent in the scheme of things. Similarly, Douglas ultimately asks us to believe in the reality of natural production, replacing the abstractions of credit with a correlation between the production of money and the production of wealth. The fundamental error is to invoke once more the naturalistic metaphysics of the "real world," overlooking the question of ontology, and the conditions of possibility of belief. And questions of ontology, politics, and credit meet in the sphere of theology.[43]

## The Politics of Money

When the "real economy" collapses and all values are devalued, the abstract economy may not: the money-form, speculation, entering into liabilities, and the creation of debts may still be possible, so long as they still command credence. In order to determine an effective relation between ontology and practice, it is necessary to inquire into the nature of the nonhuman power expressed in the politics of money.

According to the naturalistic illusion it would appear that money, as an inert commodity, is politically neutral: if society is to be organized for the sake of profit, it would appear that this would hold no power over other modes of social organization, unless we exercise power on its behalf. And indeed, history is filled with examples of the exercise of power through violence, exploitation, appropriation, imperialism, and neoimperialism for the sake of profit. This description is inadequate, however, for many of those who exercise power today, such as executives of TNCs (transnational corporations), banks, governments, and international financial organizations, are not simply "wicked men" seeking power and profit; instead, just as they externalize costs of production, they also succeed in externalizing the moral responsibility for violence and appropriation through which they profit onto others further down the chain, whom they may justly condemn; or else they may justify violence in the interests of the all-too-fragile system as a whole, the alternative of economic collapse being worse. It is important to note that the exercise of power through fragility as well as the externalization of moral responsibility are crucial elements of human power relations in the contemporary capitalist system. They depend on the perceived political and ethical neutrality of money and the economic system. Here, however, there is a theoretical danger: one can repeat this externalization of responsibility by theorizing the global capitalist system as an impersonal empire.[44] In contrast to this, I believe it is vital to separate the capitalist system as such, with the distinctive forms of power exercised within it due to the unique ontological status of money, from the forms of state power with which it is allied, and which are exercised in its name. This is the fundamental political message of Deleuze and Guattari's *Capitalism and Schizophrenia*: that capitalism is a different regime of signs, a different organization of belief and desire from the state, and if one contests the forms of state power without which capitalism would have no substance, one does not contest capitalism as such, which will merely preside over the rebirth and regrowth of these state powers faster than they can be defeated. Resistance, revolution, and emancipation, in response to state power, do not become viable political options without addressing the distinctive power of capital itself.[45] They remain human, all too human.

Let us therefore examine the distinctive power of money. In the first place, monetary wealth, as effective demand, attracts credibility because of the promises it offers to the individual: liberation from the control of nature and material need; liberation from social obligation and dependency on others; and freedom to pursue one's own desire. Each of these promises depends upon the unlimited becoming effected by capital. Yet since accumulation of such effective demand is achieved only by expansion of the capitalist economy, including its sphere of property and appropriation, these promises are implicitly dependent on the externalization of costs: freedom from material need is bought by plunging others into vulnerability before their subsistence needs; freedom from social obligation is bought by employment as wage slavery, where social obligation becomes concentrated into serving the demands of one's employer; and freedom to pursue one's desire may be bought by subjecting others to one's desires—epitomized, in contemporary capitalism, by all dimensions of the burgeoning sex trade. The promise of wealth is thus always accompanied by a threat: if one fails to secure financial independence, one may be exposed to the struggle for survival, to wage slavery, or to sexual exploitation. Promise and threat are thus the first modes of its power.

In the second place, once within the capitalist system, and subject to market imperatives, one has little choice but to exercise power on its behalf. For wealth gives access to power in a competitive market, whether through mobilizing weapons and workers, through improved access to transport, communication, and information, through advantages of scale, or through liberation from the imperatives of survival.[46] And since demand is only as effective as the amount of money one can afford to back it with, then the supreme demand is for money itself. The unique feature of money is that it prioritizes itself, sacrificing all existing values to the demand for money. Moral values gain a partial resurrection, however, in the form of those qualities required for participation in the market: freedom, respect for the rule of law (i.e., of the laws that support market relations), respect for property, fulfilling of contractual obligations, maximizing one's opportunities, holding grand dreams or desires, "family values" (where the family is one of the few institutions no longer being mediated by market relations, other forms of social trust and obligation being replaced by trust in money), and defense of "civilization" against "terror." The self-positing of money as the supreme value is the second mode of its power.

In the third place, money as speculation is based on a projection of the future as an imagined present—the imagined present that belongs to the actual present, rather than engaging with the real future. Investments and speculations are made on the basis of projections about what particular assets will have been. In this respect, the greater the optimism, the greater the speculation, the greater the rise in value of assets, and the greater the profits. Markets are essentially governed by collective credit. In this respect, the difference between a "bull" and a "bear" market would appear to be purely subjective; what is striking here, however, is the "objective" reality of this subjectivity. Few market actors can successfully control the direction of the market. Now, while market actors tend to fall into the naturalistic illusion and assess value by what it will "have been," the value of the particular asset at that future date remains determined by new expectations about what value it will have been at a further date. Once assets become perpetually exchangeable, then the future never comes, and the day of reckoning is always postponed. This deterritorialization of the financial economy from the "real" economy occurs on the basis of reflexivity,[47] by means of a reterritorialization upon itself. Absolute deterritorialization operates likes this: for example, the movements of the mouth become deterritorialized from the body and reterritorialized on the mutual relations of sounds with each other, so that the structure of language determines the words that one speaks, at the same time as these are determined by movements of the mouth. In absolute deterritorialization, whether of the genetic code, of language, or of economics, a new metaphysical layer acquires an autonomy as an immanent cause. In economics, the financial economy gains its autonomy from the "real" economy at the same time as being entirely determined by it. If the human sphere is defined in terms of physiological events and linguistic meaning, then a posthuman sphere is constituted, beyond consciousness, in the Real of the global financial economy. Autonomous in relation to our political activity, yet actively determining it, humanity is already enslaved to the "abstract machine."

Now, while we have already considered the way in which wealth gives access to a quantitative advantage in competitive market transactions, the duality of promise and threat introduces a qualitative difference: there is a fundamental class or power difference between those who speculate, who simply seek a profit and may thus be satisfied by any number of alternative transactions, and those who seek subsistence, who are compelled to seek out a particular utility. The fundamental class difference would appear to lie between speculators and householders. Yet even speculators may be partial "householders" for their corporations, struggling for the profits that will enable them to survive (the legal fiction of limited liability introducing a crucial limitation on this, however).[48] Thus, in relation to the demands of market imperatives, speculators are subject to a further class difference between themselves and the nonhuman power of the Real. The effect of the reintroduction of nature into economic considerations means that capitalism functions by natural selection: while one may engage in heroic resistance to market imperatives, those who survive, prosper, grow, and replace others are those who act in line with market imperatives. Capitalism generates a spiral of growth and inequality that may eliminate alternatives by growth and longevity.

The final power we may consider is the growth of the capitalist economy through creation of money by fiat. Even when confidence falls among speculators in the stock market, consumer credit may fuel the economy, as in the United Kingdom over the past two years (where lending to individuals is increasing at 13.6 percent). Ultimately, credit functions as the Real fuel that feeds the economy, as necessary for production as energy from the sun. Autonomous in relation to both natural production in the "real world," and flows and tendencies among social forces, credit is the missing dimension of ontology.

## An Eschatological Ontology

The various stages in the ontology of money parody the stages of the univocity of being according to Deleuze. In the first place, money, as a universal equivalent, institutes the univocal world of economics where all production and commodities are measured in terms of their exchange-value. One gains a quantitative determination of all beings as a price. Moreover, money functions in practice as the mediation between essence and existence because, as effective demand, it is the condition of possibility of production. Like univocal being for Duns Scotus, money remains abstract and neutral in relation to exchange.[49] What this abstract world does not include, for liberal economics, are the personal choices of rational economic agents, and what abstract rational choice theory does not notice is that such choices are constrained by promise, threat, credit, and debt.

Once subject to speculation, however, money becomes the supreme, self-positing substance—like that of Spinoza, it is the pure good, subject to pure self-affirmation. Its existence flows from its essence. Then the final stage is when money replaces itself as a differential, reflexive flow. Money has no substance, being nothing in itself; only the rate of profit determines values and determines what money is. Here, money has become the repetition of difference, reflexive self-determination: only the eternal return of money upon itself gives being to becoming. Thus, one has to subtract or destroy the "unity" of the substance of money in favor of its pure being as return.

What we find here, and throughout modern critical thought, is a univocal ontology of process or production: in the words of Daniel Defoe, "Employment is Life, Sloth and Indolence is Death; to be busy, is to be chearful, to be pleasant."[50] While the precise meaning of being may vary, its specification in terms of becoming does not. This emphasis on the production of flows runs from Thomas Hobbes ("Life it selfe is but Motion"),[51] through Marx's "Theses on Feuerbach" and the labor theory of value, to Deleuze and Guattari: "Beliefs and desires are the basis of every society, because they are flows and as such are 'quantifiable'; they are veritable social Quantities."[52] Now, this whole field of critical ontologies is partially confirmed, but also called into question, by our preceding analysis of the metaphysics and politics of money. For, in the singular case of money, being is not simply a flow, an object of speculation; it is not merely social, temporal, or historical. Money is also essentially credit and creation. We must consider credit and fiat as crucial determinations of the Real alongside ontology and practice, or being and becoming. And if credit may lead to creation, then, in a reversal of ideology critique, *what we are may be determined more fundamentally by what we believe than by what we do.* For what we do is composed of tendencies that change direction, interact, ebb and flow; it may tell us little about what we will have been should our true ontological status be revealed, either progressively through history or suddenly at its end—should there be anyone left to comprehend it. This is well illustrated by the impossibility of predicting abrupt, major climate changes, which could result from the interaction of a variety of variables, leading to temperature rises of several degrees in the space of a decade.[53] Thus tendencies may trigger, but not constitute, what we will have been.

Capital is not merely a flow because it is always also an anticipation of an imagined future—whether we are concerned with speculation or credit, it is always an anticipated rate of return that determines how much money there will be. What there is now is dependent upon what we believe there will be: our eschatology determines our mode of being, whether one adopts the Enlightenment eschatology of perpetual progress that is essential to economic growth, the American eschatology of creating the kingdom of God on earth by force, the Augustinian eschatology of human imperfection supplemented by divine grace, or the environmentalist eschatology of imminent apocalypse. Once credit is linked to fiat, an eschatology is capable of calling matters into being.

The universalizing power of the capitalist system derives from the way in which it is able to call beliefs, desires, and modes of production into being. On the one hand, an eschatological expectation of a better future relativizes and undermines all existing values; at the same time, the bill of exchange, the promise of future reward, galvanizes productive activity. At one and the same time, it removes the limits of finitude as well as traditional customs and livelihoods. As Hutchinson comments: "Economic 'progress' has created the illusion that translating every decision into market values is more rational and efficient than personal judgments based upon notions of right livelihood and personal responsibility to the local community."[54] Rationality and efficiency are technical matters concerned with real rates of growth; in economics, moral issues appear irrelevant. Where traditional beliefs gained credence on the basis of experience, custom, and tradition, modern beliefs offer a solid, physical guarantee of their truth, in the form of measurable quantities. Once metaphysics is separated from finite goods or the Platonic Good within capitalism, a belief in a nonmoral conception of being emerges; it guarantees its truth because its essence is a guarantee of truth. "To be" is to justify credit. Yet one of the central paradoxes, as Douglas explores, is that this technical discourse concerning production is supported by a moral discourse of reward and punishment invoked independently of the determination of social reality: wars occur because people are wicked, poverty, because people are idle, crime, because they are immoral.[55] The highly paid are said to require higher pay to make them work, while the poor must be deprived of incomes to make them work.[56] Or the moral discourse may be composed of the market values of freedom and rights: letting others make the most of their opportunities and resources, or in other words, putting no constraints on the power exercised in "free trade." What we have here is not simply a right-wing or liberal ideology concealing reality, but the very eschatology of reward and punishment, promise and threat, upon which the capitalist system is based. There could be no money if there were not the threat of social exclusion for those who either refuse to accept it or who do not acquire it. There could be no credit without someone undertaking a liability. This is the vital conceptual difference between belief and credit. For where beliefs, whether about what is real, about possible futures, or about political strategies, are subjectively held, credit acquires an objectivity insofar as someone else undertakes the liability of demonstrating that the belief will be true— by backing the demand with money. And it is this dimension of evidence, or liability, that gives capitalism greater credence than any religious or social beliefs founded on justice. For in capitalism, being itself is translated into offering evidence or a guarantee for credit.

The eschatological illusion particular to capitalism is that one can separate fulfillment of a promise from associated contractual liabilities. The future of freedom from natural and social constraint promised to those who acquire wealth is bought at the expense of those who will have to work to guarantee those freedoms. Indeed, every credit transaction affects the interests of all, either through its effect on prices or through the direction of energies available for production.[57] Now, it would appear that in capitalism, subject to market imperatives, one is a long way from economic democracy, understood as collective control of conditions of existence.[58] Democracy, if it is to be real and not merely formal, requires that the demands of all citizens are rendered effective. Yet it is precisely this conception of the citizen, as one who has needs and makes demands, which is produced by the capitalist promise of fulfillment of desire. Indeed, in the consumer society, we have a partial "democratization of credit" — it being accessible to all who are believed to be able to pay back the loan (although, once repaid, the money created by the loan as well as the interest belongs to the bank that offered it). The bankers' slogan, "Don't wait. Have it now!" (this is the current NatWest slogan in the United Kingdom) actually creates the demand, "discovered" in the recesses of the liberal consumer subject, as what they had wanted all along.[59] Just as socialism is caught in the capitalist illusion of the possibility of an unlimited productivity, democracy is caught in the capitalist illusion of the possibility of an unlimited demand. To define the people in terms of their drives and interests is to separate their demands from the liabilities required to render demands effective. In short, democracy is a belief system based on an eschatological resolution of conflicting demands that does not reckon with its conditions of possibility.

It is the same problem as that which holds with popular beliefs in life after death. Misfortune and injustice in this life motivate people to believe in an afterlife. At the same time, misfortune and injustice in this life constitute the "problem of evil," the problem of reconciling the existence of a God who could provide a heavenly reward with our actual experience in this world. Theodicies typically invoke a "greater good" on the one hand, consisting of the advantages of moral freedom or moral progress that would be unavailable in a "perfect" world, together with compensation in eschatological fulfillment on the other. Yet, on this argument, a heaven without misfortune and injustice would be the "perfect" world that God should not have created; it would be entirely devoid of moral value and conduct. In heaven, nothing would ultimately matter; heaven exists only on the basis of this world, and as a disavowal of this world. Similarly, democracy is the heaven of politics, the eschatology of political belief: no one has ever seen it, yet one constantly awaits its arrival. It consists in a disavowal of the natural and eschatological imperatives and forces that make individual demands possible. Civilization requires not only a renunciation of sexual and aggressive drives, but also the incurring of liabilities. What is disavowed, in a liberal conception of democracy, is that anything really matters: if there are indeed various modes of the good life and human flourishing, then it matters more that these should be achieved than it does that people should be subject to the demands of their inner drives. While it may indeed be the case that a certain degree of self-determination is essential to the good life, it is a fiction to believe that such self-determination is independent of the interests of others, just as it is a fiction to believe that the self-interest and self-determination of the individual is entirely compatible with the common good of society, without someone else paying any price.[60] The good life necessarily includes natural and eschatological constraints.

What our study of the metaphysics and politics of money has disclosed is that the creation of money by fiat is the singular point where ontology and practice are folded together. Such creation takes place on the basis of a meeting between demand, trust, and the undertaking of a liability. In spite of the absence of logical proof, what we have here is an instantiation of an ontological argument whereby thought leads directly to existence. Kant's critique of the ontological argument failed because, assuming existence is not a predicate, Kant lacked any mediation between thought and existence. What Kant overlooked is that when one considers "that than which nothing greater can be conceived," or "the most perfect being," or the value of all values (money), one is not simply considering a representation. For a representation can be of anything; it does not matter which—no greatness, perfection, or value being implied. Yet if one thinks of that which matters, one is constrained to think of it as mattering; if one thinks of existence, one is constrained to think of it as existing. And one cannot think of that which matters or that which exists as a representation, for the latter does not matter or exist. In short, if one lends credence to that which matters or that which exists, one is liable to think of it seriously, as mattering or existing. At the same time, however, that matter or existence is not guaranteed. It remains eschatologically suspended. One might have misunderstood what matters, or what exists. Indeed, there is a paradox involved in eschatological ontology that can be illustrated by the dilemmas of Christology.

Those Christians who proclaim Jesus as the Christ or the Son of God— as eschatological fulfillment—need to interpret the meaning of the ultimate on the basis of a preexisting expectation, whether the fulfillment of messianic prophecy, or a preexisting historical or metaphysical conception of God. This is particularly evident in the imperial conceptions of power that often become incorporated into such a Christology, yet were explicitly denied by Jesus (e.g., Mark 10:42–45). If, however, Jesus were to be the eschatological fulfillment, then he would replace such provisional expectations with the true revelation—the powers of empire and money being replaced by the power of faith, for instance (e.g., taxes to be rendered to Caesar, but prayer rendered to God; disrupting the book-keeping money fashioned in the Temple mint; faith being able to "move mountains," etc.). Yet the truth of this true revelation would remain invisible if the hermeneutic background against which Jesus is interpreted is a given set of preconceptions; even a purely formal theology of eschatological revelation fails here. Indeed, the preconceptions would be given eschatological significance by their confirmation in Jesus. This is why there have been no true Christians—no one truly knows what "Christ" or "Son of God" might mean. Of course, the witness of Christ's followers is meant to be supplemented by the Holy Spirit—but here, again, the eschatological significance of the Spirit's teaching will not be manifest until the end. Thus by proclaiming Jesus as the ultimate one betrays Jesus because one necessarily conceals the eschatological dimension of whatever revelation he brings.[61] In this respect, the precise nature of the "kingdom of God" proclaimed by Jesus remains a mystery, despite the best efforts of historical scholars and systematic theologians, for it can be interpreted only in continuity with some preexisting historical context or systematic theology.

In relation to eschatology, then, failing knowledge, one can proceed only by faith.[62] What faith lacks is the evidence of firm, quantifiable results. Even so, one moves from thought to existence, short circuiting the Real, if one stands liable to fulfill the faith of another. Yet the question is not whether or not one will have faith in anything; faith is inevitable—it is an ontological dimension, if what we are is determined by what we hope for. The question is that of whether one will have faith in anything that matters, and whether one's faith will be such as to bring about that in which one believes. In short, what liability can be found in the Real for our misguided ventures in faith?

## Conclusion

Let us conclude, therefore, with some remarks about ontology, practice, and credit. There are three dimensions of reality: land, labor, and credit—or the natural realm of ecological and subsistence cycles, the human realm of production, politics, and unlimited becoming, and the spectral or eschatological realm of credit, nonhuman imperatives, and creation. These reflect four ontological dimensions of being, becoming, credit, and creation. The essential move of a capitalist ontology is to evacuate all moral questions of what matters from being, in order to present us with a dualism between a nonmoral, inert, quantifiable substance that serves as evidence to generate belief, and a transcendent or extraneous morality imposed upon being that judges life as productivity. This dualism or transcendence is the source of a profound mystification. Moreover, within capitalism, any earlier moral ontology that is revived, and recommended as an object of belief, will come to seem like a transcendent source of mystification imposed dualistically upon the capitalist "real world and real people," because it will lack the neutral guarantee of its own value that belongs to the universal equivalent.

An ideological critique, drawing a contrast between what is believed and what is done, can unravel the contradictions that occur within capitalism.

For the essence of capitalism is contradiction—or, more precisely, it is dualism, the separation of promise and threat. Yet an ideological critique, in the name of a historical ontology, cannot recover the ethical dimension of being without depending on some notion of demand, power, or temporality that is called forth by capitalism. Only an immanent critique, which seeks out the mediation between ontology and practice, can take capitalism to the limit where the fiction of its "real world" is disclosed as an object of belief. Henceforth, not only must we regard ourselves as temporal, existential beings, instead of eternal essences or plain facts, but we must also regard ourselves as participating in modes of credit or piety, eschatological expectations that actually bring about what we will have been. And if we direct our attention to that which matters, instead of to future profits, then we will reintroduce ethical dimensions into being.

In regard to practice, at present, the power of the natural and nonhuman realms is growing, leaving just a narrow band for human political activity. Any materialist politics must give priority to restoring cycles of subsistence and sustainability that provide our conditions of existence. Here, options are severely restricted: possibilities of escape lend themselves to recuperation and recapture in an ever-expanding capitalist market; possibilities of resistance to the human and state powers of capitalism may win minor concessions but are confronted with more formidable powers than ever before in the alliance between the military-industrial complex, finance capital, corporate media, informationalized knowledge, and consumerized subjectivity. If the history of the past few centuries can teach us anything, it is the extraordinary power of capital to override political will. Only when this vast assemblage reaches its internal limits and dies through lack of natural energy and lack of credit will it be possible to act decisively once more. Any politics that is to become credible must fully explain the fate of capitalism, as well as offering a credible alternative. And one vital component of that politics must be attention devoted to the conditions of credit.

What this entire debacle known as the history of capitalism may teach us, however, is that there is such a possibility as creation. The right eschatological expectations, the right mode of credit may call into being new systems of subsistence and production, new dimensions of subjectivity, and new modes of social association. Precisely what such an eschatology might be is well beyond the scope of this essay. But it is clear that alongside critique we require construction; alongside theory and practice we require credit; and alongside credit, we may find creation.

## Notes

1   For such a materialist history, inspired by Gilles Deleuze and Félix Guattari, see Manuel de Landa, *A Thousand Years of Non-Linear History* (New York: Zone Books, 1997).

2   See Frances Hutchinson, Mary Mellor, and Wendy Olsen, *The Politics of Money: Towards Sustainability and Economic Democracy* (London: Pluto, 2002), 180. See further Maria Mies and Veronika Bennholdt-Thomsen, *The Subsistence Perspective: Beyond the Globalised Economy* (London: Zed Books, 1999), and Maria Mies and Vandana Shiva, *Ecofeminism* (London: Zed Books, 1993).

3   For a full discussion of oil depletion, see Richard Heinberg, *The Party's Over: Oil, War, and the Fate of Industrial Societies* (East Sussex: Clairview Books, 2003).

4   See the Baker Institute Report, "Strategic Energy Policy Challenges for the 21st Century," www.rice.edu/projects/baker.

5   There is some celebration of a future "hydrogen economy" that will replace the faltering hydrocarbon economy, as well as democratizing the production of power; see Jeremy Rifkin, *The Hydrogen Economy* (Cambridge: Polity, 2002). It is important to emphasize that hydrogen is not a naturally occurring fuel on this planet; made from a primary energy source via electrolysis (or extracted from natural gas), it is merely a means of storage, transportation, and accessing energy—a function analogous to that of money. Since renewable energy sources are unlikely to keep pace with rising energy demand, we face a period of several decades where demand for primary energy will outstrip supply, which, along with the mountain of consumer, business, and government debts, will squeeze the economy in a pincer movement that renders much current economic activity unviable. Thus I would predict a major global economic collapse within the next thirty years, probably in about ten to fifteen years' time.

6   Slavoj Žižek, *The Fragile Absolute, or Why Is the Christian Legacy Worth Fighting For?* (London: Verso, 2000), 15.

7   Derived from Jacques Derrida, *Spectres of Marx*, trans. Peggy Kamuf (London: Routledge, 1994). For my reading of this spectral Real in Derrida and Deleuze, see Philip Goodchild, "Spirit of Philosophy: Derrida and Deleuze," *Angelaki* 5.2 (2000): 43–58.

8   Žižek, *The Fragile Absolute*, 16.

9   See Foucault's essay on Kant and Enlightenment for the derivation of a "historical ontology" from the Kantian project, "What is Enlightenment?" in *The Foucault Reader*, ed. Paul Rabinow (Harmondsworth, U.K.: Penguin, 1991).

10  Žižek, *The Fragile Absolute*, 17–18; Hutchinson, Mellor, and Olsen allude to a defective ontology in socialism when they argue that calls for ownership and control of the means of production *as defined by capital* miss the point; see *The Politics of Money*, 73.

11  I have made this case in Philip Goodchild, *Capitalism and Religion: The Price of Piety* (London: Routledge, 2002).

12  Aristotle, *Politics*, I.1257a, ed. Stephen Everson (Cambridge: Cambridge University Press, 1988), 12.

13  See, for example, Mervyn K. Lewis and Paul D. Mizen, *Monetary Economics* (Oxford: Oxford University Press, 2000), 12.

14  See Glyn Davies, *A History of Money from Ancient Times to the Present Day* (Cardiff: University of Wales Press, 1994), 230.

15  Hutchinson, Mellor, and Olsen, *The Politics of Money*, 53.

16  Immanuel Kant, *A Critique of Pure Reason*, trans. Norman Kemp Smith (Basingstoke, U.K.: Macmillan, 1929), 505.

17  See Terry Eagleton, *Ideology: An Introduction* (London: Verso, 1991).

18  See Jean-Joseph Goux, *Symbolic Economies after Marx and Freud*, trans. Jennifer Curtiss Gage (Ithaca, N.Y.: Cornell University Press, 1990).

19  Hutchinson, Mellor, and Olsen, *The Politics of Money*, 74–76.

20  This is the principal cause of poverty and cycles of depression, according to Henry George and his successors. See Henry George, *Progress and Poverty* (New York: Robert Schalkenbach Foundation, 1998). Hutchinson quotes Marx's dismissal of George in *The Politics of Money* 101–2; nevertheless, the limitations of George's theory should not be allowed to obscure the continuing centrality of land in contemporary economic practices, as well as the centrality of speculation, which has developed far beyond its status as envisaged by Marx.

21  Karl Marx, *Capital III*, ed. Frederick Engels (Chicago: Charles Kerr & Co., 1909), 470–78. In a credit economy, the statistically defined money supply consists mainly of the liabilities of financial intermediaries such as banks, rather than central bank money. See Mizen and Lewis, *Monetary Economics*, 15.

22  Marx, *Capital III*, 469–70.

23  Hutchinson, Mellor, and Olsen, *The Politics of Money*, 63.

24  Marx, *Capital III*, 475.

25  Hutchinson, Mellor, and Olsen, *The Politics of Money*, 63, 65. Gilles Deleuze and Félix Guattari make much of a return to a Marxist theory of money. See *Anti-Oedipus: Capitalism and Schizophrenia*, trans. Robert Hurley, Mark Seem, and Helen R. Lane (London: Athlone, 1984), 229–30.

26  Marx, *Capital III*, 471.

27  Francis Hutchinson and Brian Burkitt, *The Political Economy of Social Credit and Guild Socialism* (London: Routledge, 1997), 43.

28  Clifford Douglas, *Economic Democracy* (Suffolk, U.K.: Bloomfield Books, 1974), 72. Douglas points out that the difference has to be made up either by export, as in the theory of continual accumulation developed from Marx by Rosa Luxemburg, or by imperial control of the future, as in debt slavery. See also *The Monopoly of Credit* (Suffolk, U.K.: Bloomfield Books, 1979) for the A+B theorem, and the account given in *Social Credit* (available at www.mondopolitico.com/library/socialcredit/socialcredit.htm) of the shortage of purchasing power resulting from production of goods without production of money.

29  Hutchinson and Burkitt, *The Political Economy of Social Credit*, 37.

30  See Michael Rowbotham, *The Grip of Death: A Study of Modern Money, Debt Slavery and Destructive Economics* (Charlbury, U.K.: Jon Carpenter, 1998).

31  Hutchinson, Mellor, and Olsen, *The Politics of Money*, 64.

32  Hutchinson, *What Everybody Really Wants to Know about Money* (Charlbury, U.K.: Jon Carpenter, 1998), 105–6.

33  Quoted by Douglas, *Economic Democracy*, 47.

34  Mizen and Lewis, *Monetary Economics*, 22.

35  Hutchinson, Mellor and Olsen argue that it was not technical innovation, but the use of bills of exchange and other credit instruments that gave rise to agrarian and industrial capitalism. *The Politics of Money*, 60.

36  The economic textbooks, taking a nominal liabilities-to-reserves ratio of 5:1, describe how a deposit of $1,000 can be multiplied, not by a single bank due to adverse clearing balances, but progressively — the first bank keeping $200 and lending $800, the banks receiving these new deposits of keeping $160 and lending $640, until total new reserves are $1,000, and new loans are $4,000. See E. K. Hunt and Howard J. Sherman, *Economics: An Introduction to Tra-*

*ditional and Radical Views* (New York: Harper and Row, 1990), 505–8. In practice, however, a bank can learn from experience of the demands of clearing balances what kind of limits to lending are safe to keep; moreover, in a large economy where there are few clearing banks, the vast majority of clearing transactions will tend to cancel themselves out. Total figures for the United Kingdom in December 2002 indicated $M_4$ at £1,004 billion and $M_0$ at £31 billion, a ratio of 32:1.

37  Hutchinson, Mellor, and Olsen, *The Politics of Money*, 62.

38  Ibid., 48.

39  Ibid., 57, 73.

40  Ellen Meiksins Wood, *The Origin of Capitalism* (New York: Monthly Review Press, 1999), 7; cited in Hutchinson, Mellor, and Olsen, *The Politics of Money*, 71.

41  Among Douglas's own writings, see *Economic Democracy, The Monopoly of Credit,* and *Social Credit.*

42  See Hutchinson and Burkitt, *The Political Economy of Social Credit,* 40–41.

43  Theology is understood here as the study of the veracity, value, significance, and construction of religious thought—the definition operable in the secular university where I work.

44  See Michael Hardt and Antonio Negri, *Empire* (Cambridge, Mass.: Harvard University Press, 2000).

45  In spite of its many advances, in this respect, Hardt and Negri's *Empire* seems to be a retrograde step in relation to the work of Deleuze and Guattari. While I have made some attempt to explore the political possibilities opened up by Deleuze and Guattari's work myself, I must admit that these have always seemed limited. See Philip Goodchild, *Deleuze and Guattari: An Introduction to the Politics of Desire* (London: Sage, 1996).

46  See De Landa, *A Thousand Years of Non-Linear History,* 48.

47  See George Soros, *The Crisis of Global Capitalism* (London: Little, Brown & Co., 1998).

48  Hutchinson describes limited liability as "an ingenious invention to enable people to borrow money on the strength of an uncertain future and not be responsible for paying it back if expectations are not fulfilled." *What Everybody Really Wants to Know about Money,* 154.

49  There has been considerable confusion in reading Deleuze and Scotus on the question of univocity, which reaches its apogee in Alain Badiou, *Deleuze: The Clamor of Being,* trans. Louise Burchill (Minneapolis: University of Minnesota Press, 2000). Scotus's principal task was to separate philosophy and theology, for if God could be understood by the human mind, then the unconditioned could be conditioned by the conditioned. His metaphysical proposal was designed precisely in order to avoid Neoplatonic strands of Aristotelianism that united Being with the One by arguing that the determinable concept of Being and the ultimate differentia such as the One are primarily diverse, so that one includes nothing of the other; see Duns Scotus, *Opus Oxoniense,* book 1, d. 3, q. 3, *Philosophy in the Middle Ages,* ed. Arthur Hyman and James J. Walsh (Indianapolis: Hackett, 1973), 618. One no longer approaches God through the concept of Being; Being is an abstract, neutral, insignificant term; even philosophy is concerned primarily with the "transcendentals," rather than Being. Being is thus "univocal," not in the sense that it is subordinated to one sense, but that it does not distinguish between "the knowledge of *whether a thing is* and *what it is*" (*Opus Oxoniense,* book 1, d. 3, q. 1, 605). This abstract and neutral realm of Being may thus be distinguished from individuating differences or *haecceities.* Deleuze, by contrast, follows Spinoza in making Being a subject of affirmation or existence, and saying it only of individuating differences or haecceities (going against the grain of conventional readings of Spinoza that prioritize essence over existence, following the nominal definitions).

Instead of simply affirming multiple haecceities, however, without addressing the question of the mediation of their mutual relations, Deleuze invokes the Bergsonian concept of the virtual so as to make these differences actualizations of a temporal flow. This leaves Deleuze with the problem of change and communication within the virtual, which is unresolved in *Difference and Repetition*. Since the virtual is the unthought within thought, the vanishing mediator, Deleuze attempted in *A Thousand Plateaus* to think the virtual in terms of multiplicity as a set of machinic relations, flows, and thresholds. Although this attempt remained incomplete, this tendency toward choosing the individuated as real leads to a reductive misreading of Deleuze that ignores the continuity of Bergsonian duration, as exemplified by Manuel de Landa's excellent yet flawed *Intensive Science and Virtual Philosophy* (London: Continuum, 2002); the alternative tendency, manifested in Deleuze's final essay on immanence, focuses instead on "a life, power, beatitude"—which, taken as the sole real, leads to Badiou's brilliant yet misguided Neoplatonic misreading. Each arises from imposing the alternative "one or multiple" onto a philosophy of mediation. The virtual plays a similar role to analogy in metaphysics as a mediation between terms, but instead of being a merely theoretical or speculative mediation, it is a temporal, existential, and active mediation between multiplicities.

For the correct exegesis of Deleuze on univocity, see Daniel W. Smith, "The Doctrine of Univocity: Deleuze's Ontology of Immanence," in *Deleuze and Religion*, ed. Mary Bryden (London: Routledge, 2000), 167–83; for a refutation of Badiou on univocity, see Nathan Widder, "The Rights of Simulacra: Deleuze and the Univocity of Being," *Continental Philosophy Review*, 34 (2001): 437–53. For a critique of Deleuze's adoption of univocity, constructed on the basis of a Scotist theology, see Philip Goodchild, "Why Is Philosophy so Compromised with God?" in Bryden, *Deleuze and Religion*, 156–66.

50   Cited in Milton L. Myers, *The Soul of Modern Economic Man: Ideas of Self-Interest* (Chicago: University of Chicago Press, 1983), 16.

51   Cited in ibid., 31.

52   Deleuze and Guattari, *A Thousand Plateaus*, 219.

53   See the National Academy of Sciences report, "Abrupt Climate Change: Inevitable Surprises," 2002, available on the Web at http://www.nap.edu/books/0309074347/html.

54   Hutchinson, *What Everybody Really Wants to Know about Money*, 4.

55   Douglas, *Social Credit*, chap. 1.

56   Hutchinson, *What Everybody Really Wants to Know about Money*, 150.

57   Hutchinson and Burkitt, *The Political Economy of Social Credit and Guild Socialism*, 37.

58   Hutchinson, Mellor, and Olsen, *The Politics of Money*, 73, 95.

59   See the discussion in Žižek, *On Belief* (London: Routledge, 2001), 117–21.

60   This is the founding ideology of classical economics. See Myers, *The Soul of Modern Economic Man*.

61   This is one of the few points where Nietzsche was indeed correct about St. Paul betraying Christ, though the sharp contrast he draws cannot be maintained on historical grounds.

62   In this respect, St. Paul, conscious of his inevitable betrayal, remained entirely faithful to his eschatological vision of Christ by relating to Christ through faith, without pretending to have ultimate knowledge.

William Desmond | Neither Servility
nor Sovereignty:
Between Metaphysics
and Politics

## Between Metaphysics and Politics

IF THERE ARE RELATIONS between metaphysics and politics, they are not immediately self-evident but seem more mediated and indirect. Yet a hidden metaphysics can influence how we think of politics, just as certain political arrangements can either hinder or enable a genuine metaphysical openness of mind. What happens in the apparently empty ether of thought may come down to earth, and a masked metaphysics come to walk the streets — or stalk. For monsters too might float in the Empyrean, coming to earth with gifts glittering and poisoned. The walkways of politics are eagerly hospitable to the arts of equivocation. What we mean by "metaphysics" and "politics," as well as relations between them, is not any the more univocal.

These relations are even less easy to discern and articulate given that today we are often said to be denizens of a "postmetaphysical" time, with the words "post-metaphysical" being bandied about with all the assurances of the self-evident. Is it evident that we know what metaphysics is? If that is not so evident, how less evident will be the relations of metaphysics and politics. And whence the self-assurance about our identities as being postmetaphysical? And is there not some irony in the fact that worry about *this* identity is not enough in evidence, despite claims that all identity is in question in our supposedly postmetaphysical time of nonidentity?

One is tempted to reply with another question. What space is there that post-metaphysical thinking might occupy, since all thinking, whether it attends to it or not, whether it knows or acknowledges it as such, is informed by basic presuppositions about, and orientations toward, the meaning of what it is "to be"? If this is so, to be postmetaphysical is to make a metaphysical claim, in the sense that some such basic presuppositions and orientations inform this claim too. To be human is to be; to be human as a thinking being is to be constituted by certain powers of the "to be," powers marking the complex integrity of one's being, as well as allowing complex intermediations between oneself and what is other. And all of this is at play, even when one lives thoughtlessly. The important consideration for metaphysics as a philosophical discipline is our moving, by the proper discipline of attentive mindfulness, between the more implicit and the more explicit, the more recessed and the more expressed. What seems remote, namely, metaphysics, may turn out to be more neighboring than expected.

I will first speak of metaphysics and come to some considerations about the political in due course. I have made efforts to develop what I call a metaxological metaphysics, bearing on, among other things, some of the problems of sameness and otherness, identity and difference that we have inherited since the time of idealism. I have also tried to articulate something of the ethical view that would go with this metaphysics.[1] This will inform what I try to say here, and it will be a judgment call as what to presuppose as given, what to explain more overtly.

One can live, more or less, without being a metaphysician in the explicit sense, but one cannot be a good philosopher without being more or less a metaphysician, in the sense of bringing to bear on what is at play in being an attentive mindfulness for the basic presuppositions, sources, and orientations toward the "to be." To be this or that is to be a particular concretion of the sourcing powers of the "to be." To be as mindful, that is, as human, is both to live from these sources but also to try to be attentively mindful of them. One does not have a choice about being an *animale metaphysicum*. The issue is not being a post-metaphysician but being a good metaphysician — under the call of truthful fidelity to the sourcing powers of the "to be." This does not mean that metaphysics is everything, but it does mean that in all our thinking some metaphysical presuppositions about the "to be" are at play. Let these be mostly unacknowledged, not only by common sense and science but by postmetaphysical philosophy; nevertheless, metaphysics as a philosophical discipline is a form of reflective thinking under fidelity to the truth of what is thus at play. (One wonders if this point about the postmetaphysician, namely, the impossibility of evading metaphysics, applies analogously to the "postreligious" person, namely, the inescapability of being religious. This also has implications for how we think of politics, as I will later suggest.)

Granted, it may well be that a certain picture of metaphysics is being criticized or rejected in this talk of the postmetaphysical. In the main it seems to come down to some version of Platonism. I would call it Nietzsche's cartoon version, a cartoon which has had multiple afterlives. Plato will be an important point of reference in what is to follow, though the dear Nietzsche himself knew well the difference between Plato and his "Platonism." "In my hands Plato tends to become a caricature": Nietzsche himself had the honor to confess this. In this caricature we find the univocal fixation of (metaphysical) difference in terms of rigidly separated worlds: the world here and the beyond world. "Metaphysics" deserts the world here for the beyond world. Interestingly for our concerns, the Greek *meta* can mean both "in the midst" as well as "beyond," a point to which I will come back. But in the cartoon version no sooner is the "meta" of metaphysics intoned and we are shooting out beyond, yonder, somewhere over the rainbow. We are to be brought back to earth. Being beyond metaphysics may have "transcending" but it must be this-worldly. If for postmetaphysical thinking there is any transcendence, it must be entirely immanent.

Of course, the postmetaphysical claim of unsurpassable immanence is not unconnected with its own version of the political and with how immanent social powers take form or are to be organized, whether in terms of sane, everyday distributions of powers, or spontaneous eruptions of repressed forces, or plotted rebellions or revolts or regime changes, and whether all these take shape under the sign of totality, or "difference." For there is a totalitarian immanence and an anarchistic immanence, and a socially concerned or compassionate immanence, and a neoliberal immanence, and an edifying pragmatic immanence. There are the capitalist postmetaphysicians who are "post" only in the accidental sense that their unrelenting engrossment in the dominion of serviceable disposability has blanked out as "useless" most metaphysical considerations, or intimations, or misgivings. This blank is itself the result of certain metaphysical presuppositions about the human being. We are units of self-interested, self-serving desire, and nature as other is the to-be-possessed reserve of resources to further the projects of economic and commercial organizations of such units, officially said to further the individual power of the consumer, de facto showing power more or less global in the potential outreach of its exploitation. There are postmetaphysicians on the left, Marx perhaps being one of the first of them; and even though the ideal banner of social justice is hoisted above, out on the streets or on the barricades or in the polemical pamphlets, there is a not-so-well dissimulated metaphysics of social will to power.

It might seem that the previously mentioned "Platonic" version of metaphysics has nothing to do with politics, and that postmetaphysical thinking would allow us more lucidly to get political actualities in focus. After all, politics has a bearing on, among other things, our social organization of immanent powers, guarding immanent order here and now, either affording or resisting tyranny here and now, and in the daily moderate middle, trying to sustain an immanent peace, such that people can go about their everyday business, be it in the life of the family, or in economic businesses, or in cultural services, either artistic or religious, that take us beyond the instrumental serviceability of utility. Politically minded people delight in the realism of their reminding the metaphysical dreamers: this all is here and now, not over there, all to be done now with feet on the ground, not with heads in the clouds, and with longing for somewhere over there, a nowhere other world.

I think it is not so simple, and not so easy to get the political into wise focus, if the sense of the "beyond" of politics is lost, or betrayed, and the "political" is tempted to assume sole sovereignty for the immanent organization of the powers of the "to be." Quite to the contrary, the loss of the beyond of metaphysics, as going with the immanent absolutization of the political, tends to lead to the loss of the wisdom of the immanent that is the genuine art of the political, a wisdom that lives by its worldly discernment of the relative. Wise discernment of the relative is not really possible without some intimation of the lacking nature of all counterfeit claims to absoluteness. This wise discernment of the genuinely political must be practiced in the art of detecting idols, and dealing prudently with the immanent havoc they threaten. Is this possible without some intimation of the metaphysical, one shaped by the doubleness of the *meta* — in the midst, and hence immanent, and yet over and above, beyond, and hence a sign of transcendence as other?

I suspect that in modern philosophy metaphysics becomes a form of ontology in which there comes to be the loss of this doubleness and the feel for its basic significance. I will below say a bit more about metaphysics and such an ontology. But one can see the rationale for these changes in modern philosophy, if the cartoon version of Platonism is the truth of metaphysics. For then we are dealing with the philosopher's escape from reality, not his or her more deep engagement with it. Of course, even this escape has political consequences, but on the surface they seem eviscerating to the excellences of immanence, and hence also to the wise discernment of immanent powers. I would say, however, that we can see the matter with more nuance, with less of the univocalizing of the dualistic "either/or." There have been metaphysicians who, in fidelity to an intimation of the "beyond," would want to relativize the absoluteness of immanent power, but this entails no denial of the necessity of wise discernment of immanent excellences. I tend to agree with them, and for reasons not unconnected with a different interpretation of Plato.[2] But with Plato we are ever confronted with the great paradox that this great Satan of metaphysics was strangely obsessed with politics and the vision of the best regime. For one who would quit immanence as quickly as you could exclaim *exaipnes*, we witness an odd loving lingering with the fluctuations of power in immanence. In the cave here and now, we need an almost heroic patience for discerning the "packs and sects of great ones that ebb and flow by the moon," as King Lear put it. Lear also speaks of becoming "God's spies," but such a spy is not engaged in espionage. He or she seeks simply to behold, to comprehend with compassion. Perhaps there are "after-worldsmen"—human beings, so to say, posthumous to will to power—who have great care for this world.

But what kind of care? If we take, for instance, a Hobbes or a Machiavelli as setting the trend, we will become political spies of the "mortal god" and opt for a self-proclaimed "realism" of politics, against the dreaming or self-deluding "idealism" of a Plato, even an Aristotle. Again, is it so simple? If humans and their communities, political, as well as prepolitical and transpolitical, are *between* "real" and "ideal," then we risk a brutal amputation, if our realism is crude—that is to say, lacking finesse for the traces of a transcendence that is more than even the superb excellences of immanence. Clearly our care for the excellences of immanence will be different when one has the intimation that there is more at stake than a self-sufficient immanence, when signs of something beyond have entered one's sense of the equivocal play of immanent powers, and not only the temptations to tyranny that we know here but also our intoxications with what is good now. One's care will be different if the excellences of immanence, in the enjoyment and joy they offer, are also signs of what cannot be exhausted by immanence. Least of all will one's care be to turn immanence into a project of our power to make itself absolute, as absolute as possible, and more than anything else absolved from transcendence as other. This will seem as a treason to the excellences of immanence rather than their last apotheosis.

## Metaxological Metaphysics and Modern Ontology

Let me say a word or two about metaphysics and ontology. Metaphysics is certainly concerned with immanence in terms of its mindful discernment of the multiple equivocities of our being native to the world. We might think of metaphysics in terms of systems, and to be sure this is an ideal found often, from early modern rationalism through to Hegel. But one can be systematic without claiming to possess the system. Indeed there are practices of metaphysics that might well display a certain diffidence about system, about the theory-building of Laputan thinkers, especially in its modern guise. We find a tendency especially present in modern philosophy to seek an ontology defined primarily by the self-determination of rational thought, to the detriment of the interruptions of surprising otherness that break in on the speculative dreams of reason, musing out of itself alone. Hegel is the high point of this tendency to system, offering us as metaphysics a speculative logic that is a categorical logyontology. I think of metaphysics less as the system of categories defined by the self-circling of thought determining itself, as a fundamental reflection on the basic senses of being, or to be, none of which we can speak about without mindful openness to what actuality as other communicates intelligibly to us. There is an openness to what is beyond self-determining thought in this understanding of metaphysics, an openness more consonant with the more original experience of wonder or astonishment we find, for instance, in the Greek *thaumazein*.

If I refer to Hegel, one might also refer, with suitable qualification, to Heidegger's fundamental ontology, which like the idealistic immanence of thought thinking itself, is still too a philosophy of immanence. Even given talk about the everydayness of *Dasein*, one suspects there is at work what one might call a "postulatory finitism" that has the effect of closing thought off from thinking the signs of transcendence as other to immanence. Again I mean metaphysics in a more Platonic sense, not in terms of the cartoon version (one suspects at times that Heidegger fell under the spell of this cartoon). Such a metaphysics asks for a practice of philosophy that, even in the immanences of everyday life, recalls us to a porosity to transcendence as other. Is there a philosophical seeing, a beholding that is neither servile nor sovereign?

I find it helpful to distinguish four basic senses of being: the univocal, the equivocal, the dialectical, and the metaxological, as I call the fourth. I will not say much about these four senses other than this general remark. While the univocal sense tends to emphasize determinate sameness and identity, the equivocal tends to stress difference that escapes univocal sameness, sometimes even to the point of the loss of any mediation between sameness and difference, identity and otherness. By contrast, the dialectic sense seeks to mediate differences, differences sometimes equivocal—not by reduction to a simple univocal sameness but by transition to a more inclusive unity or whole, which, it is claimed, contains and even reconciles the differences. Finally, the metaxological deals with the interplay of sameness and difference, identity and otherness, not by mediating a more inclusive whole but by recurrence to the rich ambiguities of the middle, and with due respect for forms of otherness that are dubiously claimed to be included in the immanence of a dialectical whole.

The modern sense of ontology is often shaped by univocal and dialectical responses to the equivocities of being, whether seeking a set of clear and distinct categories to diminish or dissolve all ambiguity, or a totality of thought-determinations claiming to exhaust the intelligibility of being. I agree with some of the postmodern hesitations about the traditional language of the whole. I would put the primary accent less on "deconstructing" the whole, as on our being in-between; and on our thinking as an intermediating that, once again, is directed primarily not to an inclusive whole of thought thinking itself but to a mindful porosity to the transcendence of being, as both other and yet in intimate relation to us. I think that metaphysics, most fundamentally, is metaxological, and that mindful attention to the equivocities of given immanence is one of its important tasks. I would also say that this mindful attention is a cousin to the mindful discernment needful for political discrimination of the powers of immanence. For politics is not a "theory" but requires also a practice of phronetic discernment in the domains of relatives.

One might distinguish ontology and metaphysics in this respect. If ontology deals with being as immanent, it tends to culminate in something like Hegel's system of self-determining thought, or perhaps the existential recoil back to human immanence in terms of fundamental ontology. Metaphysics, by contrast, is more metaxological in the sense of opening mindfulness to transcendence by means of an exploration of the signs of irreducible otherness, even in immanence. This is not a matter of the system, but it is a matter of systematic thought. Hegel closes systematic thinking into the system, but there is no a priori necessity that thinking systematically has to take this very modern form. There are rich networks of interconnections already at work in being, but these networks do not constitute a closed or completed system to be discursively expressed by philosophy; the networks are concretized by open intermediations marked by sameness and otherness, identity and difference. I think a metaxological metaphysics must try to make intelligible sense of these concrete intermediations by way of the fourfold sense of being sketched above. Dynamic integrities of being take form as stable but open constancies; our minding of these shows the living energy of thought that opens beyond closure to what is other to thought alone.

Modern dialectic tends to interpret the passages between same and other, identity and difference, and so on, in terms of self-determining thought. The intermediations of being tend to be characterized in terms of a variety of rational self-mediations that circle around and back on themselves, resulting with idealism in a closure of the immanence of thought on itself. The story is not entirely different with those postidealistic philosophies marked by an antipathy to dialectic. Insofar as the practice of philosophy is marked by postulatory finitism, the result is a not dissimilar immanence, beyond which there is nothing further to be thought. In that space of radical immanence one might dialectically sublate, one might deconstruct dialectic, one might celebrate the earth with Dionysus, but there is nothing beyond that space.

From a metaxological perspective, there is more to be said. If speculative self-mediation is taken as the true intermediation, it does not do full justice to the passages between same and other, where otherness as other is just as basic, if not more, than self-determining thought. And by contrast with anti-idealistic immanence, a metaxological metaphysics discerns in the very onto-logical robustness of immanent otherness an original communication of an even more radical otherness, hyperbolic to the terms of immanence alone. This between is the milieu of thought where metaphysics as a philosophical practice arises and takes form. As itself a form of intermediated thinking, this practice of philosophy is not for itself alone. Its own self-determination is not the absolute point. Its mindful discernment of what is hyperbolic in immanence points to what is hyperbolic to immanence.

So such a practice of philosophy asks a porosity of mindful thought to what exceeds complete determination in terms of immanence alone. It is a participant in this middle, does not overarch it from the outside, and if it is, as it were, lifted up from within, it too is always defined by passages in the between. In one sense, there is no return to the *metaxu*, since we never leave it, but there is a return in the sense of being awakened to what we are in, and to what is recessed in what we are in, and in realizing the porosity of the medium of finite life to what cannot be exhausted by finite immanence. If there is a return to the recalcitrances of given immanence, in their other-ness to self-defining thought, there is also a searching of the "more" of the given world, as charged with signs of what exceeds immanence alone. Read-ing the signs of this "more" as communicated in the saturated equivocity of the given world is intimate to the vocation of metaxological metaphysics.

I want to say that the doubleness and the sense of the between of metaxo-logical metaphysics must yield a different relation to politics than does an ontology oriented wholly toward immanence. The latter orientation tends to be defined by the language of the whole, whereas, metaxologically speak-ing, we must consider again the *meta* of metaphysics as double. As I said, this *meta* can be taken to refer to what is "in the midst," and here it links with the metaxu; it can also be taken to refer to what is "beyond," over and above, and here it refers the metaxu to what is super(ior), to what is *huper*. We are referred both directly to what is hyperbolic in immanence and indirectly to what is hyperbolic to immanence.

Ontology, by contrast, as a *logos* of *to on*, is tempted to shortchange this doubleness, tempted always by a kind of univocity of immanence, and this can take different forms. It might be defined in terms of the immanence of self-determining systems, or in terms of the immanence of postulatory finitism such as informs fundamental ontology, or in terms of the immanence of the scientistic univocity that informs many projects of science and technology, or in terms of the rhapsodic univocity of Dionysian immanence, Nietzschean or postmodern, or in terms of a studied naturalizing pragmatism shorn of the more suggestive intimations of something other that we do find in a Charles Peirce or a William James. For there are many forms of this univocity of immanence: scientistic in the technological will to conquer the equivocities of given being and subject creation to the homogeneity of a projected human measure; moral through the immanence of absolute autonomy in Kantianism; calculative in the homogeneous reckoning of hedonistic bliss in utilitarianism; speculative and political in the dialectical immanence of Hegelianism and its state; dialectical or revolutionary in the political immanence of post-Hegelian totalitarianisms, be they Marxist or fascist; antidialectical and Dionysian in the immanent Nietzschean world that is "will to power and nothing else besides," and we ourselves also "will to power and nothing else besides."[3]

Modern ontology is tempted to bind politics to a language of the immanent whole, beyond which there is nothing. Those postmoderns who deconstruct this whole do not quite deconstruct this immanence; postmodern immanence is still immanence, even if now racked or tortured with itself. One must ask if immanent difference is difference enough, difference enough for transcendence as other to us, and not only for immanent self-transcendence. If it is not, as I think follows from a metaxological thinking, one has to wonder whether the silence on this in postmodern politics signals a decayed, skeptical, cynical form of the modern version of totalizing immanence. The particular strain may have mutated and may not look at all like its ancestor, but it is of the same gene pool. And if this gene pool is immanent will to power (as we suspect after the last revelation of Nietzsche), the totalitarian form may have mutated into a pluralistic form or an anarchistic form, but it is still will to power and "nothing else besides." Finally again, the circulation of immanence is only around itself, and to the occlusion or exclusion of signs of transcendence as other. One wonders if, from a metaxological viewpoint, this circulation is the mimicking of ultimate transcendence in immanence. What this means for the communal intermediation of social power is that politics is asked to be more and more the mimicking of religion, even as a certain politics would put religion more and more on the compost heap of history.

I will shortly turn from what might seem high abstractions to different forms of concrete human community, but I need to make this last point. If metaphysics reflects on the fundamental senses of the "to be," and if this "to be" is metaxological, the finite "to be" cannot be described in entirely immanent terms: it manifests a between, both in an immanent sense, and in a sense that is porous to what is other to it. There is a finitude and openness to the between in which we come across communications of what exceeds the immanent terms of what is given "in the midst." There is something hyperbolic to the between communicated in the between. There are many expressions of this, but one of importance for our consideration here is the charge of the good immanent to the givenness of the finite "to be." Modern ontology tries to give a logos of *to on*, but it seems to be of one mind with the development of modern science in this regard, namely, that given being is stripped of the signs of qualitative value and determined in terms of a homogenous sameness.

Granted, there are reactions against this, but the main point is important in that we do find at the extreme a divorce of being and the good. The consistent outcome of this divorce is nihilism: the objectification of other being, the subjectification of the human being, and the development by the latter of a project of will to power to make the homogeneity of the former serve the homogeneous heterogeneity of its own desires.[4] I say homogeneous heterogeneity since in the end there turns out to be no principle of qualitative discrimination between higher and lower, and hence the heterogeneity becomes a mere diversity, but this is indistinguishable from homogeneity: everything different finally comes to the same thing. Thus a philosophy of extreme difference easily reverts to a monism of sameness that it ostensibly has rejected or overcome. We see this with those pleas of tolerance that, mirabile dictu, can quickly become quite intolerant when it is the "wrong" kind of difference that is before one. What determines the discrimination of "wrong" difference? One suspects mere dissidence with one's own will to power, nicely masked in the niceness of one's preaching of diversity.

Yet there does seem to be one form of the good of the "to be" that is still hard not to affirm. I mean the good of the "to be" granted in the will to preserve and perpetuate one's own being. This granting may be an expression of the subjectification of the human being, but the will to be of the latter is at least granted a value in a sense not controverted. Every being seeks to preserve and perpetuate its own being. Let it be expressed in Hobbesian or Spinozistic terms, in utilitarian terms, or neoliberal: there is a basic value to the "to be" in that fact that I and you continue to affirm our own existence, in the face of threats, and more positively, in advancing the guaranteed satisfaction of our recurrent desires. In other words, at a primitive level in our own singular being something of the intimacy of the "to be" and its being good to be is acknowledged in ourselves. This is right. But it is wrong, if this is taken as the last word, or even the first. We then no longer have an adequate sense of the good: the good not as the good of my "to be," but of the "to be."

I know this needs to be further articulated (and I have made some efforts in *Ethics and the Between*), but the point is that there is a metaphysical-ontological meaning to the good of the "to be," constituting an ethos of being within which the human effort to be, and to be good, is situated. This, however, will not be seen to be our situation if we claim that the whole of what is other to us is a neutral homogeneity. Then the good of our "to be" is self-asserting in a void of value, with respect to the ethos of being as other to us; and hence inevitably we cannot but take a posture of revolt against this ethos. For this worthless otherness, worthless without our imposing our value on it, must finally be hateful, must be negated to be made good — good on a scale that mirrors our own self-affirmative will to be. Neutral homogeneity is thus only a lull or pause in the onslaught of will to power on being as other that in itself is thought to be valueless. There are only too many political expressions of this. Revolutionary politics too often fits the profile. The untrammeled calculative exploitation of the earth in a capitalist mode is not ontologically different in a qualitative sense. One might feel some sympathy with songs of defiance hurled in the face of the absurdity, or even systems of moral value such as the ethics of autonomy that try to raise self-affirmation to a higher ideal level. The devalued ethos of being underpins all. That is to say, it underpins nothing, and nothing is underpinned. Politics becomes a project that must exploit the devalued being to further the preservation and continuation of humans, individually or collectively, either keeping in check the excess sleeping in human self-assertion, or seeking to release it when established orders prove not to satisfy.

The devalued ethos of being is occupied by one being that is not immediately devalued: the human being in whom the good of the "to be" expresses itself. This language may not be used, but I would say this answers to a certain self-mediating logic. And it is not false, but it is at most only half-true, and hence also at best half-false. The good of the "to be" is both self-mediating, and hence related to the process of selving, and also intermediating, and hence it informs our relations to others in diverse forms of community, be these ethical or political. A metaxological metaphysics has to do justice to both these self-mediations and social intermediations, in their interplay and proper balance, and to both as grounded in an ethos of being that is not the devalued otherness we have come to take for granted in modernity. It is not enough just to revolt against this. For there are revolts that risk only a reversal of who now is sovereign, who now is servile. The regime of will to power is not altered by filling the empty throne with a new invested sovereign; nor is it altered by leaving the empty throne empty, if there is nothing *beyond* that throne, whether filled or empty. We need something beyond sovereignty and servility.

## The Between and Communities

Reflection on the good of the "to be" is metaphysical and ethical, but it is also political. Political community bears on diverse orders of the sourcing powers of the "to be," as marked by diverse values and senses of what is worthy. It bears not just on the power to be, but of the good of the "to be," in its human forms, both individual and social, and as enabled to be in the given ethos of being. There is a perhaps more normal sense of politics as having to do with the intermediations of communal sovereignty; there is also a sense of the political that must take into account the relations of the different social intermediations of the good of the "to be."⁵ I know some would want to separate ethics and politics, but while the two might not be identical, a metaxological philosophy of the between will emphasize a certain porosity between them. All forms of community, be they called ethical or political, ultimately bear on what we love, as Augustine stresses, and how our loves are expressed and organized in ways of life. The metaxu, coupled in Plato's *Symposium* with eros, refers us to a form of love, and what is love if it does not direct itself to what is good or worthy? Eros is a between, and neither a god nor a beast, both of whom have no need of politics. Human beings need politics because they are, so to say, between earth and heaven. But love, like intermediation, is plurivocal. Diverse forms of giving and receiving, as well as their corruptions, go on in the between. Their discrimination is part of the task of philosophy. The art of politics, at its best, is involved in an analogous discrimination.

The *Symposium* refers to the power of eros as an intermediary to bind up *the whole*, but in line with what already has been said, I would stress less the whole as *the porosity of the between* to what is beyond the immanent whole. I note again a certain *doubleness* of eros, underscored in all its political resonances in Plato's dialogues: the difference of *eros turannos* and *eros ouranios*. To refer to *eros turannos* is to name something already redolent with political significance.⁶ Plato speaks of *penia* (poverty) and *poros* (resource) as at the origin of eros. I would relate this *poros* to a kind of *porosity*: porosity is a condition of our being open to what is other and beyond us. The original energy of our being as a given power is a paradoxical mix of lack and plenitude. Our intermediate being is, I would put it, both a passion of being (*passio essendi*) and an endeavor to be (*conatus essendi*). But the *passio* is itself a porosity: at once a kind of "nothing" or opening, and also a fullness or power or plenitude. If once again we have need of a double description, one might think this is constitutive of our equivocity, but this need not be understood in an entirely negative sense. Tyrannical politics, at the extreme, is an organized outrage to the passio essendi, in the name of a self-absolutizing conatus essendi, insisting on its own absolute immanence, insisting on itself as the whole. This is one extreme that reduces the doubleness to a usurping univocity. Properly the doubleness refers to both our self-surpassing power and our potential for limitless reception. Ultimately our porosity to the other is related, I think, to the promise of agapeic self-transcending in human existence, not just the desire for erotic sovereignty, but this is at the opposite extreme to tyranny.

It may help to give a brief summary of the different forms of communal intermediation I discuss in *Ethics and the Between*.[7] There I have tried to show how communities in the between range from the more intimate, to the more instrumental, through more erotic forms, to touch on the agapeic. The four forms of community I discuss are these: first, the ethical community of the family, where the intimacy of being is more important; second, the network of utility, where economical and instrumental values often dominate, and where today we find too much of what I call an ethos of serviceable disposability: things must serve us, be serviceable for us, but once they have served their use, they are disposable (this attitude can treat human persons also as items of serviceable disposability); third, the community of what I call erotic sovereignty, where the intermediation of social and political power is to the fore; fourth, and finally, what I call the community of agapeic service, where our ethical and religious service to our neighbors and fellow humans is most important.

In these diverse social formations of loves, trust is basic, and the interplay of trust and distrust. This trust is ontological, in being bound to an enigmatic, given confidence in good of the "to be." It is also human, and hence ethical and political, in that out of it emerge the diverse forms of being in relation to others and to ourselves, none finally separable from the incognito work of this grounding trust. There is something equivocal here too, and an openness of freedom in which trust can mutate into distrust, love into hate, the friend into the enemy.[8] These different communities are all forms of metaxological intermediation, which diversely mix self-serving and service of the other. In the third there come to the fore more explicitly political considerations. But politics has the care for the just support, formation, and advancement of the other worthy forms of community also.

First, the ethical intermediation of the *family* is the most elemental. This is very important. If the seeds of ethical intermediation are not well sowed at this intimate level, it is difficult to see our participation in a more public political space as being marked by genuine ethical openness to others. I would say that a public philosophy has to foster mindfulness of what is proper to the family, since this provides the first intermediation between the intimate and the larger social world in which we will all inevitably participate. There is also a two-way porosity between the family and that larger world. If the ethical health of the latter is questionable, it may affect the intimacy of the family also. I must refer to the fuller discussion in *Ethics and the Between* (chap. 13).

Public intermediation, by its nature, tends to turn us away from the intimate, just so far as others call us out from self and enjoin our participation in the shared between. There are different ways of participation. If the family remains more in touch with the intimate, there are more objectifying participations that might be called our living in the *commons*. What is a commons? A commons constitutes a public space of intermediation wherein a plurality of participants are together, either joining freely or being enjoined, whether through external compulsion, secret suggestion, exploitative use, or persuasive solicitation. The milieu of being, charged equivocally with value and diversely stressed by different ethical potencies, is the primal ethos; a commons crystallizes a more particular formation of these potencies. (There is an extensive discussion of what I call the ethical potencies in *Ethics and the Between*.) A commons shapes its own derived ethos and is marked by its own purposes or common good, by its normalized ways of acting and its standards.

Here intermediation in the public space is more accentuated than the intimate. A more embracing sense of commons can be dominated or overlaid by more particular commons — which contracts the promise of the larger commons. Ethos, in the derived sense, is always a mix or mixing. Thus pure utility is an abstraction, expressing a human self-understanding, the strengths and deficiencies of which are reproduced in the character of the commons. The dominion in our time of this abstraction, which is socially real, merits some notice. There comes to be a *gap* between the intimate and the space of the commons. When this happens, the between can seem to be "neutralized" into a particular public domain. Ultimately the notion of a neutral between is a sheer abstraction; indeed, it makes no sense. For in the between we always find a complex dialectic of trust and distrust in a commons. The others, to some degree, are always strangers. They do not know me as my family does. Their ambiguity makes one more recalcitrant to the giving of trust. How are we to know if the other is hostile or hospitable? We cannot always be certain. We learn to be wary, on guard. A commons is both a togetherness serving shared purposes and the possibility of hostile otherness. Both are reflected in forms of intermediation not attuned to the intimate. In this mixture of trust and distrust, the social between can appear thus as more objectified and externally determined. Likewise, a more determinate self emerges, insecure and over against the others. This intermediation with the possibly hostile stranger shapes the social milieu in which I come to stand over against the other. There are a number of resulting configurations of intermediation. There is the process of *education* (formal and informal) that a society offers to its members, by which is effected the transition from the intimacy of family to a more public space of togetherness.

Turning more directly to the *second* communal intermediation, the network of utility and what I call *serviceable disposability* (*Ethics and the Between*, chap. 14), we find here a commons of public importance in relation to the *world of work*. This constitutes a web of useful intermediations, in turn fragile, powerful, and entangling. For though driven by the exchange of instrumental goods and services, it is yet an interconnecting of self and others. In our time a dominion of use-values pervades the ethical milieu and infiltrates all the levels of social intermediation. The necessity of such values is undeniable, but it is not finally sufficient; indeed, it can be pernicious when totalized relative to the ethos. It tends toward a univocal instrumentalization of the ethos and an ambiguous contraction of human transcending. Its exploitation is proximately directed to the shifting ambiguities of the intimate and the aesthetic, but when it is totalized, human beings cannot see beyond use-values. Not only is everything other in nature reduced to its instrumental value, but so also are human beings. There are too many signs of this in our world that are troubling.

This use-full intermediation cannot attain a fully ethical comportment vis-à-vis the good of the other, or indeed of self, despite the surface pervasiveness of self-interest. There is something necessary about it vis-à-vis pragmatic affairs, but this necessity is governed by useful expedience rather than excellence beyond expedience. Its relativization of the good to use-values is, in the end, dissembling, since were there a complete occlusion of inherent ends, there would be precipitated an inexorable slide toward nihilism. The togetherness of the many may have many purposes, but it would also have no purpose. There would be no point to it as a whole, other than the infinite multiplication of finite satisfactions, none of which proves satisfactory in the end.

In a word, a community lacks ultimate purpose if the business of serviceable disposability exhausts its creative energies. Its freedom refashions itself into a bondage to the products it consumes to slake its own emptiness. The omnivorous devouring of worldly resources does not, cannot slake this emptiness. Something more is needed: a different gathering of creative power, another release of freedom transcending serviceable disposability. Such would give it a purpose more inclusive than the expenditure of power on the useful. This something "more," I suggest in *Ethics and the Between*, is intermediated by the communities of erotic sovereignty (chap. 15) and agapeic service (chap. 16).

The third form of social intermediation, the community of erotic sovereignty, is directed to the intermediation of *excellence beyond utility*. Politics is always more than economics, even if too often many political representatives are snagged by the puppet strings of the money dealers. The statesman is more than an economic manager. Nor is sovereignty just a matter of something like an individualistic aristocratism, such as we find in Nietzsche. At issue is a distinctive intermediation, hence an interplay of selves and others, hence something always communal, even when the flower of the intermediation might be an extraordinary individual. The political intermediation of the sources of social power, whether recessed in the general eros of a people or expressed in the shared forms of activity, is effected through its sovereign representatives, who, at best, help to give some exemplary expression of the immanent excellences of a people. This may not be quite bread and butter politics, but there is more than bread and butter to politics.

If work is mostly bound to the web of utility, sovereignty is a kind of play of power, a freer power beyond utility. Sovereignty is not servile. It lives in a transcending to positions of "being above." "Being below" is not fully in accord with the full release of our power to be. In "being above" we seek to come into our own (though there is more). This freedom of "being above" is more than the network of utility can define, where everything is a means and nothing, in the end, a supreme end. To be sovereign is to approach the supreme and useless—beyond serviceable disposability. It is useless, but as such may be more supremely useful, if it gives use the *self-justifying excellences* the network of serviceable disposability lacks, and without which the whole seems finally pointless. This worth beyond serviceable disposability can take different forms, but primarily what is important is an intermediation of social power into a community of purpose beyond utilitarian goals. Again, despite claims that the world is ruled by multinational corporations, there is a politics of statesmanship that finally is more sovereign than economics. I cannot give here more than a hint and can only refer the reader to the fuller treatment of the matter in *Ethics and the Between*.

The political intermediation of social power in the community of erotic sovereignty is always stressed between the requirements of justice and power. In the tension of these two, there can be a tilt to power unconstrained by justice in some cases such as tyranny; in the best cases, there is a balance and harmony of the two. There is a dynamic process at work in which power can serve justice as a communal expression of immanent excellence, but power can also be self-serving. For instance, a people may want to rest in itself and its excellences and seek to constitute itself as a self-justifying immanent whole. Absolute justice is not to be found in any political community, but justice is still to be found there. And there is still something more. Sovereignty, one might say, often finds itself in a tempting middle space between *eros turannos* and *eros ouranios*. Beyond servility and sovereignty, I think, is the *community of agapeic service*. This is the *"meta,"* the "beyond" of immanent excellence, but it is also the *"meta"* as "in the midst," and as such it can help purge power and transform justice. This is the *fourth* form of communal intermediation I treat, and it is really on the boundary between the ethical and the religious, but essential to its political significance is that it most ultimately serves to absolve human power of its temptation to being an *eros turannos*.

Suppose we were to contrast the *sovereign* and the *ethical servant*. If the sovereign is beyond servility, the ethical servant is beyond servility and sovereignty. We could say that both the sovereign and the ethical servant are moved by the self-surpassing energy of transcendence. Both ambiguously move on the border between human transcending as reaching for the ultimate and the good as transcendent. If in the sovereign there is an ambiguous mixing of the power of self-transcending and transcendence itself, in the ethical servant there is more of transcendence itself than of self-transcending. In the middle between transcending and the transcendent, the sovereign tilts to the former, the ethical servant to the latter. In the middle ethos, as always, there is no complete eradication of ambiguity. A sovereign may be a secret servant of the transcendent good, though appearing as lord of will to power; an ethical servant may be a double creature whose great devotion to the transcendent good is incompletely freed from human-all-too-human self-insistence. Even Jesus prayed: let not my will but thine be done.

I connect this community of agapeic service with the metaxological intermediation of the good, beyond will to power. If erotic sovereignty deals with immanent excellences, agapeic service deals with transcendent good. It is most released to ethical care for the other as other. It releases something of the promise of a more universal love of being, both in respect for the value of nature as other, and for other human beings with whom one shares the gifts of the between. We do not create this community through ourselves alone, or through any form of our own self-mediation. This final community is not just at the end, but is our participation, most unminded, in the always already effective communication of the agape of the good. As there is a community beyond use, intermediated by sovereignty, there is a community beyond sovereign power, and beyond politics. I think that this is the apotheosis of the bond of trust inherent in all forms of communities; it is at the ultimate, at the extreme, in relation to origin and end. It intermediates trust in good in an ultimate sense, and in relation to the extremes of life: birth and death, and the ordeal of suffering. In face of our coming to nothing, it is trust in the good, by love of those who are as nothing, in facing their nothingness. It is community seeking to live in absolute service of the good.

We might put it this way (with a bow to Dostoyevsky): Christ is beyond the Grand Inquisitor and Caesar. But I do not mean to confine agapeic service to the Christian tradition or to the religions of the Bible. Signs of this ultimate community are not exclusive to one and only one tradition. This would again be to univocalize the ultimate community. Thus the story is told: a prince, groomed to be king, an erotic sovereign, comes to leave the palace of his father. Beyond its cushion, he is shocked by the suffering he sees, shocked into a different mindfulness of the between as the universal impermanence of all finite things. He abandons the place of regal power, abdicates the claim of the erotic sovereign to rule. He becomes a wandering beggar, homeless, seeking a way. The way, in time, enlightens, and the wanderer becomes the Buddha. At a certain boundary, do we need a politics that can make way for such an abandonment?

## Neither Servility nor Sovereignty

I suggested earlier that a point about the post-metaphysician, namely, the impossibility of evading metaphysics, might apply analogously to the postreligious person, namely, the inescapability of being religious. If metaphysics and being religious indicate something beyond servility and sovereignty, implications follow for how we think of politics. In a final reflection, I offer some remarks on the following four considerations: first, the temptation to absolutize politics; second, the art of discrimination and the necessary seriousness of politics in its relativity; third, the issue of politics, nihilism, and the good of the "to be"; fourth, the question I will now just indicate with the word "porosity."

FIRST CONSIDERATION

Rather than absolutize politics in terms of immanent sovereignty, politics asks to be absolved from immanent idolatry. It would require an extended study to indicate why modernity and its politics find it difficult to quite place properly the requirements of the fourth intermediation of agapeic service. This is something beyond servility and sovereignty, but one of the sources of the modern difficulty is the wars of religion in which the solicitation of agapeic service was betrayed in religion itself, with the result of something of the blame falling on religion per se, as if it were too a masked form of will to power, seeking its own erotic sovereignty. Betrayal of agapeic service makes space for certain political forms of erotic sovereignty to claim the immanent whole as its dominion, since it will now be argued that agapeic service is only a disguised form of erotic sovereignty, one using the rhetoric of service to further its sovereignty. If what is beyond servility and sovereignty is obscured, so also the political is tempted to its own self-absolutization.

If the premodern sense of politics sometimes risked collapsing the difference of the third and the fourth communal intermediations from the standpoint that claimed the fourth, I am inclined to think that the modern sense of the political tries to put the fourth out of play, with the result that there is a certain contraction of the difference of the third and the fourth, but from the side of the political understood in terms of an immanent whole. This must risk making politics, in an immanent sense, absolute. We find this on the totalitarian "left." There is also a very modern contraction of difference, most to be found on the capitalist "right," when the dominion of serviceable disposability becomes the form of relation to the whole, and everything is made subject to its instrumental requirements. Then not only politics, but also ethics and religion, are made to speak the language of serviceable disposability. They are suborned to witness to their use, and in the process the meaning of what is worthy beyond use is driven into recess.

Even if we try, as did the Marxists, to offer a vision of politics beyond capitalist serviceability, given the devalued soil of otherness in the ethos, given the contraction—nay, destruction—of the difference between political sovereignty and agapeic service, the divinization of human politics is always shadowed by the will to power of the dominion of serviceable disposability, but now more explicitly totalized in a communal sense. Hence the intermediation of erotic sovereignty is also at risk of losing the sense of immanent and intrinsic value in favor of a voracious instrumentalism, whether individualist or communist, in which everything finally is disposable—not only the citizens of a polity but the politicians also. The family is ruined by the same attitude of serviceable disposability—an attitude blithely preached, though misery is created for those who treat familial others and themselves thus. The family is invaded by a set of relatively arbitrary arrangements, now sanctioned by economic profitability and political institutionalization, as if we were all freelance autonomists, with no inherent ties and loyalties to others, loyalties that properly enlarge a freedom beyond solitary self-assertion, but which are now censured as hang-ups curbing self-expression.

When it is made whole, the sense of the political generates a diminished sense of the metaxu in a number of ways. There are the diverse finite metaxus that constitute the tissue of different intermediations in immanence itself. There is also the metaxu at the boundary of immanence—both in the inward otherness of the singular human, and I think also in the deep intimacy of a family—and the metaxu that is between immanence and transcendence as other,'and that is signaled by the difference of the communities of erotic sovereignty and agapeic service. Both of these metaxus are meta: in one sense shaped in the midst of political community, but also beyond, over and above, since political community provides the conditions that make possible their maturing, but does not constitute it; in that regard, they are also both transpolitical. We have difficulty thinking of the transpolitical, except as a retreat into suburban cocooning, or else an entire break with the political. But even were one to see such a break, say, in the way the desert fathers shook the dust of the city off their sandals, this break is also a symbolic political act enacted in terms of a higher loyalty, a higher fidelity to the community of agapeic service. When Augustine wrote the *City of God*, its composition was both transpolitical and yet immensely influential in a political sense, since it mediates our understanding of different powers and their proper intermediation, without reduction of the City of God to the City of Man, as happens with Hegel and his successors.[9] With the latter there is a difference crushed dialectically, a difference now forgotten in the urge simply to reassert difference in the face of this speculative crush. But there is a finesse for differences of community on which we can effect neither a dialectical construction nor an antidialectical deconstruction. An absolved politics would not close off porosity to the community of agapeic service.

SECOND CONSIDERATION

I said that in the third communal intermediation political considerations come to the fore more explicitly, and yet that politics has the care for the other worthy forms of community also. Given the complex porosities and intermediations between different forms of community, the task of politics cannot be defined immanently through itself alone, but must itself have some finesse for the discriminations that differentiate and relate these different communities.

The art of discrimination must have a political finesse for differences, not least in holding firm to the doubleness between the communities of erotic sovereignty and agapeic service. Though these in concrete living are in fact mixed up, we should not mix them up, in the sense of mistaking one for the other, or collapsing their difference into expressions of one whole. They must not be mixed up, but in the between, they must be mixed up, in allowing their porosity in living itself, an entirely different matter. This is coherent with metaphysics as metaxological, which means we are not dealing with an Eleatic ontology, or an idealistic speculative holism, or a deconstructive immanence. We are in the midst but also beyond. This is a double posture that might well be captured in the advice to be in the world but not of it, to be true to a kingdom that is in this world though not of it. Is this the double contradictory thing that Maurice Merleau-Ponty criticized? Perhaps only if it is an evasive servility, then it will only ever produce the miscarriage of immanent sovereignty. But suppose it is neither servile nor sovereign. Yes, it is a sign of contradiction, but a contradiction to immanence at home with itself, and hence to a politics that would absolutize itself. The accusation of contradiction risks invoking what amounts to an immanent univocalism when it suits it, though otherwise it might fruitfully offer us more finesse for the equivocities of finitude. Metaxological finesse for these equivocities reads the sign of contradiction in terms neither servile nor sovereign.

There is a sense, perhaps known better by ancient and medieval thinkers, in which metaphysics is beyond politics, and yet there is nothing antipolitical in recognizing this. Raphael's *School of Athens* captures the balance perfectly between the vertical pointing of the finger of Plato and the horizontal, even hand of the moderating Aristotle. The moderating hand reminds us of just care for the *"meta"* as defining our "being in the midst"; the finger pointing upward recalls us to the *"meta"* as "over and above" the moderate middle, reminds us of the exceeding of our self-transcending and the excess of transcendence itself. Who would deny that there are tensions between these two senses of the *"meta,"* but is this not both the suffering and the glory of our being in the between? And is there not a suffering beyond servility and a glory beyond sovereignty?

Each human being is a metaphysical being, in whom the sourcing powers of the "to be," both those most intimate and those most self-transcending, are at the boundary of the political, even in the political itself. A good politics lets those boundaries be. Metaphysics as a philosophical discipline of mindfulness can be close to this beyond in this sense: as a practice of what I have called agapeic mindfulness—an admiring openness to the given worthiness of the "to be," freed from will to power, and, so to say, a released theoria beyond the tyranny of theory.[10] There is a beyond in the form of a kind of posthumous mindfulness, mindfulness posthumous to erotic sovereignty, not servile but released in a purer service of the true. Lest what I say be misconstrued as antipolitical (it is not), I think there are seeds of this service beyond servility and sovereignty in politics itself, even if often masked in many (sometimes necessary) equivocations. Politics as needing an art of discrimination has to have finesse for these equivocations, and for the mask. Notwithstanding this, there is a public service, a political service that is for the good of the community, and its form is not a self-fulfilling sovereignty. I mean it again in the sense in which one could say that the genuine statesman is beyond the erotic sovereign. I mean also that many of the daily servants of the common good, whose work remains incognito, are themselves servants of this political good, though they make no headlines.

The necessary seriousness of the political resides in its care for the importances of the relative. I am speaking of the relativity of a public space hospitable to the flourishing of the other intermediations of value. It does not create them, but rather enables them in this space. If there is a governing of them, it need not be a dominating. There is something about them that is not just servile to political sovereignty and yet not entirely sovereign in their own right. Consider thus the intimacy of the family at one end and the transcendence of the religious at the other, with practical invention and entrepreneurship in between. Each of these is a necessary serving of essential value but not necessarily servile or sovereign per se. Politics has to do with public goods and their distribution, more often than not in terms of organizing the institutions governing everyday life. There is more to it than this, since it also can offer a people an intermediation with itself, in terms of its self-understanding, and sense of what it is to do and be—and perhaps even its sense of destiny, if it has one. A people's symbolic sense of itself is hyperbolic to the merely instrumental since it has its sources in the general eros, and intimate to this are excesses no one can quite know or master. The intermediation of a people to itself can take many forms (see *Ethics and the Between*, chap. 15), and this manyness has to be taken with more seriousness than is allowed by drumbeats about "democracy," as if the invocation of that holy name were enough to put this manyness in its proper perspective. Politics is more than the organization and administration or higher management of economics. The power of the "to be" as good is open to a multiplicity of communal expressions. Politics requires its own finesse, prudential and visionary, for this diversity of powers.

THIRD CONSIDERATION

Politics is a therapy against nihilism, a hedge, a house against the temptation to think of the "to be" as worthless. True, sometimes it does this by organizing distractions, by filling time, sometimes by dreaming great enterprises. Yet it must guard against the fall of the moderate middle into meaninglessness. In this regard, politics has an intimate relation to the good of the "to be." In this too it is not exhausted by an imperium of will to power. Indeed, this last is itself a powerful, violent hedge against the worthlessness of the "to be," but it perpetuates the worthlessness. Tyranny and nihilism go hand in hand. Nothing is of inherent worth for tyranny, beyond the perpetuation and expression of its own will to power. But this too finally comes to nothing. Wars may even be organized as diversions from this "coming to nothing," though they must, and will circle back to the nothing they only seem to escape. Premodern political thinkers, such as Plato, Augustine, and Aquinas, bring us to face this better than many modern thinkers, certainly in this absolute essential: they do not renege on the ontological good of the "to be."

I know that the best of politics seeks to make good in the more moderate middle, but I do think the problem of tyranny merits special mention, in its oblivion to the possibilities of an agapeic service beyond sovereignty and servility. Tyranny is rooted in eros, individual or general, as the self-transcending sweep of the human power to be. There is an intensification of its self-affirmation to an extreme such that what is other counts only as a means for this self-affirmation. The doubleness of eros, as both *poros* and *penia*, is deformed: the power to be is expressed as an unlimited conatus essendi claiming absolute sovereignty, while the passio essendi has been rendered servile to the unbridling of the self-affirming endeavor to be. The compassion of being, *com*passio essendi, is mocked and hated. But the power to be is the power to be good, and moreover, we are first empowered before we power ourselves. Power is based on a porosity, and an endowment given by the origin. What endows politics? Nothing but our own will to power, if some are to be believed. They are not entirely wrong if, for instance, we grant that powerful nations or peoples always risk the mutation of their general eros into an *eros turannos*. But everything hangs on the interpretation of this mutation. The view beyond servility and sovereignty suggests this, however: we cannot endow ourselves in the first place; we must first be endowed to be able to endow. But this means again a relativization of the claims of the eros turannos, which follows from the distortion of the passio essendi — something has been forced into recess, thrust into a false reserve, silenced. Tyranny involved the self-expression of will to power that instrumentalizes the power of the "to be" as good: this good is made to be my good, our good, and all other goods are harnessed to the end of serving the power, my power, our power, which claims to be "number One." Tyranny can also take democratic form when the people claim to be "number One."

The claim to be "number One" can be sustained only by means of violence by any being who is not God. There is only one One, and that is God. Everything else is a relative one, in the sense of a one in relation to others.

With human beings, the one in relation to the others is in an ethical relation, which transforms the meaning of power: the power of the "to be" as good. If we understand the one One as the agapeic God, it is not that being in relation has no claim. Quite to the contrary, agapeic service beyond servility and sovereignty is the consummate relation of endowing goodness that gives to and for the other as other. It is as much prior to self-affirming will to power as beyond it, in the end. Granting this, we will have a relation to the political that communicates from the opposite extreme to tyranny. Tyranny is the seizure of the immanent excellence of the erotic sovereign who battens on the endowment of the good of the "to be" and usurps its communicative power. The God who is agapeic is at the opposite extreme of goodness to this usurpation. There is the communicative endowing of the good of the "to be"; there is no usurpation in relation to the other; there is the freeing and enabling of the power of the finite "to be."

I speak of the extreme temptations. Without God as the agapeic One, one wonders if the extremes defining the between turn out, in the end, to be either a totalitarianism or anarchism, each nihilistic. What of the moderate middle? Without God, the moderate middle becomes, one fears, the tepid middle of the last men. The last men are the middling ones, ones who are an extremity in mediocrity: spiritual lassitude touches a lowest happy low, for our self-satisfaction here is our unnamed despair. In these extreme instances, the only countervailing powers seem also immanent, and likewise come from the extremes. In the case of the individual, the immanent otherness of self proves to be an-archic. In making itself the absolute, self comes to know that there is nothing there that is absolute. There is an inward otherness beyond our self-determination, but this here will not be understood in a more religious manner. Postulatory immanence issues its countermanding insinuation: no, if our immanent otherness resists the absolute self-mediation of immanence, let our self-absolutizing mean self-implosion, perhaps even self-explosion, for I am not a man, I am dynamite. In the case of the communal whole, totalitarianism would be the extreme. The totalized power of the social whole becomes the absolute strange power claiming to be the absolute intimate power, whose intimacy is intrusively enforced as transcendence absolutely incarnate. In truth, the intimacy of the incarnate it cannot absolutely reach, for this is hyperimmanent: it is the gateway of porosity between the human and the divine, and no politics can ultimately answer for this in its radical ontological intimacy: its being shut in, or opened out: its freedom to consent to the ultimate porosity, or to close or fold its own porosity in on itself alone.

In all of this we find the diversion of our immanent porosity away from transcendence as other, but in this diversion we are always meeting something we cannot determine on the terms of our own immanence. In pointing beyond servility and sovereignty, a metaxological metaphysics looks beyond the temptations to idolize the whole, or the idolatrous human self. If immanent politics is always tempted by the power plays of servility and sovereignty, the agapeic God beyond the immanent whole deabsolutizes such a politics. This dedivinization of politics might perhaps make the divine more intimate to politics, but in the mode of the agapeic servant, and not the erotic sovereign. The erotic sovereign is relativized by the agapeic servant but relativized by a different being in relation—not by an autarchic absoluteness that squats on top of the others as a higher tyrannical power. The endowing good endows power but the good of the "to be" it endows is more than will to power. God beyond the immanent whole relativizes the idolatry of the totalitarian whole, and the idolatrous say-so of self-asserting an-archism.

FOURTH CONSIDERATION

Let me conclude with a remark on the matter I named with the word "porosity." In speaking of extremities, I should reiterate that when I refer to transcendence, I mean it in a sense other than the cartoon version of Platonism, referred to earlier. We are dealing not with a univocal dualism of the here and the "beyond," but rather with a between that communicates what is beyond by its leavening of immanence. There in immanence, the play of servility and sovereignty may be much in evidence, but in immanence there also is a porosity to something more. Perhaps more than anything else, the community of agapeic suggests that being religious is lived out of a certain primal porosity between the human and the divine. We might understand this, for instance, in terms of the life of prayer, or the rituals of liturgy that make us porous to praise, or as a life enacted in care for the other, and indeed care for self who too is to be loved as agapeically as possible. Without religious finesse for the primal porosity, is the art of politics weakened in its wise negotiation of immanent porosities and boundaries in the finite between? Is it tempted to make itself the replacement for the primal porosity, or at least the secular porosity between immanent power and power that ceaseth only in death?

In the given middle there are complex porosities and intermediations between the different forms of community, distinguished above, and hence the task of politics cannot be defined immanently through itself alone. The notion of anything in the finite between being defined immanently through itself alone is called into question by a metaxological philosophy. Especially in the fourth community, ethical openness to the other as other is at its most pronounced even though this ethical-religious community cannot be reduced to the terms of the political community; it has to find its way in terms of the empowerments and constraints often marking the political community. Finesse for the porosity of the two is needed, and diversely needed by those who would be just political leaders, as well as those who are in service to the holy. Porosity between the two certainly does not mean the takeover of one by the other, whether from one side in terms of a self-absolutizing secularism, or from the side of a religious putsch that rides on the holy as a vehicle of a will to power that is deviously as equally immanent as that of a self-absolutizing secularism.

Beyond servility and sovereignty, a metaxological philosophy asks for finesse in negotiating boundaries. We between-beings are creatures passing and in passage. Thus, for instance, we might distinguish between local politics and international politics, but both are forms of being between: between members of a nation, and between (inter-) nations. If the stress must fall on the between, it must do justice to the passages in the between and to the porosities that allow passing. This means a loss of absolutely secure boundaries. There are no such boundaries. One of the tasks of politics is a concern to determine boundaries, but none can be absolute. To take the ultimate case: in the between as offering a primal porosity between the human and the divine, there can be no absolute walls that can confine the communication and passage of the endowing good. Of course, postures of defense and offense can take place along different borders, and hence shape the communication of good and evil in the porosity. But the porosity as such makes one ontologically vulnerable to the other. Keeping the porosity unclogged means a fidelity to our being as a passio essendi. This is also a fidelity to endowing good. But just the vulnerability might make one to revert to self-asserting conatus, and we make the endowing good of the "to be" mutate into offensive will. If the other on the boundary is suspected of will to power, fear of one's violation by an intruding power, they will seek protection in a boundary without porosity.

One might situate here the definition of politics in terms of foe and friend. This is an important consideration, but the sources out of which this distinction emerge have to do with the primal porosity, the poros and penia of eros, the immanent passage in our being between passio essendi and conatus essendi. To do justice to these requires ontology and metaphysics—the former to discern the forms of immanent dynamic powers, the latter to see the openness to transcendence that these powers enable. But to identify that distinction with the political as such runs the risk of stipulative say-so, one that makes a condition of war more absolute than the porosity of being; for then finally everyone is a partner in woe, in war, even when my ally.

The porosity, in truth, is more ultimate, for without reference to it, we cannot understand the happening of enmity and the condition of war, much less the promise of the power of the "to be" as endowing good.[11] The distinction of friend and enemy is not arbitrary, but to identify it with what is essential to politics does risk an arbitrary decisionism. Willful say-so to determine ultimately self-serving differences overrides the patient art of political finesse. A much more deep-going reflection on the porosity, and all it entails, will bring us to the difference of the erotic sovereignty and agapeic service. This too is no arbitrary difference. And there are considerations of immanent excellence with erotic sovereignty that do not fit into the distinction of friend and foe. If what is essential to the political is defining the enemy, politics becomes the violent settlement of boundaries that tries to close down the porosity. This is inherently unstable, even self-defeating, since there is no closure of the ultimate porosity, for it allows the stream of human self-transcending, whether on this side or the opposite side of any boundary that we try to fix. We remain stuck in the primitive definition of justice in Plato's *Republic*—helping one's friends and doing harm to one's enemies. Beyond this the *Republic* passes far. Passing even further beyond servility and sovereignty, doing good even to one's enemy, is enjoined by the agapeic relation.

There is a nonviolent universal in the call of the agapeic relation. The home of the call of this universal is religion, and not primarily politics. In a sense, there are no absolutely universal politics, since for us in the world of immanent powers there must be boundaries drawn in which the porosity is given determinate form. This does not mean that a universal call does not continue to resound within any boundary so drawn, and hence the political is always made to sway or tremble in the hearing of this transpolitical call. The desire for a universal politics without the boundary, and without ethical and spiritual finesse for the religious, tends to generate counterfeit doubles of the agapeic community. Further, the appeal to absolute porosity in absolutely immanent terms tends to veer from an inflated idealism of expectations to a brutal deflation of reckoning. The other, previously the absolutely lovable, becomes now the absolutely suspect. The general eros tries to inflate itself as an absolute porosity but instead creates an absolute conatus that seeks to bring down all boundaries that mark our finite porosity to finite others. Good fences make good neighbors. Without the fitting boundary, and its appropriate negotiation, we risk an explosion of self-inflating tyranny, followed by implosion, and in the extreme, the murder of the others, as they are drawn into the retraction of the emptiness into its self-created void. The porosity of the between allows also that we make of it this desolation.

On the one hand, then, one might say we need to heed the lessons of

Shakespeare's *Macbeth*: there is much bearing on the porosity and boundaries, and indeed much of incognito metaphysic, in this great dramatic study
of tyranny.[12] There is the porosity of the elements, for the earth has bubbles
even as the water has; there is porosity of the powers, the porosity between
the living and dead, for the murdered come back to disturb our feasts; there is
the repulse to the human porosity of pity, symbolized by the child, the naked
newborn babe, striding the blast; there is Macbeth's impatience with time,
and his will to overleap the boundary between the present and future, indeed
the life to come; there is no letting of what is, and what is to be; there is his
seizure of "solely sovereign sway and masterdom," in a world steeped in the
half-truth, the half-lie of equivocity, for fair is foul and foul is fair; there is the
shriveling of the passio essendi under tyranny's power, and the engorgement
of the conatus essendi; there is the intimate bond of the family desecrated,
with "the near in blood, the nearer bloody"; there is the setting at naught
of the bound of measure, in the exceeding of measure; there is erotic sovereignty warping into eros turannos, and then there are no friends anymore,
only foes, and with this the way of life is fallen into the sere, the yellow leaf.

On the other hand, we need to heed the lessons of political romanticism.
This, in its own way, reminds us of our porosity to what exceeds finite measure in immanence. And yet, from adolescent good will we have seen many
graduate, so to say, to Pol Pot. Imagine there's no heaven, the song sings,
imagine there is no religion, imagine no countries, no boundaries. And then
the singing stops, the screaming begins and, horrible *dictu*, death is loosed
in the boundless whole, and on it. Politics is the necessary art of intermediary boundaries in the porosity. Without this art, and the moderation of an
ethical discipline, and the finesse of religion, the porosity can be turned to a
formlessness of chaos, where the idiotic sources of human selving release a
madness—not a divine but a murderous madness. An ethical and religious
finesse moderates the darker excesses in the intimate and offers measure in
the exceeding of measure, such as marks the infinite restlessness of human
self-transcending. Any religion of politics is a false religion; it doubles and re-
doubles itself in a counterfeit whole. We need different services of the everyday. The everydayness of politics can be a sacred service: not an administration of the banal, but a safeguarding of just measure, with the guidance of
exemplars of practical wisdom who have something about them beyond servility and sovereignty.

Once again, the extreme calls of human existence are not to be denied,
and my own focus in this present reflection does not slight them, but to identify these with the political is dangerous. No doubt there are dangerous politics in exceptional circumstances, but political theologians under the spell of

the "mortal god" will not save us, or the between. They do not do a good job in keeping before us the reminders of a higher measure that comes from the community of agapeic service. Secular politics may disguise theologies (an insight developed very differently by Carl Schmitt and John Milbank), as well as disguise metaphysics; but as we need good metaphysics, we also need good theology (a task assumed by Milbank but not by Schmitt).[13]

And there can be ways of treating the political-theological problem that lead to a counterfeit double of the political and a debasement of the theological. These ways are attractive to tough men who think life is hell, but they are univocalists of the dark. In the equivocal play of light and dark, the dark is the more favored. They think that the world is as Macbeth made it to be by his sacrilegious murder, and they supplement this murder with their subtle rationalizations. Falling under the spell of King Death, they desert the equivocal field of powers where political finesse is most needed, and needed with remembrance of the measure of the Good beyond finite determination, such as we find in Plato's Good or in the God of Biblical personalism. They canonize a world of darkness that has been secreted by dark men and the candle they light gives the honor to the darkness. Their thinking has reconfigured the equivocal field of politics in the dark light of this honor. These hard men of life's hell might even see themselves as superior sons of heaven, but Shakespeare is the superior in seeing something beyond servility and sovereignty. And though they may well be the familiars of Macbeth, Macbeth also was their superior, for he did not blink the sticky evil he had done in undoing the good of the "to be." While Macbeth fought to the death, he did not deny that what he had wrought was a world without blessing, a world wherein sleep was murdered, a world wherein *amen* sticks in the throat. "Out, out, brief candle": his outcry comes clean about what he himself cannot cleanse. No honor now more to the darkness wrought and in which he too is also undone. Life falls into the sere, the yellow leaf, but Macbeth at least does not equivocate the truth that it is he himself who has wrought this fall, and the last fall of usurping power into unredeemed, and unredeeming, death. King Death makes claim to govern all, but death can crown no king.

## Notes

1   See, respectively, William Desmond, *Being and the Between* (Albany: State University of New York Press, 1995), and *Ethics and the Between* (Albany: State University of New York Press, 2001).

2   For a less dualistic reading of Plato, see *Art, Origins, Otherness: Between Philosophy and Art* (Albany: State University of New York Press, 2003), chap. 1; see also Catherine Pickstock, *After Writing: On the Liturgical Consummation of Philosophy* (Oxford: Blackwell, 1998).

3   Friedrich Nietzsche, *Der Will zur Macht* (Leipzig: Kröner Verlag, 1930), 697; *The Will to Power*, trans. W. Kaufmann and R. J. Hollingdale, ed. W. Kaufmann (New York: Random House, 1967), 550.

4   On this more fully, see *Ethics and the Between*, especially chap. 1; see also Conor Cunningham, *The Genealogy of Nihilism: Philosophies of Nothing and the Difference of Theology* (London: Routledge, 2002).

5   A metaxological metaphysics reflects not only on the question "What does it mean to be?" but also on the question "What does it mean to be good?" *Being and the Between* addresses the first question, *Ethics and the Between* responds to the second.

6   See my "Tyranny and the Recess of Friendship," in *Amor Amicitiae: On the Love that is Friendship: Essays in Honor of the Rev. Professor James McEvoy*, ed. Thomas A. Kelly and Philipp W. Rosemann (Louvain: Peeters, 2003), chap. 6.

7   The discussion of these four communities constitutes the fourth part of *Ethics and the Between*: chap. 13 is "The Familial Community of the Intimate: The Ethical Intermediation of the Idiot"; chap. 14 is "The Network of Serviceable Disposability: The Instrumental Intermediation of the Aesthetic"; chap. 15 is "The Community of Erotic Sovereignty: The Intermediation of Immanent Excellence"; chap. 16 is "The Community of Agapeic Service: The Intermediation of Transcendent Good." Part 3 deals with ethical selving: the stress is more on ethical self-mediation than on communal intermediation.

8   On this more fully, see my "Enemies," *Tijdschrift voor Filosofie*, 63 (2001): 127–51.

9   See *Hegel's God: A Counterfeit Double?* (Aldershot, U.K.: Ashgate, 2003), esp. chap. 7.

10  See *Perplexity and Ultimacy* (Albany: State University of New York Press, 1995), chap. 4.

11  On this, see "Enemies."

12  See my "Sticky Evil: On *Macbeth* and the Karma of the Equivocal," in *God, Literature and Process Thought*, ed. Darren Middleton (Aldershot, U.K.: Ashgate, 2002), 133–55.

13  See Carl Schmitt, *Politische Theologie: Vier Kapitel zur Lehre von der Souveränität* (1922; Berlin: Duncker und Humblot, 1996); trans. George Schwab as *Political Theology: Four Chapters on the Concept of Sovereignty* (Cambridge, Mass.: MIT Press, 1988); John Milbank, *Theology and Social Theory: Beyond Secular Reason* (Oxford: Blackwell, 1990).

Simon Critchley and | Of Chrematology:
Tom McCarthy | Joyce and Money

Der Geist, der aus der Ornamentik der Banknoten spricht.
— Walter Benjamin, *Kapitalismus als Religion*

MONEY MAKES THE ROUND go a-world, as Joyce might have said. Certainly,
*Finnegans Wake*, his book of wandering and return, of "aloss and again," is
awash with money.[1] There are English pounds, "shelenks"(8) and pence,
American bison nickels, French louis, Russian kopecks, German grosch and
"dogmarks" (161). "Woodpiles of haypennies" (11), the "sylvan coyne" (16) designed for Ireland by William Wood, circulate alongside "ghinees" (16), "tenpound crickler's" and "tinpanned crackler's" (82). Money crinkles, clunks,
and rings throughout this novel in which nothing's free, this novel in which
roads have tolls, museums entry fees. Belchum solicits "tinkyou tankyou sil-
voor plate" (9); Kathe barks "Tip!" (8). Before he'll tell Jute anything, Mutt
must be bribed with "trink gilt" (16); on receiving this he shows him "selveran
cued peteet peas of pecuniar interest," pellets that make the "tomtummy's
pay roll" (19)—then demands the cost of tram fare. Money is the prerequi-
site for the passage of signs: "You will never have post in your pocket unless
you have brasse on your plate" (579). If *Finnegans Wake*'s very content is, as its
first page reminds us, "retaled" (3), then the space of recirculation in which
this retaling occurs is, as Jones suggests in book 1, chapter 6, an "economantarchy" (167).

Our aim in this chapter is simply to read *Finnegans Wake* by following the
chains of coinage that litter the text: of credit, credibility, credence, debt, indebtedness, reneging on debt, bankruptcy, profit, loss, inflation, deflation,

and counterfeit. *Finnegans Wake* opens with a prophetic allusion to the Wall Street Crash of 1929 ("the fall . . . of a once wallstrait oldparr," 3) and we would like to view the text as if it were some vast financial system. We will try and establish what we call a *chrematology* in this economantarchy, that is, pick out the monetary logic in Joyce's text. Our deeper, darker purpose in all this is not just to show that literature is haunted by economics, in the manner of classical Marxism and contemporary Marxist mannerism. Rather, our hypothesis is that in Joyce and elsewhere (where Joyce might be seen as the index for an elsewhere of absolutely modern literary, visual, and musical art), economics is raised to the level of cultural form.[2] For us, artworks are aspects of an agon as to the irreducible determination of contemporary life by economics, engaging us in a process of reflection that might, at best, achieve some distance from the fact of that determination.

Joyce himself, of course, had a strange and intense relationship with money. His parents had been rich but met with financial ruin; his mother would pawn furniture to send James money while he lived in Paris. Continually poor, he nonetheless retained expensive tastes, taking his family to eat in the best restaurants when they couldn't pay the rent on their accommodation, tipping theater ushers ten pounds when the ticket had cost less than one. It is almost as though he willed himself into debt. He borrowed incessantly. He liked to boast that he owed money to every single person he knew. His situation is reflected in that of *Ulysses*'s Stephen Daedalus, who, when asked by Deasy whether he could say of himself "I payed my way," runs through a mental list of everyone to whom he is indebted: "Mulligan, nine pounds, Curran, ten guineas, McCann, one guinea, Fred Ryan, two shillings. Tempel, two lunches. Russel, one guinea, Cousins, ten shillings, Bob Reynolds, half a guinea, Koehler, three guineas, Mrs MacKernan, five weeks' board."[3]

For Deasy, not owing is a measure of one's subjectivity, one's sovereignty. The Englishman can boast this sovereignty precisely because he can say: "I paid my way." For Deasy, this is not unconnected to the fact that England never let in the Jews, a race (as far as anti-Semites such as Deasy are concerned) of usurers and wanderers. Stasis and self-sufficiency are the lynchpins of Deasy's credo. Stephen falls very short of meeting this credo's terms, and so did Joyce, an exile living on perpetual credit, extended against or guaranteed by some vague promise that he'd one day write a masterpiece and become rich.

What better place to discuss this theme than Trieste, the city described by Joyce as "Europiccola." Is it a more Joycean city than Dublin? Obviously not, but it is intriguing to entertain the thought. As Joyce said, "Trieste ate my liver" or "Trieste était mon livre." In Jan Morris's clear, still prose, Trieste becomes many things: a crepuscular, melancholy city swept by the *bora* wind and enwrapped in an ecstasy of the poignant; the capital of nowhere, of wistful meditation, a Triesticity located at the intersection of the cultural plate tectonics of Latinity, Germanity, and Slavicity.⁴ The place where the young Freud tried the locate the testicles of eels, from where Adolf Eichmann dragged his unexpungeable guilt away to South America and which was described by Filippo Tomasso Marinetti as "la nostra bella polveriera," "our beautiful powder-magazine." But, above all, Trieste is a money town, the port of Vienna, a place of trade, of human and inhuman cargo, of capital, of profit and (since 1918) of loss. The monumental Hapsburg structures of the Piazza Unità and the shoreline simply testify to the wealth that poured through Trieste. Who knows, but Joyce's errant, economantarchic preoccupations might have been better served had he set *Ulysses* in Trieste rather than Dublin.

But what is money? Many things. It is, of course, the coins and notes rattling in our pockets, as well as the piles of real and virtual stuff lying in banks, or the smart money that tends toward disappearance and increasing immateriality, being shuffled electronically along the vectors of the financial networks.

This might serve as an empirical definition, but what is the logic of the concept of money? The core of money is trust and promise: "I promise to pay the bearer on demand the sum of . . ." on the British pound, the "In God we trust" of the U.S. dollar, the *BCE-ECB-EZB-EKT-EKP* of the European Central Bank that runs like a Franco-Anglo-Germano-Greco-Finno-Joycean cipher across the top of every Euro note. In other words, the legitimacy of money is based on a sovereign act, or a sovereign guarantee that the money is good, that it is not counterfeit. Money has a promissory structure, with an entirely self-referential logic: the money promises that the money is good; the acceptance of the promise is the acceptance of a specific monetary ethos, a specific, yet often flexible monetary geography.

This ethos, this circular "money promising that the money is good," is underwritten by sovereign power as its transcendent guarantee. It is essential that we believe in this power, that the sovereign power of the bank inspires belief, that the "Fed" has "cred," as it were. Credit can operate only on the basis of credence and credibility, of an act of fidelity and faith, of con-fid-ence. The transcendent core of money is an act of faith, of belief. The legitimacy of money is based on the fiction of sovereign power, and in this connection one can speak of a sort of monetary patriotism, which is particularly evident in attitudes in the United States to the dollar, particularly to the sheer materiality of the bill, and in the United Kingdom's opposition to the Euro and to the strange cultural need for money marked with the queen's head.

In a deep sense, money *is* not. It exists empirically, but it is not essentially there at all. All money is what the French call *escroquerie*, swindling; it is a virtual or at best conceptual object. It is, in the strictest Platonic definitional sense (forget Baudrillard), a *simulacrum*, something that materializes an absence, an image for something that doesn't exist. Money is delusionary, and faith in money is a form of collective psychosis. In the godless wasteland of global capitalism, money is our only metaphysics, our only ontotheology, the only transcendent substance in which we truly must have faith. It is this faith that we celebrate, we venerate, in commodity fetishism. Adorno makes the point powerfully,

> Marx defines the fetish-character of the commodity as the veneration of the thing made by oneself which, as exchange value, simultaneously alienates itself from producer to consumer. . . . This is the real secret of success. It is the mere reflection of what one pays in the market for the product. The consumer is really worshipping the money that he himself has paid for the ticket to the Toscanini concert. He has literally "made" the success which he reifies and accepts as an objective criterion, without recognizing himself in it. But he has not "made" it by liking the concert, but rather by buying the ticket.[5]

Marx describes money as the universal form of equivalence by virtue of which capitalism can exist, that goods can be exchanged. In the imperial space of what Hardt and Negri describe as "network sovereignty," money becomes the general form of life, it constitutes the fact of Empire and money's absence defines Empire's opposite: the multitude are poor.[6]

For us, here and now, money has no outside, there is no pure form of economy, no barter system, somehow unsullied by money's circulation. You are always already locked into a monetary ethos, part of a contour line upon a financial cartography. There *is* only the sully of money. All money is dirty. From a Freudian perspective, money is deeply anal, it is shit rather than bread, you can use it to buy shit, and a general obsession with money is why people talk so much shit. For the infant, the little Freudian child, shit is money, which is why it is so proud of its soft, smelly currency. In the proto-Lockean world of anal sadism, shit is the first form of property ownership; the labor theory of value begins in your diapers. Let's not forget, Freud is a kind of anti-Midas: where, for Midas, everything natural was transformed into gold, for Freud, all that glitters is transformed into shit. Freud touches a familiar object and suddenly — poo! — you wonder where the smell is coming from. Our favorite Freudian neurotic, the Rat Man, is obsessed with money, with repaying a misconceived debt. He is also highly aware of money's dirtiness, and anally obsessed, his fears of rat torture (in which a rat eats into one's anus) verbally linked to shame about his "Spielratte," his father's gambling debts. His very neurosis is described in economic terms by Freud, who writes, "In his obsessional deliria he had coined himself a regular rat currency. Little by little, he translated into this language the whole complex of money-interests which centered around his father's legacy to him."[7]

Of course, money is also indexed to desire, and there is a strong association between money and the *dépense* of *jouissance sexuelle*, and not only when you have to pay for it. Money is power, sex is power, power is sexy and so is money. And let's not forget the profound link between psychoanalysis and payment. With the exception of Karl Marx, were there ever creatures on earth more obsessed with money than psychoanalysts? Of course, they are right and the core of the analytic pact is a monetary union, a monetary act of trust: one has to pay, whatever it is that you can afford, otherwise the analysis begins to lose credibility. One cannot do analysis for free. The faith and trust of the transference, which is the key to the analytic relationship, is guaranteed by money; the promissory trust of therapy is secured through monetary exchange.

Jouissance brings us back by a commodious vicus of recirculation to Joyce. Lacan, who was unnaturally obsessed by *Finnegans Wake* throughout the 1970s, writes, "Joyce is in relation to *joy*, that is, *jouissance*, written in *lalangue* that is English; this en-joycing, this *jouissance* is the only thing one can get from the text. This is the symptom."[8]

For Lacan, it is the joy in Joyce that enjoys, just as it is the *Freude* in *Freud* that *freut sich*. This is what one feels in reading Joyce, "Read *Finnegans Wake* without trying to understand . . . One usually reads it *because one can feel the presence of the writer's jouissance*."

It is the sheer pressure of this presence that suffocates and oppresses the reader of *Finnegans Wake* because, as is well known, Lacanian jouissance is not pleasure but suffering, an excitation or excess that is too much for the organism to bear. En-Joyce-ment, or what Joyce calls "joyicity" (414), is not enjoyable. Perhaps this is why many people think that the *Wake* is unreadable—is it not rather simply *unbearable*? Its seeming trifles are traces of psychic pain. One might go a little further with Lacan and say that jouissance is the kernel of psychotic suffering, a kernel that is nonanalyzable and which cannot be symbolized. For Lacan, it is this writing of psychotic jouissance that Joyce enacts: "Joyce manages to bring the symptom to the power of language, yet without rendering it analyzable."

A very common behavior of psychotics is the forging of neologisms or fresh linguistic coinages, and to this extent the writing of *Finnegans Wake* might be viewed as some vast psychotic case history. Of course, the psychotic suffering here is not just that of Joyce (although Lacan asks, "When does one start to be mad[?] . . . Was Joyce mad?"), but also that of his daughter Lucia, whose psychotic sayings and diagrams litter the literature of *Finnegans Wake* (260–308).

In a wonderful formulation, Lacan remarks that Joyce was "désabonné à l'inconscient," namely that he abandoned or gave up his subscription to the symbolic order. In ugly Lacanese, this means that Joyce affirmed the lack in the big other and experienced the jouissance of the real. In more everyday parlance, we might say that Joyce progressively shed the legitimating narrative conventions and expectations of the nineteenth-century realist novel. For some, literature might be understood as the draining of the excitation of jouissance, the *zuider zee* of the unconscious in Freud, or the Dionysian womb of being in Nietzsche. Literature symbolizes or gives beautiful Apollinian form to the chaos of desire. As such, *Finnegans Wake* is literature in reverse, a writing of the symptom that attempts to attend to the clamor of *jouissance* that subtends literary creation and which cannot be dammed up. This reversal is mirrored linguistically in Lacan's punning distinction between language (*la langue*) and *lalangue*. If the symbolic is the order of language, which is given priority in Lacan's earlier structuralist-inspired work, then *lalangue* is his nickname for an experience of language that is itself a form of jouissance and sheer material affect that precedes and resists symbolization: "What I put forward, by writing *lalangue* as one word, is that by which I distance myself from structuralism." We want to read the planned Babel of *Finnegans Wake* as a monetary *lalangue*, a chain of crazy coinage that both subtends and ruins the symbolic universe of literature, reducing letter to litter.[9]

Only one town, perhaps, could rival Trieste in its claim as ideal host for this discussion: Dublin — not Dublin, Ireland, but rather Dublin, Georgia, USA. This city, founded on the River Oconee in Laurens County by Irish emigrant Peter Sawyer, finds its way into the *Wake*'s first complete sentence, whose second clause reads: "nor had topsawyer's rocks by the stream Oconee exaggerated themselse to Laurens County's gorgios while they went doublin their mumper all the time" (3).

Topsawyer's rocks are a formation on the Oconee's banks; "rocks" also means both testicles and money. "Ochone!" is the Gaelic for "alas!" The image here is of mothers wailing as their sons, fruits of their father's swollen loins, depart across the waters in an effort to win wealth and status in the new world, to swell their coffers. Joseph Campbell and Henry Morton Robinson, always keen to emphasize the "story" of the *Wake*, interpret the passage thus: "A successful son of HCE emigrates from East to West, as his father before him. Settling in America, he begets a large progeny and bequeaths to them a decent, even gorgeous, prosperity."[10]

Joyce's own son was, of course, Giorgio. Downstream of Topsawyer's Rocks, the biologic and the economic blur together, much as they do in Shakespeare's sonnets, where "from fairest creatures we desire increase," "increase" being both economic profit and physical reproduction. What is "doublin their mumper"? Rocks: balls, wealth, world in the sense of place and populace. The town motto of Dublin, Georgia is "Doubling all the time," and Joyce keeps doubling Dublin into "Dyoublong" (13), "durlbin" (19), and "*Dybbling*" (29).

So many of the *Wake*'s themes are touched on in these twenty-three words. So, too, perhaps, are the workings of the novel's very text. *Finnegans Wake* is an accumulative novel, a novel in which characters, events, reports, and interpretations multiply incessantly, doublin their mumper all the time. Mutt, discussing the relation between printed "papyr" and the significations generated by it, tells Jute: "You need hardly spell me how every word is bound to carry over threescore and ten toptypsical readings throughout the book of Doublends Jined" (20).

Meaning itself, it seems, is an accumulation: profit, a return on a text's investment to the tune of 7,000 percent, of threescore and ten—also, coincidentally, the average return (in years) on the investment of biological existence.

What we have here, then, is a glowing annual report, a multileveled tale of profit. But lurking between the lines of this report is another, contradictory one, a tale of loss. To return to our opening twenty-three words, the Latin *exaggerare* may mean to pile up, but the English *exaggerate* suggests that the wealth is overstated, perhaps even nonexistent. Hiding inside the "mumper" of fertile rocks is mumps, an illness that makes men infertile. The book's next sentence shows us not aggrandizement but collapse, the fall of "a once wall-straight oldparr" (3)—a reference to Wall Street crashes. The great crash of 1929 was lurking round the corner when Joyce wrote the passage. Values, now as then, have plummeted, "one sovereign punned to petery pence" (13). The opulent, accumulating landscape of Laurens County gives way to a retreating one whose length "lies under liquidation," whose typical inhabitant, "living in our midst of debt," will "loan a vesta and hire some peat and sarch the shores her cockles to heat and she'll do all a turfwoman can to piff the business on" (12). The line separating gorgeous bourgeois splendor from frugal poverty, as Joyce knew all to well, is thin.

*Finnegans Wake*, then, is a tale of two economies, two coexisting ones: one characterized by surplus, profit, wealth, and another characterized by bankruptcy and debt. This is true semantically as well: alongside a great glut of meanings runs a continual failure to establish any: "The unfacts, did we possess them, are too imprecisely few to warrant our incertitude, the evidencegivers by legpoll too untrustworthily irreperible . . . our notional gull-

ery is now completely complacent, an exegious monument, aerily perenni-
ous" (57).

In the *Wake's* negational language, "Sense" becomes "sinse" (83)—without (*sin*) sense, *senza*: "Enquiring" becomes "unquiring" (3); *Fiat* (it was thus)
becomes "fuit" (it eluded us, escaped, 128) and, eventually, "pfooi" (125):
"rubbish!" "In this scherzarade of one's thousand one nightinesses," we are
told, "that sword of certainty which would indentifide the body never falls"
(51). The book fails to return its readers' investment with fixed dividends of
meaning, instead "borrowing a word and begging the question and stealing
tinder and slipping like soap" (93), sliding further and further into the red of
indeterminacy.

*Finnegans Wake* is a tale of two economies in more ways than one. Not
only do the economy of surplus and that of loss tussle with one another for
supremacy: so, too, do two differing versions of economy itself. We will call
these versions "economics" and "chrematistics," respectively. The distinction
is borrowed from Aristotle, where, crudely stated, it is the difference between the good, natural economy of the *oikos* and the bad, artificial economy that arises when money (*to khrema*) appears on the scene. Derrida, in
a fascinating passage from *Donner le temps, La fausse monnaie*, summarizes
Aristotle's distinction between economics and chrematistics thus: "For Aristotle, it is a matter of an ideal and desirable limit, a limit between the limit
and the unlimited, between the true and finite good (the economic) and the
illusory and indefinite good (the chrematistic)."[11]

Economics comes from *oikos*—home, hearth, seat of the family, the
household, indeed of all those things that Derrida lists under "the proper,"
the sovereign—and "chrematistic" from *to khrema*, money, the unlimited exchangeability of goods that occurs when money appears on the scene. The
distinction between economy and chrematistics is reflected not only in that
between the limited and the unlimited but also in that between, continuing
the above quote, "the supposed finiteness of need and the presumed infinity
of desire." Once money, to khrema, has appeared on the scene, the infinity
of desire will always transcend the finitude of need. Money is the desire of
desire itself, a priori unsatisfied by any object one might actually need—
behold, the logic of shopping! The fact that Derrida's language recalls that
of Levinas (need/desire, finitude/infinity) is perhaps not accidental, for in
opposition to an antimonetary tradition in philosophy that begins with Aristotle and culminates with Marx (recall that a communist society would be a
society without the spectrality of money), Levinas is one of the rare thinkers
who reserves a privileged place for money in his work. He writes in *The Ego
and Totality*, "Money then does not purely and simply mark the reification of

man. It is an element in which the personal is maintained while being quantified—this is what is proper to money and constitutes, as it were, its dignity as a philosophical category."

And further on the same page,

> Money allows us to envisage a justice of redemption to be substituted for the infernal or vicious circle of redemption or pardon. We cannot attenuate the condemnation which from Amos II, 6 to the *Communist Manifesto* has fallen upon money, precisely because of its power to buy man. But the justice which must save us from economy, that is, from the human totality, cannot negate its superior form, where the quantification of man appears, the common measure between men, for which money, whatever be its empirical form, supplies the category. It is indeed shocking to see in the quantification of man one of the essential conditions for justice. But can one conceive of a justice without quantity and without reparation?[12]

Connecting this line of thought with Derrida, he continues the passage with a gesture that will be familiar to readers of his work: "As soon as there is the monetary sign—and first of all the sign—that is, *différance* and credit, the *oikos* is opened and cannot operate its limit." Money, in effect, is deconstruction, opening the closure of the *oikos*, what Levinas calls totality, to the unrestricted "economy" of desire where money circulates and where wealth is accumulated or squandered.

However, we would like to go a little further and think of deconstruction as a monetary sign—indeed, to think of money as one of the names for that incalculable excess that precedes any restricted economy of meaning. In this sense, money might even be thought of as a quasi-transcendental structure rendering the activity of a restricted economy of the proper both possible and impossible. It is with this thought in mind that one might redescribe grammatology as *chrematology*, as a logic of money. Money is a kind of deconstruction, opening the totality of the proper's economy, but is not the reverse of this proposition also plausible, namely that deconstruction is a kind of money? For what is money if not a specter, namely the spectrality of difference that haunts the "real" value of the notes and coins in our pockets, the spectrality that has been at the heart of so many of Derrida's texts, particularly his reading of Marx's political economy? Doesn't the force of Derrida's argument against what he sees as Marx's essentializing "ontology" of life, praxis, labor and the organicism of community, entail a commitment to what he coins the "hauntology" of money, and thereby capital itself? What is deconstruction, on this account, if not a cipher for capital?[13]

Turning back to Joyce, this movement from the oikos to to khrema, breaching the possibility of home rule in all senses of the term, occurs constantly in *Finnegans Wake*. HCE, the patriarch, "Highup Big Cockywocky Sublimissime Autocrat," finds himself repeatedly turned inside out, "all-aroundside upinandoutdown" (612). His private life is made public, subject to speculation. He is tried, fined, bankrupted. He has to pawn his furniture, the landscape of his *oikos*. It gets auctioned off—that is, assigned value according to how much and how many other people desire it; it becomes currency. He becomes currency himself: people, first blackmailing him and then selling his story, make money from him (from *him*, they *make money*). He is coined, stamped, circulated, sent abroad and then called back again. As a fallen, broken ur-god (Humpty Dumpty, or "Hump Cumps Ebblybally," 612) he becomes a tip, a scrapheap full of items of "pecuniar interest" (19) through which other people sift. His fall, a fall into both sin and debt (the German *Schuld*, combining both these terms, crops up in several guises), makes him "oblious autamnesically of his very proprium" (251): it is a fall from the limited propriety of economics into the aneconomic openness of chrematistics. *Finnegans Wake* is a retale that is retailed—again and a gain—a story of "one sovereign punned to petery pence": the sovereign economy of meaning punned chrematistically into grubby public circulation.

This rupture of the limits of economics, which are the limits of the family, hearth, and home rule, makes possible, writes Derrida, "the chance for any kind of hospitality . . . the chance for the gift itself. The chance for the event."[14] Derrida is suggesting here that money is the possibility of a form of aneconomic giving, for a donation without return, for an event. As a long and intriguing footnote to *Donner le temps* makes clear, the word *event* is to be understood in its Heideggerian sense as *das Ereignis*. Derrida associates money, to khrema, with *der Brauch* or usage, *to khreon*, which, according to Heidegger, names Being as the presencing of the present in early Greek thinking. Thus, the possibility of money, that is to say, the possibility of *"différance* and credit," breaking the restricted economy of finite need, is also the possibility of the gift, of another ethicality of the gift, hospitality. What Joyce calls "creed crux ethics" (525) might be replaced with a new "ethical fict" (523)— and here a further series of connections with Levinas's work might be imagined.

*Finnegans Wake*, like many of Shakespeare's plays—or, for that matter, Hergé's *Tintin* books—abounds in instances of host-guest encounters, often fraught. As Hosty, publican perhaps of foreign origin, HCE plays host to people who, turning on him, become an alien host; Mutt, playing host to Jute's Danish invader, "trumple[s] from rath" (16). It also abounds in instances in which a gift is sought, a line of credit opened. One of the primal events of *Finnegans Wake* is the encounter in the park between HCE and the cad. The episode is replayed at least twice (in book 1, chaps. 2 and 4). It is based on a report Joyce found in a regional Irish newspaper, *The Connaught Enquirer*, which told of how a drunk accosted another man demanding money, and a scuffle followed, after which the other man agreed to lend him some. This small news item caught Joyce's eye, as it echoed a story his own father had told him about being accosted by a tramp (whom John Stanislaus described as a "cad") in Phoenix Park one evening. Joyce told Frank Budgen that these twin events—or, rather, twin secondhand accounts, formed the basis of the novel.[15] In Joyce's versions of the incident (or incidents, the one which "pre-repeated itself," 81), HCE plays the lender. In the second, the accoster is described thus: "Whereupon became friendly and, saying not, his shirt to tear, to know wanted, joking and knobkerries all aside laying, if his change companion who stuck still the invention of his strongbox, with a tenacity corrobberating their mutual territorial right, happened to have the loots change of a tenpound crickler about him at the moment, addling that hap so, he would pay him back the six vics odd" (82).

HCE replies:

> Woowoo would you be grossly surprised, Hill, to learn that, as it so happens, I honestly have not such a thing as the loo, as the least chance of a tinpanned crackler anywhere about me at the present mohomoment but I believe I can see my way, as you suggest, it being Yuletide or Yuddanfest and as it's mad nuts, son, for you when it's hatter's hares, mon, for me, to advance you something like four and sevenpence between hopping and trapping, which you might hust as well have, boy baches, to buy J. J. and S. with. (82–83)

In the first account of the encounter, too, HCE is well-to-do, "billowing across the wide expanse of our greatest park" (35)—billowing like Antonio's ships' sails, but also, like the overstretched Antonio, bill owing. The cad asks him for the time—a veiled demand, perhaps, to hand over his watch, for time is money. HCE asks the cad to "credit" him in believing that there is no truth "in that purest of fibfib fabrications" (36). What fibfib fabrication? It seems HCE is giving over more than he was asked for—and, in doing so, rendering himself *accountable, indebting* himself.

What's at stake in this encounter? HCE's reputation, certainly, as well as his money, his watch, and his life. The cad's next drink is in the balance too: J. J. and S. denotes Jameson's whiskey. But it also denotes James Joyce and Son. There's a sense that Joyce is writing his own history, opening a line of credit, the continuum in which his mumper can be doubled. The cad's words, "I have met with you, bird, too late, or if not, too worm and early" (37) echo those Joyce claims to have said to Yeats on their encounter ("I have met with you too late to help you")[16] folding literary history itself, its struggles of succession and anxieties of influence, in which pretenders to the literary crown are recipients of "loans" unwillingly made by—and unlikely to be returned to—their predecessors, into the mix.

The cad asks for ten pounds and is offered four and sevenpence: the encounter involves not just indebtedness and impropriety (*Schuld*) but also bartering, like the bartering Heidegger describes when discussing the Anaximander Fragment. Beings come, then go back whence they came, thus rendering justice and paying penalty to one another for their injustice, according to the ordinance of time, the fragment tells us. "Thus," Heidegger writes, "they exhibit a kind of barter system in Nature's immutable economy."[17] What the fragment, an incomplete account from deep, deep in the past— just like the *Wake*'s accounts of the encounter, or encounters, of which Joyce himself only received partial accounts—represents to Heidegger is the dawn of that destiny whereby Being, the presencing of what is present, is sent to us—the dawn, that is, of the possibility of the *Ereignis*, the event, "in which the history of the Western world comes to be born out, the event of metaphysics."[18] *Finnegans Wake*, the book of history, of knowledge and of ignorance, of rereadings, repetitions, and exegeses, turns around the possibility of the event: of the event that might have happened way back in the park, or might happen again, or maybe is continually happening and has never stopped—and round the possibility of understanding it, of finally containing it in thought. In Joyce's text, the event unfolds as possibility, as destiny. It comes round again and again; it is retaled. But what it brings round is not Being, presencing, and presence—rather, it reopens all lines of difference and credit around a monetary sign, an event of economic exchange. It is a tale that is retaled, again and a gain. Joyce's *Ereignis* is not that of presence, but rather of *différance*. In it, *es gibt Sein* becomes *es gibt Geld*.

Joyce believed that *Finnegans Wake* would be the last book, the one in which the destiny of literature realized itself. We would argue that he was exactly wrong: *Finnegans Wake* is the first book, the very possibility of literature become visible as letter and as litter. One could almost say that it *is* money, the currency (to khrema) that has haunted literature's home and hearth since its beginnings, enabling its various closed economies (the Homeric epic, the picaresque adventure, the nineteenth-century novel, etc.) as it lays them waste.

The way in which *Finnegans Wake* is offered to us is economic: it is not just retailed but also *entailed*. The second sentence of the novel's second paragraph tells us this, with a further allusion to Wall Street crashes: "The great fall of the offwall entailed at such short notice the pftjschute of Finnegan, erse solid man" (3).

What is the meaning of this word "entailed"? The *Oxford English Dictionary* defines "entail" as "the settlement of the succession of a landed estate, so that it cannot be bequeathed at pleasure by any one possessor; the securing (an office, dignity, privilege) to a predetermined order of succession; to carve, sculpt, engrave." It seems we are being treated, right from the outset, to a drama of inheritance, a drama of inheritance engraved in writing. This drama, acted out around the struggles between Shem and Shaun, is alluded to as soon as the first paragraph, in which we are told that "not yet, but venisoon after, had a kidscad buttended a bland old Isaac" (3).

The reference is to Jacob ("Shem is as short for Shemus as Jem is joky for Jacob," 169) robbing Esau of his inheritance by bringing a lamb to his blind father Isaac while dressed in a hairy sheepskin: Isaac felt the hair, thought Jacob was Esau, and gave him his estate. Wile, trickery, and subterfuge will make themselves felt throughout the struggle.

Let's take a closer look at Shem and Shaun, these twin representatives of economic poles. Shaun is dubbed "the Post," the one controlling the economy of messages, of signs, of currency. He is wealthy. Shem, by contrast, is poor, and constantly in debt. He "lives off loan" (173). He is prodigal, a spendthrift, "foe to social and business success" (156), "making encostive inkum out of the last of his lathings and writing a blue streak over his bourseday shirt" (27). As Burrus, Shaun inherits bread and honey; as the Ondt, he smokes "Hosana cigals" (417). Shem, as Caseous, inherits shit; as the Gripes, he relies on "the fortethurd of Elissabed" (156), the poor relief law or, as it was known, the Forty-third Statute of Elizabeth. Biographically, Shem corresponds to James, Shaun to Stanislaus Joyce. Shem is a penman, a writer. He is also a forger. For Joyce, the two are synonymous: ever since *Portrait* it has been axiomatic for him that art is forgery. Shem's literary apprenticeship is one and the same as his development as a forger: perusing other writers' work, he decides to "study with stolen fruit how cutely to copy all their various styles of signature so as one day to utter an epical forged cheque on the public for his own private profit" (181). The "epical cheque" denotes Joyce's own novel, the shady trading zone in which all literature becomes chrematized currency.

Identity and difference, twin principles of money. That money—every single penny, zloty, dinar, lira, and shekel—must be exactly the same as another and yet different. Money's sameness is constituted through a repetition that makes it distinct: again and a gain. And Shem and Shaun are almost twins; it is suggested that what occurred in the womb was not a splitting of the egg but rather superfetation, the fertilization of a second egg while the first was already gestating: doubling mum (superfetation also means profit, accumulation). As children, they are twinlike, "jimminies" (23). "Why do I am allok alike two poss of porterpease?" the Prankquean asks Jarl van Hoother/HCE as she swaps them for one another under his very nose (22).

This problem of identity versus difference comes to a head in book 1, chapter 6, as Shaun/Jones answers his eleventh question: Would you give money to an exiled, wandering beggar to save his soul? No, replies Shaun/Jones, before launching into an elaborate explanation in which time and space are discussed in terms both economic and concerned with principles of equivalence and likeness. In his "cash-dime" speech Shaun/Jones starts by belittling Bergson ("the sophology of Bitchson"), Einstein ("the whoo-whoo and where's hairs theorics of Winestain"), and Proust ("who the lost time we had the pleasure we have had our little *recherché* brush with," 149). They are all temporalists and all Jews, and hence, by "Deasian" association, wanderers, exiles, as is Professor Levy-Bruhl ("Professor Loewy-Brueller," "Professor Levi-Brullo, F.D. of Sexe-Weiman-Eitelnaky"), whose work on *les mentalités primitives* and the experience of the mystical is dispatched on the next pages, "by what I have now resolved to call the dime and cash diamond fallacy" (150). This preoccupation with time, Shaun/Jones argues, is solipsistic and sentimental, in another swipe that makes Proust's madeleine crumble:

> *When* Mullocky won the couple of colds, *when* we were stripping in number three, I would like the neat drop that would malt in my mouth but I fail to see *when* (I am purposely refraining from expounding the obvious fallacy as to the specific gravitates of the two deglutables implied nor to the lapses lequou asousiated with the royal gorge through students of mixed hydrostatics and pneumodipsics will after some difficulties grapple away with my meinungs). Myrrdin aloer! As old Marsellas Cambriannus puts his. But, on Professor Llewellys ap Bryllars, F.D., Ph. Dr's showings, the plea, if he pleads, is all posh and robbage on a melodeontic scale since his man's *when* is no otherman's *quandor* (Mine, dank you?) while, for aught I care for the contrary, that all is *where* in love as war. (151–52)

Which is to say the following: an intense memory of eating a madeleine does not entitle its author to claim insight into all of human experience. The fact that Proust can hold up his two bits, his tiny dime, does not mean that he owns all the world's time, its thought-wealth, for dime is money. In arguing this, Shaun/Jones claims, Shem is a mere cashdime . . . to this graded intellektuals dime *is* cash and the cash system (you must not be allowed to forget that this is all contained, I mean the system, in the dogmarks of origen on spurios [dogmas of spurious origin; Deutschmarks of dodgy origin; dog marks, i.e., shit; and Darwin's *Origin of Species*], means that I cannot now have or nothave a piece of cheeps in your pocket at the same time and with the same manners as you can now nothalf or half the cheek apiece I've in mind unless Burrus and Casseous have not seemaultaneously sysentangled thmselves, selldear to soldthere, once in the dairy days of buy and buy. (161)

Thus, juggling the questions of likeness, self-sameness and difference that currency brings into play, Shaun refutes Shem's claim to his wealth. It is he, and he alone, who will inherit. One Dubliner will be doubling his mumper, while the other will be doubled with mumps.

Shaun repeats this claim in book 3, chapter 1. There, setting out his own "last will intesticle" (413), he "spinooze[s]" (414) the fable of the Ondt and the Gracehoper. Shaun reinvents himself as the industrious Ondt, a truly anti-Schellingian idealist with "a schelling in kopfers," whose "raumybuilt" riches contrast strongly with the Gracehoper/Shem's "jungle of love and debts" (416). Encountering the Gracehoper while he, the Ondt, smokes "a spatial brunt of Hosana cigals," he mocks him with what Joyce calls his "comfortumble phullupsuppy": "Flunkey Footle furloughed fould, writing off his phoney, but Conte Carme makes the melody that mints the money. *Ad majorem 1.s.d!* [pounds, shillings, pence] *Divi gloriam* [divi as in dividend paid in former time by the Co-Operative Society, a share or portion]" (417–18).

The Gracehoper/Shem admits defeat, his capitulation also expressed economically:

> As I once played the piper I must now pay the count . . .
> I pick up your reproof, the horsegift of a friend
> For the prize of your save is the price of my spend

He ends, though, with a caveat:

> As I view by your farlook hale yourself to my heal . . .
> Your genus is worldwide, your spacest sublime
> But, holy Saltmartin, why can't you beat time? (418–19)

Shem/Gracehoper, down to his last dime, is countering that Shaun/Ondt may inherit space, the "sees of the deed" (416) the exiled Gracehoper has "twicycled," the "vico's onto which he's 'tossed himself'" (417), but the time in which the world goes round remains the preserve of the artist.

Which of these two claims does Joyce's text prefer? Ultimately, neither. Each time Shaun and Shem's battles over inheritance replay themselves, they fade away to be replaced by Isabelle, Issy, Nuvoletta, Margareen: the sons give over to the daughter. And what does the daughter do? Long for the father, his "roturn," "I go back to you, my cold father, my cold mad father, my cold mad feary father." She longs not for the world to come around to her, but for the round to go a-world again, "Onetwo moremens more." For the ISA figure, HCE is experienced not as an economic legacy, a fortune or a debt-mountain to be inherited, but rather as a gift, an accumulative gift, a donation without return, "Till thousendsthee." This is how the novel ends: with an invocation of the gift, its recirculation. The last complete sentence in the novel consists of a single word: "Given!" (628). The next phrase tails off incomplete, unclosed, improper, entailing the pftjschute of Finnegan, erse solid man, once more, bequeathing one more time his debris, his pecuniary litter, the unconverted currency that makes the round go a-world, as gain and loss, again.

## Notes

1  James Joyce, *Finnegans Wake* (London: Faber, 1939), 18. Subsequent references to the work are cited parenthetically in the text.
2  We borrow this formulation from Peter Osborne.
3  James Joyce, *Ulysses* (London: Penguin, 1968), 25–26.
4  Jan Morris, *Trieste and the Meaning of Nowhere* (London: Faber, 2001).
5  Theodor Adorno, "On the Fetish-Charcacter in Music and the Regression in Listening," in *The Essential Frankfurt School Reader*, ed. A. Arato and E. Gebhardt (New York: Continuum, 1982), 278–79.
6  Michael Hardt and Antonio Negri, *Empire* (Cambridge, Mass.: Harvard University Press, 2000).
7  Freud, *Case Histories*, vol. 2 (London: Penguin, 1972), 63.
8  Quotations from Lacan are from his 1975 paper, "Joyce le sinthome 1," here translated by Lorenzo Chiesa (unpublished typescript).
9  See also "Joyce le symptome," in *Autres Ecrits* (Paris: Seuil, 2001), 565–70. Our interpretation of Lacan's reading of Joyce is deeply indebted to a paper by Lorenzo Chiesa, "Writing Enjoyment: Lacan, Artaud," given at the University of Essex, June 2002.
10  Joseph Campbell and Henry Morton Robinson, *A Skeleton Key to Finnegans Wake* (New York: Viking, 1967), 32.
11  Jacques Derrida, *Given Time: 1. Counterfeit Money*, trans. P. Kamuf (Chicago: University of Chicago Press, 1992), 158.
12  Emmanuel Levinas, "The Ego and Totality," in *Collected Philosophical Papers*, trans. A. Lingis (Dordrecht: Kluwer, 1987), 45.
13  Derrida responded to our thoughts, with scepticism but good grace, during an extensive discussion of the function of money in his work. The debate is published in *De l'argent* (Paris: Albin Michel, forthcoming).

14   Derrida, *Given Time*, 184.
15   We are grateful to Finn Fordham for drawing our attention to this.
16   Richard Ellmann, *James Joyce* (Oxford: Oxford University Press, 1959), 101.
17   Martin Heidegger, "The Anaximander Fragment," in *Early Greek Thinking*, trans. D. F. Krell and F. A. Capuzzi (New York: Harper and Row, 1984), 20.
18   Ibid, 51.

Daniel M. Bell Jr. | Only Jesus Saves:
Toward a Theopolitical
Ontology of Judgment

FOR A TIME IT WAS fashionable in some revolutionary circles to suggest that liberation was to be found only beyond the confines of ontology. If humanity was to overcome the afflictions of this present age, then a genuinely revolutionary politics must eschew, indeed escape, the constrictions of ontology. Thus began the quest for a politics shorn of the master narratives of modernity, the grand ontological schemata peddled by the likes of Hegel, Marx, Freud, and their epigones. Now, however, on the far side of the end of history that has opened onto a horizon of terror, the dismissal of ontology is being reconsidered. While totalizing discourse may be anathema and practice celebrated, it is recognized that liberation hinges upon a prior ontology that maps the trajectories of the constitutive power of life.

For a time it was also popular to espouse a militant atheism, to insist that liberation, if it is to be truly liberative, reject appeals to transcendence (and its handmaid, theology) in accord with the received prejudice that transcendence was but a species of opiate. In recent times, this too has been reconsidered. Seeking to ward off a reductive materialism that cannot account for hope, would-be revolutionaries have sought to circumvent the antinomy of God and Man[1] by means of a material vitality (frequently equated with transcendence or theology) conceived in terms of identity, or the Other, or event, and so forth.

There is much right in the recent effort to recover ontology and overcome the divine-human problematic. The struggle against savage capitalism must be waged at the level of ontology, for capitalism advances not merely by economic victory but by ontological capture. And the divine-human antinomy must be overcome, lest resources of struggle be overlooked and matter be dismissed either as mechanical or inert, and finally nonmeaningful.

But, of course, not just any political ontology will do. Nor will just any effort to incorporate the vitality of transcendence in the material realm succeed in avoiding the dead ends on which modernity's engagement with the finite and infinite foundered, namely inert matter and immaterial theology. Indeed, I will argue that only a robustly theological ontology can found a politics of resistance and hope. However, even this remains insufficient. Too many false friends today invoke a kind of transcendence (even, in some cases, "Christ") that can be little more than the figment of a Feuerbachian imagination. Thus, I argue specifically that only Jesus saves. The good news is that in Christ's offering of himself, a political ontology unfolds, a line of flight is opened up beyond the depredations of capitalist organization.

The foil for my argument is the work of Gilles Deleuze. His work garners such attention for several reasons. First, to Deleuze's substantial credit, he was never taken in by the ill-fated efforts to shed ontology. "The death of metaphysics or the overcoming of philosophy," he wrote with Félix Guattari, "has never been a problem for us: it is just tiresome, idle chatter."[2] This is to say, he was among the earliest to recognize that the struggle against capitalism had to be waged at the level of ontology. Second, in a similar vein, before the futility of the modern episteme was widely acknowledged, he was laboring to articulate a hylozoism, an ontology that ascribed creative power to matter itself, which he called "pure immanence." While Deleuze's political ontology of pure immanence merits attention in its own right, there is yet a third reason for engaging his work. In a lesser-known essay, "To Have Done with Judgment," Deleuze cuts to the heart of the matter: resistance and liberation turn on the judgment of God. A corollary of the assertion that Jesus saves is that redemption is a gift that exceeds (although it does not arrive simply from outside) *humanum*, even the über- or parahuman.[3] As the venerable Fathers of Chalcedon rightly noted, redemption appears in the truly human, the true human, Jesus Christ. In the aforementioned essay, Deleuze recognizes that salvation hinges upon Christ as the instantiation of divine judgment on the world. Of course, Deleuze holds that salvation is contingent upon *refusing* Christ and the judgment he embodies and enacts; liberation entails turning on God and God's judgment. And so the gauntlet has been thrown down.

In what follows I will suggest that only in Christ are we finally done with judgment and that Deleuze's vision of pure immanence, far from fleeing judgment, can only subject us to the harshest judgment, one that may exceed even that of capital. Accompanying this effort will be an outline of how the practice of the end of judgment that Christ inaugurates opens a space of liberation from the bondage of savage capitalism.

## The Metaphysics of Madness and Cruelty: Deleuze, Capitalism, and Desire

Because it sets the stage for the constructive argument so well, we begin with a brief consideration of Deleuze's political ontology of pure immanence. Precisely because it is a forthrightly *political* ontology, perhaps the best way into it is at the point of political struggle, so this survey begins with Deleuze's account of capitalism and desire.

### CAPITALISM AND DESIRE

As revolutionary currents crested and then were turned back in the late 1960s and 1970s, Deleuze devoted his intellectual acumen to reenvisioning revolutionary politics. Perceiving the inadequacy of both social democracy and actually existing socialisms as means of generating and sustaining resistance to and liberation from the advancing capitalist order, he began to explore new ways of conceiving human relations and revolutionary practice. The result of this effort was a history of capitalism and desire,[4] a history that suggested contemporary capitalism's dominion was not merely an economic affair—concerning modes of production, the efficient manipulation of labor, and the creation of wealth—but was ontological. This is to say, Deleuze develops an account of capitalism and its advent that displays its triumph as a matter of the successful capture and disciplining of desire, the constitutive human power. Capitalism, Deleuze asserts, extends its dominion at the level of ontology, disciplining desire in accord with the golden rule of production for the market.

The recognition that capitalism advances in the ontological and not merely economic register threatens to undo much revolutionary practice. Indeed, Deleuze's history of capitalism is intended in part as a critique of visions of resistance to the capitalist order that amassed their resources on the political-economic front while ignoring the greater horizon on which the ontological struggle was waged (which Deleuze called the "state-form" and which I unpack in more detail elsewhere as "technologies of desire").[5] In particular, it was intended as a critique of then-current revolutionary politics that were circumscribed and hence crippled by the "social unconscious"[6]— that ensemble of ideas, institutions, and social arrangements erected and propagated by state, party, and class but attributed a certain fixed, unquestioned status as a "given." Specifically, Deleuze's account of capitalism and desire was meant to dislodge the unquestioned assumption that politics and therefore revolutionary struggle against capitalism is a matter of statecraft — that social and political power rests in the state and therefore the key to change is seizing the state and wielding its power for revolutionary ends.

Of course, the suggestion that capitalism's victory is much more insidious and pervasive than mere control of things economic is not necessarily good news to those who seek to throw off its yoke. For it threatens to undo not only much but all revolutionary practice as the realization that by forming and shaping desire, capital binds us ontologically, tempts us to a pessimism that severs the nerve of liberative practice. That capitalism is indeed total, as its advocates proclaim; it is not welcome news to those who would resist its advance. Yet Deleuze certainly intends this analysis of capitalism and desire to aid revolutionary practice. An explanation entails turning more directly to his political ontology of pure immanence.

## PURE IMMANENCE

A helpful approach to Deleuze's political ontology passes through the archeology of knowledge he borrows from Foucault.[7] In *The Order of Things*, Foucault maps three *epistemes*: the classical, the modern, and what was for him a yet-to-be-disclosed future formation. According to Deleuze, the classical formation was characterized by infinity, perfection, the God-form. Everything, including humanity, was cast on a continuum of development that strove to transcend the finite toward the infinite. With the advent of the modern episteme, humanity undergoes a mutation as transcendence is eschewed (and God-talk is subjected to suspicion) in favor of finitude. Now humanity is shaped by wrestling with the forces of finitude (life/biology, labor/political economy, and language/linguistics). Under the sign of modernity, the God-form gives way to the Man-form. The passing of the modern episteme delivers us to the site/time of Deleuze's work. This final episteme is characterized by the dissolution of the antinomies of God-Man/infinite-finite and the emergence of Nietzsche's superman — "the advent of a new form that is neither God nor man and which, it is hoped, will not prove worse than its two previous forms."[8] Here the preoccupations of modernity, namely the forms of finitude, give way to what Deleuze calls an "unlimited finity." This unlimited finity is marked by the proliferation of flows of aleatory, anarchic desire continuously effecting mutations and combinations, multiplicity and difference. It is the realization of a nonreductive materialism, an ontology of pure immanence that attributes to matter an inherent, intrinsic vitality or power. Appreciating the revolutionary potential of this ontology requires delving a bit deeper into what Deleuze calls the "micropolitics of desire."[9]

In constructing his ontology of aleatory desire, Deleuze draws on the medieval theologian Duns Scotus, who erected an ontology around the univocity of being. Put simply, that being is univocal means that "being" has only one sense and is said in one and the same sense of everything of which it is said.[10] For medievals such as Scotus, this meant that God is deemed "to be" in the same univocal manner as creatures.[11] At first glance, this would appear to be a rather odd way to establish an ontology of difference that celebrates multiplicity, becoming, and flux. If being is univocal, then what could the difference between beings be? Deleuze answers, again echoing Scotus, that difference is a matter of degrees of power, or, rather, degrees of desire.[12] Everything is desire, flows of desire. What distinguishes desire, what renders desire distinct, singular, is a matter of degree. Univocal being, desire, is differentiated by degrees of intensity: "Between a table, a little boy, a little girl, a locomotive, a cow, a god, the difference is solely one of degree of power in the realization of one and the same being."[13]

What renders the univocity of being politically potent for Deleuze is the additional fact that this univocal being, the flux of desire that constitute the material realm, is productive. Production constitutes the immanent principle of desire. Thus, desire, according to Deleuze, should not be mistaken for a lack, deficiency, or absence.[14] Desire is not a desire for something; it is not a matter of acquiring or grasping an object. It is not about possession. Nor is it a matter of meeting needs or seeking pleasure; this too would be a lack. Rather, desire produces; it gives. It works. It creates.[15] Desire is a positive force, an aleatory movement that neither destroys nor consumes but endlessly creates new connections with others, embraces difference, and fosters a proliferation of relations between fluxes of desire.

The world, then, is constituted by flows of intensities of desire. The world is constituted as various machines (social machines and their formations of power, semiotic machines and their regimes of signs) capture and organize flows of desire into bodies and institutions and languages. For example, society is an assemblage of desire. A given society or social formation is nothing other than productive desire under determinate conditions. The subject, likewise, is an assemblage of desire. The subject is an assemblage of intensities of desire; it is the result of the capture of desire by a particular regime of subjectification.

We are now in a position to apprehend the revolutionary potential of Deleuze's political ontology of pure immanence. Every society, every social formation, every subject is constituted by flows of desire, differentials of intensity, that render every assemblage of desire inherently tenuous and every capture congenitally uncertain. Simply by virtue of its being the intrinsically productive, creative, anarchic force that it is, desire is antagonistic to every attempt to capture and assemble it. Univocal, productive desire, reveling in the ceaseless proliferation of new connections and relations, resists any and every end or telos, any and every organization and assembly. Resistance and revolution, therefore, are always possible. At any moment desire may discover a line of flight, a crack in a given order, and explode it. Every organization, every social formation, every subjectivity is thereby rendered a contingent, unstable assemblage, whose duration is uncertain—lasting a day, a season, a year, a life—and order is nothing but a temporary check on disorder, stability nothing but variation within tenuous limits.[16]

Accordingly, the recognition that capitalism's dominion is extended by ontological capture is not grounds for despair. To the contrary, Deleuze's analysis discloses capitalism's inescapable vulnerability. That capitalism is an always unstable assemblage of flows of anarchic, aleatory desire should reassure all who seek the end of capitalism's reign. Likewise, that power is not finally contained in a center such as the state but is dispersed across the *socius* is reason for hope insofar as it means that resistance can begin at any place and may erupt at any moment. In other words, that capitalism is an ontological and not merely economic discipline does not mean that its victory is in fact total; rather the ontological nature of the struggle broadens opportunities for resistance insofar as it opens up a plethora of fronts on which capitalism may be contested. Deleuze's political ontology opens a horizon of micropolitics, of microrevolutions. How such politics may usher in the end of capitalism is our next concern.

MADNESS AND CRUELTY

Desire is restless. As the anarchic, creative force that it is, it resists every capture, it eludes every end. And this applies to all desire, not merely to some specifically "revolutionary" desire or privileged subject (generals, workers, academics, the poor). "Desire" writes Deleuze, "is revolutionary in its own right."[17] Even now, in the midst of the triumph of global capital, desire continues to resist (thereby constituting a "war-machine"), eluding capture (thus called "fugitive"), seeking cracks in the system and creating lines of flight (hence, named "the nomad").

Thus, revolution, as Deleuze envisions it, is a matter nurturing these flows of desire, encouraging desire's becoming a war-machine, fugitive, nomad.[18] But this revolution has a peculiar characteristic. In keeping with the productive, creative nature of desire, escape from capitalism is not a matter of destruction but of creation, addition, intensification. Liberation is a matter of overwhelming capitalism's ability to capture and adapt desire to the axiomatic of production for the market. Thus, the path beyond capitalism is not one that destroys capitalism so much as it exceeds it. Revolution, in other words, is a matter of achieving absolute deterritorialization. Capitalism advances by means of a pincer movement of deterritorialization and reterritorialization. Capitalism deterritorializes desire, releasing it from prior social formations and codes, only to reterritorialize desire by disciplining it in accord with the axiomatic of production for the market. Hence, although capitalism does liberate desire from various assemblages, it does not permit desire to attain genuine freedom — the anarchic, creative, experimental movement that is the consequence of absolute deterritorialization and that Deleuze labels "schizophrenia." Instead, capitalism's profound potential for absolute deterritorialization is always curtailed by its concomitant reterritorialization of desire.

In its voracious deterritorializing, observes Deleuze, capitalism is a form of madness, and as a way beyond the madness of capitalism, he proposes intensifying the madness, continuing the process of deterritorialization, intensifying the proliferation of aleatory flows of desire, until every order and organization is simply overwhelmed and implodes: schizoid desire, pure *autopoesis*.[19]

At this point, we might ask, But what has this to do with judgment? How does this political ontology of pure immanence, schizoid desire, turn on the practice of judgment, and in particular, on the judgment of God? In the essay "To Have Done with Judgment," Deleuze presents the case against judgment and, in particular, against the Christian doctrine of the judgment of God. There he sketches the development of a "doctrine of judgment" from the ancient Greeks through modernity. In its infancy, Deleuze observes, the doctrine of judgment declared that the gods gave lots to men, and that men, depending on their lots, were fit for some particular form or end.[20] Under this early regime, judgment confines one to one's appointed lot or form and punishment falls swiftly on deviance or transgression. Christianity soon overtook the Greek doctrine and intensified its effect. Under Christianity, "we are no longer debtors to the gods through forms or ends, but have become in our entire being the infinite debtors of a single God" (129). By this Deleuze means that with the arrival of Christianity, judgment becomes total, infinite, eternal. It is total and infinite in the sense that the debt under which we finite beings toil is now raised to the level of infinity, thereby rendering us totally and infinitely in debt. With the Christian transformation of judgment, there is no longer any sanctuary from judgment; even the restricted space of a lot or form that previously offered some shelter is foreclosed as judgment becomes our lot. Christ's appearance announces "nothing is left but judgment," and even the apparent acquittal that is effected through him is in actuality but an "unlimited postponement" that ironically extends judgment to the infinite degree (129, 127).

What renders such judgment problematic, according to Deleuze, is that it is synonymous with the capture and confinement of desire. The judgment of God, in particular, has served the West as one of the principal paradigms for and instigators of the organization of desire. "Judgment implies a veritable organization of the bodies through which it acts . . . and the judgment of God is nothing other than the power to organize to infinity" (130). Judgment restrains and restricts desire, blocking the proliferation of new connections and relations between flows of desire by subjecting it to transcendent norms or values. In the end, Deleuze declares, "judgment prevents the emergence of any new modes of existence" (135).

As an alternative to judgment Deleuze develops a "system of cruelty." What distinguishes this system from judgment is not that whereas the latter hinges on debt, the former is founded on the forgiveness of debt or debt relief. To the contrary, the system of cruelty also functions according to a logic of debt. Indeed, Deleuze praises Nietzsche for having recognized that exchange between bodies is necessarily a creditor-debtor relation (128). Rather, what differentiates the system of cruelty is that its debt-cycle is strictly *finite* in scope. One promises and becomes indebted not to a god but to a partner, and redress is obtained through finite relations in the course of time. This, says Deleuze, amounts to a justice "according to which bodies are marked by each other, and the debt is inscribed directly on the body following the *finite blocks* that circulate" (127–28). Under this system, not only is the judgment of God abolished, but even the judgment of man is dissolved as the law is ceaselessly displaced through the vendetta that draws blood or pays with it. This merely finite vendetta Deleuze identifies as combat. Combat, however, should not be equated with a will to destroy or dominate. Rather, the combat of cruel justice is a matter of "a powerful, nonorganic vitality that supplements force with force, and enriches whatever it takes hold of" (133). The example he gives is that of the obstinate, stubborn, indomitable will of a baby — one whose relation to its surroundings is sheer affective, impersonal vitality.

At this point, the connection between the madness that exceeds capitalism and the cruelty that would have done with the judgment of God is apparent. Judgment is but a form of control that would bind desire, just as capitalism disciplines desire for the sake of the market. Both judgment and capitalism restrain the anarchic vitality of desire. And the madness of cruelty or the cruelty of madness is desire released from every such discipline, every such order or organization.

BEYOND MADNESS AND CRUELTY

We are compelled, however, to ask, Are madness and cruelty the way beyond the madness and cruelty of capitalism? Or does such a revolutionary course, such madness intensified, finally collapse in the black hole of nihilism, where vitality becomes necrophilia and an absolute violence is unleashed? Perhaps madness is simply madness and the cruelty that would be done with the judgment of God simply cruelty? Perhaps schizoid desire is nothing but the far side of the madness that is savage capitalism, which makes it that much more savage, and the justice that would be guided neither by God nor human law but only the force of love and hate, the highest injustice?

Deleuze, of course, would vehemently reject such conclusions and counter that his vision is one of affirmation and creativity, not dominion and destruction. Indeed, it was this affirmative desire that prompted him to begin his political ontology with a rupture, with a certain "capture of being."[21] As noted previously, Deleuze recovers from Scotus an ontology of the univocity of being, which is a rupture with the Thomistic *analogia entis* or "analogy of being," and is a capture of being in the sense that it renders being knowable, calculable, an "object." The appeal of the univocity of being for Deleuze is precisely the way it secures difference (as degree, intensity) and the interplay of difference that he characterizes as love, joy, playing, and dancing by releasing it from the gaze of a God who imposes a transcendent norm or hierarchical order on being.[22]

Yet Deleuze cannot get to where he wants to go, starting from where he starts; consequently, his madness is distinguishable only as a difference of degree from the madness that is savage capitalism, and his justice is indistinguishable from terror. It is as if Deleuze has forgotten his own insight — that capitalism's victory is ontological. Hence, by beginning with the univocity of being, he has already suffered ontological defeat. He has already conceded the crucial capture, the capture of being, that leaves desire vulnerable to the ravages of capitalism.

This is the case because relations of desire in the univocal mode can finally only degenerate into the violence of conflict and conquest.[23] In rejecting the analogy of being that preserves ontological difference while nevertheless permitting participation of one in another, Deleuze is left with discrete singularities for whom relations are always external and never constitutive of identity.[24] As a consequence, these singularities can relate to one another only through the formal mechanism of contract (between producer and consumer, between victor and vanquished). Once captured in the univocal code, singularities become "objects," and relations between objects are a matter of capture and possession — combat and sheer assertion. This follows from the fact that the discrete individuals Deleuze celebrates, precisely as discrete individuals, are intrinsically unrelated on account of the absolute and un-bridgeable difference (of degree or intensity) that distinguishes them and, hence, they can form relations only by either forcing themselves on others (by piercing the sacrosanct veil of analogically unmediable difference and seizing the other) or entering into a contract with the other (which as a purely external or formal relation rooted in the aleatory coincidence of the calculi of discrete individuals' wills remains a kind of possession).

The inescapable violence of Deleuze's vision rooted in univocity is per-haps easier to ascertain when approached from the angle of desire's being shorn of any teleology. The development of the univocity of being sundered notions of the good, of love, of justice from the active power of being.[25] Thus it is no surprise when Deleuze definalizes desire, casting it as an experimen-tal, anarchic force that defies every telos and resists every organization. The question is on what grounds does he assert that when this self-creating, self-asserting desire is released from every organization, the resultant flows of liberated desire will enter into joyful, harmonious relations? From whence cometh the confidence that the flows of desire, deprived of any shared end and barred from analogous participation in the other (which entails desire be understood not merely as assertive or creative, but also as receptive), will not simply collide in absolute war? How does he generate the innocence to assert that justice left in the hands of individuals will not quickly usher in an age of terror, where the only limit to the marking of bodies and drawing of blood (be it in the form of justice or injustice) is finite death? And would this not be the harshest judgment? As was perhaps most famously pointed out by Thomas Hobbes, the sort of nominalist-voluntarist account of desire that Deleuze advocates requires a teleology (whether divinely given or im-posed by a secular state) to avoid a state of *bellum omnis contra omnem*. Lack-ing a shared end and ontologically incapable of entering into nonpossessive relations, univocal desire does indeed resemble a "war-machine" and life a cruel combat that is made all the more cruel by insisting that it be called just. Deleuze's assertion otherwise becomes a plea for the miraculous,[26] which re-mains eternally unanswered because, transcendence having been banished, the heavens are empty. Thus, Deleuze's championing of assertive, creative desire looks more like the advancement of arbitrariness, and it portends not the proliferation of joy and harmony but the endless spilling of blood and shedding of tears.

Having embraced the univocity of being, Deleuze is delivered to an ac-count of desire that in the name of securing difference insures that relations of desire will be conflictual. In this way, Deleuze does not escape capitalist discipline, for capitalism has so construed the market that it too mediates all relations of desire agonistically. Capitalist discipline distorts desire into a competitive force—competing for resources, for market share, for a living wage, for the time for friendship and family, for inclusion in the market, and so forth. Of course, Deleuze's capitulation to savage capitalism comes as no surprise, given that, as his analysis masterfully shows, capitalism is erected on the same ontology of univocal desire shorn of any particular telos.

In the end, then, Deleuze's vision does not dismantle capitalist discipline. But this was never really his goal; his objective was to envision a way beyond capitalism, and there is a sense in which he has accomplished this. The revolution of schizoid desire, of absolute deterritorialization, promises to surpass capitalism in the sense that were it to succeed, we would be delivered to a world that exceeds even the savagery of savage capitalism. *Bellum omnis contra omnem.* Absolute war. After all, there is some truth to the long-standing claim that capitalism has a pacifying effect. Deleuze's revolution would leave us without even this, and as terrifying as capitalism is, this is a truly hideous prospect.

If Deleuze finally does not free us from madness, neither does he succeed in being done with the judgment of God. Far from being done with it, he only sets it aside, leaving us to our own deadly devices, to the (in)justice of our loves and hates. But there is a judgment of God, and we are not left to our own devices. And there is a way to be done with that judgment, although that occurs not by setting it aside but only by passing through it. And it is in this passing through that desire discovers the hope of escaping the cruel madness that is capitalism. To the hope that is ours by having done with the judgment of God we now turn.

## Christ and the Judgment of God

The "doctrine of judgment" Deleuze sets forth, which reaches its climax with debt being extended infinitely and judgment totalized in Christianity, is a truly horrific spectacle. In this, Foucault offers, it is of a piece with the exposition of the Christian practice of judgment, confession, which reveals a logic of torture, death, and self-destruction.[27] Confronted with such an account, the temptation is to dismiss it out of hand as a caricature of Christian theology. After all, one might note, in vain does one search the corpus of Deleuze's work for sustained and vigorous engagement with orthodox Christian thought. Such a dismissal, however, would be disingenuous. For the ethos of debt and judgment he portrays permeates significant segments of the Christian population. Moreover, as a host of modern and contemporary theologians will attest, such a logic of infinite debt and judgment does ring true to the orthodox heart of the Christian faith. In particular, such a logic finds a prominent niche in the Christian imagination by way of St. Anselm's (in)famous account of the atonement of Christ. Indeed, in his treatise *Cur Deus Homo*, the doctrine of divine judgment constructed around an infinite debt is laid out with such stark clarity that one cannot help but wonder if, although never mentioned, Deleuze had Anselm in mind when he set out to have done with the judgment of God.

### CUR DEUS HOMO REVISITED

In his treatise, Anselm sets forth how the judgment of God is brought to bear on the world through Christ. In summary form, the well-known argument unfolds something like this: As creatures, we owe the Creator perfect obedience. The failure to render this obedience is an offense against God's honor, thereby increasing the debt infinitely, since the one offended against is infinite. Because God must uphold justice, God cannot simply remit the debt. Indeed, humanity is required to restore more than was taken in order to make satisfaction. But, alas, finite humanity possesses nothing with which it might satisfy this infinite debt. In this circumstance, only a God-man will do: one who as God can make an infinite payment and who as man needs to. Thus, Christ emerges to pay the infinite debt on the cross with a compensatory death that satisfies divine justice. As a result, anyone who has faith in him, and abides in that faith, may avoid the infinite judgment of God.

Here we have all the components of the doctrine of judgment that Deleuze set forth: totalized judgment (creatures subjected to a regime of perfect obedience); a debt raised to infinity; and an acquittal become unlimited postponement—in the sense that a loss of faith entails the reinstatement of the regime of judgment. If this is indeed what Christ is about, then there is no escaping Deleuze's judgment. Nor will it do to invoke a heterodox current of the Christian tradition, for such a move would be only an evasion of and not a refutation of Deleuze's charge. Deleuze must be confronted head on. Does an orthodox understanding of atonement, as articulated by Anselm, embody a doctrine of judgment founded on the logic of infinite debt and omnipresent judgment?

Recently, theologians such as David Hart and Hans Urs Von Balthasar[28] have offered readings of Anselm that suggest precisely to the extent that his account of the sacrifice and death of Christ on the cross has been used to underwrite a doctrine of infinite and totalized judgment, it has been distorted—its aneconomic logic of charity, plenitude, and ceaseless generosity transposed into an alien and merely economic logic that trades on debt, lack, and loss. This is to say, read rightly Anselm displays the beauty of sacrifice, of life in the mode of donation and gift, which promises to free us from the horror of the merely economic, from the terror of capitalism and the cruelty of justice.

Read rightly, Anselm's account of the atonement is finally not economic. It is not a matter of debt, of juridical equity and restitution, of compensatory loss or penal suffering. As Anselm says, in accord with the standard precepts of medieval theology, God needs nothing and no necessity compels God to act as God does in redeeming us from sin.[29] Likewise, God does not demand bloodshed, divine justice is not in conflict with divine mercy, and God's power and dignity cannot be diminished by human insurrection.[30] That Anselm continues to be read in terms of this economic logic (debt, equity, retribution) and these distinctions (justice versus forgiveness) reflects less the deficiencies of his Augustinian vision of sacrifice than it does the way we modern readers of Anselm have been disciplined by an economy that functions in accordance with such logic and such distinctions.[31]

Shorn of such economic distortions, Anselm's account of the atonement reveals the splendor of the aneconomic bounty of God's goodness. God became human not to satisfy an infinite debt, but so that humanity might be restored to the place of honor that God from the beginning intended for humanity, namely, participation in the divine life. The injury to God's honor that is effected by sin is a matter of the absence of humanity from full communion with its creator.[32] Thus, rightly understood, God's honor is not a barrier to humanity's reconciliation with God, one that creates an infinite debt; rather it is the origin of God's free act to provide humanity with a path to renewed communion.[33] The atonement, the judgment of God, is about not a juristic reckoning stretched to infinity, but ontological union.[34]

As such, it displays not the scarcity of finitude in the face of the infinite but the plenitude of divine charity, of God's giving and giving again. God has always given to humanity in the form of love, and when humanity rejected that gift, God gave again in the form of love incarnate, which is the Son.[35] Christ's work is that of giving again, of communicating God's love and grace (which has never ceased to flow) to humanity again (and again). The work of atonement is God in Christ bearing human rejection and extending the offer of grace again, thereby opening a path for humanity to recover beatitude. In this sense, Christ's faithfulness even to the point of death on the cross marks not a divine demand for retribution, not the settling of a debt, but a divine refusal to hold our rebellion against us. (In this sense, pace Deleuze, the Book of Life is the book of *life* precisely because it does not record debt.)[36]

The atonement is not about infinite debt and totalized judgment, but about the instantiation of the gift that enables us to return to our source. It is about humanity's being taken up into the divine life of the Trinity through participation in Christ. There is a sacrifice involved in this atoning work, and there is a substitution. But these are not positioned in an economy of debt and retribution; rather, they find their true meaning in the aneconomic order of divine plenitude and superabundance where life recovers its true modality of gift, donation, and unending generosity. Thus Christ's sacrifice becomes the donation of obedience and praise (the return of love) offered by the Son to the Father, and his role is substitutionary in that the Son offers the worship that we cannot. As Hart explains,

> As Christ's sacrifice belongs not to an economy of credit and exchange, but to the trinitarian motion of love, it is given entirely as gift, and must be seen as such: a gift given when it should not have been needed to be given again, by God, and at a price that *we*, in our sin, imposed upon *him*. As an entirely divine action, Christ's sacrifice merely draws creation back into the eternal motion of divine love for which it was fashioned. The violence that befalls Christ belongs to our order of justice, an order overcome by his sacrifice, which is one of peace.[37]

In sum, God became human as a gift that exceeded every debt, that exploded the very calculus of debt and retribution and set in its place an aneconomic order of charity that recovers life in the mode of donation and lavish generosity. In Christ, we are done with the judgment of God; in Christ we reach the end of judgment.

TRUE GOD AND TRUE MAN
It is worthwhile to linger a bit longer over Christ's atoning work, for Christ's enactment of the judgment of God as the end of judgment is the ground of our hope for being free of the bondage of capital. Previously it was noted that contemporary efforts to articulate a political ontology could be mapped in terms of several epistemes. Deleuze, we will recall, positioned his work beyond the antinomy of the infinite and finite, God and Man, such that the vitality of transcendence is reclaimed for the material via the pure immanence of the über- or, more accurately, parahuman. In turn, my critique suggested that the effort to articulate a pure immanence on the basis of the univocity of being could only deliver us to the worst violence, the harshest judgment. Now it is time to indicate how Christ, and only Christ, overcomes the antinomy of God and Man in a manner that is full of the promise of freedom, which is to say, that neither sacrifices the finite to the infinite (a concern that drives both Deleuze's critique of the "doctrine of judgment" and his ad-

vocacy of a schizo desire beyond every order and organization) nor abandons
the finite to the agony of unlimited, if still only finite, combat and cruelty.

Following the Apostle Paul's lead when he wrote, "God was in Christ reconciling the world to himself" (2 Cor. 5:19), at Chalcedon (451 CE) the Church
stated once and for all that what it professed when it professed Jesus Christ
is precisely that in this particular person the antinomy of God and Man that
Foucault traced has been definitively overcome. Jesus Christ, the fathers of
the Church declared, is "perfect in divinity and perfect in humanity," "truly
God and truly man." In him are found two natures which "undergo no confusion, no change, no division, no separation." Elaborating on this, they state,
"at no point was the difference between the natures taken away through
the union, but rather the property of both natures is preserved and comes
together into a single person and a single subsistent being; he is not parted or
divided into two persons, but is one and the same only-begotten Son, God,
Word, Lord Jesus Christ."

Here the antinomy of God and Man is overcome, not by a defeat of one
at the hand of the other nor by means of a synthesis that creates a hybrid (although in the long argument anteceding and proceeding the council, such
victories were attempted and such mutants proposed). God and humanity
(two *ousias*) come together in one person (*hupostatsis*), Jesus. Moreover, here
God and humanity are joined in the unsurpassable closeness and intimacy
("no division, no separation") of a single life ("he is not parted or divided . . .
Jesus Christ") and they are united in a manner that nevertheless preserves
the difference ("no confusion, no change . . . properties of both natures preserved") peaceably. Here is the interplay of difference without agony, combat, conflict—a difference that in Deleuze's univocal pure immanence can
be only imaginary, virtual.[38]

More needs to be said, however, about Jesus's overcoming of the divine-
human antinomy, if it is to surmount the inevitable rejoinder, one that
Deleuze would surely issue, that this orthodoxy is but another form of organization, another transcendental theory that descends from on high to enclose all of reality in its grasp by means of a divine discipline. Does this not
reveal salvation to be just another totalizing discourse that imposes a fixed,
transcendental template (order) on an unsuspecting finitude? If so, then the
definition of Chalcedon notwithstanding, Christ is but the instantiation of
the defeat of the human and finite at the hands of the infinite and no freedom is forthcoming.

A response entails attending to the implications of Chalcedon's claim that
redemption comes through the particular person Jesus. That redemption
happens in this particular person means that redemption is not a generalized state of affairs that is ineluctably happening to us.[39] Redemption is not

a generalized process, a fixed order that is always already around all of us acting on us all, to which Jesus is uniquely transparent, as some sort of symbol, or which Jesus manifests in an unusual degree, as an example or leader, perhaps. Although such general theories of salvation, with corresponding images of Jesus as symbol or exemplar, are popular in some theological tributaries, it finds no repose in the orthodox Christology of Chalcedon, where salvation is associated not with a generalized process but with the goings on of a particular person. Said differently, redemption is not the capture of finitude within a given totality; it is not the setting of finitude in its assigned place according to a predetermined, transcendental order of fixed essences. Rather, redemption is what happens in the life, death, and resurrection of one particular person, Jesus Christ. This is to say, redemption is tied to the one whom Von Balthasar calls the "concrete universal."[40] The particular, concrete human, Jesus, by reason of his being the same person who is the second person of the Trinity, is of universal significance. And this significance is made known—redemption is incarnate—not by means of a transcendental capture or overcoding that is laid upon us all simply by virtue of our being finite beings who live in the inescapable shadow of the infinite but rather as finite beings enter into relation with this concrete, particular one. In other words, redemption is not imposed from above or outside the contingencies of history but rather unfolds in the midst of, by means of, the contingent encounters of particulars with this particular one named Jesus. In this regard, it is worth recalling Anselm's assertion that no necessity compels God as a reminder that redemption does not proceed by a fixed organization but by the contingent proliferation of relations with Christ in history.

Granted all of this, there is still the question of freedom. Even if redemption is not imposed from above, a fixed template pressed onto humanity, it remains to be seen how this redemption does not entail a loss of freedom and so still a defeat of the finite by the infinite. Does it not remain an order, organization, or discipline that restricts the movement of desire, even if it advances only immanently, contingently? As previously indicated, the definition of Chalcedon is careful to state that the redemption effected in Christ's person does not destroy the ousia therein united. In him is found true humanity, and it is not lost in its being brought near to divinity. In Christ, finitude is neither lost nor eclipsed but is provided a new way of existing (of which Deleuze's "unlimited finity" is finally only a parody). In Christ, finitude is lived in a new way. In particular, and of particular relevance to the matters at hand, in Christ finitude can be lived peaceably: "My peace I give to you" (John 14:27). In Christ, finitude no longer need be scarred by agony, conflict, combat. Rather, finitude can be lived in peace with God and one another (Eph. 2:14).

At this point, in order to spell out how this new way of living finitude does not eclipse freedom but instantiates it (Gal. 5:1), it is necessary to supplement Chalcedon with Thomas Aquinas on the *analogia entis*, the analogy of being. Deleuze embraced the univocity of being in the name of nurturing difference and freedom. Yet as Aquinas lays out the analogy and univocity of being in the *Summa Theologica*, it becomes clear that the univocity of being cannot preserve difference—at least it cannot preserve difference peaceably, which means that it cannot preserve freedom. Either univocal being does not bring beings closer (insofar as differences can be maintained only by the distance of differing degrees of intensity) or it dissolves difference altogether (as univocal beings meet they melt together, thus effacing difference). The only mediating position for univocal being is conflict, competition, combat. Univocal being can maintain difference in relation only by means of a friction (agony) created between different degrees of intensity that necessarily mediates the encounter and clash of otherwise univocal beings.

In contrast, the analogy of being maintains difference in a way that allows differences to be drawn into a relation while preserving (and in the case of the human, enhancing) the freedom of both. Only the analogy of being permits differences to draw near in a mode other than competition and conflict such that in this embrace of intimacy neither being nor its properties are lost (recall Chalcedon, or the Thomistic principle that grace does not destroy but perfects nature). How is this so? Aquinas's account of the analogy of being begins with what at first glance would appear to be a univocal claim, namely that all created beings participate in God, who is the first and universal principle of all being.[41] This, however, is not univocal pantheism, for Aquinas is quick to point out that God's presence to all things is not as a univocal agent (I.4.2); rather, the relation is one of analogy (I.4.3). What Aquinas accomplishes by positing a qualitative (analogy) and not quantitative (univocal) difference of being is the drawing near of God and humanity without competition. This is the case because the analogy of being does not posit God and humanity on a single plane, with the result that they are locked in a sort of zero-sum competition as the act or will of one delimits the freedom of act or will of the other. Instead, the analogy of being permits God an immediate intimacy unavailable to univocal being.[42] It enables God to draw nearer to all things that they are to themselves (to paraphrase Augustine). Thus, "God is in all things, and innermostly. . . . No action of an agent, however powerful it may be, acts at a distance, except through a medium. But it belongs to the great power of God that he acts immediately on all things. Hence nothing is distant from him" (I.8.1). Moreover, this immediate intimacy does not compromise finite freedom (if it did, this would mark a fall to univocity).[43] For God is present to things according to their mode of being (I.8.1). Thus,

God's drawing near does not overrule human freedom but enables it: "Just as by moving natural causes He does not prevent their acts being natural, so by moving voluntary causes He does not deprive their actions of being voluntary: but rather is He the cause of this very thing in them; for He operates in each thing according to its own nature" (I.83.1).[44] Under the influence of this immanent and immediate power that Aquinas calls charity — love — desire moves out beyond itself to embrace others in an ever-broadening expanse of friendship, a dance of conviviality that takes place in the very heart of the Triune God.[45] Here, finally, is desire, not disciplined and defeated but healed and set free: Beatitude.

### THE TRUE SACRIFICE

Aquinas's account of the analogy of being provides a way of envisioning the interplay of difference that maintains difference and freedom yet is full of the promise of peace, of the genuine communion that eludes the madness and cruelty of Deleuze's pure immanence. But Aquinas's account of the analogy of being is no general theory of salvation. For Aquinas, no less than for Anselm and the fathers of Chalcedon, the possibility of the free and peaceable communion of difference is anchored in the concrete universal, Jesus Christ. So we are compelled to inquire: How do we joint this dance? Where do we enter into the aneconomic fold of plenitude opened up by Christ's sacrifice? When do we encounter the particular one who is of universal significance, yet who died some two millennia ago?

The orthodox claim is that the one who died on the cross as an atonement for sin was raised from the dead and through the Spirited fire of Pentecost gathered unto himself a community, the Church, that eucharistically becomes his body and as such continues his atoning work in the world. This is to say, we meet the one who redeems in the particular, contingent event of the Eucharist. Augustine describes this encounter, and the union thereby effected, in a profound passage from book 10 of *The City of God*. There he is discussing the nature of true sacrifices, and about them he writes that they are "done that we may be united to God in holy fellowship" and they have as their reference "that supreme good and end in which alone we can be truly blessed." Then he continues with a lengthy description that takes us to the altar:

> Since, therefore, true sacrifices are works of mercy to ourselves or others, done with a reference to God, and since works of mercy have no other object than the relief of distress or the conferring of happiness, and since there is no happiness apart from that good of which it

is said, "It is good for me to be very near to God," it follows that the whole redeemed city, that is to say, the congregation or community of the saints, is offered to God as our sacrifice through the great High Priest, who offered himself to God in His passion for us, that we might be members of this glorious head, according to the form of a servant. For it was this form he offered, in this He was offered, because it is according to it He is Mediator, in this He is our Priest, in this the Sacrifice. . . . This is the sacrifice of Christians: we, being many, are one body in Christ. And this also is the sacrifice which the Church continually celebrates in the sacrament of the altar . . . in which she teaches that she herself is offered in the offering that she makes to God.[46]

Here the strands of my argument come together in a manner that gestures toward a conclusion. Christ's work of atonement is the true sacrifice, which did not pay a debt but rather draws us unto God. As the true sacrifice, Christ is the mediator, the one who overcomes the antinomy of God and Man in a way that delivers beatitude. Moreover, this beatific communion is realized through the contingent encounter with one person, Christ, whom we do meet and with whom we are intimately joined (but not lost) in the Church's celebration at the altar.

Yet there is something odd about Augustine's account. Christ, the true sacrifice, does not stand alone, in stark solitude, a transcendent totality that has no room for mere finite sacrifices. To the contrary, the one true sacrifice unleashes a multitude of sacrifices, not only in the proliferation of eucharistic enactments, but also, Augustine notes, as the Body receives the form of a servant who enacts other true sacrifices.

To the sacrifices of this servant, and how such sacrifices, nonidentical repetitions of the one true sacrifice, extend the effect of this sacrifice—like a rhizome of redemption across the rough terrain of sin—we turn. For herein lies the promise of freedom from capital.

## Practicing the End of Judgment: Sacrifice and the End of Capitalism

Christ enacts the judgment of God as the end of judgment, overturning the economy of debt, loss, and death, healing the breach between the infinite and finite, opening a horizon of harmonic concord. In the celebration of the Eucharist we are joined to Christ and consequently released from judgment for communion. But this release takes a peculiar form. Insofar as we are set free, we become a servant who extends the effect of the one true sacrifice by making true sacrifices. But is this not a contradiction? By Christ's final and sufficient sacrifice (Heb. 7:27; 10:10-12), we are done with judgment, and yet now we go forth to sacrifice? Are we then truly done with judgment? (And has not the infinite debt reappeared?) This is to say, is not to sacrifice to be reinscribed in the agonistic logic of debt and retribution and so of the very economic order we seek to escape? How, then, is it that such sacrifices portend the fall of capital?

PRACTICING THE END OF JUDGMENT

For the beginning of an answer we return to Anselm's aneconomic reading of Christ's work of atonement. His account of the atonement revealed that Christ bears God's judgment, but he does so in such a way that God's judgment marks the end of judgment. Christ, in other words, is God's judgment of judgment. If judgment is as Deleuze holds, a matter of debt, loss, and compensatory agony, then Christ's sacrifice is God's refusal of every such a judgment. God's judgment then is paradoxically revealed to be a nonjudgment precisely because it refuses to record debts or exact compensation.[47] In nonparadoxical terms, echoing Augustine's suggestion that true sacrifices are ultimately about mercy, we might call this a judgment of mercy or grace, which contravenes the logic of infinite as well as merely finite debt and retribution.[48] In more traditional theological language, this judgment of mercy, which is the end of judgment effected by Christ's sacrifice, is named "forgiveness."

How does this forgiveness that is the end of infinite judgment come to bear on the finite agony of capital? How does the end of judgment that is forgiveness contravene both the logic of infinite as well as merely finite debt and retribution? Recall that even as Deleuze rejects infinite judgment (whether rendered by a god or human law), he embraces a purely finite justice. Yet because he cannot unthink the economic logic of debt and retribution, he can think only of a different economy, which is to say, the difference between infinite judgment and finite justice can be only a difference of degree or intensity (the only kind of difference his univocal ontology permits). Thus, his alternative to infinite judgment is finite cruelty—the vendetta—and in the end, this is no escape from judgment; it is only judgment of a different degree or intensity. And, as argued previously, it is no escape from the economic logic of capital.

If Deleuze's univocal ontology finally traps him in a logic of judgment—albeit the finite judgment of a cruel justice—Christ sets us free from infinite judgment and finite justice insofar as his true sacrifice inaugurates a flow of forgiveness in the form of the finite sacrifices of those pneumatologically connected to him at the altar. In place of an economy of justice, Christ's Spirit releases the aneconomic flow of forgiveness (thus, contra Foucault, confession and penance are not an embodiment of judgment, but its end). At first glance, this appears an absurd claim. After all, Christianity has not forsaken justice; indeed, it is one of the cardinal virtues! This objection is deceptively true. It is such because what Christianity calls justice is a justice that has been transformed or redeemed by its being relocated from the univocal order of combat to an aneconomic order of charity. As a result, it would no longer be recognizable as justice at all to the likes of Deleuze. What is forsaken (absolved) is the economic justice founded on scarcity, debt, and retribution and that founds combat and cruelty. What is given in its place is a justice formed by charity, tempered by mercy, that nurtures the sociality of desire in love precisely by absolving debt, instead giving. For this reason, both Aquinas and Anselm insist that there is no opposition between divine justice and mercy; mercy implements perfect justice (Aquinas) and the rule of God's justice is mercy (Anselm).[49]

What, then, happens at the Eucharist as we are provided a new way of living, which includes the poetic continuation of true sacrifices, is not the reinstatement of an order of judgment or justice that adjudicates debt, loss, and retribution. Rather, insofar as these sacrifices flourish as a consequence of a pneumatological connection with the one true sacrifice of Christ, they repeat (although nonidentically, because the particular, contingent finite matters, which is to say, because the finite is a difference that is not obliterated by this connection but preserved in accord with the analogy of being) or extend the line of flight from the economic logic of both judgment and justice that was initiated by Christ and is sustained across time and space by his Spirit. In other words, true sacrifices are the continuation of the end of judgment. They are the practice of the end of judgment. To make true sacrifices is to have done with judgment, in both infinite and finite forms.

### SACRIFICE CONTRA CAPITAL

Anselm's aneconomic reading of Christ's atonement also provides several intimations of how true sacrifices, the practice of the end of judgment, may fund resistance to capitalism. It does so as it creates a space that allows us to distance true sacrifice from all pernicious forms of sacrifice, all forms of sacrifice that correspond to an economy of debt, scarcity, and competition.[50] According to such an order, all sacrifice is implicated in violence as it necessarily entails a loss—a loss of self, a loss of dignity, a loss of identity, a loss of life. Pernicious sacrifice is always a giving up or a surrender of the lesser to the greater—the present to the future, women to men, men to the state or corporation, all to the greater good (the market). Thus, morality under the sign of modernity oscillates between egoism and altruism, between self-preservation and self-sacrifice. And, perhaps unsurprisingly, modern Christian ethics has tended to embrace altruism and "self-sacrifice."[51] But in so doing, it is rightly censured by liberationists and others, for altruism and self-sacrifice remain circumscribed by scarcity, loss, and death — sacrifice always entails a loss. For this reason, as Ayn Rand reminded us, altruism is immoral.

Conversely, Deleuze's univocal *autopoesis* gravitates toward the other pole, egoism, as it refuses the participation in the other offered by the analogy of being and consequently construes relations as effects of sheer self-assertion. Indeed, Deleuze's account of difference in combat, again in spite of his hopes otherwise, cannot avoid becoming Darwinian struggle for self-preservation. And here too we see how Deleuze's economic logic cannot resist but only surpass the madness of capital.

Yet Anselm's account of Christ's sacrifice suggests that true sacrifice is not pernicious. The sacrifice of Christ, and hence of those who would follow him, does not belong to an economy that forces one to decide between self and neighbor, with a decision for one necessarily entailing a loss of the other. To the contrary, Christ's sacrifice births an aneconomic space where the divine plenitude spills over with the result that sacrifice becomes gain (Luke 9:24; John 12:25) and we can give ourselves as a gift of love to our neighbors without end and without loss (Matt. 22:39; Mark 12:31). In Christ's sacrifice nothing is lost and everything is gained. Through his sacrifice, sin, which as *privatio* is precisely nothing, is lost. The "nothing" that is lost is the modern illusion of the isolated, alienated self (or postmodern dissolute self) that has the eyes to see and ears to hear the sacrifice of love only as loss. The "nothing" that is overcome is the masculine fantasy of an absolute self-possession that can only be lost in giving, sharing, participating in and receiving from others. What is gained in Christ's sacrifice is abundant life,[52] life lived as donation, as the ceaseless giving (and receiving) of the gift of love, life as participation in the dance of charity that is the Trinity.

Moreover, to cling to the economic vision of pernicious sacrifice is to refuse the aneconomic gift of Christ's sacrifice. Said ethically, it is to renounce the gift of the theological virtues of faith, hope, and love that animate Christian sacrifice. For it is precisely the theological virtues that save us from the futility of pernicious sacrifice. It is faith in Christ's resurrection (1 Cor. 15:17) and the hope that we shall share in it (Rom. 6:5) and the love that casts out all fear (1 John 4:18) that sustains us in the conviction that infinite self-giving is truly an expression of the fullness of love and is not gratuitous self-annihilation or masochistic self-renunciation.[53]

We can now appreciate how Christ's work of atonement creates the possibility of release from capitalism. Through Christ's sacrifice a path is opened up beyond the iron cage of sin, of capitalism, and of the Hobbesian/Weberian world where both appear to rule. In Christ we are liberated from all that would prevent us from giving, that would interrupt the flow of divine plenitude that continues through our enactment of love. We are freed from captivity to an economic order that would subject us to scarcity, competition, dominion, and debt, that would distort human desire into a proprietary and acquisitive power. We are released from the agonistic logic of rights that envisions only a world where atomistic individuals compete for access to the goods necessary for the pursuit of private ends.

This is to say, the only way to defeat capitalism is to embrace the gift given in Christ, which is nothing less than the superabundance of grace that repositions our lives within the aneconomic order of love. So repositioned (redeemed) by love, we are enabled to give ourselves, to enact true sacrifices without loss or end, even in the face of an economy that would eclipse gift and plenitude through the imposition of a regime of scarcity, debt, and dominion. Christ's sacrifice defeats capitalism as that sacrifice, and every true sacrifice that flows from it, opens a way for desire to be healed of its economic distortions and renewed in the mode of donation, of perpetual generosity. Capitalism is overcome as human relations are redeemed from the agony of competition and dominion and revived as the joyous conviviality of love that is the fruit of the proliferation of non-proprietary (that is, participatory) relations. Capitalism is defeated as fear is cast out—the fear of my neighbor that compels me to possess more tightly and acquire more compulsively, the fear that in giving I can only lose, the fear that death and the cross is the end of every sacrifice.

## WORKS OF MERCY

In terms of specific aneconomic practices, the practice of the end of judgment that is true sacrifice prompts us to reassess the Christian practice of charity. Of course, by charity I do not mean the anemic contemporary practice of contributing two or three percent of one's disposable income to worthy causes, which many rightly critique as falling short of the gospel. Likewise, charity as the concretion of life lived as an outpouring of the divine donation has but the faintest resemblance to tech millionaires pledging the "earnings" they accumulate from a day's "play" on the stock market (Mark 12:41–44). Rather, again recalling Augustine ("true sacrifices are works of mercy"), charity as an incarnation of true sacrifice takes shape in the ancient tradition of the Works of Mercy, at the heart of which are almsgiving and hospitality. Accordingly, charity as an aneconomic practice animated by the theological virtues is manifest not in the hobby of philanthropy, but in lives lived in accord with Matthew 25:31–45, one of the traditional Scriptural warrants for the Works of Mercy. Although it does not compare to the witness of the lives of countless saints, from Francis and Clare to Day and Romero, Martin Luther captured the profundity of the aneconomic life of charity as well as anyone when he wrote, "We should devote all our works to the welfare of others, since each has such abundant riches in his faith that all his other works and his whole life are a surplus with which he can by voluntary benevolence serve and do good to his neighbor."[54] Having received all that we need in Christ, we are freed to devote our lives in their entirety to meeting the needs of others. By opening our hands to give freely of our resources to those in need and by welcoming them into our homes and communities, by becoming, as the Latin American liberationists say, "friends of the poor," we display the aneconomic order of divine charity that is overcoming the agony of the capitalist economy.[55] It is worth noting, however, that placing the emphasis on the Christian embodiment of charity via the Works of Mercy does shift the focus of Christian confrontation with economic sin away from where it is principally located today, namely, in public policy pronouncements by bureaucratic arms of ecclesial bodies that do not themselves adhere to their own "official" pronouncements. Instead, it suggests that Christians confront economic sin, systemic and otherwise, first by enacting (or receiving) this aneconomic order in their own life together.

At this point, some may object that, to paraphrase Jon Sobrino, speaking of charity and works of mercy is too soft, even too dangerous, an expression of what those who suffer under the capitalist economy need.[56] Interestingly enough, Adam Smith did not share those doubts concerning the potency of the church's aneconomic practice of charity when he penned his famous economic treatise, *The Wealth of Nations*.[57] There he noted that the hospitality and charity of the church were very great, maintaining the poor of every kingdom, and he laments that those practices "not only gave [the church] the command of a great temporal force, but increased very much the weight of their spiritual weapons." Indeed, he goes on to observe that the church constituted the most formidable obstacle to the civil order, liberty and happiness that the free market could provide. But, alas, he is glad to report that eventually improvements in "arts, manufactures, and commerce" not only conquered the great barons but undercut the church as well, weakening both its spiritual and temporal authority by rendering its charity merely economic, that is, more sparing and restrained.

Beyond capital there is plenitude. Beyond madness there is hope. Beyond cruelty, joy. Beyond judgment, peace. At that altar of God we approach this "beyond." There we behold the true sacrifice—the Lamb of God who takes away the sin of the world—and beholding, we are beholden. But this implies no debt, for this sacrifice is a pure offering, defying every necessity, exceeding every economic calculus. This mutual beholding is the gaze of love—beatitude—that fires a multitude of other true sacrifices. And as this conflagration spreads, blowing where it will, we are set free.

A fading, flickering neon sign interrupts an urban moonscape announcing a rescue mission to the nomad, the fugitive, the veteran, to the homeless and destitute: Jesus saves. Only Jesus overcomes the hostility between God and humanity, the infinite and finite, in a way that is full of promise, that is full of the promise, not of the nihilistic madness and cruelty postmodernity barely wards off, but of the joyous conviviality that is love.

## Notes

1 See Michel Foucault, *The Order of Things* (New York: Vintage, 1973).
2 Gilles Deleuze and and Félix Guattari, *What Is Philosophy?*, trans. Hugh Tomlinson and Graham Burchell (New York: Columbia University Press, 1994), 9. In the course of this essay I refer to several works in which Deleuze collaborated with another author, the most notable example being his work with Félix Guattari. I do not attempt the futile task of sorting out the voices; instead I will simply refer to the texts as being Deleuze's. For Deleuze's remarks on his collaborative efforts, see Gilles Deleuze and Claire Parnet, *Dialogues*, trans. Hugh Tomlinson and Barbara Habberjam (New York: Columbia University Press, 1987), 16–19; and Gilles Deleuze and Félix Guattari, *A Thousand Plateaus: Capitalism and Schizophrenia*, trans. Brian Massumi (Minneapolis: University of Minnesota Press, 1987), 3.
3 The concept of the "parahuman" is taken from Kenneth Surin, "Liberation," in *Critical Terms for Religious Studies*, ed. Mark C. Taylor (Chicago: University of Chicago, 1998), 183. It is helpful because it points to Deleuze's disassembly of the very notion of a distinctly human subject. It gestures toward the tendency in Deleuze's work in the direction of the cyborg, which is a result of his critique of organic thought and organism.
4 Deleuze and Guattari, *A Thousand Plateaus*. For a synopsis, see Kenneth Surin, "The Undecidable and the Fugitive: *Mille Plateaux* and the State-form," *SubStance* 66 (1991): 102–13.
5 See Daniel M. Bell, *Liberation Theology after the End of History: The Refusal to Cease Suffering* (New York: Routledge, 2001), 12–32.
6 The phrase "social unconscious" comes from Philip Goodchild, *Deleuze and Guattari: An Introduction to the Politics of Desire* (Thousand Oaks, CA: Sage, 1996), 3.
7 Foucault, *The Order of Things*. For Deleuze's use of this, see his *Foucault*, trans. Seán Hand (Minneapolis: University of Minnesota Press, 1988), 124–32.
8 Deleuze, *Foucault*, 132.
9 Deleuze, *Dialogues*, 17; Deleuze, *A Thousand Plateaus*, 203.
10 Gilles Deleuze, "Seminar Session on Scholasticism and Spinoza," trans. Timothy S. Murphy, www.imaginet.fr/TXT/ENG/140174.html (accessed August 6, 1999).
11 For a fuller account of Scotus's theology and its consequences, see Catherine Pickstock, *After Writing: On the Liturgical Consummation of Philosophy* (Malden, Mass.: Blackwell, 1998),

121-66. For Deleuze's treatment of Scotus and the emergence of the univocity of being along the trajectory of Scotus, Spinoza, and Nietzsche, see Gilles Deleuze, *Difference and Repetition*, trans. Paul Patton (New York: Columbia University Press, 1994), 35-42. For a helpful narrative of Deleuze's philosophical development in this regard, which unfortunately does little with Scotus, see Michael Hardt, *Gilles Deleuze: An Apprenticeship in Philosophy* (Minneapolis: University of Minnesota Press, 1993).

12    Deleuze, "Seminar Session on Scholasticism and Spinoza," 4.

13    Ibid.

14    Deleuze, *Dialogues*, 91; see also Deleuze, *A Thousand Plateaus*, 154.

15    By positing the ontological primacy of productive desire, Deleuze runs the risk of sounding like a vulgar Marxist who reduces everything to the economic forces of production and their shadows. Indeed, the emphasis on production resonates with the traditional Marxist focus on the modes of production, a focus renewed in Marxist circles in the 1960s and 1970s. However, Deleuze's account of productive desire does not equate, in any uncomplicated way, productive desire with the modes of production. Rather, desire produces the modes of production. Productive desire is what makes the modes possible. Drawing the facile equation "productive desire equals modes of production" overlooks the way in which Deleuze's ontology of desire collapses any distinction between a productive base and a nonproductive superstructure. Everything is desire, hence everything is productive: productions of productions, productions of consumptions. The economy produces, but so too does culture, and religion, and the family, and so forth. See Gilles Deleuze and Félix Guattari, *Anti-Oedipus: Capitalism and Schizophrenia*, trans. Robert Hurley, Mark Seem, and Helen R. Lane (Minneapolis: University of Minnesota Press, 1983), 4.

16    Brian Massumi, *A User's Guide to Capitalism and Schizophrenia* (Cambridge: MIT Press, 1992), 58-59.

17    Deleuze, *Anti-Oedipus*, 116.

18    See ibid., esp. 246.

19    Ibid., 373.

20    Gilles Deleuze, *Essays Critical and Clinical*, trans. Daniel W. Smith and Michael A. Greco (Minneapolis: University of Minnesota Press, 1997), 128.

21    The claim that "politics precedes being" is an instantiation of the univocity of being because it implies a distinction similar to Scotus's "formal distinction," marking a virtual reality between essence and existence, a possible that is not yet actual, a possible that through an act of the will (politics) becomes actual (being). See Deleuze's discussion of Scotus in *Difference and Repetition*, 39ff. I owe the phrase "capture of being" to Éric Alliez, *Capital Times*, trans. Georges Van Den Abbeele (Minneapolis: University of Minnesota Press, 1996), 197.

22    Deleuze, *Anti-Oedipus*, 347; Gilles Deleuze, *Nietzsche and Philosophy*, trans. Hugh Tomlinson (New York: Columbia University Press, 1983), 194; Gilles Deleuze, *Expressionism in Philosophy: Spinoza*, trans. Martin Joughin (New York: Zone Books, 1992), 246; Gilles Deleuze, *Spinoza: Practical Philosophy*, trans. Robert Hurley (San Francisco: City Lights Books, 1988), 126.

23    My understanding of the impact of Scotus and the univocity of being relies heavily upon the treatments in Alliez, *Capital Times*; Pickstock, *After Writing*; and Kenneth Schmitz, "Is Liberalism Good Enough?" in *Liberalism and the Good*, ed. R. Bruce Douglass, Gerald M. Mara, and Henry S. Richardson (New York: Routledge, 1990), 86-104.

24    The proliferation of relations in Deleuze would appear to be more accurately described

as a proliferation of "expressions." Desire enters into relations as it expresses itself. The other in this situation resembles a canvas upon which desire expresses itself. Furthermore, the extent to which univocal desire can be genuinely creative is questionable, since new relations are only the old with more added. The already given is simply rearranged.

25   Alliez, *Capital Times*, 211–12; Pickstock, *After Writing*, 157.

26   Pickstock, *After Writing*, 132.

27   Michel Foucault, "About the Beginning of the Hermeneutics of the Self: Two Lectures at Dartmouth," *Political Theory* 21 (1993): 215.

28   What follows draws heavily on D. Bentley Hart, "A Gift Exceeding Every Debt: An Eastern Orthodox Appreciation of Anselm's *Cur Deus Homo*," *Pro Ecclesia* 7 (1993): 333–49; Hans Urs Von Balthasar, *The Glory of the Lord, Volume II* (San Francisco: Ignatius, 1984); as well as John Milbank, "Forgiveness and Incarnation," in *Questioning God*, ed. John D. Caputo, Mark Dooley, and Michael J. Scanlon (Bloomington: Indiana University Press, 2001): 92–128.

29   Von Balthasar, *The Glory of the Lord*, 240, 245, 250, 246.

30   Von Balthasar, *The Glory of the Lord*, 262, 247; Hart, "A Gift Exceeding Every Debt," 343, 349.

31   Note that Milbank, in "Forgiveness and Incarnation," suggests that Anselm does at times attempt too much and thus is guilty of occasionally slipping in the direction of this economic logic. He goes on to argue that one must read Anselm aesthetically, which is precisely what Von Balthasar does: one of the sections of his treatment of Anselm is labeled "aesthetic reason."

32   Von Balthasar, *The Glory of the Lord*, 248.

33   In this regard, Alasdair MacIntyre notes that with the loss of a thick conception of the common good, the notion of "honor" degenerates into merely a "badge of Aristocratic status." See his *After Virtue*, 2nd ed. (Notre Dame, Ind.: University of Notre Dame, 1981), 232.

34   Thus we can see why sheer negative "pardon," although possible as Anselm and others such as Aquinas make clear, is nevertheless not "fitting." And it explains Anselm's intriguing claim that he would prefer to be in hell without sin than heaven with sin. Sheer negative pardon would result in humanity gaining entrance to heaven but still in need and thus devoid of blessedness. As a result, heaven would be hell. Conversely, hell with complete virtue would be heaven. See Von Balthasar, *The Glory of the Lord*, 249.

35   Technically this is incorrect. As John Milbank points out, God does not give anything to anyone but establishes all that is as sheer gift. See "Can A Gift Be Given? Prolegomena to a Future Trinitarian Metaphysic," *Modern Theology* 11 (1995): 134–35.

36   Deleuze, *Essays Critical and Clinical*, 128.

37   Hart, "A Gift Exceeding Every Debt," 348.

38   Univocal difference is not a difference of being, thus it is virtual. On this, see Daniel W. Smith, "The Doctrine of Univocity: Deleuze's Ontology of Immanence," in *Deleuze and Religion*, ed. Mary Bryden (New York: Routledge, 2001), 179.

39   David Yeago, "Jesus of Nazareth and Cosmic Redemption: The Relevance of St. Maximus the Confessor," *Modern Theology* 12 (1996): 177. Much of what follows draws from Yeago's insightful analysis.

40   Hans Urs Von Balthasar, "Characteristics of Christianity," in *Explorations in Theology*, vol. 1 (San Francisco: Ignatius, 1989), 170.

41   In-text references are to the *Summa Theologica*, trans. Fathers of the English Dominican Province (Westminster, Md.: Christian Classics, 1981).

42   This is so because were a univocal being to have an unmediated relation, that is, an immediate relation with another univocal being, the "otherness" or difference would dis-

solve, rendering them one. At which point it no longer makes sense to speak of a relation between different beings. There would no longer be difference or beings, only one being.

43  In this regard it is worth noting that Deleuze fears thinking God will impose a transcendent measure on finitude. Aquinas notes that such could only happen with God thought in the univocal key, that God in analogical relation to creatures is not their measure (I.13.5).

44  As Hans Urs Von Balthasar puts it: "He allows the individual his own will, his choice, his freedom. He does not impose himself from without, but works in the inner source of the created spirit, not as "another" but as one exalted above all otherness . . . so immanent that he is indistinguishable from the natural spirit." *A Theology of History* (San Francisco: Ignatius, 1994), 102–3.

45  Note that the being of finite created beings in relation to other finite created beings is univocal, and their difference is finally quantitative. Two observations spring from this. First, what enables these differences to interact with one another in nonagonistic ways is precisely their mutual participation in God, whose call (in the sense of gathering and sending) both mediates and maintains those differences peaceably. Second, it is these differences in created being that underwrite what are often pejoratively called "hierarchies" among created beings, but when rightly understood and practiced, such relations are nonhierarchical precisely because hierarchy enacts not simply difference but distance, and the analogy of being maintains difference *without distance* insofar as it permits God an immediate intimacy with all created being—an intimacy that all created beings share with one another via their participation in Christ.

46  Augustine, *The City of God*, trans. Marcus Dods (New York: Modern Library, 1950), X.6.

47  Note that this opens the space for accounts of final judgment that suggest such judgment is not something that finally God inflicts, but rather is self-inflicted by the sinner in the sense that it is not God's turning away from the sinner but the sinner's final refusal of God's eternal offer.

48  See L. Gregory Jones, *Embodying Forgiveness* (Grand Rapids, Mich.: William B. Eerdmans, 1995).

49  See Daniel M. Bell, "Sacrifice and Suffering: Beyond Justice, Human Rights, and Capitalism," *Modern Theology* 18.3 (2002): 349–51.

50  I am indebted here to John Milbank, "Stories of Sacrifice," *Modern Theology* 12 (1996): 27–56.

51  See Linda Woodhead, "Love and Justice," *Studies in Christian Ethics* 5 (1992): 44–61.

52  John Milbank, "Midwinter's Sacrifice: A Sequel to 'Can Morality Be Christian?'" *Studies in Christian Ethics* 10 (1997): 31.

53  John Milbank, "Socialism of the Gift, Socialism by Grace," *New Blackfriars*, no. 77 (1996): 546.

54  Martin Luther, "The Freedom of a Christian," in *Martin Luther: Selections from His Writings*, ed. John Dillenberger (Chicago: Quadrangle, 1961), 74.

55  The risk in positing charity as the central aneconomic practice of the faith is that it may appear to treat symptoms of injustice and poverty while overlooking (systemic) causes. Charity and the Works of Mercy rightly practiced, however, do not preclude but rather demand confronting sin. One of the spiritual works of mercy, for example, is "admonishing sinners." In this regard, I find the lives of the saints, such as Romero and Day, the best "explanations" of Christian charity.

56  Jon Sobrino, *The Principle of Mercy* (Maryknoll, N.Y.: Orbis Books, 1994), viii.

57  Adam Smith, *An Inquiry into the Nature and Causes of the Wealth of Nations* (Chicago: University of Chicago Press, 1976), V.1.3.3.

PART 3    Infinite Desire and
          the Political Subject

*Antonio Negri* | The Political Subject and
Absolute Immanence

CAN ONE PROVIDE an ontology of the political subject outside of all teleology and within the postmodern conditions of absolute immanence?
This is the subject that we want to confront here, a subject that is all the more important in the face of the fundamentalist infection, whether it be Islamic or Western and/or Christian, which risks wiping out the great secular values of tolerance to which we have grown accustomed.

I will situate the problem within the debate on the "multitude." To begin with, in *Empire*, the concept of the "multitude" is defined against that of the "people." It is defined there as a set of singularities bearing inalienable rights, and thus in contrast to what we encounter in the process of constitution of the modern state. Second, the multitude is defined against the traditional ideas of "class" and of the "masses." If we can say that the multitude works, if one of its fundamental qualities consists in its expressing living labor, the set of singularities that the multitude is cannot be reduced to an indistinct unity, whether we call this unity "class" or "mass." Rather, the valorization of production derives from the capacity of singularities to produce value. Third, the multitude is given, on the ontological plane, as constitutive power:[1] the social and the political, united in the biopolitical, together form the genealogical basis and product of the multitude.

Having said that, we have still not said how the multitude is capable of becoming a political subject. That is, a political subject at a remove from any theological basis concerned with essence or identity, but a political subject situated in absolute productive immanence. Many of those who agree with the concept of the multitude as it is expressed in *Empire*, asserting its correctness from the productive and the political standpoint, go on to pose the question of how this multitude can express itself as subject, as force, as capacity for decision. Evidently we are not speaking of definitions of Power à la Carl Schmitt; rather, we are engaged with the forces and desires that give life to the multitude. And yet we must try and understand what it is that gives substance to the actions, to the project and to the capacity of the multitude to construct history.

## Spinoza's Conjecture

It is well established that Spinoza's discussion of the strategy of *conatus* (striving) represents the linear course of an argument that proceeds from the phenomenology of a multitude of subjects to the definition of democracy. It is a line of argument that leads from *cupiditas* (desire) to *amor* (love), from the expression of desire to the transformation of co-operation into the "common," and from the anthropology of singularities to a political ethics. Thus, in Spinoza, the conditions of the political subject are included in the power of *conatus*: they unfold through various degrees of ontological perfection, from the imagination to the material recomposition of bodies, from singularities to the collective and from the affirmation of the individual to the universal. Here we see how the expressive process of being develops. Ancient materialist ontology established the passage from singularity to value through the insertion of the *clinamen*. With Spinoza, materialist ontology is traversed and founded anew by desire. It is a living force that unfolds in the world so as to construct it as divine. Freedom translates the continuity of an absolute productive immanence, of a *vis viva* that develops, from physical conatus to human cupiditas to divine amor. Ethics constitutes the physical world before it interprets the human and sublimates itself in the divine. Eternity is lived as presence. The collective subject is born in the shape of a common subject; it is produced by the passion that stirs up and constructs both the world and the divine. The immanence of Spinoza's argument is thus complete. It dares to oppose itself (and succeeds in so doing) to the transcendental presumptions of modern political thought, countering the modern state with the aim of absolute democracy. The goal of Spinoza's state is the establishment of liberty. Let us paraphrase this Spinoza of ours: the state is not established in order to keep Man in a state of fear (as Hobbes wished); in fact, the reverse is true. The civic state is established in order to liberate individuals from fear, so that they should live better in security; or more precisely, so that they should maintain, without causing harm to others, their natural right to act and to exist. Thus, the end of the state is freedom.

As we have said, this process is described not simply from the metaphysical standpoint. Both in the *Tractatus Teologico-Politicus* and in the *Ethics*, this process is directly related to the constitution of bodies, from the single body to the collective and common body. It is the productivity of the *bios* that is at stake here. In Spinoza we have the basis for a definition of biopolitics.

## Spinoza's Infinite and the Blockage of the Investigation

The shift in the problematic of materialism (and of immanence) from its classical form (the Lucretian materialism of the *clinamen*) to the Spinozian one (a materialism of the passions) is a powerful one. But we must also indicate the limits of this position. It harbors a residue of infinity; there is always a mark of teleology, a measure that blocks (and presumes to shape) the power of Spinoza's materialist ascesis. The relationship of singularity to multitude is one that, in some ways, cannot be pursued within the ambit of Spinozism. The idea of the infinite and the teleology of measure even spurt some of their venom onto the new radicalism of Spinoza's materialist procedure. Spinoza's materialism, which posited the concept of the multitude in such real and forceful terms, is, nevertheless, unable to show us political subjectivity within the fabric of absolute immanence. The force of liberation from the measure of being, from the prefiguration of being, that characterizes ascesis is only partially successful. If we bear in mind that the common is subject to the same measure as the passion of the singularities, we are unable, with Spinoza, to draw upon such a force. Indeed, we experience its blockage and are, therefore, in thrall to an ethical and ascetic illusion: the blockage of what serves as the measure of the modern; that is, the blockage represented by the infinite. The measure of modernity renders the relationship between singularity and totality tautological.

Thus, to the infinite of modernity we must oppose the eternity of creation, or what we now call (postmodern) expression. So it is not by materialist physics (in the form Spinoza gives it) opening itself to the question of the common (through the exploration of the passions) that the question of the political subject can be considered resolved. The question of the political subject calls for another approach. It demands that the tautology of measure (of the subject and the totality) be overcome and that the conception of the common be sustained by the genealogy of innovation. The problem is not that of grasping the passage from singularity to the common but of grasping the innovation, novelty, and creativity that constitute it. Communication among subjects is not enough to construct a world. This world must comprehend novelty, openness, expressivity, and surplus.[2]

Some postmodern thinkers have sought this creative opening on the margins of the totality formed by the action of the singularities. But the margin represents a liminal transcendence: it is an immanence that is almost transcendence, an ambiguous place in which materialist realism and ascetics end up bowing to a form of mysticism. Jacques Derrida endlessly peruses the margin of being; Giorgio Agamben, the artist of paradoxes, fixes upon it as though it were a power of the negative. Perhaps it is merely a case of waiting for the other, and, as in Emmanuel Levinas, this waiting for the common transpires into mysticism. There are also those who have tried to pursue this teleology (from the subject to the common and from the multitude to its subjectivation), projecting it onto a thousand plateaus of singular power. Here, in Gilles Deleuze and Félix Guattari, the edge of being is rent asunder but the appearance of the singularities takes place in a circuit from which there is no exit.

All of which suggests that we must reaffirm the question we posed at the beginning of our discussion, only this time we will be setting off from a new assumption: the multitude will be able to become a subject only when its common becoming is presented as a surplus, as a new creative articulation of ontology. The singularization of the multitude posits the immeasurable: it is not universal but common, it is not infinite but eternal, it is not the substance of temporality but the arrow of time, and it is not the accumulation of singularities but rather a proliferation of ontological expressions.

*Another Example: Aporias of the*
*Biopolitical in Agamben*

As we have already noted, Giorgio Agamben has attempted to find a new positivity on the negative margin of the world. He attempts to construct an ontology of the margin, complicating the constitutive process of the immanent subject by contrasting it with the singular difference and the negative repetition of experience. According to Agamben, an event is determined: it is an exteriority that suffers, on the limit, but is unable to break off. It is a difference that persists and resists politically. Thus, Agamben, far from giving us a new definition of the political subject, presents us with a new ontological possibility. In fact, the core of Giorgio Agamben's reasoning in *Homo Sacer* consists in the construction of a concept of biopolitics (and of biopower) set in contrast to the concept of modern sovereignty. If modern sovereignty can be defined as a set of Powers, Agamben aims (in his anti–Carl Schmitt) to perfect and *overturn* that concept. And there is no doubt that here we are touching upon a central element of the definition of modernity and of the political. In the context of the 1970s and the political crisis that characterized it, Agamben perceived this problem perfectly. Today, however, he seems to have retreated from this insight. Indeed, the process whereby he forms his definitions avoids, from the start (and thus prevents one from attaining), the productive dimension of the *bios*, which is to say, the materialist moment of innovation. If the first definition of the political is to be sought in the biopolitical, if "Western politics is co-originally biopolitics," how can Agamben say that "the decisive political conflict that governs every other conflict is, in our culture, that between the animality and the humanity of Man"?[3]

Summing up this first transition, we can conclude that, for Agamben, biopolitics is not immediately productive. Indeed, before rooting the analysis in the biopolitical, Agamben wrestles with the modern concept of sovereignty, that is, with the concept of sovereignty as "state of exception" that Carl Schmitt had proposed as the transcendental schema of political reason. He absorbs and retains this determination of sovereignty. In this way, though, he finds himself unable to account for the productive dimension of the *bios* and ends up blocking the *bios* on a naturalistic plain (life as *zoè*) or on a generically anthropological negativity (sacredness, bareness, exclusion, or camp, without any historical determination). Consequently, since for Agamben biopolitics is not productive, he finds himself with only two possible alternatives: either naturalism or an existential conception with a nihilist tinge, marked by a limit, a separation, an insoluble strain. Here the subject becomes a mystery.[4]

However, Agamben has two ways out from this ambiguous line of thought. The first is represented by Bartelby, for whom the negative becomes refusal and the refusal becomes absolute. This negative becoming-absolute of the refusal appears almost to represent the place of the mystical. In order to understand this passage one must bear in mind *Language and Death: The Place of Negativity*, which forms the backdrop of Giorgio Agamben's thinking.[5] The positive aspect of this book lies in Agamben's problematizing of the *krisis* of the foundation: of his doing away with all definitions of it in terms of destiny, against all the interpretations that in the mid-1970s reiterated a radical pessimism (e.g., Massimo Cacciari). In contrast to these authors, Giorgio Agamben situates himself within the place of the negative, nevertheless refusing nihilism, tirelessly asking himself what relationship there could be between reality and history, between being and practice. If Agamben will never cross the threshold of the positive construction of being, he is, nevertheless, able to propose, through ontological critique, an aspect of existentialist pessimism (and of the nihilism of this school of thought) that had, until now, been interpreted in entirely superficial terms.

But there is nothing to say that Agamben must come to a halt on this funereal conception of being that we have described so far. Indeed, in *The Coming Community* Agamben interrupts the oscillation of the nondecision between humanity and animality (and he somehow overcomes the one between Heidegger and Benjamin).[6] Agamben proposes here that formidable concept of "whatever subjectivity" that appears able to establish itself within an ontological and materialist dimension, beyond a drift into conceptions of belonging and identity, and toward a project of metamorphosis, hybridization, and liberation. In *The Coming Community*, Giorgio Agamben comes very close to this idea of a constitutive subjectivity.

But Agamben abandons the course steered in *The Coming Community* as, in *Homo Sacer*, he returns to the theme of the negative and even develops further his analysis of the figure of Bartelby in that of "the Muslim."[7] Summing up this passage, which is typical of postmodern thought, we can conclude that:

1. Agamben *hits squarely the problem* of the margin, that of the *exit from a materialist physics* and from the tautology of value in pantheism.

2. The way out, as defined by Agamben, is never through an operation of *verticalization* of being, that is, through an operation by which value is founded in the sphere of transcendence and theology. The operation carried out by Agamben is always *horizontal*. We may, occasionally, encounter a wavering in Agamben, an opening that alludes to theology, but the verticality of the theological solution is never adopted, contrary to what occurs in certain tendencies of phenomenology (as Janicaud has extensively shown).

3. However, the solution that Agamben gives to the problem, despite having correctly defined its site, will be powerless. Indeed, it will not be through Bartelby's refusal or the stronger refusal represented by "the Muslim" that we will be able to grasp being. Nor will it be Benjamin's desperate utopia (which reverberates throughout *The Coming Community*), and which still has so distinct an echo of nineteenth-century communism about it. In effect, the fundamental limit consists in taking the biopolitical as nonproductive, as "bare life." Now "bare life" will never, as we have seen, be said to be theological or vertical, although it leads us into a blind alley because life is never naked but always clothed. Life can present itself as monstrous but never as bare. In the biopolitical, that which clothes life is never separate but always organically connected to the body.

All this to say that "bare life" is the opposite of Spinozian power and joy of the body. One cannot place oneself ambiguously between Spinoza and Heidegger. Spinoza systematically overturns all the ontological positions that characterize *Dasein* as unproductive. Just as Spinoza opposes amor to angst and to *Umsicht* (the look that grasps the environment), he opposes *mens* (the reason that opens passion to the absolute); so to *Entschlossenheit* (the decision that encloses), he opposes *cupiditas* (the desire that creates); to *Anwesenheit* (*ousia*, present being), conatus (the force always open to the being to-come), to *Besorgen*, he opposes *appetitus*; and to *Möglichkeit*, he opposes *potentia*.

## Power and Poverty

The conclusion we can draw from this lengthy discussion and from this example is that if we want to pose the problem of the construction of a new political subject (constituting it according to the flows of the ontology of immanence), we must not cross the margin but must rather take up a position within the biopolitical fabric. That is, we must elucidate the common dimension of the productive *bios*. It is there that we must dig so as to avoid crushing any emergent subjectivation by determinism, and in order to elevate subjectivation to the immeasurable, elevate it to the position of a surplus with respect to even the materialist experience of the world. This is true of the imagination just as it is of the rational schematization of the construction of the world. The only chance for subjective opening, the only possibility for giving direction to the multitude, lies in engaging with it as immeasurable and thereby qualifying the common that characterizes it as creation.

It is for this reason that I propose to set out from *poverty*. For Agamben, in the light of a political Power defined in a one-dimensional manner, the only possible reaction, as an alternative to Power, is that of "bare life" — the extremity, the margin of life. But here we remain caught within modernity, or more precisely, in the narrow-minded 1930s definition of Power as ideological *à la* Carl Schmitt. In contrast to this position, we understand Power in biopolitical terms: we are immersed in Power; we are within Power and harbor no illusion of being outside out of it or being on the margins. But if biopower is an invasion of life, the exercise of Power shows itself to be essentially exploitation. Here, then, the poor person emerges and is revealed in a clear light. It is the poor person that requires an explanation for the concept of the political to be constructed, and not vice versa, as Agamben would prefer. At present, the experience of poverty occurs within a common that knows no "outside," within a dense common that has neither spatial fissures nor temporal suspensions of time. *In postmodernity the poor are the excluded, and this exclusion is "within" the production of the world.* But in this situation, to be excluded is a logical paradox: in a linguistic community, exclusion is only a pathological fact and, in biopolitical production, it is materially impossible. Here we see the emergence of the first features that characterize the scandal of the experience of the poor in postmodernity. One is the poorest of the poor because one is the most integrated in the common, in the commonality of life, of language, of production and of consumption. One is excluded within the biopolitical, in that same biopolitical that he produces and in which one is subjectively produced. Poverty is thus a being *inside*. Is it also a being *against*? This is what is revealed by the resistance of the poor. This is what is revealed by the fact that this resistance is productive of new spaces of creation and circulation; that thus the resistance of the poor person rises up as surplus. The poor are excluded from the world that they produce, but that power becomes resistance and resistance nourishes new power. When we speak of poverty, it is therefore not a case of "bare life" but rather of a power to create the world; this power is constrained, excluded, and must reappear as resistance. Poverty is entirely redefined due to its existing within the *bios*, and it stays within the bios because there is no longer an "outside"; it remains within the bios because exclusion affects but does not nullify power. Thus resistance expresses itself as excess and immeasurableness.

BIOPOLITICS AND MOVEMENT

In order to sum up the operation of disarticulation of linear materialist physics that we have carried out here—in the course of our investigation into the elements of subjectivation that enable us to consider the multitude as a *dispositif* of decision—let us secure the following points:

1. The productive fabric of biopolitics is fundamental, whatever the limits and the politics to which it is subjected. The *tempus potentiae* that traverses biopolitics is its central characteristic.

2. One can test out the strategy of conatus in this framework but only if one does not consider it in linear fashion but thinks of it, instead, as an interweaving of different threads, which are in a state of permanent agitation and rise up in untimely fashion. Otherwise, we fall back into the univocal dimensions of modern materialism.

3. The *prise de conscience* of the multitude passes through the proliferation of singularities that constitutes it. Put in these terms, the task of teleologically recomposing the multitude, of constructing it as political subject, is unrealizable. This failure does not affect the substance of the problem, it demands only that we displace it.

4. The *displacement* consists in a refusal to incorporate the formal characteristics of constitutional and/or institutional engineering into the problem of the organization of the multitude. The element upon which to concentrate the entire debate is solely that of poverty. Poverty does not represent merely the content of the resistance of the multitude but also the site where its power reveals itself. Poverty is the extremely radical capacity to overturn

the biopower that puts power to work so as to exploit it, exclude it and enslave it. *Poverty is the multitude in action.*

## Notes

Thanks go to Alberto Toscano and Juliet Rufford for much improving this translation.

1   Translator's note: Negri makes a crucial distinction between *potere* and *potenza* in his *The Savage Anomaly* that he derives from Spinoza's distinction between *potestas* and *potentia* and that is missed in the English translations of Spinoza's works. I have followed Michael Hardt's rendering of these two terms in his translation of *The Savage Anomaly* as "Power" and "power" respectively. The distinction is both a political and an ontological one, in that *potere* (Power) stands for a centralized transcendent force of command, while *potenza* (power) denotes rather immanent and local constitutive forces. For a succinct discussion of this distinction, see the introduction to *The Savage Anomaly: The Power of Spinoza's Metaphysics and Politics*, trans. Michael Hardt (Minneapolis: University of Minnesota Press, 1991).

2   Translator's note: I translate the notion of *eccedenza* as *surplus*, although one should always bear the notion of *excess* in mind. It is not a reference to the notions of "surplus labor" and/or "surplus value" of the classical Marxist tradition but it refers one rather to the notion of "immaterial labor"—the form of labor that predominates under post-Fordism—developed by Negri, Maurizio Lazzarato, Michael Hardt, and others. Speaking of immaterial labor and of its "product," Negri insists that its fundamental characteristic is that it is not exhausted when consumed, it is not eroded and mutilated whether in the labor process itself or in the consumption of the product. It does not then disappear but is always augmented, forming an excess or surplus. It can be consumed endlessly, thereby producing a new affective range in the subject, and in the extension of its consumption it produces a broader audience, its affective forces resonating out, producing a surplus for new creation, new consumption, and new common forces of subject formation.

3   Giorgio Agamben, *L'aperto. L'uomo e l'animale* (Torino: Bollati Boringhieri, 2002), 82.

4   Ibid., 95: "Once again the *mysterium coniuctionis* from which the human is produced undergoes an unprecedented deepening of the practical-political mystery of separation."

5   Giorgio Agamben, *Language and Death: The Place of Negativity* (Il linguaggio e la morte. Un seminario sul luogo della negatività) (Torino: Einaudi, 1982).

6   Giorgio Agamben, *The Coming Community*, trans. Michael Hardt (Minneapolis: University of Minnesota Press, 1990).

7   Giorgio Agamben, *Homo Sacer: Sovereign Power and Bare Life*, trans. Daniel Heller-Roazen (Stanford: Stanford University Press, 1995).

*Kenneth Surin*  | Rewriting the
Ontological Script
of Liberation: On the
Question of Finding
a New Kind of Political
Subject

THERE IS A CONVENTIONAL wisdom in the history of philosophy regarding the more or less intrinsic connection between the metaphysical-epistemological project that seeks an absolute ground for thought or reason, and the philosophico-political project of finding a ground in reason for the modus operandi of a moral and political subject. According to the lineaments of this well-seasoned narrative, the essential congruence between the rational subject of thought and the complementary subject of morality and politics was posited by Plato and Aristotle, and this unity between the two kinds of subject then found its suitably differentiated way into the thought of Hobbes, Locke, Spinoza, Leibniz, Hume, Kant, and Hegel (among many others). The core of this narrative is expressed by the somewhat Kantian proposition, characteristic of the Enlightenment in general, that reason provides the vital and indispensable criterion by which all judgments concerning belief, morality, politics, and art are to be appraised. On this view, reason is the faculty that defines and regulates the thinking being's activity, while this activity is in turn the essential means for reason's deployment in any thinking about the world, for the thinking being's capacity to describe and explain the world in ways that accord fundamentally with reason's precepts, precisely because reason is the irreducibly prior and enabling condition of any use of this capacity. Reason, in other words, constitutes the thinking being, and the activity of this being in turn enables reason to unfold dynamically (to provide a somewhat Hegelian gloss on this initially Kantian proposition). In the topography of this unfolding of reason, both thought and politics find their foundation.

The philosophical tradition provides another way of delineating this connection between the subject of thought and the political subject, one that also derives its focal point from Kant. Using the distinction between a *subjectum* (the thing that serves as the bearer *of* something, be it consciousness or some other property of the individual) and a *subjectus* (the thing that is subjected *to* something else), the tradition has included among its repertoire of concepts a figure of thought taken from medieval philosophy that hinges on the relation between the *subjectum* and the *subjectus*. Etienne Balibar, in his fascinating essay "Citizen Subject," uses this distinction to urge that we not identify Descartes's thinking thing (*res cogitans*) with the transcendental subject of thought that very quickly became an ineliminable feature of modern epistemology. Nothing could be further from the truth, says Balibar, because the human being is for Descartes the unity of a soul and a body, and this unity, which marks the essence of the human being, cannot be represented in terms of the *subjectum* (presumably because the *subjectum*, qua intellectual simple nature, can exist logically without requiring the presupposition of a unity between soul and body).[1] As the unity of a soul and a body, the human individual is not a mere intellectual simple nature, a subjectum, but is, rather, a subject in another quite different sense. In this other different sense, the human individual is a subject transitively related to an other, a "something else," and for Descartes this "something else" is precisely the divine sovereignty. In other words, for Descartes the human individual is really a *subjectus*, and never the *subjectum* of modern epistemology (which in any case owes its discovery to Locke and not to Descartes). For Balibar, therefore, it is important to remember that Descartes, who in many ways is really a late scholastic philosopher, was profoundly engaged with a range of issues that had been central for medieval philosophy, in this particular case the question of the relation of lesser beings to the supreme being, a question which both Descartes and the medieval philosophers broached, albeit in differing ways, under the rubric of the divine sovereignty.

The Cartesian subject is thus a *subjectus*, one who submits, and this in at least two ways that were significant for both Descartes and medieval political theology: (1) the subject submits to the Sovereign who is the Lord God, and (2) the subject also yields to the earthly authority of the prince who is God's representative on earth. As Descartes put it in his letter to Mersenne (April 15, 1630): "Do not hesitate I tell you, to avow and proclaim everywhere, that it is God who has established the laws of nature, as a King establishes laws in his Kingdom."[2] From this passage, and from his other writings, it is clear that the notion of sovereignty was at once political *and* theological for Descartes, as it had been for the earlier scholastic philosophers. This is not the place for a detailed discussion of Balibar's argument, which in addition to being a little sketchy is also not entirely new — G. W. Leibniz, Antoine Arnauld, and Nicolas Malebranche had long ago viewed Descartes, roughly their contemporary, as a follower in the footsteps of Augustine who found philosophy's raison d'être in the soul's contemplation of its relation to God, and who therefore took the dependence of lesser beings on the supreme eminence as philosophy's primary concern.[3]

But if Locke is the inventor of the modern concept of the self, who then is the real author of the fully-fledged concept of the transcendental subject, if Balibar is right to insist that it is not Descartes? The true culprit here, says Balibar, is not Descartes, but Kant, who needed the concept of the transcendental subject to account for the "synthetic unity" that provides the necessary conditions for objective experience. Kant chose to foist onto Descartes something that was really his own "discovery," and with Heidegger as his more than willing subsequent accomplice in this dubious undertaking, the outcome of this grievous misattribution has been momentous for our understanding (or lack thereof) of the course taken by the history of philosophy.[4] Kant, however, was about more than just the "discovery" of the transcendental subject. The Kantian subject had also to prescribe duties for itself in the name of the categorical imperative, and in so doing carve out a realm of freedom in nature that would enable this subject to free itself from a "self-inflicted tutelage" that arises when we can't make judgments without the supervision of an other, and this of course includes the tutelage of the King. The condition for realizing any such ideal on the part of the enlightened subject is the ability to submit to nothing but the rule of reason in making judgments, and so to be free from the power of the despot when making one's judgments entails a critical repositioning of the place from which sovereignty is exercised: no more is this place the body of the King, since for Kant this "tutelage" is stoppable only if the subject is able to owe its allegiance to a republican polity constituted by the rule of reason and nothing but the rule of reason.

Whatever criticism Balibar levels at Kant for the (supposed) historical mistake he made with regard to Descartes, the philosopher from east Prussia nonetheless emerges as a very considerable figure in Balibar's account. For Kant also created the concept of a certain kind of practical subject, one who operates in the realm of freedom, and this practical subject, whose telos is the ultimate abolition of any kind of "self-inflicted tutelage," had to destroy the "subject" of the King (i.e., the subjectus of Descartes and medieval political theology) in order to become a "self-legislating" rational being. Kant therefore simultaneously created the transcendental subject (i.e., the subjectum of modern epistemology) and discredited philosophically the subjectus of the previous philosophical and political dispensation. The concomitant of Kant's philosophical evisceration of the "subject" of the King was thus the political emergence of the republican citizen who from 1789 onward would supplant the subject/subjectus of the previous epoch. In the process, Descartes's philosophical world of subjects who submit to the laws of God and King was dislodged by Kant's world of "self-legislating" rational subjects who engage in this legislation precisely by adverting to the notions of right and duty. This new subject is the embodiment of right and of the operation of practical reason (right being for Kant the outcome that can be guaranteed only by the proper use of practical reason), and furthermore the subject is considered a citizen to the extent he or she embodies the general will, in which case the only laws worthy of the name are those framed to reflect "the united will of the whole nation."[5] Sovereignty is thus glossed by Kant through a recasting of the Rousseauian social contract. Laws are rationally promulgated only when they exemplify the general will, and this exemplification of the general will is possible only if there is a perfectly just civil constitution. The outcome, as the philosophy textbooks tell us, was a crucial separation of the earthly from the heavenly city. However, if Kant is the inaugurator of the Citizen Subject, then for Balibar Michel Foucault is the great theorist of the transition from the world of kingly and divine sovereignty to the world of rights and duties determined by the state and its apparatuses, and Balibar concludes his essay with the following observation: "As to whether this figure [the Citizen Subject] like a face of sand at the edge of the sea, is about to be effaced with the next great sea change, that is another question. Perhaps it is nothing more than Foucault's own utopia, a necessary support for that utopia's facticity."[6] I would like now to address the Foucauldian question left by Balibar for future consideration and pose the question of the current destination or fate of the Citizen Subject. To do this we have to look again at Kant.

The reason that constitutes the subject is perforce a Transcendental Reason. The Kantian inflection here is not accidental, because the reason that grounds the subject is not a reason that can be specified within the terms of the activity of the subject: this reason is the basis of this subject's very possibility qua subject, and by virtue of that, reason is necessarily exterior to the subject. Reason in this kind of employment is thus the activity of a single and universal quintessence whose object is reason itself, so that reason has necessarily to seek its ground within itself, as Hegel noted.[7] Reason, by virtue of its self-grounding, is perforce the writing of the Absolute.[8] The subject's ground, which has to reside in Reason itself, is therefore entirely and properly metaphysical, and any crisis of Transcendental Reason unavoidably becomes a philosophical crisis of the subject. Kant himself was the first to realize this, though it was left to his philosophical successors in the movement known as "early Romanticism" (*Frühromantik*), to make the acknowledgment of this crisis of Transcendental Reason into a starting-point for philosophical reflection.

With Nietzsche, however, the hitherto radical figure of the transcendental subject is propelled into a crisis, and with this crisis the fundamental convergence between the metaphysical-epistemological subject and the philosophico-political subject is denied plausibility. We all know from the basic textbooks in the history of philosophy that reason, insofar as it operates on both the understanding and the will, is placed by Nietzsche entirely within the ambit of the *wille zur macht*, so that power or desire becomes the enabling basis of any epistemological or moral and political subject, thereby irretrievably undermining or dislocating both kinds of subject. As a result of the intervention represented by Nietzsche, truth, goodness, and beauty, that is, the guiding transcendental notions for the constitution of this epistemological and moral and political subject, are henceforth to be regarded merely as the functions and ciphers of this supervening will to power. The same conventional wisdom also assures us that Marx and Freud likewise "undid" the two kinds of subject and thus undermined even further any basis for their essential congruence. The constellation formed by Nietzsche, Marx, and Freud (and their successors) shows both the transcendental subject and the ethico-political subject of action to be mere conceptual functions, lacking any substantial being (Kant of course having already argued in the *Critique of Pure Reason* that the subject of thought is not a substance).

This hackneyed narrative about the collective impact of the great "masters of suspicion" is fine as it goes; what is far more interesting, however, is the story of what had to come after Nietzsche, Marx, and Freud, of what it is that was going to be done with the ruins of the epistemological and moral and political subject who ostensibly had reigned from Plato to Hegel before receiving its quietus in the latter part of the nineteenth century. It is interesting that Balibar, who is as resolute a Marxist as anyone could be in these supposedly post-Marxist days, appears not to take on board Marx's critique of bourgeois democracy in "Citizen Subject" but instead regards Foucault as the thinker who, more than any other, registered the crisis of this subject. Be that as it may, it is hard to deny that the transcendental subject of modern epistemology suffered calamitously at the hands of Nietzsche (and Heidegger after Nietzsche), and that political and philosophical developments in the twentieth century cast the Citizen Subject adrift in a rickety lifeboat headed in the direction of the reefs mapped by Foucault.

But can the course of this stricken lifeboat be altered, and the functions and modes of expression typically associated with the Citizen Subject be reconstituted in some more productive way, so that this subject, or its successor (but who would that putative successor be?), would be able to meet the political and philosophical demands generated by the presently emerging conjuncture? Here one senses a certain ambivalence at the end of Balibar's essay, a wish that Foucault was perhaps not going to be right when it came to a final reckoning of the fate of the Citizen Subject, and that new and better times will somehow come to await a radically transformed Citizen Subject. But what could the shape and character of this new life for the Citizen Subject be? Balibar has an emphatic proposal: the Citizen Subject will live only by becoming a revolutionary actor. I want to take Balibar's proposal as the starting point for the discussion that will occupy the rest of this paper. There is also the question of the theoretical "space" that used to be occupied by the transcendental subject of epistemology. While we may not quarrel with Balibar's suggestion that the Citizen Subject supplanted the subjectus that owed its fealty to the sovereign monarch and sovereign deity, it has also to be acknowledged, and Balibar himself is certainly aware of this, that Kant placed under the category of *Right* not merely action, but also knowledge: the Kantian subject is both the Citizen Subject who acts and the epistemological subject who reflects in accordance with the principles of Reason. This subject may have been displaced or finally extinguished in the latter part of the twentieth century, but the question of the "right use" of Reason remains, or at any rate, the question of the place of a hoped-for right use of Reason still poses itself. This question is therefore one that demands to be addressed.

Whatever Foucault may have said about the supersession of the postclassical episteme, and the death of Man-Citizen that accompanied this supersession (I take Foucault's Man-Citizen to be coextensive with Balibar's Citizen Subject), it is obvious here that the subsequent mutation of classical liberalism into a globalizing neoliberalism and the disappearance of socialism to form the basis of a new conjuncture—a conjuncture some have called the "postpolitical" politics of the time after 1968—represents an added inconvenience for the already punishing trajectory taken by this Citizen Subject or Man-Citizen. The culmination of this trajectory in the postpolitical politics of the last few decades seems at one and the same time to reduce the weight of the critique represented by Nietzsche, Marx, and Freud (the subject's apparent superfluity in this postpolitical dispensation undermines the very need for its critique; with the effacement of the object of critique, critique also finds itself fading into nothingness), while at the same time making more urgent the question of the ontological status of the subject of this postpolitical politics (is it still some kind of vestigially effective subject, a barely breathing remnant of the Man-Citizen of Foucault's modern episteme or Balibar's Citizen Subject of the time after 1789?); and if so, what powers (if any) reside in this brute remnant, or are we left today with nothing for the metaphysical constitution of the possibility of politics but the sheer acknowledgment of the power of the body, the power of bare life (as proposed by the thinkers of the "inoperative" community and the community to come), or the appeal to some kind of undeconstructable justice (as proposed by Derrida and his epigone)? We don't have to hear too much along these lines in order to recognize that the practices and orders of thought associated with the "societies of control" limned by Deleuze, and those of the domain of the biopolitical identified by Foucault, but also developed by Agamben and Hardt and Negri, each derives their saliency from this postpolitical conjuncture. The centrality of the problematic of the postpolitical for any putative project of liberation can therefore hardly be gainsaid.

By the 1960s and 1970s it had become clear, or clear enough, that the politics of the last two hundred years was no longer able to manage the complex and uneven movements of force that had been unleashed by the newest regimes of capitalist accumulation. Although many periodizations take 1789 to be the emblematic starting point for this politics—which by the 1970s and 1980s had become more and more clearly visible as a "previous politics"—by such a politics we mean both a politics based on centrally planned economies of the party-state (i.e., the system of government that existed in the former eastern bloc) and one predicated on the market-oriented liberal-democratic state (associated in a complementary way with what is however still called "the West"). This politics, even in countries of the former Soviet bloc, was always the politics of a particular phase of capitalist development. As indicated, it lasted from 1789 until the first unravellings of this international system in the early 1970s.[9] As has also been noted, the metaphysical heart of this politics was a particular conception of sovereignty and of the political subject ideally subsumed under the benison of this sovereignty through the principle of representation. With the new capitalist dispensation that came into being in the 1960s and early 1970s, a dispensation now described and analyzed under several familiar titles ("post-Fordism," "disorganized capitalism," "flexible accumulation," "worldwide integrated capitalism," "late capitalism," "empire after the age of imperial empires," "the domain of the biopolitical," and so forth), such notions of sovereignty were progressively enervated or circumvented. These unprecedented transformations in the capitalist order were accompanied by an attenuation and deracination of the "classical" political subject, that is, the subject who up to now had been at once enabled and constrained by the principles of sovereignty embodied by the previous political dispensation.[10] To put it somewhat schematically, if Nietzsche, Marx, and Freud undid this classical epistemological and political subject, and in the process undermined its philosophical rationales, then the move to a postpolitical politics associated with the latest stage of capitalist development has had, ostensibly, the effect of doing away with the very need for such a classical Citizen Subject as well as the accompanying philosophical rationales provided on its behalf.[11] The thing rendered equivocal and otiose by Nietzsche, Marx, and Freud, but still needed by the politics that had lasted from 1789 up to the 1970s, had by the 1970s become a sheer relic.

Transnational capitalism and the neoliberal ideology identified with its current ascendancy simply have no need for the classical Citizen Subject, just as they have no need for the ideology of modernization that was an intrinsic component of the first or classical liberalism and the various socialisms and communisms that rivaled this liberalism. One does not have to be Naomi Klein, Will Hutton, or Ignacio Ramonet to acknowledge that, however complex the processes that led to the emergence of the current phase of capitalist development, it is virtually undeniable that consumers, corporations, and markets have now gained in legitimacy and power at the expense of the Citizen-Subject and the accompanying notion, integral to the "previous" politics just referred to, of a sovereignty lodged unconditionally in the state and its constituent administrative agencies. The historical and social conditions that served to legitimize the state and its functions, as well as the figure of this citizen-subject, were severely undermined in the episteme instituted by transnational late capitalism, whose influential proponents in the overdeveloped economies of the North now administer everything in the name of capitalist accumulation. Enron and other energy companies effectively police the U.S. government's energy policy, Italy's government is in the pocket of one of its richest men (who bought his way into the prime ministership of his country), Tony Blair's entourage at the recent Johannesburg Earth Summit included the boss of one of Britain's biggest corporate polluters, weapons manufacturers are so completely in league with ministries of defense in the advanced industrial countries that this is no longer reckoned a scandal, and so forth. In the place of the Citizen Subject posited as an ideal by the political systems of the nineteenth- and twentieth-centuries by and large stands a new kind of ideal subject, to wit, a consumer-subject cajoled and tutored in this country by Disney and *USA Today*, and in place of the ideal of the sovereign state by and large stands a state formation that has been transformed over the course of the last few decades into a more loosely amalgamated bundle of functions and apparatuses (economic, political, ideological, military, and so forth), with some functions and apparatuses demanding relatively high concentrations of state power for their operation, and others not.

It is important not to exaggerate the outcomes and implications of this postpolitical politics for state-formations, tempting though it is to declare that the state has no place in today's "borderless world." The truth in regard to state formations is quite different: in some domains, state-power has been drastically weakened, in others it has been more or less effectively neutralized, but in still others it has, if anything, been strengthened (globalization notwithstanding). State projects, to use Bob Jessop's helpful term, are constituted more and more through multiple and even contradictory armatures and their associated structural and strategic capacities. There are states that are and aren't nations (France being an example of the former and Cyprus of the latter); there are nations that are and aren't states (France again being an example of the former and Kurdistan of the latter); there are states that are functional and those that exist precisely in order not to be functional (Switzerland being an example of the former and Somalia of the latter); there are cities that are states (Hong Kong and Singapore) and there are continental regimes that encompass several different kinds of state (NAFTA, the EU); and where forms of state governance in the advanced industrial countries are concerned, there are Keynesian welfare states and those that are Schumpeterian workfare states (the United States being an example of the latter, Germany of the former); and there are also emerging forms of a parastatial civil society not delimited by national boundaries, as when the indigenous peoples of Australia form linkages with those of Mexico and New Zealand.[12] But this variety and complexity notwithstanding, state projects and their associated conceptions of citizenship are today permeated by a powerful neoliberal sensibility that glorifies the convergence of a minimalist state with a deregulated economy and insists implacably that the rate of profit be maximized at every turn.[13] The economic and political logic behind this convergence has come to be questioned in the last few years, especially since the bursting of the 1990s U.S. speculative bubble, but this mistrust of neoliberalism is never, in itself, going to be able to restore the classical Citizen Subject. The demise of this subject was one of the outcomes of the cluster of conditions responsible for the subsequent emergence of neoliberalism, and it will take the removal of these prior enabling conditions, and not just the passing of neoliberalism per se, to put in place a new kind of political subject. For these new conditions to come into being, a new kind of state practical logic for dealing with the state will first have to materialize: nothing less will suffice.

The state, no matter how weak or powerful, is not, however, a mere arrangement of apparatuses or functions. As Sean Sayers and Phil Corrigan point out in their somewhat neglected book *The Great Arch*, the state never stops speaking.[14] The state speaks to and from its idea before it even becomes the "thing" that is embodied in institutions, constitutions, legal protocols, and the activities of functionaries: the ability to "imagine" the state is something that has to exist before the state can be brought into being, and the state begins speaking the moment it can be imagined. In the past the state used to speak by using the compelling and simultaneously inhibiting social power of the sovereign (or its cognate forces) to subdue the ineffective and wasteful power of the citizen-individual. When this was accomplished, the state became fully-fledged, and the practical exercising of its sovereign principle was able to unite, more or less decisively, the many potentially recalcitrant individual wills into a collectively harmonious power of the people or the body politic (or so it was maintained). The state, on this view, is external to the body politic: as the constituting force and arbitrator imposing order on the disorganized elements of the body politic, which it does through the various organs of representation available to it, the state stands above the jumbled panoply of individual wills ranged below it. Hobbes, Locke, Pufendorf, Spinoza, Rousseau, Kant, Sieyès, and Hegel were the primary philosophical architects of this conception of the state as the architectonic force that created a single polity out of the contending elements lodged within it, and this conception regulated the political dispensation that lasted until the 1970s.[15]

While we may seek a more contemporary understanding of this "speaking" of the state by resorting to the Althusserian notion of an "interpellation" of its subjects by the state's ideological apparatuses, or Deleuze and Guattari's conception of the state as an immense, criss-crossing apparatus that mobilizes a repertoire of codes to regulate every possible kind of entity (linguistic, monetary, military, political, educational, racial and ethnic, etc.), and while the state continues to speak even in the postpolitical order that emerged in the last few decades of the twentieth century, it no longer does so by privileging the kind of rational and political subject who becomes an object of representation through the implementation of the principle of a people's sovereignty. Instead, in today's postpolitical politics the state effectively eviscerates or dispenses altogether with the principle of this sovereignty, and speaks, more or less straightforwardly, the language of an all-encompassing hedonistic capitalism (one recalls here George W. Bush's passionate appeal in the days after the destruction of the World Trade Center that Americans make it their patriotic duty to begin shopping again).

The postpolitical state coddles this hedonistic capitalism by harnessing it to a populist lowest common denominator that preempts real criticism of capital or state. This populism, which pervades the state's mode of social regulation, is typically expressed in such nostrums as "The government does not create wealth, it only taxes it," "There is no such thing as society, there are only individuals," "When guns are outlawed, only outlaws will have guns," "America: love it or leave it," "If the United States has a national health-insurance system, a bureaucrat will choose your doctor for you," and so forth. The principle of representation, integral to the "previous" politics and its Citizen Subjects, has nowadays been pretty much reduced to a shuffling and reshuffling of the seating arrangements in congressional and parliamentary chambers. However, by inserting itself strategically into the realm of the popular consciousness, and by in effect becoming the metacorporation that safeguards the other corporations, at least where the promotion of capital accumulation is concerned, the postpolitical state situates itself willy-nilly within the political field: unlike the "previous" politics that in principle presumed the externality of the state to this field, the current postpolitical dispensation has reduced the distinctiveness of state formations, so that the state has now tended in certain domains to become one institutional agent among others, or at any rate is now more easily decomposed into its component functions, each of which can be hived off or outsourced to other social and economic agents, invariably with a view to maximizing the profit rate. The state today in most countries runs prisons, radio and television stations, schools, hospitals, asylums, airlines, railways, laboratories, telephone systems, banks and pension funds, and farms, but then so do private companies, often side by side with their state-owned counterparts, or sometimes in conjunction with the state. As many commentators have noted, this trend toward a "market-friendly" economic policy is frequently coupled with the espousal of a populist modus operandi in the state's administration of culture and the social mores: populist positions are widely prevalent in policy debates in the advanced industrial countries concerning immigration, law and order, education, privatization policy, governmental inefficiency (whether merely perceived or otherwise), environmental issues, social welfare provision, foreign aid, free trade, rural life, religious freedom, hunting, gun control, and so forth. By often casting its positions in these debates in a populist vein, the state is drawn inexorably into the political field, and these positions are then susceptible to challenges in ways not conceivable when the state constituted itself as the absolute arbiter of politics by purporting to stand firmly above the political fray.[16]

The postpolitical state, as much as it espouses "market-friendly" and populist policy positions in all its activities, has however to retain a considerable state capacity, since it is also a competition state whose rationale is the pursuit of competitive advantage over its rivals. The securing of competitive advantage can then be translated into tangible monetary assets, the possession of which enhances the power of the state, so that whereas in the previous phase of capitalist development states sought power in order to gain competitive advantages that could then be translated into wealth, nowadays states acquire wealth that can be transmuted into power. This accounts for a novel and peculiar feature of America's current hegemony, namely, that the United States and its economic allies assure their preeminence primarily by keeping the rest of the world in debt, debt that is denominated in strong U.S. dollars, so that the less-wealthy countries are trapped in endless spirals of debt repayment and can never challenge this hegemony. This is the postmodern equivalent of the debt peonage that characterized premodern societies, the only real difference being that whereas in premodern societies it was a peasant who was indebted a landowner, now it is whole countries that are indebted in ways that redound to the colossal advantage of the wealthier nations, and especially the United States. So for all that globalization is purported to amount to, the prevailing mode of capitalist accumulation is still premised on the effective functioning of the various national capitals. The system in which states struggle for competitive advantage is thus one that still has individual nation-states as its primary units.

The postpolitical state is still therefore very much a national state, and it finds its raison d'être and fulfills itself precisely by serving as a "model of realization" for capital in this competitive system.[17] It does this by mobilizing a range of sectors and their agents, which are sorted and aligned according to the wealth they can realize, as well as demographic considerations, the availability of natural resources, trade and industrial policy, levels of technological development, the relation of national-capital to world-capital markets, and most important of all, the existing configuration of social relations. The claim that the state transcends politics is therefore true in one sense: for the state to mobilize capital through its control of the system of social regulation, the state has to be a field in which class contradictions and conflicts can be resolved and social compromises forged, and as the "container" of these antagonisms and architect of the resultant compromises, the state has to appear to be "above" politics.[18] Today, in other words, the postpolitical state is both "above" politics (in the sense just specified) and at the same time an agent, indeed the principal agent, within the political domain. The action of the state in the political domain invariably does not appear as such but rather takes the form of a direct administration of social formations and the cultural forces sustained by these formations. The state uses its resources of power and coercion expressly to transform cultural traditions and social structures, while appearing all the time to be the "thing" that is above any actual and specific exercise of governance, and in this way it can profess to be acting "in the common interest."

The postpolitical state and the capitalist regimes of accumulation authorized by it thus have explicitly cultural objects and cultural identities, as much as stocks and bonds, as their currency. Through the relentless administration of culture, the state reconstitutes social subjects and market participants (and nonparticipants), who by virtue of this reconstitution become the agents and bearers of the capitalist state's "substance." In the course of expressing the capitalist state's "substance," these subjects are constrained by the state and its component organizations (on this issue the Frankfurt School is perhaps more right than ever), even as they exercise varying degrees of command on behalf of the state (and ipso facto of capital). But the power of the state is really and ultimately only that of a radical disempowerment, since the capitalist state can maintain itself only by neutralizing as thoroughly as it can any force capable of undermining the state and its capitalist raison d'être. The capitalist state has of course always been in the business of holding down living labor in order to empower the various capitalist regimes of production and accumulation.

In the past—before the current postpolitical constellation—the capitalist system had to undertake this regimentation of living labor against the backdrop of an active and effectual politics, one which, regardless of how circumscribed or disorganized it was, at least afforded its protagonists the possibility of differentiating meaningfully between a political left and whatever it was that stood in opposition to that left. In that "previous" politics, both the left and the right had to confront each other as their respective exteriorities precisely as a condition of engaging in politics. There was in principle the viable option of an emancipatory or a reactionary politics, or at any rate, the conflicts and contradictions between the two kinds of politics were discernible at the level of the state's structures and strategies. And beyond the somewhat more immediate and limited exteriorities of day-to-day politics, with left posed against right on this or that issue, lay the "space" of the one superordinate exteriority, that is, the absolute possibility of being able to strive for a decisive alternative to any and all existing political arrangements ("revolution" in other words). Integral to the "previous" politics, therefore, was the possibility of setting aside the old order in the name of an entirely new social reality. Today, by contrast, a liberation that seeks to turn things upside down seems pervasively unrealizable: as my colleague Fredric Jameson has remarked, it's easier for us nowadays to contemplate the total destruction of the earth through some ecological catastrophe than it is to believe that capitalism will come to an end. Where left and right were once able to contend, there is now a void in which any real distinction between left and right is blurred, and the demarcation between the dominant and the marginalized, central to the previous politics (and indeed to *any* politics), is harder to locate if not effaced altogether.[19]

The question of this exteriority to the political as it is presently constituted is a crucial one for thought today. It is the overarching framework for Derrida's reflections on today's unavoidable "spectralization" of Marx, and for Hardt and Negri's understanding of empire ("empire" being for Hardt and Negri the political order of a worldwide capitalism that has subsumed every conceivable space around it), while Slavoj Žižek and Alain Badiou have both argued that the twentieth century was the age of the great and overwhelmingly powerful revolutionary transformations, transformations that occurred on the right as well as the left. Politics today is postpolitical precisely to the extent that there is no such exteriority to the political as it actually exists, no enabling point in the so-called liberal democracies from which to pose a genuine social democracy against the regnant liberalism, let alone one that will overturn the system in its entirety. The project of liberation can be viable only if it is predicated on the need to find this exteriority once more. Only then will there be an alternative to the mutually reinforcing relationship that exists between this neoliberal conjuncture and world-integrated capitalism.

Three basic kinds of exteriority are involved here: (1) that in which there is the bare possibility of establishing a political alignment beyond something that is currently left or something that is currently right (exteriority as the political boundary between left and right); (2) that in which it is possible for the entirety of the political field to be superseded by a completely new configuration of possibilities, such as a radically new mode of production, a completely overturned system of governance, and so forth (exteriority as the space of revolutionary transformation); and (3) that exteriority in which it becomes possible for desire to surpass itself in ways that desire itself cannot know or anticipate (exteriority as the threshold of ontological transformation or exteriority as a new regime of truth or encounter with the [Žižekian] Real). These exteriorities, at the very least (1) and certainly (2), have necessarily to be on the agenda for any project of liberation that cannot be collapsed into actually existing liberalism and world-integrated capitalism, while (3) is the sine qua non of any revolutionary change capable of finally negating the forms of self-justifying power that are integral to the maintenance of the capitalist system and its liberal-democratic appurtenances. In fact, it could be argued that the exteriority expressed by (3) is the one that guarantees the potential efficacy of those contained in (1) and (2).

There seem these days to be four main options for organizing a politics directly motivated by the quest for liberation: the politics of identity, the politics of subjectivity, the politics of the Event, and the politics of the multitude. Of these possible bases for launching the project of liberation in any substantive sense, we can discount more or less immediately the politics of identity, since it seems to be little more than an extension of the actually existing liberal democracy that dovetails so smoothly into actually existing capitalism. Nearly thirty years ago the late Robert Nozick argued, in his *Anarchy, State, and Utopia*, that the minimalist state propounded by him in that book was entirely compatible with a whole range of communal options, with the sole proviso that individuals should be free to join and free to leave these communities. In this "utopia of utopias" (the phrase is Nozick's) there will be communities that consist of "visionaries and crackpots, maniacs and saints, monks and libertines, capitalists and communists and participatory democrats, proponents of phalanxes (Fourier), palaces of labor (Flora Tristan), villages of unity and cooperation (Owen), mutualist communities (Proudhon), time stores (Josiah Warren), Bruderhof, kibbutzim, kundalini yoga ashrams, and so forth."[20] As long as they adhere to the absolutely unobtrusive framework of rights that overarches these communities, "anyone may start *any* sort of new community (compatible with the operation of the framework) they wish. (No community may be excluded, on paternalistic grounds, nor may lesser paternalistic restrictions geared to nullify supposed defects in people's decision processes be imposed—for example compulsory information programs, waiting periods.)" The supervening minimalist regime of rights and rules remains impartial and detached from these communities, and their members simply get on with their lives. So in this utopia there is no politics, and moreover there can be no need for politics.[21] It would not be unfair to view Nozick's proposals for a utopia as the culminating-point or utopia for any identity politics, and at the same time as the integral *reductio ad absurdum* of identity politics. These proposals also show graphically the ultimate bankruptcy of any rights-based regime not accompanied by a substantive conception of human well-being. Slavoj Žižek has been the most trenchant recent critic of this identity politics, and I see no reason in principle to disagree with the import of his critique.

Less easy to dismiss is the politics of subjectivity, which we can associate with any politics premised on the notion of a reciprocity between a subject and its other. Derrida is the most notable exponent of the thought of such a politics, though where Derrida is concerned Levinas is of course very much the background force inspiriting this line of ethico-political thought. A detailed argument is needed to press home a compelling critique of the politics of subjectivity, especially since Derrida has scrupulously insisted on the need for a thoroughgoing renovation of the discourse of the subject.[22] Nonetheless, I think Simon Critchley is right in claiming that for all Derrida's firmness in maintaining that the "post-deconstructed" subject begins with a constituting nonidentity with itself, and that its underpinning as subject comes precisely from a call made by the other (justice then being defined as one's irreducible responsibility for the other in the face of the undecidability that pervades one's relationship with the other), there is still an unavoidable sense in which the politics that comes from this conception of the subject is a politics of decision vitiated by Derrida's inability to tell us how the (seemingly always solitary) subject moves from ever-present undecidability to concrete political decision.[23] Toni Negri did not mince words in his response to Derrida's *Specters of Marx* when he said that Derrida's insistence on "solitary transcendental horizons" when expounding his conception of justice means that Derrida had nothing really to say about exploitation and the forms of capitalist regulation that subtend this exploitation. Negri is absolutely right—the tragedy of the politics of subjectivity (at least the Derridean version thereof) is that it has no way of inserting the subject into the domain of the actually political.[24] We are left instead with a paralyzing Kierkegaardian pathos that provides no way of imagining resistance at the level of a politics of collective action.

The politics of the Event, associated here with Alain Badiou and (to a lesser extent) Slavoj Žižek, finds the possibilities of a reinvigorated militancy in the political reorientation opened up by a particular kind of singularization, one stemming from an encounter with the Real or a truth-event (the primary exemplars of this kind of singularization being such figures as St. Paul or Lenin). From these remarkable and distinctive singularizations there emerge possibilities of a rupture with the baneful reality of the present, and in turn with such ruptures come potential anticapitalist political interventions. Several of his commentators have noted that Badiou's truth-events tend to be august and rather splendid (St. Paul's conversion, 1789, 1917, May 1968), as well as being associated with charismatically distinctive personages (Lenin, Mao, St. Paul), and Simon Critchley and others have criticized him for this political romanticism. The other problem with a politics of the exceptional event is that it is the right that is now using the category of the exceptional event to mobilize the very considerable resources of power and coercion that are at its disposal after September 11. September 11 is clearly the right-wing obverse of Badiou's 1968 truth-event, as evidenced by such claims as "things can never be the same again in America" or "from now on everything is different," used by George Bush and his handlers to mobilize American public opinion not just as a response to al-Qaeda, but also to promote the Republican Party's overall right-wing agenda. The left's attempts to mobilize a countervailing power to this right-wing truth-event have to involve the insistence that some things really have remained the same; that, for instance, the exigent claims of justice, the cause of equality, and so forth, have not been abolished or shelved by the events of September 11. As the country singer Steve Earle reminded an audience in London a few days after September 11: "George W. Bush did not stop being stupid on September 11."[25] If September 11 is the truth-event par excellence for us today (and this proposition is entertained here as a posit), then this is its profoundly fundamental truth, its "axiomatics": that the world will not be a better place for the majority of human beings as long as those who lead us continue to provide forms of psychic relief for the bewildered and confused, as well as the plain nasty, even though these forms (inducing a war fever over Iraq in the case of George W. Bush, conducting a xenophobic campaign against asylum seekers in the case of the Australian Prime Minister John Howard, making specious humanitarian appeals and riding the Princess Diana or Queen Mother "effect" in the case of Tony Blair) are utterly disabling, even in the shortest of short runs. A countervailing politics should not seek to predicate itself on the event of exception, and in this way would seek to organize signs in new ways, as well as finding new theoretical operations and formulations; it would discover novel and sometimes disturbing styles for organizing gestures and actions and expressing dissatisfactions, in many places and in many times. After all, even as tacit structures for the disclosure of revolutionary possibility taken in the most abstract sense, St. Paul and 1968 mean nothing for most of the inhabitants of the earth. The import of these notions may be implicitly universal, but they are not pragmatically available to those who lack a basic familiarity with the foundations of Christianity or the thwarted revolution of 1968. Finding ways, in their specific locations and contexts, of getting rid of the shah of Iran, or Margaret Thatcher, or George W. Bush, or the local tyrant, on the contrary possess a saliency that is politically less elusive. To accomplish such things urgently needed and sought-for patterns of revolutionary opportunity will have to be sought, and hopefully found, in theoretical formulation as much as on the streets. But it is not clear that we need the singularization of an exceptional event for such a politics.

The politics of the multitude, which can be identified with Deleuze and Guattari's nomadology and Hardt and Negri's *Empire*, has the two primary virtues. First, unlike its counterpart politics of the exceptional event, it does not rely on the extraordinary event to provide the basis for the convergence of collective agents around a project of liberation. The crowds who seemingly emerged out of nowhere to restore Hugo Chavez to the presidency of Venezuela after he had been deposed in a coup, or the similar crowds of protesters at the Genoa G8 summit, both constitute multitudes whose actions are regarded by some as harbingers of significant future political transformations.[26] Second, and in a more philosophical vein, multitude theory has the great merit of bypassing the problematic of representation identified earlier with the "previous" politics' model of sovereignty—the model that requires an orchestration, primarily through the mediation of the state, of the mass of individual wills into a single collective will or body politic. This assembling of the hodge-podge of individual wills into "the people" is then regarded by proponents of this political tradition as the essential, indeed transcendental, condition for effective political action. In multitude theory this axiom of political action is totally dispensed with, and this because the logic of the multitude's political being cannot but be structurally autopoetic: the multitude directs itself according to its own powers and its own history. It should be noted that overlaps are possible between multitude theory and the politics of the event, this convergence being very evident in the work of Deleuze and Guattari, for instance, whose nomadology provides the logic for a project of struggle, but who also accord certain events (the foundation of the paleolithic state, May 1968, and so forth) a decisive political significance.

It would be wrong to assume that we are behooved to choose between these different practico-theoretical models for a project of liberation. Of course, it does appear that multitude theory possesses fewer disadvantages than its rivals, and that in my admittedly sketchy account identity politics and the politics of subjectivity are virtual nonstarters in comparison to the alternatives against which they are ranged. But—and this is the suggestion I wish to develop now—the primacy we are likely to accord one or the other of these models for a project of liberation can be determined only ontologically. That is, this primacy can be determined only in relation to the "space" of an exteriority in which, as was said earlier, it becomes possible for desire to surpass itself in ways that desire itself cannot know or anticipate. What in principle are the conditions that allow this exteriority to exist and to be effective?

A number of candidates deserve the title of this exteriority. A prime candidate is the "universal pacified myth" of the vision of Christianity underwritten by the Radical Orthodoxy movement. Two reservations come to mind, however, when considering this proposal advanced in the name of Radical Orthodoxy.

The first is Radical Orthodoxy's reliance on the *via analogia*, as opposed to a Scotist, Spinozist, or Deleuzean univocity. The following set of claims will be hugely tendentious in the eyes of some, but the espousal of the via analogia ostensibly militates against Christianity's "universal pacified myth" in at least one respect, namely, that the via analogia necessarily introduces a hierarchy among beings, this hierarchy being specified in terms of a being's proximity in principle to the Godhead (angels being nearer the Godhead than humans, and so forth), so that there is the inevitable possibility of the sad passions arising when ontologically a being is lower down the hierarchy. For with analogy there is always a primary and a secondary analogate, so that some kind of *via eminentiae* becomes absolutely unavoidable, with one subject (the primary analogate) "producing" the other (the secondary or derivative analogate), at any rate "conceptually," through the unavoidable mechanism of the analogy of concepts. Christianity forestalls this pathos of ressentiment by retaining its Platonist philosophical antecedents, this Platonism in effect allowing a relationship of "peaceability" to be maintained between the primary and the derivative analogates, so that the eminence of the primary analogate does not ensue in a violence of intractable "difference" between it and its derivative analogates. But the price of this has to be the incorporation into Christianity of a version of the doctrine of preestablished harmony.[27] By sanctioning the equivalent of a preestablished harmony between levels of being, the unavoidably Platonized Christian mythos obviates the pathos of ressentiment that is bound to exist between the different levels of being (which, of course, an analogical doctrine is required to posit). But do we want to adopt some version of the doctrine of reestablished harmony?

Christianity's "peaceableness" is thus guaranteed only when there is logically prior commitment to the ontological requisites of a preestablished harmony (in fact acceptance of this divinely ordained harmony becomes an ontological condition for being a Christian), since this is the only way to preempt absolutely the occurrence of the sad passions. This preestablished harmony is thus vital for Christianity—its ineluctable weddedness to the great chain of being, without which it cannot operate the via analogia, is at once its power and its weakness. As was said, this problem for Christianity's "universal pacified myth" arises because hierarchies necessarily impose difference. But it could be argued that difference in itself is not necessarily to be identified with an inevitable ontological violence, since there can always be a peaceable difference (in the eyes of Radical Orthodoxy, this is precisely the ontological core of Christianity's "universal pacified myth") because, on this account, only Christianity is capable of providing a metaphysical legitimation of a difference that does not ensue in ontological violence. On this view, only Christianity can furnish an ontological backing for hierarchy that does not involve a recourse to terror, but if I am right, it can make this claim only because of its prior adherence to some version of the doctrine of preestablished harmony. There is an interesting implication here, because it has to follow from this that difference as difference will be peaceable only when all become Christians, for only then will there be the possibility of a peaceable acceptance of difference. The Christian mythos will work only when all are guided or constrained by it, which means that the via analogia can plausibly serve as the basis for Christianity's "universal pacified myth" only when the whole world is converted or somehow drawn toward the Christian mythos.[28] Christianity bestows harmony through "essence," which raises the question whether harmony can be given in this way, or whether, as urged by the Scotists, harmony can come only from the striving of collectivities whose efforts are organized by the operation of a will guided by eros (this a question I shall return to shortly). Univocity, the Scotist doctrine par excellence, is of course disavowed by Radical Orthodoxy, but it could be argued that it alone is capable of securing the principle of an accord among beings without overriding difference in the process, because for univocity (at least in its Scotist-Deleuzean rendition) difference resides purely and simply in the repetition of singularity, with there being no hierarchy among the singularities.[29]

Second, there is the matter of what comes first: the universal myth that founds peaceable difference, or the solidarity with other human beings, out of which comes the development and consolidation of a rationality that enjoins peaceability. The Christian mythos requires the first of these alternatives, whereas the Stoics and Hume, as well as Deleuze and Guattari, are to be aligned with the second of these choices. The problem with the immanentism of the position identified here with stoicism, Hume, and Deleuze and Guattari (which happens also to be my own position) is that solidarity is never attainable by desiring solidarity as an end in itself (the desire for solidarity for its own sake seems to be an inherently tragic desire, as when one seeks absurdly to make friends merely for the sake of having friends), so that a politics that never gets beyond politics is doomed to futility. Christianity is founded on a logic that affirms the rationality of a desire grounded in something beyond that which we know and desire, and to this extent it is ontologically disposed to acknowledge the exteriority premised on self-surpassing desire, the desire that gets beyond what desire itself can know or anticipate. This is a truly remarkable ontological asset (if one can speak of it in this way), since it enables Christianity ceaselessly to move beyond the limits necessarily constituted by the given (this movement being another name for the exteriority adverted to in this paper), and this of course is something that liberalism never really can do. Žižek is therefore quite right to insist that

Christianity and Marxism are the only two real metaphysical alternatives to liberalism. Faced with the ultimately spurious choice of harnessing Marxism to the ontological lineaments of Christianity, or trying somehow to make Marxism compatible with liberalism ("the management of difference that has always to be placed within limits in order to facilitate this bureaucratic administration of difference"—this aptly expresses liberalism's metaphysical nucleus), Žižek has clearly opted for the former. But are we confined to two, and only two, alternatives: on the one hand, a Marxism functioning concordantly with Christianity in the manner advocated by Žižek; or, on the other, a Marxism that, because it has no real way of engaging with its exteriority, can become only an approximation to liberalism (albeit one with a bit more struggle tacked on)? How is the project of liberation to come to a proper acknowledgment of the exteriority constituted by this self-surpassing desire? Here we should end where we began, that is, with the figure of Kant.

Kant broke with his scholastic precursors when he declined to view "being" as the transcendental of the transcendentals, and instead made "truth" and "judgment" function in place of "being" in his first *Critique*. Kant failed to see, however, that the notions of "truth" and "judgment" can't perform this surrogate function, for two reasons: first, making judgments always presupposes other judgments, and these in turn presuppose yet other judgments, and so on;[30] and second, the use of the notions of "truth" and "judgment" to serve as quasi-transcendentals depends in any case on a harmony of the faculties that simply can't be justified by reason.[31] So "imagination" (i.e., aesthetics) displaced judgment in the third *Critique*, as Kant made the *Critique of Judgment* complete the transcendental argument that could not be completed by his first *Critique*. Feeling (*Gefühl*) was initially kept outside the boundary delimited by the critical philosophy but inevitably became the organizing principle for completing the transcendental argument, since only feeling can harmonize the faculties. Just as important is another consequence of this Kantian shift from judgment to the imagination and feeling, which is that the sublime, necessarily lodged in the noumenal for Kant, becomes for him the only place for the properly ontological. German idealism then took over this axiom regarding the imagination as the proxy for the transcendental of transcendentals, and it is perhaps noteworthy that the contemporary interest in the "unpresentable" (the writings of Lyotard, Lacoue-Labarthe, Derrida, and Nancy come readily to mind in this connection) is really an extension of the exemplary philosophical pattern established by Kant. But this pattern has now run its course: today what is presentable in the popular culture is precisely the "unpresentable" as it is displayed in the phenomena that go under such labels as "panic culture," "trauma culture," "hyperreality," and so forth.

But how does one philosophize this momentous transformation, important as it is for any thinking about the absolute exteriority that is the metaphysical (though not the practical!) place from which any kind of movement toward a revolutionary transformation will have to issue as thought? What lies beyond this historic change, which in effect requires the very presentability of the sublime, where its being the sublime (i.e., the unpresentable) has become paradoxically the precise condition of its presentability? With the now normative reinsertion of the sublime into the realm of feeling and sensibility in this paradoxical movement (Kant in any case having prepared us for this shift with his linking of the sublime to time), the imagination has to yield to the sensibility (or so it would seem); or, more precisely, it would appear that feeling and the passions have supplanted the imagination at the level of the faculties. Kant's faculties, if we retain them, now necessarily relate to each other through affectivity and the structures of affect.

Kant's circumscription of reason had thus effectively broken down by the time he got to the third *Critique*, when he was forced to concede that the faculties cannot be regulated in their employment. Henceforth there could be no preestablished harmony of the faculties. Deleuze has a passage on the ground-breaking implications of Kant's "emancipation of dissonance" that is worth quoting:

> This is no longer the aesthetic of the *Critique of Pure Reason*, which considered the sensible as the quality that could be related to an object in space and time; nor is it the logic of the sensible, nor even a new logic that would be time. It is an aesthetic of the Beautiful and the Sublime, in which the sensible takes on an autonomous value for itself and is deployed in a pathos beyond all logic, and which will grasp time as it bursts forth (*dans son jaillissement*), at the very origin of its thread and its vertigo. This is no longer the Affect of the *Critique of Pure Reason*, which linked the Self to the I in a relationship that was still regulated by the order of time; it is a Pathos that lets them evolve freely in order to form strange combinations as sources of time, "arbitrary forms of possible intuitions." It is no longer the determination of an I, which must be joined to the determinability of the Self in order to constitute knowledge; it is now the undetermined unity of all the faculties (the Soul), which makes us enter the unknown.[32]

This unconstrained deployment of all the faculties inevitably politicizes any undertaking involving knowing, feeling, and doing, although this is a conclusion that Kant himself failed to draw. A very significant philosophical opportunity opened up by the "dissonant accords" (the phrase is Deleuze's) introduced by Kant in the *Critique of Judgment* comes with the accompanying acknowledgment that it is not reason which leads us to the real, but rather the will guided by eros, so that reason is produced as an effect that emerges from the will's striving. Kant thus opened a way that led back to Scotus and Spinoza, and from these figures a trajectory could be launched that takes us forward to Deleuze. The Scotist axioms that reality is to be approached by the will guided by love, and that reality is constituted by worlds of singularities, events, and virtualities, and not of subjects and objects, allows all these items to be "expressively" distributed: all kinds of possible worlds, extending to a potential infinity, can express the same singularity, event, or virtuality, so there is from the beginning a complete preemption of any bureaucratic administration of these "expressive" distributions and the worlds in which they are located. The very constitution of reality is politicized, but not in the sense that involves, necessarily and from the beginning, a coercive reigning-in, a management, of this multiplicity by the negative power of the state/sovereign. The distribution of expressivities is governed by a logic of ceaseless proliferation, one freed from any ontological dependence on the categories and principles of classical representation and the anthropological presuppositions that guided the previous architectonic of reason and the politics it sustained. With this uncontainable production of expressivity, there is an absolute "beyond" for all that is given. As the horizon for the critique of anything that is given, this "beyond" is precisely the exteriority needed for any viable project of liberation.

This infinity of expressivities and their associated possible worlds is rigorously immanent and materialist. Without being transcendent (there being no universal subject and universal object for it to transcend), it serves as a transcendental field for the becoming of new multiplicities, each new multiplicity being potentially another name for a new kind of political agent living for a liberation that the old sovereignties are now unable to forestall. The ontological script that can be written out of this delineation of the immanent field of the multiple is certainly compatible with a Marxist conception of liberation. We cannot be sure that it is compatible with Christianity, which seems irreducibly to be wedded to an ontology of the transcendent. But the possibility of Christianity's being able to incorporate an ontology of unqualified immanence is one that cannot be ruled out *tout court*. (Someone someday is going to write a dissertation on this!) Or it may be that we cannot after all obviate the transcendent, despite what I have been arguing for, in which case Christianity's ontological preeminence is guaranteed. But either way, I think we know that it is possible for us to delineate convincingly the terms of a conceptual basis for a notion of liberation that is unrelentingly immanent.

What this actually portends for conceptions of liberation so far premised on transcendence is really another story. For the moment, the immanent ontology of liberation certainly bypasses liberalism, but, as I said, we cannot be so certain that it does the same with regard to Christianity.

*Notes*

1 See Etienne Balibar, "Citizen Subject," in *Who Comes after the Subject?*, ed. Eduardo Cadava, Peter Connor, and Jean-Luc Nancy (London: Routledge, 1991), 33–57. In another work, Balibar goes on to argue that it is Locke and not Descartes who invents the modern concept of the self as that which the "you" or the "I" *possesses*. See Balibar, *Identité et différence* (Paris: Seuil, 1998).

2 For Descartes's letter to Mersenne, see René Descartes, *Philosophical Essays and Correspondence*, ed. Roger Ariew (Indianapolis: Hackett, 2000), 28, also in *Oeuvres de Descartes* (Paris: J. Vrin, 1987), 1:145. Balibar refers to this letter on page 36 of "Citizen Subject."

3 The importance of the Augustinian tradition for Descartes is stressed in Stephen Menn, "The Intellectual Setting," in *The Cambridge History of Seventeenth-Century Philosophy*, ed. Daniel Garber and Michael Ayers (Cambridge: Cambridge University Press, 1998), 69. See also Nicholas Jolley, "The Reception of Descartes' Philosophy," in *The Cambridge Companion to Descartes*, ed. John Cottingham (Cambridge: Cambridge University Press, 1992), 393–423.

4 According to Balibar, the notion of the transcendental subject arose from Kant's modification of the Cartesian *cogito*, with the Lockean self beginning a second tradition that circumvents Kant before ending up with William James and Henri-Louis Bergson. See Etienne Balibar, "Je/moi/soi," *Vocabulaire européen des philosophies* (Paris: Seuil, 2001).

5 For this, see Immanuel Kant, "On the Common Saying: 'This May Be True in Theory but It Does Not Apply in Practice,'" in *Kant: Political Writings*, ed. Hans Reiss (Cambridge: Cambridge University Press, 1991), 71.

6 Balibar, *Identité et différence*, 55. Balibar says a great deal more about the Cartesian and medieval-theological *subjectus* than can be indicated here, rightly pointing out that a notion that had evolved over seventeen centuries from Roman times to the period of the European absolute monarchies is not easily encompassed in a single definition. He also rightly indicates that the supposed *novum* of the Citizen Subject has to be regarded with some skepticism, since under the aegis of bourgeois democracy this subject was always going to retain some traces of the old subjectus.

7 For Hegel's (early) view on the operation of "speculative" reason, see *The Difference Between Fichte's and Schelling's System of Philosophy*, trans. Horton S. Harris and Walter Cerf (Albany: State University of New York Press, 1977), 88. For excellent commentary on this aspect of Hegel's relation to Kant, see Terry Pinkard, *Hegel: A Biography* (Cambridge: Cambridge University Press, 2000), 160ff.

8 The essential correlation between Reason and the Absolute entails that every operation of consciousness, practical as much as theoretical, is necessarily one that falls within the remit of the Absolute. The subject of thought then has to be the subject of morality and politics and vice versa—a connection previously established by Kant when he moved from the *First Critique* to the *Second Critique*, that is, from the subject's understanding to the subject's willing and acting.

9   A case therefore exists for saying, where periodization is concerned, that the short twentieth century which began in 1918 really ended in 1968 or the early 1970s. For this view, see Antonio Negri, "The End of the Century," in *The Politics of Subversion: A Manifesto for the Twenty-First Century*, trans. James Newell (Cambridge: Polity, 1989), 61–74.

10  For accounts of some of these epochal transformations and their impact on notions of sovereignty and the place and role of the political subject, see Saskia Sassen, *Losing Control? Sovereignty in an Age of Globalization* (New York: Columbia University Press, 1996); and John Braithwaite and John Dranos, *Global Business Regulation* (Cambridge: Cambridge University Press, 2000).

11  It is important here to distinguish between the conditions of *possibility* that underlie the emergence and demise of the citizen-subject (these having essentially to do with the historical and social conditions associated with capitalist development), and the conditions of *intelligibility* that underpin the philosophical rationales ("the knowledges") that sustain this subject. The two kinds of conditions function on different logical levels, and conditions of intelligibility serve a very different purpose than do conditions of possibility. We can follow Foucault in using the notion of the episteme to bridge the two sets of conditions, so that conditions of possibility allow an episteme to exist, and the existence of the episteme in turn enables discourses to be constructed that provide conditions of intelligibility for knowledges, and so forth. On this, see Gilles Deleuze, *Foucault*, trans. Seán Hand (Minneapolis: University of Minnesota Press, 1988), 47ff.

12  As Michael Kitson and Jonathan Michie put it: "The globalisation that has occurred has not necessarily meant a reduction in national differentiation." See "The Political Economy of Globalisation," in *Innovation Policy in a Global Economy*, ed. Daniele Archibugi, Jeremy Howells, and Jonathan Michie (Cambridge: Cambridge University Press, 1999), 163–83, esp. 178. The proposition that the contemporary state is not entirely without power nor has it been totally deprived of legitimacy is strongly defended in Linda Weiss, *The Myth of the Powerless State: Governing the Economy in a Global Era* (Ithaca, N.Y.: Cornell University Press, 1998); Eric Helleiner, "Explaining the Globalization of Financial Markets: Bringing States Back In," *Review of International Political Economy* 2 (1995): 315–41; Michael Mann, "Has Globalization Ended the Rise and Rise of the Nation-State?" *Review of International Political Economy* 4 (1997): 472–97; and Robert Wade, "Globalisation and Its Limits: Reports of the Death of the National Economy are Greatly Exaggerated," in *National Diversity and Global Capitalism*, ed. Suzanne Berger and Ronald Dore (Ithaca, N.Y.: Cornell University Press, 1996), 60–88. For the distinction between the Keynesian welfare state and the Schumpeterian workfare state, see Bob Jessop, "Capitalism and Its Future: Remarks on Regulation, Government, and Governance," *Review of International Political Economy* 4 (1997): 561–81. For Jessop's use of the term "state projects" see his *State Theory: Putting Capitalist States in Their Place* (Cambridge: Polity, 1990). On the emerging civil society of indigenous peoples, see Duncan Ivision, Paul Patton, and Will Sanders, eds., *Political Theory and the Rights of Indigenous Peoples* (Cambridge: Cambridge University Press, 2000). On the multinational state, see Alain-G. Gagnon and James Tully, eds., *Multinational Democracies* (Cambridge: Cambridge University Press, 2001).

The notion that certain crucial historical events can pose an epochal challenge to an existing state form is central to Hegel, whose *Phenomenology* can be seen as an attempt to answer the question of the challenge posed by the French Revolution to the failing and militarily ineffective Holy Roman Empire, with its hodgepodge of German principalities appended to the Austrian *Reich*. On this, see Terry Pinkard, *Hegel: A Biography* (Cambridge: Cambridge University Press, 2000), 147ff.

13    On this neoliberal system, see Gérard Duménil and Dominique Lévy, "The Nature and
       Contradictions of Neoliberalism," in *Socialist Register 2002: A World of Contradictions*, ed.
       Leo Panitch and Colin Leys (London: Merlin, 2001), 43–71; "Costs and Benefits of Neolib-
       eralism: A Class Analysis," *Review of International Political Economy* 8 (2000): 578–607; and
       especially *Crise et sortie de crise: Ordre et désordres néolibéreaux* (Paris: Presses Universitaires
       de France, 2000). See also Colin Leys, *Market-Driven Politics: Neoliberal Democracy and the
       Public Interest* (London: Verso, 2001); Guy Standing, *Beyond the New Paternalism: Basic Secu-
       rity as Equality* (London: Verso, 2002); and Graham Dunkley, *The Free Trade Adventure: The
       WTO, the Uruguay Round and Globalism—A Critique* (London: Zed Books, 2000).

14    Phil Corrigan and Sean Sayers, *The Great Arch: English State Formation as Cultural Revolu-
       tion* (Oxford: Blackwell, 1985).

15    Spinoza constitutes an important exception to the position taken by Hobbes, Rousseau,
       and Hegel, since his notion of the power of the multitude is very different from the notion
       of the people who become the people only when their individual wills have been harmo-
       nized through the exercise of sovereignty. For this reading of Spinoza, see Antonio Negri,
       *The Savage Anomaly*, trans. Michael Hardt (Minneapolis: University of Minnesota Press,
       1999), 194ff.

16    The exemplary analyses of Mrs. Thatcher's "authoritarian populism" by Stuart Hall and
       his associates come to mind here. For these analyses, see Stuart Hall, *The Hard Road to Re-
       newal* (London: Verso, 1988).

17    On the state as the instrument for the realization of capital, see Gilles Deleuze and Félix
       Guattari, *A Thousand Plateaus: Capitalism and Schizophrenia*, trans. Brian Massumi (Min-
       neapolis: University of Minnesota Press, 1987), 221.

18    For this reason Nicos Poulantzas thought the state could not be an independent actor in
       the political field. Here I think he was wrong, though given that he was writing twenty-
       five years ago some license can be afforded him. For Poulantzas, see his *State, Power, So-
       cialism*, trans. Patrick Camiller (London: New Left Books, 1978). Poulantzas was not in a
       position to take into account the emergence of what Gilles Deleuze has called "societies
       of control." For Deleuze, see "Societies of Control," in his collection *Negotiations*, trans.
       Martin Joughin (New York: Columbia University Press, 1995), 177–82.

19    For some suggestive thoughts on the importance of this constituting boundary between
       the left and the right, see Gerassimos Moschonas, *In the Name of Social Democracy: The
       Great Transformation, 1945 to the Present*, trans. Gregory Elliott (London: Verso, 2002).

20    Robert Nozick, *Anarchy, State, and Utopia* (Oxford: Blackwell, 1974), 316.

21    David Runciman has noted this with regard to Nozick in "The Garden, the Park and the
       Meadow," *London Review of Books*, June 6, 2002, 7–11.

22    Derrida argues for a recasting of the notion of the subject in "'Eating Well,' or the Calcu-
       lation of the Subject: An Interview with Jacques Derrida," in Cadava, Connor, and Nancy,
       *Who Comes after the Subject?*, 107–8.

23    For Critchley's strictures, see his essays "Post-Deconstructive Subjectivity?" and "Decon-
       struction and Pragmatism: Is Derrida a Private Ironist or a Public Liberal?" in his collec-
       tion *Ethics-Politics-Subjectivity: Essays on Derrida, Levinas and Contemporary French Thought*
       (London: Verso, 1999), 51–82 and 83–105 respectively.

24    See Antonio Negri, "The Specter's Smile," in *Ghostly Demarcations: A Symposium on Jacques
       Derrida's Specters of Marx*, ed. Michael Sprinker (London: Verso, 1999), 5–16.

25    On Earle's remark, see Nick Cohen, "And Now the Trouble Really Begins," *New States-
       man*, November 19, 2001, available at www.newstatesman.co.uk.

26    For an application of multitude theory to the events that led to Hugo Chavez's restoration

as president of Venezuela, see Jon Beasley-Murray, "It Happened on TV," *London Review of Books*, May 9, 2002, 6–7. For the Genoa demonstrations, see Antonio Negri, "Italy's Postmodern Politics," *Le Monde diplomatique* (English edition), August 2002, 5.

27    Leibniz, who made this doctrine the lynchpin of his philosophical system, and who saw it as the expression of Christianity's philosophical core is thus by virtue of this the great modern Christian philosopher.

28    One is not talking here of conversion in the empirical sense, involving such absurdities as forced baptism. Rather, conversion here refers to an ontological state of affairs in which all are somehow drawn into being adherents of the Christian mythos, whether consciously or implicitly.

29    Objections to univocity argue that, unlike Christianity's "good difference," it can only legitimize a "bad difference," since univocity has as its necessary concomitant immanentism, casting difference entirely as phenomenality, in which case difference is negotiated only on the basis of the power of those who see things *this* way and not *that*, and so forth. According to these critics of immanence, in absolute immanence everything has to replicate the given (because ontologically this is all there is to replicate), and this then becomes the source of an unavoidable ontological violence. Univocity holds beings on the same plane through sheer and naked power, which then has perforce to destroy peaceability. I am indebted to John Milbank for many discussions on this topic.

30    Howard Caygill has dealt brilliantly with this aspect of Kantian judgment in his *Art of Judgment* (Oxford: Blackwell, 1989).

31    Gilles Deleuze has stated this problem perspicaciously: "Now we see Kant, at an age when great authors rarely have anything new to say, confronting a problem that will lead him to an extraordinary undertaking: if the faculties can thus enter into variable relationships in which each faculty is in turn regulated by one of the others, it must follow that, taken together, they are capable of free and unregulated relationships in which each faculty goes to its own limit, and yet in this way shows the possibility of its entering into an *indeterminate* [*quelconque*] harmony with the others" (emphasis original). See Deleuze, "On Four Poetic Formulas That Might Summarize the Kantian Philosophy," in his collection *Essays Critical and Clinical*, trans. Daniel W. Smith and Michael A. Greco (Minneapolis: University of Minnesota Press, 1997), 33–34.

32    Ibid., 34.

*Anthony Baker and Rocco Gangle*    Ecclesia: The Art
of the Virtual

If anything "outside" creation is to emerge from God's concealment and to supplement this limitless infinity of the divine creative power, liberated once and for all, in the direction of a coupling of that infinity with the factual unity, then it must be something which contains enough drive to traverse all the widespread infinity of divine power little by little. It has to be, that is, something inherently growing, inherently augmentable. — Franz Rosenzweig, *The Star of Redemption*

THE CAREER OF PHAENARETE, the mother of Socrates, deserves attention. As recounted by Socrates himself in Plato's *Theaetetus*, this skillful woman takes upon herself the vocation of midwife after having given birth to her divinely gifted son and then subsequently passing beyond the age of fertility. In following this sequence Phaenarete adheres to the sovereign decree of the goddess Artemis: fertile women ought not to become midwives, but neither should women who have never given birth — since the latter lack direct experience. Of course, in his own way Socrates goes on to become a midwife of knowledge and virtue to the citizens of Athens and to subsequent history. Through this legacy Phaenarete's role in the destiny of Athens becomes twofold: she serves the city directly in her later years through the art of midwifery, but she also serves history by giving birth during her fecund years to the fated infant whose wisdom will come to be proclaimed unparalleled and whose influence will extend far beyond the walls of Athens.[1]

The life of Phaenarete plays a role in the future of her city on at least these two distinct levels, yet her direct involvement in Athenian politics is nil — not least because of the stark gender division in ancient Greek society. The question thus arises of the relation of Phaenarete's actions (her natural act of birth and her hybrid social-natural practice of midwifery) to the eventual political destinies of her son Socrates and the other children whose births she assists. Is Phaenarete responsible for the later histories of the lives she initiates into the Athenian polis? Are the lives thus engendered obligated or answerable to Phaenarete's original gift? As the Socratic legacy is handed down through history, what is its relation to Phaenarete — who remains independent of its development yet has made it possible?

Translated into the register of the more general philosophical question of human freedom, these concerns touch upon the ultimately ontological and theological grounds for any sustained reflection upon the essence of politics. Contrary to the Rousseauian tradition, politics is not the self-grounded and autonomous result of a collective decision. The doctrine of the social contract presupposes what it needs to explain: the emergence of human freedom within history and the uncovering of the ground for that freedom. To seek freedom's ground is to attempt to expose the transcendental conditions for the essentially unconditioned. In the modern period the paradox at work in such an attempt has been reflectively developed from Kant's second and third *Critiques*, through Fichte, Schelling, and Hegel, to Heidegger and beyond, as above all a question about time and the ecstatic or self-transcending character of all temporal becoming. In this philosophical trajectory, the terms of the problem remain oriented within the tension between two poles: on the one hand the infinite and unconditioned essence of freedom, and on the other the historical conditions of finite existence.

For theology this question of freedom comes to be asked in terms of the human possibility of realizing a free and communal relationship to the world's divinely creative ground as that ground has been revealed to and within history. Finite, historical freedom must be coordinated with the act of divine creativity without thereby losing its free character. As the epigraph from Rosenzweig's *The Star of Redemption* suggests above, the realization of any such relationship would require the radical deceleration of God's infinite creativity into the finite dimensions of history's slow development. This deceleration would constitute the event of revelation itself and the history of that revelation's reception. If this reception is itself to be characterized as a freely creative response, the event of revelation to which it answers must be developmental and dynamic in its very essence. It must be "something inherently growing, inherently augmentable."[2]

For both philosophy and theology, then, the question of human freedom is always also a political question: the question of sovereignty. Particularly since Hegel, the issue of political sovereignty has become indissociable from the concern with temporal becoming and its concomitant philosophy of history. In Hegel's conception genuine sovereignty—the freedom of Absolute Spirit—must engender itself, must come to itself across a process of historical and institutional development. True freedom can be actualized only as a result of this process. In Hegel's well-worn narrative, the original asymmetry of the consciousnesses of Master and Slave is overcome through the movement and labor of history itself. True sovereignty consists at last in the mutual recognition of particular and historically conditioned consciousnesses as they attain symmetry within the spiritual and universal medium of language.³ Since at this ultimate moment—which consummates the *Phenomenology of Spirit* and initiates the posthistory of the *Science of Logic*—the equation of thought and being has been accomplished, this form of sovereignty requires, and includes, nothing outside its own immanent circulation.

In this historical development, however, each step of history's dialectical movement is logically entailed by the state of consciousness or spirit that immediately precedes it. No step is free, but each is logically and sequentially necessary (even if this necessity becomes visible only from a later vantage point). The ultimate state of absolute knowledge as attained in mutual recognition can alone be designated as truly embodying or expressing sovereign freedom, yet this final state of freedom can result structurally only from an essentially unfree movement of Reason within history.

The main features of this common reading of Hegel follow in broad strokes Alexendre Kojève's lectures on the *Phenomenology of Spirit* given in the 1930s at the École des Hautes Études in Paris.⁴ This series of lectures, which had a tremendous impact on the next generation of French philosophers, had a particularly traceable influence on the work of Georges Bataille. In the later analyses of "general economy," Bataille draws certain extreme social and political consequences that bring to light shortcomings in Hegel's concept of historical freedom. Here, as well as in the three volumes of *The Accursed Share* and his *Theory of Religion*, he follows Kojève in strictly identifying temporal duration with the historical dialectical processes of Reason, though Bataille hypertrophizes this reading to the point that even the mere endurance of consciousness through time, across even the shortest segment of continuous duration, necessarily subjects the sovereignty of consciousness to the utilitarian, conservative, and productive forces of Reason. Subjected to these forces, sovereign freedom inverts into its opposite, becoming a mere instrument of abstract Reason. Reason is thus expressed as a principle of pure utility coextensive with time itself. The movement of consciousness or spirit in history serves only to effect the efficient coordination of means and ends, and the ultimate end of this process is none other than total rational efficiency itself.⁵

On this view the apparently sovereign moment of mutual recognition in Hegel as forgiveness in freedom and the overcoming of the universal/particular antinomy can be read as no more than a subjective illusion that a purely formal process of Reason exploits as a means for its own extension. Here Bataille follows Kojève's logic more strictly than Kojève himself. If the movement of Reason—coextensive with the movement of time—is essentially formal and unfree, then the appearance of any state of freedom that endures through time must be nothing other than a further means for Reason's own development. In the face of this potentially all-pervasive instrumentality, true sovereignty shrinks to the ecstasy of a dimensionless instant. Genuine freedom can then exist only in opposition to time and knowledge. Sovereignty itself becomes durationless, unknowable, and hence, in Bataille's term, an ecstatic experience of "NOTHING."[6]

Such a conception of sovereignty is obviously not conducive to a viable conception of politics. In fact, at the close of the third volume of *The Accursed Share*, Bataille asserts that the only genuine political alternatives available to contemporary humanity are Communism and Nietzscheanism. Since Communism appears doomed to relapse inevitably into the productive state model of Stalinism, a Dionysian politics—a politics of the delirious Nietzsche at Sils-Maria—seems to be the only real option remaining.[7] For Bataille, nothing but a relentlessly consumptive and exorbitant politics as confined to the sovereign, durationless instant could possibly escape the dialectical utility of Reason in history. Gratuitously destructive acts beyond any recuperation of pleasure or purpose would be the only conceivable expressions of genuine political freedom.

Bataille's extremist political conclusions follow directly from his failure to challenge the Kojevian-Hegelian identification of temporal duration and Reason.[8] If sovereign freedom cannot endure across time without compromising itself, Bataille's conclusions about sovereignty would seem inevitable. Yet a different model of temporality and freedom exists that draws on sources and themes very near to Hegel yet avoids Bataille's political conclusions. By effectively *equating* freedom and duration, this model—first apparent in Friedrich Schelling's philosophy of art—rejects any definitive or final production of freedom as the result of an unfree process. Instead, it relates temporal freedom to an excessive and transcendent "virtuality" which is in itself an infinite and unlimited becoming. We will see how the early-twentieth-century Russian Orthodox theologian Sergei Bulgakov makes use of this model and draws upon Schelling's thought in working through the question of historical freedom on a Trinitarian basis.

For Schelling, a kind of sovereign ambiguity characterizes the role of the artist vis-à-vis the production of the work. Every genuine creation "is capable of being expounded *ad infinitum*, as though it contained an infinity of purposes, while yet one is never able to say whether this infinity has lain within the artist . . . or resides only in the work of art."[9] Like Hegel, Schelling argues that the radically historical work of art can no longer be conceived as the copying within time of a fixed, eternal model, but in sharp contrast to Hegel's *Aesthetik*—which sees no way around mimetic representation except that of abolishing the archetype altogether—Schelling supposes that the artist herself shares in the eternal archetype: without looking to any predetermined prototype, she sculpts—in time and utter freedom—a form that is itself dynamic and eternal.[10] Rather than a mimetic copying, the artist's work accomplishes the eternalization of this form precisely by means of its production within time. The slow work of the sculptor brings an infinitely self-varying, or virtual, form into history, clarifying it into finite actuality. The labor involved in the creation of the work serves thus to catalyze the virtual form's subsequent unfolding through actual history. Here sculpting is a kind of temporal deceleration of the eternal and virtual form, the *eidos*, which the work itself presents. The actual "finished" work is thereby in no way final or closed, since it itself endures through time only insofar as it continues to be received, interpreted, and extrapolated further in new historical contexts.

Independently of the artist, the work begins to transmit its form—the decelerated labor of eternity by which it was produced—into the new and continuous creation of its subsequent history. In this ongoing history of reception and new production, the artist him- or herself is no longer directly present, yet his or her artful labor constantly renews itself therein and spawns its own unforeseeable inventions. It would be useless to ask at which exact moment the work becomes freely and independently creative in this way, since its creative freedom consists precisely in the extended duration of its making. Over the course of its conception, creativity and reception become strictly indistinguishable. Open throughout this conception onto the whole of its ensuing and unforeclosed history, the artist's act of creation is equally the reception of an eternal and virtual form; on the other hand, the work's historical reception functions as an ongoing creative act.

Where the Hegelian model of freedom remains predicated upon the possibility (and indeed the supposed actualization) of a completed historical state in which the telos of all previous history would be realized definitively, the Schellingian model of the work of art allows for freedom's unlimited and pluralistic development. Freedom here is not the end result (always subject to suspicion) of an essentially unfree course of development; instead it subsists throughout the durational process itself. The conception of the work of art is an expression of freedom precisely insofar as that process *does not* complete itself in a definitive closure but rather continues to extend and differentiate through time. Its freedom is a freedom to endure and proliferate.

Hegelians will try to accuse Schelling's conception of falling into the trap of a "bad infinite." If the future is truly unending, is it not the case that actual, historically realized freedom remains endlessly deferred? Is not an "unlimited development of freedom" nothing more than freedom's eternal postponement? No, since any "moment" or "segment" of duration, including the final "moment" of the actualization of the absolute state, cannot really be construed independently of the infinite virtuality from and in which its temporal flow derives its impetus and momentum. The apparent isolation of any particular event within time is always artificially constructed, as the event itself has its "home" in the virtual.

The work of art, then, is brought forth ("delivered," one might say, pace Phaenarete) within a nonarrestable virtual form, a form embodied by the work even as it endlessly exceeds the work on every side. But what is this eternally proliferating virtual, and how does it mediate itself into the historical?

Sergei Bulgakov offers a possible thesis for the ontology of the virtual, taking cues from Schelling, especially from the mystical Schellingian theology of Vladimir Solovyov. For Bulgakov, the being of all within God implies an excessiveness that is at the heart of God's own being. This is first of all the case because of the specific form of self-knowledge that characterizes the triune God. For God, consciousness of self has no cognitive "gap," a period of self-ignorance that must be overcome by knowledge. Nor is it static, as an I that subsists immediately in the denial of an other. Rather, God's personality is *kinetic*, consisting of the eternal affirmation—the Holy Spirit—of intradivine alterity—the Son. As Trinity, God knows himself only as an eternal "exiting of himself in penetration of the other." The *unity* of God appears only in this penetration, and in fact *is* only this penetration. In this sense, the single *ousia*, the unity of God that is not ruptured even by internal alterity, is eternally manifested to God in the movement of Father, Son, and Spirit.[11]

Beyond the love that the Hypostases reciprocate between themselves, however, it is also the case that the entire Godhead as a whole is enraptured by this "discovery" of divine unity. In this light, the kinetic manifestation takes form as the intrinsic subsistence of an extra-Trinitarian "companion," an other to God that is identical to God's desire for this nonidentical unity: that is, the Godhead together desires unity as if it were an extradivine being. Further, as the love of the Hypostases for each other is irreducibly an exchange, both given and returned, the love that characterizes the Godhead as a whole is likewise reciprocating. God not only desires the manifest unity but desires to be desired by it. Hence for Bulgakov, the Christian God (in contrast to the Plotinian One) is, "prior" to any question of creation, always already a God in relation. The "absolute" is always already the "absolute-relative";[12] not simply internally relational as Trinity, but also, and by virtue of this, relating as a Godhead to an "imaginary" exteriority, to a beloved companion who springs from the love that is the intrinsic essence of God himself. This companion is God's beloved wisdom, "the Divine Sophia."[13]

In terms of God's kinetic personality, we might define Sophia as a "divine rapture." The Spirit "beatifies" the Son to the Father, resting upon him in such a way as to reveal him to be "of the same essence as the Father." The self-revelation within God thus discloses his unity, as if God eternally discovers the truth of the Shema: "The Lord is One." This timeless moment is God's joy at the eternal discovery of his unity: *essence* is revealed to God, and, as revealed, radiates.[14] There is in this sense a kind of brilliance to the kinetic Trinity, an excessive explosion of a joy that is not collapsible into any of the three hypostases. And, as desired reciprocity characterizes God's relation to his *raptus*, God "personifies" this raptus itself as eternal and dependent object of God's favor: Sophia, the eternal "bride" of God.

For Bulgakov, the unboundedness of the Triune God implies that this intradivine excess enfolds all time and being within the eternal instant. In the formulation of the Church Fathers, all *logoi* are bound up within the Logos in infinite simplicity, so that his beatification by the Spirit is, simultaneously, the beatification of "the all." In the transcendent—and only here—being and beauty perfectly coincide. This coincidence, however, is no more static than the intradivine relations themselves: played out in a cycle of manifestation and rapture in the excess of the divine, Sophia possesses an infinite and absolute dynamism, her timeless movement in and through the divine Hypostases.

To say that the excess is the ontological all is not to say that all "possible worlds" are contained in God, as in the Scholastic Franciscan hypothesis. Eternity is beyond possibility, and even the simple Sophianic All has a certain actuality, which, extracted from time, is identical to God's own actuality. Within God's being as pure act, however, this excessive companion displays a certain virtuality: as if her beauty is, in the formulation of Solovyov, an eternal summons to God to give her own actuality, her own being in the form of temporal becoming.[15] There is no sense here of a disinterested detachment of God to a field of possibility that might rise up to actuality: instead, the Sophia entreats God to allow her to decrease, to surrender the infinite speed of divine companionship and enact her love for God "at her own pace." Divine excess is the eternal rapture in God that contains this plea for a created sphere, a world of decelerated excess. This then is the theological virtual: the excess of the Trinitarian relations, a "virtual world" to itself, eternally manifest to God in the midst of God's rapture.

But how is the plea actualized? That is, if sovereignty within the historical is a matter of the mediation of this kinetic virtuality, the virtuality itself must "decelerate" to finite proportions. The Divine Sophia, as God's timeless celebration of the beauty of the all, must itself achieve a transferal into time, now as *historically* and *independently* actual: in short, as an "earthly Sophia." How then does the earthly come to participate in the divine?

Perhaps nowhere is a deceleration of precisely this kind more clearly dramatized than in the Gospel of Luke's account of the Annunciation. In Gabriel's encounter with Mary, the archangel charges her with the dual task of the natural birth and the social, cultural, and religious formation of Israel's Messiah, who is also the universal Incarnate Logos of God. As Gabriel articulates Mary's mission, all of heaven hinges on her reply, as if the infinite movement of the heavenly virtual—the Divine Sophia—is in this narrative contracting to a pause, anticipating her reception by history. A significant element of the "blessedness" of the Virgin in ecclesiastical history is the recognition that, while she is presented by the gospel as unquestionably free in her submissive response, it is at the same time quite out of the question that she might have refused.[16] (And in this she is perhaps even more attuned to the divine than her son, who hesitates and appears even to contemplate a refusal when confronted with his "cup.") Mary's freedom is not a voluntarism, as if she were disinterestedly perched between a yes and a no;[17] it is precisely in her acceptance of the invitation to *affirm* the full actualization of God's "companion" in history that her own complete freedom appears: Mary is free to bear God into the world, to generate divinity through human, historical "labor."

This dynamic is manifested in El Greco's well-known painting of the Annunciation. As Gabriel makes his impassioned plea to Mary, an angelic orchestra hovers above, perched to begin the symphony. One angel sits holding a recorder, but his face is turned away from the mouthpiece, with one ear turned toward the conversation below. Another angel has her hands already at the keys of a harpsichord, but a third seems to tell her to wait, as the conductor stands before them, hands hovering in the air. A path opens through space (or is it time: a way from the eternal into the temporal, a way perhaps constituting the very essence of the temporal?) from the angels to the young virgin, a path seemingly lined with souls, and it is down this path that the dove descends. The transcendent, where Sophia dwells as timeless virtual, waits to see if history will "magnify the Lord" in and through itself: absolute being pauses in its eternal symphonic activity to see if it will in fact become in time.

In some recent critical literature the Annunciation is taken as a prime case of negative gender typing: the mundane female is made to submit to the power of the supramundane male, such that Mary's self-effacing submission becomes the Church's paradigm of ontologically female discipleship. Interestingly, however, her acquiescing *verbum* "be it unto me" comes only *after* the angel Gabriel seeks her out and announces that she has "found favor in the eyes of the Lord" (Luke 1:26-38). Is it not significant that God at the very least "notices" her, and his gaze is drawn to what he sees? If there is no indication in text or traditional readings that Mary could have refused, there is *also* no indication that God could have done without Mary, that Mary was pure instrument (as if any functioning uterus would have done the trick). She was chosen, and divinity itself is contingent on her response. In this light it is no longer absolutely clear just who the "handmaiden" in the narrative is: the Spirit of God waits on Mary, submits to her submission.

To extend the image of divine deceleration further through history, we might observe that the original choice to enfold the divine is offered not only to Mary, but originally to Israel as an entire people. Again in this case a refusal is quite out of the question,[18] and, again, there is no hint in the Torah that just any people at all would have sufficed to be Chosen. In this sense Mary's "divine attraction" invites a retroactive appeal to the world that crafted her: Sophia waits for Mary, Sophia waits for Israel. The chosen (people, virgin) are given the freedom to make divinity within time, and divinity itself can only rest its fingers at the keys while the choice is made.

The telos of the heritage of Israel-Mary is the birthing of Sophia. The practical art is itself a kind of secret knowledge pervading the activities of Abraham and Moses as well as the orations of the prophets: it would appear that there is a kind of *techne* for the birthing of the divine. Anticipating the Pauline extension of Mary's "work of art" in the direction of the eschaton, we might call this *techne* "ecclesia," recognizing that its prevalence throughout history suggests that the infinite movement of Christ's church is in no sense the first or only instance of divine birthing in history. Israel and Mary are not *necessary* moments that feed into a later *freedom* of life in the finality of the eschatological church; rather, their singular submissions are perfectly free repetitions of an eternal and virtual craft, utterly free events of ecclesia.[19]

Mary, in short, with Israel before her, is a midwife for the divine Sophia. Like Phaenarete's two "labors," Mary's vocation also places her in a dual role, though for her both come through a single event. The Marian assent affirms both the actual conception of Christ, and through his "Socratic" career, the deferred birth of the heavenly city, the new Jerusalem. (And it is significant that this city does not ascend from time to eternity, as we might expect a more Hegelian church to do if history's final product were to be posthistorical sovereignty. In the Revelation of St. John, the heavenly city descends to earth, suggesting that the political craft had all along been making the true form, but in an infinitely "slower" mode.)[20]

Sophia, the timeless rapture of the Godhead, is therefore precisely the pure freedom that must wait on the handmaiden. Again, the El Greco: heaven is a wealth of kinesis now in hesitation, pausing the unpausable symphony while it strains to hear Mary's response, and remaining in pause—or better, in a profound ritardando—as it waits upon ecclesia. (Is the angel with his hand up telling the harpsichordist to stop, or to ease the tempo? Is the angel at the viol to the conductor's back attending to a deceleration in the lead of the orchestra?)[21] Sophia is not subject to history in her virtual being, as God's immediate "symphony," yet in her actual becoming she is *only* historical. Her being is the eternal form, the ever-kinetic virtual; her becoming—the excess and fulfillment of this being—is the actual event of "birthing" the form in time. Divine sovereignty is therefore thoroughly mediated by the art of ecclesia, given not in the immediacy of the heavenly, but as *logoi spermatikoi*—the virtual seeds of the Logos—unborn but through the artful hand of the midwife.[22]

At stake here is the continuity of God's incarnational event in relation to the social, political, and historical contexts in which that event takes shape. Can an absolute line be drawn prior to which God is *not yet* revealed or incarnate and posterior to which God *has been* revealed or made flesh? Even if the difficulties of determining such an instant seem insurmountable, one might argue that such a definitive instant has to be posited in principle. If incarnation is to mean anything at all, it needs to have clear conceptual limits; as a historical event it must have a clear before and after. Yet this way of thinking presupposes to one degree or another an autonomous or neutral field of historical being into the logic of which God's incarnational revelation would *enter*. To say that the Incarnate God *develops* out of such a field would clearly be incoherent. If, on the other hand, the field of historical being is always already Sophianic (though perhaps not yet fully affirmed as such), and if temporal movement can never be other than a finitely realized deceleration of the Divine Sophia's own infinite velocity (both less than and in excess of—because *the* excess of—intra-Trinitarian relations), then incarnational eventfulness would characterize time as such. Time in its essence would already be historical, and history already incarnational. The freedom of the human polis—the freedom to organize, shape, and reproduce the human *bios*—would extend indefinitely toward its fulfillment in ecclesia.

Phaenarete remains the original figure—womanly, Athenian, and nearly forgotten—of a birth that becomes an art. Her creative act extends beyond her own local circumstances and develops beyond itself into an historical destiny. In a separate context, Mary's affirmative response to Gabriel repeats Phaenarete's act with this important difference: Mary affirms the *whole* of the virtual with her "yes," and with this seemingly paradoxical affirmation she initiates the full, historical actualization of the virtual (that is, Sophia herself *as* history). Since the virtual exists only as an excess or transcendence of the whole, Mary's embodied "yes" also repeats in act the Divine Sophia's eternal relation to the Godhead, thereby constituting the very substance of human history and politics as the labor of rapture.

In what sense, however, can the whole of the virtual be fully actualized within the limits of history? Is the form not, as Hegel suspected, complete only *after* history? Indeed, scripture strongly implies a postponement of this sort. Israel is the womb called to bear a young virgin who will, in her turn, bear God. Once born, however, *Christ* takes over the laboring process, as he is, in Gregory of Nyssa's image, responsible for "giving birth" to himself.[23] Even Christ himself cannot finish the job and ultimately passes the finalization of his form to his followers, so that St. Paul can say the many members (throughout the ensuing centuries, we can surmise) *are* the Body. In this way the specific art form originating in Israel is passed along through a series of artists and will seemingly be deferred indefinitely, until the "final form" of history or ecclesia.

Added to this seemingly problematic deferment is an element of excess within the temporal itself: for Mary, as for Phaenarete, the form that is born from her body overtakes her actual laboring, and the son becomes more than she could have expected—perhaps even hoped.[24] In the case of Christ as well, who, like Socrates, is more clearly a barren, "Artemian" midwife ("*I* have come that *they* might have life"), the canvas upon which he works escapes his human reach, and the life-form he begins to create has to be completed in his absence. The *corpus verum* stretches out through history, almost infinitely overreaching the *corpus historicum*. For each "artist" (Phaenarete or Socrates or any given Athenian, Israel or Mary or Jesus, or any given disciple), the virtual form overflows the historicized actual, and all the midwific efforts to make it appear in its fullness finally come up short. If the virtual is in itself dynamic and augmentable, it would seem to resist any complete actualization, and thus the totally affirming assent to its full, historical realization would appear to be impossible.

There is thus a dual protest to our thesis that the historical birth is a true moment of eternal sovereignty. On the one hand, the form is passed down from one "midwife" to another, never complete. On the other hand, even the work of a single midwife seems to detract from her "freedom," insofar as it overtakes her direct intentions and escapes her grasp. This protest leaves one of two options open for us: either Mary herself is not free, not really birthing the divine, and can be called Theotokos only from the perspective of the posthistorical end (call this the Hegelian option), or Mary, Israel, Christ, and the Pauline body, together *are* actually bearing God, in that their historical mediation of the virtual is never isolated from this virtual; only in this precise sense is their craft "sovereign" in the midst of history (call this the Schellingian/Bulgakovian option).

According to this second option, the only genuine form of political sovereignty would be one that, like Mary's, embraces the whole of the virtual in a contingent act of affirmation mediated through continuity with its past and future embodiment. This temporal act would affirm the virtual infinite as the only real Event of freedom possible and would craft itself within this ontological space as a historical ritardando. As a slowing of God's virtuality, political sovereignty is neither a thing sacrificed for the sake of the common good, nor a destructive ecstasy, nor an impossible telos of the historical state but rather the historicity of political life itself: more directly, it is the techne that understands all invention and reinvention within the polis to be a repetition of divine rapture, a free and earthly passage of divinity, under the care of the midwife, into the life of the city. Such an art is the enraptured labor of mercy. Still, the pains of birth remain great even in the care of the most practiced midwife: as Schelling understood in his own day, "this is still a time of struggle."[25]

## Notes

1   See Plato, *Theaetetus*, 149–150b, in *Plato: Collected Dialogues*, ed. Edith Hamilton and Huntington Cairns (Princeton, N.J.: Princeton University Press, 1978), 853–55.

2   Franz Rosenzweig, *The Star of Redemption* (Notre Dame, Ind.: University of Notre Dame Press, 1985), 159.

3   G. W. F. Hegel, *Phenomenology of Spirit* (Oxford: Oxford University Press, 1977), 392–409, 479–93.

4   A collection of these lectures in available as Alexandre Kojève, *Introduction to the Reading of Hegel*, ed. Allan Bloom (Ithaca, N.Y.: Cornell University Press, 1996).

5   See Georges Bataille, *The Accursed Share, Vol. I* (New York: Zone Books, 1991) and *The Accursed Share, Vols. II and III* (New York: Zone Books, 1991) as well as *Theory of Religion* (New York: Zone Books, 1998).

6   Bataille, *The Accursed Share, Vol. III*, 197–211.

7   Ibid., 368. It is interesting that here Bataille himself understands the Nietzschean option as a direct challenge to the model of theological sovereignty.

8   Bataille notes in another context, "I don't have the necessary strength[;] in my mind Hegel

is not in question." See *The Unfinished System of Nonknowledge* (Minneapolis: University of Minnesota Press, 2001), 271.

9   F. W. J. Schelling, *System of Transcendental Idealism* (Charlottesville: University of Virginia Press, 1997), 225.

10  *Hegel: On the Arts. Selections from G. W. F. Hegel's Aesthetics or the Philosophy of Fine Art*, abridged and trans. Henry Paolucci (New York: Frederick Ungar, 1979); F. W. J. Schelling, *The Philosophy of Art*, ed. and trans. Douglas W. Scott (Minneapolis: University of Minnesota Press, 1989). See also Andrew Bowie, *Schelling and Modern European Philosophy: An Introduction* (London: Routledge, 1993), 52–54.

11  Sergei Bulgakov, *Agnets bozhii: O bogochelovechestve, Chaste I* [The Lamb of God: On the Divine-Humanity, Part 1] (Paris: YMCA Press, 1933), 112–24. Translated into French by Constantin Andronikof as *Du Verbe incarné (agnus dei)* (Paris: Aubier, 1943), 7–20.

12  Sergei Bulgakov, *Uteshitel: O bogochelovechestve, Chaste II* [The Comforter: On the Divine-Humanity, Part 2] (Paris: YMCA Press, 1936), 253–54. Translated into French by Constantin Andronikof as *Le Paraclet* (Paris: Aubiers, 1944), 211–12.

13  Bulgakov, *Agnets bozhii*, 130–40 (French trans., 21–38).

14  Ibid., 122–24 (French trans., 18–20).

15  Vladimir Solovyov, *Lectures on Divine Humanity*, trans. Boris Jakim (Hudson, N.Y.: Lindisfarne Press, 1995), chap. 7.

16  See Sergei Bulgakov, *Kurina neopalimaia: Opyt dogmatischeskogo istolkovaniia nekotorykh chert v pravoslavnom pochitanii Bogomateri* [The Burning Bush: A Dogmatic Interpretation of Some Features of the Orthodox Veneration of the Mother of God] (Paris: YMCA Press, 1927).

17  And in this, clearly, the responses of Jesus and Mary to their missions are identical: even if more hesitant, the son is beyond question not contemplating an acceptance or refusal of the cup, just whether "drinking of it" is the only way to obey God.

18  See, for example, Emmanuel Levinas's reading of Talmudic commentary on Exodus 19:17 in "'The Temptation of Temptation," in *Nine Talmudic Readings* (Indianapolis: Indiana University Press, 1994), 30–50.

19  For a parallel treatment of Mary and Israel, see Hans Urs von Balthasar, *Theo-Drama: Theological Dramatic Theory*, vol. 3, *The Dramatis Personae: The Person in Christ*, trans. Graham Harrison (San Francisco: Ignatius, 1992), 175–78.

20  See Bulgakov, *The Bride of the Lamb*, trans. Boris Jakim (Grand Rapids, Mich.: Eerdmans and T&T Clark, 2002), 263–64. This volume is the third and final part of his Divine-Humanity trilogy.

21  The authors appreciate the assistance of Eric Baker, a church musician in Indianapolis, in identifying these instruments of the Baroque.

22  Bulgakov, *Uteshitel*, 244–51 (French trans., 203–9). We wish to acknowledge the gracious assistance of Boris Jakim, who provided us with a proof of this chapter in his excellent English translation. This full volume as well as the third and final in the trilogy are both forthcoming, in Jakim's translation, from Eerdmans.

23  Gregory of Nyssa, *Vita Moysis*, 2.3, in *Gregory of Nyssa: The Life of Moses*, trans. Abraham J. Malherbe and Everett Ferguson (New York: Paulist, 1978), 56. The direct reference in this text is a typological reference to Moses as Christ. Nyssa's Christology follows this theme of self-generating quite closely. See *Ad Theophilum adversus Apollinaristas*, in *Gregorii Nysseni Opera*, vol. 3, part 1 (*Leiden*, 1958–).

24  Consider, for instance, her baffled acquiescence in the wedding feast of Cana (John 2:1–

11), or the estranged relationship when she tries to visit him in the house in Galilee and he refuses her (Mark 3:31–35). Of course, the ultimate event of Mary's loss of her son is the crucifixion itself, which, along with these other instances, is foreshadowed in the words of the prophet to Mary at her infant's presentation in the temple: "A sword shall pierce your own soul too" (Luke 2:34–35). ·

25  F. W. J. Schelling and Slavoj Žižek, *The Abyss of Freedom/Ages of the World* (Ann Arbor: University of Michigan Press, 1997), 120. The quotation is from the end of Schelling's 1813 introduction to book 1 of *Weltalter*, "The Past." The authors wish to acknowledge the many conversations on Schelling and Bulgakov out of which this essay developed, including especially those with Creston Davis, Angel Mendez, and Willis Jenkins.

Catherine Pickstock | The Univocalist Mode of Production

HAVE WE REALLY ENTERED a "postmodern" phase of history? And if so, is this to be celebrated or regretted? If the modern is progressive, then is the postmodern inevitably reactionary at heart, for all its clever disguises? In what follows, I will examine the relation of the postmodern to the modern through a double perspective. In the theoretical sphere, I will focus on the conjoined philosophical legacy of univocity and representation which can be taken as the ultimate presupposition of modern thought. In the practical sphere, I will focus on the category of "civil society" which is normally regarded as the core of a secular public space in modern times.

In his book We Have Never Been Modern, French philosopher of science Bruno Latour exposes the falsity of the myth that there are absolutely irreversible breaks in cultures through time.[1] This observation bears strongly upon the theme of the present essay, for in tracing certain theoretical and practical transformations from the later Middle Ages to the early modern period, one can see that aspects of late medieval theological thought underpin later characteristically "modern" ideas, even though much in the Enlightenment may also be seen as a qualified reaction against these changes. It has been common to account for the origins of modernity in terms of the vague edifice of "the Enlightenment," and to see modernity as coextensive with the rise of the secular modern state needed to quell the Wars of Religion, together with the rise of systematic organization of medical, educational, and penal institutions. But given that attempts to improve society in a secular way via the state and market have so visibly failed, perhaps this revised genealogy that stresses the legacy of a distorted religious theory and practice could also point us indirectly toward a more serious alternative future polity than the liberal and postmodern critiques.

But one can go even further than this. Against the one-dimensional "modern" vision of progress without a genuine *novum*, postmodern philosophers and cultural theorists have protested in the name of the diverse, the more than human, the incommensurable. In doing so, some of them (in particular Gilles Deleuze, Alain Badiou, and Jacques Derrida) have explicitly appealed back to Duns Scotus for their alternative vision. They regard his leveling of the infinite and the finite to a univocal being, his unleashing of the virtual and unmediably discontinuous, as permitting a radical break with a totalizing rationalism. But it has recently been argued that all these Scotist innovations themselves lie at the inception of modernity. How then can they provide the key to a break with modernity? Surely they betoken a radicalization of, and a return to, the very origins of modernity?

Duns Scotus's flattening out of actual necessity (an "aesthetically" necessary order shown only in actual existence, not proceeding from logical possibility) to pure virtuality, and of being to the bare fact of existence, a modern "rationalist" move that undergirds the primacy of epistemology over ontology, does indeed suggest a radicalization of the modern in a more anarchic direction that renders all possibilities in their limitless range equally valid, and all existence merely phenomenal and ephemeral, lacking altogether in depth, or any symbolic pointing beyond itself toward either eternal truth or abiding "human" values.

This suggests that one way to understand the postmodern is as the "late modern," or the intensification of certain trends established within modernity. The invocation of Duns Scotus and the later Middle Ages by Gilles Deleuze, Alain Badiou, Jacques Derrida, and many others is a crucial part of what is best understood as a revised understanding of the nature of modernity itself.

In the philosophical sphere, modernity used to be characterized by the turn to the subject, the dominance of epistemology, and the guaranteeing of secure knowledge by the following of a reliable method. Today, following tendencies beginning early in the twentieth century with the work of Étienne Gilson and climaxing in the rigorous scholarship of Jean-Luc Marion, J.-F. Courtine, and Olivier Boulnois, we have become aware of the way in which both the Cartesian and the Kantian moves depended upon shifts within Latin scholasticism, to such an extent that one can now validly say that both Descartes and Kant remained to a degree "scholastics."[2]

In particular, it can be seen that these two thinkers did not simply transfer allegiance for objectively critical reasons from an unwarranted claim to know being as it really is, to an attempt to define true knowledge and even being in terms of the unequivocally graspable and internally consistent. Rather, a prior change in the understanding of being, a prior reorientation of ontology, was necessary in order to make possible the move from ontology to epistemology. As long as the Greco-Arab and then Western Catholic synthesis of Aristotle with Neoplatonism remained in place, a turn toward epistemology could have possessed no critical obviousness. Within this synthesis, every abstraction of properties—such as "being" or "truth" or "good" or "entity"—from the real was still concerned with their instance *as* universal elements within the real (as opposed to logical abstractions), while even the act of abstraction was regarded as an elevation toward that greater actuality and perfection that characterized a more purely spiritual apprehension. The working assumption was that the finite occurrence of being (as of truth, goodness, substance, etc.) restricts infinite being in which it participates. When knowledge grasps finitude in its relatively universal aspects, it does not simply mirror finitude but rather fulfills its nature in achieving a certain elevation of its reality.[3]

To conceive of knowledge, by contrast, as a mirroring, or as "representation," requires that one think of the abstraction that is clearly involved in all understanding in an entirely different fashion. To abstract must not involve any elevation but rather uses a kind of mimetic doubling. It is now regarded as a demand of rigor that one keep a "transcendental" universality strictly distinct from "transcendent" height and spirituality, logical abstraction from spiritual ascesis. This is what Duns Scotus achieves by reading Pseudo-Dionysius and Augustine in his own fashion, which was sometimes alert to ambiguities within their texts, and at other times seemingly almost willfully perverse. His new and explicit deployment of perfection terms as "common" both to God and creatures was nonetheless anticipated by Bonaventure and was decisively undergirded by central elements of Avicennian metaphysics.[4] For Scotus, Being and other transcendental categories now imply no freight of perfective elevation.

Instead, finite creatures, like the infinite creator, nakedly "are," as opposed to "not being" in a punctiliar fashion—they are "the same" *in quid* as regards existing that belongs to them as an essential property, just as substance and accident, genus, species, and individuality all exist in the same fashion, in quid. Only *in quale*—as regards specific differences of a qualitative kind, including the difference between finite and infinite, and the differences between the transcendentals (since Duns Scotus denies their full convertibility: being is not of itself entirely true)[5]—is there no univocity, but rather, it seems, something like pure equivocity. This provides a very

complex and notoriously subtle picture, but, put briefly: as regards the pure
logical essence of *esse*, there is univocity between all its instances, while as regards ultimate differentiating qualitative properties there is equivocal diversity. Thus although *esse* is univocal in quid, in the fully determined quiddative
instance there is always something existentially present that is over and above
pure univocity and appears indeed to be entirely "different." Nevertheless,
because differences are instantiated only in things that are, Scotus declares
that uncreated being and the ten genera of finitude are all included "essentially" within being as univocal and as a quasi-genus (it is not a proper genus,
for Scotus, because for him genera only divide the finite, and not because, as
for Aquinas, being cannot, like a genus, be extrinsically determined). Moreover, even the specific differences of finitude, the property of infinitude and
the *passiones* or transcendentals are "virtually" included within being as univocal. This makes it clear that while, indeed, univocity is first of all for Scotus a semantic thesis regarding the constancy of meaning through diverse
predications, all the same he tends to semanticize the field of ontology itself,
through his thesis of essential and virtual inclusion.[6] In effect this implies that
being as a semantic or logical unit is also a real, formal element of the make-
up of any existential reality; although Scotus does not explicitly speak of a
"formal distinction" between being and essence, later Scotists logically did so.

When Scotus speaks of analogy, as Boulnois concludes, this seems to reduce either to the equivocal, or to degrees of "intensity" upon a quantitative
model.[7] Although, indeed, Scotus allows that an infinite degree transcends
the quantitative, this excess is once again conceived in an equivocal fashion,
while the model of intensive ascent itself remains quantitative in its paradigm, as is shown by Scotus's insistence that the idea of "more good" does
not—*contra* Augustine—affect our very grasp of the meaning of "good."[8]

The position of the analogical, as a third medium between identity and difference, whereby something can be like something else in its very unlikeness
according to an ineffable cobelonging, is rejected by Scotus because it does
not seem to be rationally thinkable.[9] What remains is a semantic world sundered between the univocal and the equivocal. Scotus's refusal, in contrast
to Aristotle and Aquinas, to conceive of a semantic analogy within grammar
and logic inevitably influences his conception of the metaphysical field also,
since the new autonomy he grants to the semantic is itself a metaphysical
move: purely logical existence, including purely punctiliar essential univocal
being in quid, now belongs entirely to the real and can always be "virtually distinguished" within its more complex concrete binding together with
other elements in quale. Far from this outlook displaying an unquestionable
rigor, it would seem that the idea that abstraction opens upon its own neu-

tral quasi-ontological realm of virtuality that is independent of any ascent to the concretely spiritual amounts simply to the following through of one hermeneutic option.

Since finite being is now regarded as possessing in essence "being" in its own right (even though it still requires an infinite cause), when the mind abstracts being from finitude, it undergoes no elevation but simply isolates something formally empty, something that is already in effect a transcendentally a priori category and no longer transcendental in the usual medieval sense of a metaphysically universal category that applies to all beings as such, with or without material instantiation. For this reason, it now represents something that is simply "there," without overtones of valuation, although it also represents something that must be invoked in any act of representation and is in this new sense "transcendental." Scotus here echoes the Avicennian view that the subject of metaphysics is being and not the first principle (as Averroës held), for "Being" can now be regarded as (for our understanding) transcendentally prior to, and also as "common to" both God and creatures.[10] In one sense, this inaugurates ontotheology and so is modern and not postmodern. But in another sense, Scotus opens up the possibility of considering being without God, and as more fundamental (supposedly) than the alternative of finite versus infinite, or temporal versus eternal. This space is occupied as much by Heidegger, Derrida, and Deleuze as it was by Hegel. Here, Scotus's protomodernity involves also the postmodern.

Something similar applies to the Scotist impact upon theology. As a protomodern thinker, Scotus's contributions had implications for the alliance between theology and the "metaphysical" (in the broad sense, not meaning ontotheology). For within the prevailing theologico-metaphysical discourse of participated-in perfections, there was a ready continuity between reason and revelation: reason itself was drawn upward by divine light, while, inversely, revelation involved the conjunction of radiant being and further illuminated mind. Here, as we have seen, to rise to the Good, before as well as within faith, was to rise to God. But once the perceived relationship between the transcendentals has undergone the shift described above, to abstract to the Good tells us nothing concerning the divine nature. To know the latter, we wait far more upon a positive revelation of something that has for us the impact of a contingent fact rather than a metaphysical necessity.

One can interpret the latter outcome as modern misfortune: the loss of an integrally conceptual and mystical path. Already before Duns Scotus (even in Bonaventure, perhaps), the business of "naming God" was beginning to change; it was gradually losing the accompanying element of existential transformation of the one naming. This tends to be a consequence of an aprioristic reading of Anselm by the Franciscans, for which perfection terms already start to denote abstraction rather than elevation.[11] But with Scotus, the mystical dimension is lost, and Augustinian divine illumination of the intellect (in all human knowing) is reduced to the divine causal instigation of the natural light of the agent intellect (more so than for Aquinas, for whom the entirely "created light" of the individual human agent intellect was still a self-exceeding light).[12] In this way a path was opened for a historical transition from Platonic recollection (in its many mutations) to modern apriorism.

The above verdict on Scotus is strongly contested by Orlando Todisco and Isiduro Manzano.[13] These writers do not question the Radical Orthodoxy (henceforward RO) view that Scotus stood at the center of a paradigm shift in the late twelfth century. The argument here concerns evaluation rather than exegesis. I tend to view negatively, they view positively.

In particular, Todisco and Manzano reject my view that Scotus's ideas led to a diminution of the scope of theology. For Todisco, just the opposite is the case: by reducing metaphysics to a bare ontology that defines the *ens* in terms of the law of excluded middle, Scotus ends rather than inaugurates ontotheology, ensuring that thenceforward our discourse concerning God and his relation to the world will be much more radically derived from the sources of revelation. The RO writers are, furthermore, guilty of ignoring the fact that even univocity of being is a theological as well as a metaphysical thesis. Because of our fallenness, *in statu ipso* the first object of knowledge seems to be a material creature, mediated to us by the sensorily imagined phantasm. Only revelation of our previous unfallen condition opens up the hidden truth that by its original, integral nature our intellect is attuned to the metaphysical before the physical: that it properly grasps first the ens qua ens, in abstraction from either material or spiritual designation. In this way, and on account of this neutral abstraction, revealed theology itself paradoxically makes available the space for metaphysics as a science in its own right, purified of any Aristotelian coreference to God as subject matter along with Being. Conversely, a metaphysics redirected toward thinking about ens as such in indifference to cause and relation reciprocally opens up the space of revealed theology in two different ways. First of all, it helps to show the contingency of our perverse fallen condition, where, contrary to natural governance, the senses lead the mind. Second, it reveals a natural precondition for the reception of supernatural grace—namely, the neutral possible orientation of our mind as much to infinite as to finite being.

Both Todisco and Manzano rightly consider that this indeed subtle and creatively brilliant schema allows for a kind of benign dividing and ruling. Strict reason is more fully acknowledged than with Aquinas, since univocity permits a proof of God's existence without reference to a higher cause beyond our grasp, and so within the terms of strict maintenance of a mediating identity as required by syllogistic proof: one can see with certainty that infinite must be ontologically prior to finite being only because the middle term *being* retains a univocal identity. By contrast, Aquinas, following Averroës, knows that his always somewhat "physical" (though also metaphysical, unlike Averroës) "proof" of a first highest cause falls short of strict demonstration.[14] In the Proclean-derived schema of analogy of attribution and metaphysics of participation, a mystical supplement to pure reason would appear always to be required. However, Scotus goes still further in seeing this schema as rationally deficient: he argues that it violates the law of the excluded middle. Thus, one may contend, participated esse at once is and is not the divine esse: if a thing is "like" what is higher than it, and this is irreducible to its being like in some ways (univocally) and unlike in other ways (equivocally), then it must be at once present as something that exists and yet also present as not this thing—and in the same way and the same respect.

On the other hand, reason is more chastened for Scotus than for Aquinas. Our fallen reason is properly attuned to the finite, and for this reason finite causes form a closed system, otherwise they would disperse into uncertainty (the foreshadowing of Kant is clear). God cannot be demonstrated from physical causes, and the ontological proof of his existence concludes only to a bare infinite without further determination purely qua infinite (whereas for Aquinas the infinite in its simplicity also equals esse and all the other transcendentals). Above all, for Scotus, the ontological difference between esse and ens will not capture the difference between Creator and creature, since this difference cannot logically and so (for Scotus) ontologically be construed in terms of participation. Esse is nothing in itself (a "vicious abstraction," as Richard Cross terms it) and is exhaustively instantiated in the same way in all the punctual occurrences of *entia*. The latter do not share an eminent elevation but something common and equal that they alone determine. Nevertheless, Todisco argues, this shared ontological dimension much better reveals the ontological distance of God than does the Thomist real distinction of esse from essentia. For as we have seen, one cannot rationally know the eminence or causality or excellence of the infinite.

In this way, univocity, unlike analogy—which can only open upon distance by also insinuating a likeness—leaves us radically open to divine grace. No extrinsicism is involved here for Todisco, since, quite to the contrary, Scotus saw the extrinsicist dangers of Aquinas's view of cognition: reason that is naturally (and not just *pro statu ipso*) confined to the *conversio ad phantasmata*, is not at all prepared for the reception of grace. Nor does univocity encourage an arbitrary voluntarism: what it favors is charitable gift, not tyranny.

For Aquinas the sharedness of esse, whereby divine omnipresence concerns a certain emanation of his esse as such, suggests a necessitating of God in creation, and indeed the divine reason for Thomas takes precedence over his will. In the Thomist cosmos some realities—like the orbiting stars—are "necessary," and only some others purely contingent. Likewise creatures possess "natural ends," which it seems they arrive at ineluctably. By contrast, for Scotus, the Creation is a pure-willed free gift. It is incited, beyond reason, not by a will to dominate but by charity, which freely gives a space of freedom to the other. In the Scotist cosmos every creature qua creature is contingent, and in being what it is, reveals that it might have been otherwise. Instead of possessing "natural tendencies," human creatures are endowed with open capacities (recognized by the doctrine of univocity) to which divine grace may condescend.

Corresponding with the new primacy of charity, however (and here Todisco and Manzano are in a kind of negative agreement with the RO authors), is a certain arena of created autonomy. This shows clearly that all parties agree that while univocity is rooted in formal logic, it has ontological and theological consequences. Univocity of being allows for Scotus a reading of divine/human concurrence in freedom in terms other than those of Aquinas—whose notions of a fully determined creaturely freedom can seem contradictory: what is an entirely determined freedom? Even if, for Scotus, the divine election is irresistible, our response still has some formal space of its "own," its own integrity grounded in the logical law of identity ( just as, as one might mention, for the Franciscan tradition culminating in Ockham, property rights are a matter of absolute formal ownership and not built upon "appropriate use," as for Aquinas—in such a way that the life of religious poverty requires the abandonment of material ownership by a will still nonetheless "owning itself").[15] Since God freely gives gifts of finite being to us as "others," he can also enter into covenanted bonds with us that are sensitive to our freedom. As free we especially exhibit the image of God, but this God of freedom whom we reflect is no despot; to the contrary, the Thomist *potentia absoluta* is dangerously undetermined and rendered just and true only under the auspices of *potentia ordinata*. For Scotus, however, the two potencies display one single will to charity—both in what God actually does and in what He might do.

The same formal goodness is shown in human beings: they do not require extrinsic teleological determination in order to be accounted good by nature, nor do they await any mode of cultural determination. Aristotelianism, to the contrary, requires that human beings be teleologically fulfilled in the life of the *polis*. But for Scotus human beings are not political or social animals, as they are for Aristotle and Aquinas respectively. Instead, they are able to negotiate culture as a work of freedom, and the only "common good" one should recognize is a contractually produced state of empirical peace. This Scotist "proto-liberalism," on Manzano's account, meshes exactly with his protoempiricism and modest rationalism. Scotus maintains both the latter two elements because he also foreshadows (one can add to Todisco and Manzano) a Baroque division of knowledge between "truths of fact" and "truths of reason" confined to the little that follows from the law of identity.

The perspective Todisco and Manzano present with great lucidity offers an extremely attractive theological program. If one takes modernity back to its Scotist roots (and even where Todisco and Manzano protest this thesis, their own exegesis tends to confirm it), one can retain what is valid in the modern world purged of its secularity. Thus empiricism, a strict use of reason, and political liberalism all sit nicely with an apophatic attention to revelation and a theology focused upon charity and the gift.

It is a very Anglo-Saxon program, and why should some contemporary British and American authors question it? If, for the moment, I were permitted to be somewhat expansive, I would say that this is in part because of doubts about the "modern" Anglo-Saxon project that have arisen from within this project itself. Wilfred Sellars, W. V. O. Quine, Richard Rorty, and John McDowell have all questioned the possibility of empiricism and rationalism by questioning the possibility of distinguishing the sources of our knowledge as clearly either fact or reason, synthesis or analysis, or fact or value.[16] The epistemology of "representation" whereby the mind can "image" reality (in either an empiricist or rationalist/idealist variant) has been in this way challenged. Likewise, the liberal politics of "representation" of supposedly originally isolated and fully autonomous individuals through the objective artifices of contract, money, politeness and parliamentary election has been challenged by the work of MacIntyre and Sandel and many others (MacIntyre's work being very much Thomistic in inspiration).[17] So if, as both RO and Todisco with Manzano seem to agree, epistemological representation and political liberalism have roots in univocity, then an "anglo-saxon" questioning of univocity is not so surprising: it would appear logically to be next on the postempiricist agenda. And one might add, to conclude this digression, that it may be a welcome sign of the recovery of a truly European culture that British defenders of a southern Italian Norman find themselves in debate with Latin defenders of a man born in a small town in the Scottish borders.

Can this defense of Scotism be adequately answered? In responding to it, it is important to stress that the present author is not simply advocating the autonomy and wide compass of theology. Rather, the present critique of Scotus has more to do with the separation of faith from reason, grace from nature, will from reason, and theology from metaphysics and physics.

One cannot (as most contemporary commentators agree) really exonerate Scotus from the charge of ontotheology. The distance of the infinite is not difference from the ontic, and univocity requires that God and creatures "are" in the same albeit spectral ontic fashion. Scotus's treatment of a vast range of issues from human freedom (as we have just seen) to questions concerning Adam, Christ, Grace, and the Eucharist tends to show that this logical/ontological minimum still makes a considerable conceptual and practical difference. Common to all these instances is the idea that a being as self-identical and so recognizable must be free from all "internal relations" (to adopt a later terminology). It must be thinkable in abstraction from all cause and constitutive cobelonging with other realities. This position tends to encourage both epistemological and political atomism. If each finite position does not occupy the problematic (even, one can admit) contradictory space of participation, then it is identical with its "own" space, and univocity involves necessarily a logic of "self-possession" that may be at variance with the theological notion that being in its very existence is *donum* and not the mere ground for the reception of a gift—even for the gift of determination of this ens as finite. For even the latter reception allows a certain formal ground to persist outside gift, as in the case of the Scotist conception of the human will. This "self-possessed" space is frequently considered by Scotus as if *per impossibile* God did not exist, and so *etsi Deus non daretur*. Being can be treated purely "metaphysically" (for the first time) in abstraction from "physical" issues of cause and moving interactions. Yet does not this approach in some slight way impugn divine omnipotence and render God a being alongside other beings, even if this "alongside" is a nonnegotiable gulf (and even because it is a nonnegotiable gulf)? Todisco and Manzano do not really engage this issue. Todisco in particular obfuscates the point that while, for Scotus, Being and not God is the subject of metaphysics, God is nonetheless included in the first subdivision of this subject-matter, as infinite being, whereas for Aquinas God, as cause of *ens inquantum ens* (and not just of being qua finite) can be invoked only as the inaccessible principle of the subject-matter of metaphysics, unknowable by metaphysics itself.[18]

If, in this fashion, God is somewhat reduced to ontic status and included within the consideration of metaphysics, then the greater autonomy allowed by Scotus to theology in relation to metaphysics appears ambivalent. In particular, the conceptual space for revelation is predetermined in its nature by philosophy—just as much (and arguably more so) as with analogy of attribution. Since revelation is seen to be removed from every mode of compellingly intelligible necessity, it has to fall within the scope of pure contingency and pure factuality. It will inevitably favor the "truths of fact" pole within a facts/reason a priori alternative supplied solely by philosophy. The danger is clearly one of revelational positivism: that we know in advance that all that God can show us is positive facts and unambiguous information. For example, it does not seem good enough to say, with Manzano, that only by divine freedom are bread and wine appointed to be sacramental vehicles. Of course this is true, but it does not preclude a certain insight into their "convenience" or one might say "aesthetic necessity"—how otherwise should spiritual writers be able to meditate, for example, on the significance of the color, liquidity, and intoxicating power of the wine? It is hard to make sense of this sort of limited but real insight into revelation without invoking certain ideas about analogical ascent (and also extending those notions to encompass theories of metaphor).[19]

Univocity appears to encourage dualities without mediation: God is unknowably and equivocally remote as regards His being in quale; this gap can be bridged only by positive revealed disclosures—yet this means that the space of revelation is philosophically predetermined as a space of facts or empirical propositions. By contrast, while it seems that analogy already by reason intrudes upon the space of revelation (since any rational advance is ultimately lured forward by a grace-granted anticipation of the beatific vision), nevertheless the paradoxical presence of unlikeness within likeness in analogy, which also governs revealed discourse, ensures that the mysterious unlikeness of the revealed truth is sustained, not just with regard to content, but even with respect to formality. An analogical participating reality is neither simply a reason nor simply a fact, neither simply universal nor simply particular. The participating analogue exhibits not a full rational account of its cause (it cannot furnish us with a syllogistic proof of its cause) but only a partial one, by way of its concreteness as an effect—its very factuality, which declares its cause only by exhibiting more clearly its own concrete character. And yet this "fact," in pointing toward its more excellent cause, embodies a kind of "reason." Only this analogical perspective ensures that revelata are not reduced to objects or items of information. It allows more scope to revelation than does univocity, since revelata now bear with them not just their own historical contingency but also their own logic, which reason without revelation cannot fully anticipate. To put this another way: the space for the Logos to amend even our logic may be somewhat lacking on Scotist premises.

So might it be that analogy more than univocity presents the autonomy of the logic of revelation? One can note that it was Aquinas and not Scotus who wrote many commentaries upon scripture imbued with the principles of fourfold allegorical exegesis.

This is not at all to deny that for Scotus univocity is a theological as well as a metaphysical category. It does indeed have profoundly to do with Scotus's theology of grace, as Todisco insists. Since, for Scotus, we are fallen, we have lost the possibility of our orientation to the infinite in the beatific vision. At the same time, redeeming grace permits us a minimal recovery in "neutral" terms of the natural orientation of the intellect to being—but without yet allowing us, like Adam, by grace also to see angels and God as easily as trees and rocks—and facilitates our reorientation via grace to the infinite. Nevertheless, this beguiling circle relies heavily upon Scotus's Avicennian (and ultimately somewhat Plotinian) view that knowledge is not for us by nature mediated by the senses.[20] And this would appear to qualify the verdict that Scotus more than Aquinas allows this world to be true to itself on its own terms, since here something that clearly belongs to our embodiment—our full conceptual grasp only of the sensorily mediated—is reevaluated. Everything that depends upon this mediation—science, the arts, philosophy, even the sacramental practice of religion—must partake of this reevaluation. The entire sphere of culture, like politics, for Scotus can figure only as a kind of semi-sinful emergency measure.

By contrast, Aquinas was able to combine a certain materialism with our natural orientation to a supernatural end. His affirmation that, even in Eden, we first understand the materially instantiated ens requires no extrinsic supplementation in the order of grace (as Scotism suspects), because Aquinas also thought that being as such was the first object of the human understanding. The coprimacy depends entirely upon Thomas's esse/essentia metaphysics as supervening upon his form/matter, spirit/body metaphysics. Since every essence participates in esse and discloses it, the material thing renders being as partially transparent to our gaze as does the spiritual thing. In this way the embodied creature can be as near and far from the beatific vision as the angelic one. It is for this reason that Aquinas, elaborating on several of the Fathers, could so vividly grasp that the degraded following of our senses by the reason after the Fall was subverted by the Incarnation into the instrument of our redemption. Here it is, after all, Scotus who permits a pathway to extrinsicism because of his cognitive Plotinianism: Adam was oriented to the beatific vision not by nature but only by special grant of grace; Christ's humanity possessed grace not intrinsically but only by special fiat; Christ's dead body in the tomb was divine by virtue of the formal distinction, yielding separability of his body from his whole substance (whereas for Aquinas it was divine by virtue of its substantive inclusion via the *persona* of the Logos and single esse granted by the *Logos* instead of the normal unity of substantive form); our desire for beatitude is not entirely natural except according to a nature "elicited" by grace.[21]

The theological dimension of univocity tends to problematize rather than assist an integral vision. But leaving questions of revelation aside, does logic nevertheless ineluctably commit us to a univocal vision, whatever the consequences for the theological realm? Todisco argues that this is the case. One can concede to him that our finite minds are inclined by their very *modus cognoscendi* to thinking that everything that "is," including God, "is" in the same fashion. The forms of language we are obliged to use tend to imply this, and it is impossible for our logic altogether to escape such a conception. This circumstance, as both Aristotle and Aquinas recognized, is part of the categorical boundedness (at once ontological and logical) of our finite circumstances. However, this inescapable "univocal moment" concerns being as fully transparent to our logic, or mode of thinking. But this does not mean that logic by itself obliges ontology to follow its lead, unless one has already assumed an ontological priority of rational possibility over actuality. Just because, for the most transparent logic, existence is an either/or and the notion of "degrees of being" makes no sense, it does not follow that actual existence necessarily enshrines this logic. Moreover, disclosures of being other than the logical—in aesthetic, ethical, and contemplative experience—may suggest to us that being can undergo a qualitative intensification. For actual existence—the circumstance that there is anything at all—exceeds the a priori notion of existentiality as the condition of the possibility for things being this or that. Although everything that is given to us is a being, this still involves a disclosure that existence itself is a given mystery. And since the a priori grasp of ens qua ens as bare possibility cannot of itself generate a single actuality, we cannot know what being itself is, nor that it is predatory upon the prior repertoire of the possible; to the contrary, since the possible is always only the possibility of the actual, it makes more sense to assume the ontological primacy of actuality.

For these sorts of reasons, Aristotle's metaphysics asks, What is being, and in what diverse ways can it occur? Neoplatonism dealt with the resulting aporia—Is being primarily a first causal source or primarily the most general categorical circumstance?—with the notion of a scale of emanations, construed by Proclus more Platonically as also participations and imitations (albeit finally of the One beyond Being).[22] Without this resolution, one is left either with the notion of a highest ontic being, which does not explain being as such and invites infinite regression, or else with an Avicennian/Scotist notion of an acausal being in general, which tends toward the mystery of an original *res* indifferent to something or nothing—in the long run this allows the possibility of "Scotist" nihilism as evidenced by Deleuze. The Proclean (but also Augustinian, Dionysian, and Thomist) hierarchy of participation and attribution avoids both of these problems. But is it merely senseless? Here one can venture that no finite logic can rule out the idea that the actuality of finite being includes always a greater and lesser intensity. Indeed, according to a certain traditional logic, only the instance of a lack in appropriate being at any level makes sense of notions of falsity and evil. Likewise, according to a certain traditional ontology, only the notion of degrees of being makes sense of the facts of autonomous life that can accommodate more being and exhibit a "self-advancing" being, and of the comprehensive powers of cognition that "is in a manner all things" according to Aristotle. Most crucially, the doctrine of Creation forbids theology to think in terms of "bare existence." If being as such is created, then to be a finite being is causally to receive a measure of being. To say that one can think being univocally outside the realm of causality weakens the doctrine of Creation — hence, in the wake of Scotus, a residue of Avicennian Neoplatonism remarkably resurfaces in Ockham: for the latter, at least in principle, the intelligences may create beings below their own level.[23] The idea that created being is only a gift bestowed by infinite esse, not an a priori something/nothing that any creature might posit, is here dismissed.

Logic does not therefore oblige us to assume an univocal ontology. However, does analogy in logic violate the principle of noncontradiction? One must concede to Todisco that it does. So at this point the present author becomes a Thomistic heretic: Scotus was rigorous and correct in this respect, but maybe this is exactly why Nicholas of Cusa, who sought (unlike the Baroque "Thomists") to salvage the Proclean heritage in the face of Terminism, decided to question the law of identity itself? The recourse to coincidentia oppositorum is legitimate because of the ontological difference, which is also for Aquinas the infinite/finite difference. Just as there can be only pure identity and simplicity in the infinite — since finite things are always composed and shifting — so, inversely, there can be no mere logical identity in the unlimited, since this notion makes sense only by reference to limitations. For Aristotle (for whom it was still a relatively ontological, and not purely logical principle), the law of excluded middle applies because there is such a thing as (for him always limited) "substance" (even though inversely the law also ensures that there can be such a thing).[24] If God, as according to Aquinas, lies beyond limited substance, then the law loses its field of application.

In a similar fashion, the law of excluded middle cannot readily apply to participation of the bounded in the unbounded. For the finite to enter into participation in the infinite is to enter into identity and nonidentity, and this coincidence is reflected and doubled in the circumstance that the finite here becomes at once finite and infinite. (And the finite can be construed either as the complex and nonidentical or as the bounded self-identical.) This provides the contradictory dynamism of analogy which exceeds that of Hegelian dialectics (also indebted to Proclus), since the contradictory tension is not really a conflict in search of an elusive return to formal identity but a higher harmony beyond logical opposition that inspires an increase and intensification of a tension which mediates and resolves in and through its apparent contradictoriness. One may protest that here language has taken a very long vacation indeed. But does it make any more workaday sense that God is omnipresent and yet the world is not God? That for Augustine we are "of ourselves" nothing and are something only from God and yet are not God? That (as for Aquinas) our created freedom is entirely determined in the very formality of freedom and yet is incomprehensibly determined as free since God is the absolute author of the existential, including the existentiality of freedom? (If he is not, then, as David Burrell has argued, there is a competition between God and creatures in a "zero sum game" that loses divine transcendence in an ontic parity.)[25]

The doctrine of Creation seems to impose these mysteries, and the incomprehensible logic of analogy seems sensitive to them. According to a Scotist perspective, however, they undergo a demystification. This perspective appears to prioritize the mystery of freedom, yet pure freedom is so open as to cancel mystery. It is already emptily determined as the supposed opposite of rational determination, but this allows to the divine absolute freedom the status of a pure free "thing" alongside us only insofar as our reason can comprehend this. Every voluntarism is but the reverse face of a rationalism: what one has here is not a benign dividing and ruling, but instead a collusion generated by a questionable dualism. This dualism tends not to allow God the status of a freedom that is equally (and incomprehensibly) something rationally determined and also (again incomprehensibly) able to allow "another" space of freedom that is still *non aliud*. Inversely, reason and determination, once robbed of a freedom intrinsic to their being, are left to their own merely formal and ultimately tautologous devices. The mediation of the beautiful between goodness and truth is here impeded, and whereas an aesthetic is always secretly fundamental for Aquinas (as also for Bonaventure and other Franciscans), in Scotus it tends to be converted at once into an empirical aggregate (a consequence of the Avicennian view that there can be a multiplicity of forms in a single substance) and to analyzable proportion. (This somewhat anticipates the much later eighteenth-century tension between empirical and rationalist approaches to aesthetics, neither of which were capable of capturing the Beautiful—a circumstance that helped precipitate the romantic reaction against the Enlightenment.)[26]

One can say in opposition to this that unless we can formally distinguish truth and goodness in God, our use of these words no longer makes any sense. But this confines theological discourse to the inert and nonmystical. The Thomistic counter to this objection is that we already partially integrate in our lives the cobelonging of truth and goodness, and by mystical advance we are asymptotically but essentially drawn to the divine point where the difference between the two really vanishes.

Moreover, the Scotist determination of the divine difference by infinity alone is ontologically insecure once the infinitization of the finite opens to view in the Renaissance (though this was anticipated by another great British Franciscan, Robert Grosseteste, in *De luce*). Once this has happened, Scotus's ontological primacy of the infinite over the finite (which may be a true thesis) is perfectly compatible with a pantheistic immanentism. At this point it was only a continued subscription to attributive ascent and to ontological difference (between simple *complicatio* and composed *explicatio*) that prevented Cusa from becoming a Bruno or a Spinoza. (Alternatively there is a direct passage from Scotism to a Spinozistic postmodernism.)[27] As Cornelio Fabro has argued, only participation secures simultaneously transcendence and immanence. But only the God who is simultaneously both is the transcendent God, since infinity without participation and so simply "beyond" and "outside" the finite can be recruited to pure immanence alone. So participation is not merely a "Greek" thesis alien to the Biblical legacy, it is a framework perfectly compatible with free creation ex nihilo.[28]

Nor does Aquinas's idea that certain created structures are relatively "necessary" and others relatively contingent negate the freedom of the divine creative act. It rather augments divine freedom to point out that he can build into creation such a distinction, for the free contingency of the creation is ontological and not ontic and therefore more transcendentally free. This means that even the most apparently necessary structures within the cosmos are nonetheless contingent in their ontological dependency, just as the most apparently free creatures in the cosmos are fully determined in their existentiality. To say, by contrast, with Scotus, that all creatures are equally contingent in their ontic instance, thereby taking contingency always to mean that "a thing might have been otherwise" rather than to mean (ontologically) "a thing did not have to be," is to reduce the actual to our logical apprehension and to claim too much insight, despite the apparent mood of empirical piety or pious empiricism. How do we know that water, trees, fire, and so forth merely instantiate "possibilities" from an infinite repertoire? Might they not instead disclose to a small degree the mysterious (not simply rational) necessities of the divine mind and will? Aquinas never separates these two realities. Aquinas, unlike Scotus, for whom a formally distinct will in the human instance is open to the possibility of an incomprehensible "pure" choice, altogether without inspiring reasons.

We have explored some of the negative consequences of univocity and its alliance with the formal distinction of will from reason. But is there nothing in the idea that the reduction of metaphysics to a minimal ontology actually frees theology to be a practical discourse about charity that is truer to the priorities and exigencies of the Christian life? Certainly this perspective allows Scotus to articulate a rich theology from which valuable insights may sometimes be gleaned. Nevertheless, as both Todisco and Manzano reveal (inadvertently or not), the danger here is of a drift into formalism. If God's will is inherently charitable and this quality enjoys a certain subtle priority over and independence from his intellect (with which indeed it harmonizes yet does not altogether coincide), then what is the content of charity? It will tend to become a free respecting of the freedom of the other; the gift will be simply of freedom, and such giving will be set at variance with the mutual agreement of covenant and contract. (Even though for Scotus the second table of the Decalogue republishes the natural law, its extra force as direct divine law still depends on willed institution and formal agreement.)[29]

This secures what one might see as a typically modern duality of private "free" gift over against contract, and Manzano appears to endorse (though to evaluate differently) my reading of Scotus that allies him with an emerging market society and the rise of the nation-state. But why should Christian theology endorse with Todisco (and Scotus?) the assumption that people properly pursuing their own legitimate interests will naturally and nondeliberately be in a hostile relation to one another? Is this compatible with Augustinian frameworks of the natural harmony of the creation and the possibility of a substantive (not just formally and contractually contrived) human peace? And why, for Manzano, are notions of "the common good" any more obscure than the shared values of the public library, or the shared pleasures of the public piazza — and why allow Oxford professors (in this case J. L. Austin), with their remarks about trousers, cats, and teacups ("the common good" is an ambiguously forking "trouser phrase"), to deprive us of such palpable actualities? Does not the shared piazza exhibit an irreducibly collective good in so far as it involves a kind of *state* of charity, a reciprocal give-and-take within a shared horizon, rather than the empty one-way gift of freedom and the contractual achievement to enjoy such gifts in solitary self-pleasuring? Such an exchange of freedom amounts to a reduction of gift to contract, since the gift is given only within the mutual agreement to respect each other's freedom; by contrast, a contract is like the passing in the night of two "free" gifts that never acknowledge each other or discover a mutual appropriateness.

Manzano's abandonment of Catholic social teaching (for which the notion of "the common good" is scarcely dispensable) in favor of the today still emerging liberal market-state must ensure that the realm of human cultural choices has little relevance to transcendent goodness and truth. If indeed Scotus went this far in the direction of contractualism, then the thesis concerning the secularizing tendency of univocity is all the more confirmed.

I am not at all contending instead, as Manzano suggests, for "natural law fundamentalism." To the contrary, I take the view that Aquinas's natural law, beyond the minimum that we share with animals (self-preservation, care of the young, and so forth) concerns the prudential judgment of equity and not the reading-off of norms from a pregiven nature (a perspective that may indeed result in prejudicial views concerning women, as Manzano suggests). To deny, with Manzano, our natural orientation to sociality beyond the family does nonetheless appear to ignore certain facts (such as the fundamental role of sympathy, for example, as noted by that other great philosophical Scottish lowlander, David Hume). But the fact of our orientation to agreeable association can nonetheless be interpreted only by increasing theoretical and practical insight into the value of association and just what it is that makes it agreeable. Teleology is not closure, if it equally avoids formal openness. But then, even the eschaton can be somewhat anticipated — otherwise it may as well be threat as promise.

Neither Aquinas nor Scotus possessed an adequate ontology of culture or history.[30] However, the semivoluntarist perspective of the latter promises less in this domain than the semi-intellectualism of the former. If culture is merely the work of will, then it is irrelevant to reason; it is still irrelevant to reason if it is half the work of will and half the work of a rational *mathesis*. For neither is intrinsically cultural. Culture is taken seriously only where it is seen that both reason and desire are possible only in terms of language and other humanly constructed products that in turn construct humanity. The Scotist denial that human knowledge naturally concerns primarily sensorily intuited things cannot support this sort of insight. Much is made of Scotus's "historicist" attention to the *status lapsus*. Yet this exhibits only a concern with salvific metahistory, whereas the denial of the materiality of knowledge before the Fall is also by implication a denial of the natural historicity of human understanding — namely, the rootedness of our thoughts in concretely embodied occasions and circumstances.[31] By contrast, the Thomist model of both human and divine understanding seems more promising. God's intellect at one with his will responds to a kind of intrinsic aesthetic necessity, since Aquinas does not yet subscribe to anything like Leibniz's idea of God as submitting to sufficient reason and a calculus of the best possibilities. This necessity is present only in the Trinitarian emanation of the *Verbum* and the procession of the *Donum*. (Although this embodies the potentia ordinata, it properly expresses the potentia absoluta, which coincides with divine wisdom, although this infinite potency and wisdom cannot be adequately embodied in any particular finite order. Nevertheless, since the particular ordained order perfectly expresses an infinitely wise absolute power, the latter does not virtually suspend the finitely incomparable "justice" of the actually ordained order, reducing it to a mere possible instantiation of an infinite repertoire, as it tends to do for Scotus.)[32]

For Aquinas our utterance of the inner word and directing of desire participates in the Trinitarian processions. In the seventeenth century, the Portuguese Dominican Juan Poinsot (John of St. Thomas) expanded the theory of the concept as inner word into an account of our necessary cognitive deployment of culturally instituted signs that were nonetheless in continuity with natural signs.[33] The Trinitarian reference was preserved through a recognition that a sign like the Trinitarian person falls under a "real relation" within the domain of *esse intentionale* and as such is as objective as a real relation in the substantive universe (material or angelic). This means that for Poinsot (making use of the category of real relation, which Scotism and Terminism had tended to reject), human knowing and willing are possible only within the cultural and yet objective edifice of signs, which itself participates in the divine Verbum and Donum and so in divine esse. (Poinsot's grasp of participatory metaphysics and analogy was not strong, but his account of signs is Thomistic and compatible with such a metaphysics.)[34]

One could argue that the potential of Thomism to generate an ontology and theology of culture is linked with its Proclean dimension. Proclus, as a "theurgic" Neoplatonist, insisted that recollection of the transcendent realities was possible only via their descent into culturally instituted ritual forms; even in his treatment of geometry he insists on the technological and pragmatic mediation of geometric theorems.[35] I would concur with Benedykt Huculak's stress upon an Aquinas-Proclus alignment versus a Scotus-Plotinus alignment.[36] However, Proclus's interest in recollection, participation (despite Huculak's denial of this and conflation of Proclus with Plotinus at this point) and insistence upon the abiding of the finite soul in time seem closer to Plato than does the Plotinian legacy. It is partly on this basis that one might see Aquinas as "more Platonic" than Scotus. One could also add that Augustine had also reacted to Plotinus in a manner somewhat analogous to that of Proclus: in the *Confessions*, although the soul measures time, it remains within created time; recollection plays a role in Augustine's articulation of divine illumination, reinvoking the *Meno* problematic of seeking for what we somehow already know; God must descend in the Incarnation and the Eucharist if we are to see the divine ideas; "interior" vision is contained within the vision of a sacral cosmos.

Are the usual alignments and contrasts (Plato versus Aristotle; Plotinian Augustine versus Proclean Aquinas) really reliable? Can we not sometimes read Aquinas as more Augustinian than medieval Augustinians much influenced by Plotinus via Avicenna? This is not necessarily to deny that Franciscan mediations of Augustine can balance Aquinas's perhaps not always sufficient stress on intellect as intrinsically desiring. However, Augustine was himself far more Platonically intellectualist than the standard interpretations often suggest. (Huculak cites Fabro as saying that Thomist participation proved incompatible with Augustinianism. However, the passage cited concerns merely Thomist refusal of the "Augustinian" idea that finitude equates with materiality — Augustine's view here being arguably more complex than this characterization.)[37]

It is declared by Scotus that the way of denial, or *via negativa*, only removes finite imperfections from the positively-known quality "infinity," deemed to be properly "convenient" for God in a more absolute sense even than intellect and goodness and so forth.[38] By this concept of a positive infinite, one "grasps" an absolute void of mystery. Within the framework of Pseudo-Dionysian and Thomist negative infinitude, by contrast, one does not grasp mystery, but one might say that the mystery was such that one is positively initiated into it — according to the Pseudo-Dionysian dialectic of the apophatic and cataphatic that mystical theology embraces. The comprehended infinite void is akin to the Plotinian-tinged Avicennian infinite One, taken by Scotus as formally preceding the divine qualitative perfections ("good," "true," and so forth), which themselves formally precede the divine intellection: at *Quodlibetal Questions* 5 a 3 Scotus speaks of these orderings as "quasi-emanations." (This ontological priority of a positive infinite over any substantive qualities seems more or less to legitimate the use of the term *void* here.)

To say, as many do, that Scotus retains, in his own fashion, a form of apophaticism is somewhat misleading. For Augustine and Aquinas, negativity introduces us to a mysterious and yet palpable darkness, which in refusing our analysis still welcomes us. This remains the case even when perfection terms are negated, as with Pseudo-Dionysius and Eriugena, because this negation is always driven by a superexceeding, not a skeptical suspension.[39] But Scotus offers us instead the positive presence of a kind of fetishized infinite absence. This could be seen as an anticipation of the Kantian sublime that is alien to an infinitude of the *forma* of the beautiful. This shift in the mystical component toward the absolutely empty effectively delivers theology over to the ineffable authority of the Church hierarchy, and, later, alternatively, to that of scripture.[40]

One can also read Duns Scotus as offering a theological anticipation of postmodernity: by foreclosing the scope of theological speculation, he demoted intellect in general and opened up theology as the pure discourse of charity. We receive the loving will of God and respond to this with our answering will.[41] Between the reading of Scotus as surrendering the mystical heart of Catholicism and the reading of Scotus as inaugurating a kind of Pascalian way of charity, recent French historians of philosophy seem to hesitate — and with perfect legitimacy. There is certainly a sense in which the Scotist distinguishing between the ethical goal of happiness and the goal of pure justice, linked with an obedient and correctly intending will, rather than a beatified intellect, leads not only toward Kant, but also (as he recognizes) toward Jean-Luc Marion's disinterested charity and unilateral gift. In like fashion, Scotus's separation of revelation from mystical ascent points forward both to Karl Barth's hermeneutics of the pure word of God and Marion's phenomenology (without metaphysics) of the revealed word. Both seem to be linked to a loss of the mediating vision of analogy, even though, contradictorily, Marion's defense of the Pseudo-Dionysian *via antiqua* against the Scotist inauguration of ontotheology seems to require the via antiqua alliance of revelation with metaphysics in the broader sense, and a more emphatic sense of analogy and participation than Marion affirms (although establishing his position on this is very difficult indeed).[42]

It becomes illogical to uphold the postmodern Scotus while denouncing the modern Scotus, and this applies both in philosophy and theology. If one cannot countenance Scotist ontotheology, one must also question a "pure" philosophy concerned with a nondivine being, since this is ultimately grounded in univocity and the refusal of analogy in any sense consistent with the pseudo-Dionysian naming of God. In this way, Heidegger comes into question. Likewise, if one is wary of the Scotist separation of abstraction from elevation, or, rather, his particular refusal of the mystical, one must be wary also of his semivoluntarism. For the very same separation, applied by Duns Scotus to Augustine's discourse on the Trinity, ensures that one must interpret the divine intellect and divine will as univocally similar in character to the human intellect and will. Such a predilection is reciprocally reinforced by Scotus's Franciscan rejection of a distinguishing of the persons of the Trinity by substantive relations.

This rejection is allied to an Avicennian assumption that divine essence, and then intellect, and later still divine will, are quasi-emanations that precede in some fashion the entire Trinity. This tends to disallow the idea that the Verbum simply "is" an original aspect of the divine intellect in conjunction with the Donum, which in turn simply "is" an original aspect of the divine will. Duns Scotus sees the Verbum as simply "declaring" an understanding fully present in the Father as Father, in principle not requiring any generation in order to be understanding; likewise with the Holy Spirit in relation to paternal and filial volition.[43] This is inevitable, because if essence and intellect and will are all "prior" to the Trinity, and formally separate from it, then all three realities are essentially nonrelational.

If relation has no root in the divine essence, then the persons that spring from the divine essence, understanding and will, cannot have their most fundamental identity in relation. They require instead some preceding respective "principles" to ground their distinctive personhood. For Scotus, such principles are found in originating essence, intellect, and will. The divine intellect, for Scotus, in contrast to Aquinas, can be intellectual only if it "represents" something that precedes it: since what it represents is the divine perfections (in contrast to the absolute simplicity of the divine infinite essence which can be represented only as perfect), the latter are formally distinct from the divine intellect as well as the divine essence (whereas, for Aquinas, divine ideas in no way abide outside the divine intellect any more than the divine essence).[44] Because the intellect is ineluctably compelled by the perfections, it is a "natural" response, and the Verbum is said to proceed *per naturam*. This compulsion is formally independent of the will, again in contrast to Aquinas (the supposed intellectualist), and this inaugurates a separation, in Scotus, of judgment from teleology. Concomitantly, the divine will in Scotus is somehow wrenched away from the inner lure of desire, and the procession of the Spirit is grounded in a pure nonnatural and, it would seem, arbitrary procession *per voluntatem*.

Without recourse to substantive relation in identifying the persons of the Trinity, the attribution of intellect to the Son, and will to the Spirit, ceases to be remote analogical naming—since we cannot really grasp pure relationality—and becomes the means of literal distinction. The Son proceeds per naturam (in "declaring" as words do thought, the Father's ineluctable representations) but the Spirit per voluntatem. In this way, God is psychologized in an unequivocal fashion foreign to Augustine—yet scarcely because of Western "perversions," since neither substantive relation nor the *filioque* is anywhere in sight. Indeed, a reading of Scotus tends to show that none of the typical textbook categorizations of the history of Trinitarian doctrine is valid: for example, Scotus has a strong doctrine of the paternal *monarchia* as prior to generation and spiration because he also has a strong view of the divine *essentia* as characterizing Godhead, rather than Trinitarian relations. Such a view is found neither in Augustine nor in Aquinas, whose writings have weak (but sufficient) accounts of the *monarchia*. The oft-trumpeted Franciscan "alternatives" in Trinitarian theology, it seems, result from the subordination of the Christian Trinity to a Neoplatonic trinity lurking in the ontological shadows.

The Scotist mode of distinguishing the persons by the natural/voluntary contrast in turn ensures that will is regarded as a movement of pure sponta- neity outside the heteronomy of the laws of motion (a movement is always from another, according to Aristotle) and independent of the recognitions of the intellect.[45] If the latter now simply "represents" a neutral being, without evaluation, then concomitantly "will" begins its career of the pure positing of values without foundation. This is the inauguration at once of pure piety and pure irresponsibility.

The issue does not involve a contrast between the modern and the post- modern. It is rather that both represent a certain middle ages (with roots that reach back before Duns Scotus in his Franciscan forebears and in Avicenna) within which our culture still mostly lies, and whose assumptions we might want to reexamine.

It is not that the postmodern aspect of Scotism is now to be perceived as the most fundamental one. So far, I have pursued such an argument, but this is too one-sided. It is true that the reign of representation (or epistemology) assumes univocity of being, but it is equally true that the latter assumes rep- resentation. In reality, one cannot assign a priority, either in logic or in his- torical fact; not in logic, because while representation assumes the formality of abstraction that univocity guarantees, this univocal formality is recipro- cally established when it is assumed that the mind's ability to abstract some- thing common mirrors something in the real, rather than doing something to the real. Not in historical fact, because the moves toward univocity were permitted by the Avicennian and later Franciscan doctrine that there can be many substantive forms within the entity, rather than merely subordinate forms integrated under one overriding form, as for Aristotle. This position arises because a new ontological weight is accorded to the mind's ability to isolate and abstract different elements—the source of the Scotist "formal distinction." In addition, Olivier Boulnois has shown how Roger Bacon's re- ception of Arab optics (or "Perspective") encouraged the view that physical realities are generated through an exact imaging or copying of prototypes, in a fashion that tends to reduce the Arabic stress on *convenientia*—or ineffable aesthetic rapport of all beings to each other (a theme taken up by Aquinas)—to exactly measurable proportion and equivalence.[46] This account of optics then tended to encourage Bacon's account of the linguistic sign either as assisting a mental copying of something either real or imagined, or as arbitrarily invoking an ontic equivalent in algebraic fashion without the mediation of reflective understanding (so resisting the Aristotelian sequence of sign > concept > external thing understood). Such a perspective tended to undo the Aristotelian view of knowledge as "realizing" spiritually a materialized form, and this shift is sustained through Scotus up to William of Ockham.

We have seen that the paradigm of representation had another source. This may be equally or more fundamental. This is in relation to the *divine* intellect. As we have seen, Scotus shifts notions of divine understanding away from simple identity with essence, and, in consequence, away from the idea of its being archetypal art—a supreme "maker's knowledge"—rather than a kind of self-mirroring. For Scotus, the divine ideas of the divine perfections that are the first exemplars arise only as "representations" of perfections that in some sense precede cognition. So, just as for Aquinas finite knowledge by identity (the species of a thing being realized in our understanding) is grounded in the supreme divine identity that is simplicity, so for Scotus finite knowledge by representation is grounded in divine self-representation. In this double fashion, realism gradually gave way within the Middle Ages to modes of empiricism, skepticism, and even idealism (though there were many examples of hybrids of knowledge by identity and knowledge by mirroring).[47]

The complex and gradual shift toward representation also tended to render less distinct cases of mere logical predication from real invocation. As we have already seen, the domains of logic and semantics began to dominate and predetermine that of metaphysics. This process was begun in Avicenna himself: for the latter, logic deals with universals, and physics with particulars, while metaphysics concerns pure forms or essences indifferent to either universal or particular. But this tends to turn the subject of metaphysics into certain inherently abstract entities that hover in a no-man's-land between the logical and the real, the mental and the actual. Inevitably, this suggests a further logic of that which is not necessarily universal, and metaphysics is here placed on its Kantian course of concern with a "transcendental logic." (Perhaps Kant—the preeminent "modern"—also remained with a certain Middle Ages?)[48]

Another way to express this would be to say that Scotus increased the tendency to logicize and semanticize metaphysics. Prior to his writings, being had usually been considered to be univocal within logic, equivocal within physics and analogical within metaphysics. It is true that Aquinas's theological analogy plays subtly between metaphysical and logical analogy, where the former (*ad unum ipsorum*, or "proportionality") denotes a real ineffable "sharing" in one principle through *convenientia* by two other realities (as substance and accident share in being), and the latter (*ad unum alterum*, or "proportion" or "attribution") denotes a mysterious link strictly in terms of semantic priority with no necessary foundation in the real—as both medicine and the body are healthy; the latter primarily so, yet the former in a causal manner. Nevertheless, attribution still assumes, following the Proclean legacy, an ontological foundation; as in this case the matter of occult sympathies, etc. Thus Aquinas also talks of *proportionalitas*, a parallel sharing in "health" between medicine and the animal body.[49] Without this metaphysical dimension, attribution would collapse into equivocity. In theology, for Aquinas, the metaphysical aspect of analogy preserves the real affinity, while the logical aspect preserves the dimension of mystery: how is God good? And how is medicine healthy? Yet the ontological assumption is made that God is preeminently good.

In this way, Aquinas begins somewhat to qualify metaphysics with logic in theology. His analogy, as Alain de Libera has suggested, can be seen as analogical to a second degree, since it lies between the relative univocity of metaphysical analogy and the relative equivocity of logical analogy.[50] Nevertheless, the interweaving of a logical moment tends to favor the metaphysical interpolation of participation within the schemes of ordered proportionate causality.

Scotus also gives logic and grammar a newly accentuated place in theology. But he goes much further. Earlier in his career, he had presented being as logically equivocal; later he saw it as logically univocal, mainly under the pressure of the need to ground the possibility of predication by finite creatures concerning the infinite, once participated-in perfections had been abandoned. The univocity of being within logic is here held to govern also the character of being as a transcendental formality. Every existing thing, whether finite or infinite, is univocal in quid, where being is taken to mean an essential "not not-being." Specific and virtual differences remain, however, as we have seen, purely equivocal. Gilles Deleuze was right: univocity releases equivocal difference—but it suppresses analogy.[51] Ultimately, the warrant for this move is not objectively rational; rather, it is grounded in the refusal of any existential and evaluative freight to the process of abstraction.

Can one sustain any notion that postmodernity is a more fundamental matter than modernity? It is really simply an advanced phase of modernity, where univocity and representation now become inseparable. But, one might object, modernity is very difficult to identify, so much so that there is perhaps little point in engaging in the Quixoticism of trying to resurrect the premodern. There is no modern, and so there is no premodern. Instead, there is a certain middle ages that has been dominant. Where, in the midst of all these epochs, which turn out not to be straightforward epochs after all, are we to look? Perhaps, many people—from French Catholics to midwestern exiled evangelicals (such as John Hare)—seem to suggest, we need to retheologize modernity by returning it to its roots in Avicenna, Henry of Ghent, Bonaventure, and, supremely, Duns Scotus. But then, if so, how should one describe Aquinas's challenge to Avicenna (deploying Averroës, Pseudo-Dionysius, and Proclus, rather than Avicenna's Plotinus, and a de-Avicennised Augustine)? Not, surely, as an invocation of the premodern, but as something like an avant-garde innovation against the modern already begun in the name of a deepening of the patristic tradition?

Somewhat parallel considerations apply in the cultural domain. One might focus upon such themes as individual rights, bureaucratic formality and abstract economic equivalence as characterizing "the modern." By contrast, one might take an emphasis upon style and the subtle conformity of fashion as denoting "the postmodern." However, from the outset, modernity concerned the rise of civility as a substitute for "liturgy."[52] All that is occurring in our own epoch is the increasing slide of fixed manners into temporarily fashionable idioms of behavior. But in many ways this augments the formal lack of underlying rationale and shows an equally increased need for surface reliability, rendering what goes on behind the surface not so much irrelevant as nonexistent.

From the outset of modernity, civility undergirded rights just as univocity undergirded representation. The "representation" of subjects as formal bearers of equal rights was possible only once their humanity had been abstracted from their creaturehood without any concomitant advance toward deification, a movement that was in parallel with the Franciscan shift toward an immanent leveling of perfection terms. Whereas, in the Middle Ages, deification involved, among other things, a cultivation of the virtue of "cleanness," which for monks and knights encompassed both spiritual purity and physical integrity with bodily hygiene, from the Renaissance through to the eighteenth century the "human being" became increasingly a literally dirty bearer of an abstract nominal spiritual essence of detached reason and indeterminate freedom. Included within the continuing medieval "Platonic" practice of preventative medicine (greatly reinforced by Arabic influence) was the continued devotion to the Roman practice of bathing, sometimes indeed within old Roman baths. In the later Middle Ages and the Renaissance, by contrast, public bathing came to be viewed as a threat to morals, and water as itself possibly contaminated. For the generalized "baptism" of lustration was now substituted the frequent change of clothes and resort to cosmetic concealment: a bodily equivalent of the art of dissembling that the new civility was specifically recognized as often concealing. This can be seen as culturally equivalent to the perspective of ontological anarchy opened up by the formal distinction. (In the nineteenth century, certain neo-Gothic texts, such as Pugin's *Contrasts*, specifically recognized the lost cleanliness of the medieval monastic, ecclesial, and urban civic order, comparing for example public fountains to mean and sordid parish pumps. In 1928 Lynn Thorndyke confirmed that the nineteenth century may well have been far less hygienic than the Middle Ages.)[53]

The medieval "clean" universal humanity, just as it reached down into the body, also reached up into the sphere of transcendence. With St. Paul, after Christ, there was now a universal humanity and no longer just Greek and Jew, male and female, slave and free, because all human beings were no longer merely human, since God had entered humanity. Therefore, human beings became human beings only by elevation beyond humanity, just as to recognize the good (prior to Bonaventure and Scotus) was to advance toward God in one's substantive being. By contrast, within modernity, human beings could be human beings without transformation: as simply thinking (representing) or willing (positing values). This new mode of formal recognition implied a shift in social ontology. No longer was society seen in terms of the liturgical body of Christ (the trace of God ceasing to be only God, which inaugurated humanity as no longer humanity).[54] Initially, it had been only by this mythos of divine descent ("the glory of God is humanity fully alive") and theurgic ascent ("the life of a human being is the vision of God," to complete Irenaeus's couplet)[55] that general human interrecognition was first established — as Hegel realized. But now, with the advent of civility as quasi-liturgy, a general humanity was given merely in the uniform practice of empty formal codes. So, to sum up: once upon a time there was only generality beyond locality via universal myth and ritual. Later, there was only generality where all styles were measured in conformity and equivalence with one another and in the same ever-dictated and appropriate circumstances. And today? Today, a general humanity where all wear the same back-to-front unmediable styles in the same spans of time.

This general legal and "democratic" representation (the abstraction of the general will so that it can constitute a single mirroring mind of government) presupposes civility, in the same way that cognitive representation presupposes univocity. And here also there is a reciprocal foundation.[56] Civility presupposes formal representation. Even if there must be orderly behavior and handshakes between rivals if there is to be an election or a court trial, the hidden presupposition of civility is abstract equality and formal negative freedom. All may use forks (a Renaissance innovation) and wear their conforming or alternative styles or be dirty or externally clean (now without any symbolic resonance) in manifold conventional or subversive fashions;[57] it denotes nothing and therefore nothing (or everything) is affirmed or subverted in the fullest conformity. If all are to be free and to aim for anything, then, paradoxically, behavior must be made more and more predictable; but, inversely, an essentially contentless behavior always proclaims freedom and the sublime gesture. "Postmodern" civility and "modern" representation therefore continuously spring up together. And they both conform to a certain middle ages: a middle ages tending to privatize devotion and separate clerical from lay power—thereby immanentizing the latter.

Civility and rights coalesce around the idea of a normative formalism. Rights allow an appearance of peace through regularity that disguises the *agon*—beyond any defense of a substantive cause—of the marketplace and competing state bureaucracies. Civility prevails in the space of "civil society" or of free cultural intercourse that is supposedly aside from state mechanisms and not wholly subordinated to the pursuit of abstract wealth. Any radical analysis of contemporary society must expose these twin formalisms as disguising the operations of concrete if self-deluded interests. Do postmodern discourses attain to such radicalism?

One can here isolate three tendencies associated with the names of Emmanuel Levinas (and to a large extent Jacques Derrida), Gilles Deleuze, and Alain Badiou respectively.

First of all, a Levinasian perspective tends to bring together the perspective of rights with the perspective of civility. A Kantian formalism regarding the generalized other is supposedly exceeded at the point where a legal acknowledgment of freedom passes over into the non-legislatable style of regarding the other's specificity. This is a matter of cultivating a manner, rather than simply following a rule. And apparently this is a liturgical idiom, because respect for the other is described by Levinas in terms of the worshipful acknowledgment of the absolute Other, in his irreducible absence.[58]

At this point, Badiou objects to Levinas's assertion that such a religious perspective mystifies and obscures human relationships. If every human being presents to us the absolute distance of God, then we are always asked to respect the ineffable in mortals, and nothing is said regarding how we are

to respect the actual appearing attributes of mortals, save vacuously, insofar as they contain a "trace" of the unsoundable. This trace is not at all an
"image" that can be in some ways—if not exhaustively—characterized (as
is the case for the human *imago Dei* within Christian theology).[59] Here the
merging of rights with the protocols of sublime civility toward others in fact
draws one even further away from a characterization of those others, whose
noumenality now exceeds even the rationality and freedom of the Kantian
bearer of rights. It is not clear that this sort of respect for the other rules out
any act of violence that one might commit against appearing bodily subjects,
since nothing that appears is here regarded as a token of what warrants absolute respect, and, furthermore, the realm of appearing is for Levinas always
necessarily—beyond the whit of politics—contaminated by totalizing oppression. Because of this latter perspective, Levinas does not seem to deny
that an instrumentalization of human life and human bodies is unavoidable
in the world of human labor and striving (as a moment's reflection will show),
but then has no means of teleological discrimination between acceptable and
unacceptable instrumentalizations. In consequence, the most diabolical instrumentalization could still present itself as compatible with respect for the
nonappearing other.

With good reason, Badiou avers that this is just what the West tends to do
with the discourses of rights and pluralism: when respect for the other harmonizes with the power of a capital-owning minority, liberalism is affirmed;
when this particular mode of arbitrary power is threatened by relatively non-
capitalist forces, liberalism is suspended and all sorts of terroristic acts and
torturings are legitimated.[60]

Ultimately, the hopeless formalism of Levinas's ethic is determined by its
reactive character. The ethical impulse is for Levinas born with our "perse-
cution" by the sufferings of others. That is to say, his ethic assumes death
and violence as the fundamental facts of ethical relevance; such a perspective
is perfectly compatible with nihilism, and in some ways Levinas appears to
offer an ethic for nihilists. This negativity means that as, again, Badiou says,
for Levinas the only shared attribute of human beings beyond ineffability is
the fact that we are all going to die. Against this perspective, Badiou suggests, in some ways in keeping with Augustine, that the good has primacy
over evil, and that the good for human beings arises in those acts of imagination whereby we conceive of noble projects that transcend our mere animality and mortality. Evil is therefore more or less privative (though Badiou
obscurely backs away from precisely this position) and not the radical positive force that wields the instrument of death in the name of totalization, as
for so many of the followers of Levinas, Derrida, and even Žižek.[61]

One might say that for Levinas the best one can do is to exercise a kind of metaphysical politeness in the face of death. However, Badiou surely over-simplifies matters in saying that Levinas illustrates the danger of letting ethics be contaminated by religion. One could argue that Levinas also commits the opposite error: transcendence is reduced to the essentially immanent dis-tance of the subjective other, who occupies the same univocal space as our-selves. Certainly the identification of the horizontally encountered face with vertical height tends to mystify that appearing; but, equally, the identifica-tion of vertical height with the human subject of respect reduces mystery to civic formula. Later we will see that Badiou's own philosophy seems al-most to require a more plenitudinous transcendence that constantly arrives through grace to unfold new concrete possibilities for human coexistence. The space of the religious beyond the ethical matters to politics, because it reminds us that the circumstances of good social blending rely to some de-gree on "chance" and "coincidence," and are not simply under the command of the private moral will.

If Levinas can be construed as the contemporary philosopher of rights and civility, this is in no way obviously true of Gilles Deleuze. A Deleuzian per-spective recognizes that notions of civil society tend to conceal from view the playing out of power disputes. It is not an abstract respect for rights that is promoted by Deleuze, but rather a Spinozistic wider and wider combin-ing of active forces in order to permit mutual flourishing.[62]

For Deleuze, such forces manifest no basic drives or possibilities but are themselves the play of surface simulacra that conceal no real original essences. A certain Nietzschean distance from pure Marxist orthodoxy (although this does not forbid a reworking of Marxist categories) is indicated by what is in effect a refusal to read the late capitalist "society of the spectacle" (as the more Marxist Guy Debord and the situationists already described it in the sixties)[63] in terms of an augmentation of the role of the spell of the fe-tishized commodity as an element in sustaining conformity. For Deleuze, as for most of the post-sixties generation marked by Nietzsche, there can be in a sense only fetishes, and the specifically capitalist illusion concerns the con-finement of the play of substitution and divergence by abstract fundamental norms, rather than the older substantive norms of transcendence. This is the holding back of complete "deterritorialization."[64]

Nevertheless, the modern capitalist order still represents for Deleuze an important, and even, it would seem, fated stage of deterritorialization within the historical process. Where Deleuze's position appears truly incompatible with Marxism is at the point where it would seem that pure deterritorializa-tion can never arrive, any more than Derrida's pure gift, or pure difference and deferral uncontaminated by presence. For "territory" in Deleuze's philosophy is constituted within the space of epistemological representation. Beyond this space, and always governing it, and undoing it, resides the virtual, which does not represent but constitutes new regimes of the event, and is not mere "possibility" because of its anarchic unpredictability. However, just as for Heidegger, the history of Being ensures that there must be ontic illusion that is "folded back" into Being, so also for Deleuze, as Badiou points out, there must be the realm of representation and of temporary territorial illusion that is "folded back" into the virtual.[65]

It follows that one can say that whereas Aquinas questions the instance of the Avicennian (and later Scotist) regime of representation, Deleuze affirms its sway within a realm of the real. Again, as with Heidegger's Being, this is because for him the virtual has no real ontological content. Just because this absolute is not God, it is in fact paradoxically parasitical upon the very set of temporary orders that it institutes and ceaselessly undoes. The absolute speed of positive difference is too fast for being and understanding; their secondary illusion arrives always too late, but just for this reason belatedness is inescapable, and all that remains is the conformity of the vacuum of empty retardation.

Moreover, as Badiou argues, this would appear to be but a variant of the Plotinian metaphysics of the One—so determinative for Avicenna's metaphysical innovations, and therefore for the modern outlook in general. The One has to emanate; in a sense it only is one within and over against the many that it constitutes. For the Plotinian One is itself beyond being—not like the Platonic good with a hyperreality of the irradiating ideal, but rather with an ineffable emptiness of perfect simplicity. Likewise, for Deleuze, the virtual does not possess in itself even the latent being of the possible; it exists only in those regimes that disguise it in manifesting it, since their manifestation of the new also restricts the power of innovation.

However, if the virtual is in this way oddly impotent, it is also true that the various multiple regimes are strictly subordinate to the singleness of the virtual. For this reason, Badiou makes the seemingly astonishing complaint that there is too little difference in Deleuze, who is after all a Platonic metaphysician of the One. (Later we will see the ambivalence of this accusation; for Badiou, all philosophers are Platonists.) Deleuze's statement that the many always manifest the same univocal being in their differences can be read in a substantive Neoplatonic fashion. This is because the specificity of their diversity belongs entirely to the economy of representation; at a higher level of reality they are constituted conjointly in being/truth (in such a way that representation is only a game within a cunningly contrived hall of mirrors) by the virtual. But this means that, before and after difference, difference collapses back into the One.

Part of Badiou's quarrel with Deleuze here is a political one: isn't all this Scotist apparatus of univocity, virtuality, and formal distinction (whereby anything can be composed with anything else and anything equally can get unraveled) likely only to usher in a nonrevolutionary politics of relative speeds, where the theorist is simply the spectator of fated conflicts between territorial politicisms and presidents, on the one hand, and deterritorializing terrorists and mavericks, on the other, which only obscurely allow some mode of ingress for a vision of justice and freedom? Deleuze's metaphysical framework does not allow any place for clean breaks — or even for discontinuous ruptures of any kind. At best it would seem to allow for the development of civil protocols of temporary balance between restraint and emergence — while one would always have the suspicion that the real manners pertaining between emperors and nomads occurred according to a predetermined and impersonal code.

What is Badiou's third alternative to Levinas and Deleuze? And does this offer a postmodern escape from the coils of civility?

In one sense it does. Badiou's manners are much more those of revolutionary rupture. He celebrates the pure event or arrival of innovation in the spheres of politics, cosmology, art, and eros.[66] Compared with Deleuze, this event of arrival is given no ontological underpinning — not even the contradictory underpinning of emergence from a virtuality that it simultaneously cancels or contradicts. In this sense Badiou's claim to have broken with Hegelianism is much more convincing than that of Deleuze. At the same time, however, the event in Badiou's philosophy ceases to have the sense of the plural fragment that still clings to Deleuzian and Derridean difference. To the contrary, Badiou insists that the revolutionary event in any sphere is universally compelling for all humanity, and he combines this with a traditionalist Marxist (or Maoist) impatience at the politics of ethnic, racial, and sexual difference.[67]

In this fashion, for Badiou, the universal emerges from a singularity, not from a hidden background of Neoplatonic unity. Though he shares Deleuze's affirmation of univocity, he declares that, if he were forced to choose between the univocal and the multiple, he would choose the multiple. And, for Badiou, events occur not against a background of the henological virtual, which generates an agonistic play between movement and stasis, but rather against a background of meaningless multiplicity. Here he develops a fundamental ontology on the basis of the Cantorian theory of infinites.[68] All that there is is an infinite set of multiples that endlessly break down into infinite sets and subsets. All these monadic universes, one could say, enshrine the mirror play that allows the illusion of representation, but in contrast to Deleuze, these universes are originally there, and therefore the possibility of representation is more primary and lies in a noncontradictory relation to fundamental ontology. What stands in contrast to representation now arises not before but after it, in the field of the pure event, which is a kind of surface countercurrent to ontology, governed by the Platonic priority of the Good over Being; but with the Good now defined in terms of the radical imagination of new possibilities.

The pure event is held to break with the static, given "situation" that embodies some set or other of the multiple. Here Badiou appears much closer to the situationists and their surrealist legacy than Deleuze, because the break with the spectacular universe of the commodity is seen as absolute, and the pure event performed with integrity as a genuine origination uncontaminated by secondariness or mimesis. There is no longer any need for a civil or well-mannered social governance of an unavoidable ontological agon between what totalizes and what breaches and innovates. Thus, politically, Badiou advocates militant industrial disturbances plus removal from parliamentary processes, and yet, at the same time, pressure on the state to force it to make destabilizing concessions. He claims, against Deleuze, that nothing in his ontology renders impossible the realization of the socialist hopes that drive such stances.[69]

This political approach has its parallel in Badiou's deployment of religious analogues. We have already seen that he is critical of Levinas for his religiosity, and he is a far more militant atheist than Derrida — and perhaps even than Deleuze or Nietzsche, since in place of the Spinozistic substantive void, or the Dionysiac will to power (the "will of a god," perhaps literally, for Nietzsche), we have instead the pure Mallarméan random throw of the cosmic dice.[70]

And yet it is possible to claim that this purer atheism is less obviously nihilism, less obviously the worship of a dark God. For, in Badiou's philosophy, the random and agonistic are in no way subtly affirmed and fated by a more primary virtuality or Being into which they are "folded back." As with Mallarmé, the hope here persists that a single throw or series of throws may yet somehow defeat the desert of chance itself:

Excepte
à l'altitude
peut-être

aussi loin qu'un endroit
fusionne avec au delà
hors interet

    .    .
une constellation.[71]

This would appear to be a humanist hope, and there is far more residue of
Sartrean humanism in Badiou than in other of the *soixante-huitards*, however
he might protest this. Yet this is not entirely accurate: Badiou retains the tinc-
ture of transcendence in the Mallarméan hope. It would seem indeed that
he must do so, if he is to explain how the singular event can have the lure of
the universal: how, for example, the French Revolution or Cubist painting
or Cantorian mathematics or the cult of romantic love should rightly elicit
the admiration of all humanity and yet be entirely self-founded, appealing
to no pregiven ontological or epistemological circumstances.

Here Badiou proclaims himself still Platonist, offering a "Platonism of the
multiple" that expresses the radical thrust of the later Platonic dialogues.
Refreshingly, Badiou points out that all the "anti-Platonic" and "antimeta-
physical" moves against Plato that appeal to difference and indeterminacy
are anticipated by Plato himself. Not only that, he suggests that Plato's self-
critique is the more thoroughgoing because the tendency of Heidegger and
Deleuze (in ways that we have seen) is to retreat into the monist or dualist
(or both at once) cosmologies of the pre-Socratics. If everything is really the
flux of difference, then the life of the city—mathematics, erotic encounters,
exchanges in the agora, the shaping of statues of the gods—becomes epiphenomenal and illusory. Plato, however, was for Badiou the first philosopher as opposed to cosmologist, because he said, quite simply, that there is
the cosmos, and there is love and politics and art and mathematics, and then
asked what reality comprises all of this. This is why true philosophers can
proffer only "Platonisms." Plato's own answer, according to Badiou, eventually half-acknowledged the primacy of the multiple in both cosmos and city
but also struggled to explain why certain humanly contrived practices were
absolutely and universally compelling.[72]

And yet Badiou (too hastily perhaps) rejects the continuing role of the
Forms in the later Plato, together with his account of *methexis*. He ascribes
without warrant to Plato a recognition of the univocity of being. This leaves a
flattened-out ontology of the multiple, in multiple combinations. In this cosmos the absoluteness of human practices is not guaranteed by participation
in the forms, in Being, in the One, or in God. But how then can something
with a singular beginning represent more than the arbitrary of power? In ask-

ing this question, Badiou remains in effect postmodern yet appears to break with postmodern nihilism and enthronement of the agon of difference.

And the only possible answer is that the event is the event of grace. This is exactly what Badiou declares, and he is forced to see the event of the advent of Christianity as one crucial paradigm of the event as such; this is set out in his book on St. Paul.[73] Yet of course this is grace without God, an event of grace that delivers its own grace and yet only arrives by a grace that seems to exceed its merely empirical or mathematical instance as a member of a pre-given set or situation. One may well find such a conception contradictory, since if an event in order to be a universal event must bear an excess over itself, the notion of an "elsewhere" seems inescapable. In line with such a consideration would be a further question: since Badiou acknowledges that the arrival of Christianity was not just one more event, but rather the first event of the arrival of the field of events (singularities that inaugurate a new universal), how can he subtract from the religious content of this event without losing its concreteness and reducing the principle of all universality (which this event first supplies) to something ahistorical and so "eventless"?

If Badiou commendably escapes from the infinite/finite dialectics of "folding" and refreshingly points out that Heidegger's Being/beings and Deleuze's virtuality/representation schemata are simply variants of traditional metaphysical dualisms and monisms, and not "post-" anything whatsoever, then all the same he seems to offer instead a stark neo-Cartesian and Sartrean dualism without mediation. His cosmos of infinite sets is simply "there," like Cartesian space hovering in a virtual void somewhere between geometry and the genuinely physical, and it lacks, as compared with Deleuze, any account of the forces involved in its genesis. As with Sartre, the emergence of another meaningful urban reality from this bleak cosmic rural idiocy is left an unsoundable mystery. And the return to the notion of uncontaminated pure origins seems to lose the valid force of postmodern critique: as historical beings, we do indeed dwell in secondariness, and every apparently new thing is indeed to some extent a copy, and so on, running back ad infinitum. If we may applaud the refusal of that postmodern despair which sees every rupture as doomed to retotalize, we may nonetheless stand aghast before the adolescence of a perspective that thinks there is a neat distinction to be made between politically repressive "situations," on the one hand, and liberating "events" supposedly without any antecedence, on the other.

If Badiou genuinely lacks civility, he merely offers us an unredeemed rudeness, which at times aspires to a kind of liturgy but does not fully envisage it. All too readily one surmises that followers of acclaimed "events" would demand absolute universal submission to the implications of those events

of which they would regard themselves as the privileged *avant-garde* interpreters. The proviso that no event should declare itself the absolute event
and Badiou's sincere horror at the upshot of the activities of the Red Guards
are insufficient to placate this concern.[74]

The pluralist criterion to prevent a slippage into evil only opens again
the postmodern prospect of potentially unmediable difference, this time between possibly rival universals. While clearly Badiou will view the event of
Incarnation/Ecclesia as a falsely self-absolutized event, could not this be to
fail to ask whether it is just the event that seeks to be open to all events in
audaciously offering to them not the perspective that subsumes them, but
rather the impossible idiom of their cobelonging? Without such an event of
events, it would seem that Badiou's laudable desire to restore universality
in the face of a fixation upon diversity cannot possibly be accomplished.
Badiou's insights into the possibilities of a liberal totalitarianism should therefore not blind us to the stark opening to an old-fashioned illiberal totalitarianism in his own philosophy, whose reverse face is itself a continuing postmodern liberalism.

We have seen that postmodern politics offers variants of modern civility,
if sometimes in the negative mode of incivility. How can we think beyond
this? Can there be a more substantive mode of civil blending that goes beyond the formal distance of polite respect?

In accepting the postmodern sense that all is simulacrum, we still need
to be able to distinguish a fake from a true copy, and in this way to locate
Badiou's event of universal import. The way to do so is to suppose that there
may be nonidentical repetition without rupture, and at times an instance
of a positive relation between the virtual and that which the virtual provides. In this way, there would be no folding back of the event into the virtual that would entail its cancellation. But by the same token one would not
countenance Badiou's absolute contrast of event and situation: every creative
event would rather be seen as developing the hidden and repressed seeds of
a largely diabolical past, just as the New Testament is taken by Christianity
as fulfilling in an unexpected way the fragments of antiquity.

To say this is not at all to deny that often, or even most of the time, Deleuze
and Badiou's diverse pictures do correspond to historical reality. For the most
part, history, including the history of the Church, is indeed the violent interplay between stasis and movement, or the alternation between fixed situations and revolutionary breaks (though Badiou's picture is the less realistic one). The point rather is whether this historical reality reflects the
ultimate ontological situation, and whether, if it does not, there can at times,
if fleetingly and fragmentarily, be historical processes that disclose other,

nonagonistic possibilities. It may be that such rare sequences of events are, for all their paucity, more "compelling" than the overwhelming weight of terror, in rather the way that Badiou intimates.

If they are so compelling, and if true events are not in total discontinuity with situations, then this requires an ontological grounding. It must be that nature contains the seeds of more than the random, but rather also the sources of the meaningful, as Deleuze (in a distorted way) affirms. But if general situation and singular event can occur in harmony, it must further be the case that there is a higher ground for both these aspects of higher reality. This higher ground cannot be the Neoplatonic One, nor the merely virtual, realized in what it cancels, but rather is a plenitudinous, infinitely actual Being expressed in a certain measure in the finite being that it provides or lets be.

This notion of participation in the source of all situations and events that is an infinite unified multiple implies that what truly emerges as event is a gift, since it is good in its harmony and as good expresses toward us a good will — how can we detach the notion of goodness from the notion of an intention of beneficial providing as coming toward us? For this reason, participation requires that the event be the event of grace. At the same time, however, it also requires that the mystery of the source be preserved, since in seeing that the event is a gift from a higher source we recognize that source only in its self-manifestation as inexhaustible by us and infinitely reserved. Participation is always in the impossible; grace declares to us the unknown god.

By comparison, postmodern thought is unable to hold together grace with the *via negativa*. Characteristically, it seems to search for secular equivalents to theological themes. Levinas and Derrida present us with a secular negative theology, Badiou with a secular account of grace. Yet, as we have seen, the former delivers only a formalism of civility that is more formalistic than the Kantian formalism of rights and can equally serve as a mask for terror. Inversely, the latter ascribes to a mystique of avant-garde self-grounding that renders grace a mask for pure human affirmation without possibility of redress, analogical mediation, or appeal to a higher authority.

Could one not say that one requires both grace and negative theology? Then political ethics could cease to be reactive, and we could accord primacy to the projects of the human imagination that combine appearing bodies and do not just futilely acknowledge invisible subjects. But equally we could retain suspicion of these projects as only partially and inadequately displaying what we can never fully command, while also acknowledging that that mystery was somewhat present in human beings never reducible to players in civic processes. The secular equivalent of both grace and the via negativa would in this way think beyond either the idolatry of the humanly instituted, or the more subtly idolatrous hypostatization of the unknown "beyond being." It would rather conceive the appearance of the withheld or the withholding within appearance. This thought also requires the liturgical practice of searching to receive as a mystery from an unknown source that grace which binds human beings together in harmony.

But to think this is to think theologically; the "secular equivalent" fades into the thinking of incarnation and deification and the search for a liturgical practice that would allow for the continuous arrival of the divine glory to humanity. It transpires that the postmodern secular theologies predicated upon Scotist univocity are nothing really so grand. They are like Scotism itself, but partial theologies after all.

## Notes

For a development of Scotist univocity in this essay, please see the present author's forthcoming essay in *Modern Theology*. I would like to thank Lluis Oviedo for granting permission to reprint this essay.

1    Bruno Latour, *We Have Never Been Modern*, trans. Catherine Porter (New York: Harvester Wheatsheaf, 1993).

2    It has become fashionable to contest any interpretation of Duns Scotus that seeks to place him in any instrumental relationship with the kind of genealogy here; see, for example, David Ford's review of *Radical Orthodoxy* (London: Routledge, 1999) in *Scottish Journal of Theology* 54.3 (2001): 385–404, 423–25. See also my response essay to his review in the same issue of that journal (405–22). My interpretation of Duns Scotus and his historical significance, especially in relation to Aquinas, are scarcely controversial. See further Étienne Gilson, *Jean Duns Scot: Introduction à ses positions fondamentales* (Paris: Librairie Philosophique J. Vrin, 1952); but, more explicitly, Olivier Boulnois, "Quand commence l'ontothéologie? Aristote, Thomas d'Aquin et Duns Scot," *Revue Thomiste* TXCV.1 (1995): 84–108, *Etre et représentation* (Paris: P.U.F., 1999), and *Duns Scot: Sur la connaissance de Dieu et l'univocité de l'étant* (Paris: P.U.F., 1990); J.-F. Courtine, *Suarez et le système de la métaphysique* (Paris: P.U.F., 1990); Éric Alliez, *Capital Times: Tales from the Conquest of Time*, trans. Georges Van Den Abbeele (Minneapolis: University of Minnesota Press, 1996), 197–239; Michel Corbin, *Le Chemin de la théologie chez Thomas d'Aquin* (Paris: Beauchesne, 1972); J.-Y. Lacoste, "Analogie," in *Dictionnaire Critique de Théologie*, ed. J.-Y. Lacoste (Paris: P.U.F., 1998); Bruno Puntel, *Analogie und Geschichtlichkeit* (Fribourg: Herder, 1969); G. Prouvost, *Thomas d'Aquin et les Thomismes* (Paris: Éditions du Cerf, 1998); C. Exposito, *Introduzione a Suarez: Meditazioni metafisiche* (Milan: Rusioni, 1996); Gilbert Narcisse, O.P., *Les Raisons de Dieu: Arguments de convergence et esthétique théologique selon St Thomas d'Aquin et Hans Urs von Balthasar* (Fribourg: Herder, 1997); David B. Burrell, *Knowing the Unknowable God: Ibn-Sina, Maimonides, Aquinas* (Notre Dame, Ind.: University of Notre Dame Press, 1986); Mark D. Jordan, *Ordering Wisdom: The Hierarchy of Philosophical Discourses in Aquinas* (Notre Dame, Ind.: University of Notre Dame Press, 1986), and *The Alleged Aristotelianism of Thomas Aquinas* (Toronto: Pontifical Institute of Mediaeval Studies, 1992); John Inglis, "Philosophical Autonomy and the Historiography of Medieval Philosophy," *Journal of the History of Philosophy* 5 (1997): 21–53,

and *Spheres of Philosophical Inquiry and the Historiography of Mediaeval Philosophy* (Leiden: E. J. Brill, 1998); H. Möhle, *Ethik als Scientia Practica nach Johannes Duns Scotus, Eine Philosophische Grundlegung* (Münster: Aschendorff, 1999). The significance of Duns Scotus's contribution is not that he is the sole inaugurator of transformations in theoretical speculation, but rather that he is one figure among many—although a crucial one—in a general shift away from a focus upon the metaphysics of participation (which he tended to reduce to a matter of external imitation rather than intrinsic "sharing in"), and he is noteworthy in particular because he gave attention to these issues in a comprehensive fashion. No scholar could deny that such a shift occurred: see, for example, such diverse figures as Gilles Deleuze and Richard Cross: Gilles Deleuze, *Différence et répétition* (Paris: P.U.F., 1968), and Richard Cross, *The Physics of Duns Scotus: The Scientific Context of a Theological Vision* (Oxford: Clarendon Press, 1998), and *Duns Scotus* (Oxford: Oxford University Press, 1999). Richard Cross is a critic of the present author's own interpretation of Duns Scotus, although the reader is asked to note that, despite the former's protestations, it is not so much that the two analyses of Duns Scotus stand in a hostile relation, but that the negotiations of these analyses differ greatly; see, for example, Cross's critique in "Where Angels Fear to Tread: Duns Scotus and Radical Orthodoxy," *Antonianum* LXXVI (2001): 1–36. See especially 13–14 n. 40. Whatever one's position with regard to specific texts, one must perhaps take a position in relation to this generally acknowledged shift away from participation and its relative importance or otherwise. Put briefly, the present author's own position is that Duns Scotus and his successors, within an approach seeking (after the post-1270 condemnations) for complex reasons to emphasize the sovereignty of God and the primacy of scripture, opened a space for univocal treatment of finite being without regard to theology, rational or revealed. Although this space was not immediately exploited in a secularizing fashion, in the long run this came to be the case.

3   Duns Scotus, *Ordinatio*, I d. 8 q. 3 nn. 50 and 86, and I d. 3 q. 3, and see Boulnois, *Duns Scot: Sur le connaissance*, 379 nn. 192 and 193; Boulnois, *Etre et representation*, 308–14, 457–505.

4   Alain de Libera, *La Philosophie médiévale* (Paris: P.U.F., 1994), 404–6, *Penser au Moyen Age* (Paris: Éditions du Seuil, 1991); Alain de Libera and Maurice-Ruben Hayoun, *Averroës et l'averroësme* (Paris: P.U.F., 1991); Boulnois, *Etre et representation*, 293–327. Richard Cross seems both to admit and to evade this issue concerning the shift in the meaning of removed universality and perfection terms. He rightly says that for Aquinas the concept of being was not an abstraction, but a matter of concrete elevation and participation ("Where Angels Fear to Tread," 13). However, he also says that for both Aquinas and Scotus the concept of Being (and other transcendental terms) constitutes a concept "common" to both God and creatures: "there is a concept under whose extension both God and creatures fall, just as there is a concept under whose extension both cats and dogs fall" (18). Once things are set up like this, Scotus is bound to seem the more lucid thinker. Demonstrative theology using common concepts will clearly require univocal ones. However, since Aquinas admits that demonstration in general requires univocity, one can only assume (unless he uncharacteristically overlooked something rather crucial) that for him, as for Averroës, demonstration of God is not genuinely apodeictic (related to syllogism) but more dialectical (allowing probable assumptions). Likewise for Aquinas the only "common" concept of being is that of *ens commune*, which applies to created being alone. (Cross neglects to note that for Aquinas, as for Scotus, "God" does not fall directly under the subject of metaphysics, which, after Avicenna's modification of Aristotle, they see as concerning *ens inquantum ens*: for Aquinas this is ens commune, for Scotus, univocal esse,

conceptually indifferent to created and uncreated). For Aquinas, the conceptual transition from creatures to God works (ontologically and epistemologically) through the ineffable *convenientia* of analogy of attribution, without any isolatable, univocal medium that can be considered to be "in common." (God himself is the ultimate ground of what is held in common between beings, so he cannot himself be an item within this set.)

This means that for Aquinas the mode of signification/thing signified contrast as regards knowledge of God distinguishes between the divine *res* or reality, which is also infinite thought, on the one hand, and our *modus* or limited access to this reality, which is at once cognitive and existential, on the other hand. But Cross reads this distinction in post-Fregean terms as somewhat like a distinction of focal sense and multiple existential contexts. Without textual warrant this gives "being" and not *Deus/Esse* as the res, and then variable finite or infinite *modi*. But this scheme already allows being to be abstracted without perfective elevation—and, of course, if one thinks in these terms, Scotus is likely to appear superior to Aquinas. But the important point is that Scotus inaugurates the conceptual sphere in which Fregean logical universes and Kantian transcendental categories can safely orbit.

Cross ensures that Scotus must beat Aquinas at a Scotist game. Does not his disdain for historicism in this instance of profound epistemic transformation prevent him also from considering a possibly viable philosophical alternative? Nor is Cross consistent in this disdain. He indicates that he knows well that most thinkers up to and including Aquinas did not regard "being" as merely a "vicious abstraction," for reasons bound up with notions of abstraction as involving real ontological elevation. It seems rather as though Cross thinks of the alternative view of the concept of "being" as simply not worth discussing. Fortunately, it would seem, Scotus put a stop to all this nonsense. Yet if he did call a halt to obfuscation, then it would seem that, indeed, "Radical Orthodoxy" is right to see him as a revolutionary, at least in this respect.

Cross is again inconsistent about whether or not he is prepared to acknowledge historical change in relation to the question of analogy (another aspect of the handling of perfection language). In places he seems clearly to allow that for Aquinas analogy is grounded in participation (14), while in other places he asserts (28) that for Aquinas "the likeness of analogy is just the likeness of imitation." For Cross, the reduction of participation to imitation is in line with nominalist common sense (participation "confuses" the essence of a property with its imitability, 14), but he fails to reflect that this common sense, if it be such, is also idolatry. Creation cannot simply be "part" of God, since God is not a divisible object, but nor can it simply "imitate" God, since there can be no third real medium between God and creatures that could confirm the truth or falsity of this copying. Only God himself provides the medium. Hence to imitate (somehow) God is also to share (somehow) in God, since God alone establishes and confirms the veracity of the imitation. For this reason, traditional "participation language," from Plato onward, hovers between literal mimesis and literal "being a part of." Thus, for Aquinas, "to participate is to take a quasi-part" (*In Boeth. De Hebdom.*, 2.24). Yet Cross insists that the tradition was always secretly nominalist and adhered to the criteria of Anglo-Saxon common sense, reducing a real sharing-in to an empirically observable "likeness."

This is no more than anachronism, whatever one's opinion as to the coherence of "participation language." Moreover, Scotus's innovation in reducing participation to imitation is seen in his reduction of the language of *imago Dei* to an intensified instance of *vestigium*, in the context of his discussion of Trinitarian theology. By contrast, Aquinas had seen the vestigium (always seen as more like an empirically observable causal imprint of literal but relatively "thin" likeness, a "footprint" showing mainly God's might) as a weak instance of the *imago* (which is an ineffable showing-forth in a weak degree of the divine essence). See *Ordinatio* I d. 3 Pars 2 q. unica; Aquinas *S.T.* I q. 93 a. 2.

5  See for example, Scotus, *Ordinatio*, I d. 3 q. 1 and d. 8 q. 3 nn. 112–15.

6  Ibid., I d. 3 q. 3 nn. 31–151.

7  Boulnois, *Etre et representation*, 290–91.

8  Scotus, *Ordinatio*, I d. 3 q. 4 nn. 358–60.

9  Duns Scotus, *In Elench*. q. 15 para. [8] (22a–23a); *In praed*. q. 4 para. [5] (446b–447a) and para. [6] (447a); see also Boulnois, *Etre et representation*, 246–47.

10  Ibid., 327–405, 457–93.

11  Alain de Libera, *La Philosophie médiévale*.

12  Thomas Aquinas, *De spiritualibus creaturis*, a. 10: "Now it does not matter much if we say that intelligible things themselves are participated in from God or that the light that makes them intelligible is participated in from God."

13  Orlando Todisco, ofm conv, "L'univocità scotista dell'ente e la svolta moderna," *Antonianum* LXXVI 2001): 79–110; Isidoro Manzano, ofm, "Individuo y sociedad en Duns Escoto," in the same issue, 43–78.

14  De Libera, *La Philosophie médiévale*, 116ff.

15  Oliver O'Donovan, *The Desire of the Nations* (Cambridge: Cambridge University Press, 1996), 248: "Promoting a mendicant idea of absolute poverty [the Franciscans] posited a 'right of natural necessity' (Bonaventure) or a 'right of use' (Ockham). Though dissociated from real property, the right still carried proprietary overtones. Gerson invoked the term *dominium* to describe the right of self-preservation and indeed initiated the tradition of conceiving freedom as a property in one's own body and its powers." O'Donovan here radicalizes the discussion of the ambiguity of poverty in John Milbank, *Theology and Social Theory* (Oxford: Blackwell, 1990), 16.

16  John McDowell, *Mind and World* (Cambridge, Mass.: Harvard University Press, 1995); Wilfred Sellars, *Science, Perception and Reality* (London: r.k.p., 1963); Willard Van Orman Quine, "Two Dogmas of Empiricism," *From a Logical Point of View* (Cambridge, Mass.: Harvard University Press, 1994), 20–47; Richard Rorty, *Philosophy and the Mirror of Nature* (Oxford: Blackwell, 1980).

17  Alasdair MacIntyre, *Whose Justice? Which Rationality?* (London: Duckworth, 1988).

18  In defense of Scotus on this matter, see Leonardo Sileo, ofm, "I 'soggetti' della teologia e il 'soggeto' della metafisica," *Antonianum* LXXVI (2001): Fasc 2 207–224. See also Boulnois, *Etre et representation*, 457–505.

19  Nacisse, *Les Raisons de Dieu*.

20  Boulnois, *Etre et representation*, 55–107.

21  Olivier Boulnois, "Duns Scotus, Jean," in Lacoste, *Dictionnaire critique de Theologie*; Rowan Williams, "Jesus Christus III: Mittalalter," *Theologische realencyclopedie* 16 (1987): 748–53; Cornelio Fabro, "Participation," *Catholic Encyclopedia* 10 (1967).

22  Proclus, *Elements of Theology*, trans. E. R. Dodds (Oxford: Oxford University Press, 2000), propositions 13, 25, 29, 55.

23  William of Ockham, *Quodlibetal Questions*, 1.1.

24  Aristotle, *Metaphysics*, 1005B 16–1009A 37.

25  David Burrell, *Freedom and Creation in Three Traditions* (Notre Dame, Ind.: University of Notre Dame Press, 1993), 94.

26   Duns Scotus, *Opus oxoniense*, I d. 17 para. 3 q. 13. See also Umberto Eco, *Art and Beauty in the Middle Ages* (New Haven, Conn.: Yale Nota Bene, 2002).

27   Nicholas of Cusa, "On Learned Ignorance," in *Selected Spiritual Writings*, ed. L. H. Lawrence Bond (New York: Palist Press, 1997).

28   See 2 Peter 1:4, where we are clearly said to be "sharers in the divine nature."

29   Duns Scotus, *Rep. Paris.*, I IV d. 28 n. 6.

30   Javier Andonegui, OFM, "Escoto en el punto de mira," *Antonianum* 76 (2001): 145–91.

31   This might seem to be contradicted by Scotus's assertion that there is an individuating factor in things — *haeccitas* — beyond negative material determination, which the intellect can intuit. See here Antonio Conti, "Alcune note su individuazione e struttera metafisica della sostanza prima in Duns Scoto," *Antonianum* 76 (2001): 111–44. However, the Scotist account of individuation involves a somewhat incoherent "formal" element in matter (as if it could potentially exist of itself in an unformed state) and an ineffable principle of *haecceity*. One could here agree with Gilson that the Thomist account of the concrete act of esse supervening upon essential form gives a more adequate account of individuation (and a more relational one). However, Conti argues against Gilson that since being is the act of essence (the entire nature of a thing) and not of form (which is an aspect of the thing insofar as it informs matter), this leaves Aristotelian individuation, which concerns the activation of matter by form — matter supplying negatively the individuating factor — unaffected. Hence Gilson's argument that the concrete existence of the thing gives a new primacy to the individual beyond Aristotle will not work. However, one might argue that the equal creative actuation by esse of matter and form, substance and accident, ensures that material individuation occurs only through its share in esse. This tends to turn the negative individuation into something positive. Moreover, Aquinas makes it clear that the esse/essentia dimension is not just a topmost, "added-on" layer. Its analogical economy extends to the interrelations of genus, species, and individual. See Fabro, "Participation." It is also the case that the frequent expression in Aquinas *forma dat esse* suggests some equation of *forma* with essentia. The "negativity" of matter seems the best way to understand it, and compared with Aristotle, Aquinas accentuates its nonpositivity: matter exists through form. This leaves external (nonangelic) limitation itself a gift or created mystery.

32   Aquinas, *S.T.*, I q. 25 a. 5 *resp.*

33   John of St. Thomas (John Poinsot), *Artis Logicæ secundæ*, pars. 581B 24, 582A 16, and 574B 35, 575A 5.

34   Ibid.; John Deely, *New Beginnings: Early Modern Philosophy and Postmodern Thought* (Toronto: University of Toronto Press, 1994), 65–109; Jacques Maritain, *The Degrees of Knowledge*, Gerald B. Phelan (Notre Dame: Notre Dame University Press, 1995), 75–145.

35   Proclus, *A Commentary on the First Book of Euclid's Elements*, trans. E. R. Morrow (Princeton, N.J.: Princeton University Press, 1970); Jean Trouillard, *La Mystagogue de Procles* (Paris: Les Belles Lettres, 1982); Gregory Shaw, introduction to *Theurgy and the Soul* (Pennsylvania: Pennsylvania University Press, 1995).

36   Benedykt Huculak, "De mature Augustiniano opere Joannis Duns Scoti," *Antonianum* 76 (2001): 429–79.

37   Ibid. On Augustine's intellectualism, see James Wetzel, *Augustine and the Limits of Virtue* (Cambridge: Cambridge University Press, 1992).

38   Scotus, *Ordinatio*, I d. 8 q. 3 n. 49.

39   On illumination, see ibid., I d. 3 q. 3 a. 5. On negation, see I d. 8 q. 3 n. 49, and nn. 70–86. On the formal distinction of divine perfections and divine intellect, see I d. 3 q. 4. See also

Olivier Boulnois, *Sur la connaisance de Dieu et l'univocité de l'étant* (Paris: P.U.F., 1988), 111–81, and Boulnois, *Etre et representation*, 308–14, 457–505.

40  Duns Scotus, *Quodlibetal Questions*, 5 a. 1. See George Tavard, *Holy Writ and Holy Church* (New York: Harper and Row, 1959).

41  Duns Scotus, *Ordinatio*, I d. 8 q. 4; and see Boulnois, "Duns Scotus: Jean."

42  See Jean-Luc Marion, "Une époque de métaphysique," in *Jean Duns Scot ou la révolution subtile* (Paris: Éditions Radio-France, 1982), 62–72.

43  Scotus, *Ordinatio*, I d. 3 q. 4 n. 387 and d. 13 q. 1 n. 45; *Quodlibetal Questions*, q. I a. 3.1 57–80; q. 8 a. 1.27; Boulnois, *Etre et representation*, 107–14.

44  Aquinas, *S.T.*, I q. 14 a. 4 *resp*; a 5 *resp*; Scotus, *Ordinatio*, I d. 30 q. 1 nn. 11–53; Boulnois, *Etre et representation*, 405–32.

45  See Boulnois, *Etre et representation*, 107–114; and Scotus, *Ordinatio*, d. 3 q. 3 a. 4. See also Scotus, *Quodlibetal Questions*, q. 1 a. 3; q. 2 a. 2; q. 3 a. 2; 5 a. 3.

46  Boulnois, *Etre et representation*, 55–107. Richard Cross interprets the formal distinction (*The Physics of Duns Scotus*, 28) in terms of the idea of features distinguishable within an entity but not separable from it. I wonder, however, whether this somewhat misses the point. For Aquinas such features are distinct either in a certain way (like one's arm from the rest of one's body) or only intellectually (like God's truth from God). Scotus, however, presents this in a different way: an intellectual distinction without total separation must have some real foundation of separability as well as holistic unity. One might say that he is a more realist thinker. For Scotus the arm is no mere real part: in one (overly?) holistic respect, the "arm" is pulled back into ineffable *haeccitas*, where its separability lies dormant. In another (overly?) atomistic respect, the arm is a kind of virtual prosthesis, ready to take on a life of its own. In relation to God there is only the latter danger: divine simplicity is compromised by Scotus. His Neoplatonic language of "quasi-emanations" to describe the ontological succession of formal distinctions in God tells against Cross's reading of this doctrine.

47  Boulnois, *Etre et representation*, 17–107, 405–453. Cross speaks of Scotus's epistemic theory as if it simply followed common sense. However, once again he equivocates: at times Aquinas is also supposed to have a representational theory of knowledge (*The Physics of Duns Scotus*, 53), yet finally Cross concedes that Scotus innovates in shifting to *esse representivum* as the basis for knowledge, and that this inaugurates a modern epoch in thought about thinking.

48  H. Möhle, *Ethik als Scientia Practica nach Johannes Duns Scotus, Eine Philosophische Grundlegung* (Münster: Aschendorff, 1999); Étienne Gilson, *Jean Duns Scot: Introduction à ses positions fondamentales* (Paris: Librairie Philosophique J. Vrin, 1952).

49  Aquinas, *S.T.*, I q. 13 a. 5 *resp*.

50  De Libera, *La Philosophie médiévale*, 408–11.

51  Deleuze, *Différence et répétition*.

52  Pickstock, *After Writing*, 135–67.

53  Lynn Thorndike, "Sanitation, Baths and Street Cleaning in the Middle Ages and Renaissance," *Speculum* 3 (1928): 192–204. See also the Gawain Poet's "Cleannesse," in the *Pearl Manuscript*, ed. Malcolm Andrew and Ronald Waldron (Exeter: Exeter University Press, 1994), 111–85; A. W. Pugin, *Contrasts* (London: C. Dolman, 1841).

54  Henri de Lubac, *Corpus Mysticum: L'Eucharistie et L'Eglise au Moyen-Age* (Paris: Aubier-Montaigne, 1949).

55  Cited by Archbishop Rowan Williams in an interview conducted by David Cunningham, "The Converging Worlds of Rowan Williams: Living the Questions," *Christian Century*, April–May 2002, 21.

56  Éric Alliez, *Capital Times*.

57  John Bossy, *Christianity in the West, 1400–1700* (Oxford: Oxford University Press, 1985), 121–22.

58  Emmanuel Levinas, *Autrement qu'être ou au-delà de l'essence* (Paris: Kluwer, 1984).

59  Alain Badiou, *Ethics: An Essay on the Understanding of Evil*, trans. Peter Hallward (London: Verso, 2001).

60  Ibid., 18–40.

61  Ibid., 40–90.

62  Deleuze, *Différence et répétition*.

63  Guy Debord, *La Société du spectacle* (Paris: Gallimard, 1996).

64  Gilles Deleuze and Félix Guattari, *Capitalisme et schizophrénie*, vol. 2, *Mille plateaux* (Paris: Éditions de Minuit, 1972).

65  Alain Badiou, *Deleuze: The Clamor of Being*, trans. Louise Burchill (Minneapolis: University of Minnesota Press, 2000), 82–91.

66  Alain Badiou, *Manifeste pour la philosophie* (Paris: Éditions du Seuil, 1989).

67  Badiou, *Ethics*, 18–30.

68  Alain Badiou, *L'Être et l'événement* (Paris: Éditions du Seuil, 1988); *Court Traité d'Ontologie Transitoire* (Paris: Éditions du Seuil, 1998).

69  Badiou, *Ethics*, 95–145.

70  Badiou, *Deleuze*, 74–5.

71  Stephan Mallarmé, "Un coup de dès," in *To Purify the Words of the Tribe*, trans. Daisy Alden (Huntingdon Woods, Mich.: Sky Blue, 1999), 122–65.

72  Badiou, *Manifeste* and *Deleuze*.

73  Alain Badiou, *Saint Paul: La Formation de l'universalisme* (Paris: P.U.F., 1997).

74  Badiou, *Ethics*, 58–145.

PART 4　Reenchanting the Political
beyond Ontotheology

*Graham Ward* | The
Commodification
of Religion, or
The Consummation
of Capitalism

CORNELIUS CASTORIADIS, commenting critically upon the Marxist under-standing of economic development, particularly the process of accumulative reification that Marx saw was inevitable with the increasing alienation of the worker's labor from the products of that labor, writes:

> Reification, the essential tendency of capitalism, can never be wholly realized. If it were, if the system were actually able to change individu-als into things moved only by economic "forces," it would collapse not in the long run, but immediately. The struggle of people against reifica-tion is, just as much as the tendency towards reification, the condition for the functioning of capitalism. Capitalism can function only by con-tinually drawing upon the genuinely *human* activity of those subject to it, while at the same time trying to level and dehumanize them as much as possible.[1]

It is a curious statement to make for Castoriadis, and I will develop just why in a moment. But first, allow me to make four clarifications.

First, for Marx, reification [*Verdinglichung*] is not a synonym for the pro-duction of commodities [*Produktionprozess der Waren*], for reification (as Cas-toriadis rightly demonstrates) is associated with Marx with what happens to human beings.[2] Commodification is what happens to the products of human labor when they are placed in systems of exchange—although Marx him-self never used the word "commodification" and there is no German equiva-lent. Nevertheless, these are the two fundamental processes of capitalism. They are intimately related, so if reification can never be completed, according to Castoriadis, neither can commodification. Second, reification cannot be completed because of the residual and resistant humanity that prevents that completion and, in that prevention, opens up space for the continuing process of producing commodities. That is, human beings remain free and independent from the processes of capitalism—and this freedom ensures a future for the capitalist system. Third, this freedom and independence is rooted in the fact that individuals are not (a) turned in things and (b) turned into things "moved only by economic 'forces.'" And fourth, capitalism requires the freedom and independence of human agents in order to continue as a process and not collapse immediately.

What is so surprising about Castoriadis's statement is that he is more than aware that "the individual is a social institution."[3] In other words, what is human is a social fabrication. It is not some essential thing independent of society. And while he is critical of certain attempts to erase the subject—the poststructural "death of the author"—for he wishes to emphasize all hope of social transformation lies in the ability to act both individually and socially, what is "genuinely human" is never established. Subjects are in possession of what he terms a "radical imagination." They construct notions of their own identity and make sense of the world on the basis of a magma or "incessant flux in and through which anything can be given . . . this thick and continuous flow [of representations] which we ourselves are."[4] Humanisms are institutions of this order; they are continually undergoing a process of modification. Even capitalists are of this order; capitalists are made:

> For someone who lives in a capitalist society reality is what is posited by the institution of capitalism as constituting reality. This reality is, in any case, that of a host of second-level institutions, of socially categorized individuals (capitalists and proletarians), of machines and so forth—social-historical creations held together by the common reference to a magma of imaginary social significations which are those of capitalism, and by means of this common reference these significations actually *do exist* and exist as *what* they are both in general and for each individual. This reality as a social-historical creation, includes within it, and would be impossible without, the social fabrication of individuals who *are* capitalists.[5]

Whence then is this "genuine humanity" that struggles heroically against the humiliations and atomizations of capitalist hegemony?

This is not an essay on Castoriadis, but I suggest his reasoning on reification (and, by extension, commodification) in capitalism is symptomatic. It is symptomatic of a certain tension with respect to critiques of reification, a tension that focuses around an understanding of what it is to be human. For, on the one hand, there is no place outside the immanent cultural logic of production, while, on the other, in order for there to be real transformation of and critical engagement with this production, a point has to be insisted upon that does lie outside this immanence—namely, here, "genuine humanity." The question of what is genuinely human is in fact the crux of the matter. In order to vouchsafe a resistance, the logic of capitalist production must be circumscribed. Its structure must be dialectical. It cannot be allowed to be a logic that subsumes all things, even the possibility of dialectic. But the very inability to give an account of what is genuinely human raises the question of whether the immanent logic of capitalist production must necessarily subsume all things. The consummation of that logic is in fact the subsumption of all possibility of there being an externality, a transcending means of resistance, a dialectical other. Marx himself writes: "The *inherent* tendency of capitalist production does not become *adequately realized* . . . until the specific mode of *capitalist production and hence the real subsumption of* labor has become a reality" (1037). Antonio Negri argues convincingly that this "real subsumption" that "reduces dialectical possibilities to zero" now has occurred.[6] So what I am wondering, in effect, is what Castoriadis would have made of a film like *The Matrix.* For capitalism (and ironically later in his book he adds socialism) to be possible, human beings must be impossible to reduce to productive-economic abstractions. In Marx's terms, neither they nor the products of their labor can simply become bearers [*Traeger*] of exchange-value. And of course this is precisely what Morpheus makes Neo see in the film: that human beings do need saving from their advanced reification and the advanced commodification that maintains all their illusions of being free, autonomous individuals making significant choices about lifestyles. The truth is that human beings are farmed in order to be used as batteries to power a matrix that generates their own false consciousness of living in a Western liberal democracy.

Allow me then to make three observations. First, that the Wachowski brothers, along with other directors like Oliver Stone in *Natural Born Killers*, Fernando Meirelles in *City of God*, Quentin Tarentino in most of his films, are portraying how human agency in the West and Westernized cities across the world is increasingly dominated by economic "forces." The contemporary reenchantment of the world is a virtual reality generated by the hegemony of capitalism. Second, that because of this the reification of human beings as laborers (energy outputs) and the commodification of all things is becoming ever more realized. Third, that capitalism as a system is not about the collapse because of this realization (though it may be overturned by an alternative system). The basis upon which I make these three observations is Marx's own analysis of how the process of commodification is profoundly associated with the development of a religious worldview, an enchantment of the material conditions for sociality. Commodification, for Marx, is religious. So the commodification of religion itself is a late stage in the process of commodification as it begins to feed upon its most essential character. Therefore, if religion is enmeshed in the production of commodities, then the processes of both reification and commodification are (pace Castoriadis) almost complete and the matrix for generating virtual reality almost established. These are enormous claims, polemical claims, to which I will add two more. First, to my mind, there has never been a greater need to rethink Marx on economics, motion, and history. And second, that there has never been a greater need to develop a theological anthropology that can challenge both the frailty of Marx's humanism[7] and the reduction of human beings by capitalism to units of productive power. Let me start now to back up these outrageous claims.

There will be two stages in my defense. The first and longest stage will examine the nature of the production of commodities and the reification that ensues. The second will address the question: In what ways does the commodification of religion now differ from its commodification in the past? The answer to this question will bear upon the advanced reification and social atomization that increasingly militates against the shared practices of a religious culture. With this second question I am acknowledging that commodification has always been constitutive of religion, but that we have now entered into a more advanced mode of this process.

I begin an analysis of commodification with Marx's classic examination of value in the first part of *Capital*. What I wish to demonstrate in my reading of these statements is how the process of commodification fosters a tropology, a worldview dominated by various forms of figurative representations, theatrical spectacle, or what Marx calls "personifications" that float free from and veil material reality, transposing the world of material and natural forces into a highly wrought allegory controlled by capitalist hoarding. I wish to demonstrate that this is so and point also to the complexity of what is involved here by drawing out four points about the nature of a commodity as Marx observes them and adding a critical, even theological comment.

First, the production of a commodity must be understood in relation to desire, for materials are worked upon and become commodities in order to satisfy a human want. At this point I will not distinguish a difference in human wanting between desire and need, for at the level of production the differences between desire and need become confused. But the significance of the association of commodity and desire, for my thesis, is twofold; first, it announces a politics, for some objects enter the exchange system and become commodities and others do not, remaining either objects of utility or potential objects of exchange for which there is no demand as yet; second, this politics is a politics not of objects but of desires. We can ask then: What is the relationship between objects and desire such that some objects are chosen and, by implication, some are not? Furthermore, are all desires with respect to objects the same? If they are not the same, then the commodity that emerges through the process of desiring is not the same either. The production of a religious artifact, a crucifix, say, can then be interpreted differently — an aid to worship, on the one hand, or a piece of costume jewelry, on the other. But the way it is interpreted and desired (and in a moment I shall demonstrate the profound association of interpretation and desire) will affect the manner in which that object is or has become a commodity. Demand determines exchange-value. But all demands are not homogeneous, so all values are not identical and, more importantly for Marx, who insists that capitalism requires a law of equivalence, some demands and values are incommensurate. What I am suggesting here and will return to later is that the production of commodities does not necessarily belong to one single economy, the capitalist. There are other economies, other forms of exchange, and therefore other systems of exchange-value.

Second, the relationship between the process of producing a commodity and desire is affected through the manner in which a manufactured thing's use-value is exceeded by its exchange-value. As Marx observes, the character of this relationship [*zufaelliges Verhaeltnis*] continually changes with time, place, and the technologies of production, such that the valuation of an object can seem mysterious or arbitrary (126). This opens two further questions. The first relates to the various forms of production that may be, like demands and desires, incommensurable rather than equivalent. The second relates to the question of forms of exceeding that arise as a consequence of this relation, and the possibility, again, of different economies of exchange generating different forms of excess-value. Marx makes clear that no value can stand autonomously: it stands in a matrix composed of the "motley mosaic of disparate and unconnected" (156) relative values of other commodities and under an equivalent value that acts as the common denominator of evaluative system, a benchmark value. But the point to be made here is the infinite flux within which the "bodies of commodities" come to be marked by values instituted from forms of exchange and affected by the various means of production — values that are not transparent to themselves, so that "the isolated expression of A's value is thus transformed into the indefinitely expandable series [*verlaengerbare Reihe*] of different simple expressions of value" (154).

What generates this verlaengerbare Reihe? Marx is aware it is not the exchanges themselves (156); rather it is value that regulates exchange. I suggest,
and perhaps Marx does also, that desire generates value—the verlaengerbare
Reihe issues from *verlangen*. Excess-value is the product of desire. Values have
to be made transparent by submission to a law of equivalence and a final
translator of all equivalences: money, or gold. This is the "dazzling" commodity, the commodity that cannot be looked upon and whose character
therefore can be most concealed while omnipresent: like God. I am going
to develop this association of capitalism and theology in a moment. Values
then have to be interpreted according to a univocal calculus, where interpretation means evaluation and evaluation means coming to an understanding
of. To this extent Marx's unveiling of the metaphysics of the commodity par-
allels Friedrich Schleiermacher's investigations in hermeneutics, for both are
concerned with how we come to understand, evaluate, make judgments.
And for Marx, as for Schleiermacher, the "One has only understood what
one has reconstructed in all its relationships and in its context"[8]—an infinite
task that turns interpretation into a creative "art." The analysis cannot then
be scientific or based upon a claim to an objective space. The analysis is itself
an art form, an interpretation, an evaluation of value. Marx's evaluation of
values is then profoundly interrelated with the conditions it is describing. I
will say more about this interrelationship and the problem it raises later. For
now I wish to emphasize only that the object of that interpretation is not the
commodity and its evaluation, but the desire governing the production of
the weighting [*tragen*] given to the "body of the commodity" [*Der Koerper der
Ware*]. And what prolongs [*verlaegen*] the endless task of such interpretation
if not the circulations of desire composing the social relation [*gesellschaftliche
Beziehung*]?

A third observation follows from this: the process of producing commodities not only dematerializes the world—"Not an atom of matter enters into
the objectivity of commodities as values" (138)—it establishes the social order
as an allegory: "Here the persons exist for one another merely as representatives and hence owners of commodities. As we proceed to develop our investigation, we shall find, in general, that the characters who appear on the
economic stage [*die oekonomischen Charaktermasken*] are merely personifications of economic relations; it is as the bearers [*Traeger*] of these economic
relations that they come into contact with each other" (179). Marx's allusion
here, as the German makes plain, is to the theater of classical Greece and the
ornate masks or personae worn by the actors. The allegory, like all allegories,
is a tissue of rhetorical operations that represent and symbolize by various
forms of figurative speech—metonymic acts of substitution lie at the heart

of the system of relational and equivalent values; all relations between commodities are analogical, governed by the univocity of money/gold; reification is personification, and the operative relations between commodities are anthropomorphized as objects become "endowed with a will and a soul of their own" (1003). Exchange-values are "mode[s] of expression" and "form[s] of appearance" (127). Capitalism, then, generates virtual realities as "value . . . transforms every product of labor into a social hieroglyph" (167).

The unmasking, literally, of the *die oekonomischen Charaktermasken* is necessary in order for there to be a society at all, for society as such under capitalism is what Benedict Anderson termed an "imaginary community"—a fiction. Marx's project is to rescue the social, establish its materiality, which now is concealed beneath the allegorizing. The tool for this job is interpretation, judging "the bearers [*Traeger*] of these economic relations," but the project is endless. Rules then for the interpretation of this continuing allegorization are needed; and this is what he is attempting to provide. The hermeneutical rules attempt to re-establish an object in the nakedness of its use-value only. But the rules and the evaluations made in and through devising them perpetuate the allegory, for they cannot escape the rhetorical operations that they too perform. This is what I pointed to in my last observation: the analysis is not executed in a neutral or objective space, it is profoundly interrelated with the conditions it is evaluating.

Marx's writings, Marx's books are themselves implicated in the production of commodities and therefore the extension of "die oekonomischen Charaktermasken." What this means is that the social value and the use-value of objects that pass between and constitute the social are never there as such; their materiality—so necessary for judgments to be made and true understanding to be recovered from "beneath" false states of consciousness—are always deferred. There is no escaping the matrix generated by capitalism's virtual reality: to establish the materiality of social relations (not *als gesellschaftliche Beziehung*, but *als gemeinschaftliche Beziehung*) becomes a secularized eschatological task comparable to the establishment of the kingdom of God. The task becomes Messianic—nothing less than the overthrowing of the idols.

For—and this is the fourth and final observation on the opening part of *Capital*—all commodities are characterized by their fetishism. The idol and the fetish establish a religious worldview; they are the necessary obverse of the icon and the sacrament. Capitalism generates then what Marx calls the "mystical [*geheimnisvolle*]" or "mysterious" or "enigmatic [*raetselhafte*]" or "fantastic [*phantasmagorische*]" forms of relation between things, whose only analogy is "the misty realm [*Nebelregion*] of religion [*die religioese Welt*]" (165). Capitalism generates a world of "metaphysical subtleties and theological niceties" (163) in which all things are subjected to the authority of "the universal commodity," money. Money is not a regulative but a constitutive transcendental. In the religious world of commodity-values it wears the mask of the antichrist—the beast of the Book of Revelation (which Marx cites, 181). The apocalypse of capitalism is being challenged then by the eschatology of a new community or a restored community—since Marx believes that once in history this community existed—in which relations no longer exist in "reciprocal isolation and foreignness [*wechselseitiger Fremdheit*]" (184). As such, capitalism is inseparable from gnosticism—only there is a subtle inversion with respect to the body and the soul, an inversion that is worthy of Foucault. For capitalist evil that moves through history like Hegel's *Absolute Geist* and imprisons the goodness of the material order; the body is captive to the soul in the production (understood both in terms of economic process and theatrical staging) of commodity-values. And like Hegel's *Geist*, the magic of the money fetish (Marx's language) lies in its power to vanish, "leaving no trace behind." It erases its own presence by becoming "visible and dazzling to our eyes" (187), like Jean-Luc Marion's idol, which can only reflect the desire and retroject the values projected onto it.[9] Money not only has the "appearance of value," like other commodities, it is the "form of appearance of the value of commodities" (184). It participates in a Platonic metaphysics in which its abstraction is consummated by its disappearance. The power of capitalism lies in the omnipresence of an absence that circulates in and through desire and constitutes desire, an absence that is at once demonized and adored. What the power of capitalism effects is a trade in bad faith, winning allegiance, through seduction, to the incantatory credo of credit.

Having then examined the nature of the production of commodities and the reification that ensues, the correlation between capitalism and the fabrication of a religious worldview clarifies itself. And Marx's analyses of the elements and the processes involved furnish us with that clarification. But let me return to a point I made earlier about the possibility of economies of exchange, other modes of desire, other systems of evaluation, and the production of values that, while unable to disengage themselves completely from the production of commodities, fetishism, and reification, nevertheless remain incommensurate to the seductions of capitalism. As we have observed, the *religioese Welt* that issues from fetishism is parasitic upon, a mimicry of, a more authentic set of symbolic practices, artifacts, and beliefs. The idol is made possible by the icon—and vice versa. This mimetic rivalry becomes important when trying (a) to assess the contemporary commodification of religion with respect to past forms of the same and (b) to answer the question concerning what, if anything, is different between past and present forms.

While recognizing and agreeing with Marx's seventh thesis on Ludwig Feuerbach—"the 'religious sentiment [*Gemuet*]' is itself a social product"— religion is not simply a matter of feeling or sentiment. This is a very disembedded understanding of religion. It is a view of religion, fostered by pietism and early Romantic thinkers like Schleiermacher, that plays directly into the religious world issuing from fetish commodities—a world of abstractions, enigmas, and swirling mists. It is a very individualistic understanding of religion forged by Protestantism, as Marx himself acknowledges: "Christianity with its religious cult of man in the abstract, more particularly in its bourgeois development, i.e. in Protestantism, Deism etc., is the most fitting form of religion" (172). But this is a highly distinctive view of religion that fails to recognize and take account of the material practices of a faith, the technologies for the forging of persons as social and theological agents, the communities of believers, the circulation of sacred texts and artifacts. If these aspects of religion are taken into consideration, it is possible to see that while religion always remains a social product, the processes of its socializing and the economies of its desires are excessive to the ideologies of a hegemonic capitalism and bourgeois liberal humanism ("the cult of man"). In some ways the products of this socializing and its technologies may be not only excessive but resistant to the generation of commodity-values, desiring and promoting alternative commodity-values that, in turn, constitute commodities differently themselves. Indeed, such communities of believers may already constitute, or be closer to constituting, the material sociality that is the aim of Marx's critique of capitalism. What then would be the difference and the relation between this religious world and circulation of its desires and the realms of mystification conjured by the dazzling magic of money and "the *perpetuum mobile* of circulation" (226) that issues from "gold as [society's] Holy Grail, as the glittering incarnation of its innermost principle of life" (230)?

Let me return to the contrast between the icon and the idol and suggest that while the icon is a symbolic representation of a transcendent horizon, indeed, a symbolic performance drawing viewers beyond themselves and toward that horizon, the idol symbolizes nothing. The idol is a representation, but it is not a symbol. It reflects back only what is projected onto it—like the dazzling fetish of money. It does not signify. It does not communicate. It remains a representation, a sign endlessly reflecting back on its own status as sign. It produces nothing. It reproduces only itself. Allow me to call this fetish not a symbol but a simulacra—I evidently have the work of Foucault, Deleuze, and Baudrillard on simulacrum in mind. And I am aware that their understanding of what constitutes simulacra is not identical—though they are close and Foucault's account is evidently indebted to Deleuze's. Simulacra announce, to quote Deleuze, "the failure of representation . . . the loss of identities";[10] "The problem no longer has to do with the distinction Essence-Appearance or Model-Copy. This distinction operates completely within the world of representation. Rather it has to do with undertaking the subversion of this world—the 'twilight of the idols.'"[11] Simulacra seduce, argues Baudrillard. They dazzle in such a way that any object they are the index of disappears in the spectacle so that "signs are exchanged against each other rather than against the real."[12] Marx does not develop an order of signs. But his observations on the uninterrupted flow of commodity metamorphoses (244) that emerges from the bourgeois desire for money ("As the hart pants after fresh water, so pants his [the bourgeois's] soul after money," 236) clearly indicate that the fetish of gold produces a world of simulacra governed by a rampant libidinal drive ("passionate desire," 227). Money or gold is "capable of being replaced by valueless symbols of itself [blosse wertlose Zeichen seiner selbst]" (225–26). Paper money is a symbol of a symbol, the circulations of which encourage imaginary expressions of quantities of gold that never materialize as such (225). It is the alienating and alienable commodity, "because it is all other commodities divested of their shape, the product of their universal alienation." It makes commodities as such disappear by "mirror[ing] itself in the bodies of all . . . commodities [spiegelt sich so in allen Warenleibern]," conjuring a world of imaginary prices (205).

Commodification produces a spectogram or hologram of religion, a bloodless and disembodied "religious cast of mind [Gemuet]," a fantasy of religion that, like an atmosphere, demands only that we breathe it in. We cannot say the real is enchanted, for there is no place locatable outside this enchantment. Marx continually depicts the immanent laws of this world in religious metaphors such that his own representations mirror the mirroring of all commodity fetishism. He cannot then find a place for an alternative social world, materially grounded, for his own writing circulates within and fosters the production of the orders of simulation and simulacrum, the theater of spectacle. What is produced by this simulation is not simply the religion of commodification, the pop-transcendence of capitalism, but the commodification of religion—the metamorphosis or transubstantiation (Marx's two favorite words for describing what takes place through commodity-exchange) of those socially and culturally embedded practices of faith into a misty Lord of the Rings realm, eine Nebelregion. His critique of capitalism, which is simultaneously a critique of religion, is made possible only by taking up a position that mirrors from within the body of religious discourses, turning it into a bourgeois commodity. The communist can announce himself only in and as a capitalist; the atheist can announce himself only in and as one initiated into the mysteries of religion. The immanent circulations of desire only fold back upon themselves in an eternal reoccurrence of the same. This is the order of simulacrum.

We can now return to that observation made by Castoriadis about reification and the presuppositions that bolster the confidence of his proclamation: "Reification, the essential tendency of capitalism, can never be wholly realized." My analyses of Marx's account of the operations of capitalism suggest this is mistaken: everything is already commodified and all things already compose a virtual reality within the circulations of capitalism. No "genuinely human activity" can be located within the order of simulation and simulacrum; a genuine and material sociality is still to be founded and is continually deferred. The last object that capitalism commodifies is the object that constitutes its inner identity: religion. In the commodification of religion, capitalism narcissistically consummates itself: autofellatio. While Marx wrote, and for a long time afterward, embedded practices of faith resisted this consummation, resisted the marketing of religion itself. But the processes of capitalism, as Marx saw, continually erode this alternative, resistant sociality in its march toward "universal alienation," the "personification of things and reification of persons [*Personifizierung der Sachen und Verdinglichung der Personen*]" (209). I predict, on the basis of my examination of Marx, that the reenchantment in contemporary Western culture, which takes place in and through the marketing of the resources of religion (its artifacts, its myths, its symbols, its vocabularies, its cosmologies, its beliefs, its technologies) will only develop further. We are entering a profoundly postsecular age. The messianic mission in *The Matrix* is a case in point: Are you the one we have been waiting for, Neo?

The order of simulation and simulacrum that fosters, as we have seen, dematerialization, atomism, the disappearance of things and universal alienation, will become increasingly pervasive. A culture is rapidly being produced and disseminated that is profoundly religious, profoundly capitalist, and, because of both of those events, profoundly virtual. We are entering not the twilight of the idols but the dawn of an unprecedented idolatry, when "false Christs and false prophets shall rise and show signs and wonders to seduce, if it were possible, even the elect" (Mark 13:22). Marx points the way here, and that's why we need him. Only a counterculture, based within practices and desires that are excessive to capitalism, can resist the immanent vortex of this *Zirkulationsprozess*. No socialist "cult of the human" ever will resist it, for socialism's discourses, technologies, and practices are made possible only by being parasitic upon capitalism. All socialism's moves have already been predicted, checked, and absorbed within capitalism, as Slavoj Žižek has recently reminded us: "Capitalism and Communism are not two different historical realities, two species of 'instrumental reason'—instrumental reason *as such* is capitalist, grounded in capitalist relations; and 'actually existing Socialism' failed because it was ultimately a subspecies of capitalism, an ideological attempt to 'have one's cake and eat it,' to break out of capitalism while retaining its key ingredient [pure unleashed productivity]."[13] This situation is made evident in the fact that socialism has always remained chic. I suggest that is why we need critical theologies—theologies as critique and theologies able to be critical about themselves;[14] theologies that advance alternative socialities and ways of being human that are not merely human.

But as a concluding coda, let me emphasize that theological discourse, however critical, does not bear the Holy Grail across the wastelands of late capitalist democratic culture. It is not the antidote to commodification, or even reification. As I said at the outset, commodification has always been constitutive of religion—fetishism is first and foremost a religious phenomenon. And this leads me to recognize that there is the smell of moral self-righteousness throughout this essay, if not throughout the whole series of lectures on commodification of which this was originally a part. For what seems presupposed is that commodification (and reification) are bad things, evidence of corruption in the social body. Castoriadis evidently believes this and pits his own humanism against such wicked forces. But commodification is not only inevitable—Marx is clear that even among primitive nomadic tribes, imperial Rome, and Christendom's Middle Ages, the circulation of commodities becomes necessary—it is not in itself a social evil. Moral enquiry and moral debate are possible only on the basis of evaluations of goods, situations, and behaviors; the operation of a judiciary requires both the atomization of individuals within larger social groupings and their reification. Commodification and reification are not in themselves wrongs, nor are they simply the products of capitalism. Capitalism produces certain forms of the circulation of commodities, certain forms of the reification of persons. Theological discourse, and theological praxis more generally, cannot escape either commodification or reification. Escape is not the point. Rather, the point is to produce forms of the circulation of commodities and the reification of persons that critique and resist the social and cultural effects of rampant capitalism. Christian theology is a case in point, for some of its key doctrinal moments weave notions of exchange, debt, repayment, and redemption into accounts of "making good." Capitalism does not have the monopoly on economics, on *oikonomeo*—and in that lie all our hopes for cultural transformation.

## Notes

1 Cornelius Castoriadis, *The Imaginary Institution of Society*, trans. Kathleen Blamey (Cambridge: Polity, 1987), 16.

2 Karl Marx, *Capital*, vol. 1, trans. Ben Fowkes (Harmondsworth: Penguin Books, 1976), 1054. Further references to this work are cited parenthetically in the text.

3 Castoriadis, *The Imaginary Institution of Society*, 247.

4 Ibid., 331.

5 Ibid., 319.

6 Antonio Negri, *Time for Revolution*, trans. Matteo Mandarini (London: Continuum, 2003), 41.

7 I am aware of some of the debates concerning this "humanism." Certain French structuralists like Louis Althusser wish to see Marxism as a profound antihumanism, giving scant attention to any account Marx might have of "human nature" or agency. More recently, scholars like W. Peter Archibald (*Marx and the Missing Link: "Human Nature"* [Basingstoke: Macmillan, 1989]) and Sean Sayers (*Marxism and Human Nature* [London: Routledge, 1998]) have sought to excavate an anthropology in Marx that is philosophical, sociological, and even psychological. I am persuaded from my own reading that despite Marx's attacks on liberal bourgeois humanism—in *German Ideology*, for example—and his method of abstraction, he does work with a presupposed account of what it is to be human. Furthermore, this account, indebted both to Hegel and Feuerbach, is a development of the Enlightenment's "man of reason." It is this account that I term his "humanism."

8 Friedrich Schleiermacher, *Hermeneutics and Criticism*, trans. Andrew Bowie (Cambridge: Cambridge University Press, 2001), 228.

9 See Jean-Luc Marion's analyses of the idol in *L'idole et la distance* (Paris: Grasset, 1977; 2d ed., 1989) and *God Without Being: Hors-texte*, trans. Thomas A. Carlson (Chicago: University of Chicago Press, 1991).

10 Gilles Deleuze, *Difference and Repetition*, trans. Paul Patton (New York: Columbia University Press, 1994), xix.

11 Gilles Deleuze, *Logic of Sense*, trans. Mark Lester (London: Athlone, 1990), 262.

12 Jean Baudrillard, *Symbolic Exchange and Death*, trans. Iain Hamilton Grant (London: Sage Publications, 1993), 12.

13 Slavoj Žižek, *The Fragile Absolute* (London: Verso, 1999), 19.

14 I owe this insight and even the terminology to Dr. Michael Hoelzl.

*Mary-Jane Rubenstein* | The Unbearable
Withness of Being:
On the Essentialist
Blind Spot of
Anti-ontotheology

FOR BETTER OR WORSE, a good deal of the work of contemporary academic theology entails justifying its own existence in the face of charges of dogmatism, primitivism, and irrelevance. From its shifting place on the margins of the purportedly secular academy, modern theology at its best is able not merely to testify to its own intellectual rigor, but to unveil the repressed theologies and hidden ontologies animating the very social sciences and humanities that would doubtless be more comfortable if it would just go away. One particularly fervent (and increasingly prolific) sector of this modern theological landscape includes those scholars who seek, in response to Heidegger's call (especially as mediated through Derrida) to wrest free of "metaphysics as ontotheology." A postmodern reconfiguration of premodern apologetics, post-Heideggerian theology seeks above all to demonstrate its own possibility within the fiercely anti-"religious" arena of contemporary critical theory, insisting that truly rigorous theology can escape (and in fact, helps to dismantle) the anthropomorphic, presentist, logocentric determinations of ontotheology.[1]

The conviction that true theology is not ontotheology is grounded in and articulated through the primary conviction that God is not "God"; that the God who is dead is not our God; that the "God of Abraham, Isaac, and Jacob," the God before whom we dance and pray, is wholly other than that sterile, conceptually stable *summum ens*, "the God of the philosophers." Echoing Heidegger's claim that metaphysics has mistaken beings for being-itself, anti-ontotheology maintains that metaphysics has confined God within the categories of its all-too-human, calculative-representational thought, making

God a superhuman object that confers a neat dialectical identity upon the human "subject." "Metaphysics" as ontotheologically constituted thus takes place within a hall of mirrors, the omnipresent *cogito* and *causa sui* reflecting and securing one another's inviolable autonomy. "Overcoming metaphysics," then, would be a matter of shattering the idolatrous glass presuming to encapsulate the divine — of freeing God from human projections of God and "letting God be God." And so these antiontotheological efforts set forth various neoapophatic strategies in order to break through the philosophical looking glass to the God of faith, the God beyond "God," the God without Being, the God without God, the *khôra* otherwise than the God beyond the God without Being.

As much as I am committed and indebted to this particular theological trajectory, I would suggest that most of the contemporary post-Heideggerian conversation suffers from two major shortcomings. The first is its failure to dismantle what Mark C. Taylor calls "the proper theological self": "The solitary self, whose self-consciousness assumes the form of an individual 'I' that defines itself by opposition to and transcendence of other isolated subjects. Such a self is primarily and essentially a *unique individual*."[2] As antiontotheology goes about overcoming "God," crossing him out, unsaying him, striking him through, saving his name, and capitalizing his Otherness, it neglects to interrogate the rational, autonomous (and inevitably raced, sexed, classed, and nationalized) subject whom "God" images.[3] In other words, the self of this neonegative theology is never annihilated in its voyage to the God beyond God. Left perfectly intact by its own philo-theological framework, this self-constituted individual effectively proceeds to make himself a new subjective Guarantor, so that even the God of Abraham, Isaac, and Jacob, antiontotheological superstar, becomes just another means of securing human meaning — just another, more tortuously constituted "God of the philosophers."

The second failure of post-Heideggerian theology is its unwillingness, or inability, to ground a politically engaged ethos. Ultimately, most antiontotheology amounts to an eloquent mystical escapism, the resecured theological self tying logic up in knots, sneaking off to merge with the divine, and leaving the violent, unjust, idolatrous world to its own devices. I would argue that these two problems disabling post-Heideggerian theology — subjective essentialism on the one hand and an evasion of ethico-political commitment on the other — are symptoms of the same disease: a refusal to take relation seriously.

To be fair, it can be argued that Heidegger himself makes the same mistake. Perhaps the most significant discovery of his existential analytic is that being-there, insofar as it is irreducibly in-the-world, is always also with-others; *Dasein* as *in-der-Welt-sein* is *Mitsein, Miteinandersein, Mitdasein*. Da-sein, in other words, is never essentially itself but rather is constituted and deconstituted in and through its relations with others. Yet almost as soon as *Sein und Zeit* opens ontological relationality in this manner, it closes it off through the "authenticating" attunement of being-toward-death. Dem-onstrating this properly, not to mention evaluating the finality of such non-relationality, would require at least a full volume's study, but far too briefly, *Sein zum Tod* uncovers the structural groundlessness of Dasein. Dasein's own death, which Heidegger insists cannot be shared or substituted, reveals Da-sein's ownmost possibility; that is, the impossibility of any possibility's being Dasein's "own." In being-toward-death, Dasein is therefore delivered from the self-grounding delusions and undifferentiated cultural repetitions of *das Man*[4] into the open air of resoluteness (*Ent-schlossenheit*), whereby Dasein ceases its efforts to cover over its structural meaninglessness, groundless-ness, and inessentiality. By locating Dasein's authenticity in an attunement he insists is "nonrelational" (*unbezügliche*),[5] however, Heidegger cuts off the structural withness of Dasein. To be sure, this "individualization" is no re-consolidation of the autonomous "subject," for what is ownmost to a par-ticular Dasein is precisely its inability to constitute itself, but insofar as it faces its own groundlessness, Dasein is isolated from other Daseins: "The non-relational character of death individualizes Da-sein down to itself... It reveals the fact that any being-together-with what is taken care of and *any being-with [Mitsein] the others fails when one's ownmost potentiality-of-being is at stake.*"[6]

Insofar as this foreclosure of *Mitsein* carries through to Heidegger's later work and ultimately prevents the "way back into the ground of metaphysics" from opening onto a viable *ethos*. This is not to deny that Heidegger's search for "another beginning" stems from a profoundly ethical critique. It is cer-tainly not some lofty concern for conceptual purity that motivates Heideg-ger's call to think being-itself, but rather a suspicion of the concrete effects of philosophy's overvaluation of the ontic. According to Heidegger, meta-physics' increasing privilege of certitude over unconcealment corresponds to an increasing privilege of beings over being, actuality over possibility, pres-ence over *ecstasis*, and the human will over every other force. This anthro-pocentric trajectory finds its consummation in modern technology, through which humanity bends being-itself to its own design, creating a whole world that conforms to its will. Heidegger thus exposes the philosophical scaffold-ing of modern technology, revealing its violent, dehumanizing, and instru-mentalizing force as the effect of a particular metaphysical stance. He calls this stance *Ge-stell*, an epoch in the history of being in which being-itself is overcome by beings. Under the reign of the Ge-stell, the call of being is heard as a call to subjugate the earth, the whole world a mere stockpile for man's techno-calculative domination of the globe. It is therefore no philosophical abstraction, but rather "the collapse of the world characterized by metaphysics, and at the same time . . . the desolation of the earth stemming from metaphysics"[7] that prompts Heidegger's call to think being-itself.

In these later works, by contrast with *Sein und Zeit*, Dasein is construed as being essentially *removed* from the truth of Being. This distance is not so much a function of Dasein's being turned the wrong way around, but rather of being's having withdrawn from Dasein. The task of thinking, then, cannot simply be a matter of Dasein's hauling itself out of inauthenticity, a matter, of course, which was never that simple. Abandoned by being and disconnected from the truth, the most Dasein can do is to let itself be "drawn into the withdrawal. . . . Socrates did nothing else than place himself into this draft, this current, and maintain himself in it."[8] Thinking, in other words, requires a relinquishing of the very will that dominates and sustains metaphysics — a radical receptivity that Heidegger calls *Gelassenheit*. In Gelassenheit (a reworking of *Ent-schlossenheit*), Dasein resists representational thinking — that is, the desire to comprehend or totalize Being within stable, predetermined, conceptual categories. It is precisely by renouncing this will toward calculation that Dasein might finally begin to *think*; by giving up the various conceptual strangleholds it has placed upon being, Dasein might finally let being give itself to be thought.

As Jacques Derrida has shown, however, Heidegger ends up falling into the very ontotheological logic he tries to subvert, installing being as "Being"; that is, yet another permanent, self-identical presence beyond the ontic fray.[9] Accordingly, as Hannah Arendt has suggested, the self that remains attuned to this otherworldly being-beyond-beings — the self in Gelassenheit — must maintain its position beyond the ontic fray as well. For Arendt, Heidegger embodies the misguided Platonic philosopher who, having grown accustomed to the light of the Good, cannot manage to readjust his eyesight to the shadowy delusions of the cave. Dwelling "in his singularity" outside the particular, material contingency of the ontic, the Platonic Heideggerian becomes incapable of forming concrete political judgments.[10] This is the reason, for Arendt, that so many philosophers have mistaken dictators for saviors, beginning with Plato himself, who tried to get to Sicily in order to teach philosophy to the tyrant of Syracuse. "As to the world," she continues, "[Heidegger] was served somewhat worse than Plato, because the tyrant and his victims were not located beyond the sea, but in his own country."[11] Here too, then, Heidegger closes off the very possibility he opens up, disabling the ethico-political commitment that compelled his critique of metaphysics pre-cisely by configuring the self in Gelassenheit as nonrelational.

The task of a post-Heideggerian theology would therefore be to find a way to resist at all turns this insistent ontico-ontological essentialism that plays itself out as ethico-political impoverishment. Both with and against Heideg-ger, theology must reopen (and keep open) the space of Mitsein, sustain-ing a relentlessly antiessentialist critique by beginning with—and remaining with—being-with.

In a long essay entitled "Being Singular Plural," Jean-Luc Nancy boldly under-takes a complete rewriting of "first philosophy," grounding it in an (anti-) ontology that starts not from the identity of being-itself, but "from *being-with* (*l'être-avec*)."[12] There is, in fact, no being independent of being-with, no pri-mordial essence to which multiplicity is secondary. Multiplicity, to the con-trary, goes all the way down to the "original alterity" of origins; to the "origi-nary coexistence" of existence itself.[13] This originary coexistence constitutes the inessential essence of "being-itself"; being *is* being-with, and as such, is never "itself": "The singularly plural constitutes the essence of being, a con-stitution that undoes or dislocates every single, substantial essence of being itself."[14]

The stubborn inessentiality of being in turn grounds groundlessly the in-essentiality of all that is. There can be no question here of the philosophi-cal "subject" insofar as subjectivity names a substance's infinite relation to itself. (In fact, to the extent that it *is*, the existent does not subsist at all; it ex-ists.) The fracture of the essentially continuous subject, however, condi-tions the emergence of the *singular*. The singular takes place as "just once, this time (*une seule fois, celle-ci*),"[15] as both synchronically and diachronically distinct from every other singular event of Being. In this manner, every event of being is utterly new, utterly *surprising*. And precisely because it ex-ists as spatio-temporally severed from the (Scotist) undifferentiated ontological continuum, the singular *is* as related to others—not continuously, but con-tiguously—across both time and space. Nancy reminds us that the Latin *sin-guli* literally means "one by one" and exists only in the plural.[16] There is, he insists, no singularity that is not always also plurality, for a singularity always takes place in relation to other singularities: "One equals more than one, be-cause 'one' cannot be counted without counting more than one."[17]

Singular existence, then, is fully coextensive with "being-in-common." Again, that which is held in common is no substance—no essence—no racial or sexual or national identity—but the inessentiality of being-itself. Under-stood as a common substance or essence, being can only become trapped within a relentless and undifferentiated immanence: "In fact, a pure identity would not only be inert, empty, colorless, and flavorless (as those who lay claim to identity so often are), it would be an absurdity. A pure identity cancels itself out; it can no longer identify itself. Only what is identical to itself is identical to itself. As such, it turns in a circle and never makes it into existence."[18] When being is being-with, however, nothing can be simply itself; the very being of beings takes place as *partage*—as the sharing and splitting between, among, and within existents that constitutes ex-istence as perpetually beside itself. Being, then, is radically inessential, but precisely for this reason, it is *not nothing*. The "essence" of being is not meaninglessness, nothingness, or voidness, but ex-istence, coessence, surprise, transcendence.

In one of Nancy's earlier works, this inessential essence of existence is thematized somewhat differently as "freedom"—the *Ungrund* or *Abgrund* that deconstitutes what it constitutes and unfounds all it founds. Freedom brings existence into being in the very act of freeing existence from all determinations of essence; freedom (in-)essentially frees. Freedom takes place as "the inappropriable burst (*l'éclat*) from which the very existence of the subject comes to the subject, with no support in existence . . . the burst of a 'there exists' that nothing founds or necessitates . . . that makes it exist *without allotting it any essence* . . . [the subject] is therefore not an essence, but the free burst of being."[19] This free inessentiality, however, is not easy to sustain. Horrified by the groundless ground of its own existence, unable to bear the persistent surprise of a being that is never its "own," the existent may (and usually does) seek to stabilize itself, to render itself self-identical and secure. This denial of inessentiality, this "free renunciation of freedom" played out as a "frenzied" attempt to become a "substantial entity," is what Nancy understands as evil.[20] Evil is "acting in order to wipe away the condition of being unconditioned"; it wants existence to mean stable essence, and commonality to mean common substance (in race, nature, or nation). Wanting unshakable foundations, evil makes itself its own foundation, gradually effecting the ascendancy of essence (*this* people, *this* nation, *this* idea) over existence (being-with) and taking refuge in its own positivity.[21]

In "Of Being Singular Plural," this free renunciation of freedom finds expression as the desire to pin down Being, the Origin, God, or the Other. This reconfigured death drive is a desire for simple location, a desire for "the Position itself"[22] that would put an end to the relational interconstitution of inessential existence. With this in mind, the effort to privilege, respect, or save the unmediable difference of "the inevitably 'capitalized Other'"[23] looks like little more than a glorified attempt to resecure "individuality" through a denial of one's primordial relation to (lowercase) others. The Wholly Other (along with the self it secures) becomes a mere *"punctum aeternum* outside the world,"[24] a "pure" essence that, by definition, does not ex-ist.

The alternative to this maniacal will toward fixity is what Nancy calls singularity as "decided existence." Singularity must be "constantly renewed"[25] through a decision at each moment for singularity; that is, for the freedom, groundlessness, coessentiality, and constant surprise of existence as being-with. This decision, made at every moment (for each moment is the origin, each moment creation when each one is "just this once"), is marked by a certain restraint: "Only decided existence withdraws from the essential 'self' and properly holds back its possibility for devastating fury."[26] In this decided mood, which Nancy calls "grace," the chimerical, other-worldly Other is given up for the sake of others, *each of whom* reveals in fleeting instants the irreducible otherness of being: "This 'other,' this 'lowercase other,' is 'one' among many insofar as they are many; it is *each one*, and it is *each time* one, one *among* them, one among all and one *among* us all. . . . Whether an other is another person, animal, plant, or star, it is above all the glaring presence of a place and moment of absolute origin, irrefutable, offered as such and vanishing in its passing."[27]

It is crucial to emphasize the stubborn incompatibility between this omnipresent alterity, which sustains precisely the relationality that positing an other-worldly Other forecloses, and Derrida's interpretation of Levinas's "dictum": *Tout autre est tout autre.* The difference of each other is not the same as that of every other other; to the contrary, the being-with that gives existence, and which each existent momentarily reveals, is utterly different—utterly surprising—each time. For this reason, being-with demands a thinking that can abandon numb recitations of Grounds and Principles and remain perpetually open to each event and possibility of being as entirely different from the different differences of every other event and possibility of being. Far from closing down the space of ethical discernment, then, an ontology of withness *opens* onto ethics precisely by dismantling all categorical, universal, or prefabricated "ethical" machinations.

A friend in religious studies recently told me that in the face of resurging global fundamentalisms and their attendant violence, nationalism, and anti-intellectualism, she had come up with a new motto: "I want my secularization hypothesis back." To be sure, the very collapse of atheist humanism that has conditioned (and necessitated) the transformed reemergence of theological critique within the academy has simultaneously summoned an onslaught of the most dangerous breed of religio-political dogmatism. This, then, is no time to practice triumphalist theology. In fact, if theology is truly to become an effective political ethos, it will need constantly to unsettle the self-certain proclamations and stable identities that consolidate and popularize the "bad theology" overtaking so much of the modern world. To this end, a thinking theology must continually decide to give up trying to ground itself, fix its *Fons et Origio*, or save its theological self from the ontic mess. This means that it cannot know from the outset where it is going, or what its tools will be. But its task will be to think *with*: to think with others (even those harboring bad theologies), to think with those who suffer injustice, to think with the victims of theology's own unspeakably violent history, and most fundamentally, to think withness itself. For what would theology be if not the perpetually doomed endeavor to think that which forever exceeds thought? And it is withness that smashes all conceptual idols, withness that unsettles every furiously held identity, withness that dismantles all logical certainties and pokes ecstatic holes through all immanentist pretensions. It is withness that, at every moment, presents new possibilities for thought, for justice, for being-in-common, through the continually renewed surprise of being that is always, and only, being-with.

## Notes

1  The major voices in this conversation include (but are by no means limited to): John C. Caputo, *The Prayers and Tears of Jacques Derrida: Religion without Religion* (Bloomington: Indiana University Press, 1997); Thomas A. Carlson, *Indiscretion: Finitude and the Naming of God* (Chicago: University of Chicago Press, 1999); Kevin Hart, *The Trespass of the Sign* (Cambridge: Cambridge University Press, 1989); Richard Kearney, *The God Who May Be* (Indianapolis: Indiana University Press, 2001); Jean-Luc Marion, *God without Being*, trans. Thomas A. Carlson (Chicago: University of Chicago Press, 1991); Merold Westphal, *Overcoming Ontotheology: Toward a Postmodern Christian Faith* (New York: Fordham University Press, 2001); and Charles E. Winquist, "Postmodern Secular Theology," in *Secular Theology: American Radical Theological Thought*, ed. Clayton Crockett (London: Routledge, 2001), 26–36.

2  Mark C. Taylor, *Erring: A Postmodern A/theology* (Chicago: University of Chicago Press, 1984), 130.

3  There have been efforts on the self-identified feminist fringes of contemporary theology to set forth an antiessentialist understanding of "subjectivity," but these fall into the opposite (which is ultimately the same) problem by neglecting to deconstruct the "God" that has traditionally secured essentialist notions of human identity. By leaving "God" firmly in place to reconsolidate the (white, male, upper-middle-class, etc.) subject, these projects reessentialize the whole solipsistic ontology they seek to overcome. See Ellen T. Armour, *Deconstruction, Feminist Theology, and the Problem of Difference: Subverting the Race/Gender Divide* (Chicago: University of Chicago Press, 1999), and Mary McClintock Fulkerson, *Changing the Subject: Women's Discourses and Feminist Theology* (Minneapolis, Minn.: Fortress, 1994).

4   Joan Stambaugh renders *das Man* as "they theyself," rather than "the one" (trans. John Macquarrie and Edward Robinson) which, although a more literal translation, is less helpful for these purposes than Stambaugh's, insofar as Dasein's flight from das Man is ultimately also a mistaken flight from plurality (and thus relationality) *tout court*.

5   Martin Heidegger, *Being and Time*, trans. Joan Stambaugh (Albany: SUNY Press, 1996), 240; Martin Heidegger, *Sein und Zeit* (Frankfurt am Main: V. Klostermann, 1977), 345 [259]. (Page numbers from the German text will henceforth be given in square brackets.)

6   Heidegger, *Being and Time*, 243 [263]; emphasis mine.

7   Martin Heidegger, "Overcoming Metaphysics," in *The End of Philosophy*, ed. and trans. Joan Stambaugh (Chicago: University of Chicago Press, 2003), 86.

8   Martin Heidegger, "What Calls for Thinking," in *Basic Writings*, ed. David Farrell Krell (London: Routledge, 2000), 374, 382.

9   Jacques Derrida, "Violence and Metaphysics," in *Writing and Difference*, trans. Alan Bass (Chicago: University of Chicago Press, 1978), 79–153.

10   Hannah Arendt, "Philosophy and Politics," *Social Research* 57 (1990): 100.

11   Hannah Arendt, "Martin Heidegger at Eighty," in *Heidegger and Modern Philosophy*, ed. Michael Murray (New Haven, Conn.: Yale University Press, 1978), 302. Countless volumes have been written about Heidegger's commitment to National Socialism in 1933, which he called "die grösste Dummheit" of his life, but which he never formally revoked. See Philippe Lacoue-Labarthe, *Heidegger, Art, and Politics*, trans. Chris Turner (Oxford: Blackwell, 1990).

12   Jean-Luc Nancy, "Of Being Singular Plural," in *Being Singular Plural*, trans. Robert D. Richardson and Anne E. O'Byrne (Stanford, Calif.: Stanford University Press, 2000), 26; emphasis original. Jean-Luc Nancy, "De l'être singulier pluriel," in *Être singulier pluriel* (Paris: Editions Galilée, 1996), 45. (Page numbers from the French text will henceforth be given in square brackets.) It should probably be noted from the start that Professor Nancy would be less than sympathetic to a theological engagement of his thought, yet it could be argued that the project of setting forth an antiessentialist theology must in a certain sense proceed antitheologically, much in the way that setting forth an antiessentialist ontology proceeds antiontologically.

13   Nancy, "Of Being," 11, 12 [29, 30].

14   Ibid., 28–29 [48]. Throughout their translation, Richardson and O'Byrne have capitalized *being*. I have not retained this interpretation here, not only because "l'être" remains in lower case throughout the original text, but also because of Nancy's conviction that capitalizing Otherness always signals a break in relation to others.

15   Nancy, *The Experience of Freedom*, trans. Bridget McDonald (Stanford, Calif.: Stanford University Press, 1993), 66. Nancy, *L'Expérience de la liberté* (Paris: Editions Galilée, 1988), 91. Throughout most of *The Experience of Freedom*, Nancy prefers the term "existent" to "subject," insofar as subjectivity is usually understood as a self-identically constituted substance in solipsistic relation to itself. It is clear enough from the context in which this word appears, however, that Nancy is referring to something more like a "subject without subjectivity."

16   Nancy, "Eulogy for the Mêlée," in *Being Singular Plural*, 156 [180].

17   Nancy, "Of Being," 39 [60].

18   Nancy, "Eulogy," 153 [178].

19   Nancy, *Freedom*, 58 [81] (emphasis in original).

20   Ibid., 16 [21]; Nancy, "Eulogy," 147 [173].

21  The "positivity" of evil should be read both as the self-certainty of evil and as the substantiality of evil, effected through the free renunciation of freedom as insubstantial. This will be difficult for proponents of Augustinian privation to swallow, and in fact Nancy contests evil as privation in *The Experience of Freedom*, but it should be noted that these apparently contradictory arguments are in fact quite similar. In Augustine, evil finds its inauguration in the turning away from the plenitude of God/the Good, who/which alone *is*. In Nancy, evil emerges as a flight from the groundlessness (but not nothingness) of existence. In both cases, evil is the revolt against is-ness itself.

22  Nancy, "Of Being," 20 [39].

23  Ibid., 11 [30].

24  Ibid., 13 [31].

25  Ibid., 9 [28].

26  Nancy, *Freedom*, 140 [180].

27  Nancy, "Of Being," 11, 20 [30, 39]. Were this written by someone else, one might just mistake it for a radically incarnational theology.

*Eleanor Kaufman*  |  "To Cut Too Deeply
and Not Enough":
Violence and the
Incorporeal

WHEN TERROR WOULD seem to be all around us, terror equated with the
threat of physical violence, it is all the more imperative to articulate what it
is that makes violence violent. On a certain level, it is obvious: when there
is bodily injury or destruction, there is violence; but beyond that, there is
the abstract and less overtly corporeal violence of a state or a multinational
class that dominates those who are less powerful. This, too, is violence, but a
violence less predicated on the immediately physical. It is not unlike Michel
Foucault's distinction between premodern sovereign societies, in which a
monarch held the power of life or death over his subjects, and modern disciplinary societies where subjects are kept in line less by the direct threat
of death than by a disciplinary structure such as the prison or school where
those in power have visual if not physical sovereignty over those they govern.[1]
The point is to show not that one system is better or worse, but that they
are different mechanisms of organizing power—each relying on violence of
a particular sort. Rather than elaborate this distinction between immediate
corporeal violence and more systemic, structural, and incorporeal violence,
I wish instead to examine the incorporeal attributes that lie at the heart of
the most destructive corporeal actions. This will entail a turn to both an ontology and a phenomenology of nonhuman objects.

No one has gone further than the phenomenologists in delineating (often
in spite of themselves) the secret life of objects. One has only to turn to almost any page of Sartre, Beauvoir, or Merleau-Ponty to see a world inhabited
by rocks, coffee cups, inkwells, paper cutters, and the like. Though it is rarely
stated as such, there is always an implicit attempt to broach the barrier of

nonhuman ontology, to pose the question of what ontology might look like from an object's perspective. Simone de Beauvoir captures this conundrum in her 1943 novel *She Came to Stay* when the central character Françoise tries to imagine her old jacket being cognizant of its existence:

> [The jacket] was old and worn [*fatigué*] but it could not complain as Françoise complained when she was hurt; it could not say to itself "I'm an old worn jacket." It was strange; Françoise tried to imagine what it might be like if she were unable to say, "I'm Françoise, I'm six years old, and I'm in Grandma's house." Supposing she could say absolutely nothing; she closed her eyes. It was as if she did not exist at all; and yet other people would be coming here and see her, and would talk about her. She opened her eyes again; she could see the jacket, it existed, yet it was not aware of itself. There was something irritating, a little frightening, in all of this. What was the use of its existing, if it couldn't be aware of its existence? She thought it over; perhaps there was a way.[2]

This passage presents an object—the old jacket—as being absolutely devoid of a human consciousness, yet everything it "experiences" is articulated at the level of the human: "It could not say to itself 'I'm an old worn jacket,'" or "it existed, yet it was not aware of itself." On the one hand, we might interrogate Françoise's assumptions and ask if this is how the jacket would really describe itself to itself (would it see itself as old and worn, or is this just Françoise's perspective?). Furthermore, how can Françoise know for sure that the jacket does not realize its existence? It might not realize its existence on her terms, but perhaps it has other terms for self-realization, terms that might not entail attributes of oldness and wornness or even of a human ontology. Might the object somehow have its own object ontology that is not even perceptible by the human as such?

On the other hand, the passage above is already replete with markers of recognition that something is amiss: "It was strange"; "there was something irritating, a little frightening, in all this." What is so strange and irritating and frightening? That the jacket cannot articulate its existence or that Françoise cannot formulate an object ontology on anything but human terms that somehow miss the mark? Françoise's overt recognition of this impasse comes out most forcefully with the provocative yet undeveloped statement "perhaps there was a way." It is this pointing to another way, to another ontology positioned at the limit of the human, that is so mesmerizing in the work not only of Beauvoir but also of Merleau-Ponty and especially of Sartre.

Sartre is at once the most resolutely human-centered of the phenomenologists and the one who most radically envisions an alternate universe where inert, inanimate objects hold sway. His oeuvre, and especially his two lengthy philosophical studies—*Being and Nothingness* and *Critique of Dialectical Reason*—are marked by an extreme dualism where the human is distinguished from and set off against the nonhuman. Any relation that obtains between the two sides is predicated on a fundamental separation. This is perhaps most clearly illustrated in *Critique of Dialectical Reason*, where the entire work is structured around the opposition between the practico-inert and praxis. Like the dualism of the In-Itself and the For-Itself that undergirds *Being and Nothingness*, the first term is at the same time distinguished from and in relation to the second; moreover, the first term is the more static, less animate, and ultimately less desirable of the two terms.

The practico-inert is used in conjunction with a network of oppositionally defined terms in the *Critique*. Foremost among them are the pairings *series/group* and *anti-dialectic/dialectic*. The series is epitomized by Sartre's famous example of people brought together solely because they are waiting for the same bus. Each has taken a number in advance that determines his or her place on the bus, a number that is itself determined by the order in which the passengers arrived and by no other intrinsic quality of the person. The people waiting for the bus are equivalent or exchangeable insofar as they are related to each other by their difference of number. Yet their relations with one another are passive, precluding any real possibility of reciprocity or active community. Albeit a complex and structured process, seriality falls short of a more spontaneous and dialectical group formation:

> On this basis, it is possible to grasp our relations to the object in their complexity. On the one hand, we have effectively remained general individuals (in so far as we form part of this gathering, of course). Therefore the unity of the collection of commuters lies in the bus they are waiting for; in fact it *is* the bus, as a simple possibility of transport (not for transporting *all* of us, for we do not act together, but for transporting each of us).[3]

Because the waiting for the bus is done equally but separately, it constitutes a *serial* and not a *group* structure. The serial formation is constituted externally, passively from the outside, whereas the group is formed through a less regulated but more dynamic internal logic, the only formation that for Sartre is properly historical and worthy of the name of praxis—and the name of dialectic.

Beyond mapping out these sets of distinctions, what is striking and of significance here is how active a role objects and inorganic matter play in Sartre's dialectical system, even in their role as the negative term. For it is these objects that animate Sartre's philosophy, and often, it would seem, in spite of him. What Sartre's thought paradoxically makes possible, as he states in the passage above, is "grasp[ing] our relations to the objects in their complexity." This complexity appears in the lines immediately following, when Sartre writes that "the unity of the collection of commuters lies in the bus they are waiting for; in fact it *is* the bus." For one so careful to demarcate the human from the inanimate, this marks an odd ontological slippage, where the collection of the commuters *is* the inanimate bus, and their being is on some level indistinguishable. Though Sartre is clearly at pains to articulate a human ontology, in the process he also articulates a striking ontology of objects.

On the next page of the *Critique*, Sartre repeats the same gesture of drawing an ontological equivalence between inanimate objects and something that might seem intuitively incomparable (such as the people waiting for the bus in serial fashion). In the passage that follows, the temporal concept of future possibility is equated with inorganic matter. Still referring to the bus example, Sartre writes: "And whatever ordering procedure is used, seriality derives from practico-inert matter, that is to say, from the future as an ensemble of inert, equivalent possibilities . . . : there is the possibility that there will be one place, that there will be two, or three, etc. These rigid possibilities are inorganic matter itself in so far as it is non-adaptability."[4] Once again, an inanimate object and a conceptual category are related at the level of their being: "These rigid possibilities *are* inorganic matter itself." Although both terms are relegated by Sartre to a secondary and not fully realized status, this is nonetheless achieved by a willingness to imagine the nonhuman in a language generally reserved only for the human. This is the double movement of Sartre's work, that in the process of making rigid distinctions he inadvertently opens a way to go beyond the limitations of these very distinctions. What I hope to suggest is that Sartre provides the tools for thinking a continuity between the human and the nonhuman, even and in fact because he is simultaneously arguing for their radical separation.

Throughout the *Critique*, Sartre highlights (and here quite literally underlines at the level of the text) the words or phrases that suggest an absolute link between human and nonhuman even while he is dismantling or, as in the passage that follows, qualifying that linkage: "Normally, at the present level of our investigation, the human object and the inanimate tool do not *become identical*; rather, an indissoluble symbiosis is set up between the humanised matter of the material ensembles and the dehumanised men of the corresponding human ensemble."[5] On the one hand, the very notion of the "indissoluble symbiosis" between human and thing is already anticipating a strain of thought customarily linked with thinkers as varied as Maurice Merleau-

Ponty, Gilles Deleuze and Félix Guattari, Jean-François Lyotard, and Donna Haraway.[6] In this sense, it could be argued that Sartre is closer than is customarily thought to those thinkers generally regarded as reacting against him and that furthermore he anticipates antihumanist theories that are the mainstay of so-called poststructuralist thought.[7] While this position is certainly defensible, my more extreme claim is that, precisely in the underscored disavowal, Sartre actually goes further than the thinkers who follow him in *imagining*, at the phenomenological level, a continuity between persons, concepts, and things.

Sartre, like Beauvoir in the example of the jacket, continuously imagines encounters between persons and inanimate objects. Often, as in the following sentence, such an encounter is expressed in the conditional: "Man lives in a universe where the future is a thing, where the idea is an object and where the violence of matter is the 'midwife of History.' But it is man who invests things with his own *praxis*, his own future and his own knowledge. If he could encounter pure matter in experience, he would have to be either a god or a stone."[8] In expressing the impossibility of the human ever truly experiencing pure matter, Sartre nonetheless envisions a limit situation where this very impossibility might take place—the virtually unthinkable scenario of the human actually *being* a stone (*caillou*),[9] as it is here presented in the conditional tense. If the human might actually experience (i.e., *be*) pure matter, then this is a pure matter inextricably bound to violence and history: here, in another jarring equation, the "violence of matter" is none other than the "midwife of History." Insofar as Sartre explores the boundaries between the human and the nonhuman, he also suggests new ways of conceptualizing the complexity of the relation between matter and violence.[10]

Just as Sartre provides, when read against the grain, the parameters for thinking the continuity between the human and the nonhuman, he also provides the conceptual structure for thinking the continuity between the violent and the nonviolent. This can be extrapolated from his notion of the radical break constituted by the act of cutting. In an elaborate explication in *Being and Nothingness* of the way nothingness is the point of separation or cleavage between past and present, Sartre injects (almost as if it were a parenthetical aside) a counterexample of a knife cutting a piece of fruit in two. Sartre here describes how *nothing* slips in between a prior consciousness and a present state. He then contrasts this nothing that separates past and present from the act of cutting:

> If we consider the prior consciousness envisaged as motivation we see suddenly and evidently that *nothing* has just slipped in between that state

and the present state. There has been no break in continuity within the flux of the temporal development. . . . Neither has there been an abrupt interpolation of an opaque element to separate prior from subsequent in the way that a knife blade cuts a piece of fruit in two. . . . What separates prior from subsequent is exactly *nothing*.[11]

Although Sartre takes great care in arguing that it is *nothing* and not an *object* that separates past from present, he nevertheless constructs a model of temporal continuity that is continuous precisely because *nothing* intervenes to separate previous from subsequent. What, then, is so entirely different about the knife cutting the fruit? It seems that the parallel structure of the fruit example secretly gestures to the same response: *nothing*. Yet there is a violence, even at the level of the verb, about the act of cutting (and this even if the thing cut is not human), a violence that does not seem equivalent to the nonviolence in the alternate possibility of *nothing* separating prior from subsequent. But what if, here too, we were to suggest a fundamental continuity between violence and nonviolence, terms that are separated, like the parts of the fruit, by the act of cutting—the act of violence—itself?

Before returning to this question, it is interesting to note that such a counterintuitive logic has been much more elegantly elaborated in mathematics, and in fact had the force of a breakthrough when it was outlined by Richard Dedekind in 1873. In his small pamphlet entitled "Continuity and Irrational Numbers," Dedekind sets out to construct an arithmetic proof to explain continuity, something usually accounted for in differential calculus only by geometric explanations. He goes about this by proposing the notion of the cut, for he argues that it is only by hypothesizing an absolute break in the rational numbers or along a straight line that the continuity of the line can be established. He writes:

> The above comparison of the domain $R$ of rational numbers with a straight line has led to the recognition of the existence of gaps, of a certain incompleteness or discontinuity of the former, while we ascribe to the straight line completeness, absence of gaps, or continuity. In what then does this continuity consist? Everything must depend on the answer to this question, and only through it shall we obtain a scientific basis for the investigation of *all* continuous domains. . . . I find the essence of continuity in the converse, i.e. in the following principle:
>
> "If all points of the straight line fall into two classes such that every point of the first class lies to the left of every point of the second class, then there exists one and only one point which produces this division of all points into two classes, this severing of the straight line into two portions."[12]

In order to prove continuity, Dedekind relies on the notion of the cut. He further elaborates this proof—what he calls the "principle of continuity" (also known as "the Dedekind cut")—by linking it to theorems of infinitesimal analysis, or the study of what constitutes infinity. As Alain Badiou writes of Dedekind in *Le Nombre et les nombres*, "Dedekind is a true modern. He knows that the infinite is *more simple* than the finite, that it is the most general attribute of being, an intuition from which Pascal was clearly the first to draw the radical consequences with respect to the site of the subject."[13] In addition to envisioning the infinite as an *attribute* of being—something that will be discussed in what follows with regard to the concept of the *incorporeal*— there is also an implicit relation of continuity established between the finite and the infinite, in other words between two distinct logical systems.

It seems that Sartre, much like Dedekind but less explicitly, provides a way of thinking continuity between the human and the nonhuman, between the animate and the inanimate, between the past and the present, and between the violent and the nonviolent, precisely because he is able to think the radical separation of these terms, to make a cut between them.

I wish to turn now to the discussion of violence in Walter Benjamin's celebrated "Critique of Violence" and trace a submerged subtext—that of the nonhuman—that at once helps elucidate the implicit distinction between the violent and the nonviolent and also opens up the possibility of theorizing the nonviolent with a rigor that is customarily reserved only for the question of violence. Building on Georges Sorel's *Reflections on Violence*,[14] Benjamin distinguishes between two kinds of violence, *mythic violence* and *divine violence*; the first works in the service of the law and the state, while the second poses a threat to the very foundations on which the law and the state are built. As Benjamin writes, "If mythical violence is lawmaking, divine violence is law-destroying; if the former sets boundaries, the latter boundlessly destroys them; if mythical violence brings at once guilt and retribution, divine power only expiates; if the former threatens, the latter strikes; if the former is bloody, the latter is lethal without spilling blood."[15] Following Sorel, Benjamin takes the political strike as the example of mythical violence and the proletarian general strike as the disruptive divine violence that aims not at a specific injustice in one part of the system but at an overhaul of the entire system in the name of justice itself. Benjamin continues by relating this distinction to two different notions of life: "Mythical violence is bloody power over mere life for its own sake, divine violence pure power over all life for the sake of the living." Here, Benjamin makes a subtle distinction between two kinds of life, what Giorgio Agamben has characterized as *zoē* (naked life) and *bios* (form-of-life), life that is only about the act of being alive versus life that is in some sense an exploration of its own form and potential, an opening to the future.[16] Benjamin applies this distinction conditionally to nonhuman forms of life:

> Man cannot, at any price, be said to coincide with the mere life in him, no more than with any other of his conditions and qualities, not even with the uniqueness of his bodily person. However sacred man is . . . , there is no sacredness in his condition, in his bodily life vulnerable to injury by his fellow men. What, then, distinguishes it essentially from the life of animals and plants? And even if these were sacred, they could not be so by virtue only of being alive, of being in life.[17]

The reference to the plants and animals foregrounds the embattled oppositional logic that structures the entire essay, a logic that is not far removed from what we have seen in Sartre. There is a strong opposition between the two forms of life, similar to that between the two forms of violence, with life for itself and mythical violence taking a subordinate position to "sacred" life and divine violence. It is worth noting that, whereas for Sartre only praxis and the group formation are properly dialectical and hence superior, for Benjamin it is mythical violence that is caught up in a dialectic between law-making and law-enforcing violence and only the superior divine violence that is outside of the dialectic. In both cases, however, the conditional phrasing of the example exposes a hidden dialectic between the human and the non-human that is foregrounded at the very moment when it is called into question (as when Sartre writes "if [man] could encounter pure matter in experience, he would have to be either a god or a stone"). So, too, the conditional dialectic appears in Benjamin's cryptic sentence "even if [plants and animals] were sacred, they could not be so by virtue only of being alive, of being in life." On the one hand, plants and animals are different from the human, but on the other hand, if they were hypothetically sacred in the same way, their form of life would follow the same structure.

This is the great impasse that both thinkers—as well as Beauvoir, in the opening example of the jacket—inadvertently confront: given that the human and the nonhuman are fundamentally separate, can one even use an example taken from the realm of the nonhuman in the service of an admittedly human logic? And, by the same token, if it is imaginable that both human and nonhuman function in similar fashion, is there not a greater continuity between them? While it is the latter position that, in the spirit of Dedekind's principle of continuity, is the stake of my argument, it is a position irreparably haunted by the problem of the limit, the problem that any attempt at confronting the nonhuman must entail the recognition that, from a human perspective, the nonhuman can only ever exist at the limit of what it is possible for the human to think. But this limitation does not foreclose the imperative of posing the question and attempting an answer, for interrogating how we perceive violence to objects might give us a new way of perceiving violence to humans. Insofar as we can perceive different forms of violence and different forms of life, such distinctions open to a rethinking of the less theorized realms of the nonhuman and the nonviolent.

In his reading of Benjamin's "Critique of Violence," Derrida employs the double logic outlined above, which both distinguishes human violence from nonhuman violence and in the very mode of distinction employed points to a possible and unexplored continuity between the two terms. He writes the following by way of a provocative aside:

> In the space in which I'm situating these remarks or reconstituting this discourse one would not speak of injustice or violence toward an animal, even less toward a vegetable or a stone. An animal can be made to suffer, but we would never say, in a sense considered proper, that it is a wronged subject, the victim of a crime, of a murder, of a rape or a theft, of a perjury—and this is true *a fortiori*, we think, for what we call vegetable or mineral or intermediate species like the sponge.[18]

Although this passage overtly situates the human as distinct from the animal or vegetable in that violence is a uniquely human category, so many of its subtle phrasings qualify, and by qualifying undermine, the categorical nature of the distinction being outlined. When Derrida writes "In the space in which I'm situating these remarks," he also implies that in another space the distinctions would be different. His remark "we would never say, in a sense considered proper, that [an animal] is a wronged subject" suggests that in some improper (but perhaps desirable?) sense it would be. And when he writes "and this is true *a fortiori*, we think, for what we call vegetable or mineral or intermediate species like the sponge," he implies that what "we think" might be inaccurate and what "we call" might be a misnomer.

Derrida in fact concludes this meditation with a convoluted though ultimately damning deferral of these questions:

> I will leave these problems aside for the moment, along with the affinity between carnivorous sacrifice, at the basis of our culture and our law, and all the cannibalisms, symbolic or not, that structure intersubjectivity in nursing, love, mourning and, in truth, in all symbolic or linguistic appropriations. . . . If we wish to speak of injustice, of violence or of a lack of respect toward what we still so confusedly call animals— the question is more topical than ever, and so I include in it, in the name of deconstruction, a set of questions on carno-phallogocentrism—we

must reconsider in its totality the metaphysico-anthropocentric axiomatic that dominates, in the West, the thought of just and unjust.[19]

Such a remark undermines any exclusive link between violence and the human, suggesting that violence and injustice are possible regarding the nonhuman as well—that indeed Western thought and civilization have been blind to such violence and injustice. It also suggests that the anthropocentric terms in which these questions are necessarily posed are never outside or beyond performing the violence they would hope to confront. As Derrida suggests in the interview "Eating Well," every act of incorporation is an act of violence, and what is crucial is how to perceive such an act and how to do it well.[20] For example, we cut and eat fruit all the time and don't think anything of it, but to cut or eat people is one of the ultimate violent actions. Obviously there is a difference, but in what does this difference consist? What I wish to suggest is that there is a violent and a nonviolent, or a corporeal and an incorporeal, aspect to both kinds of cutting.

In conclusion, I will explore this nonviolent potential as it is figured in the notion of the incorporeal. In his extraordinary study of the incorporeal in Stoic philosophy, Emile Bréhier outlines the way in which the Stoics perceived a radical division between the body (*corps*—what I will refer to as the *corporeal*) and the *incorporeal*. What is truly radical about this division is that it does not allow for a relation between the two terms but instead insists that they are not of the same kind and thus not comparable. Yet, as Bréhier points out, the signal shortcoming in the Stoic logic is that it is unable to entirely eliminate the need for relation. Bréhier emphasizes this in his summary of the Stoic position with respect to Plato and Aristotle. Whereas Plato and Aristotle explain such things as the finite and the infinite through their relations, the Stoics imagined two distinct domains that cannot act upon each other.[21]

Bréhier's study highlights how the emphasis on nonrelation marked a significant break from Plato and Aristotle, yet in spite of this the question of relationality never failed to haunt the Stoics. By the same token, it is the nonrelation that haunts those philosophers who write in the wake of Plato and Aristotle, which is of course everyone under consideration here. As I have suggested, the examples from Beauvoir, Sartre, Benjamin, and Derrida of nonhuman objects set off against a human counterexample all secretly foreground the problem of nonrelation. Can the nonhuman, even if presented in contradistinction to the human, even be posed on the same terms? It seems that only a recognition of the nonrelational relation between the human and the nonhuman will allow for a thinking of the continuity between the two.[22]

Bréhier's study is particularly useful for the examples it provides of a non-relational logic embedded in that which seems readable only as a violent corporeal action. The examples that follow are dependent on a notion of what Bréhier terms an *incorporeal attribute*. The attribute expresses aspects of reality but is not equivalent to reality itself. Bréhier elaborates this through the example of the scar's relation to the wound:

> In a proposition of this genre: "If there is a scar, there was a wound," the wound in itself is clearly something in the past, but it is in no way the wound, but rather the fact of having had a wound that is signified; of this present fact, the sign is this other fact of having a scar that is equally present. . . . Thus the relation of sign to signified is between two incorporeal terms, two expressibles, and not at all between two realities. But could it be said that this relation between expressibles supposes a relation between the things (here the wound and the scar). In their semeiology at least, the Stoics are concerned only with the first relation and never with the second.[23]

This is not to assert that the wound and the scar are not real, but that they operate on a level that is simultaneously incorporeal. Because they seem so thoroughly corporeal in nature, this other level is difficult if not impossible to perceive. Leaving the sticky question of the relation or nonrelation between the two levels aside for the moment, the great insight of the Stoics is to perceive that there are two levels at all.[24]

Gilles Deleuze's *The Logic of Sense* is none other than a manual for learning to perceive incorporeal attributes. The degree of its indebtedness to Bréhier's study has rarely been remarked upon (Bréhier was, interestingly enough, the director of Merleau-Ponty's thesis on Plotinus).[25] In the opening pages of *The Logic of Sense*, Deleuze cites a lengthy example from Bréhier that is similar in its import to the example of the scar and the wound. To cite Deleuze citing Bréhier:

> When the scalpel cuts through the flesh, the first body produces upon the second not a new property but a new attribute, that of being cut. The *attribute* does not designate any real *quality* . . . it is, in fact, neither active nor passive, for passivity would presuppose a corporeal nature which undergoes an action. . . . [The Stoics distinguished] radically two planes of being, something that no one had done before them: on the one hand, real and profound being, force; on the other, the plane of facts, which frolic on the surface of being, and constitute an endless multiplicity of incorporeal beings.[26]

Deleuze goes on to develop the concept of incorporeal events as surfaces distinct from bodies, and he does so in a more sustained fashion in this work than in any other. Drawing on Lewis Carroll's *Alice's Adventures in Wonderland* and *Through the Looking Glass*, he carefully outlines a system based on the disjunctive or alogical logic of the Stoics. It is a system that allows—through the concept of the incorporeal event, or the surface effect—what might seem to be contradictory or perhaps imperceptible qualities to coexist. To return to the permutations of violence outlined above, the Stoic notion of the incorporeal attribute allows for the opening question to be posed with greater precision: what might it mean to envision not only a divine (and in some sense nonviolent) violence as distinct from a mythical violence, but beyond that to perceive even at the center (the ground zero) of the most vulgar and mythical violence (the act of terrorism), the simultaneous existence of another level, that of incorporeal effects? This in no way diminishes the violence of the act. If anything, it makes it more real, precisely because it gives rise, and has given rise, to a whole series of surface effects. It is not my project here to outline what those effects might be, but rather to insist that the corporeality of an event not blind us to the eventfulness of its incorporeality.

The nonhuman objects that populate phenomenological writing help to express a conundrum that has both human and nonhuman implications. When you cut a jacket or a piece of fruit or human flesh, is it a violent or a nonviolent action? Deleuze helps us see that it is always both/and—it is always both at once. This continuity between the violent and the nonviolent is itself made perceptible only by a rigorous system of difference (which we have seen in its finest form in Sartre), one that might—provocatively—be termed a dialectics. Deleuze writes:

> The Stoics discovered surface effects. . . . The infinitely divisible event is always *both at once*. It is eternally that which has just happened and that which is about to happen, but is never that which is happening (to cut too deeply and not enough). The event, being itself impassive, allows the active and the passive to be interchanged more easily, since it is *neither the one nor the other*, but rather their common result (to cut—to be cut). . . . Perhaps the Stoics used the paradox in a completely new manner—both as an instrument for the analysis of language and as a means of synthesizing events. *Dialectics* is precisely this science of incorporeal events as they are expressed in propositions, and of the connections between events as they are expressed in relations between propositions. Dialectics is, indeed, the art of *conjugation*.[27]

Echoing Derrida in "Eating Well," Deleuze observes with respect to *Alice in Wonderland* that one is always doing violence to both the inanimate and the animate other, and the question is how to do it ethically. Deleuze writes:

> To eat and to be eaten—this is the operational model of bodies, the type of their mixture in depth, their action and passion, and the way in which they coexist within one another. To speak, though, is the movement of surface, and of ideational attributes or incorporeal events. What is more serious: to speak of food or to eat words? In her alimentary obsessions, Alice is overwhelmed by nightmares of absorbing and being absorbed. She finds that the poems she hears recited are about edible fish. If we then speak of food, how can we avoid speaking in front of the one who is to be served as food? . . . How can we avoid eating the pudding to which we have been *presented*?[28]

To cut too deeply—to cut and incorporate and not enough—to touch only the surface of things: both are at the same time violent and nonviolent. Rather than respond in kind to violent acts, it is perhaps more important to think the conjugation and the implication of violent and nonviolent events, events that coexist yet, in dialectical fashion, are fundamentally different in kind.

## Notes

My thanks to Rocky Gangle, Fredric Jameson, Toril Moi, and Danny Siegel for providing invaluable references.

1   See Michel Foucault, *Discipline and Punish: The Birth of the Prison*, trans. Alan Sheridan (New York: Pantheon Books, 1977).

2   Simone de Beauvoir, *She Came to Stay* (New York: W. W. Norton, 1954), 120 (translation modified). For a discussion of the pivotal role of the jacket episode both in *She Came to Stay* and in Beauvoir's own life, see Elaine Marks, "The Old Jacket: Intimations of Nothingness," in *Simone de Beauvoir: Encounters with Death* (New Brunswick, N.J.: Rutgers University Press, 1973), 12–21.

3   Sartre, *Critique of Dialectical Reason*, trans. Alan Sheridan-Smith (London: NLB, 1976), 262.

4   Ibid., 263. For an analysis of these same issues with a greater emphasis on temporality, see Eleanor Kaufman, "Solid Dialectic in Sartre and Deleuze," *Polygraph* 14 (2002): 79–91. For an excellent discussion of dialectics and temporality in Sartre, Bergson, and Husserl, see Gerhard Seel, *La Dialectique de Sartre* (Lausanne: Editions L'Age d'Homme, 1995), 172–93. See also Raymond Aron's study of the *Critique*, *Histoire et dialectique de la violence* (Paris: Gallimard, 1973). Aron proposes that Sartre's notion of praxis from the *Critique* is a substitute for the For-Itself of *Being and Nothingness* (19) and furthermore considers Sartre's concepts of *praxis, totalization, temporalization*, and *dialectic* to be interchangeable (39).

5   Ibid., 185. Sartre expresses a similar position just before: "If materiality is everywhere and if it is indissolubly linked to the meanings engraved in it by *praxis*, if a group of men can

act as a quasi-mechanical system and a thing can produce its own idea, what becomes of *matter*, that is to say, Being totally without meaning? The answer is simple: it does not appear *anywhere* in human experience. At any moment of History things are human precisely to the extent that men are things" (180).

6 See Maurice Merleau-Ponty, "The Intertwining—The Chiasm," in *The Visible and the Invisible*, trans. Alphonso Lingis (Evanston, Ill.: Northwestern University Press, 1968), 130–55; Gilles Deleuze and Félix Guattari, *A Thousand Plateaus: Capitalism and Schizophrenia*, trans. Brian Massumi (Minneapolis: University of Minnesota Press, 1987); Jean-François Lyotard, *The Inhuman*, trans. Geoffrey Bennington and Rachel Bowlby (Stanford, Calif.: Stanford University Press, 1991); Donna Haraway, "A Cyborg Manifesto: Science, Technology and Socialist-Feminism in the Late Twentieth Century," in *The Cybercultures Reader*, ed. David Bell and Barbara M. Kennedy (New York: Routledge, 2000), 291–324.

7 This is suggestively proposed but not extensively developed in Bernard-Henri Lévy's *Le Siècle de Sartre* (Paris: Bernard Grasset, 2000). See the chapter "L'Existentialisme est un antihumanisme," where Lévy sets the lineage of Leibniz-Spinoza-Merleau-Ponty-Deleuze against that of Descartes-Husserl-Levinas-Sartre. Yet he prefaces this by referring to remarks Deleuze once made to him about his indebtedness to Sartre and adds, with a nod to Foucault's famous statement that someday the century will be known as Deleuzian, that "the century was only Deleuzian because it started by being Sartrean" (260, my translation). See also 259–68. Similar remarks by Deleuze are published in *Dialogues*, trans. Hugh Tomlinson and Barbara Habberjam (New York: Columbia University Press, 1987): "Fortunately there was Sartre. Sartre was our Outside, he was really the breath of fresh air from the backyard. . . . And Sartre has never stopped being that, not a model, a method or an example, but a little fresh air—a gust of air even when he had just been to the Café Flore—an intellectual who singularly changed the situation of the intellectual" (12).

8 Sartre, *Critique*, 181–82.

9 While *stone* is here translated from *caillou*, there is a remarkable frequency of the word *pierre*, both as rock and as proper name, in Sartre's literary and philosophical characters and examples. For an extended study of the philosophical resonances of stone, see John Sallis, *Stone* (Bloomington: Indiana University Press, 1994).

10 For more on the relation between violence, history, matter, and surplus value, see Pierre Verstraeten, "Violence éthique et violence dialectique" in *Violence et éthique: Esquisse d'une critique de la morale dialectique à partir du théâtre de Sartre* (Paris: Gallimard, 1972), 397–413.

11 Sartre, *Being and Nothingness*, 63–64. It is interesting to note that elsewhere Sartre uses the extended example of a paper cutter as an object whose essence precedes its existence. This is set off against the more privileged human subject, whose existence precedes his or her essence. See "The Humanism of Existentialism," in *Existentialism: Basic Writings*, ed. Charles Guignon and Derk Pereboom (Indianapolis: Hackett, 1995), 270–71.

12 Richard Dedekind, "Continuity and Irrational Numbers," in *Essays on the Theory of Numbers*, trans. Wooster Woodruff Beman (Chicago: Open Court, 1909), 10–11.

13 Alain Badiou, *Le Nombre et les nombres* (Paris: Editions du Seuil, 1990), 46. My translation.

14 See Georges Sorel, *Reflections on Violence*, trans. T. E. Hulme (New York: AMS, 1975).

15 Walter Benjamin, "Critique of Violence," in *Reflections*, trans. Edmund Jephcott (New York: Schocken Books, 1978), 297.

16 See Giorgio Agamben, "Form-of-Life," in *Means without End: Notes on Politics*, trans. Vincenzo Binetti and Cesare Casarino (Minneapolis: University of Minnesota Press, 2000), 3–12.

17   Benjamin, "Critique of Violence," 299. This citation is prefaced by a strange defense of a
     quote from Kurt Hiller that advocates the prioritizing of existence itself (naked life) above
     all: "The nonexistence of man is something more terrible than the (admittedly subordi-
     nate) not-yet-attained condition of the just man." The terror of nonexistence expressed
     here has striking affinities with Beauvoir's expression of terror at the jacket's nonexistence.
     In his reading of this passage, Jacques Derrida emphasizes the call for a future justice and
     links this to Judaism: "And while noting that these terms 'Dasein' and 'life' remain very
     ambiguous, [Benjamin] judges the same propostition [from Hiller], however ambiguous
     it may remain, in the opposite way, as full of a powerful truth . . . if it means that man's
     non-being would be still more terrible than man's not-yet-being just, than the not yet at-
     tained condition of the just man, purely and simply. In other words, what makes for the
     worth of man, of his Dasein and his life, is that he contains the potential, the possibility
     of justice, the yet-to-come . . . of justice, the yet-to-come of his being-just, of his having-
     to-be just. What is sacred in his life is not his life but the justice of his life. Even if beasts
     and plants were sacred, they would not be so simply for their life, says Benjamin. This
     critique of vitalism or biologism, if it also resembles one by a certain Heidegger and if it
     recalls, as I have noted elsewhere, a certain Hegel, here proceeds like the awakening of a
     Judaic tradition" (53–54). See Jacques Derrida, "Force of Law: The 'Mystical Foundation
     of Authority,'" in Deconstruction and the Possibility of Justice, ed. Drucilla Cornell, Michael
     Rosenfeld, and David Gray Carlson (New York: Routledge, 1992), 3–67.
18   Derrida, "Force of Law," 18.
19   Ibid., 19.
20   See "Eating Well, or the Calculation of the Subject: An Interview with Jacques Derrida,"
     in Who Comes after the Subject?, ed. Eduardo Cadava, Peter Connor, and Jean-Luc Nancy
     (New York: Routledge, 1991), 96–119.
21   See Emile Bréhier, La Théorie des incorporels dans l'ancien Stoïcisme (Paris: J. Vrin, 1970), 51:
     "For Plato and Aristotle, the world contained both the limited and the unlimited, stable
     mathematics and the indeterminate. It is in their relations that things are explained. In
     altering both the meaning itself of these elements and their relations, the Stoics sought to
     isolate them from one another, not in the fashion of Plato and Aristotle by considering
     them as distinct elements of a whole, but in giving them a nature that prevents the action
     of one on the other. The finite is the corporeal, limited, determined, acting in its move-
     ment and containing its own principles of action. The infinite is the incorporeal, emptiness,
     that which adds nothing to being and receives nothing, unlimited nothingness remaining
     in perfect indifference. We have seen how they were nevertheless unable to suppress this
     relation." My translation.
22   No one has gone further than Maurice Blanchot in creating a philosophy and a literature
     of nonrelation. See especially The Infinite Conversation, trans. Sue Hanson (Minneapolis:
     University of Minnesota Press, 1993).
23   Bréhier, La Théorie des incorporels, 32.
24   Just as Bréhier credits the Stoics with being able to perceive a generally imperceptible dif-
     ference, he also notes that they did not perceive other differences that are now seen as
     commonplace: "The Stoics, like the other Ancients, did not have the notion of the inertia
     of matter, a fundamental postulate of the materialism of our era" (6).
25   This is noted in Dermot Moran, Introduction to Phenomenology (London: Routledge, 2000),
     392. The importance of Bréhier to Deleuze's discussion of the Stoics in The Logic of Sense is
     outlined in the first part of Anthony Uhlmann, "'The Ancient Stoics,' Émile Bréhier, and
     Beckett's Beings of Violence," Samuel Beckett Today Aujourd'hui 11:1 (March 2002): 351–60.

26  Gilles Deleuze, *The Logic of Sense*, trans. Mark Lester with Charles Stivale (New York: Columbia University Press, 1990), 5. See also the longer passage in Bréhier from which this is taken, 12–13. I discuss this passage and its connections to Sartre in more detail in Kaufman, "Solid Dialectic in Sartre and Deleuze."

27  Deleuze, *The Logic of Sense*, 7–8.

28  Ibid., 23.

*Hent de Vries*

The Two Sources of the "Theological Machine": Jacques Derrida and Henri Bergson on Religion, Technicity, War, and Terror

IN RECENT YEARS, we have seen increasing attention turn toward the importance, the incredible opportunities, and the considerable downsides of globalization, global capital, and new technological media, and at the same time an unexpected, increasingly unpredictable return of religions—indeed, a turn to the religious—as a political factor of worldwide, indeed, global significance. The result seems to be an ever more globalized and, I will suggest, "global" concern with "religion"—one that is, often, dislocated, mediated, mediatized, and virtualized, yet also deprivatized or politicized, and whose implications and consequences extend well beyond the assumptions concerning differentiation, disenchantment, and rationalization held by most theories of modernization, which until recently remained unquestioned. Such "global religion" seems at least in part inaccessible to established empiricist scholarly approaches, which seek to explain this renewed —and oftentimes quite novel and, we should add, violent or even "terrorist"—presence of "religion" in terms of a turn to communal commitments or values and hence tend to privilege "local"—that is to say, familial, national, ethnic, or otherwise identitarian—contexts of origin, including their diverse forms of authority, legitimacy, and so on. By and large these approaches, which have typified both contemporary religious studies and classical modern approaches to confessional theology (including those of the progressivist-emancipatory variety, as in liberation and "genitive" theologies), leave in place a naive and at times downright essentialist—or, which amounts to the same, historicist, sociologistic, psychologistic, and, more recently, culturalist—definition and understanding of "religion."

The recent collection *Global Religions* (in the plural), edited by Mark Juergensmeyer, seems an exception to the rule.[1] It seeks to "think globally about religion," queries "religion in a global age" and "in global perspective," investigates "the global future of religion," the "global resurgence of religion," "the global religious scene," and, against this background, discusses the implications of an opposed tendency: "antiglobal religion." But this book does not concentrate on the structural features of "globality" and "the religious" that interest me here; instead it presents itself as a guide to understanding "the state of *worldwide* religion in the twenty-first century," while emphasizing the diversity — indeed, plurality — of religions even (or especially?) today. It shuns the temptation and risks of generalization and abstraction. Hence the organization of its lengthy first part, consisting of chapters devoted to the three major monotheisms (Christianity, Judaism, Islam), Hinduism, Buddhism, while adding two chapters on "African Religion" and "Local Religious Societies," respectively.

Yet the return of "religions" and "the religious" on a "global" scale could perhaps be approached quite otherwise, in a more philosophical, ontological, and, as I shall argue, minimally or, what comes down to the same, globally theological way — along with the apparent, simultaneous *emptying out* of the concept, if not the practice, of "religion" (its increasing formalization and apparent universalization, but also its reification and even commodification). Such a change in perspective can, I believe, provide insight into the more protracted yet highly volatile process of what emerges as an ongoing and ever increasing profanization — that is, simultaneous trivialization and intensification — by contrast to previous notions of an undisturbed and fairly linear narrative of secularization.

Even more so than the somewhat tired concept of secularization, this category of profanization — like all idolatry, blasphemy, fetishization, and superstition, and the kitsch — that accompanies it, remains irrevocably tied to the very tradition it tends (or intentionally seeks) to subvert or substitute for once and for all, according to a logic and dynamic whose workings and effects we have hardly begun to understand. Here contemporary philosophy, in both its so-called Continental and analytic varieties, and in "solidarity with metaphysics at the very moment of its downfall," as Adorno diagnosed the task of thinking "today," in his magnum opus *Negative Dialektik* [Negative Dialectics], still has important contributions to make, even though it cannot stand on its own. In order for such philosophical thinking to — quite literally — *work out* its concepts, that is to say, give them the material or materialist (I am not saying naturalist) grounding, as well as sufficient leeway to fit nonidentical contexts, it must engage with and learn from the very disciplines (history, anthropology, political science and economy, and studies in new media and recent biology) whose conceptual schemes, together with their limitations, it begins by pointing out.

In what follows, I will return to some of Jacques Derrida's most telling analyses of the phenomenon of "religion" to illustrate where his inquiry into its supposed "return" in the present day and age of a Christianly over-determined process of globalization and mediatization—of *mondialatinisation*, Derrida writes in "Faith and Knowledge"—might lead us. So much is clear: the result of such inquiry is not a formal analysis or reconstruction of religion "as such" (i.e., in its "essence," a priori or sui generis character) nor an apologetic (i.e., dogmatic) justification of any of its historical truth claims. In ironic appreciation of one of Adorno's central intuitions, as formulated in *Minima moralia*, I would rather claim that Derrida's version of "reflective faith" (an expression he takes from Kant) entails *minimal* reference to the theological and, indeed, the theologico-political at most.

What could this mean? How does theological or theologico-political *minimalism* pair with the supposed *globalism*, indeed, *globality* of its object or reference, that is to say, "religion," the religiosity of the so-called histori-cal, revealed or positive religions, and, perhaps, not of such religion (in this common or strict sense) alone?

The task of answering these questions is enormous, not least because whenever Derrida, in *Faith and Knowledge: The Two Sources of "Religion" at the Limits of Reason Alone*, speaks of religion—a "single word, the clearest and most obscure: *religion*"—he hastens to add that we "act as if we had some common sense of what 'religion' means through languages that we believe . . . we know how to speak."[2] Indeed, Derrida goes on to say:

> We believe in the *minimal* trustworthiness of this word. Like Heideg-ger, concerning what he calls the "Faktum" of the vocabulary of being (at the beginning of *Sein und Zeit*), we believe (or believe it is obligatory to believe) that we pre-understand the meaning of this word, if only to be able to question and in order to interrogate ourselves on this subject. Well, nothing is less pre-assured than such a "Faktum" . . . and the en-tire question of religion comes down, *perhaps*, to this lack of assurance.[3]

Even if such "minimal trustworthiness" were possible after all, it would of necessity still imply a maximum uncertainty where "religion" in its global meaning—that is to say, in its public dimension and universal aspiration—has become (once again) an issue of major importance. The discrepancy be-tween the generality of its definition and concept, and the irreducible "thick-ness" (to cite Clifford Geertz, citing John L. Austin) of its singular words, things, gestures, and powers would remain *near total*, forever challenging even the most adequate theoretical account (scholarly explanation, phenomenological description, etc.).

With the risky expression "global religion," I nonetheless seek to designate the way in which, within political liberalism and its cosmopolitan or, if one prefers, expansionist empire, no less than in its economic infrastructure, religion's proper names, rituals, practices, and institutions continue, on a globally increasing scale, to mark the present, though they do so more and more as voided or empty signifiers, mechanical gestures, or petrified structures, whose historical origin and meaning, contemporary function, and future role have become virtually unclear, irrelevant, or obsolete. The religious legacy has not quite ceded its place to secular terms, mundane forms of life, autonomous individual agency, and lay-republican political formations (as was long expected); "religion" retains a diminished yet abiding presence, intelligibility, even an explanatory force, not least in the socio-juridical, multicultural, transnational, and postcolonial realm — in short, wherever the problematic of the theological-political, in its mediatic, automatic-mechanical-technical and far more hidden (and often hideous) manifestations, periodically gains new prominence.

If the religious and theological legacies can no longer master their current valence yet have not quite faded into oblivion, what use might we still have for terms such as "religion" in describing contemporary geopolitical, globalized, and globalizing trends with the help of a terminology in which universalization and cosmopolitanism, disenchantment and neutrality or laicity are no longer the dominant feature and cede their place to an altogether novel relation to "the world," "worldliness," that takes the place of traditional and modern interpretations of "the profane" (and hence of idolatry, blasphemy, and the like)? Why risk an even more excessive expression, "global religion," in an attempt to capture religion's continued or renewed manifestation and significance — displaced yet recited and recycled, evanescent yet ever more insistent, at once promising and pernicious? Redescription of historical "revealed" or "positive" religion — marked by the utmost respect and disrespect at once — can still (and, I believe, especially at this particular juncture in time) be of *strategic* use in bringing out some of the problems that "secularism" sought to theorize and to realize, without falling prey to its reductionist naturalism, in epistemology and method no less than in politics.

I thus offer the term *global religion* as a heuristic and, admittedly, provisional understanding in order to account for and respond to the simultaneous pluralization and, as it were, virtualization of public spheres and lifeworlds said to be taking place today, within the circulation and concentration of capital, the "informationalism" of the "network society" (as Manuel Castells would have it in his trilogy on the "information age"), and so on. This term, understood here in a strategic and slightly ironic sense, seeks to capture the qualities of a dislocation and deterritorialization that increasingly tend to characterize a terrain that has lost all fixed boundaries (such as those of, say, "Europe" or "the West") and that we can begin to explore under the heading of "religion" for historical and analytical, conceptual and, perhaps, sentimental-existential reasons, as a fact, as it were, not just of the "life world," of increasingly diversified as well as unified "forms of life," but of "life."

Interestingly, a transposition and translation of the religious into the secular, the profane, the exoteric, and the public constitutes at once a purification and an *intensification* of its supposedly ultimate concern and the trivialization or profanation of religion itself: a global or globalized religion, but a merely global—that is, a minimally theological—sense of what "religion" once meant. Yet there are no historical or conceptual means for deciding whether this "secularization" does not, in the very process of minimizing religion, realize it in a more fundamental and promising way—that is to say, whether profanation and heterodoxy are not, after all, the "kernel" and final consequence of orthodoxy. Conversely, there are no historical or conceptual means for deciding whether this process—by merely repeating the same, in a seemingly senseless, nonformal tautology—does not produce something radically new as well: the heterology of some undeterminable—as Derrida would say, undecidable—now religious, now nonreligious—other.

Derrida points out that the turn to—or return of—"religion" and "the religious" is not simply a given, which could be ascribed to an irreducible fact of human nature, an a priori of history and culture, a perhaps long forgotten ideal that has now resurfaced, and as such further proof that there is fundamentally "nothing new under the sun," nothing but business as usual (in spite of or, rather, thanks to its capitalized and expansionist exportation into supposedly nonreligious territory). Derrida clearly does not agree that this recent upsurge is merely an epiphenomenon, an anomaly within modernity: "The said 'return of the religious,' which is to say, the spread of a complex and overdetermined phenomenon, is not a simple *return*, for its globality and its figures (tele-techno-media-scientific, capitalistic and politico-economic) remain original and unprecedented."[4]

What seemed old presents itself not merely in a new guise but *as* new, not as renewed but in novel terms or forces. The old vocabulary is coined anew, not merely adjusted. Conversely, what seemed new reveals itself to be old, outdated, outwitted, indeed "outbid" (to cite a concept Derrida deploys).

To explain this paradox of the old-new and new-old—a phrase that in the form of the "old-new enigma of sovereignty, notably the sovereignty of the nation-state"⁵ that informs Derrida's recent interrogation of democracy in relation to the "world," in *Voyous*, as well—it may be helpful to rethink two important and interdependent motifs scattered throughout *Faith and Knowledge*. First, the newly—and now religiously and theologico-politically—coined term for globalization, *mondialisation*, which transmutes into *mondialatinisation*, aptly translated by Sam Weber as "globalatinization" (a); second, the intriguing and quite elliptical reference to a well-known title by Henri Bergson, *Les Deux Sources de la morale et de la religion* (*The Two Sources of Religion and Morality*). Bergson's thought may provide an important key to Derrida's central argument—the "theo-logic"—in the text under consideration (b). I will spell out these motifs and their respective implications and end with some more tentative general conclusions (c).

First, Derrida defines "globalatinization" as the "strange alliance of Christianity, as the experience of the Death of God, and tele-technoscientific capitalism."⁶ Following the Christian interpretation of the theologico-political order of people and things to its logical extreme—in "elective affinity," as Max Weber might have said; as the executor of its testament, Derrida seems to add—the specific "formations of the secular" (to cite the title of Talal Asad's recent book)⁷ is "at the same time hegemonic and finite, ultra-powerful and in the process of exhausting itself."⁸ Speaking of this "strange phenomenon of Latinity and of its globalization," Derrida adamantly insists that we should not be thinking here of "universality" or even of an "idea of universality," but merely of "a process of universalization that is finite but enigmatic": "Well beyond its strictly capitalist or politico-military figures, a hyper-imperialist appropriation has been underway now for centuries. It imposes itself in a particularly palpable manner within the conceptual apparatus of international law and global [*mondiale*] politic rhetoric. Wherever this apparatus dominates, it articulates itself through a discourse on religion" (66–67 [47]).

It often does so by surreptitiously introducing a minimal referent, an "elementary act of faith," the "elementary condition, the milieu of the religious, if not of religion itself": "We speak of trust and of credit or of trustworthiness in order to underscore that this elementary act of faith also underlies the essentially economic and capitalistic rationality of the tele-technoscientific. No calculation, no assurance, will ever be able to reduce its ultimate necessity." (81 [68–69]).

Just as often, the "discourse on religion" is explicitly theologico-political. I will not revisit the intricacies of this term here, many of which are analyzed in exemplary fashion by Gil Anidjar in *The Jew, the Arab*, but draw attention only to one feature of this syndrome and symptom: namely, the fact that—for example, when one speaks of Islam, even political Islam, and rightfully distinguishes it from Islamism—"directly or not, the theologico-political, like all the concepts plastered over these questions, beginning with that of democracy or secularization, even of the right to literature, is not merely European, but Graeco-Christian, Graeco-Roman" (46 [14–15]). Questioning this legacy means not doing away with it but interrogating it with the help of a "cautiously designated" and "unreserved taste," if not unconditional preference, for what, in politics, is called republican democracy as universalizable model, binding philosophy to the public "cause," to the res publica, to "public-ness [publicité] . . . to the enlightened virtue of public space, emancipating it from all external power (nonlay, nonsecular), for example from religious dogmatism, orthodoxy, or authority (that is to say, from a certain rule of the doxa or of belief, which, however, does not mean from all faith)" (47 [17]). Here, as in Voyous, Derrida's critical gesture would seem based on "a messianic act of faith—irreligious and without messianism."⁹

As Derrida, citing Kant as his witness, insists: there is an irrevocable, reasonable and responsible "faith"—"reflective faith, to be precise"—whose minimal creed one could hope to spell out only by respecting its tendential virtuality and pressing actuality. This "faith," doubled at its source, self-contradictory and inflicting violence upon itself with the very pronunciation, expression, or instantiation that it must nonetheless incessantly seek (as long as it is faithful to its name and, indeed, reflective)—such faith would by definition be in search of its definition, redefinition, or, as Levinas would say, "infinition," inserting itself surreptitiously into the order of the finite, into finite orders, ad infinitum, without any hope for any possible realization and, therefore, without any hope, any salvation. In its inevitable conceptual and figural idolatry, blasphemy, and profanization—and without this being virtually nothing, indeed, the opposite of which it means and calls for—it would be almost indifferent, uncertain in all respects.

Although Derrida emphasizes the irreducibility and inescapability of a certain structure of religiosity, of "bare faith"—thematized in earlier contexts under such headings as "originary" or "double affirmation" or as "the mystical postulate"—there is no implication here of the "groundless belief" or "fideism" that some interpreters believe to be the quintessence of the later Wittgenstein's views, notably in On Certainty. "Faith," Derrida writes, "supposes, in its purity, that nothing is assured, probable, or believable."¹⁰ The barest minimum of faith is intrinsically contested—indeed, is aporetic, marked by "a certain absence of way, path, issue, salvation"¹¹—due to a logic that Derrida now analyzes in terms of "auto-immunization." Autoimmunity functions here as a "non-synonymous substitution" for what was previously formalized in terms such as "ineluctable contamination,"[12] the "pharmakon," and, of course, "difference," "supplementarity," "the trace," and the like, just as much as it inserts itself in the earlier series of the "double bind," the "aporia," and the "non-dialectizable internal-external antinomy that threatens to paralyze and therefore calls for an event of interruption decision."[13] The new term—hardly a neologism, but nonetheless deployed in singular ways—stands for what, in the medical sciences, is seen as a "terrifying biological possibility," to wit: that "a living organism destroys the conditions of its own protection," in other words, that the body "destroys its proper defenses or organizes in itself (and the question here involves generic writing and reading in the large sense) the destructive forces that will attack its immunitary reactions."[14]

That autoimmunitary "overdetermination" and "inevitability"[15] involve "generic writing and reading in the large sense" simply means that its aporetic logic and effect does not limit itself to the organic contradictions observed in the domain of the life sciences and of medicine. Derrida writes: "Despite their apparently biological, genetic, or zoological provenance, these contradictions all concern . . . what is beyond living pure and simple. If only because they bear death in life."[16] Examples of this abound—mechanical repetition and reification, not least of the religious, being the most prominent among them.

Thus, Derrida illustrates: "When religion shows itself on television, wherever it manifests and deploys itself in the 'world,' in the 'public space,' it at the same time increases its power and its power to self-destroy, the one *as* the other, to the same degree."[17] Again, speaking of the state in the present-day simultaneously globalized and particularized, ever more divided world: "The state is both self-protecting and self-destroying, at once remedy and poison."[18]

Globalatinization exemplifies the same process. Maximal globalization would, by its own logic, stumble upon its own limit, that is to say, on an irreducible and infinitely, if not necessarily infinitesimal minimal creed that absolves itself from all capitalization, commodification, fetishization, indeed, universalization, and expresses itself (if at all), now from within, then from without, in any case, in barely audible, legible, or otherwise noticeable ways.

While "Faith and Knowledge," in addition to referring to Hegel's text with the same title (*Glauben und Wissen*), revisits the premises and redraws the contours of Kant's *Religion within the Limits of Reason Alone*, in ways that I tried to analyze elsewhere and will not repeat here,[19] it provides an even more interesting reference to yet another (as Derrida writes, "Latin") book, namely

Henri Bergson's 1932 study *Les Deux Sources de la morale et de la religion.* This work, Bergson's last, which, Derrida reminds us, appeared "between the two world wars and on the eve of events of which one knows that one does not yet know how to think them, and to which no religion, no religious institution in the world remained foreign or survived *unscathed, immune, safe and sound."* [20]

As in Kant's *Religion within the Limits of Reason Alone* and, indeed, "as today," Derrida adds, the central issue for Bergson—"that great Judaeo-Christian"—would seem that of "thinking religion, the possibility of religion, and hence of its interminable and ineluctable return." From Bergson's title, echoed and mimicked, as are Kant's and Hegel's, in the careful wording of *Faith and Knowledge* and its undertitle *The Two Sources of "Religion" at the Limits of Reason Alone,* Derrida jumps almost immediately to the text's famous closing lines, which he cites and scantly interprets in a remarkable, if somewhat enigmatic, way: "Already in speaking of these notes [the aphorisms that make up 'Faith and Knowledge'] as of a machine, I have once again been overcome by a desire for economy, for concision: by the desire to draw, in order to be quick, the famous conclusion of the *Two Sources* towards another place, another discourse, other argumentative stakes. The latter could always be—I do not exclude it—a hijacked translation, or a rather free formalization. The book's concluding words are memorable." [21]

Let me quote, picking up from an earlier moment, the Bergson citation that follows. Bergson writes: "Mankind lies groaning, half crushed beneath the weight of the progresses it has made. Mankind does not sufficiently realize that their future depends on her. . . . Hers [is] the responsibility, then, for deciding if it wants to merely live, or to make just the extra effort required for fulfilling, even on the refractory planet, the essential function of the universe, which is a machine for the making of gods." [22] What could that possibly mean?

Part of the answer lies in an equivalence between the "mystical" and the "mechanical"—indeed, a corresponding and complementary summoning up of these terms—which Bergson analyzes a few pages earlier in the text. It relies less on the assumption of a process of increasing rationalization fed by abstractive, formalizing tendencies of thought that, tragically, get caught up in a paradoxical logic of reification and mystification (as Max Weber and the Frankfurt School claimed in their analysis of the cultural logic capital and the ensuing dialectic of Enlightenment). Instead of deploring the reversal of disenchantment into re-enchantment, Bergson assumes a certain identity of mysticism and the mechanical at the source—that is to say, of religion at its most dynamic and technology and, indeed, ever newer media. Not only for Bergson is there "no doubt that the earlier features of what was destined later to become mechanization [*machinisme*] were sketched out at the same time as the first yearnings after democracy,"[23] a "connection," he continues which becomes "plainly visible" in the heydays of the Enlightenment, in the eighteenth century; also, rather than fearing a "new polytheism of incompatible values" (or value-spheres), as did Weber and, in his footsteps, the Neo-Marxists of the Frankfurt School, Bergson welcomes the chances—well beyond the democratic project in its ancient and modern forms, but not necessarily incompatible with them—that the universe may still have in store for us, if only we prove to be inventive and resourceful enough:

> Man will rise above earthly things only if a powerful equipment supplies him with the requisite fulcrum. He must use matter as a support if he wants to get away from matter. In other words, the mystical summons up the mechanical. This has not been sufficiently realized, because machinery . . . has been switched off onto a track at the end of which lies exaggerated comfort and luxury for the few, rather than liberation for all. We are struck by the accidental result, we do not see mechanization [*le machinisme*] as it should be, as what it is in its essence . . . What we need are new reserves of potential energy—moral energy this time. So let us not merely say . . . that the mystical summons up the mechanical. We must add that . . . mechanism should mean mysticism. The origins of the process of mechanization are indeed more mystical than we might imagine. Machinery will find its true vocation again, it will render services in proportion to its power, only if mankind which it has bowed still lower to the earth, can succeed, through it, in standing erect and looking heavenwards. (329–31 [309–10])

Let me not attempt to further interpret this passage, which is as enigmatic as the conclusion of the *Two Sources* that Derrida chooses to cite and both radicalize and reinterpret instead. I will note only two things. First, for Bergson, this coimplication of mysticism and the mechanic is based on the fact that the technological is, as it were, internal to the problematic of body and mind, so that the perversion of mechanization and its (perverse but therefore no less major, "special") effects becomes, for him, a matter of adjustment alone—a point on which neither Max Weber nor the members of the Frankfurt School, nor, I think, Derrida, convinced as they are of the paradoxes or rather aporias of so-called modernity, seem likely to agree:

> If our organs are natural instruments, our instruments must then be artificial organs. The workman's tool is the continuation of his arm, the tool-equipment of humanity is therefore a continuation of its body.

. . . A spiritual impulsion had been given, perhaps, at the beginning: the extension took place automatically, helped as it were by a chance blow of the pick-axe which struck against a miraculous treasure underground. Now, in this body, distended and out of proportion, the soul remains what it was, too small to fill it, too weak to guide it. Hence the gap [vide] between the two. Hence the tremendous social, political and international problems which are so many definitions of this gap, and which provoke just so many chaotic and ineffectual efforts to fill it. . . . the body, now larger, calls for a bigger soul [un supplement d'âme]. (330 [309–10])

In close proximity to Spinoza, Bergson would seem to suggest that we do not yet know what a body—our body and, perhaps, even the collectivity of ours bodies or body politic—is capable of.[24] Derrida, attempting to dislodge the theological-political premises—and, perhaps, the very concept—of sovereignty, seeks a new figure beyond any appeal to a quasi-biological notion of filiation, whether that of the *corpus mysticum* or that of the modern body politic, the brotherhood, and so on. The place and function of the body is taken by the demos, no longer taken as the fuller and universal expression of humanity, more in particular of life's ownmost "aspiration towards love," the "vital impulse," but "*at once* the incalculable singularity of anyone, before any 'subject,' the possible undoing of the social bond by a secret to be respected, beyond all citizenship, beyond every 'state,' indeed every 'people,' indeed even beyond the current state of the definition of a living being as living 'human' being, *and* the universality of rational calculation, of the equality of citizens before the law, the social bond of being together, with or without contract, and so on";[25] just as much as it is tied to a notion of force and power, a "-cracy" that is no longer identified with an instinctual "social pressure," as in Bergson's understanding of "moral obligation," nor merely with law but with a concept of "justice" exceeding the limitation of the Kantian (or, for that matter, Rawlsian and Habermasian) regulative idea. Needless to say, such notion of a never present—and, in a sense, nonpresentable and not merely representational—"democracy to come" could "ultimately" no longer be designated as a "political regime,"[26] as had been the case in the Greco-Christian and Latin world. Indeed, as if conjuring up the early medieval theologico-political construct of the "king's two bodies" (as described by Ernst Kantorowicz), Derrida reminds us, almost in passing, that the "the democratic, becoming co-substantially political in that Graeco-Christian and globalatinizing tradition, appears indissociable in modernity after the Enlightenment with an ambiguous secularization (and secularization is always ambiguous because it liberates itself from the religious while remaining marked, in its very concept, by the theological, even by the onto-theological)."[27] But then, a democracy "to come" could by no means mean "a future democracy that will one day be 'present'"; on the contrary, the at best minimal—as Benjamin said, "weak messianic"—"force" of this notion would be that of "a promise that risks and must always risk being perverted into a threat."[28]

This brings us back to Bergson's contrasting position, for the outcome of the adjustment of larger body and bigger soul that we found earlier has a peculiar—again, Spinozist—ring to it, as well: "Joy [as opposed to 'comfort,' 'luxury,' and 'pleasure'—and we are reminded of the final distinction in book 5 of the Ethics] would be that simplicity of life diffused throughout the world by an ever-spreading mystic intuition; joy, too, that which would automatically follow a vision of the life beyond attained through the furtherance of scientific experiment."[29] Here, a certain undivided purity of the vital impulse would seem to be disseminated undisturbed, unaffected, in principle, by technological mediation, even though it finds its origin in the "mysticity" of genial individuals (heroes, prophets, saints, notably in the Christian tradition). True, Bergson writes that we must "ascertain whether the spirit of invention necessarily creates artificial needs, or whether in this it is not the artificial need which has guided the spirit of invention," but he immediately adds that the second "hypothesis" is "by far the more probable."[30] As we will see below, it is by no means excluded that the mechanical reproduction of meaning is not, precisely, protective of—and conducive to—that very same meaning that it would seem to threaten as well, once again according to an autoimmunitary logic, of sorts.

What does it mean that Derrida forces Kant's and Bergson's titles together in his own subtitle, while knowing very well that Bergson considered his philosophical project to be resolutely anti-Kantian (as is testified nowhere more clearly than in the famous "Introduction to Metaphysics," published in La Pensée et le mouvant) and on the whole entertained a complicated relationship with German Idealism, notably in its Hegelian variety? Moreover, in what sense could the Bergson of The Two Sources—more precisely, of its merely elliptically cited final words, evoking the "machine for the making of gods"—be said to be of even greater importance to Derrida's central intuitions, perhaps, than the Kant of Religion within the Limits of Reason Alone (or, for that matter, the Hegel of Faith and Knowledge)?

One reason might, indeed, be a "desire for economy" in the ambition to sketch a more than simply psychodynamic, psychoanalytic, or even mass-psychological account of "resistance," "reaction," and "resentment"[31] and to do so with the help of an alternative energetic or quasi-biological model based, as we found earlier, on a "non-dialectizable internal-external antinomy."[32] As if Bergson's concern were Derrida's own, we read in "Faith and Knowledge" that "the reaction to the machine is as automatic (and thus machinal) as life itself."[33] In fact, the more than simply analytical distinction and even certain opposition between the machine and "living spontaneity"[34] seems to govern Derrida's text throughout. What resists and reacts is not external to what it resents, but the fruit of an "ineluctable contagion," according to which "no semantic cell can remain alien." This is the role of the autoimmunitary logic for which *pharmakon* was "another name, an old name"; one could see it at work, Derrida suggests, virtually everywhere, but nowhere more clearly than in the present age of "terror," that is to say, "in the inevitable perversion of technoscientific advances (mastery over living beings, aviation, new informational teletechnologies, e-mail, the Internet, mobile phones, and so on) into weapons of mass destruction, into "terrorisms" of all kinds. Perversions that are all the more quick to occur when the progress in question is first of all a progress in speed and rhythm."[35]

Just as certain "events," Derrida says in indirect dialogue with Jürgen Habermas, can become singled out, not just by their obvious major nature (or, indeed, quite special effect on bystanders and viewers), but by an "index pointing to this date, to this date, the bare act, the minimal deictic, the minimalist aim of this dating," is in many cases—and "September 11," or "9/11," would be one of the most telling and best known as well as mediatized recent examples since the violences and violations during the time of the twentieth-century world wars—also marked by "something else."[36] This "something else," Derrida writes, is the no less obvious—if not always televised and publicized—fact that "we perhaps have no concept and no meaning available to us to name in any other ways this 'thing' that has just happened."[37] In other words:

> "Something" took place, we have the feeling of not having seen it coming, and certain consequences undeniably follow upon the "thing." But this very thing, the place of this "event," remains ineffable, like an intuition without concept, like a uniqueness with no generality on the horizon or with no horizon at all, out of range for a langue that admits its powerlessness and so is reduced to pronouncing mechanically a date, repeating it endlessly, as a kind of ritual incantation, a conjuring poem, a journalistic litany or rhetorical refrain that admit to not knowing what it is talking about.

The least we could say is that this "major event" was nothing short of a "perverse effect"—all too special, indeed—that should not so much be attributed to a determinate, single, and foreign "axis of evil" but rather to an effect of the autoimmunitary logic (and, we should add, theo-logic) itself: the fact that its attempted "repression in both its psychoanalytic and in its political sense" of the archaic, the mythological, and the religious "ends up producing, repro-ducing, and regenerating the very thing it seeks to disarm." In other words, the "impression" that a single recent "major event" marked the very "criti-cal essence" of a certain "hegemony," namely "the greatest technoscientific, capitalist and military power," revealing it to be "today more vulnerable and threatened than ever," constituted in many different ways a "properly global effect." It cannot, Derrida goes on to suggest, be easily "dissociated from all the affects, interpretations, and rhetoric that have at once reflected, commu-nicated and 'globalized' it, from everything that also and first of all formed, produced, and made it possible" (99).

Thus, Derrida writes: "When Bush and his associates blame 'the axis of evil,' we ought both to smile at and denounce the religious connotations, the childish strategems, the obscurantist mystifications of this inflated rheto-ric. And yet there is, in fact, and from every quarter, an absolute 'evil' whose threat, whose shadow, is spreading. Absolute evil, absolute threat, because what is at stake is nothing less than the *mondialisation* or the worldwide move-ment of the world, life on earth and elsewhere, without remainder."[38] Re-pression of the theologico-political and, indeed, of the legacy of the "Latin" in *globalatinization*—the very premise upon which the tradition of early and later modern liberalism is based[39]—simply reproduces what it, in vain, tends to suppress, ignore, or relegate to internal or external, but no longer public sphere (private conscience, on the one hand, the anomaly of fundamental-ism, on the other).[40]

Needless to say, important differences between Derrida and Bergson need to be noted as well, especially since in the second, post–World War half of the twentieth century and at the beginning of the twenty-first "things have really gotten somewhat better" (as Habermas once said in distancing himself from the bleak diagnosis of his predecessors, Max Horkheimer and Theodor Adorno in their *Dialectic of Enlightenment*),[41] but, then again, "have also really gotten far worse" (as Derrida, somewhat more realistically, seems to be eager to add).

Well beyond this difference in *Zeitgeist* and political climate—which by themselves might already have largely sufficed to draw Bergson's words "to-wards another place, another discourse, other argumentative stakes" (see above)—Derrida does not assume a simplicity of (or at) the source or sources, nor does he postulate an initial or ultimate indivisibility of the vital impulse or, rather, of the "living spontaneity" whose original duality and "elliptic(al)" nature he, on the contrary, brings out. More importantly, for all its centeredness around with the concept of life—in the "double postulation" of "respect for life" and the "sacrifice" of (some of) that same life—religion's dual source, Derrida points out, is nonetheless preoccupied with what he calls an "instance of the non-living," of the "death in the living."[42] More specifically, it is with a certain, formalizable, *mechanical* and *technical* insistence (repetition, regularity) that the religiosity of the religious aspires for what in life transcends life, for what in the absolute value of life is more than that; or, at least, of what is "beyond the *present* living."[43] On Derrida's view, the dual source of religion (and of morality, the political, etc.), of its "pressure" and "aspiration," is thus hardly "in essence biological,"[44] to be explained by a metaphysics or new philosophy of life. It is no accident, therefore, that "the possibility of religion" is seen as the "link" *between* the absolute "value of life"—at least in its Kantian "dignity" and Bergsonian hypostasis—on the one hand, and the "theological machine, the machine to make gods [*la machine théologique, la 'machine à faire des dieux'*]" (with which Bergson, perhaps somewhat surprisingly, concludes) on the other.[45]

Nor, finally, do Derrida's concepts of reaction outbidding, of resistance revenge,[46] or, more broadly, of autoimmunization fit the biological model of dichotomization and bifurcation upon which Bergson's understanding of creative evolution and its "*movement en spirale* [spiral movement]"[47] is based.

True, not unlike Derrida, Bergson highlights the first upsurge of ("primitive" and "static") religion as "a defensive reaction of nature against the dissolvent power of intelligence" (122 [127]); he also sees a link between religion and automatism and technology, more generally, or more particularly, as he titles the concluding part of his book, between "mysticism and the mechanical," just as he assumes a relationship between religion and the political, indeed, the theologico-political, implying that mysticism, if not necessarily "true mysticism," reveals itself at (and as) the source of colonization and decolonization, imperialism and nationalism, sovereignty and democracy.

Mysticism, like and beyond "dynamic" religion, is a driving force—indeed, the vital impulse or *élan vital*—behind the "open" as distinguished from the "closed society"; it pushes us to consider "humanity" and its beyond (animality, the cosmos) rather than the, however extended, circle of the communitarian and identitarian group (family, city, nation, etc.), which, for all its intended inclusiveness, remains premised upon some major principled and practical exclusion.

More broadly and, perhaps, more importantly, mysticism would open up the very source or "source [*fond*] of sociability and unsociability," which would be "perceptible to our consciousness if established society [*société constitué*] had not imbued us with habits and dispositions which adjust us to it.

Of these strata we are no longer aware save at rare intervals [more precisely, we have a revelation of them only from a distance, *Nous n'en avons plus la révélation que de loin et de loin*], and then in a flash. We must recapture that moment of vision and abide by it" (272 [292]). We could even interpret this as the moment and always momentary—now monumental, then banal—instantiation of a certain reserve, of a possible holding back on which the very possibility of political judgment (of approval or disapproval) rests: "The original state of mind [*l'ancien état d'âme*]"—to be found in its "simple original sketch [*schéma simple*]" through the study of "primitive people [*des 'primitifs'*]," "children," and, most of all "introspection"—

> survives, hidden away beneath the habits without which indeed there would be no civilization. Driven inwards [or, rather, repressed, *refoulé*], powerless, it yet lives on in the depths of consciousness. If it does not go so far as to determine acts, yet it manifests itself in words. In a great nation certain districts may be administered to the general satisfaction; but where is the government that the governed go so far as to call a good one? They think they have praised it quite enough when they say that it is not so bad as the others and, in this sense only, the best. (275 [292–93])

If true mysticism were kept in mind, we would not only realize its incompatibility with all domination and imperialism that have characterized the body politic internally and externally, but also that such mysticity "cannot be disseminated without encouraging a very special 'will to power.' This will be a sovereignty [empire], not over man, but over things, precisely in order that man shall no longer have so much sovereignty over man" (311 [332]).

But there is something intrinsically instable and disturbing with the proper logic or movement of instinct, intellectual, and will—in short, agency and freedom—as well. Thus, Bergson also asserts that "all prolonged action . . . brings about a reaction in the opposite direction" and adds: "Then it starts anew, and the pendulum swings on indefinitely." But the nature of these "alterations of ebb and flow [*alternances de flux et de reflux*]" (292 [311]) are interpreted in different terms and according to an altogether different law—and tendency—of life: a "law" whose "vital tendency is to develop fan-wise, creating, by the mere fact of its growth, divergent directions, each of which will receive a certain portion of the impetus" (293–294 [313]). There is, Bergson adds (recalling one of his earlier views), "nothing mysterious about this law. It simply expresses the fact that a tendency is the forward thrust of an indistinct multiplicity, which, is, moreover, indistinct, and multiplicity, only if we consider it in retrospect, when the multitudinous views taken of its past undivided character allow us to see it composed of elements which were actually created by its development" (294 [313]). Although there is "nothing mysterious" here, since the source—the vital impetus, the *élan vital*—is fundamentally, at the source, "undivided" and thus one (if not the "Same"), Bergson leaves no doubt that its tendency thereby propels life in directions that are unfathomable: "An intelligence, even a superhuman one, cannot say where this will lead to, since action on the move creates its own route, creates to a very great extent the conditions under which it is to be fulfilled, and thus baffles calculation" (296 [315]).

The concluding elliptical references in the final remarks on "Mechanics and Mysticism," invoking "telepathic phenomena," the "immensity . . . of the *terra incognita*" that remains for "us" to "divine," and the prospect of once (in our days?) being able "to turn into a live, acting reality a belief [*croyance*] in the life beyond, which is met with in most men, but which for the most part remains verbal, abstract, ineffectual" (316 [337-38])—all these courageous, somewhat wild speculations (immediately preceding the reference to the universe's "essential function" being that of a "machine for the making of gods") underscores the perspective of tragedy, despair, and "pleasure" overcome by "joy," that is to say, by "that simplicity of life diffused throughout the world by an ever-spreading mystic intuition, which automatically follows a vision of the life beyond attained through the furtherance of scientific experiment" (317 [338]).

In Derrida's view, there is an interminable scansion between simultaneous processes of "abstraction" (for good and for ill, for the best and for the most radical of evils), on the one hand, and of "anthropological re-immanentization," on the other, each of which reacts to—that is to say, resists and resents—the other moment, the other movement. "Heterogeneous," the two are also "indissociable," meaning that their relation is governed by irresolvable contradiction and an unbridgeable gap, one that only "resolve" (in, for example, "decision" or "responsibility") and a leap or, rather, "act" of "faith" could make liveable (or make life worth living). Opening oneself to the coming of the other, to the "spontaneity of life," to the impossible possibility of "living together," would necessarily mean answering in some determinate way, "giving *something determinate*." This "determination," Derrida adds, "will thus have to re-inscribe the unconditional into certain conditions. Otherwise, it gives nothing. What remains unconditional or absolute (*unbedingt*, if you will) risks being nothing at all if conditions (Bedingungen) do not make of it some thing (Ding). Political, juridical, and ethical responsibilities have their place, if they take place, only in this transaction—which is each time unique, like an event—between . . . the unconditional and the conditional."[48] Reification (*Verdinglichung*, if you like)—but also: sedimentation, incarnation, crystallization, institutionalization, archivization, materialization, and, we might venture, even trivialization, profanization, and, as it were, naturalization—belongs to the very heart of even the most reflective, most reserved, bare and minimal faith. For all its globality, it requires this local inscription, a translation and betrayal, of sorts.

How should we think the place of repetition in this general economy of the divine, whose salutary and no less infernal—indeed, terrorizing—effects tend to become virtually indistinguishable? How should we think "repetition" if the temporality and/or rhythm of the autoimmunization is that of the instant, of instantaneousness, of a split (second of) simultaneity, as it were?

There is no easy answer to this question, neither in Bergson nor in Derrida. I wanted merely to show the striking resonance between two alternative—neither compatible nor simply incompatible—interpretations of the relationship between "mysticism and mechanics," "faith and technoscience," both of which are inscribed into a concept of living—the "vital impulse" and the "living spontaneity," the "living together"—that is neither vitalistic, in the metaphysical sense of the word, nor biological in the scientific-scientistic meaning of the term, but nonetheless takes on cosmic, universal, worldly, and global proportions, whose implications we do not yet well understand.

Their respective engagements with "religion" and the "world" complicate matters even more. No small theology, limiting itself to particular religions, creeds and dogmatic edifices, can help untie the knot. But it is with minimal theology, thinking religion "globally"—indeed, in the most worldly and yet more than merely secular sense of the term—that we may have to make do.

Bergson seems to suggest as much when he evokes a more than simply moral or religious but, in essence "metaphysical"[49] and, indeed, mystical perspective by asking: "How . . . could humanity turn heavenwards an attention which is essentially concentrated on earth? If possible at all, it can only be using simultaneously or successively two very different methods. The first would consist of presumably intensifying the intellectual work to such an extent, in carrying intelligence so far beyond what nature intended, that the simple tool would give place to a vast system of machinery such as might set human activity at liberty, being, moreover, stabilized by a political and social organization which would ensure the application of the mechanism [machinisme] to its true object" (235 [249]). To pursue such method, Bergson acknowledges, would be a "dangerous method, for mechanization, as it developed, might turn against mysticism: nay more, it is by an apparent reaction against the latter that mechanization would reach its highest pitch of development. But there are certain risks which must be taken" (235-36 [249-50]).

The second, "successive" but also "very different" method, means, or way, would consist "not in contemplating a general and immediate spreading of the mystic impetus, which was obviously impossible, but in imparting it, already weakened though it was, to a tiny handful of privileged souls which together would form a spiritual society" (236 [250]). This does not exclude that "religion," more especially Christian religion, can diffuse mysticism and contribute to "high-level popularization [*une vulgarisation noble*]," just as, conversely, mysticism plays the role of "an intensifier of religious faith [*un intensification de la foi religieuse*]" (238–39 [253]). Indeed, whereas Bergson's Judeo-Christian conception seems to tilt to one side in particular, he does hesitate to note that "Christianity, which succeeded Judaism, owed largely to the Jewish prophets its active mysticism, capable of marching on to the conquest of the world."[50]

The second option indicated by Bergson would seem largely, if not totally, absent from Derrida's horizon (unless, of course, we recall his engagement with the apophatic way and his awareness of it being steeped in a problematic of secrecy, having nothing to do with election, but with initiation into a secret, albeit one whose diffusion can never be excluded or avoided; unless, also, we are willing to see his concept and politics of a denaturalized and defamiliared concept of friendship, premised on a limitation of number, as spiritual small society, of sorts).

On the first view, however, automaticity, mechanicity, and technicity might come to be viewed not merely as that which diverts from the integrity and authenticity of faith, belief, and morality, nor as its substitution, functional equivalent, or stand-in. Both Bergson and Derrida would seem to analyze a more complex relationship between the process of mechanization — but also circulation, formalization, commodification, and fetishization — on the one hand, and that of authentication or, as Derrida says, "verification," on the other. By the same token, Bergson writes,

> we should not . . . disparage religions born of mysticism, which have generalized the use of its formulae and yet have been unable to pervade with the full measure of its spirit. It sometimes happens that well-nigh empty formulae, the veriest magical incantations, contrive to summon up here and there the spirit capable of importing substance to them. An indifferent schoolmaster, mechanically teaching a science created by men of genius, may awaken in one of his pupils the vocation he himself never possessed, and change him unconsciously into an emulator of those great men, who are invisible and present in the message he is handing on.[51]

For Derrida, the logic and rhetoric of the theologico-political would seem to function in similar ways. For good and for ill, since the best and the worst might still come to pass in the, so far, interminable wake of the religious, of mysticism, and whatever takes its place. In Derrida's words: "It cannot be said that humanity is defenseless against the threat of this evil [i.e., of the 'perverse effect' of the autoimmunitary logic]. But we must recognize that defenses and all the forms of what is called, with two equally problematic words, the 'war on terrorism' work to regenerate, in the short or long term, the causes of the evil they claim to eradicate."[52] Ineradicable evil, the perverse effect would belong to the essence or structure—indeed, the very life—of perfectibility and moral-political perfectionism as such.

## Notes

1 Mark Juergensmeyer, ed. *Global Religions: An Introduction* (Oxford: Oxford University Press, 2003).

2 Jacques Derrida, *Foi et savoir: Les deux sources de la "religion" aux limites de la simple raison* (Paris: Seuil, 2000), 11; trans. Samuel Weber as "Faith and Knowledge: The Two Sources of 'Religion' at the Limits of Reason Alone," in *Acts of Religion*, ed. Gil Anidjar (New York: Routledge, 2002), 44. Translations are cited below with the page number of the English translation followed by that of the French text in square brackets.

3 Ibid., emphasis mine.

4 Derrida, "Faith and Knowledge," 78 [65].

5 Jacques Derrida, *Voyous* (Paris: Galilée, 2003), 12.

6 Derrida, "Faith and Knowledge," 52 [23].

7 Talal Asad, *Formations of the Secular* (Stanford, Calif.: Stanford University Press, 2003).

8 Derrida, "Faith and Knowledge," 52 [23].

9 Derrida, *Voyous*, 14.

10 Derrida, "Above All No Journalists!" in *Religion and Media*, ed. Hent de Vries and Samuel Weber (Stanford, Calif.: Stanford University Press, 2001), 56–93, 70.

11 Derrida, "Faith and Knowledge," 43 [10].

12 Ibid., 66 [48].

13 Derrida, *Voyous*, 60.

14 Derrida, "Above All No Journalists!" 67.

15 Derrida, "Autoimmunity: Real and Symbolic Suicides—A Dialogue with Jacques Derrida," in *Philosophy in a Time of Terror: Dialogues with Jürgen Habermas and Jacques Derrida*, ed. Giovanna Borradori (Chicago: University of Chicago Press, 2003), 85–136, 119 and 121.

16 Ibid., 119.

17 Derrida, "Above All No Journalists!" 67. It might seem that such diagnosis and its subsequent analysis is hopelessly abstract, unable to tackle the problems of real people in a through and through material world. However, to counter such objections it suffices to refer to authors like Mark Juergensmeyer who in his topical study, entitled *Terror in the Mind of God: The Global Rise of Religious Violence* (Berkeley: University of California Press, 2001) addresses different instances in the modern world in which Christian, Jewish, Muslim, Hindu, Sikh, and Buddhist individuals and groups *acted out* an excessive violence in what he terms the drama of a "cosmic war." In this scenario and, literally, theater of war an explicit or implicit notion of martyrdom of fallen heroes and demonization—"satanization," he writes—of the primary or secondary enemy go hand in hand. The verbal expres-

sion *acting out* is used deliberately here. Juergensmeyer offers an interpretation, if not explanation, of these instances of religious violence—of religiously motivated violence, that is, and of violence empowering, indeed staging religion—in which the so-called performative moment and momentum are central. Just as Hannah Arendt had already insisted that violent acts and protest do not so much "promote causes, neither history nor revolution, neither progress nor reaction," but had added that it "can serve to dramatize grievances and bring them public attention" (Hannah Arendt, *On Violence* [San Diego: Harcourt Brace Jovanovich, 1970], 79), so also Juergensmeyer—in critical discussion with the work of sociologists like Pierre Bourdieu and comparatists such as René Girard—stresses that the violence of, say, terrorist attacks should be understood not as part of an elaborate calculation or *"tactics* directed towards an immediate, earthly or strategic goal," but as "performance violence," as the performance of *"dramatic events* intended to impress for their symbolic significance"; as such, Juergensmeyer concludes "they can be analyzed as one would analyze any other symbol, ritual, or sacred drama" (*Terror in the Mind of God*, 123). Religious violence or the violence that takes on religious qualities would be "performance violence" (124), whose paradoxical goal is a (posthistorical) peace and whose modality and motivation should not be confused with a political act or elaborate theory—a political theology, say—in disguise. The reason why "violence has accompanied religion's renewed political presence" would have everything to do with the fact that "the religious imagination . . . has always had the propensity to absolutize and to project images of cosmic war. It has also much to do with the social tensions of this moment of history that cry out for absolute solutions, and the sense of personal humiliation experienced by men who long to restore an integrity they perceive as lost in the wake of virtually global social and political shifts" (242).

18    Derrida, "Autoimmunity," 124.

19    For a discussion of Derrida's reading of Kant's text, see Hent de Vries, *Religion and Violence: Philosophical Perspectives from Kant to Derrida* (Baltimore: Johns Hopkins University Press, 2002), chap. 1.

20    Derrida, "Faith and Knowledge," 77 [63].

21    Ibid., 77 [63–64].

22    Henri Bergson, *Les deux sources de la morale et la religion* (Paris: Presses Universitaires de France, 1997), 338; *The Two Sources of Morality and Religion*, trans. R. Ashley Audra and Cloudesley Brereton, with the assistance of W. Horsfall Carter (Notre Dame, Ind.: University of Notre Dame Press, 1986), 317, translation modified.

23    Ibid., 328 [307].

24    See Pierre Trotignon, "Bergson et Spinoza," in *Spinoza au XXe siècle*, ed. Olivier Bloch (Paris: P.U.F., 1993), 3–12.

25    Derrida, "Autoimmunity," 120.

26    Ibid., 121.

27    Derrida, *Voyous*, 51.

28    Derrida, "Autoimmunity," 120.

29    Bergson, *The Two Sources of Morality and Religion*, 317 [338].

30    Ibid., 304 [324].

31    Derrida, "Faith and Knowledge," 81 [70].

32    Derrida, *Voyous*, 60.

33    Derrida, "Faith and Knowledge," 81 [70].

34    Ibid., 82 [71], 67 [48].

35    Derrida, "Autoimmunity," 124.

36   Ibid., 86. For the motif of "onze septembre 2001," see also Derrida, *Voyous*, 12.

37   Derrida, "Autoimmunity," 86.

38   Ibid., 99. On the "axis of evil" motif, see also Derrida, *Voyous*, 21 and 23.

39   Pierre Manent, *Histoire intellectuelle du libéralisme* (Paris: Calman-Lévy, 1987), chap. 1.

40   The need to denounce the "religious connotations" in the appeal to the—apparently single, that is to say, unique and unambiguous or undivided—"axis of evil" cited in our epigraph should, therefore, not lead us to forget Derrida's insistence on a certain "permanence of the theologico-political" (to cite Claude Lefort's phrase). Let me give an example from "Capital Punishment" ("Peines de mort"), a central chapter in the dialogue with Elisabeth Roudinesco, *De quoi demain . . . Dialogue* (Paris: Fayard, Galilée, 2001), 223–67. Derrida observes that "it is impossible to treat the question of the death penalty without speaking of religion, and of that which, through the *mediation* [emphasis mine] of the concept of sovereignty, secures the right to religion." (And without the principle of sovereignty, Derrida claims from the outset, the death penalty would have "no chance.") What intrigues me in his analysis, indeed, his *working through*—an *impossible* working through, for, lest we forget, the concept of mourning and its paradoxes is never far from these reflections—is his formulation that a "theologico-political" or "theologico-juridico-political *alliance*" [emphasis mine] is the "basis or the principle of the death penalty, as it is being set to work." Intriguingly, this reference to the theologico-political or the theologico-juridical is immediately qualified and distinguished from all linear or historicist genealogies or causal explanations, and thus from any facile reductions. Furthermore, the religious (its Scripture and imagery, archive and institutions), although it supposedly conditions capital punishment—that extreme of the criminal law (or is it its heart)—is not simultaneous and coextensive with the criminal law. The two realms (say, political sovereignty and its *ultimate ratio*, its first and final recourse) do not simply map onto each other. Their relationship is one of "alliance" and of a "basis" or "principle" that is "set to work," is "welded" and "cemented" together, nothing more, nothing less.
     To complicate matters further, Derrida goes on to assert that the invocation of the theologico-political or the theologico-juridical does not "rely on an *already available* theologico-political concept that it would suffice to *apply* to the death penalty as one of its 'cases' or examples." Instead, he says, it is the other way around. No simple relationship of primacy or priority, deduction or foundation is at work here: indeed, "one cannot begin to think the theologico-political, and thus the onto-theologico-political, *except* [emphasis mine] from this phenomenon of criminal law that is called the death penalty." But just as capital punishment is not retheologized or even transcendentalized (its relationship with the theological being one of "alliance" and of "setting to work"), the exceptional importance given to the "phenomenon" of the death penalty does not imply that the theologico-political or theologico-juridical is historicized or inscribed into the tradition of law: the fundamentally pagan-Roman, Catholic tradition of the *jus talionis*, of "canon law," and, eventually, of modern penal codes. Moreover, where the death penalty is concerned, these legal formations themselves cannot be rigorously historicized and archived, because they are premised upon (or "allied" with) a notion of the theological and the transcendental that, in turn, cannot be reconstructed in its purity, its integrity, even its intelligibility.
     In fact, Derrida writes, what is involved in capital punishment is "less a phenomenon or an article of criminal law than, in this tradition, the quasi-transcendental condition of criminal law and of law in general." The death penalty is the *transcendental* of the law, "at once *internal*, included: the death penalty is an element of criminal law, one punish-

ment among others, a bit more severe to be sure; and *external*, excluded: a foundation, a condition of possibility, an origin, a non-serial-exemplarity, hyperbolic, more and other than a penalty." These terms could also be reversed: criminal law is at once internal and external to the penalty (or rather giving) of death, whose stakes are much higher, and whose foundation, tightly though it cleaves to the principle of sovereignty and its quasi-theological foundations, precedes and, as it were, exceeds the law (or at the least its positive, legal codification, its jurisprudence, etc.). Thus no simple, unilateral conditionality, whether of causation or conceptual implication, exists between capital punishment and the theologico-political; rather, they are held ("welded") together in a relationship of "alliance," a "setting to work" of a "basis" and "principle." Let me explain: the theologico-political must be the "transcendental" of capital punishment, in that it is at once internal and external to it. In consequence, the death penalty is at once internal and external to the theological, to the history of religion whose essence it seeks to capture theoretically, dogmatically.

Contrast to this the hypothesis, the disturbing "fact" that throughout the history of Western philosophy, no philosopher "in his or her role as philosopher, in his or her own, strictly and systematically philosophical discourse," has ever "*as such* contested the legitimacy of the death penalty," and one is left with a puzzling question. Should not the resources—both conceptual and rhetorical, figural and pragmatic—for abolishing capital punishment instead be sought elsewhere, perhaps in the very religious tradition that delivered its theologico-juridico-political alibi and justification in the first place? Might not the source and the cure be one and the same? Like religion, the death penalty "undoubtedly will survive for a long time yet, despite its general retreat in the world" (3). But are these "retreats" congruous? If they are not fully cotemporaneous, but, say, in delay and retreat with respect to each other—and the metaphors of "alliance" and "welding" suggest nothing else—might not one also outlast and even undo the other? That capital punishment is not the prerogative of religion, even of the theologico-political, seems clear; it is equally clear that it does not allow one to think the phenomena of "mass killing (extermination or genocide)," which, Derrida notes, require different "categories" altogether. Most philosophers have been no less silent about these categories. Should we not perhaps rely, then (or rely once again, albeit it otherwise), on a *not yet available* theologico-political concept, not in order simply to *apply* it to the death penalty as one of its "cases" or examples, nor as a "prosthetic artifact" that keeps capital punishment "upright," but as the necessary tool for its abolishment, as well as for the abolishment of killings that shame the very concept of legal punishment, and for which no categories are as yet available? To vary and parody Camus (cited by Derrida): could there be any hope of abolishing the death penalty in a fully secularized world, in a world, that is, in which the "right to religion" and the sovereignty on which it relies would be countered by a consequent immanentism, a world, finally, that would no longer trust Christianity's "other resources of internal 'division,' self-contestation, and self-deconstruction."

41   See Hent de Vries, *Minimal Theologies: Critiques of Secular Reason in Adorno and Levinas* (Baltimore: Johns Hopkins University Press, forthcoming 2004), part 1.

42   Derrida, "Faith and Knowledge," 86 [78].

43   Ibid., 87 [79]; emphasis mine, translation modified.

44   Bergson, *The Two Sources of Morality and Religion*, 101 [103].

45   Derrida, "Faith and Knowledge," 87 [79–80].

46   Ibid., 88 [81].

47  Bergson, *The Two Sources of Morality and Religion*, 292 [311].

48  Derrida, "Autoimmunity," 130.

49  Bergson, *The Two Sources of Morality and Religion*, 234 [248].

50  Ibid., 240 [255]. See also Henri Gouhier's *Bergson et le Christ des évangiles* (Paris: Fayard, 1962; Paris: Vrin, 1987, 1999).

51  Bergson, *The Two Sources of Morality and Religion*, 215 [227–28].

52  Derrida, "Autoimmunity," 100.

PART 5 | Theological Materialism

*John Milbank* | Materialism and
Transcendence

ONE PROMINENT ASPECT of French and French-influenced *Marxisant* thought since the 1950s has been its attempt to supply Marxism with a more adequate ontology than was contained within the writings of Marx and Engels themselves. Partly because continental thought tends to distinguish itself from a perceived scientistic bias of analytic philosophy, this attempt is marked by the search for a nonreductive materialism. Reductive materialism imagines matters as atomistic, mechanical, passive and inert, and tends to explain away meaningful action and volition as illusion. Nonreductive materialism imagines matter as that which can itself occasion subjectivity and meaning, because it is the site for the emergence of a spontaneous and unpredictable energy. Since the history of materialism is mostly the history of reduction, with the exception of the Stoics, Spinoza, and Nietzsche, those in quest of a nonreductive version must characteristically borrow from Platonic-Aristotelian, Idealist, and even theological thought if they are to develop a sufficiently enriched version of material processes. (The Stoics, Spinoza, and Nietzsche also made these problematic borrowings.) This quest seems inevitable and justified: even though there is a British tradition of reductively materialist Marxism, it is difficult to reconcile this with Marx's absolute valuation of subjects freely reaching their full productive and expressive potential. Nor can one simply dispense with ontology in order to concentrate upon practice: Marxism, and indeed every socialism, requires an account of human nature and of the role of human beings within the cosmos; otherwise it is not clear why there is something now lacking that needs to be emancipated, nor why one should suppose that we live in a reality within which such emancipation is possible.

Must such an ontology indeed be a materialist one? Yes, in the sense that socialism sees earthly justice as crucially concerned with material distribution. Yes, also in the sense that Marxism is right to see all human knowledge as linked with human conventions of justice, and so as inseparable from historically arising patterns of production and exchange.

This connection of notions of truth with notions of the good was earlier understood by Catholic theology in terms of the "convertibility" of such "transcendental" concepts. A link between Marxist historicism and Catholic metaphysics can be provided by the axiom of the eighteenth-century Catholic thinker Giambattista Vico, who proclaimed (in its full version) that the transcendentals *verum* and *bonum* also convert with a new transcendental, the *factum*, meaning the historically and even eternally "constructed." (Vico was cited but weakly understood by Marx.) Much later, and in the wake of Marx, the Orthodox theologian, socialist, and sometime Marxist economist Sergei Bulgakov made a similar affirmation: the Christian East has failed to include within the work of "deification" (as the East describes "salvation") the collective process of historical construction, while the West has falsely seen this as a secular, transcendentally indifferent work of the merely human will, not as a synergic working with God that seeks through making (art and labor) itself the telos of the good and the vision of the true. It followed that for Bulgakov human knowledge as well as human virtue was an entirely economic matter, collectively possessed in the rhythms and dispersals of exchange and production.

In this way one has a mode of historical materialism. Yet for Bulgakov the human general economy (of signs and numbers, as well as commodities and prices) participates in and is guided by the divine *economia* of Orthodox theology: the entire "distribution" of God's eternal being in the single work of creation and redemptive re-creation.[1]

If one looks by contrast at recent secular attempts to develop a materialist ontology that will undergird socialist aspirations, then it is striking that even in these cases an appeal is increasingly made, not just to idealist philosophy — to Hegel, to Schelling, and to their heir (despite everything), Heidegger — but also to theology: to notions of the *via negativa*, of the absolutely other, of grace, hope, and agape. What is the reason for this? I shall venture an explanation. If matter is to be more than inert, and even capable of subjectivity and meaning, then it must be innately more than a spatially or mechanically limited substance; it must rather be forcefully self-transcending. Our only human access to the notions of force and self-transcending development involves experiences of volition and meaning: hence self-transcending matter is inevitably conceived as somewhat etherealized and idealized. This may be perfectly consistent with materialism, since we have no ultimate notion of what matter consists in: to imagine it as only dense and inert is merely to confine it to *one* mode of ideality that forms a background for volition — namely the negative *hyle* that shaping ideation and determined purposeful intending always presuppose.

However, if matter is totally etherealized and idealized, then real material processes become epiphenomena of logical processes, or else the magical outcome of pure willing, or again some combination of both. As soon as one says something like "matter" can, in certain instances, think and, in certain instances, will, then the unthinkable background of hyle tends to fade away, bearing with it all the irrational and latent impulses of nature and humanity that help to shape historical occurrences, in favor of what we think we can fully grasp, namely meaningful intending processes. In which case, one must say that materialism is lost in idealism and humanism.

Yet one cannot prevent this lamentable outcome by the reduction of all subjectivity to the blind urgings of hyle. For in that case, conversely, the desire of humanity for emancipation is itself reduced to an epiphenomenal illusion that conceals what is really going on: viz meaningless evolutionary processes. In that case, one cannot will the true human future in the name of the fulfillment of the real — except as an entertaining illusion — but can see it only, at best, as an honest collapsing back of the human illusion into prehuman sequences. Since these are mechanical or else obscurely impulsive, they certainly cannot sustain anything like the reality of peace or justice: viewed anthropomorphically, they seem to sustain rather the rule of Heraclitean violence. If this is reality, then it is capitalism that gets nearest to acknowledging it without ever quite doing so, since it reduces the meaningful goal to an agon round an empty fetish, which in this case, far from being finally an illusion, as classic Marxism would have it, would rather be the closest possible willed and meaningful manifestation of the real reign of the blindly nonmeaningful. The forces of so-called progress — science, rationalism, and materialism — are far more precisely allied to capitalism than Marx realized. Hence an ontology that legitimated socialism would have to discover a way of locating ideality in matter without idealizing matter away or finally canceling ideality tout court.

This means that many of the notions characterizing German idealism become inappropriate, since they tend to involve either or both of a purely transparent realized logical process and/or where they admit an inaccessible presupposed ground or foundation, something like a purely autonomous self-sustaining, inexplicable action or willing, that is, in this way again transparent *and* self-explanatory. In either case, the closure and transparency of thinking and willing must both negate and foreclose their mysterious energies and potentials. What one needs instead are notions of thought and of willing that *themselves* sustain an excess of reference beyond themselves, that involve unpredictable creativity and the lure of a self-exceeding desire. "Thinking for oneself" in an exercise of Kantian autonomy will cancel material density; likewise exercising purely your own spontaneous choice for good and evil à la Kant will also cancel this density: in either case we exit from muddy appearances to dwell in the crystalline spheres of the noumenally monadic. By contrast, if thought is open and assertive and does not quite know what it is that it thinks, and if accompanying will is obscurely compelled before and beyond itself, then the density and fathomless force of matter are sustained.

Where though, can one derive such notions of thinking and willing? The answer must be in theology and in modes of philosophy (such as Neoplatonism) that make reference to the transcendent. This is because theology alone posits both that there is an ultimate principle which is thinking and willing and that this principle is, for our thought and volition, only remotely accessible. As purely unified, as *esse* rather than *ens*, this principle does indeed "think itself," yet not after our mode of doubling self-reflection, which would contradict its simplicity. Indeed this simplicity can be thought of as having something of the nonhuman purity of a rock, to whom the Bible frequently compares the deity.

In consequence our thought and volition become *gifts* that are received from something that is higher than thought or volition. And as gifts from the supraintellectual, they therefore remain more consonant with our bodies which are *clearly* things that we have received and never entirely master. Likewise our thought and volition, when taken as remote echoes of an entire infinite and simple nonreflective thought and volition, can be seen as unselfgrounded and obscure to themselves. Just as we do not know what our bodies are finally capable of, so we do not know the entire implications of what we think, nor what we ultimately will when we will. Here abstraction and the grand gesture both expand and yet reassert our obscure embodiment. (This accords much more with the Aristotelian account of *eide* and *hyle* as well as *psyche* than with any idealist dialectic of idea and ground.) Our thought is in the first place characteristically creative, rather than reflective, and yet in creating we always transform matter, and we cannot command the arrival of a transformative idea. Ideas come to us by inspiration, as if from on high, and for this reason they are well received by latencies of the material ground.

In this way, the theological appeal to transcendence alone sustains a nonreductive materiality and is the very reverse of any notion of idealism. In fact, idealism is always most at home within immanence, for its essentially pagan Greek horizon (sometimes gnosticized) is to do with the confrontation between active logos and chaotic hyle within a single closed cosmos. Without the gods or the Platonic forms, however, this pagan immanence is more perfectly realized by German idealism: logical processes outworking themselves through time are not received gifts, but the unfolding of autonomy, albeit through contradiction and return. Although this principle of autonomy stands in contrast to the alien self-enclosure of matter, nonetheless it is included with matter within the same cosmos, and for just this reason it is in a dualistic rivalry with the material principle, even if it must posit it from the outset, à la Fichte, as its enabling other. To assert the self-origination of immanent ideation is ultimately at the expense of the material ground.

By contrast, genuinely theological notions of thinking and willing do not regard thought and matter as poles in dialectical tension after the manner of Fichte, Hegel, and the early-to-middle Schelling. Instead, in the manner we have seen, they are blended through ultimately shared proclivities. If, in the end, both thought and matter exhibit a resistant density and an excessive potential, then this is because their combined meaningful finitude is together an arriving gift, which if regarded as such, indicates an ultimate creative source. Since finite logos is every bit as created as finite hyle, thought and matter are here leveled and equated with reference to a transcendent source, without this equation abolishing their relative real difference, nor even abolishing the relative hierarchical superiority of thought over matter. For the ultimate creative source of an entire hierarchical series is not simply "on top" of that series in the way that ideas lie "above" matter for idealism; rather, since (unlike the topmost rung of the series) the source *gives* the entire series, it tends from the absolute point of view to level what nevertheless remains, within the series, hierarchically distinguished. In this way, it is only the monotheistic doctrine of creation (to which nonetheless Proclean Neoplatonism closely tended) that allows a nonreductive materialism in theory and in practice, which allows us, for example, to value humanity above the cosmic and animal, and yet also in a more ultimate gesture to proclaim that the highest value lies in establishing all these three in peaceful harmonious perfection. This is exactly the gesture made by Dionysius the Areopagite's Christianizing of Proclus, who had already insisted that the simplicity of matter in a way *more* reflected the simplicity of the first principle than did the reflexivity of intellect. (Dionysius echoed this in his remarks about the apophatic suitability of seemingly gross symbols for the Godhead.) And this perspective alone allows us the vision of a nonfascistic, non-anti-human ecology.

One can also go a little further. An infinite thought, an infinite volition, which is entirely "simple" (in no way, even formally, distinguished within itself), as Thomas Aquinas put it, and also self-sustaining, cannot, as we have just seen, be truly akin to any finite thought or volition that we are familiar with. First of all, as self-sustaining, it has a certain property that *we* can imagine only in somewhat material terms, as for us individual material substances appear nearer to being self-sustaining (if not self-initiating, like thought, which, however, inversely lacks by comparison in relative self-standing). Second, as infinite, and therefore nonbounded, it must sustain, yet without imperfection, a certain nonbounded "incompletion," or rather it must sustain a "completion" beyond any concept we have of the complete, which always involves the bounded. In this way, the kinship of our finite thought with matter, as mysterious, noncommanded, and boundless in potential, is in a certain paradoxical way sustained in that which is replete and absolute—just because it is infinite. It is important to remember here that the attribution of this "disorganized" principle of the in-finite to the One or to God arose in philosophy only with the Neoplatonists and the Church Fathers—it was not allowed by the ancient Greeks. Finally, one can note that the Church Father Tertullian, even though he was orthodox and in no way a pantheist, affirmed that God's lack of a bounded body does not imply the *immateriality* of God. For Tertullian, just as the Creator God was boundless thought and will, so also he was boundless materiality.[2]

To achieve an adequate ontology, therefore, materialist socialism needs to invoke theology. Perhaps this is why Walter Benjamin thought that, in future, philosophical thought would have to sublate itself into theology, rather than, as Hegel thought, the other way around. I am not, however, trying to say that recent French or French-influenced Marxisant thinkers explicitly argue in the way that I have done above. Instead, I am claiming that this is an implicit logical horizon that is drawing them forward unawares, and which they grasp so far in a thoroughly fragmentary and partial fashion. Nevertheless, this logic is shown in their reasonings so far: Derrida sustains the openness of signs and the absoluteness of the ethical command by recourse to (or as he supposes—wrongly, in my view—by way of a radicalization of) negative theology; Deleuze sustains the possibility of a deterritorialization of matter and meaning in terms of a Spinozistic virtual absolute; Badiou sustains the possibility of a revolutionary event in terms of the one historical event of the arrival of the very logic of the event as such, which is none other than Pauline grace; Žižek sustains the possibility of a revolutionary love beyond desire by reference to the historical emergence of the ultimate sublime object, which reconciles us to the void constituted only through a rift in the void. This sublime object is Christ.

In the case of Badiou and Žižek, a further feature has become notable.[3] They are rightly discontented with the submergence of the socialist left in a liberal celebration of plurality and otherness. Such celebration, they correctly aver, is inauthentic, because it usually wants nothing actually to do with the exotic other—this is why it insists that the ultimate ethical gesture is a visual presentation of exotic otherness at a distance. Likewise, this tendency admits the other to ethical significance in the guise of victimhood: this means that we have only human solidarity in our weakness, rather than in our positive creative aspirations. One can object here that such an ethical stance may well desire that the other substantively fulfill herself; however, if this fulfillment does not concern our human project in common, then its content is, for the regarding other, a matter of ethical indifference: once again this moral agent lapses into the character of a mere, anemically detached spectator.

Socialism instead requires our solidarity in the name of the project of positive affirmation of life and more abundant life: we are to love others as active expressive affirmers and not, or not primarily, as victims. As theology puts it, we are to love people because—and even only insofar as—they display the image of God. But such a love involves mutual recognition of our positive realizations and capacities. Therefore what is valued here in every case is not the ineffably and inexpressibly different, but rather what is universally acclaimable and shareable, albeit precisely because it is unique and particular. Only *as* unique and particular does a value clearly "stand out," but this standing out renders it sometimes universal and also participable—albeit in the mode of non-identical repetition.

This new concern for the question of the universal, for what binds us together, goes beyond the Levinasian/Derridean concern with an irreducible plurality beyond totality. Totality is not here reinstated, because we are united not within a total complete cosmos, but rather around uniquely arising events, whose new logic, whose new rhythms, we all come to embrace. This shift has a very marked impact upon the attitude of Marxisant thought toward religion.

For Derrida so far, a secularized negative theology suggests a more radical removal from the specificities of religious tradition, and the emergence of a rootless and nomadic postmodern religiosity orientated toward a negativity upheld by no finally positive infinite ontological pole. Since, for Derrida, the deconstructive urge has never performed its work, this rootless religiosity is only ceaselessly parasitic on all the various religious traditions that are all more or less affirmed, even if notable prominence is given to Judaism and Christianity.

By notable contrast, Badiou and Žižek's suspicion of the politically correct discourse of pluralism causes them also unequivocally to favor the example of one religion over that of all the rest, and this religion is, of course, Christianity. This new favoring of Christianity is an integral part of their desire to reassert the human universality and singularity of the socialist project beyond all received historical traditions, over against postmodern liberal political pluralism, whose last word is "respect difference" and whose religiosity is scarcely distinguishable from the new age recommendation of self-cultivation in negative removal from given social processes.

Why is an attention toward Christianity so integral in this fashion? The answer is that Christianity is seen as, uniquely, the religion of universalism. Badiou and Žižek are perfectly correct about this, and they expose thereby all the incipient triviality of recent theological talk about a particular "Christian language game," which is just as valid or invalid as all other language games, and so forth. Once again theologians have been caught out in their inauthentic pusillanimity. In deference to liberal fashion, they have foresworn Christian claims to uniqueness, to a transcending of the Jewish legacy and so forth. Now they are wrong-footed by Marxist atheists who recall us to the facts of historical phenomenology: Christianity was the very first enlightenment, the first irruption of an absolutely universal claim. The Greeks were mostly uncertain whether women and barbarians could philosophize and certain slaves could not; the New Testament, by contrast, asserts that all—slave and free, male and female, Jew, Greek, Roman, and barbarian— can recognize God in the resurrection of Christ and moreover insists that this potential of universal recognizability alone qualifies a truth as a universal truth. The merely substantively universal truth of Greek philosophy is thereby disqualified in its universality, and therefore in its truth, after all. It is certain, of course, that Judaism already displayed a universalizing drift; however (and this is continued even by Islam), it never quite makes recognition of its particular laws a condition for the universal recognition of the God of all nations. In this way it does not quite enact a universal *event*, which has the consequence of relativizing in practice cultural particularity and allowing a universal human association.

The objection here that surely Christ is more utterly specific than the Jewish law entirely misses the point (as Hegel realized, albeit in an insufficient mode). Christ is *so* specific as to be immediately the most general. We can all identify with the adroit, fluid, savage, gentle, wise, miracle-working, and suffering man, just as we can all—from pole to pole—identify with Charlie Chaplin or Buster Keaton but cannot easily identify with, say, the *actants* within the Japanese conventions of politeness. Both St. Paul and Kierkegaard were in a way right (though also in a way wrong, as I have just implied) to elide the specifics of Christ's life from our purview: what matters is to know that God was manifest not in any human state or notion of generality, but in one — which is to say as a *dependent* consequence in any — human life, death, and resurrection. Precisely because Jesus escapes any general framework, given that any general set can always be subsumed in a further set, Jesus is universal. The universality of Christianity is not therefore a matter of subjective opinion or of faith in the first place; it is rather a matter of logic. Christianity is universal because it invented the logic of universality; it constituted this logic as an event. Such an invention and constitution could not have consisted in a mere discovery of universal truth, as the Greeks mostly supposed (though arguably *not* Socrates and Plato), because philosophy failed adequately to grasp the logic of universality. As Badiou argues, philosophy (but again, not really Plato on Badiou's reading) seeks to place everything within its right place within a given totality, a finite (not infinite) cosmos. However, this means that every thing and every person must identify with its fixed place in the cosmos and can only, for an ultimate gesture, relate to the cosmos as a whole, for, since the cosmos is a whole, it has no relation outside itself and therefore has itself no place and no identity. It might as well be a void. Thus in Hinduism, there are plural ethics appropriate to specific hierarchical position, but there is no general universal good: at the general level, as the *Bhagavad Gita* teaches, all ethics are relativized, and the only thing that is shared is nirvana — but that is not really shared, since at such a point of elevation things cease to be shared, as there are no longer any subjects of sharing.

Likewise (to shift the compass perspective rapidly from the Far East to the Farthest West, old and new), Alexis de Tocqueville remarked, in *Democracy in America*, that in an aristocratic society like England's, no one is interested in general ideas and indeed finds them almost impossible to grasp, as ideas are always relative to the rules and manners of class position (this is still somewhat true today), whereas in Democratic America (still also true?) they *are* interested in general ideas, because people see themselves as all humans in general.[4] However, one can add to Tocqueville here that there would be no American idea of humanity in general outside the constant repetition of the specific event of the American Revolution, nor indeed (as Tocqueville himself made clear) outside the repetition of the universal man Christ, in religiously constituted American civil society. One could even argue that Tocqueville unwittingly displays the truth that universality emerges only from the event: without the impulse toward free association generated by religion, he argues (one could say without its impulse toward collective repetition of religion's founding event), American democracy tends to dissolve into myriad individualisms and particularisms that will cancel out any sense of common humanity: in its place there will emerge the sway of propagandistic fashion at once over and yet on behalf of the majority — we today can well term this "fascism." Hence Tocqueville's arguments regarding America and the danger of capitalistic corruption of its project recognize implicitly not only the generation of universality by an event, but also the religious dimension of this logic.

Philosophy, placing things in a cosmos, does not then establish the universal. But an event that *exceeds* the given totality establishes itself as more than a specific place or position. Rather it exhibits itself as a universal non-identically repeatable possibility. Such an event can only arise in time, as only in time can established totalities be sundered. Yet in order to be valued as universal, the event must also be regarded as "eternal" in the sense of having universal pertinence: this is what Badiou argues.

We can now see how Badiou and Žižek add a new dimension to the Marxisant debate about religion. All the participants in effect turn to theology because this discourse alone permits an ideal materialism that does not result in the out-and-out triumph of idealism. However, the turn to the secularized via negativa, because it does not admit any real transcendent superabundant plenitude within which religious performances might remotely participate, never recognizes any degrees of more-or-less correct manifestation of the absolute, or any advance toward the absolute that is not equally and inversely a regression. Since all religious images fail equally, all religiously ideal discourses are validated in their very invalidation. In this way, the mysterious "surplus" in the ideal that allows it to be fused with matter and not to conceal matter is merely handed over to the absolutely and impotently negative, which, unlike the true theological negative of Dionysius the Areopagite, is not really going anywhere. This leaves the positive aspect of religious ideality — the attempt at *Cataphasis* — paradoxically replete in its very failure. Hence religious ideas, for this pluralist ideology, remain at the level of ideality, even though they compose no inexorable logical train, save the *absolutely* inexorable one of mechanical deconstruction. Thus if one values primarily the other, this means the other taken in the place of God is purely negative, in such a fashion that a hypostatized negativity going nowhere *is*, in effect, a replete and autonomous idea that effaces all material appearing. (Alternatively, one values the other in his totalized idiosyncratic specificity, closed off from the mysterious negative surplus in which he does not participate — and so once again one has a replete, abstractable idea. Such an option is rightly refused by Levinas and Derrida, but they never consider the third possibility of a negative surplus mediated by the phenomenally manifest.) This is why Derrideanism is idealist.

In the face of this idealism, Badiou insists that a powerful human thought or idea is not something replete and inert, and therefore cannot be unmediably diverse in its contingency, but rather is universal by virtue of that very contingency. It follows that one must not merely negate its positivity in a Derridean fashion, as though such positivity always threatens to congeal into a presence of a general sway at variance with the idea's contingent particularity. This imperative holds for Derrida, since true difference is by him considered to be only the about-to-happen of difference and sustains itself as different only in the moment of negation of prior sedimented difference that has always lapsed back into presence in the very instance of its occurrence. Yet for Badiou the positivity of the idea need not be negated in this manner, because the idea acquires an "eternal" presence not by suppressing its specificity, but precisely by asserting it. Its presence is that not of something static and closed, but rather of something forever-after fertile, generating endlessly further insights that more and more disclose its originally latent depths.

For this reason, Badiou first of all celebrates not—ironically, à la Derrida—the plurality of religions, but the singularity of the absolute religion, Christianity, which emerged as the event of that which elicits universal recognition. The event of universal love, the event of life-over-against death, the event of the universal offer of forgiveness and reconciliation, and a new mode of sociality based upon the reciprocal exchange of this offer. It makes no sense to refuse this event, at least as a horizon of possibility. Debate and dialogue at this point would be ridiculous, short of the emergence of some more universal horizon. For these are the very conditions of universality, as we in the West imagine it.

In the second place, Badiou stresses not the movement of signifying or forceful negation, but the arrival of grace as that which interpellates us as subjects in the first place. Not absence then, but a superabundant and always specific presence. Whereas for Derrida, we can keep trying to surrender an illusory self-autonomy in relation to a constitutive absence, death, contentless gift, and so forth, for Badiou we are, in our original self-present contingency, clearly *not* self-possessed and autonomous, but indeed given—given in our very concrete materiality, which sustains our conscious action and reflection. And whereas, for Derrida, all religions might be the staging places for negation, for Badiou only Christianity offers divine grace, in the sense that Christianity simply *is* the thought that we are redeemed or liberated by the arrival of grace, which we can all share in our bodies as loving people, and not by human systems of law or human philosophies and mystical practices—even that of absolute negation.

Do Badiou and Žižek, insofar as he concurs, get it right? I have so far described ways in which they do: ways in which Christianity is aligned with materialism, ways in which socialist universalism requires Christian universalism, and not, by contrast, postmodern pluralism or new age gnosis. However, I do not think this goes far enough. To put it briefly, I think that their atheistic, essentially Hegelian versions of Christianity sustain very well an ontology of *revolution*, but not an ontology of socialism. I think, furthermore, that despite their respective intentions, what they still offer us is gnostic Christianity, negative dialectics, and captivity to an inexorable law. By contrast, I believe that to think the possibility of the socialist future, we have to travel much further out of the idealist captivity of the logos, beyond dialectics, beyond tragic gnosis, beyond mystical nihilism. We have to reinvoke much more of the spirit of the ancient Greeks, of the Latin South, of the Slavic East, of pre- and anti-idealist Germany and of the Celtic-Scandinavian-Saxon north. Finally, we have to strip ourselves of a million prejudices and false historical conceptions and consider again the radical content of orthodox Catholic Christianity. In the end this tradition and materialist socialism require each other.

Let us consider briefly, in more detail, the proposals of Badiou and Žižek. First of all, let us begin with Badiou. More than any others of the *soixante-huitarde* philosophers, he has traveled some distance in the direction that I think is required. This is ironic, because of all these thinkers he is in a way the most militantly atheist. But just because he is such, he is the most free of the taint of what can be called "mystical nihilism." That is to say, Badiou rejects what he rightly identifies as the concealed Plotinianism of both Derrida's and Deleuze's thought—namely the idea that there is a kind of "real" absolute absence, or void, or virtuality from which everything emerges, and back into which everything dissolves. This is all too like Plotinus's One, which (unlike the Platonic "Beyond Being" which was superexistentially present as the Ideal), was truly formless and in a way "there" only in the compulsion to emanate diverse existences. Badiou finds the same historical echo in Heidegger's temporal Being that is identical with nothing. In all these instances, I would add to Badiou, one has the logic of a "double shuttle" between two nullities. Heidegger's ontic, Derrida's presences, Deleuze's local territories of mirroring epistemological representation, are less than fully real, indeed are somewhat illusory, and are therefore *nothing*. But behind them lies the real absolute nothing that is Heidegger's Being, Derrida's absence or pure gift, Deleuze's virtual or impossible absolute deterritorialization. This absolute nothing is only there at all, only insists in its absoluteness, *through* its giving rise to the lesser nothings that are illusions. Badiou is the first continental philosopher to point out the pretensions of this charade. There is really nothing postmetaphysical going on here; rather, these are all typical examples of metaphysics, and as Conor Cunningham has shown in his remarkable book *Genealogy of Nihilism*, the same pattern of "double shuttle between two nothings" can be found already somewhat in Plotinus and Avicenna, and then certainly in Spinoza, Kant, and Hegel.[5]

Why does this matter, politically? Badiou denounces in Heidegger and Deleuze what he refers to after Heidegger as the "folding back" of illusory regimes of stable particular order into the Absolute Being/Nothing or the Virtual, since this amounts after all to an ultimate nonvaluation of finite specificities and differences. For Badiou, Deleuze wrongly depreciates "formal equilibrium" in art, "amorous consistency" in the existential sphere, and "organization" in the political.[6] (In *this respect* one can read Deleuze as the thinker of modernism in philosophy and Badiou as the truly postmodern thinker who allows a plurality of stable truths in a way that encompasses a certain neoclassicism in every realm of culture.) In the case of Deleuze, as with Derrida, differentiation that liberates is an insistence and is never perfectly accomplished (even if its mode of arrival is more positive and to a degree more *positively* realized for Deleuze as difference than is the case with Derrida). This means that he can articulate the ontological conditions for revolution, but not for an achieved, or even constantly arriving, revolution, which would be socialism—not even to any degree. One could have an advance by degrees into socialism if Deleuze admitted analogical difference, but where Being is always unmediably and immediately different, every asserted difference against territory is destined to lapse into territory in turn. Here socialism cannot arrive fully, or even by degrees.

Deleuze therefore offers us, as a kind of new Neoplatonic One, the absolute void or virtuality, which tends to fold back into itself all finite regimes of territory or representation, since these regimes *are* the only actuality of the virtual in its anarchic unfolding, such that the illusion of stable hierarchic distribution (into genera and species), is nevertheless the work—the only realized work—of nonidentical repetition, univocally conceived. But in that case, nothing finite betokens any socialist promise, just as authentic art can only be an operation of violence, cruelty and disruptive gesture.

Badiou offers us instead a notion of Being not as a forceful "virtual" prior to any logical possibility, but rather as simply the anarchic infinite set of all mathematical possibilities with their endless subsets, overlapping sets and sub-subsets that paradoxically diagonalize out of their containing sets. In none of this, however, does there reside any human promise for Badiou. Here again, he challenges all the other Marxisant thinkers: if one takes, for example, Deleuze's "Virtual" in a materialist sense, then the collapse of differences, because of their univocal manifestation of being, back into this empty univocal ground, amounts after all to a recrudescence of vulgar materialism: one gets (as described in *A Thousand Plateaus*) a purely "diagrammatic" matter without meaning, that is transcendentally prior, as a series of "abstract machines," to both substantive content and semiotic expression, both of which it distributes as sedimented states (the equivalent of the ontologically engendered yet local domains of "transcendental illusion" constituted by "representation" in *Difference and Repetition*) according to no constraint or logic.[7]

This conception of the hidden urging of abstract machines encourages Deleuzean-Guattarian fantasies about the emergence of posthuman bodies and cyborgs. The question to raise here is: In what sense are posthuman bodies "bodies" if they exceed the psychic (rendering them thereby merely inorganic and inert)? And if, conversely, they do not, then how are they posthuman, if nonreductive materialism means that we never fully know what a human body can do or how it can develop? To lose the human is here also to lose the body in favor of a subpsychic dimension that can be either only mechanically determined or random, or else (in some fashion) both. This is clearly a "reduced" matter once more, however intoxicating the formulas that seek to express it.

It is also not surprising that Deleuze and Guattari celebrate machines, albeit "abstract ones," reduced to "matter and function," so avidly, for the abstraction does not render the machine less purely material: to the contrary, as in the case of the Cartesian reduction of physical space to geometrical space, the ordinary physical machine without a unifying *eidos* or directive telos is already an abstract machine just for this reason, transferable as an abstracted idea of a process into indefinitely many physical circumstances with any possible degree of rarefaction, including (for a reductive perspective) processes of information. Thus even if the abstract machines of Deleuze and Guattari are propelled by and sustain mysterious and un-Cartesian energies, they are still, in their conjoined abstraction and lack of integrating form, actually typical modern purely physical machines after all.

So is not Deleuze in the end, asks Badiou, simply a pre-Socratic cosmologist and not a philosopher at all? Is not the philosopher rather always a Platonist who wonders how, within and yet beyond the cosmos, which is now for Badiou the futility of infinite abstract meaningless sets, there is also the city, eros, and art, as well as manifold plural proliferating realities whose universal fields are not mere arbitrary differences always doubling into theaters of representation, but fields at once unpredictably fertile yet continuously recognizable under a consistent and yet not closed formality? At this point, all Badiou can himself offer us is a neo-Cartesian or neo-Sartrean contrast between a strictly *mathematicized* material extension on the one hand and an unexplained world of subjectivity and seemingly neo-Kantian valuation on the other. The latter is, admittedly, prepared for within the ontological world of multiple sets, in those various instances where a subset exceeds its inclusion in the initial set—for example, by containing within itself rogue elements that do not belong within the scope of the original set at all. (As, to illustrate, mistletoe is an element of growth within the phenomenon "oak tree," regarded as a set of components, but not within the set of the phenomenon of "trees," including all that strictly pertains only to their growth as such, to which "oak tree" belongs.) Within such an "evental site" a process of subjectivization can emerge, through which something acquires an identity by consistently affirming a rogue instance. Yet it is never clear in Badiou just how the boundary between the presubjective chance escape of a parasite and true subjective deliberation and commitment is crossed. (Badiou himself recognizes this problem and is working to remedy it.)

So if Deleuze materially reduces meaning in a way that, as we have seen, is dialectically complicit with an idealization of matter, does not Badiou offer us a yet more emphatically idealized matter, in terms of highly abstract mathematical entities lacking even the motion of machines; a matter also without Deleuzean forces and virtual capacity, which then exhibits no appropriate ground for the emergence of the event?

It might very well be that Badiou's event suggests the possibility of a true revolutionary break more than does Deleuze's difference, since his event is not parasitic upon the infinite set of all sets, as Deleuze's difference is parasitic upon sedimented territory. However, Badiou's Avicennian ontology of pure prior possibility leaves the arising of the actual (as an arbitrary instantiation of some possibility or other) more of an unsoundable mystery than Deleuze's other Avicennian variant of a creative virtuality always seeking to actualize itself.

Nor is it so clear that Badiou himself escapes the taint of Neoplatonism he so rightly detects in both Deleuze and Heidegger. For Badiou's ontology is forced to move beyond the pure delineation of a repertoire of possibilities at the point where the actual instantiation of a set (for example, in the natural world) must actually endorse the logical operation of the production of a set that involves a "count for one" that produces always a certain effect of unity. But beneath this level, the "set of all sets" for Badiou does not really exist but is rather the irreducible remainder of "inconsistent multiplicity" also apparent in any actualized possibility and approximated by Badiou both to the Lacanian "Real" and to Heidegger's "Being as such," which is in consequence materialized. This gives rise to the critical question: do not the sets "fold back" into this original multiple being, or "void," as Badiou terms it, since this is the "reality" behind every mere effect of unity that ultimate reality in no way legitimates, even though it exists only *through* such a "count for one"? Why is Badiou's void any less like the Plotinian One that exceeds the contrast of one and many than is Deleuze's virtual and also only "is" through the lesser and imperfectly "true" effects it generates? At most one could say that Badiou's void is more like Damascius's "first principle," which had abandoned (against Proclus) any notions of the priority of unity over plurality. Moreover, Badiou would appear to face precisely an extreme immanentist version of the problematic of the last Athenian Academy: if his void is pure, then how do sets arise at all as actualized, given on the other hand that they do so arise, then must not the void itself involve a virtual insistence? (This problematic led to a positing of a "One beyond the One" in Iamblichus and Damascius.)

Without an appeal to such a virtuality and the positing of a link between its operation and the emergence of subjectivization, does not the notion of an arising absolutely presuppositionless self-originating event of truth appear simply mythical and needlessly mystifying in character? Does it not require Badiou to espouse, for example, a kind of triumphalist view of the emergence of new universal reasonings in science that takes no account of the work of historians of science and their exposure of complex hidden continuities and returns to apparently abandoned positions?

And then one must also ask: How can absolute truths in science, mathematics, art, ethics, and politics be secured for Badiou in an (often romanticized) event of subjective historical constitution and yet be absolute and universal? It is not surprising—and indeed it is wonderfully honest on Badiou's part—that here he has to have recourse to the notion of grace.

How does this recourse work? A truth arises out of an event; it mirrors no preceding reality, since, as Badiou rightly says, the most fundamental truths of art, ethics, political practice, and even of science and mathematics (which are shown only in new practices and technological performances) are new creative manifestations: "corresponding" truths, in the sense of mirroring truths, are only secondary, folded-back repetitions of these more primary truths. So if a subjectively arising truth is compelling, is taken as "true," it has to be regarded as being like a "gift" that has inexorably taken one over. For this reason, Badiou affirms St. Paul's account of truth as established in the "weakness" of pure subjective witness by assertion. This feature is exactly that which paradoxically renders it universal. A philosophical truth of placing something in its right place in a cosmos can be only particular and empirical after all, and relative to the cosmos, taking no account of the new that arrives through time. Its very generality turns out to but local and specific—confined to givenness without the gift. Likewise, the legal truths of the Jewish law can only be particular placings within a total regime of legislation, while equally Jewish prophetic "signs" can only be particular placings within an overall framework that is only one, total Jewish specificity, even if this specificity is potentially infinite. By contrast, the new subjective gesture closes the gap between law and life, sign and performance, and steps outside any given total and abstract, even if infinite, set of signs or laws (remembering that for a post-Cantorian perspective there can be infinite sets that, as sets, are still finite).

But to Badiou one can ask, How can an event bring with it its own grace, without reinscribing the principle of Kantian liberal autonomy which he rightly rejects? As he says, to see oneself as primarily a bearer of rights is to overlook and reduce in value one's given contingency that is not, and never can be, autonomously self-governed but rather implies prior specific membership of the cosmos and the collective human body. Yet if for this reason an event cannot own its own arrival, and as Badiou declares, can never know its own future capacity, then how can it actively affirm its own self-arising value? That would mean, once again, a contrast between the material unknown potential over against a neo-Kantian autonomous and ideal valuation. Once again, one would have replete and categorical ideas, and so a certain measure of idealism. And once again, the only way to save materialism from idealism is to invoke theology. If the value of the event is not transparent to a subjectivity and owned by it, because it generates the event as a self-instance in a Fichtean fashion, then like the event in its more material aspects it must arise, must be given, and must even be literally given from an eternal elsewhere, if it is to enshrine eternal value. Badiou needs to incorporate into his materialist Platonism a real affirmation of the Forms, which *are*, contra his rather dated reading, still present in the later dialogues. Already he allows that Platonism, via the doctrine of recollection, validates time positively, since it is only the arrival of the new in time that permits the recollection of the eternal beyond the cosmic totality. But he needs to realize beyond this that the value of the new event can be upheld only if really and truly one regards it as an arrival from a plenitudinous and not empty eternity.

This issue becomes heightened when one takes into account the fact that Badiou already allows that the Christian event is not just one more event, but the event of the first arrival of the logic of all events—that is, universal events—as such. Even though he thinks that this logic first of all arrived in a mythic guise and was expounded in an antiphilosophic manner by St. Paul, the latter is still taken as diagnosing, with respect to a supposed nonrational truth, the logic of universality that applies also to universal rational truths—which indeed can only now arise as events within the space of the event of the emergence of the logic of the universal as such, which is Christianity.

Was the first inauthentic mythical mode of the ingress of the universal somehow inevitable? Badiou is unclear. And what precisely distinguishes *mythos* from *logos*, antiphilosophy from philosophy? (At this point Badiou also fails to see that because for Plato truth remains enshrined in the Forms, and yet a mediation of the knowledge of the forms remains something that occurs partially by *mythos*, that Plato is in his terms as much an antiphilosopher as a philosopher).[8] Both, after all, arise from a subjective event, and both are able to repeat the founding event non-identically. Both, as to content, are able to abstract from the particular. Perhaps, for Badiou, this abstraction is more perfect in the case of reason, and he also says explicitly in his *Ethics* that a rational and ethical practice will not confuse its own inner infinity of possibility with a totalizing logic. Such a logic characteristically pretends to present the "substance" of an accidentally emergent biological or cultural situation (as with racist ideologies) rather than treating such a situation as in essence a void, thereby foreclosing the possibility of other revolutionary theories and practices emerging from other singular occurrences. For example, non-Euclidean geometry, abstract art, Lacanian psychoanalysis, and revolutionary politics should all simply lie alongside each other within the polis, without claiming a mythical identity with topos or genus.

Neither of these modes of distinguishing mythos from logos appears very convincing, however. If, in the first place, reason is more perfectly universalized than religion, then one must ask, How is this measured? If it is by degree of abstraction, then the problem with an absolute degree of abstraction would be that the universal could no longer in any sense be rooted in the contingency of an event. An idea would then fly off like a leaf from its genealogical tree. Alternatively, if the event remains, and along with the event some degree of contingency, some element of defining the idea with reference to certain initial happenings and commitments, then there is an ineliminable "anti-philosophical" and "religious" element.

In the second place, if the guarantee of ethical reasonableness is once more plurality of discourses, then something very akin to postmodernism à la Lyotard has after all returned within the heart of Badiou's thought. The fundamental social rules are once again formal, as they concern a respecting of the "rights" of the various discourses and their various exponents (although Badiou does not see the appositeness of the term *rights* here). The latter therefore become again the subjects of rights, despite the fact that Badiou has already explained (earlier in his *Ethics*) why rights cannot be ontologically or politically primary. As subjects of rights, they are no longer primarily defined by the impact upon them of events, and so they must be treating the universal practices they carry forward as fixed sedimented "situations" (to use Badiou's term for a practice grounded only in the accidental realization of a particular possible ontological set—for example, feudalism or capitalism—and not in an eventual irruption of a genuine universal "truth"; a truth can also lapse back into the condition of a situation, as when representational and perspectival art is seen as defining art as such). Once this occurs, it becomes impossible for subjects to question the foundational assumptions of practices, since these always lie either in the passively contingent falling into a situational habit that instantiates a particular set, or else in the active inauguration of a truth. To treat a "situation" as normative means ipso facto that one fails to recognize its contingency. Hence on Badiou's own logic one cannot simply be resigned to the unmediated plurality of various universal ideas and practices grounded in diverse events. This plurality must itself constitute an ideologically preserved situation or "state of affairs."

In that case, the only alternative must be to recognize that there is some discourse and practice that universally encompasses all universal discourses and so in some way participates in a qualitative and absolute infinite. For this discourse, practice can be encompassing in a nontotalizing and nondistorting fashion only if in some sense it intuits the absolutely infinite set of all sub-sets, including internally infinite sets. Yet Badiou himself seems to admit that there is a "common" logic to universalism as such, and therefore a metauniversalism. Moreover, he implicitly denies that this metauniversalism is merely formally universal, in contrast to the lesser and substantive universalisms, since he affirms that the logic of all universalism also arrived as an event in time—with Christianity.

Putting these two positions together, it would seem that Badiou must affirm an overarching universal discourse and practice that is a development of Christianity. Can this be a rationalization of Christianity, purging it of mythic and historically specific elements? No, because as we have seen, if universalism springs from an event, then to lose mythos and history is to lose the event, and so to lose the universal. Therefore if, as I have argued, the élan of Badiou's own thinking should force him to acknowledge the givenness of ideas as the arrival in time of a participation in Platonic Forms, then we have now seen why he should also acknowledge the incarnation of the Logos (which bears all those Forms within itself) in time. Given not only that every universal idea arrives as an event but also that the very idea of universality must first arrive as an event, materialism requires that this universality was initially material (or incarnate) and remains so in its later transmission and development (the perpetuation of incarnation in a yet more physical repetition which is transubstantiation and the collectively corporate *ecclesia*). Badiou's Cartesian dualism involves therefore elements of materialism and elements of idealism without integration. His duality of sets-plus-situations over against events embodies a duality of matter versus idea. On the other hand, it is equally true that this diagnosis could be inverted—his idea of given material being is wholly abstract because mathematical, while his idea of the universally valued event is wholly and ineffably concrete because it springs entirely ex nihilo. These modes of unmediated duality are inevitable within Badiou's immanentist cosmos, since it involves only a material chaotic aspect and an ideal aspect with no common transcendent source that would permit an integration. His notion of Being as the set of all mathematical possibilities cannot exceed the status of a logical fiction and assumes without warrant an Avicennian or Scotist ontological priority of the possible over the actual. Primary actuality simply *may not be* in accordance with either the ultimate logical calculus of possibilities or the accompanying primacy of an undetermined "will," whether blind or conscious. This is the Thomist counterpossibility of the primacy of a (beautiful, reasonable, desirable) *actus purus* that defeats the supposed reign of possibility (and of logicism-cum-voluntarism) itself.

The (arbitrarily) assumed ontological background of pure multiple sets in Badiou ensures that there cannot be any prior ground in these sets for the irruption of universal truths (which, it is important to stress, Badiou *really* affirms, beyond "postmodernism"). But suppose, instead, events arise somewhat less mysteriously and mushroomlike than he thinks, because something in the hidden but always specifically *actual* orderings of matter encourages their emergence?

Could there be after all an analogical ordering between (now primarily actual) sets and situations and then between situations and events? Badiou interestingly says that if he *had* to choose between Deleuzean univocity and Deleuzean difference, he would choose the latter. Yet he still clings stubbornly to univocity rather than analogy, even though his notion of an open and yet consistent truth process would seem to require an analogy at least internal to the event.

What is truly at issue here in postmodern thought as between the univocal and the analogical? The real problem in tackling this issue is that Deleuze never truly considered the claims of *analogia entis* at all.

For Deleuze, Being itself is univocal, while that of which it is said, namely individual beings, is equivocal.[9] Analogy simply inverts this schema on Deleuze's account. Being is equivocal in its nongeneric distribution among generic differences (as Aristotle says, it cannot be divided like a genus because a division of Being yields only a being which does not differentiate Being qua Being, as "tiger" differentiates "animal" qua animality). On the other hand, the specific differences of which being is said exist univocally as differences of the same genera in every case. Hence for Deleuze (ultimately after Scotus), analogy must be affirmed only in denial, in order that it may conform to the law of the excluded middle: it therefore splits into *either* equivocity or univocity at different levels. For Deleuze, at the highest level of Aristotelian ontology the distribution of Being among genera is masked in its anarchy and dubbed "analogical" only as the supposed imposition of a "judgment" (grounded in the self-thinking first mover). At a lower level, the parallel ratios between different inclusions of generically diverse species under their respective kinds (like the ratio of oak to plant compared with the ratio of tiger to animal) — or else ratios concerning the relations of individuals to species, or of accidents to substances or of effects to causes — are dubbed "analogical" only in disguise of the pure univocity that pertains to similar formal proportions (the mathematical *analogia*, for which Aristotle reserved the word).

This is the most sense that I can make of Deleuze's construal of analogy, and while his presentation pays respect to Aristotle, it bears very little relation to any scholastic discussions — of the kind to which the theory of univocity was a riposte. However, his double reduction of analogy to the equivocal Being/genera relation on the one hand, and to univocal proportions pertaining to species on the other, suggests a derivation from postmedieval neoscholastic manuals. By contrast, it is now generally admitted by medieval scholars that the mathematical "analogy of proper proportion" was subordinated to the role of "analogy of attribution" in the tradition that passed from Proclus through the Arabs and culminated in the work of Thomas Aquinas.[10]

Attribution concerns relations of ineffable affinity, especially between effects and causes, that are not available for the scrutiny of comparison. It proposes a real "medium" between identity and difference and encompasses both levels discussed by Deleuze without fracturing into either the equivocal or the univocal. This is primarily because, on the view perfected by Aquinas, the supreme source is no longer a supreme "being" like Aristotle's first cause — in consequence problematically sharing in Being with its effects — but rather is now the infinitive esse, is itself Being as such in its all — inclusive omni-determination as *essentia* (such that esse and essentia *here coincide*) and so is *itself* as source the shared medium for all beings that it generates. This has the immediate consequence that God as esse is directly *given* to every individual ens, even though genera are given to individuals only by the mediation of species, while the created common, abstracted, and so quasi-generic being (*ens commune*) that all creatures share as the "existence" which they contingently have, but might not have, is given to individuals only by the mediation of genera and species. Hence Deleuze is wrong to say that only Scotus's univocal Being (logically common to the infinite God and to finite creatures) relates directly to individual difference: to the contrary, esse in Aquinas relates to difference with equal directness (and is said to be *maius intima* in individual substances) since it is not ontic and lies above even the contrast of the ontic with the ontological (God must be, he is esse, not a contingent essentia, yet this esse as his essentia is also omnidetermined, not existentially empty). Since esse involves no intraontic difference and involves the ontological difference only insofar as it necessarily exceeds it (abstracted ens commune is imperfectly ontological in its quasi-generic abstraction), it cannot be in any way mediated in its distribution to differences; rather, this distribution is immediately mediation.

In this way the divine distribution of Being "by judgment" (as Deleuze rightly says) extends to species and individuals as well as to genera, in such a fashion that the transcending of hierarchy by the source of pure esse, which is "equally near" to every level of created being, can result, for Thomas Aquinas, in "accidental" features of individuals from a generic and specific perspective assuming priority from an existential one. In this way, within analogia entis, individual difference really could "diagonalize out" of its embedding within a general categorial framework—one could say like a crowned tiger in a fable, whose kingship exceeds in lived significance his bestiality, or Balaam's talking ass in the Bible who has become primarily a donkey-who-spoke, not a certain instantiation of donkey. Or, again, like a man become accidentally yet essentially an artist, or a woman an apostle. Or, finally, the exemplary person for a theological conception who is deified and raised to the rank of the angels.

In this way analogy of attribution involved (beyond Aristotle, who had left obscure the character of distribution between genera and the nature of certain transgeneric processes of cause and effect) no bifurcation between the essential equivocity of the distribution of Being among genera and the essential univocity of the distribution of genera among species. Rather, analogy always implied an analogy of analogies: an obscure kinship (but no measurable proportion) between the analogically judged-to-be-fitting distribution of Being among genera, and the equally analogically judged-to-be-fitting distribution of genera to species and of species to individuals. For since the division of genera is not simply predictable according to a *mathesis*, but species existentially adds something to genus, and moreover in such a way that there are no rules for determining the last crucial specific difference that fully determines integrity of form and so "gives" being (according to Aquinas), here also a moment of equivocity is redeemed only by the instance of judgment (distributively by God and perceptively by us) of *convenientia*. Likewise, analogy reaches down even to the materially individuated thing. For although, in the

Aristotelian scheme, the mere negative potential of matter individuates—so (as Deleuze rightly thinks after Scotus) rendering difference beneath reason and meaning—in Aquinas's supplementary ontology of esse, as Étienne Gilson realized, the negativity of material determination is converted into a positive instance by virtue of its assumption into the shared esse of the individual substance. Since (one needs to add to Gilson) this is a participation in a hyperspecificity, because infinite esse as such coincides with infinite essentia, material individuation must here be transmuted into an active and determined feature. For this reason Aquinas has no need of Scotus's somewhat obscure *haeccitas*; his position also implies that matter is only a kind of projected shadow of beings that are externally differentiated by species and not simply identical with their species like the angels. (In the latter case of "intellectual being," a thought of a type fully exists as such, without diverse "illustration" of the type, which requires matter.)

After such a fashion, Aquinas indirectly suggests the most extreme and perfect form of nonreductive materialism: "in itself" matter is nothing; all its positivity is granted by Being and by ideal essence. Hence it is only active and embodied precisely at the point where it is also "formed," meaningful, and sometimes psychic. The point here is that "shape" (eidos) is at once entirely concrete and entirely abstract and ideal. The tree is first inescapably there when it can also already be transplanted, drawn, imagined differently and yet still as "tree," and so forth. Such constitutive forceful variability is at once the latent negative passive potential of matter and the real existence of the latter only through the active potential of form. The unpredictable yet coherent energy of form as created or actively received (and not as an immanent ideal whose logic or willing trumps the material) casts the shadow of matter as the screen that distinguishes things through exteriority and reveals the limits of the "so far" and the uncertainty of "what is to come," whereas angels occupying each a single species are not exterior to each other in space, nor do their existences unfold in successive time. Materiality therefore is an effect of space and time, both of which it negatively sustains as the ideally projected "nether-limit" of creative emanation.

One can note that eidos as "shape" is very akin to Deleuze's "diagrammatic" medium of the abstract machines, since it mediates between content and expression: the *forma* migrates into our mind as *species*, which is actively transmuted into *verbum*, and both form and inner word can for Aquinas act as signs (a point greatly elaborated by John of St. Thomas in the seventeenth century). However, in the case of Thomist eidos, there is no duality of the formative process and the outcome of sedimentation, since the two belong in a harmonious analogical series. Because "sedimentation" is here saved and seen as issuing from the first principle (esse = essentia), difference is more radically affirmed than with Deleuze, since the positing of difference does not immediately unfold into the illusory self-affirming sphere of the Baroque monadic mirror of representation. In the Deleuzean scheme, material content and ideal expression absolutely coincide in the diagrammatic; but as we have seen, this notion at once cancels matter in the mathematical and ensures a reductive materialism such that a material flow reduced to the mathematicizable is the real final principle. By hierarchically subordinating the sedimented as an unfolding lapse, Deleuze downgrades simultaneously the stable form *and* the real concrete material body. It is the reverse of the situation with the Thomist eidos. Here to the contrary, an interplay between process and fixity also involves some interplay (instead of perfect coincidence) between the ideal and the material, since there is a difference between the communicated form (from material substance to material substance, or from material substance to mind) and the materially instantiated form. Nevertheless, this interplay is analogical and is neither dialectical nor univocal/equivocal (the latter is also, despite Deleuze, unavoidably dialectical). Therefore there is no necessary lapse nor rupture and the negative reserve of matter appears only when it works with the active reserve of form, while inversely the active reserve of form can "work" only on the mystery of created material resistance, which is never "there" and yet provides all sublunary "thereness"—the absolute ethereality of the absolutely concrete.

So we have seen that analogia entis involves a constantly proliferating analogy of analogies which reaches down toward a difference that mediates with the universal, unlike the Scotist haeccitas that is external to "common nature" (which in consequence tends to be hypostasized as "formally" distinguishable within the concrete substance), or the Deleuzean singularity whose priority is simultaneously its subordinate downfall into the dizzying abyss of reflection.

We have also seen that at every stage of its operation, analogizing means that proportions which may be abstractly envisioned in terms of patterns of univocal sameness and equivocal difference are more profoundly marked by the mysterious analogical middle between these extremes. This middle holds Being together both horizontally and vertically. Horizontally, diverse things (genera, but also the residue of otherwise equivocal diversity between species and between individuals) hold together in convenientia. Vertically, lower excellencies are included in a more eminent way in higher causes, partially and imperfectly in higher ontic causes, but absolutely and perfectly in the supreme ontological (and paraontological) cause that is God. However, this eminence is not to be conceived in the mode of proper proportion as merely an appropriately different (equivocal) excellence (as in "God's good-ness is proportionate to God as our goodness is to us, but God is infinite and so his goodness is unknown"), nor as a maximally "intense" (univocal) de-gree of excellence (as in "God's is an infinite degree of a perfection whose essence we grasp," *etsi Deus non daretur*). Duns Scotus conceived analogy in both these fashions at once, inaugurating its bifurcation, which was sustained by most later scholasticism and descends even to Gilles Deleuze. For Aqui-nas, instead, eminence implies a "supereminence" such that, for example, God's goodness is "like" the mode of creaturely goodness and yet also "un-like" this goodness in an unknown manner that nonetheless establishes the very archetype of this excellence (all this being very authentically Platonic). So in ascending the analogical scale of Being, one passes from a known to an ever-more-unknown Good, yet this difference of the unknown Good is not equivocal, since it more and more clearly discloses the nature of the fi-nite good it surpasses. Yet neither is this "shared" goodness univocal, for with this disclosure the distance of the finite from the infinite good is rendered yet more clearly apparent.

In both the horizontal and the vertical instances, one is speaking of an un-imaginable, logically impossible (for formal logic) middle between same and different, or likeness and unlikeness, where to grow different is to increase in identity, and to increase sharing is to increase hierarchical distance and "external" diversity. (This is why Aquinas stresses that the power of God in granting esse is shown precisely in creaturely independent existence and ca-pacity including freedom, even though all this is absolutely "determined" by God and sets up no totally external or autonomous reality in the ontic sense.) Thus analogical ascent guarantees at once deification and yet the persisting good of the creature as creature.

Yet Aquinas failed to recognize that the middle of analogy can only be the excluded middle of Aristotle's logic. One must agree with Scotus's demon-stration that this is the case, which resulted in a parting of the ways between the Neoplatonized Aristotelianism of analogy and participation on the one hand, and the new, more rationalist/empiricist Aristotelianism strictly fol-lowing the law of identity on the other. Since Scotus was right, no conven-tional scholastics were thenceforth really able to preserve Thomas's legacy. One must look instead to figures more tangentially linked to this legacy, espe-cially Eckhart and Nicholas of Cusa. The latter's *coincidentia oppositorum* can surely be read, not as the inauguration of dialectics, but rather as the attempt to salvage analogy in the face of Scotism and Terminism.

An affirmation of the middle as not excluded becomes possible for Nicho-las because he reckons with the participation of the finite ens even *as* finite (one property of the finite is infinite extendability or divisibility) in a sharing out even of the infinite itself. This exacerbates a sharing already recognized by Aquinas of the finite ens as finite in esse as infinite ("infinite" is often used by Aquinas to qualify esse, because it is necessary to establish nonrestriction by particular essence and essential omnidetermination). Since the sharing of Being involves an infinite/finite *proportio*, this cannot be thought in terms of identity or difference without placing infinite "alongside" finite in Scotus's ontotheological fashion. This is clear for Aquinas from the point of view of the infinite: it is not one more thing, so it belongs neither inside things nor outside them, since outside is still a relative placing. But Cusa makes it clear also from the point of view of the finite: the finite itself opens onto the infinite, and even a merely endless finite infinite involves a certain presence of the absolutely simple infinite (just as for Aquinas esse is maius intima to the thing, and for Augustine God is closer to me than I am to myself). Therefore the finite does not relate to the infinite as simply "exterior." Rather the infinite shares/does not share itself with the finite, while the finite becomes/does not become the infinite. Same and different here coincide beyond (Hegelian) dialectics, but in accordance with analogical descent, ascent, and horizontal affinity — since dialectics is merely, as it were, a formal logic exiled from formality and longing to restore it in a fashion that is indeed "contradictory" and so constitutes the law of a gnostic agon. Deleuze does not really escape this dialectics, because he thinks the infinite/virtual, finite/difference relation according to a Scotist scheme subservient to the excluded middle.

From all this it follows, against Deleuze and Badiou's rationalist classicism, that they altogether fail to consider the critical romance of Neoplatonic and Christian analogy. Although the latter is indeed a matter of judgment of the Beautiful (but of the Sublime at the same time without distinction), this involves an extracategorical, suprahierarchical, and extralegal distribution that is entirely prior to the representation of any fixed order of essences.

In this respect it is important to point out that Olivier Boulnois has in effect shown that Deleuze's association of analogy with representation is historically wrong: to the contrary, univocity and representation sprang up together (in a line extending from Avicenna through Roger Bacon and other, often Franciscan, scholastics to Scotus) because Being reduced to bare abstract existentiality (the minimum of conceivability as "a possible existence" according to the law of excluded middle), is also Being reduced to what our mind can represent to itself. Univocal Being *is* mirrored Being: so it is determined by the gaze, and not by its own prior mysterious distribution. Indeed the anarchic distribution into differences unmediated by the beauty of convenientia is simply the only mode of nonessential distribution that cold logical reason can represent to itself. If Deleuze's philosophy is not merely a creative elaboration of his taste, then it is a gigantic claim to represent reality; if it is merely a matter of taste, then his taste is after all for representation.

Nor does Deleuze really get rid of the represented hierarchies of genus and difference within his system. Rather, as we have seen, he recognizes that any order (theoretical or practical, prehuman or human) that is not impossibly vertiginous has to impose such orderings. While they are, as it were, ontologically invalid, they are also ontologically inevitable. Thus the refusal of representation by Deleuze is not the refusal of a false theory of knowledge, but rather of the ultimacy of an ontological sphere that remains inevitably governed by representation and within which alone "humanity"—for him a spectral phenomenon—arises. Deleuzean univocity therefore spells out the always somewhat futile and not finally winnable war of sheer difference (without real constitutive relation) with temporarily stable hierarchies that always merge as the only possible expression (and yet simultaneous inhibition) of difference and fold back upon themselves to shape monadic theaters of representation.

By contrast, Thomist analogy (revised in the Cusan direction) implies rather that there can be analogical continuity between the "sameness" of given hierarchy and the constant temporal intrusion of difference. By the same token, this given regime need not be reflexively self-constituting and confirming, but rather its "fold" can both be in continuity with and further help to compose the entire process of ontological dissemination. In that case "representation" is but a secondary instance and the illusion that it is a primary instance ceases to be a *necessary*, because ontologically grounded illusion, as it is for Deleuze. In social terms, this means that unavoidable hierarchies of value and command (for collective projects of thought and action) can be reduced to the educative and self-dissolving purpose (beyond the collectivist sacrifice of individuals to the social totality and the social future, which leaves hierarchies of command permanently intact) of allowing "pupils" to exceed "teachers," and so new differences to emerge and truly to flourish in webs of harmonious relation to other emergent singularities.[11]

So in reality Aquinas's analogy concerns some mediating principle that is at once like and unlike, yet with neither dialectical tension nor resulting shuttle between these two poles that results from a never really resolved contradiction. Analogy does indeed offer mediation, or what William Desmond calls "the Between," whereas in Hegel there is after all no mediation, but only an unresolved contradiction that still negatively assumes the sway of identity—this is why dialectics is already the doctrine of alienated and unre-

deemable differences, while inversely differential philosophy remains a dialectical shuttle between the univocal absent source and differential manifestation. Between Hegel, Heidegger, and Deleuze the intellectual differences
are trivial. They all at bottom refuse or fail to consider the true mediation that
is analogy. If reality is analogical, then it is possible that it "holds together"
through a concealed multiple affinity in an ineffable fashion, as I have endeavored to suggest. Ineffability need not denote idealism; it is simply unavoidable, since dialectics and univocalist differential philosophy offer their
own ineffability: the invisible *absence* of mediation between void source and
differential emergence. Since this absence is invisible, they can only assume,
beyond reason, the empty sublimity of source manifest only in the abject
differential remainder. But supposing one instead assumes that which we
sometimes appear to see: the sublime yet also beautiful proportion of the
invisible obscurely manifest in the visible? This constitutes vertical analogy,
which grounds a horizontal affinity between the material and the ideal. Then
one might allow that there could be a passage from given state to event that
involves continuity as well as rupture, since one would no longer enclose the
event in a replete ideality of utter mythical uniqueness. Then also, it would
not be necessary to erect a duality between the culture of the event of socialism on the one hand and the mere "indifferences" of various human cultures
receiving socialism and regarded as mere arbitrary "situations" on the other.
In this way, one would not need to make so abrupt a choice between socialist universal commitment and the valuing of local cultural identity. One
could thereby help to avert the danger of revolutionary terror. The analogous
ontological perspective that thinks "the between" allows (beyond Badiou)
the different cultural and religious incarnations themselves to help constitute and reconstitute universality.

The same lack of mediating analogy colors Badiou and Žižek's account of
the emergence of a universal and redeemed subjectivity. They both rightly
insist that it was St. Paul who first proclaimed the logic of such a subjectivity.
St. Paul insisted that the law — that is to say any abstract commanding imposition from a *merely* general state of affairs — elicits my willed assent yet
gives rise also to a fantastic, perverse desire to do what the law forbids. Since
the law sets itself up reactively, it assumes sin and death as positive forces
possessed of real activity and real subjective appeal. Thus in denying that the
law is the real source of the Good or of liberation, St. Paul, as Badiou notes,
said all and more than Nietzsche managed to say. The Law thereby institutes
a divided subjectivity. As Žižek, following Lacan, rightly argues, the way to
overcome such a division cannot be the "release" of my subconscious per-

verse fantasies, as a certain kind of crude Freudianism would suppose, but rather must be the *sacrifice* of my self-centered fantasies, which, however, if it is complete, will entail also a liberation from the Law that alone sustains them. Both Žižek and Badiou recognize that St. Paul first of all in history proposed a step beyond a divided subjectivity in thrall at once to the law, and by the same token to its own obsessions and illusions. (Here, indeed, Lacan Catholicized Freud's inverted Judaism.)

Nevertheless, St. Paul was much more radical than Lacan, Badiou, and Žižek. For Žižek in particular, in accordance with orthodox Lacanianism, desire is sustained at all only in response to the law's imposition, and desire is accordingly always of an impossible object: the fantasized shadow side of the impossible "real" that every law as a symbolic order must assume as its fictional reference point of absolute value—just as the laws of the United Kingdom sustain a "reality" that no one can define and is in a sense not really there, especially in the year 2005. Although Žižek rightly denies that Paul's agape excludes eros, this seems to mean for him that it involves something just like Deleuze's active force of self-expression to which also Badiou tends to reduce agape. However, the consequences are somewhat austere. First of all, in this perspective, we cannot really ever finally rid ourselves of illusory desire, since every symbolic order is akin to Paul's legal order, and yet symbolic order is constitutive of humanity as such. So are we really so far removed from Deleuze's ontological impossibilism after all? On this ontological basis one can imagine the gesture of revolution, but really no stable progress toward socialism, much less its stable achievement.

In the second place, the subject who has gone beyond both law and desire is only an austere disillusioned subject, only able to share with others a tragic consciousness of what has been transcended. This situation is compounded, not really altered, if one follows, as Žižek sometimes does in *The Fragile Absolute* (116–17), the more radical Lacan of Seminar XX, for whom there is no longer any "one" simple instituted symbolic order, but rather the ultimate reference of the latter to the impossible "real" is echoed in its multiple fragmentation. In consequence there is now a manifold of incompatible regimes of fostered desire, such that one "authority" is but a pathological "symptom" for another authority and vice versa (for example the incommensurability between the laws of male and female sexuality). This ensures that in a sense there are "only symptoms" and no laws at all. But where there is no single identifiable abstract source and system of law, then there is equally no possibility of resignation to its sway, and to its instigation of a desire that is "healthily" exercised precisely when one knows (for Lacan) that it cannot really be fulfilled even though it must never be given up. One cannot any longer here abandon oneself to the law in order to outwit it by denying the constitutive gap between legal order and the reluctant subject of always somewhat illegal desire, that alone allows legality to function. Instead, the symptomatic obsession taken in earlier Lacan to indicate a disguised seduction of the subject by law into fantasizing a finite source of fulfillment is now seen as the *original* instigation of desire in terms of a gap that is opened up by the fetishized object or theme, between itself and itself; like the classical "fetish" of anthropologists, it at once repels and entices. It becomes in this way its own hollowed-out void, just as it plays at once the role of law and irregular exception to the law.

No longer, then, can one safely be rid of symptoms without losing *even the sublime void of the real* that for the earlier, as it were "dialectically Buddhist" Lacan, saved desire even in the recognition of its impossibility. Žižek sees the newer scheme as more "Christian" according to the terms of a Hegelian death of God theology: the abject finite object of desire alone enshrines the sublime void (as God the Father is dead in Christ's dead body), and so desire cannot be saved by recognizing its illusory instance. It *is* its illusory instance: sublimity resides only in the once discarded sign of sublimity—in *shit*, the sublime object.

Yet this is in reality only an intensification of the older Lacanian scheme. In clinging onto the multiple pathological symptoms that are now seen as original and inescapable, we still attain the void, and with the crucified God-Man can "begin again" without illusion as to even the possible loss of illusions. Still more than before, we receive the Lacanian cure of not being cured.

And all this is still very Greek, not at all Pauline. Žižek's tragic subject, resigned to the supposed impossibility of sexual relationship and satisfied desire, albeit in the midst of his continuing but chastened obsessions, simply commits an utterly abandoned ego to collectively revolutionary seriousness. Such a Lacanian revolutionary subject will be committed if necessary to the violent overcoming of all still confined under the law or multiple laws/symptoms of desiring—but to what end, and so with what justification? Not to any possibility of just laws and just desiring and so not to any *real material incarnation* of socialism, given that laws and desiring are constitutive of our humanity as such. Hence the problem is not that the new Lacanian-Leninist revolutionary may will dubious means toward a just end, but rather that he or she can conceive no innately just end. What such revolutionaries share among themselves can be only the replete *idea* of a surmounting of inevitable and ultimately materially grounded processes. (Like all nihilists, they must remain idealists.) This follows, since for Žižek (unlike Badiou), the human rupture that invokes "the real" (which I am diagnosing as an "ideal" moment) and takes us beyond the symbolic (which is a materially grounded process) is nonetheless a constitutive fissure in a Heideggerean fashion, a fissure within Being and so within materiality as such. This fissure is the authentic irruption of pure Being in its ontological nullity: however, by token of this very authenticity it is destined to lapse back into the inauthenticity of the usual symbolic manifestation of materiality in all concrete appearances. Therefore the violence that such revolutionaries may visit upon the unredeemed is not the negative immanence of utopia but the usual anger of ideas against recalcitrant bodies.

In this way Žižek sustains the nihilism that Lenin, in a very Russian fashion, tended to add to Marxism.[12] He is more of a mystical nihilist than Badiou, because he sustains the Heideggerean idea of a "folding" of beings back into Being and the concomitant idea that Being as such suffers a fall and dissolution in the human realm of ontic regimes of meaning that are constituted by forgetfulness of Being.

This is somewhat worse than Badiou's relapse into immanent pagan dualism. For what one has here is, despite everything, the purest gnosticism. The heart of gnostic tradition lies not in dualism alone, but rather in a negatively mediated dualism as enshrined in the Valentinian and then Boehmenist idea that there is a kind of fall of an aspect of the absolute (or a reality just beneath it) or even of the absolute itself (in Jacob Boehme's case) into finite evil: a negative moment which is later recuperated. Hegel's thought (which, as Cyril O'Regan has firmly established, is most fundamentally grounded in the influence of Boehme) tends to see the recuperation as nonetheless also the permanent perpetuation of the original constitutive loss of the infinite in the finite, by virtue of the dialectical identity of the void of identity with the rival void of the non-identical.[13] Heidegger offers merely a variant on this gnostic idealism mutated into nihilism. Such a perspective tends to eternalize and positivize evil and to make agon an ultimate and not contingent reality. It ontologizes violence and is one version of this supreme secular gesture. As the great Russian thinkers (Florensky and Bulgakov) of the twentieth century argued, in a cosmos without ultimate meaning or order, the consequently manifest violence of the arbitrary will itself be sacralized. Nazism was but the most extreme manifestation of this implacable logic, which Leninism did not altogether escape.[14]

But it is utterly inimical to a viable socialism and cannot sustain more than a nihilist revolution. Socialism crucially recognizes, of course, that human histories of apparent peace are really histories of hidden conflict and opposition; however, it should not *ontologize* this prevailing circumstance but instead insist on its contingency. Otherwise socialism loses all hope. A hope for socialism is possible only if the cosmos is secretly such as to be hospitable to human harmony and to humanity living in harmony with the cosmos — that is to say, to (nondialectically) mediated differences. A hospitable cosmos of this kind must be an analogical cosmos, and for reasons that we have seen, an analogical cosmos is a created cosmos — a cosmos that proceeds from a simple and perfect donating source, not a first principle of absence agonistically ruptured within itself.

It follows then that if we are hoping not just for revolution or gradual transformation, but for material incarnation of socialist practice, that we require to become less austere subjects than the Lacanian ones who have advanced from the shoals of desire to the shore of a kind of disillusioned love. Such subjects, in leaving behind their false, fascinated souls, have also left behind their bodies. But we should not despair: St. Paul, unlike Lacan, does not deal in any duality of desire and love, for it is clear that for him agape is also a desiring longing both for other people (Rom. 1:11–12) and for the final vision of God (1 Cor. 13:12; Rom. 8:23). Even within the fulfillment of this vision for St. Paul, desire remains and is not cancelled, since we are told that agape abides even in the beatific vision (1 Cor. 13:8–13). This must mean agape as desire, and not as self-giving charity, since in the vision of God there can be no further need of the latter. (This is probably why, for Paul, one can give away everything to others, including one's life, and *still* lack agape — as desire and reciprocity? Rom. 13:3.)

This longing for others and for God is itself grounded in the groaning travail and longing of the material world, so that agape fulfills and does not deny the promptings of the body (Rom. 8:22–23). And why should there not be this *other sort of desire*, not elicited in response to the ban of the Law? Why should not desire be incited by the distance of the other that sustains this otherness as the very precondition of their presence to us? In that case, there must always be a surplus to presence within presence to sustain it as over against us. Certainly, we have (in Lacanian terms) to *imagine* this distance, and in doing so we are caught up in the *symbolic* webs within which alone the other can appear to us, but just what is it that causes us to assume that the unreachable obstacle of desire is therefore not real in an emphatic, fully ontological, and not Lacanian sense? And how can we know that this real and inaccessible object is not beautifully mediated to us through all our fetishistic substitutions for it, including the confronted and reintegrated abject object, whose initial exclusion is always the sign of a subordination of living desire to abstracted legal command?

Surely no psychoanalytic "evidence" could ever tell us this, since assertions concerning the unreachable — even that it cannot be reached, and cannot be mediated—can only be dogmatic and not empirical. Rather, one can suggest here that Lacan was already governed by a Kojèvian (and substantively correct) nihilistic reading of Hegel, according to which, as Žižek puts it, the only true desire that remains to us is desire of the void. But this is, after all, only one theology. *Another* interpretation of the constitutive excess and inexhaustibility of desire remains possible—another, alternative theology, of a more orthodox Catholic kind. According to such a theology, in loving others, we do indeed love them as ciphers, loving them for the signs they offer of an inaccessible true object of desire. However, if this true object is God, then in remotely loving God we do also love finite others in due measure (as both Aquinas and Scotus insisted), and *more properly* as themselves in pointing beyond themselves. All this allows more validity to certain Levinasian insights than is admitted by Badiou. However, what is involved here is somewhat more than a Levinasian nondesiring love for the infinite in the other, without analogical mediation. One has here instead a desiring love that ineffably blends us with the other insofar as we come to realize how both our imagining desire and the other's symbolic presence blend beautifully as a remote participation in a real plenitudinous infinite. Then, after all, masculine and feminine diverse desires obscurely meet and there can truly be "sexual relationship." Then, after all, the outrunning of the law by agape does not merely hypostasize the unlimited beyond taboos but constantly enacts what Paul describes as the law of love, which reaffirms in a new mode the Jewish law, in a continuing reinscribing and interlinking of temporal and bodily limits (but according to no new fixed and general rules). Then, after all, there could be socialist subjects not abandoning their material desiring specifics for human political universality but realizing that universality analogically and so harmoniously in those very domestic particularities themselves.

Equality with difference. Equality with liberty and fraternity, which, as Krzysztof Kieslowski's great film *Blue* sings out in its beginning and end, is possible to envisage only through the ontological vision opened up by faith, hope, and charity.

## Notes

1   See Giambattista Vico, *On the Most Ancient Wisdom of the Italians*, trans. L. M. Palmer (Ithaca, N.Y.: Cornell University Press, 1988), 45–53; Sergei Bulgakov, *Philosophy of Economy*, trans. Catherine Evtuhov (New Haven, Conn.: Yale University Press, 2000).

2   See Antoine Côté, "Infini," in *Dictionnaire critique de théologie*, ed. J.-Y. Lacoste (Paris: P.U.F., 1998); Amos Funkenstein, *Theology and the Scientific Imagination* (Princeton, N.J.: Princeton University Press, 1996).

3   Alain Badiou, *St. Paul ou La Naissance de l'universalisme* (Paris: P.U.F., 1999); *Ethics* (London:

Verso, 2001); Slavoj Žižek, *The Fragile Absolute* (London: Routledge, 2001) and *On Belief* (London: Routledge 2001).

4   Alexis de Tocqueville, *Democracy in America* (Princeton, N.J.: Princeton University Press, 2000).

5   Conor Cunningham, *Genealogy of Nihilism* (London: Routledge, 2002).

6   Alain Badiou, *Deleuze: The Clamor of Being* (Minnesota: University of Minnesota Press, 2001), 99.

7   Gilles Deleuze and Félix Guattari, *A Thousand Plateaus* (London: Athlone, 1988), 141–42; Gilles Deleuze, *Difference and Repetition* (London: Athlone, 1968), 367, 272.

8   Catherine Pickstock is working on a book that will provide the fullest version of this thesis so far given. *Theory, Religion, and Idiom in Platonic Philosophy* (Oxford: Oxford University Press, forthcoming).

9   Deleuze, *Difference and Repetition*, 33–39, 137–38, 302–4.

10   For this and for most of the remarks below concerning Aquinas, see John Milbank and Catherine Pickstock, *Truth in Aquinas* (London: Routledge, 2001).

11   See Olivier Boulnois, *Être et Representation* (Paris: P.U.F., 1999); William Desmond, *Being and the Between* (Albany: SUNY Press, 1998).

12   See Michael Allen Gillespie, *Nihilism before Nietzsche* (Chicago: University of Chicago Press, 1996), 167.

13   Cyril O'Regan, *The Heterodox Hegel* (Albany: SUNY Press, 2001) and *Gnostic Return in Modernity* (Albany: SUNY Press, 2001).

14   See, for example, Rowan Williams, *Sergei Bulgakov: Towards a Russian Political Theology* (Edinburgh: T. and T. Clark, 1999), 233.

*Karl Hefty* | Truth and Peace:
Theology and the Body
Politic in Augustine
and Hobbes

One of them, the earthly city, has created for herself such false gods as she wanted, from any source she chose — even creating them out of men — in order to worship them with sacrifices. — St. Augustine, *City of God*

For by Art is created that great Leviathan . . . which is but an Artificial Man; though of greater stature and strength than the Naturall . . . and in which, the *Soveraignty* is an Artificiall *Soul*, as giving life and motion to the whole body. — Thomas Hobbes, *Leviathan*

THROUGH BOTH GREEK and medieval thought runs a corpus of social and political writing that envisions the universe as "one articulated whole" and all beings within it as both wholes and parts of wholes.[1] The image of a body politic served as a predominant metaphor for describing the relation of the whole to the parts. It conveys not only a social whole analogically as a functioning body, but also a unity in which each member, without diminution of its distinct being, constitutes and participates in the whole. Sustaining this metaphor, both Greek and medieval philosophers, with few exceptions, sought to hold together in thought the good of one and the good of all.[2] This holding together cohered in part because individual and social were seen as mutually constituting and not as fundamentally dissociable or opposed categories.

By the mid-1600s, as political theorists increasingly conceived of private ends within a neutral and largely indifferent public framework, the justification of moral questions separated gradually from the justification of legal and theological ones.[3] As much as an attempt to secure peace against the risk

of domination by privileged interests, this reconfiguration of the social relied upon the fundamental epistemological assumption that human reason
somehow operated entirely independently from the movements of passion
and desire. By no means an unshackling, the bifurcation that ensued con-
signed the good to a supposedly discrete private sphere, a fixed and isolatable
province seen as devoid of social or political consequence. The cohesion of
the ensuing body politic relied for its compelling force not upon the actual
desire of its members, but upon a stoical notion of obligation, itself sustained
by the sibling fantasies of contract and consent.[4]

In this essay, I contrast Augustine's De civitate Dei and Hobbes's Leviathan,
two texts that span a wide range of philosophy concerning the body politic. I begin with a brief comparison of their accounts of human nature and
show that a seemingly compatible "realism" masks crucial differences between an Augustinian ontology that is fundamentally peaceful yet open and
a Hobbesian ontology that remains, in important ways, both violent and
closed. In the second section, I consider the manner in which both authors
relate the human person to the social body and show that their radically distinct notions of the good yield incommensurable accounts of hierarchy, proportion, and justice. In the final section of the essay, I examine Hobbesian and
Augustinian accounts of knowledge, wherein I locate and question Hobbes's
turn toward a secular body politic. I will argue that, because it wrongly separates reason from will and thus from desire, the Hobbesian political body
remains beholden to the pernicious effects of "self-interest"; unable to preserve unity amid difference, it succumbs to a vacuous conception of social
peace. Because he begins theologically, with a restoration of peace in the
human person, Augustine can be seen to retain the meaningful unity of personal and common good in a body politic that is open and creative, yet also
free from coercion and the residues of the artificial.

## Order and Nature

Hobbes and Augustine both doubt the capacity of human beings to achieve
peaceful social life unaided, but they disagree about whether peace is, or
ever has been, the natural human condition.[5] For Hobbes, notoriously, the
prepolitical, natural man abides in an immutable, asocial stasis, a "condition of Warre of every one against everyone," suffering, or haunted by fear
of suffering, poverty, adversity, and death.[6] In this condition, "every one is
governed by his own Reason" and has "Right to everything; even to one another's body" (91). This natural state of unsociability arises as a necessary
consequence of each person following his natural passions, none of which
is more pernicious than the prideful competition for self-honor.[7] Augustine,

too, laments the constant threat of "bloodshed, sedition and civil war," even where least expected, finding "treachery even in kinship."[8] Like Hobbes, he traces social chaos to the cause of pride, which he defines as "a perverted imitation of God" that seeks "to impose its own dominion on fellow men" (868, 869, 874). For Augustine, however, pride is a state of personal disorder that also disfigures the real relations between beings, which pride implicates not merely in a derivative and indifferent manner as generic obstacles to its whims, but as genuinely caught up, subjected to, and thus diminished by its ambitions. His conception of pride calls into question any notion of a merely private or limited sin.

Hobbes seeks to limit the effects of pride by the very mechanism of domination (and its correlate, fear), by a "visible Power to keep them in awe, and tye them by fear of punishment to the performance of their Covenants" (117). Augustine, however, regards all such stopgap remedies as unstable and unjustifiably optimistic. Not unlike Hobbes, he finds the polis tainted by the impossibility of just judgment, because of its inevitable situation of ignorance or incomplete knowledge. Similarly, the possibility of a peaceful universal state is ever compromised by the fact or threat of civil war. And friendship, among the most basic of social bonds, remains ultimately insecure because of its attendant fear of change or loss.[9] Even virtue, the highest among human goods, Augustine says exists only to war against vices, weakness, disease, and lethargy.

Yet, rather than revert to manipulations of fear, Augustine argues that there remains, untouched by human sin or failure, a "certain just order of nature, by which the soul is subordinated to God, and the body to the soul" (854). Peace holds priority for Augustine, for as he can conceive of life without pain but not pain without life, so can he conceive peace without war, but not war without some sort of more rudimentary peace. This foundational peace in the universe is, for Augustine, a "condition of our being" that "still connects the parts with one another" (869, 871). For Hobbes, by contrast, the first law of nature is not peace itself, but a requirement to *seek* peace, from which he derives the associated right of self-defense (92). Because he begins with a natural condition of disorder, Hobbes's solution to the problem of the body politic is not, as for Augustine, the recognition and creative perfection of a more fundamental natural order, but rather the imposition of an artificial one.

## Hierarchy, Proportion, and the Good

From these vantage points, Hobbes and Augustine envision a body politic as emerging by way of two distinct forms of hierarchical relation between beings. Hobbes brings the artificial soul of sovereign power to bear against the social body's condition of anarchy, a form of disorder. Augustine begins with a conception of justice as a form of order *within* the body and soul in right relation to God, which only then culminates in a right relation toward other creatures. We will see that, whereas Hobbes requires the dual operation of fear and domination to secure hierarchy and motivate peaceful human interaction, Augustine relies on the mutual, reciprocal work of love.

Augustine begins ontologically with the good as that to which all being has relation. Because the body does not give life to itself, it exceeds itself in soul and so already implies a social relation and a theological relation.[10] Peace and justice begin with a restoration of ordered harmony in the person, a proportion of body and soul that relates both constitutively and analogously to order in the household and in the city. "If there is no justice in such a man," Augustine argues, "there can be no sort of doubt that there is no justice in a gathering which consists of such men" (883). Domestic relations offer an example of this proportion. The relation of "head" of household to "member" is one not of sovereignty or contract, but of interested love that, while related to the good in a form of hierarchy, destabilizes the tendencies of self-interest or domination. The father serves those he appears to command, while those commanded find in their subservience a sort of freedom "by serving with fidelity of affection."[11] In this way, human bodies and the social body come to share the ultimate good as a common referent of desire and worship. According to this argument, peace in the earthly city is a provisional end that *can* serve the good of all, but is neither its cause nor its ultimate end.[12]

Hobbes considers social life based on a common object of desire or worship as an inherently unstable and tenuous arrangement, because he rejects explicitly any notion of a good that is "simply and absolutely so" (39). Humans do not share a common public and private good and are uniquely capable of manipulating any good or evil for private ends (119–20). Moreover, all objects of passion—the feared, hoped for, and desired—vary by education and are "blotted and confounded" by "lying, counterfeiting and erroneous doctrines" (10). Hobbes agrees with Augustine that we should pursue any object of desire in a deliberative rather than imperative manner; but he defines the good not as that which is desired for its own sake, but merely as that which is desired (45). By extension, all objects of human desire differ epistemologically from the "Beatificall Vision," which is "unintelligible" in the present world (46). For Hobbes, the "final cause" of man is self-preservation and maximum contentment, which is found neither in the laws of nature nor by uniting with other like-minded people in small or great numbers (117).[13] Because he mistakes will for fiat, Hobbes understands "ends" not as reference, proportion, or eros, but within the natural self-interested economy of punishment and reward, purchased by the respective currency of fear or praise.

Having rejected the Augustinian vision of the good, it is unsurprising that Hobbes enforces social peace through absolute authority. If any group of people could live sociably and justly without subjection, Hobbes argues, then all people would wish to live under such an order. Peace would arrive without subjection (118). Yet no human group gives consent to such a rule of justice without some form of coercion. Thus, underlying his turn from the good to authority, Hobbes identifies the common link between "particular Man" and "Man-kind," between the body and the body politic, not in an object of passion, but in the similitude of passions, "which are the same in all men" (10–11). From these shared passions, Hobbes purports to deduce by natural reason principles of all human behavior, of what is common among men (10, 255). For this reason, fear and self-interest serve as the ultimate unifying principles of Hobbes's social body, over which sovereign authority, a "Mortall God," serves as an artificial soul (120–21).

Supporting this argument, the Wars of Religion demonstrated that, even within the church, peaceful social life did not, in practice, emerge from a common notion of the good. Given this political setting, Hobbes's suggestion that voluntary contract offers a more just solution to the problem of ineffective authority seems compelling. However, fueling this dissent, the church of early-sixteenth-century England had inherited an untheological emphasis on authority as a safeguard against both Protestantism and an inchoate version of Enlightenment rationalism.[14] One might say further that the Wars of Religion were philosophical wars and not fundamentally theological ones, insofar as their combatants insisted upon settling for truth over against the good, upon a closed and secure realm of certainty over actual peace. In its gradual acceptance of a radical bifurcation of reason and desire, the heavenly city had already adopted the logic of the earthly one.

It is in this historical context that Hobbes redefines justice in contractual terms, as giving each his due as stipulated by contract. The contractual reduction does more than signify consent for Hobbes; it marks "a reall Unitie of them all, in one and the same Person" (120). There can be no just disobedience against the sovereign by appeal to any hypothetical higher covenant with God, for any such covenant requires "mediation by some body" (which, we will see, cannot be Christ). The sovereign may commit "injury" but not "injustice" properly understood, for he operates only by the consent of his subjects (122–24). Because instituted to establish peace, only the sovereign can "be Judge of what Opinions and Doctrines are averse and what conducing to Peace." This obviates direct conflict with church "authority," Hobbes contends, because any "Doctrine repugnant to Peace, can no more be True, than Peace and Concord can be against the Law of Nature."[15] Under this approach, the structure of human desire, rooted in disordered self-interest, remains unchanged. Worship and sacrament signify a disposition of the will toward obedience only in pursuit of private reward or out of political obligation (332, 335, 338). Self-interested desire orders worship, rather than the converse.[16]

Augustine regards contract, or the "compromise between human wills," as a provisional means to promote peaceful interaction, but only given the condition of an *absence* of justice.[17] As we have seen, for Augustine, there can be no true commonwealth united by a "common sense of right" or by a "community of interest" or by "consent to the law" without first establishing real justice within the person prior to these formations, which otherwise remain beholden to a disfigured will. Beyond the general notion of "giving everyone his due," a form of which Hobbes also adopts, Augustine defines justice as a *right ordering* rooted in faith, a service of the lower to the higher, of body to soul, passions to mind and will, and both to God.[18] Without a conception of the good as both fulfilling yet irreducible to the private projections of a human will, the body politic cannot sustain its members *as* members of a larger whole.[19] The contract of the Leviathan, which purports actually to *be* the single will of the people, makes an unwarranted presumption of true will and good intention, even and especially among those who positively endorse it. It cannot be a "real unity," which always implies difference, because its social body is comprised of *indifference*.[20] In order to discern the stoicism that sustains the concept of obligation at work in Hobbes's contract, we must consider the manner by which Hobbes assumes a division of reason and will, rather than permitting a symbiotic relation between them (256).

*Truth and Peace: The Time of the Body Politic*

Hobbes's notion of a secular body politic requires a theory of knowledge, by which it must distinguish itself from faith in order to enable a voluntary consent that is not itself a movement of faith. In an effort to ground authority (and thus hierarchy) in reason rather than revelation, Hobbes discloses an end of history for the church, with no further need for new revelation (257–58, 260). Because "Miracles now cease, we have no sign left" (259). Hobbes argues that revelation ultimately cannot contradict reason. Yet when we examine what he means by "reason," we see that he has established rules of intelligibility that derive from a mathematical model comprising parts, summations, and remainders (256). According to this model, we reason by reckoning the "Consequences of general names agreed upon, for the marking and signifying of our thoughts."[21] Apart from this method, any other mode of reason is unintelligible, because it does not begin from "settled significations" of constituent words. By fixing the domain of the intelligible in the temporal present, Hobbes banishes from the social body the "use of Metaphors, Tropes, and other Rhetorical figures, in stead of words proper." Among those prohibited, he includes "names that signifie nothing; but are taken up, and learned by rote from the Schooles, as hypostatical, transubstantiate, consubstantiate, eternal-Now" (34–36). However, in demarcating private reckoning ("marking") from public demonstration of private reckonings ("signifying"), Hobbes's reason is already a social phenomenon, both insofar as words or "general names" (even those for private use) are already "agreed upon" publicly and insofar as the act of signification is itself social. Yet Hobbes explicitly does *not* assume a social life prior to and unaffected by self-interest, for he acknowledges that, in the state of nature, each person follows his own reason. He therefore neglects to explain adequately who it is that determines agreed-upon public meanings and how these meanings escape untainted from the machinations of private interest. Without presuming peace already in operation, we must fall back upon a kind of faith, a blind trust in the intentions of the other. Of course, this trust is precisely what Hobbes wishes to resist, and this wish is precisely what the Augustinian account can be regarded as calling into question.

For Augustine, the processes of reason, however useful for understanding and persuasion, cannot reach the depths of the good, whose full expression always exceeds immediate perception. Objects of faith may prove *more* real than the "hollow realities" that result from confining the ultimate good to the present and thereby produce a false sense of security (843). Here there is no opposition between faith and reason, for Augustine is explicit that, in matters the City of God apprehends by "mind and reason," it "has the most certain knowledge," however partial; "in every case" it "trusts the evidence of the senses."[22] Yet this mode of knowledge presumes an ontological recognition of the will as an "intermediate good" and is thus at one with faith and Christian practice, for reason alone can never have perfect command over the body and its passions.[23] Augustine therefore rejects any attempt to "ground" social life in a theory of knowledge outside theology, even human self-knowledge, because ignorance, "a common affliction in the wretched condition of this life," always limits what can be truly known, either about ourselves or about the intentions of others, whom one may always suspect of ill will.[24]

We can now trace, however briefly, the complex manner in which Hobbes's creation of an artificial order *precludes* the Augustinian analogy between personal and social (335). In 1643, eight years before the publication of Leviathan, Hobbes argued that statements about God, if understood as "propositions of people philosophizing," amount to "blasphemies and sins against God's ordinance." Alternatively, if understood as "proclaiming states of mind that govern our wish to praise, magnify and honor God," Hobbes argued that our propositions "are correctly enunciated about God."[25] Given God's "unfathomable" nature and our mere propositional tools for expressing our "concepts of the nature of things," the only true proposition about God can be: "God exists."[26] Beyond this, theology can pertain only to nonauthoritative language about God.[27] The abrupt break between "the philosophical" and "the theological," between knowledge and worship, between propositional truth and states of mind, occurs even more overtly in the Leviathan.[28] The noteworthy change in Hobbes's thought involves the shift from an earlier argument in favor of a discrete theological realm, which functions to create authoritative doctrine out of otherwise nonauthoritative propositions about God, to an argument against such a realm.[29] Less obviously, this movement presumes an underlying notion of "truth" already in operation. In order to grant the Leviathan authority to determine all meanings of words, Hobbes must rely on a prior bifurcation of theological truth from all other forms of truth and, specifically, of truth that cannot be demonstrated incontestably from truth that can. This move, when coupled with Hobbes's construal of signification as immanent demonstration, has an implicit regulative content that renders it impossible to conceive of worship as a social activity, or to conceive of a heavenly city that has any bearing on the earthly one. Reduced to sanction, authority can have no real or unitive power, for it can neither invoke desire nor compel any genuine, positive submission other than involuntary servitude. Grounded in fear, its violence precludes truthful peace.

For Augustine, the earthly and heavenly cities move together from the beginning to the end of time. Augustine therefore does not secure the possibility of a just social body in law.[30] Much subsequent medieval thought would seek to articulate a body politic in the form of jurisprudence, and Hobbes was perhaps most successful in doing so.[31] But Hobbes must thereby, in a manner akin to Islam, regard Christ merely as a second Moses, who "representeth . . . the Person of God" who "from that time forward, but not before, is called the Father" (338).[32] Christ cannot disclose a transmission and reception of grace that establishes social peace in time, but can offer "only an earnest" of the future kingdom of God.[33] For Augustine, who does not define grace in terms of contract, the heavenly city lives salvation as rightly ordered fellowship in worship of God, a reconciled world of "multiplicity restored to unity" in the church: *mundus reconciliatus Ecclesia*.[34] Through participation in the love of God, social peace happens as a restoration.[35] Personal and social are held together by, indeed *are*, a single body, in all the multifarious vitality of its signification.

Does reading Augustine in this way not render current debates between "realism" and "idealism" outmoded? His theology is not one of idealism because, regarding all earthly life as open to risk, he resists the urge to procure any temporal safeguard against all threat, whether present or future. Yet his theology exceeds the category of realism, because, while he takes human sin and suffering as serious threats to happiness and to the beatific vision, they never obscure completely a still-discernable peace of being. By plumbing to its depths this question of the "*condition* of our being," he resists in a compelling way the shallow waters of the "real."[36]

Hobbes does not think that he has created a perfect state in *Leviathan* but considers it the only viable alternative to the condition of war, which a weaker power cannot abate (128). But by presuming natural disorder, by adopting an authoritarian notion of hierarchy, and by divorcing reason from will, he leaves human desire unchanged, unchanging, and unfulfilled and thereby compromises the integrity of an already artificial social body, which never comes to articulate an integral desire of its own.[37] By beginning with ontological peace and developing a notion of a restored right order within the person, Augustine unites personal and social good in a way that, though never fully realized in the present, makes intelligible the real social relation implied by the notion of a body politic. Confounding the grasping demands of the demonstrable, he holds out hope for a future city not only already in the world, but already caught up in the life of God, in whom, and in whom alone, all things have their end.

## Notes

I would like to thank Catherine Pickstock and Émile Perreau-Saussine for their helpful comments on an earlier version of this essay.

1  See Otto von Gierke, *Political Theories of the Middle Age*, trans. Frederic William Maitland (Cambridge: Cambridge University Press, 1900), 7.

2  Aristotle, *Politics*, i3.1253b1ff.; Richard Bodéüs, *The Political Dimensions of Aristotle's Ethics*, trans. Jan Edward Garrett (Albany: State University of New York Press, 1993), 42, 43. See also Cary J. Nederman and Kate Langdon Forhan, *Medieval Political Theory — A Reader: The Quest for the Body Politic, 1100-1400* (London: Routledge, 1993). The metaphor also emerges in Islamic political thought. See, for example, Alfarabi, *Selected Aphorisms*, in *Alfarabi — The Political Writings: Selected Aphorisms and Other Texts*, ed. Charles E. Butterworth (Ithaca, N.Y.: Cornell University Press, 2001), 11-13.

3  Alasdair MacIntyre, *After Virtue*, 2nd ed. (Notre Dame, Ind.: University of Notre Dame

Press, 1984), 39, 172. See Ernst Kantorowicz, *The King's Two Bodies: A Study in Medieval Political Theology* (Princeton, N.J.: Princeton University Press, 1957).

4   This shift is particularly pronounced in the account of positive law found in Marsilius of Padua, who borrows significantly from Averroes. See his 1324 *The Defender of the Peace*, in *Medieval Political Philosophy*, ed. Ralph Lerner and Muhsin Mahdi (New York: Free Press of Glencoe, 1963).

5   See Aristotle, *Politics*, I.2.1252b31–33; 1253a3–5, 29–30, in *The Complete Works, Volume 2*, ed. Jonathan Barnes (Princeton, N.J.: Princeton University Press, 1984).

6   Thomas Hobbes, *Leviathan*, ed. Richard Tuck (Cambridge: Cambridge University Press, 1996), 76.

7   As Georgio Agamben and others have made clear, Hobbes requires that the state of nature be regarded not as a "real epoch," but only as a principle "internal to the State" made evident at the hypothetical moment of its dissolution. See Georgio Agamben, *Homo Sacer: Sovereign Power and Bare Life* (Stanford, Calif.: Stanford University Press, 1998), 36, 105, 106. See also Thomas Hobbes, *De Cive: The English Version*, ed. Howard Warrender (Oxford: Oxford University Press, 1983), 79–80. One might argue that Hobbes derives the state of war epistemologically and not from any ontological supposition. On this reading, Hobbes has no need to argue that humans *are* naturally aggressive, asocial, and competitive but merely must posit the limitations of human knowledge in order to sustain the state-of-war model. Yet here ontological supposition lurks all the more furtively, for only the presumption of a human tendency toward aggression sustains the inference from a state of limited knowledge to a state of war. I am grateful to Max Whyte for conversation on this question.

8   Augustine, *De civitate Dei*, ed. Henry Bettenson (London: Penguin, 1972), xix.5. Unless otherwise noted, all following citations of *De civitate Dei* will refer to this translation.

9   Augustine, *De civitate Dei*, xix.6–8.

10  Augustine, *De civitate Dei*, xix.25.

11  Augustine, *De civitate Dei*, xix.15, 874, 875.

12  For this reason and in this sense, Markus is right to suggest that *De civitate Dei* resists "the divinization of any form of social arrangement, whether existing or proposed." R. A. Markus, *Saeculum: History and Society in the Theology of St. Augustine* (Cambridge: Cambridge University Press, 1970), xx.

13  "Whatsoever is the object of any mans Appetite or Desire; that is it, which he for his part calleth Good . . . for these words of Good, Evill, and Contemptible, are ever used with relation to the person that useth them: There being nothing simply and absolutely so; nor any common Rule of the Good and Evill, to be taken from the nature of the objects themselves; but from the Person of the man (where there is no Common-wealth;) or, (in a Common-wealth,) from the Person that representeth it" (39).

14  See Henri de Lubac, *Catholicism: A Study of Dogma in Relation to the Corporate Destiny of Mankind* (London: Burns, Oates & Washbourne, 1950), 168; Oliver O'Donovan, *The Desire of Nations: Rediscovering the Roots of Political Theology* (Cambridge: Cambridge University Press, 1996), 20.

15  "If he give away the government of Doctrines, men will be frightened into rebellion with the feare of Spirits" (127).

16  "We worship God for his favor." See Thomas Hobbes, *De Homine*, in *Man and Citizen*, ed. Bernard Gert, trans. C. T. Wood, et al. (Indianapolis: Hackett, 1991), 75.

17  Augustine, *De civitate Dei*, xix.17.

18  Ibid., xix.18, 21, 27.

19 Without such a notion of the good, it seems difficult to contrive any human relation that *both* resists collapsing the other into my own vision of the good *and* resists imagining the other as an absolute good in herself. For a thorough development of this aporia, see Conor Cunningham, "The Difference *of* Theology and Some Philosophies of Nothing," *Modern Theology* 17 (2001): 289–312, and his luminous *Genealogy of Nihilism* (London: Routledge, 2002).

20 "There can be no unity without persisting difference" (de Lubac, *Catholicism*, 186).

21 Hobbes, *Leviathan*, 32, 36, 37. This should not be seen as a proto-Brandomian scorekeeping, for the significations are here "settled" by state sanction. See Robert Brandom, *Making It Explicit: Reasoning, Representing and Discursive Commitment* (Cambridge, Mass.: Harvard University Press, 1998).

22 Augustine, *De civitate Dei*, trans. R. W. Dyson (Cambridge: Cambridge University Press, 1998), XIX.18, 947.

23 Augustine, *De civitate Dei*, XIX.27.

24 Ibid, XIX.8, 462; XIX.4 and XIX.6.

25 So, for example, "we may reverently and as Christians say of God that He is the author of every act, because it is honourable to do so, but to say 'God is the author of sin' is sacrilegious and profane" (Thomas Hobbes, *Critique du De mundo de Thomas White*, ed. Jean Jacquot and H. W. Jones [Paris: Vrin-CNRS, 1973]), ff. 396–396v, trans. H. W. Jones as *Thomas White's De Mundo Examined*, trans. H. W. Jones (London: Bradford University Press, 1976), 434.

26 Hobbes, *Leviathan*, chap. 34, 271, and *Critique*, 434.

27 This contrasts with Richard Tuck's reading, which finds that, for the early-1640s Hobbes, "All theology concerns the authoritative character of our language about God." See Richard Tuck, "The Civil Religion of Thomas Hobbes," in *Political Discourse in Early Modern Britain*, ed. Nicholas Phillipson and Quentin Skinner (Cambridge: Cambridge University Press), 123.

28 I am here arguing against Tuck's claim that "Hobbes's theological position in the early 1640s was very far removed from the kind of arguments set out in *Leviathan*." In the *Critique du De mundo* that Tuck cites, Hobbes does argue that the standard theological problems, such as "whether free-will exists," "whether the human soul is immortal," and so on, are *theological* problems, not philosophical ones. But here Hobbes does not wish to "subordinate philosophy to theology" as Tuck claims, but rather suggests that, because these are undecidable problems *beyond the realm* of "knowledge," they are the prerogative of " 'the leaders of the Church,' whose task it is to regulate all dogmas; for these will be seen to be able either to strengthen or to overthrow the fixed tenents of the faith." See Hobbes, *Critique*, f. 452v, trans. 490, and Richard Tuck, "The Civil Religion of Thomas Hobbes," 127.

29 See Hobbes, *De Cive: The English Version*, xvii, 28, 249, and *Leviathan*, 125.

30 Augustine, *De civitate Dei*, XIX.6.

31 See Gierke, *Political Theories of the Middle Age*, 29.

32 See Thomas Aquinas, *Summa Theologia*, I.XLIII.

33 Hobbes, *Leviathan*, 335; cf. 94.

34 For the crucial activity of Incarnation in Augustine's historiography, see Markus, *Saeculum*, 8, 105: "Christ's coming has created another world, where division is healed, multiplicity restored to unity and corruption to integrity."

35 Cf. Aristotle, *Metaphysics*, XII, 7, 1072b1–4.

36 Augustine, *De civitate Dei*, XIX.13.

37  We may now see, with Raymond Geuss, that "this is a highly parochial problem of a particular kind of society that has thrown itself with a will into a certain very specific process of economic and political development while being unable either fully to embrace or fully to free itself from certain remnants of the Christian worldview." But, we might reasonably surmise, does not that very specific process itself (and all of its assumptions and implications) load the question of freedom or embrace? See Raymond Geuss, *Public Goods, Private Goods* (Princeton, N.J.: Princeton University Press, 2001), 114.

*Phillip Blond*    The Politics of the Eye:
Toward a Theological
Materialism

IF ONE WERE OVERLY IMPRESSED by recent French philosophy, one could quite easily consider vision as some sort of disaster that has befallen the human race.[1] According to Derrida, such ocularcentrism opens one up to all manner of philosophical errors, chief among which would be the charge that sight, or thinking through seeing, is intrinsically metaphysical—as vision is fatally committed to presence and its *parousia*. Of course this is nonsense, but it is instructive nonetheless. It tells us that one of the characteristics of modern thinking is a mistrust of vision. But why this lack of faith in what we see and what are the consequences of this modern denigration of vision?

If we cannot see we cannot think. That at least was the belief of Aristotle, who held that all thinking requires the phantasmata produced by contact between the world and the senses. If thought is to be about something other than itself, then mind must know something besides its own activity. If thinking has to be the thinking of something, then thinking (if it is to avoid mere reflexivity) must think things. In this category of other things are both animate and inanimate beings. We would not even know of the existence of other minds unless we could hear or see them. In consequence we know other minds or other things only by virtue of the senses. Moreover, it is only by having a world and some contact with it that we can distinguish between mental fiction and rational verity.

However, popular culture doubts the efficacy of such a distinction. The contemporary idiom has decided that the very idea of any alternative to the current consensus is a platonic illusion. And, we are told, since the good, the true, and the beautiful are matters of debate, they must—if we are to avoid fascism and totalitarianism—be nothing more than matters of taste and conjecture. In the place of these displaced transcendentals is enshrined a banal utilitarian aesthetic that reduces all things to the pleasures of conspicuous consumption and commodity exchange. Such satisfactions are indispensable for current Western culture: not only do they legitimate the prevailing socioeconomic order, they also hide from us the possibility of any alternative. Politics has been redefined. Instead of postulating an alternative communal order, the liberal consensus has decreed that politics is nothing more than a public securing of the private pursuit of happiness. Thus has the public arena been privatized. We can no longer conceive of something other than this mode of life, as we practice nothing other than self-gratification.

This situation could last for generations. Perhaps we should not be surprised; most human history—until the last two thousand years or so—is marked more by stability and inertia than by change. Societies have lasted for millennia; possibly because whatever hierarchical structures marked and stabilized these societies, such structures were sacralized by the culture that framed them. What was *was* what should be, in which case what marks these cultures, and most human history, is a complete lack of politics. If change is real, it must represent an overarching and structural transformation in social relations. Change is rare and requires certain special conditions. Wars between rival kings and queens are not history. Such conflicts change very little—whoever wins the status quo is nearly always maintained. The serf, peasant, or slave merely serves a new master. One reason why the Egyptian culture of the Pharaohs, despite all its magnificent architecture, longevity, and relative world ascendancy, matters so little is that its social structure reflected—albeit on a grander scale—what had always been: what Dumézil described as a tripartite hierarchy of priests, warriors, and peasants.

Politics really began when an alternative order was envisaged—when Jewish slaves were told that their subjugation was not a natural state of affairs. Prior to the revelation of Moses on the mountain in Sinai (which itself was a continuation of those covenants given to Abraham and Noah), the gods were held to be arbitrary, representatives of a random order governed only by their requisite power. God, however, revealed himself to the Jews as lawful, and covenants were made with man that governed both him and the rest of created nature—as such the world was both redescribed and reenvisaged. No longer was the exercise of arbitrary power conducted under divine license. Power was subject to law—and law now refigured power as the servant of justice and righteousness. The priestly role was no longer the sanctifying of the existing order; it was the overthrow of arbitrary rule and the establishment of a consecrated world by a common communal practice that upheld it as such.

Israel was elected from among the multitude of nations, to be a new kind of priest to them all: "For all the earth is mine, and you shall be to me a kingdom of priests and a holy nation" (Exod. 19:5–6). "I will make of you a great nation . . . so that you will be a blessing . . . [to] all the families of the earth" (Gen. 12.2–3). However, the universal vocation of some traditions of Judaism became subject to a secondary and ultimately triumphant need: the necessity of survival. As a result of various factors (to be discussed below), Judaism lapsed into an ethnocentric faith that taught salvation for only one people. As a culture it abandoned the practice of conversion and so eschewed any genuine transformative form of politics. It was the failure of Judaism to complete and fulfill its universal mission that lead Christ to be both an inheritor of Judaism and one who transformed it into the first genuinely global movement known to man. Christ, by positing a universal *ought*, a universal that would transform all current forms of living, not only extended the law to all peoples — he also reformulated the relationship between the particular and the universal.

We know of course that Plato and Aristotle some three hundred years before Christ had already determined the presence of transcendent universals in all immanent things; they differed only in respect to the manner of this relationship. They knew that the existing order, be it social or metaphysical, was not self-explanatory. As such they knew that each particular social instantiation could not claim to wholly represent a transcendent universal warrant. Particular existent social forms, just like particular physical forms, required some further explanation as to how and why they should be so. By and large the answers the Greeks gave to the *how* were so persuasive that they have determined and framed all consequent debate. But the Greeks were always less sure as to *why* things were so. They could understand that things were like they were because of some relation to a universal, but they could not grasp why the universal was interested in the particular. If there were a God, or a demiurge, or a transcendent one, why would it bring about things other than itself? If the one were so replete, so unified, so lacking in lack, why did it create or cause the many?

It was Christianity that provided the answer to this, and in so doing it was Christianity that first constructed the condition for a radical politics. As we know, Greek society, even after Plato and Aristotle, could easily endorse a form of hierarchy such that even slavery was viewed as natural. For Christians, however, the task of the natural is to reflect the divine order, and (contra Marx) the message of the Christian priests was not division but equality. As Paul told the Greeks, "We are all his children" (Acts 17:28). For Christianity, the Trinity is not some fiction that attempts to resolve monotheism and polytheism, it is an account of the "why" of the absolute. The absolute for Christians is *already* relational; the logos was already with God (John 1:1). Thus God is not a self-identical henological Greek substance but rather a relational and loving absolute. As such the genuinely radical aspect of Christianity is that it demands that all social practices mirror and copy the divine equalitarian order. And to the extent that the exclusive hierarchy of the pagans sought metaphysical justification for enshrining division and class, it was the Christians and their priests who were the first in human history to call for the overthrow of a society based on divisions between classes: "In the one Spirit we were all baptized, Jews as well as Greeks, slaves as well as citizens" (1 Cor. 12:13).

And even if current Christian social practice has decayed to a virtual synonymy with liberal bourgeois ethics—a situation whose genealogy we can trace[2]—this should not blind us to its more radical legacy. If the left in essence is misguided in its repudiation of Christian social practice, so it follows that the left might also be misled about the Christian ontology that formed the basis for the transformative social practice of the Christian Church. Of course the eschatological hope of the Christians is that the two become the same: as practice more and more realizes in the immanent the transcendent social order, the opposition between both becomes cancelled.

In what follows I will argue that a Christian ontology is indispensable for social transformation. In this sense there is no grasping of an *ought*, of what should be, if such a state of affairs is not accessible to us. If the falseness of the world is discernable, it can be only because our minds can discern some presence or aspect of an alternative. Or to say this another way, if all good politics is in some sense founded upon a realist claim (that is, upholding the true as opposed to the false, the genuine as opposed to the illusory, and the good as distinct from evil), then we need some manner of contact with this "real." Given that we cannot dispense with our senses and leave our bodies behind in the hope of gaining a more immediate encounter with the exigencies of our material existence, we can at least say that abstraction from the world is not the mode by which we can know this earth more concretely. In which case, in terms of our ethics and politics, we might take the issue of the "senses" more seriously.

Realism, if it is worthy of the name, cannot easily dispense with the phenomenology of the world. If it were thought that appearance bore no relation to reality, then the real—and thus the true—would be hidden from us. Appearances would lie, and the things themselves would hide from us. In which case, though, we might try to grasp the real with our minds; there would be no assurance that any correspondence between our conceptions and what we were attempting to conceptualize would pertain. However, if the essence of a thing *is* its appearance, then vision would be intrinsically linked to ontology. In which case representational epistemology (which relies upon there being a gap between the mental and the material, such that mental proxies stand in for a world that cannot be presented), could be discarded as just another conceptual abstraction. That I take vision to be the prototypical sense for the purposes of this essay in no way reduces the other senses to that of sight. Nor would I deny that hearing, touch, taste, or smell (together with sight) also make the world a livable and disclosive sensorium. But the discernment that the world confronts us as a whole owes perhaps more to sight and vision than any other sense, for it is not clear that we could have a world if we did not have its visible horizon.

But it is rank foolishness to suggest that seeing the good or the true is simply a matter of clear and distinct vision. Too much modern phenomenology thinks that one need only to clean one's phenomenological spectacles to get an unambiguous look at what is the case, be it the Levinasian face or Marion's untutored intuiting of the absolute. But vision is *not* like this. And to the extent that phenomenology repudiates mind by reducing the role of the mental to that of the passive reception of an objective *positum*, phenomenology gets it all wrong.

Seeing is neither the pragmatic-cum-postmodern making whatever you want of the world, nor is it the submissive receipt of some vast objectivity already fashioned for our worship by some absent hand. When we open our eyes we neither see what we wish nor are we confronted by some ready-made truth. Both of these positions are forms of dualism, and both should be dispensed with. The myth of the given is indeed a myth, but this should not commit us to some pseudo-Kantian variant of a dynamic a priori constructivism. Mental construction and material reception occur together as part of a process of cognition broader than either vocabulary can grasp.

Leaving a description of alternative accounts of cognition until later, let me be more explicit about the political nature of sight. In the *German Ideology* Marx argues that revolutionizing the world requires an adequate conception of it. Even earlier in 1842 he tells us that "the time must come about when philosophy will get in touch with the real world of its time and establish a reciprocal relationship with it not only internally through its content, but also externally, through its *phenomenal manifestation* as well."[3]

For Marx, once consciousness has grasped the real, it understands that the real can change, for what is revealed to mind is that consciousness is nothing other than consciousness of existing practice. As such mind and world end their separate existences by discovering that they are identical products of the same process. Overcoming such a separation means the "destruction of the alien relation between men and what they themselves produce." It is here that a certain form of spontaneous naturalism emerges: human beings are restored to themselves as men abolish the gap between them and their creations such that they can enjoy a full recourse to the "all-sided production of the earth."⁴ Yet there is a problem here: on the one hand, men are nothing but a social product of the prevailing conditions; at the same time, they retain an innate (and therefore presocial) conception of their genuine needs. Thus the workers can determine a contradiction between their "intolerable" situation and their own natural needs only if they have some presocial access to what their needs are. But—and here is a further peculiarity—these natural needs as identified by Marx are on examination nothing at all, for at base Marxist anthropology posits not a natural self existing in "rural idiocy" but only a self-positing freedom. The aim of Marxist man is curiously neoliberal: the right to enjoy unfettered liberty and any and all products of voluntary activity. Division of labor is thus objected to not because it alienates man from his true nature but rather because it limits man by imposing upon him a certain sort of social fixity. Marx objects to capital only insofar as capital distributes freedom unequally, enslaving some while letting others have the benefit of the full fruits of the productive process. What is wrong with capitalism is not so much that its needs are false, but that not all enjoy them in the same measure. Far from having a natural as opposed to artificial duality, Marx exhibits—in its crudest form—an idealist legacy predicated upon the self-positing self whose only material claim is that it values only its own activity. The Marxist looks very much like the liberal bourgeois tourist of today: he determines himself at base to be summation of all his free choices.

For what is lacking in Marx is any notion of the sort of beings we *ought* to be. Outside of freedom, Marxist anthropology is wholly underdetermined. Paradoxically, what Marxism lacks is a genuine materialism, a real account of our limits and what we should want beyond the mere fact of satisfaction itself. What is unexamined in Marxism is that against which the self posits itself—the world. For Marx, nature is simply hostile and has to be subjugated as a threat or limit to human self-expression. It is part of my contention that manifestation itself can in part teach us our true needs and true nature. Marxism, however, bequeaths to us the idea of a nature without nature that makes only inasmuch as it demonstrates that it acts.

Marxism offers us not so much an alternative to the present order as its intensification. In this regard, we should not think that all the post-post-Marxism of Deleuze, deterritorialization, and desire are in any aspect an innovation in respect of Marx. Indeed, the residual sociality of Marx is increasingly eroded, as once the social has been recovered from the marketplace and true freedom is restored to all, each pursues their own end, which is only their own liberty.[5] In this regard we can concur with Alain Badiou when he calls Deleuze a thinker who cannot think relation. In Deleuze's thought, difference can be thought radically only by means of the disjunctive synthesis, which while "testifying to the infinite and egalitarian fecundity of the One" separates each individuation from all others in order to think its difference all the more acutely.[6] And as I have said, this development is not foreign to Marx, as radical spontaneity cannot think that a relationship to anything other than itself is anything but an imposition upon its own unique distinction.

In which case, as I said prior to the discussion of Marx, true and genuine politics requires an alternative to thought thinking itself. It is not just that spontaneity needs receptivity if what it thinks is to be real, nor is it that a suspension of freedom in the name of constraint should take place. It is rather that we are makers who have been made. Christianity is as far removed from the pursuit of sovereignty and autonomy as it is possible to be. All these modern thinkers have dispensed with the real or the material because they cannot think it as anything but a constraint upon self-determination. The reverse is true — only by having a created order already in some sense directed can we fulfill our nature as a creating orchestration of our world. In this manner is not just the thought of dependence. Christianity overcomes the opposition by being neither freeman nor slave. The tradition determines man both in relation to what precedes him (humanity and the world are caused) and in relation to what exceeds him (the telos of man is the beatific vision), which is nothing but the infinite practicing relationality of all creatures.

The Christian absolute (which alone offers a genuine alternative) reconciles universal and particular through the incarnation of the Christ into the material order. Appearance is thus the very stuff of relation, because it is the site of reconciliation between the transcendent and the immanent. Ever since the incarnation of the God-man, the particular contingent order has revealed itself to be the mode by which we relate to transcendent necessity (which is why the book of Revelation promises a new heaven *and* a new earth). And if the order of appearance is divine self-expression (which the tradition teaches us that it is), then the aesthetic unalienated practice we are called to is not just the complementary of the divine order, it is its very essence. The self-expression of a creator is not passivity but creativity itself. For Trinity teaches the unity within difference of the ingenerate and generate order. The particular thus becomes more universal and more singular by being not just one self-asserting uniqueness among many (the logic of the same and the one), but the uniqueness that is unique in the light of all other practice and relation. In this sense aesthetics and material ontology collide; all that *is* calls for its aesthetic discernment so that it can participate in the divine artistic practice that is creation itself. This is why appearance matters, objects give themselves so that they can be seen and thus thought, and thought in relation to what they express and so make possible.

But as we know, we are very suspicious of sight and vision. If we were being good scholars, we could trace the genealogy of this suspicion of sight to that rupture in the thirteenth century when, after the death of Aquinas, Henry of Ghent, Duns Scotus, and William of Ockham all helped to construct a voluntarist theology that drained the universal forms and structures from the world of nature. That this was done in order to prevent God's creative acts being viewed as a necessary artifice that does not detract from its disastrous consequences: the world became viewed as an arbitrary epiphenomenon of God's (possibly malign) will. Indeed, in seeking to guard against pantheism, these thinkers produced its un-Christian converse: they made (to paraphrase Nietzsche) the real world a myth. The consequence of this erasure of form or universality from visibility has dictated *virtually all* subsequent accounts of sensibility and intuition. From Descartes to the British empiricists, on up to Kant, Hegel, and beyond, sense experience is something that true knowledge has to overcome, ignore, abstract from, or add to in order to reach anything like a rational account of what it is that is seen. Even those very modern scientific discourses that claim self-explanatory appeal to the immediately evident or the clearly seen are themselves founded upon a logical abstraction from concrete entities. The truth of animals or human beings is not to be found in atoms, quanta, or even genetics, because in departing from material things in order to explain them, we forgo the evident discernment of their purpose: the visible testimony as to why such entities were formed in the first place. That is to say, one may understand the atomic or genetic structure of a flower, but neither atoms nor genetics can tell us why it is beautiful, nor defend the idea that the telos of plant blossom is to delight the human eye.

It appears then that I am crediting medieval nominalism with the denial of universals to vision (and I am) but it must be remembered that antiquity also had its doubts about sense experience. We can recall that it was Aristotle who accused Plato of being a Heraclitean for having similar doubts about the possibility of knowledge being derivable from the senses.[7] Leaving aside Aristotle's misreading of Platonic vision and ignoring for the moment all the very real complexities of the post-thirteenth-century loss of faith in appearances, and delaying for the purposes of this paper any discussion of twentieth-century phenomenology, the least that can be said about the genealogy of the history of vision is that the only period in history in which appearances appear to be valued as the manifestation of something universal is the Christian epoch itself. From St. Augustine in the fourth century to St. Thomas at the end of the thirteenth, it is Christian thinkers (in both the West and the East) who have most explicitly expressed their fidelity to vision and to the universals that appearances make manifest.

To state the obvious, it was the Incarnation that first glorified the body and thus the created order, and it was the Resurrection that redeemed the body and promised not just and not only a new heaven but also "a new heaven and a new earth" (Rev. 21.1). Once Christ assumed the human form, and Christian scripture attested to the resurrection of that form beyond sin and death, and the descent of the heavenly Jerusalem to earth then all creation and all form was — in some sense — divinized. Indeed St. Augustine so valorized appearances that much of De Trinitate is spent attempting to show that the senses can discern the presence of the Trinity in practically all of the stimulus array. Similarly, so serious a materialist or better empiricist was St. Thomas that he insisted on following Aristotle's dictum that nothing was in the mind that had not first passed through the senses.

But I have still not answered or even explicitly raised the problem implied by these first few paragraphs. Just what is it exactly to take vision seriously? Or, to put it another way, what does sight do? What is its role for human beings? Both the classical and medieval periods are in agreement on this point; vision gives us access to knowledge. Aristotle's Metaphysics opens with a eulogy on vision and its ability to apprehend the knowable and make many qualities manifest. Far from articulating a separate world of timeless forms inaccessible to or from the sensible sphere, Plato developed a form of intellectual empiricism where phenomena were seen in the light of the transcendent forms they participated in. Similarly, and most excellently, it was St. Thomas who synthesized the positions of Aristotle and Plato (a synthesis already anticipated in the work of the Academy and the Lyceum). Thomas produced a Platonic account of the cognition of form via an Aristotelian determination that such knowledge is accessible by the soul only through the knowledge of the natural world attained by the senses. So then vision is about knowledge, but what sort of knowledge, what type of things can vision know or give us access to knowing? Again, for both antiquity and the Christian epoch, there never really was a sectioning off of discreet fields of enquiry; even if (given the transcendent nature of knowledge) one could never attain a full comprehension of a thing, one either knew in some degree its nature or one didn't. In knowing a thing's nature or being, the knower would grasp the efficient and final cause of that creature. The beginning of the being and its end were cognizable, the virtues that allowed a creature to flourish and become what it was were, if a matter of debate, at least thought amenable

to human cognition. In short there was what—in the Middle Ages at least—
might be called a convertibility of the transcendentals: the good, the beautiful, and the true were thought to share identity. What is good must also
in some manner be true and beautiful.[8] Leaving precise technical discussion
aside, once again let us note the difference between such a conception and
that of the modern era. Our time is characterized by a disassociation of our
sensibility. With some notable exceptions, I would contend that the modern
tradition has separated itself from a more unified vision by failing to think
that goodness and truth are linked with each other—or even that either have
anything to do with aesthetics and its concern with the beautiful.

## The Kantian Legacy

Particularly instructive and influential in this regard is the work of Immanuel
Kant. His separation of the three transcendentals into the three critiques
alienated each transcendental from its others. As a consequence, truth telling has become a project independent of reality and relation. Doing right or
acting well has, after its separation from truth, become unable to defend any
claims for the objective value of its codes, whereas art has become merely
that—just art—a matter of taste or gratification important only to the recipients of such sensations.

Since we are concerning ourselves with beauty, it is clear that the most
perspicuous demonstration of the separation of aesthetic from moral and
cognitive worth indeed comes from Kant, who aestheticizes art by refusing
the idea that any judgment as to an object's beauty could be a cognitive one.
Consider the following remark from the *Critique of Judgement*: "A judgment
of taste is not a cognitive judgment and so is not a logical judgment but an
aesthetic one, by which we mean a judgment whose determining basis *cannot be other* than *subjective*."[9]

The origin of this refusal lies in Kant's wish to avoid a spurious choice
between, as Simon Jarvis puts it, "a rationalist and empiricist aesthetics."[10]
The rationalist operates regardless of subjective experience, believing it possible to argue someone into a position where they are forced to acknowledge
beauty. This appeal to unmediated beauty of an object becomes a dogmatic
classicism with petition to the timeless geometry of certain forms, lines, and
ratios. But such a position would locate aesthetic judgment within the object
and make of transcendental idealism an objective empiricism. Moreover, it
would run counter to Kant's primary claim that one cannot reason or argue
someone into the judgment that an object is beautiful. Claims of taste must
for Kant be separated from claims of truth or right action.

Likewise and conversely, empiricist aesthetics is merely one of subjective gratification, a description of the perceiver's feelings in the presence of an agreeable object: a type of emotivism of the eye. Kant's attempt to avoid the bad extremes of an umediated objectivism and/or subjectivism has a curious effect on his aesthetic theory. In section three of the *Critique*, he divides aesthetic sensation into two — that which expresses an interest and that which does not. For example, the sensation that produces agreeable pleasure is connected with interest; it is, as it were, a subjective (rather than objective) presentation of sense. The agreeable is not a report on the qualities of the aesthetic object, it is merely a report of our gratification by it. Those who endorse such an aesthetic "aim at nothing but enjoyment . . . they like to dispense with all judging." In this regard the agreeable represents empiricist aesthetics. Equally, the good is also connected with interest; in this respect it is not an interest for us, for "we call something intrinsically good if we like it for its own sake." In which case the good is purposive — it calls for a relationship between reason and action. Such judgment for Kant falls under a concept: "in order to consider something good I must always know what sort of thing the object is (meant) to be, i.e., I must have a determinate concept of it" (48). In short, the good fulfills the appeal to rationalist aesthetics, as it is (like the categorical imperative) clearly universalizable.

But as we have seen, Kant thinks neither is aesthetic experience just sensation (mere gratification), nor is it capable of rationalist universalization. Kant contends that "there can be no rule by which someone could be compelled to acknowledge that something is beautiful. No one can use reasons or principles to talk us into a judgment on whether some garment, house or flower is beautiful" (59). In contrast, for Kant, a judgment of taste is wholly without interest; as such, it is free of both subjective gratification and objective universalization. In this sense it escapes the Kantian schema of knowledge. Lack of interest is defined by Kant as an indifference to the object's existence: "In order to play the judge in matters of taste, we must not be in the least biased in favor of the things existence but must be wholly indifferent about it" (46). Indifference is exactly what allows aesthetic judgment to be a judgment rather than an expression of the stake or interest that one has in the outcome of beauty's discernment.

Curiously, it is exactly this lack of interest that sparks universal regard. For Kant, it is only as an object of a liking devoid of all interest that the beautiful can be presented as the object of a *universal* liking: "For if he likes something and is conscious that he himself does so without any interest, then he cannot help judging that it must contain a basis for being liked (that holds) for everyone" (54). So this disinterested delight lays claim to general assent. Yet, and at the same time, this universality cannot make universal claim through concepts, for then it would be akin to practical reason; however, if this "universality" is not to be thought through a concept, it must be received via sensation, but that would place it within the sphere of gratification. Alternatively, this conception might suggest that there could be a disinterested intuition—a *sensus communis*—of generally communicable feeling. Indeed, this is exactly what Kant argues that the beautiful represents. This subjective yet communal sense does not threaten the rest of the transcendental architectonic, as Kant holds that the beautiful represents neither a wholly subjective or objective pole but the *subjective* conditions of the possibility of knowledge, with the effect that unlike the agreeable, where no one would demand that others be of a mind with one's own, "in a judgment of taste about beauty we always require others to agree" (57). Even Kant admits there is something very strange here, for judgments are being made in respect of which universal validity cannot hold objectively but only subjectively. The feeling of pleasure or displeasure relates not to the cognitive power because the aesthetic is indifferent to the existence of its object (indeed Kant uses the example of a fabulous palace created in the mind by imagination as indicative of the feeling of beauty). It relates more to the free play of the cognitive potency: the ability of the subject to create a disinterested power that operates without a priori legislation but by means of a rule that can compel general assent— in short, the aesthetic concept of the genius.

It is important to realize that at this juncture Kant is genuinely attuned to the peculiar character of perception and its inherent resistance to monological interpretations of its nature and/or culture. This is perhaps why the only secular left—that is left—locates its last hope here in aesthetic judgment, a way out of a world where all our sensibility is conditioned and commodified by the culture industry, and all our concepts are isolated from ontological connection with the world and one another. Here I quote from Jay Bernstein's *The Fate of Art*: "Aesthetic discourse contains concepts and terms of analysis, a categorical framework, which if freed from confinement in an autonomous aesthetic domain, would open the possibility of encountering a *secular* world empowered as a source of meaning beyond the self or subject."[11] For Bernstein—and in this he follows Adorno—aesthetic judgment can attain this by virtue of its ability to displace the paradigm of knowing as a subsumption of particulars under universals, conceptualize free action through the notion of the genius as creative and legislative rather than rule following, open itself up to otherness through the sublime, and finally, with the *sensus communis*, break with solipsism and refigure an alternate community "irrevocably political in its complexion."

It is instructive at this point to note that a materialist project requires *material* if the aesthetic is to be the means by which transcendent nature can free itself from the culture of subjective domination—in which case, nature itself needs to be recovered from the Kantian indifference to its existence. As Adorno wrote, if thinking is to free itself from idealist illusion then in some manner pace Hegel "essence must appear."[12] But the difficulty in thinking materialism is that any immediate appeal to givenness free of idealism is illusory. If the model of conceptuality that the materialist wishes to escape is defined as thought, then what on earth could it mean to think materialism? Can we think an object in itself without subjecting that object to our own structures of thought, symbolization, and limit? And if there is no appeal to the objects of experience outside of our structures of experience, then it is not clear what could or would distinguish an idealist approach to the world from its materialist critique.

One way of grasping the importance for the secular left of avoiding this double bind is to acknowledge what it might mean if such a situation were true. For Adorno, it would signify the final erasure of human freedom and the disappearance of the ability to think something other than the received order and the status quo. If consciousness really is *only* the product of the social cultural process, and if it is in principle impossible to separate this commodified consciousness from the objects that it thinks, then there is no transcending the received/constructed order on the near or far side of human experience. Thus it follows that there is no possibility of a genuine experience of something other than unfreedom passing itself off as freedom; in short, there would be a complete acquiescence to the exchange value of the capitalist order.

Consequently, we can see why the art object retains a utopic focus for Adorno, as it offers, through its thought of autonomy, an account of a being in itself that is not subject to the prevailing order. Accordingly, it allows a genuine thought—and perhaps experience—of freedom and the idea that our social experience and accordingly our whole cognitive order might—one day—actually change. But again, to return to the third *Critique*, if aesthetic judgment is made cognitive, then in strict Kantian terms it will be associated with the subsumptive judgment of cognition, in which case aesthetic judgment will fall under the sway of the culture industry and forgo any of its purported independence and autonomy.

Adorno's often brilliant critique of Kantian metaphysics and epistemology indicates how he might propose to avoid such a situation. Adorno gives an account of Kant's intellectual and sensible conditions of knowledge and inverts the intellectual's primacy over the sensible by arguing that the conditions of intellectual knowledge cannot be timeless invariants of what they think are variants in time, since the variants in time are themselves conditions of possibility of what makes them possible: appearance itself. If this were not so, Kant would have no way of distinguishing between appearances and a priori conditions, for both would look the same, and Kant would be the vulgar idealist he claims not to be in the *Prolegomena*, in which case one might suggest that systems themselves are not quite the all-encompassing totalizing structures Adorno so evidently fears.

But, leaving that aside, the real strength of Adorno's critique of Kant is that he questions its very starting point. He doubts whether anything like pure understanding or pure sensibility is possible or even thinkable. As such, two unthinkables cannot produce a thought, which leaves the question of what constitutes genuine materialist thought or thought of matter very much open. I want to suggest that Adorno's account of determinate negation and mimesis are vital for any project that would liberate us from what Adorno calls an ontology of the wrong state of things.[13] If indeed, to quote Adorno, "the existing world is false to its innermost core," then an account of what is not false is required.[14] Of course, determinate negation allows thought to negate what confronts it as inevitable, and it reveals any supposed necessity to be a contingent state of affairs — affairs, moreover, whose contingency has unduly sedimented itself into thought as an ahistorical given. But Adorno's difficulty lies in the inability to negate the Kantian paradigm he considers an irreversible material condition of modern thought. In making a necessary appeal to something other than the existing state of affairs, Adorno also argues that total despair is unintelligible, in which case an account of such an unintelligibility is required that itself would be the positive loci in respect of which the world could be reordered.

That Adorno cannot think this, except in terms of the utopic function of the "art work," comes because he cannot think thought and matter together: he *accepts* the Kantian division of reason and sensibility because he is unable to give a materialist account of it. Bypassing Kant is perhaps now more possible than it was in Adorno's day; we have recovered, or are beginning to recover, the great counter-Enlightenment thinkers such as Hamann, Herder, Von Humbolt, and Jacobi, all of whom dismissed in various ways the division between mind and world and thus that between phenomena and noumena. Thanks to Husserl and Heidegger, we have the beginning of an attempt to constitute a fundamental ontology, and this may well be the same thing: a complete refusal of epistemology, a denial that the theory and practice of cognitive and political representation can in any way deliver us to a world or realm that is real.

*Materialism*

Here I want to insert a properly figured Christian theology as the only successful way in which to think the relation of matter to what is nonmaterial, as only Christianity can think the separation between concept and intuition such that their requisite dualism is cancelled. Of course, it follows from this that I do not accept that a materialism can be thought that excludes ideas, forms, or secondary qualities. In short, a materialism that does not account for the appearance of nonmaterial properties is, I believe, incoherent and ultimately unintelligible.

If there were materialism without ideal properties, presumably it would have to be some vast extended substance, which would perforce have to uphold all those nonmaterial properties or qualities. If it didn't or couldn't perform such a role, then materialism as such would lose all explicative power. And if we concede that it does not make sense to deny the existence of ideal or mental qualities, since every philosopher in the tradition has accepted their existence but disputed their nature and origin, then matter, as the upholder of nonmaterial substances, would be the only genuine materialist option. However, as I have said, I think such a materialism is neither coherent nor intelligible.

Taking the issue of basic cognitive coherence first, it is the very idea of prime matter as some sort of featureless extended substance which underpins accidents or properties that seems bizarre. We never meet with such a matter, whereas we seem to meet with qualities, properties, and attributes all the time. Yet in the venerable tradition of the British empiricists, we always give these "accidents" an independent status, as if they existed apart from the substance that underpinned them. George Berkeley first pointed out that the very idea of an independent materialism derived from the creation and separation of abstract ideas from their concrete and encountered actuality. Featureless materialism is thus for Berkeley a *mental* product of an unwarranted abstraction of "general ideas" from a particular combination of ideas, the resulting idealess residue being named as unexperienced matter, which nonetheless—in some unexplained manner—produces in human minds the effect of both primary and secondary qualities.

There are other problems for a theory of material substrata underpinning nonmaterial qualities.[15] If, for example, such substrata are conceived as place or space holders for qualities, they themselves would have to be quality-free, for if such substances were allowed to have accidents or properties, they would stand in need of material substrata themselves to enable the support of these properties. The resulting infinite regress could be terminated only by accepting substrata without properties or by meeting substrata that had properties but that required no further support. But if substrata with foundations existed, then the motivation for introducing substrata without properties would be lost, in which case any theory of material substrata is committed to the existence of propertyless substrata materially underpinning or carrying nonmaterial accidents or qualities or whatever. Yet this seems to make unintelligible any claim that matter exists in the form of a substratum, because no inference to it can be legitimately made. For example, if the defining mark of that which supports properties is that it is not a property, and if we have no access to things apart from their properties, then how can we infer the property of not being a property, and what material basis can be found for asserting that this absence of quality constitutes the foundation of all quality as such?

Moreover, materialism needs appearances, because without them it is not clear that materialism is not also a form of mental abstraction. For example, some contemporary materialists claim they are physicalists such that they can reduce all thought to the biochemical process of the brain. This reduction implies, however, that given a certain physiochemical state, a specific thought must follow. But it is exactly this linkage that is impossible to demonstrate, since it must tie each specific mental event to this specific brain state. Yet the brain state of pain is clearly realizable by any number of human and indeed animal brain states.[16] Thus if materialism posits something other than what is seen or indeed given, it always tends to a form of reductionism.

*Transcendental Idealism*

If this all suggests that matter cannot think the nonmaterial, does the converse apply? Can the nonmaterial think matter? If not, then dualism is nearer to the truth, and Kant, with his division of knowing into the separate realms of sensibility and the understanding, would be the closest to figuring how — given a dualist universe — knowledge might be possible. But even in this hope it is evident that transcendental idealism fails — for the simple reason that it cannot verify or know if the phenomena it meets with in intuition are genuine appearances (creations of matter) or subjective illusions (fabrications of mind). The great problem with Kantianism is not that it splits the object of cognition into that which we can know (phenomena) and that which we cannot (noumena), but that that which we cannot know is made the mark of all genuine experience and thus the foundation of knowledge itself.[17]

If intuition is to be distinguished from concept, we must have some means to ascertain that appearances represent something other than the activities of the understanding. That is to say, if appearances are merely the product of mind, if appearances as being-for-us reflect not being in-itself but only-being-for-us, then the connection between phenomena and noumena is sundered, in which case Kant becomes a simple idealist, for he cannot establish contact with what lies beyond the mind. If such a correspondence can be reasonably doubted, and it can, then intuitions become mental projections rather than indicators or proxys of a world beyond consciousness.

Hence, since the world in-itself is, according to Kant, inaccessible to human cognition, the question as to what the mind's representations are representative of must perforce be raised. As Manfred Frank puts it, "If objects only come about via synthetic acts of the understanding, the understanding cannot be made into the imitator of objects."[18] And if the synthesis of the understanding cannot correspond to the objects it synthesizes, then any question as to the truth of mental representations of material phenomena is both begged and found wanting.

## Idealism

If materialism fails because it cannot explain the presence of ideal properties within it, and transcendental idealism falls short because it cannot connect with (let alone explain) the material world, what philosophical options are left to us? Clearly the category that has failed in both of the aforementioned is that of relation. Materialism cannot relate to mental properties that it purports to uphold, whereas transcendental idealism cannot relate to the world whose appearances it claims to know. Perhaps secular or at least heterodox idealism is more promising. At first glance it might appear so. As Rowan Williams points out, Hegel thinks relation in such a way that there is no unmediated appeal to anything. As a result, there is no dualism to either assert or overcome, "because [for Hegel] there is no moment of pure, unmediated identity in the actual world, there are no discrete and simple objects for thought to rest in. No perceived reality is stable and self-contained for thinking. . . . Everything can be thought, nothing is beyond reconciliation," every percept makes sense in a distinctness, a uniqueness that is in harmony with an overall environment.[19]

If Hegel could make good on this promise, then he would be a resource indeed. The trouble is that Hegel (like most idealists) cannot think the individual, the unique, or the particular. That is to say, each particular is subsumed by, and into, the universal that thinks it. Sense certainty is derided in the *Phenomenology* for assuming it has knowledge of the absolute before the dialectical work of spirit has even commenced its path of reconciliation.

Likewise all matter, or rather all material form, is held to signify something higher beyond itself, in respect of which its phenomenal appearance is but a pale manifestation. By this I do not mean to suggest something silly such as Hegel is a thinker of totality, or even that Hegel subsumes all things under an abstract absolute. Rather, what I want to suggest is that Hegel can see no good *reason* for the particular, no compelling account by spirit of why there are these individual things that must be related if reconciliation is to be achieved. This is why Hegel believes almost of necessity that each particular must unfold its relationship with the universal and so self-transcend its own limitation. Such sublimation perhaps does enter into an infinite relationality, but it is still a dialectical economy whose teleology lies inexplicably beyond each and every singular manifestation. In short, from the perspective of Hegelian idealism, individual singular things are a failure, a failure to think the universality that binds, relates, and exceeds them. It follows, therefore, that there is nothing necessary about the elements that indicate necessity — one could imagine that spirit would remain happy if in some possible world there was no requirement to reconcile discreet parts to one another. A self-reliant spirit that had achieved its goals would see no logic in dividing again, no raison d'être in the dispersal of itself across the elements it had just unified, in which case Hegelianism might better be understood as an inverted voluntarist theology. While the standard voluntarist starts from God's universality and can see no reason why He invests such in the world, Hegel starts with concrete particularity and cannot explain how universality began there in each discreet worldly element. For if the claim of absolute spirit is to achieve self-knowledge, neither spirit nor Hegel can tell us why such knowledge was lost in the first place, nor indeed how the absolute came to be scattered across such a vast compass, in which case the reconciliation of the absolute with itself is made in spite of its dispersal in plurality, not because of it. It follows that plurality is neither the intention nor wish of the idealist absolute; thus, once again, an idealism of the absolute cannot explain the existence of material entities nor the value found in any relations therein. Accordingly, absolute knowing, while it involves self-consciousness of the divine, can easily dispense with consciousness of—and relationship to—the particular.

## A Christian Vision

Let us recap: I have argued that it is only in the Christian era that appearances and consequently sight as such have been taken seriously as demonstrative of the ontological nature of things. We have seen how modern cognition has marginalized sight and aesthetics by separating consideration of beauty from questions of ethics and truth. However, since the project to independently establish ethics and truth on subjective and transcendental grounds has so evidently failed, the question as to the status and role of aesthetics has returned. For Adorno and the Frankfurt school, only aesthetics can offer us a way out of the subjective domination of truth-reductive cognition and the systemic determination of subsumptive judgment, yet the purported autonomy of post-Kantian aesthetics can indicate an "alternative state of things" only if the nature of things could support such an account. If no explanation can be given as to why the things themselves would wish their essences to appear rather than be subsumed beneath falsehood and miscognition, Adorno's account remains utopic in the pejorative sense that it suggests that no such object or cognitive option exists.

In short, if we can accept that a successful materialism would have to account for appearances, forms, and secondary qualities, then a secular materialism that cannot connect appearances with the essences of things faces severe problems, as it cannot explain why objects would tell us the truth about themselves. Conversely, as I hope to have indicated, neither can a secular idealism, since according to Hegel entities reveal the truth about themselves only to escape from their particularity or individuality, for they can see no value in what they are, in which case what appears is not the entity itself but the absolute as yet unreconciled to itself. Transcendental idealism, in trying to avoid the dangers of both, unites the faults of each by producing an abstract universality that has no connection with the world it purports to judge.

But to avert to the questions I raised at the beginning of this paper, why does all this discussion about the relationship between appearances and essences matter? And what is the relation between this issue and that of vision and aesthetics? Finally, of course, what does all this have to do with God?

The question of appearance and essence matters, because if essences do not appear — if the essences of things are not capable of being known — then truth is not an option for human beings. And if truth is an illusion on the part of consciousness, then so too are ideas of any ethical or aesthetic correspondence with the nature of things and the created order as a whole. Likewise, since we human creatures can know things only according to our own structures of knowledge and experience, if the essences of things were not fully amenable to our cognition, that would suggest that truth was fundamentally hidden from us. That essence has withdrawn from us on account of our nature rather than our actions or formation would indicate that no matter what we do, think, see, or say, we are damned. Similarly, this would indicate that God had withheld Himself from us, for since we know God by His works, and since creation, if it is anything, is *His* work, then cognition of the work of God would not lead to God and we would not know our Savior. But, as St. Paul insisted, Christians worship what they know, whereas pagans worship what they do not. So if indeed God is known by his works, and if indeed, as the tradition used to hold, we need *both* the book of creation and the book of scripture to discern the work of God, then the eyes that see the work and the mind that grasps its divine nature are the means by which we know God, in which case aesthetics and vision itself are receptions of and discernments therein of the mind and work of God.

In a way, therefore, all of the philosophical problems we have discussed are able to be resolved only theologically. By this I mean that only a divine intention posited behind each and every thing could explain why the object would wish to be known by the subject. That is to say every and any theory of correspondence between mind and world will still have to explain why world would reveal itself to mind. As we have seen, no theory can really account for such a phenomenon, whereas the idea that God stands behind each and every object and intends that that object wholly and utterly gives itself to its perceiver *can* account for the appearance of essence in the human eye.

But we should not be surprised that intention itself, both on the part of the object and the subject, is theological in nature and origin. For the entire world and all that is in it is designed and destined for the human eye. What is known in each thing is its "form" or essence, and in this regard I do not think that form, being, and matter differ, as God intends there to be fleshy material creatures that *really* exist, informed by the divine idea that He has of them.[20] Inasmuch as the world is an ordered creation with differences of degree corresponding to the *scala entis* that ascends and descends from the mind of God, the form of each thing is uncompleted unless it is known by its higher complementary. The telos of each entity consists in being known, for in being known its relation with other knowables (and the known universe as such) is gained, and thereby the knower glorifies the known by placing it within that context that more perfectly reveals the Creator. Accordingly, when the being of each and every entity wishes to be known by that which is higher than it, it is elevated by being so known. This elevation consists in knowing more perfectly the nature of the thing known than the thing itself. A plant does not know that it reveals its Maker; such an imprimatur can be revealed only by the eye of man. While each thing has a teleology to be known by mind of man and God, so that in being known it can submit its unique visible testimony to the appearance of God, this knowing does not depart from a thing once it is known. Just as one keeps returning to a painting to explain it, and just as such an elucidation becomes part of the art object by increasing the knowledge and account of its aesthetic reception, so the Christian knowing of things does not depart from the thing known. And this is the true value of bringing together truth and beauty, for beauty is always an individuated and wholly irreplaceable testimony to the work of the universal. Beauty is the delight in the thing, object, action, or creature for its own sake, beauty is the visible appearance that such a work could be achieved in no other way or manner. In knowing a beautiful thing, we know its nature and thereby call others into relationship with it; in such a manner, the mind of man at its highest perfection enters into the divine mind with knowledge of the connection, relationship, and desire between all things. Man is lord of all creation because each being desires the human eye and wishes to repeat and therefore honor its naming by the first Adam at the dawn of creation. And man names creation because adding his own artifice to creation is man's way of exemplifying and demonstrating God. Man perfects nature; for the world to truly fulfill its telos man must apply the order appropriate to the natural order that nature itself cannot supply. Divine activity created the world in order that man might discharge his creative power in the light of the Trinitarian Godhead that He also will share in.

Now you might ask, Why does the knowable demonstrate its Maker? Why does God want all things to be known? Well, the knowable reveals the Creator because what is known in beings are the forms that inform each thing, making it this entity rather than that creature, that thing rather than this being. And in knowing a thing's form we know—albeit in part—an element of the mind of God. Why? Because form is *like* God insofar as it is the means, way, or manner by which creatures participate in the Creator, for each form represents a certain way that a creature's finite being can imitate God's infinite being in an analogous manner. It is not surprising then that in Book III of the *Summa contra Gentiles*, St. Thomas Aquinas uses Aristotle to proclaim that form is something divine and desirable, "forma est divinum quoddam et appetibile."[21] Now form is certainly divine and desirable in respect of matter, as matter seeks its own actualization through form, "since every being is actual through form."[22] But form is divine and desirable not only from the perspective of material potency and nonbeing but also from the position of the Highest being itself. Forms are from God, they are *of* God, and they represent the characters, grades, and determinations that God's essential goodness participates in his essential being. Form is divine in respect of potency as it represents both act and actuality, and as that which actualizes matter (even though pure matter, as we have seen, does not exist)—form is divine from the perspective of God. For form by reason of its actuality is *like* God, who is pure act: "Bodies as composed of matter and form, approach the divine likeness *because they possess form*, which Aristotle calls a divine thing."[23]

Of course this is not to say that in knowing a thing we know God completely—no, not at all. All knowing of God knows Him partially, or better yet, mediately. Even if we know God, such knowledge is asymmetrical; there is always more of God than one can know, we can know Him but not comprehend His nature. Thus, while the likeness of creatures to God is on the basis of form and *esse*, God is nonetheless not like His creatures. God is beyond all *ens* insofar as He is simple esse and indeed simple form itself. However, this distance between creature and Creator does not produce an unknown God who cannot reveal Himself to that which He has made; on the contrary, because God is infinite being itself (*ipsum esse infinitum*), He cannot fully demonstrate His goodness via one finite being or single creature. Thus many creatures and many forms are required to make manifest the goodness of God: "In order that the likeness of divine goodness might be more perfectly communicated to things, it was necessary for there to be a diversity of things, so that what could not be perfectly represented by one thing might be in more perfect fashion, represented by a variety of things in different ways."[24]

As all material and immaterial things are the result of a divine idea as to what could more perfectly reveal God's nature and Goodness, in a sense all and everything is divine mind revealing itself to itself and also, as a result of the Trinitarian promise, to us. But—and this is the crucial question—why does the divine absolute will each and every particular? Why are the divine ideas more real in their concrete instantiation than as universals in the mind of God? Because in a reversal of Hegelianism for Christian theology, particulars are *more* universal than universals, the universal is better exhibited by that which represents its concrete individuation than it is by that which returns to such universality in its abstracted state. Particulars, or better, "singulars," are the events that realize universality itself. Divine mind is more actualized in creation than it is by itself, and God's self-expression retains the higher value. In this manner, perhaps, only Christianity can explain why the universal, or rather, the absolute, would create, why it would wholly express itself in the particular instantiations of its essence. God thus stands behind the created order as that mode of divine self-expression that He wills as His most evident appearance.

A divine idealism is at the same time realism: it already encompasses and collapses the distinction between realism and idealism because it can explain both; the ideal wills the real, for the real is the ideal's more noble proxy. God makes His intentions concrete, but only we, the creating creatures of the creator God, can fulfill them: the task of man is to take his place in the Trinitarian order by making good on creation by completing the task that the Creator through the created order sets for us. Human creativity is required to make good on the intentions of God, for creation requires for its final elevation man's stewardship and aesthetic work. Human construction completes natural creation, for it adds the knowledge of artifice to the created art of God and so knows the work of creation as such.

In such a prescription beauty, truth, and knowledge are not separate but coincide. But this is not a description for this world, which is not yet paradise; there is still a gap between the *is* and the *ought*, between how things are and how they should be. I have endeavored to outline an ontology in respect of which Christian discernment can recover its aesthetic visible dimension. Part of this project would be to indicate that such judgment is indeed possible, that the nature of creation might support such an account. I have not yet even begun to outline how one might form an ethics from such a world picture, nor have I talked about the formation of this discernment, how intuition itself might be taught. This depiction will have to be given elsewhere. However, there is no avoiding ontology and accounts of how we might see its nature, not least because one consequence of the fall is the misperception of the world, a point noted by Oliver O'Donovan: "In speaking of Man's fallenness we point not only to his persistent rejection of the created order, but also to an inescapable confusion in his perceptions of it."[25] The restoration of the created order requires knowledge and previsioning of its fulfillment; this itself demands that we can account for how we might know such a thing. And if goodness and beauty have an appearance, and if we wish to make it true, then vision is, in part, a gift of the divine art in order that we might pursue what ought to be and make real its manifest warrant.

## Notes

1 See Martin Jay's *Downcast Eyes, The Denigration of Vision in Twentieth-Century French Thought* (Berkeley: University of California Press, 1994).

2 The creation of an internal, moral God of conscience and good works—pace Kant—is in large part the construction of a secular modernity that had already abandoned the external world as a source of the divine warrant.

3 Karl Marx, *Rheinische Zeitung*, July 14, 1842.

4 Karl Marx, *The German Ideology, Part I*, ed. C. J. Arthur (London: Lawrence and Wishart, 1970), 55.

5 We can see this again in the *German Ideology*, when Marx accepts that his account of the all-around dependence "can be expressed again in speculative-idealistic, i.e. fantastic terms as 'self generation of the species' . . . and thereby the consecutive series of interrelated individual connected with each other can be conceived as a single individual, which accomplishes the mystery of generating itself." Ibid.

6 See Alain Badiou, *Deleuze: The Clamour of Being*, trans. Louise Burchill (Minneapolis: University of Minnesota Press, 2000), 21.

7   See Aristotle, *Metaphysics* 1.6 987a–987b (New York: Prometheus Books, 1991).

8   There is great debate as to whether beauty in the Middle Ages ever was a transcendental in the same sense as goodness or beauty. Jan Aertsen has consistently argued that this supposition is a modern invention projected back onto the Middle Ages by modern thinkers. See Jan A. Aertsen, *Medieval Philosophy and the Transcendentals: The Case of Thomas Aquinas* (Leiden: E. J. Brill, 1996).

9   Immanuel Kant, *Critique of Judgment*, trans. Werner S. Pluhar (Indianapolis: Hackett, 1987), 44.

10  See Simon Jarvis, *Adorno: A Critical Introduction* (London: Polity 1998), 93. I am much indebted to his analysis in this volume and in his article "The Coastline of Experience: Materialism and Metaphysics in Adorno," *Radical Philosophy* 85 (1997): 7–19.

11  Jay M. Bernstein, *The Fate of Art* (London: Polity, 1992), 9, emphasis mine.

12  As quoted by Jarvis, *Adorno*, 115; Adorno, *Philosophische Terminologie* (Frankfurt am Main: Suhrkamp, 1973–74), sec. ii, 162; G. W. F. Hegel, *Science of Logic*, trans. A. V. Miller (London: Allen & Unwin, 1969), 469.

13  I take this remark from Jarvis, "The Coastline of Experience," 16.

14  Theodor W. Adorno, *Negative Dialektik* (Frankfurt am Main: Schrkamp, 1975), 22; Theodor W. Adorno, *Negative Dialectics*, trans. E. B. Ashton (London: Routledge, 1973), 11, translation altered.

15  In this regard, I am grateful to a paper by E. J. Lowe, "Form without Matter," in *Form and Matter: Themes in Contemporary Metaphysics*, ed. D.S. Oderberg (Oxford: Blackwell, 1999).

16  This point derives from Putnam's compositional plasticity thesis that quickly ended any psychoneural identity theory. See Hillary Putnam, "The Nature of Mental States," in *Mind, Language and Reality*, vol. 2 (Cambridge: Cambridge University Press, 1975).

17  "The dictum of all genuine idealists from the Eleatic school to Bishop Berkeley, is contained in this formula: 'All knowledge through the senses and experience is nothing but sheer illusion, and only in the ideas of the pure understanding and reason is there truth.' The principle that throughout dominates and determines my idealism is on the contrary: 'All knowledge of things merely from pure understanding or pure reason is nothing but sheer illusion, and only in experience is there truth' " (Immanuel Kant, *Prolegomena to Any Future Metaphysics*, ed. L. W. Beck [New York: Bobbs-Merrill, 1950], 123).

18  Manfred Frank, *Einführung in die frühromantische Ästhetik* (Frankfurt am Main: Suhrkamp, 1989), 175.

19  Rowan Williams, "Logic and Spirit in Hegel," in *Post-Secular Philosophy*, ed. Phillip Blond (London: Routledge, 1998), 119–20.

20  In this sense I repeat the early Thomistic notion that essence somehow trumps the division between form and matter because the essence of human being is to be material, rather than purely formal or spiritual. See Thomas's *De Ente et Essentia*.

21  St. Thomas Aquinas, *Summa contra Gentiles*, vol. 3, part 2, chap. 97, sec. 3.

22  Ibid., sec. 4.

23  Ibid., part 1, chap. 69, sec. 27.

24  Aquinas, *Summa contra Gentiles*, vol. 3, part 2, chap. 97, S.c.G III part ii, c.97 sec. 2.

25  See Oliver O' Donovan, *Resurrection and Moral Order: An Outline for Evangelical Ethics*, 2nd ed. (Leicester, Eng.: Intervarsity Press, 1994), 19.

# Notes on Contributors

ANTHONY BAKER is lecturer in Systematic Theology at the Episcopal Theological Seminary of the Southwest, in Austin, Texas. He is working on a manuscript entitled *The Beauty of Holiness: Christian Perfection at the End of Modernity*, which argues that a true theology of the holy has been dying since the High Middle Ages. He has published articles on theology, philosophy, and the critique of modern science.

DANIEL M. BELL JR. is assistant professor of theological ethics at the Lutheran Theological Southern Seminary in Columbia, South Carolina. He is the author of *Liberation Theology after the End of History: The Refusal to Cease Suffering* (2001), and of numerous academic articles.

PHILLIP BLOND is lecturer of philosophy at the University of Lancaster. He is the author of *Post-Secular Philosophy: Between Philosophy and Theology* (1998), as well as many academic articles.

SIMON CRITCHLEY is professor of philosophy at the New School University and the University of Essex. He is the author of many books including *On Humour* (2002); *Continental Philosophy: A Very Short Introduction* (2001); *Ethics, Politics and Subjectivity: Essays on Derrida, Levinas, and Contemporary French Thought* (1999); *Very Little . . . Almost Nothing: Death, Philosophy, Literature* (1997); and *The Ethics of Deconstruction: Derrida and Levinas* (1992).

CONOR CUNNINGHAM is research fellow at the Centre of Theology and Philosophy, University of Nottingham. He is the editor of *Divining Metaphysics* (2004) and the author of *Genealogy of Nihilism: Philosophies of Nothing and the Difference of Theology* (2002).

CRESTON DAVIS is a doctoral candidate in philosophical theology at the University of Virginia. He is an editor of New Slant, a series on religion, politics, and ontology published by Duke University Press.

WILLIAM DESMOND is professor of philosophy at the Institute of Philosophy of the Catholic University of Leuven, Belgium. Among his many books are *Hegel's God: A Counterfeit Double?* (2003), *Ethics and the Between* (2001), *Being and the Between* (1995) and *Beyond Hegel and Dialectic: Speculation, Cult and Comedy* (1992).

HENT DE VRIES is professor in the humanities at the Humanities Center at the Johns Hopkins University. He is the author of *Philosophy and the Turn to Religion* (1999), *Religion and Violence: Philosophical Perspectives from Kant to Derrida*, and *Minimal Theologies: Critiques of Secular*

*Reason in Adorno and Levinas*, all published by Johns Hopkins University Press. He is the co-editor, with Samuel Weber, of *Violence, Identity, and Self-Determination* (1997) and of *Religion and Media*, and coeditor, with Mieke Bal, of the book series Cultural Memory in the Present, published by Stanford University Press.

TERRY EAGLETON is professor of cultural theory at Manchester University. Among his many books are *After Theory* (2003), *Sweet Violence: The Idea of the Tragic* (2002), *The Idea of Culture* (2000), *The Illusions of Postmodernism* (1996), *Literary Theory: An Introduction* (1991), and *The Ideology of the Aesthetic* (1990).

ROCCO GANGLE is visiting instructor in the religion department at Oberlin College, where he teaches modern religious thought. He is currently working on a manuscript concerning the relationship between Levinasian phenomenology and Spinoza.

PHILIP GOODCHILD is senior lecturer in religious studies at the University of Nottingham. He is the author of *Difference in Philosophy of Religion* (2003), *Capitalism and Religion: The Price of Piety* (2002), *Gilles Deleuze and the Question of Philosophy* (1996), and *Deleuze and Guattari: An Introduction to the Politics of Desire* (1996). He is an editor of New Slant, a series on religion, politics, and ontology published by Duke University Press.

KARL HEFTY is a doctoral candidate in philosophy of religion at Emmanuel College, Cambridge, where he is completing a dissertation on knowledge, desire, and affectivity in Gilles Deleuze and Michel Henry.

ELEANOR KAUFMAN is associate professor of comparative literature at the University of California, Los Angeles. She is the author of *The Delirium of Praise: Bataille, Blanchot, Deleuze, Foucault, Klossowski* (2001) and coeditor, with Kevin Jon Heller, of *Deleuze and Guattari: New Mappings in Politics, Philosophy, and Culture* (1998).

TOM McCARTHY is a novelist, artist, and general secretary of the International Necronautical Society.

JOHN MILBANK is research professor of religion, politics, and ethics and director of the Centre of Theology and Philosophy at the University of Nottingham. Previously he was the Frances Myers Ball Professor of Philosophical Theology at the University of Virginia, and before that reader in philosophical theology and fellow of Peterhouse at the University of Cambridge. He is the author of *Being Reconciled* (2003), *The Word Made Strange: Theology, Language, Culture* (1997), and *Theology and Social Theory: Beyond Secular Reason* (1991).

ANTONIO NEGRI is an independent researcher and writer and an inmate at Rebibbia Prison, Rome. Among his many books are *Time for Revolution* (2003), *Empire*, with Michael Hardt (2000), *Insurgencies: Constituent Power and the Modern State* (1999), *The Politics of Subversion: A Manifesto for the Twenty-First Century* (1989), and *Marx Beyond Marx* (1989).

CATHERINE PICKSTOCK is a University Lecturer in Philosophy of Religion at the Faculty of Divinity, University of Cambridge, and a fellow of Emmanuel College, Cambridge. Her publications include *Truth in Aquinas* (2000) with John Milbank, *After Writing: On the Liturgical Consummation of Philosophy* (1998), and, as co-editor, *Radical Orthodoxy: A New Theology* (1999).

PATRICK AARON RICHES is based at the University of Virginia, where he is completing his doctorate in theology.

MARY-JANE RUBENSTEIN is doctoral candidate in philosophy of religion at Columbia University. Her articles have appeared in several journals, including *Modern Theology*, *Journal of the American Academy of Religion*, and *Telos*.

REGINA SCHWARTZ is professor of English at Northwestern University. She is the author of *The Curse of Cain: The Violent Legacy of Monotheism* (1998), *The Postmodern Bible* (1995), and *Desire in the Renaissance: Psychoanalysis and Literature* (1994).

KENNETH SURIN is based in the Program of Literature at Duke University. He is an editor of New Slant, a series on religion, politics, and ontology published by Duke University Press.

GRAHAM WARD is professor of contextual theology and ethics at the University of Manchester and executive editor of the journal Literature and Theology. He is the author of several books, most recently True Religion (2002) and Cities of God (2000). He is the editor of The Postmodern God (1997), The Certeau Reader (1998), and The Blackwell Companion of Postmodern Theology (2001). His book Cultural Transformation and Religious Practice is forthcoming from Cambridge University Press.

ROWAN WILLIAMS is the Archbishop of Canterbury. He was previously the Lady Margaret Professor of Divinity at Oxford University, before becoming the Bishop of Monmouth and subsequently also the Archbishop of Wales. He is the author of Arius: Heresy and Tradition (2001), On Christian Theology (2000), Lost Icons: Reflection on Cultural Bereavement (2000), and After Silent Centuries (1994). He is the editor of Sergei Bulgakov: Towards a Russion Political Theology (1999).

SLAVOJ ŽIŽEK is senior researcher at the Institute for Social Studies, Ljubljana, Slovenia. Among his many books are Organs without Bodies: On Deleuze and Consequences (2003), Welcome to the Desert of the Real (2002), On Belief (2001), The Fragile Absolute; Or, Why Is the Christian Legacy Worth Fighting For? (2001), On Belief (2001), The Ticklish Subject: The Absent Centre of Political Ontology (1999), and Tarrying with the Negative (1993).

# Index

LIBRARY OF CONGRESS CATALOGING-IN-PUBLICATION DATA

Theology and the political : the new debate / Creston Davis, John Milbank, and Slavoj Žižek, editors ; with an introduction by Rowan Williams.

p. cm. — (SIC ; 5)

Includes bibliographical references and index.

ISBN 0-8223-3460-7 (hardcover : alk. paper)

ISBN 0-8223-3472-0 (pbk. : alk. paper)

1. Christianity and politics. 2. Capitalism—Religious aspects—Christianity. 3. Religion and politics. 4. Capitalism—Religious aspects. I. Davis, Creston. II. Milbank, John. III. Žižek, Slavoj. IV. SIC (Durham, N.C.) ; 5.

BR115.P7T4255 2005

201'.72—dc22       2004028227